AF772287

Measuring India

Measuring India

The Nation's Statistical System

M.R. Saluja

OXFORD
UNIVERSITY PRESS

OXFORD
UNIVERSITY PRESS

Oxford University Press is a department of the University of Oxford. It furthers the University's objective of excellence in research, scholarship, and education by publishing worldwide. Oxford is a registered trademark of Oxford University Press in the UK and in certain other countries.

Published in India by
Oxford University Press
2/11 Ground Floor, Ansari Road, Daryaganj, New Delhi 110 002, India

© Oxford University Press 2017

The moral rights of the authors have been asserted.

First Edition published in 2017

All rights reserved. No part of this publication may be reproduced, stored in a retrieval system, or transmitted, in any form or by any means, without the prior permission in writing of Oxford University Press, or as expressly permitted by law, by licence, or under terms agreed with the appropriate reprographics rights organization. Enquiries concerning reproduction outside the scope of the above should be sent to the Rights Department, Oxford University Press, at the address above.

You must not circulate this work in any other form
and you must impose this same condition on any acquirer.

ISBN-13: 978-0-19-947439-4
ISBN-10: 0-19-947439-7

Typeset in Adobe Garamond Pro 11/13
by Tranistics Data Technologies, Kolkata 700 091
Printed in India by Rakmo Press, New Delhi 110 020

Contents

Tables

Abbreviations

The list consolidates abbreviations used in the book. There might be instances of duplication of an abbreviation by virtue of a difference in its full form. Readers are recommended to refer to the list contextually.

AAI	Airports Authority of India
ADB	Asian Development Bank
ADSORBS	Assessment and Development Study of River Basin Series
AFOLU	Agriculture Forest and Other Land Categories
AGM	Annual General Meeting
AICTE	All India Council of Technical Education
AIDIS	All-India Debt and Investment Survey
AIDS	Acquired Immune Deficiency Syndrome
AIES	All India Educational Survey
AISES	All India School Education Survey
ALE	Agricultural Labour Enquiry
AMA	Administrative Management Agency
ANC	Ante-Natal Care
ANM	Auxiliary Nurse Midwife
APL	Above Poverty Line
APRAD	Asia Pacific Road Accident Data
ARI	Acute Respiratory Infection
AS&FA	Additional Secretary & Financial Advisor

ASDR	Age Specific Death Rates
ASHA	Accredited Social Health Activist
ASI	*Annual Survey of Industries*
ASICC	ASI Commodity Classification
ATF	Aviation Turbine Fuel
AYUSH	Ayurveda, Yoga and Naturopathy, Unani, Siddha and Homeopathy
BCG	Bacillus Calmette–Guérin
BECIL	Broadcasting Engineering Consultants India Limited
BG	broad gauge
BMS	Basic Minimum Services
BoP	Balance of Payments
BPL	Below Poverty Line
BPSI	*Basic Port Statistics of India*
BSE	Bombay Stock Exchange Limited
BSI	Botanical Survey of India
CAB	Cotton Advisory Board
CAD	Coordination and Administration Division
CAG	Comptroller and Auditor General of India
CAPE	Crop Acreage and Production Estimation
CBHI	Central Bureau of Health Intelligence
CBR	Crude Birth Rate
CB	Commercial Bank
CCE	Crop Cutting Experiments
CCEA	Cabinet Committee on Economic Affairs
CCI&E	Chief Controller of Imports & Exports
CDR	Crude Death Rate
CDS	Current Daily Status
CEA	Central Electricity Authority
CEB	census enumeration block
CES	Coverage Evaluation Survey/Surveys on Consumption Expenditure
CFC	Consumption of Fixed Capital
CGHS	Central Government Health Scheme
CH_4	Methane
CHC	Community Health Centre
CIF	Cost, Insurance, and Freight
CIFRI	Central Inland Fisheries Research Institute

CIN	corporate identification number
CIS	Change in Stock
CIWTC	Central Inland Water Corporation
CMA	Cement Manufacturers' Association
CMFRI	Central Marine Fisheries Research Institute
CMI	Census of Manufacturing Industries
CMIE	Centre for Monitoring Indian Economy
CNG	Compressed Natural Gas
CO	Carbon Monoxide
CO_2	Carbon Dioxide
COINDS	Comprehensive Industry Document Series
COOIT	Central Organization for Oil Industry and Trade
CP	Current Price
CPC	Central Product Classification
CPCB	Central Pollution Control Board
CPD	Coordination and Publication Division
CPI	Consumer Price Index
CPSU	Central Public Sector Undertaking
CRS	Civil Registration System
CSIR	Council of Scientific and Industrial Research
CSO	Central Statistical Office
CSS	Centrally Sponsored Schemes
CUPS	Control of Urban Pollution Series
CWC	Central Water Commission
CWE	Chief Wage Earner
CWS	Current Weekly Status
CWSN	Children with Special Needs
CWWG	Crop Weather Watch Group
DADF	Department of Animal Husbandry, Dairying and Fisheries
DC-SSI	Development Commissioner, Small Scale Industries
DCU	Departmental Commercial Undertakings
DES	Directorate of Economics and Statistics
DG&CEO	Director General and Chief Executive Officer
DGCA	Directorate General of Civil Aviation
DGCI&S	Director General of Commercial Intelligence and Statistics
DGE&T	Directorate General of Employment and Training

DGFT	Directorate General of Foreign Trade
DGHS	Directorate General of Health Services
DGTD	Directorate General of Technical Development
DH	District Headquarters
DIPP	Department of Industrial Policy and Promotion
DISE	District Information System for Education
DIT	Department of Information Technology
DLHS	District Level Household and Facility Survey
DME	Directory Manufacturing Establishments
DMI	Directorate of Marketing and Inspection
DOBS	Dwellings, Other Buildings, and Structures
DPD	Data Processing Division
DPEP	District Primary Education Programme
DPT	Diphtheria, Pertussis, and Tetanus
DR	Deposit Rate
DSIM	Department of Statistics and Information Management
DSO	District Survey Officer
DST	Department of Science and Technology
DSTP	Directorate of Scientific and Technical Personnel
DTR	Daily Trade Return
DTS	Domestic Tourism Survey
EARAS	Establishment of an Agency for Reporting Agriculture Statistics
EBMC	Educationally Backward Minority Community
EDI	Electronic Data Interchange
EGS&AIE	Education Guarantee Scheme and Alternative and Innovative Education
EIAS	Ecological Impact Assessment Series
EMI	Employment Market Information
EMPS	Environment Mapping and Pollution Series
ENI	Estimates of National Income
ENI	*Estimates of National Income*
ENP	*Estimates of National Product*
EPWRF	Economic and Political Weekly Research Foundation
ESCAP	Economic and Social Commission for the Asia and the Pacific
ESS	European Statistical System
EU	European Union

FAO	Food and Agriculture Organization of the United Nation
FCRN	Foreign Company Registration Number
FDES	Framework for Development of Environment Statistics
FDI	Foreign Direct Investment
FEE	Foreign Exchange Earnings
FISIM	Financial Intermediation Services Indirectly Measured
FLS	Family Living Survey
FOB	Free on Board
FOD	Field Operations Division
FRBM Act	Fiscal Responsibility and Budget Management Act
FSI	Forest Survey of India
FSU	First-Stage Unit
FTA	Foreign Tourist Arrivals
FTSI	*Foreign Trade Statistics of India*
G2B	Government to Business
G2C	Government to Customer
G2E	Government to Employee
G2G	Government to Government
GCES	General Crop Estimation Surveys
GCF	Gross Capital Formation
GDCF	Gross Domestic Capital Formation
GDP	Gross Domestic Product
GER	Gender Enrolment Ratio
GET	Global Employment Trends
GFCF	Gross Fixed Capital Formation
GHG	Greenhouse Gas
GIS	Geographic Information System
GNI	Gross National Income
GNP	Gross National Product
GoI	Government of India
GPG	Good Practices Guidance
GPI	Gender Parity Index
GSDP	Gross State Domestic Product
GSI	Geological Survey of India
GSS	Government Statistical Service
GTKM	Gross Tonne Kilometre

GVA	Gross Value Added
GVO	Gross Value of Output
HBS	Household Budget Survey
HC	Hydrocarbons
HDPI	Human Development Profile of India
HIV	Human Immunodeficiency Virus
HTML	Hypertext Markup Language
HWMS	Hazardous Waste Management Series
HYV	High Yielding Varieties
IASI	Inter-American Statistical Institute
IASRI	Indian Agricultural Statistical Research Institute
IBM	Indian Bureau of Mines
ICAI	Institute of Chartered Accountants of India
ICFRE	Indian Council of Forestry Research and Education
ICICI	Industrial Credit and Investment Corporation of India
ICLS	Indian Corporate Law Service
ICMR	Indian Council of Medical Research
ICPF	Insurance Corporations and Pension Funds
ICPSR	Interuniversity Consortium for Political and Social Research
ICR	Intelligent Character Reading
ICS	Improvement of Crop Statistics
ICSI	Institute of Company Secretaries of India
ICT	Information and Communication Technology
ICWAI	Institute of Cost and Works Accountants of India
IDBI	Industrial Development Bank of India
IEC	Importer and Exporter Code
IFCI	Industrial Financial Corporation of India
IFS	*International Financial Statistics*
IHDS	India Human Development Survey
IICA	Indian Institute of Corporate Affairs
IIP	Index of Industrial Production
ILO	International Labour Organization
ILS	*Indian Labour Statistics*
IMF	International Monetary Fund
IMR	Infant Mortality Rate
IMYB	*Indian Minerals Year Book*
I–O	Input–Output

IOTT	Input–Output Transactions Table
IPCC	Intergovernmental Panel on Climate Change
IPP	Intellectual property products
IPS	International Passenger Survey
IR	Indian Railways
IRAD	Indian Road Accident Data
IRDA	Insurance Regulatory and Development Authority
ISCED	International Standard Classification for Education
ISD	International Subscriber Dialling
ISFR	*India State of Forest Report*
ISI	International Statistical Institute
ISIC	International Standard Industrial Classification of All Economic Activities
ISM&H	Indian System of Medicine and Homoeopathy
ISO	Information System Organization
ISSP	India Statistical Strengthening Project
ISW	Industrial Statistics Wing
ISWGNA	Intersecretariat Working Group on National Accounts
ITC HS	Indian Trade Classification (Harmonized System)
IWT	Inland Water Transport
J&K	Jammu and Kashmir
JSY	Janani Suraksha Yojana
KP	Constant Price
LFPR	Labour Force Participation Rate
LIC	Life Insurance Corporation
LLP	Limited Liability Partnership
LPG	Liquefied Petroleum Gas
LR	Lending rate
LRUR	Local Register of Usual Residents
LUCF	Land-use Change and Forestry
LULUCF	Land Use, Land-use Change, and Forestry
LUS	Land Use Statistics
MAS	Monthly Abstract Statistics
MCA	Ministry of Corporate Affairs
MCDR	Mineral Conservation and Development Rules
MDG	Millennium Development Goal
MDR	Major District Road
MES	Monthly Epidemiological Situation

MG	Metre Gauge
MGNREGS	Mahatma Gandhi National Rural Employment Guarantee Scheme
MHRD	Ministry of Human Resource Development
MID	Minor Irrigation Division
MIMAP	Micro Impact of Macro and Adjustment Policies
MIS	Management Information Systems
MISH	Market Information Survey of Households
MMF	money Market Funds
MMR	Maternal Mortality Rate
MNP	Minimum Needs Programme
MoEFCC	Ministry of Environment, Forests and Climate Change
MOSPI	Ministry of Statistics and Programme Implementation
MRTH	Ministry of Road Transport and Highways
MRTPC	Monopolies and Restrictive Trade Practices Commission
MSFTI	*Monthly Statistics of the Foreign Trade of India*
MSME	Micro, Small, and Medium Enterprises
MSMED Act	Micro, Small and Medium Enterprises Development Act
MSR	Marketed Surplus Ratio
MSW	Municipal Solid Waste
MTEF	Medium-Term Expenditure Framework
MTP	Medical Termination of Pregnancy
N	Nitrogen
N_2O	Nitrous Oxide
NAAQMS	National Ambient Air Quality Monitoring Series
NABARD	National Bank for Agriculture and Rural Development
NACO	National AIDS Control Organization
NACP	National AIDS Control Programme
NAD	National Accounts Division
NAQ	National Accounts Questionnaire
NAS	National Accounts Statistics
NATCOM	National Communication
NBO	National Building Organization
NBS	National Bureau of Statistics
NCAER	National Council for Applied Economic Research
NCDEX	National Commodity Derivatives Exchange

NCERT	National Council of Educational Research and Training
NCFC	National Crop Forecasting Center
NCO	National Classification of Occupations
NCP	National Commission on Population
NCSC	National Crop Statistics Centre
NCV	Net Calorific Values
NDCU	Non-Departmental Commercial Undertakings
NDE	Non-Departmental Enterprises/Non-Directory Establishment
NDME	Non-Directory Manufacturing Establishments
NDP	Net Domestic Product
NEERI	National Environmental Engineering Research Institute
NEP	National Environment Policy
NES	National Employment Service
NFHS	National Family Health Survey
NH_3	Ammonia
NHB	National Horticultural Board
NHP	National Health Profile
NIC	National Industrial Classification/National Informatics Centre
NIEPA	National Institute of Educational Planning and Administration
NILERD	National Institute of Labour Economics Research and Development
NKN	National Knowledge Network
NMHC	Non-Methane Hydrocarbons
NNP	Net National Product
NO_2	Nitrogen Dioxide
NOC	National Occupational Classification
NPCMS	National Product Classification for Manufacturing Sector
NPISH	Non-Profit Institutions Serving Households
NPR	National Population Register
NRHM	National Rural Health Mission
NRR	Net Reproduction Rate
NRSA	National Remote Sensing Agency
NSC	National Statistical Commission
NSDP	Net State Domestic Product

NSE	National Stock Exchange of India Ltd
NSHIE	National Survey on Household Income and Expenditure
NSI	National Statistical Institute
NSS	National Sample Survey
NSSF	National Small Savings Fund
NSSO	National Sample Survey Office
NSSTA	National Statistical Systems Training Academy
NSTMIS	National Science and Technology Management Information System Division
NTKM	Net Tonne Kilometre
NUEPA	National University of Educational Planning and Administration
NVA	Net Value Added
NVBDCP	National Vector Borne Disease Control Programme
OAD	Operational Analysis Division
OAE	Own-Account Enterprises
OAME	Own-Account Manufacturing Enterprises
OBC	Other Backward Classes
ODA	Official Development Assistance
OEA	Office of the Economic Advisor
OECD	Organisation for Economic Co-operation and Development
OMB	Office of Management and Budget
ONS	Office for National Statistics
ORGI	Office of the Registrar General of India
OWS	Occupational Wage Survey
PCO	Public Call Office
PCS	Private Corporate Sector
PDF	Portable Document Format
PDS	Public Distribution System
PFCE	Private Final Consumption Expenditure
PFRDA	Pension Fund Regulatory and Development Authority
PHC	Primary Health Centre
PIM	Perpetual Inventory Method
PIO	Person of Indian Origin
PLF	Passenger Load Factor
PMGSY	Pradhan Mantri Gram Sadak Yojana
PNC	Post-Natal Care

POSB	Post Office Savings Bank
PPP	Purchasing Power Parity
PSU	Primary Sampling Unit/Public Sector Undertaking
R&D	Research and Development
RBI	Reserve Bank of India
RERES	Resource Recycling Series
RFD	Results-Framework Document
RGI	Registrar General of India
RITES	Rail India Technical and Economic Services Ltd
RLE	Rural Labour Enquiry
RMIS	Rationalization of Minor Irrigation Statistics
RMSA	Rashtriya Madhyamik Shiksha Abhiyan
ROC	Registrar of Companies
RR	Reference Rate
RS	Remote Sensing
RTC	Road Transport Corporation
S&T	Scientific and Technical
SAARC	South Asian Association for Regional Cooperation
SC	Scheduled Caste
SCC	State Cane Commissioners
SCIS	Standing Committee on Industrial Statistics
SDDS	Standard Data Dissemination System
SDP	State Domestic Product
SDRD	Survey Design and Research Division
SEBI	Securities and Exchange Board of India
SECC	Socio Economic and Caste Census
SEMIS	Secondary Education Management Information System
SFC	State Financial Corporation
SFTIC	*Statistics of Foreign Trade of India by Countries*
SIC	Standard Industrial Classification
SIDC	State Industrial Development Corporation
SIDO	Small Industries Development Organization
SIRO	Scientific and Industrial Research Organization
SITC	Standard International Trade Classification
SNA	System of National Accounts
SO_2	Sulphur Dioxide
SPM	Suspended Particulate Matter
SPS	Special Performance System

SRS	Sample Registration System
SRTU	State Road Transport Undertaking
SSA	Sarva Shiksha Abhiyan
SSD	Statistical Standards Divisions
SSI	Small-Scale Industries
SSMI	Sample Survey of Manufacturing Industries
SSO	State Survey Officer
SSU	Second-Stage Unit
ST	Scheduled Tribe
STD	Sexually Transmitted Disease/Subscriber Trunk Dialing
STI	Sexually Transmitted Infection
STS	Science and Technology Statistics
SUT	Sustainable Urban Tourism
TDGDP	Tourism Direct Gross Domestic Product
TDGVA	Tourism Direct Gross Value Added
TFR	Total Fertility Rate
TRS	Timely Reporting Scheme
TRW	Transport Research Wing
TSA	Tourism Satellite Accounts
TSP	Total Suspended Particles
TT	Tetanus Toxoid
U-DISE	Unified District Information System for Education
UEE	Universal Elementary Education
UFS	Urban Frame Survey
UGC	University Grants Commission
UID	Unique Identification Number
UIDAI	Unique Identification Authority of India
UK	United Kingdom
UN	United Nations
UNESCO	United Nations Educational Scientific and Cultural Organization
UNFCCC	United Nations Framework Convention on Climate Change
UNIDO	United Nations Industrial Development Organization
UNME	Urban Non-Manual Employee
UNSC	United Nations Statistical Commission
UNSD	United Nations Statistics Division

UNWTO	United Nations World Tourism Organization
UPR	Usual Place of Residence
UPS	Usual Principal Status
UPSS	Usual Principal and Subsidiary Status
US	United States
USU	Ultimate Stage Units
UT	Union Territory
UTI	Unit Trust of India
VAT	Value Added Tax
VSAT	Very Small Aperture Terminal
WEO	World Economic Outlook
WHO	World Health Organization
WPI	Wholesale Price Index
WPR	Worker–Population Ratio
XBRL	eXtensible Business Reporting Language
ZSI	Zoological Survey of India

Foreword

This is a remarkable book written by one of the foremost academic experts on Indian official statistics. The author's first ever book on a similar topic, titled *Indian Official Statistical Systems*, was written in 1972. For much of that and later generation of practitioners and researchers on India, the book was a must-read. Many things have changed since then and Professor Saluja himself has been instrumental in developing much of the statistical procedures that are being followed in India today.

In this book, he has meticulously documented the current procedures so that those using Indian data can fully comprehend the current Indian landscape. The 18 chapters do not describe only the Indian government's data-collection process, but also its correspondence and compatibility with data used by various multilateral agencies to make cross-country comparisons.

I am confident that like the earlier publication, this new volume will be useful to analysts and researchers of Indian society and should be a compulsory reference book not only for students of economics and statistics, but also those engaged in various government services and the private sector.

T.C.A. Anant

Preface

Statistical data are essential for successful planning and analysis of various problems in formulating economic policy. Before using the data, however, one must know the sources and the process of collection; their reliability; and also the major limitation of these data. Without this knowledge one may be led to faulty conclusions. For example, before using a series, one must make sure that the data are comparable over time. However, in practice, data are frequently accepted without questions.

The purpose of this book is to survey the different kinds of statistics, the concepts and definitions behind them, and the existing procedures and the agencies involved for collection, compilation, and publication. The pitfalls and the gaps in the data have been mentioned wherever feasible. The subject of official statistics is very vast. I do not claim that all the topics have been covered. I have, however, tried to cover various important ones. Moreover the latest available details about different topics have been given.

In writing this book, I have used many official publications, and the mimeographed lecture notes prepared by various experts for the different training programmes of the Central Statistics Office (CSO). Officials of the various departments of the Government of India (GoI) have also been consulted for the purpose. I am thankful to all of them. They are too numerous to be acknowledged individually for their generous help. I am especially thankful to 18 experts from different government departments for reading the chapters of the original draft and suggesting improvements in the relevant chapters. As far as feasible, their suggestions have been taken into account.

I am grateful to Shubhashis Gangopadhyay, research director at the India Development Foundation, for encouraging me to undertake this project and for providing his advice at various stages of this book up till its completion.

Trina Ghosh, Snigdha Bhatia, and Moumita Deb deserve special thanks for helping me in searching the bibliography and making suggestions for improvements in the draft.

I am thankful to the CSO for their financial grant to India Development Foundation.

Introduction

Statistical data are essential for successful planning and analysis of various problems in formulating the economic policy. They are not only useful in identifying where the problem is, but also what is the nature of the problem and, hence, the types of solutions one needs to work with. Therefore, to use the data properly, one must know about the exact definitions of the variables (indicators), how they are related to each other, as well their reliability for certain types of analyses and shortcomings for others. Given the fast-changing contexts in which data are reported in recent times, and the consequent changes in data systems necessitated by transformations of the Indian economy, these issues have become increasingly important to all users of Indian data. For instance, while using time series data, one must make sure that the data are comparable over time.

Here are some examples of how definitions of terms used have changed over time:

1. For manufacturing industries, there are the concepts of organized and unorganized industries and small and large industries. For the estimation of gross value added (GVA) from manufacturing, the Central Statistics Office (CSO; earlier known as the Central Statistical Organization) used to divide manufacturing into registered and unregistered manufacturing. With the revision of the base year for national accounts to 2011–12, the division

is between organized and unorganized manufacturing. What is the connection between the two? Those in the unregistered sector that keep accounts are put in the organized sector. While using the data on GVA of manufacturing, this difference has to be taken into account. Even without this, there are other huge differences in the GVA of a number of sectors because of changes in the sources of data, among others. Table I.1 highlights some of these differences.

2. There have been changes in the concepts. In place of gross domestic product (GDP) at factor cost, as used in the series with 2004–5 as base, the basic price concept is used in the new series. Also, the term GVA is used in place of GDP for industry-wise estimates. The GVA at factor cost (earlier called GDP at factor cost)

Table I.1 Comparison of GVA of Organized Manufacturing (excluding quasi-corporations of the unincorporated enterprises) of New Series with GVA for Registered Manufacturing from Old Series for 2011–12[1] (Rs Crore)

Compilation Category	Activity	2004–5 Series	2011–12 Series	Difference (%)
6	Manufacture of beverages	15,417	28,925	87.6
9	Wearing apparel, except fur apparel and tailoring	13,509	20,341	50.6
13	Manufacture of paper and paper products and publishing, printing, and reproduction of recorded media	20,554	28,338	37.9
14	Manufacture of coke, refined petroleum products and nuclear fuel, and rubber and plastic products	95,268	1,52,710	60.3

[1] For comparison of other sectors, see Ministry of Statistics and Programme Implementation (MOSPI) (2015).

20 + 21	Manufacture of fabricated metal products, except machinery and equipment, and manufacture of machinery and equipment n.e.c. + office, accounting, and computing machinery	1,09,961	43,146	–60.8
22	Electrical machinery and apparatus n.e.c. + radio, television, and communication equipment and apparatus	46,406	1,81,652	291.4
23	Manufacture of medical, precision and optical instruments, watches and clocks + manufacturing n.e.c.	32,157	15,541	–51.7
24	Manufacture of motor vehicles, trailers, and semi-trailers + manufacture of other transport equipment	85,524	1,25,368	46.6

Source: MOSPI (2015).

Note: Changes in methodology and data sources in the new series of National Accounts: Base year 2011–12.

can be compiled from the estimates of GVA at basic prices by subtracting production taxes less subsidies. Taxes and subsidies have been divided into production and product taxes and subsidies. Production taxes and subsidies are valid in relation to production and are independent of the actual volume of production, while product taxes and subsidies are valid as per unit of production.

Why This Book?

This book has been written to help the users of data in terms of its sources, methodology used in the collection of data, and limitations, reliability, and gaps in the data. There are other problems such as duplication of data from different sources. The book clearly explains these. It makes available information regarding current publications giving different types of data. It also gives a historical view about data availability.

The subject of statistical data is vast. However, the book has tried to cover all the important topics. There are 18 chapters, each relating to different kinds of statistics, their concepts and definitions, and the agencies involved in the collection, compilation, and publication of these statistics.

In each chapter, the necessary tables providing the concepts and even the data, wherever necessary, have been given. This book will be useful for researchers, policymakers, college students, and persons aspiring for the Indian Economic Service (IES) and Indian Statistical Service (ISS) examinations.

A list of publications given at the end of each chapter relate to the data described in that chapter. In addition, the CSO, which coordinates the statistical activities and evolves statistical standard, publishes *Statistical Year Book* (previously called *Statistical Abstract*), *Monthly Abstract of Statistics* and *India in Figures*, and *Statistical Pocket Book*. These publications give detailed data on all the important economic variables in the economy.

Reference

Ministry of Statistics and Programme Implementation (MOSPI). 2015. *Changes in Methodology and Data Sources in the New Series of National Accounts: Base Year 2011–12*. New Delhi: MOSPI.

1

Indian and International Statistical Systems

There has been a major increase in the output of statistical data in various countries in recent years. This is primarily due to the demand for such data for the purposes of planning and industrial development. Current statistics on population and industrial and agricultural production are required for proper allocation and smooth functioning of an economy. Indices of production and prices give an overall picture of the state of economic conditions. The need for reliable statistical data and the consequent responsibility it places on a national statistical organization can hardly be overemphasized.

Functions of a Statistical System

Reliable and up-to-date statistics are essential for planning the economic advancement of a country. Comprehensive statistics relating to the present structure of the economy provide a sound factual basis for formulating development programmes. A national statistical system is required to organize the collection, compilation, and publication of an integrated set of statistics on a regular basis. It is the function of the system to determine the nature and extent of statistics to be collected for various purposes. The subjects on which the statistics are collected must reflect the nature of the country's economy, its stage of development, and the institutional structure. In developing an integrated set of statistical series, it is necessary for the system to study the existing gaps in statistics—both in the collection and publication aspects—and assign relative priorities for filling these gaps.

For maintaining the quality of statistics, it is necessary to evolve standards, concepts, and definitions; have standard classifications for industry, trade, and occupation, among others; and adopt a uniform standard methodology for the collection and analysis of data. The national statistical system should carry on research for evolving new statistical procedures of collection and processing of data and coordinate the activities of various statistical offices.

Another important function of the national statistical system should be to provide the statistics needed by the United Nations (UN) and its specialized agencies. In order to be useful for international comparisons, it is necessary that the statistical data conform to proper statistical standards.

Types of Statistical Systems

The types of statistical systems may be studied from various viewpoints, but the most common aspect examined is the degree of centralization involved. Centralization or decentralization, when applied to a national statistical system, refers to the degree of concentration in some person or organization of the authority and the responsibility for the collection, compilation, and publication of national statistics. Complete centralization and decentralization does not exist in any country. Although overall responsibility for collection, compilation, and publication of data may be with one organization, it is still necessary to have disassociated statistical units, particularly in the field of operational statistics. On the other hand, it is necessary to have some authority to coordinate, in some degree, the efforts of separate statistical organizations.

According to the degree of concentration involved, the following broad types of statistical systems could be distinguished.

A Statistical System with Minimum Control or Coordination

A system of this type exists when there are several offices at the national level, each responsible for the collection, compilation, and publication of data in its own field, and there is some office, group, or committee which has a watching brief on the whole field of national statistics. Such a group has no actual control of the statistical activities of the various departments other than that of an advisory nature, but it does provide a certain liaison between various statistical units.

This system provides effective coordination between departments which do appreciate the benefits of mutual consultation. This, however, may fail to cover all areas that are of statistical interest to the country and several organizations may compile conflicting data on the same subjects. As a result, there may be inconsistencies, gaps, and duplications in the collection of statistics.

A Statistical System Decentralized by Subject with Coordinating Authority

Different departments are responsible for collection, compilation, and publication of data and some office, group, or committee has the responsibility and authority to coordinate the statistical activities. Under this setup, each department can pay close attention to the special problems in its field. The central authority would eliminate major duplication and inconsistencies between offices. Standard definitions, identical coverage, and comparable time periods are more likely to be used with the functioning of such a coordinating agency, resulting in better and uniform set of statistics. In modern economy, the coordinating agency is basic to a properly functioning statistical system. Such agencies may be confined to the national level or extend down to state and local administration levels.

A Statistical System with a Major Operating Office for General Statistics and Coordinating Agency

This system is based on the idea that certain types of statistics are derived as a by-product of administrative activities of different departments, while other types are collected by the organizations specially set up for the purpose. Under this system, the latter type of statistics is collected by a major statistical office. In addition to its responsibility for collection of data for certain major fields, this office frequently acts as a coordinating agency for national statistics.

A Centralized Statistical System

This system involves one department collecting, compiling, and publishing statistical information pertaining to social and economic activities as well as activities relating to the environment, and collaborating with other departments in the compilation of administrative and specialized statistics. Under this system, specialized statistical personnel can be utilized and there can be a high degree of coordination of programmes and methods. There is considerable economy in tabulation and other such costs. One major drawback of the system is that the inadequacy of liaison with other offices may lead to a lack of interest in those offices.

Statistical Services Decentralized by Subject with No Central Control or Coordination

In many countries, before the need for statistical coordination was recognized, statistics were developed to meet the needs of individual departments and no systematic arrangements were made for the production of statistics according to the national pattern. It was only with the growth of statistics that the necessity of a central coordinating agency was felt. Under such an organizational pattern, with no coordinating agency, there are gaps in statistics, the quality of statistics varies from subject to subject, and the improvement of statistics becomes very difficult.

Development of the Statistical System in India

The history of the statistical system goes back to ancient India but the relatively modern history dates from the 1860s. The first significant development in statistics was the setting up of the Statistical Committee in 1862 for the preparation of model statistical forms for collection and compilation of a uniform system of imperial statistics. The statistics collected on the basis of the recommendation of the committee related to trade, finance, education, judicial system, population, agriculture, livestock, mining, and industry. The collection of these statistics led to the publication of the *Statistical Abstract of British India* in 1868 (published from London until 1923 and from India thereafter). The preparation of gazetteers of India containing a mass of economic data relating to various provinces, which started in 1866 with a study relating to the Madras Presidency, was another important stage in the development of statistics.

On the recommendation of the Indian Famine Commission, departments of agriculture were opened in various provinces in 1881 for collection of agricultural statistics, leading to the annual publication of the *Agricultural Statistics of British India* in 1886, which since then continued as an annual feature until Independence. In order to scrutinize and collate the enormous mass of agricultural statistics from various provinces, a separate Statistical Bureau was formed by the central government in 1895 to coordinate the agricultural and foreign trade statistics, besides being responsible for the collection of prices, wages, and industrial statistics. The bureau was headed by the Director General of Statistics.

The first complete population census was conducted in 1881 on a uniform basis throughout the country. Since then the census is being conducted regularly every 10 years. Up to the 1941 Census, a census commissioner used to be appointed before each census. There was no permanent department and no statistical organization was established for this purpose. It was only in 1948 that a permanent office of the Registrar General and Census Commissioner was created.

The other development regarding the statistical system was that the Director General of Statistics was given the additional function of enhancing liaison with the trading community. In 1914, under the reorganization of the department, the Director of Statistics was appointed to look exclusively into the work of collection and maintenance of statistics in one department. In other words, the statistics of all departments, both of the central and provincial governments, should come under the supervision of one central authority which would act as the adviser to the government in all statistical matters.

In 1925, the Economic Enquiry Committee was set up to enquire into the question of adequacy of the statistical data available, as well as the desirability and possibility of supplementing it and of undertaking an economic enquiry. The committee supported the planning of the entire statistical organization on a statutory basis by enacting a census and statistics act. Among other valuable recommendations of the committee were those for conducting quinquennial wage census in large industries and collection of statistics of output and raw material consumed in cottage industries. The recommendations of the committee could not be implemented.

The next important development was in 1934 to facilitate a further study of economic policies in India. As a result of the recommendations of the committee, the Government of India (GoI) decided to set up the Central Statistical Organization (now the Central Statistical Office [CSO]). However, due to practical and financial difficulties, this could not be done at that time.

In 1945, the GoI set up the Inter-Departmental Committee on Official Statistics with the economic adviser to the GoI as the chairperson to consider the statistical material available, to make recommendations regarding filling up the gaps, and for bringing about improvements in the existing organization. Among the organizational recommendations was a scheme for the decentralization of primary responsibility for departmental statistics, coupled with the formation of a central statistical office for coordination, institution of a statistical cadre, establishment of statistical bureaus at the headquarters of different state governments, and preparation of overall statistics for the entire country.

Thus, during the British period, statistical development was limited. A proper statistical organization in the country was not built up, although many committees were appointed for the purpose. These committees gave valuable suggestions. Some of the suggestions regarding setting up of certain departments were implemented. However, the suggestions regarding the setting up of a centralized coordinating body and departments of statistics in various provinces could not be implemented.

It was only after India became independent that the urgent need for a proper statistical organization came to the forefront. A statistical unit was set up in the Cabinet Secretariat in 1949, which was expanded in May 1951 into the present CSO. The unit was responsible for bringing about coordination in the activities of various statistical agencies in the central government and Directorates of Economics and Statistics (DESes; names may be different in different states) of the state governments, which were also being set up in all the states for similar coordination of activities of statistical agencies at the state level.

Present Structure of the Indian Statistical System

Broadly, the present statistical system in India is a decentralized one in which the authority and responsibility for the collection of statistics is divided between the central government and state governments on a subject-wise basis. At the national level, the Ministry of Statistics and Programme Implementation (MOSPI) is responsible for the coordination of all the activities of the state and central statistical agencies, while at the state level, the state statistical bureaus are charged with the function of coordination. The ministry has two wings: one relating to statistics and the other relating to programme implementation. The statistics wing, re-designated as National Statistics Office (NSO), consists of the CSO, Computer Centre, and the National Sample Survey Office (NSSO). The Programme Implementation Wing has three divisions: (i) Twenty Point Programme; (ii) Infrastructure and Project Monitoring; and (iii) Members of Parliament Local Area Development Scheme. Besides these two wings, there is a National Statistical Commission (NSC) created through a resolution of MOSPI and one autonomous institute, namely Indian Statistical Institute (ISI), declared as an institute of national importance by an act of Parliament.

Items like foreign trade, banking and currency, railways, posts and telegraphs, and population are wholly under the central government. Items like agriculture and education are under the supervision of the state governments. There are some common categories of subjects, for example, industry, where both the central and state governments operate to meet their respective requirements.

Even where states are the primary authorities for the collection of statistics, the central government acts as the coordinating authority for the maintenance and publication of data on an all-India basis. It can issue directives to the state governments for bringing uniformity in the statistics collected by them. The central government also provides guidance in day-to-day collection of statistics. At the central and the state levels, there is a further division of responsibility by subjects among the different central ministries, and among the state government departments respectively.

Some briefs of the organizations under NSO and of the NSC are given as follows:

(1) *Central Statistics Office*: The CSO, an attached office of the ministry, coordinates the statistical activities in the country and evolves statistical standards. Its activities, inter alia, include compilation of national accounts, index of industrial production (IIP), consumer price indices (CPIs) for urban/rural/combined, human development statistics including gender statistics, conducting *Annual Survey of Industries* (*ASI*) and economic census, and imparting training in official statistics. The CSO also assists in the development of statistics in the states and union territories (UTs), disseminates energy and social and environment statistics, and prepares the National Industrial Classification (NIC).

The CSO has the following five divisions:

(i) The National Accounts Division (NAD) of the CSO is responsible for the preparation of national accounts, which include the consolidated accounts of the nation and detailed accounts of public sector transactions, estimates of national income, government/private final consumption expenditure, capital formation, and savings. The division brings out an annual publication, entitled *National Accounts Statistics* (*NAS*), containing these statistics. Other important activities of the division are: (i) preparation of quarterly estimates of gross domestic product (GDP) at current and constant prices; (ii) estimation of capital stock and consumption of fixed capital; (iii) estimation of state-wise gross value added (GVA) and gross fixed capital formation of supra-regional sectors of railways, communication, banking and insurance, and central government administration; and (iv) preparation of comparable estimates of state domestic product (SDP) at current prices. The division compiles the comparable estimates of gross state domestic product (GSDP) and net state domestic product (NSDP) by economic activity and per capita income estimates, in consultation with the representatives of DESs of states and UTs.

The prices and cost of living unit under the NAD is responsible for the compilation and dissemination of CPI numbers of retail prices for rural as well as urban areas, and also the combined one for both rural and urban.

(ii) The Social Statistics Division is entrusted with the responsibility of coordinating development of social statistics, including environment statistics. The ambit of social statistics covers population, poverty, human development, employment, health, education, social justice, women's empowerment, gender statistics, disability, environment, statistical monitoring of Millennium Development Goals (MDGs), South Asian Association for Regional Cooperation (SAARC) Development Goals, and the SAARC Social Charter. In addition, the division has the responsibility of carrying out activities related to awards and fellowships for outstanding and meritorious research work in official statistics under the scheme of Capacity Development of CSO.

(iii) The responsibility of equipping the country's huge statistical personnel with newer practices in the official statistics and data management has been entrusted to the National Statistical Systems Training Academy (NSSTA) working under the Training Division of the CSO. The task is to develop an effective strategy for training, a calendar of training programme, and ways to implement it. The strategy entails conducting both induction and refresher training in-house programmes at the NSSTA and outsourced trainings in several reputed and specialized institutions.

The programmes cater to the need-based training of the statistical personnel working in the central government, namely the Indian Statistical Services officers and the Subordinate Statistical Service (SSS) officials, whose cadre is managed by the MOSPI, and the statistical officers and officials from states/UTs and public sector undertakings (PSUs) in the identified areas.

(iv) The Economic and Statistics Division undertakes the *ASI*, economic census, and IIP. The *ASI* is conducted at Industrial Statistics Wing (ISW), Kolkata. This division also issues a publication titled *Energy Statistics*, every year. The publication contains latest data available with respect to different energy sources and a brief analysis of the data on reserves, installed capacity, potential for generation, production, consumption, import, export, and wholesale price of different energy commodities as available from concerned line ministries. It also issues *Infrastructure Statistics* every year. Presently, six broad sectors—namely transport, energy, communication, drinking water supply and sanitation, irrigation, and storage—are covered under infrastructure.

(v) The Coordination and Publication Division is mainly responsible for coordinating the statistical activities of various divisions of the CSO and maintaining a liaison with central government ministries/departments, and with state governments and other statistical agencies. The division is also responsible for plan coordination of the ministry as a whole and formulation of Five Year Plans and annual plans of the ministry. Further, it looks into the preparation of the annual action plan, outcome budget, citizens'/clients' charter, and results-framework document (RFD) of the ministry. In addition, the division is responsible for carrying out research and bringing out publications. It is entrusted with the responsibility of implementing India Statistical Strengthening Project (ISSP), coordination of the Collection of Statistics Act, 2008, and coordination and follow-up of NSC's recommendations.

(2) *Computer Centre*: The Computer Centre handles the data processing jobs of the MOSPI, provides training to statistical personnel on software, and maintains the MOSPI's website and the National Data Warehouse of Official Statistics. Various types of data (in hard and soft copies) can be obtained from this office on making payments.

The central government's Allocation of Business Rules, 1961, provide for the roles and responsibilities of the MOSPI. The main statistics act under which data are collected by the MOSPI is the Collection of Statistics Act, 2008. The other most important act for collection of statistics on demographic aspects of population is the Population Census Act, 1948, which is administered by the Office of the Registrar General of India (ORGI), functioning under the Ministry of Home Affairs. Besides these two important acts, there are a number of acts, rules, and procedures that are being administered by various administrative agencies on their subjects, through which statutory returns are collected by these ministries/departments.

(3) *National Statistical Commission*: Through the GoI resolution of 1 June 2005, the government has set up a commission (the NSC) consisting of a part-time chairperson and four part-time members, one each from the fields of economic statistics, social and environment statistics, censuses and surveys, and national accounts and state statistical systems.

The secretary of the erstwhile Planning Commission is also a member in ex officio capacity. The chief statistician of India serves as the secretary to the NSC. The mandate of the NSC is to serve as a nodal and empowered body for all core statistical activities of the country; to evolve, monitor, and enforce statistical priorities and standards; and to ensure statistical coordination among the different agencies involved.

(4) *National Sample Survey Office* (*NSSO*): The NSSO, of the MOSPI, is responsible for conducting large-scale sample surveys, in diverse fields, on an all-India basis. Primary data is collected regularly through nationwide household surveys on various socio-economic subjects, *ASI* of establishments under the Collection of Statistics Act, and Enterprise Surveys, as a follow up of the economic census. The NSSO collects data on rural and urban prices and plays a significant role in the improvement of crop statistics through supervision of the area enumeration and crop estimation surveys of the state agencies. It also maintains a frame of urban area units for use in sample surveys in urban areas. It functions with requisite autonomy in matters relating to data collection, processing, and publication/dissemination of results/data based on its surveys. This is carried out under the overall guidance and supervision of NSC, which appoints working groups/technical committees comprising both official and non-official members on different subjects for finalization of survey instruments for its surveys and methodologies. The Director General and Chief Executive Officer (DG&CEO) is responsible for overall coordination and supervision of all activities of the NSSO and is assisted by three additional director generals, each one being in-charge of the divisions responsible for three distinct aspects of such large-scale surveys relating to

designing and planning, fieldwork, and data processing. For details, see Chapter 18.

Other Statistical Organizations at the Centre

Most of the other ministries at the centre have a full-fledged statistical department, a division, or a section, depending upon their needs and the stage of development of statistics in the relevant fields. Some of them, located in the administrative departments, are engaged in the processing of data, which are purely by-products of the administration. Examples of such agencies are the Income Tax Department, Central Board of Revenue, railways, post and telegraphs, and the Directorate General of Supplies and Disposals.

There are some units set up for the control of production and distribution of products in short supply. Examples of these are Office of the Textile Commissioner and Iron and Steel Controller. There are also various organizations established by the government specifically for the purpose of collecting and compiling statistical data. Some of the more important of these are briefly described in the following subsections.

Office of the Registrar General of India

Under the Indian Census Act, 1948, the ORGI was set up on a permanent basis in 1949 for organizing and conducting decennial population censuses in the country. Since 1969–70, the work of collection, compilation, publication, and improvement of vital statistics is also being done by this office. This office is entrusted with the responsibility of implementation of Registration of Births and Deaths Act, 1969 in the country. It also gives the estimates of vital statistics on the basis of a sample registration system.

Directorate General of Commercial Intelligence and Statistics

Set up in 1895, this organization was the central statistical office responsible for the collection, consolidation, and publication of important statistical series till the Second World War. With the formation of different units in different ministries during the war, many of the former functions of this office were transferred to the appropriate ministries and it was left with only the commercial intelligence and trade statistics.

Labour Bureau, Ministry of Labour and Employment

It was set up in 1946, with the functions of the collection, publication, and dissemination of labour statistics regarding employment, wages, earnings, productivity, absenteeism, labour turnover, industrial relations, and working and living conditions; evaluation of working of various labour enactments, among others; and the compilation of CPI numbers for industrial workers and agricultural and rural labour. In the recent past, it has started conducting quarterly and annual surveys on employment and unemployment.

Directorate of Economic and Statistics, Ministry of Agriculture and Farmer's Welfare

The directorate was set up in 1947 with the responsibility for compiling and publishing agricultural statistics on an all-India basis. The data cover the fields of agriculture, fisheries, livestock, and forests, collected mostly by the state governments. The main topics covered by the directorate are land utilization; estimation of production of crops; cost of cultivation studies; conduct of agricultural census; collection of retail, wholesale, and farm harvest prices; agricultural wages; and fisheries, livestock, and forestry, among others.

Central Bureau of Health Intelligence

The Central Bureau of Health Intelligence (CBHI), under the Directorate General of Health Services, is an agency involved in collection, compilation, analysis, and dissemination of information on a broad range of indicators related to health status and health services in the country. Apart from creating a credible database, it regularly brings out its annual publication, *National Health Profile*, based on the health data collected from all health directorates of states and UTs. It also has a number of other publications. A web-based application has been designed and developed covering formats regarding incidence and prevalence of disease, health risks, and performance of health systems. The data collected through this application are helping CBHI in building some of the major components of national health database/national health profile, which are of great significance to planners, policymakers, health administrators, research workers, and others engaged in raising the health and socio-economic status of the community. The system provides a wide range of state-wise/district-wise reports on morbidity patterns covering 36 types of diseases (both communicable and non-communicable).

Office of the Economic Adviser

The Office of the Economic Adviser (OEA) is an attached office in the Ministry of Commerce and Industry. It renders advice and assistance in the formulation of various policies affecting the country's industrial climate and renders advice on industrial trade, fiscal competition, and labour-related issues, and their impact on industrial performance. This office compiles and disseminates wholesale price index (WPI).

Statistical Organizations in the States

The state DESes have been set up in all the states. The main functions of these directorates are:

- coordination of statistics collected by different departments;
- publication of statistical abstracts assembling all essential serial statistics;
- organization of all enquires and surveys;
- liaison between statistical organizations of the centre and other states; and
- statistical work related to planning.

There are, however, considerable differences between the different state directorates in the areas of their responsibility for collection of statistics. In some states, the collection of statistics is almost centralized in the directorate, while in some others, the collection of agriculture, labour, and vital statistics is done by other departments. Practically all the state statistical directorates participate in the National Sample Survey (NSS) programme of socio-economic surveys. Some of the directorates also conduct enquiries on subjects of their interests and those not covered by the NSS. State statistical directorates compute state as well as district income. In most of the districts in each state, there are district statistical offices for speedy collection, compilation, and even dissemination of data. Below the districts, the data are collected by local bodies like municipal corporations and committees in urban areas, and panchayats in rural areas. Some of the states publish the aggregated data on their income and expenditure in their annual abstracts.

Besides the statistical directorates, there are other statistical units attached to various state departments which collect, compile, and publish statistics required for those departments in the states, or at the instance of their counterparts at the centre.

Other Autonomous Statistical Organizations

Indian Statistical Institute

The ISI was established in 1932. It has helped a lot in developing the Indian Statistical System. Since 1938, the institute has been holding examinations for the award of certificates and diplomas of proficiency in statistics. Until 1970, it was in charge of all technical work relating to the sample surveys conducted by the NSSO. The institute is now actively engaged in research and imparts various types of professional trainings. In December 1959, the institute was declared as an institution of national importance and was empowered to confer various degrees in statistics. It has branches in different parts of the country. It brings out a statistical journal *The Sankhya.*

Reserve Bank of India (RBI)

The RBI, set up in 1935, has a full-fledged research department which, besides processing statistics of banking activities, also maintains a division on balance of payments (BoP) statistics. The department undertakes a continuous assessment of the country's external and internal economic situation. Following are its main functions:

- monetary policy;
- regulation and supervision of the banking and non-banking financial institutions, including credit information companies;

- regulation of money, foreign exchange, and government securities markets, as also certain financial derivatives;
- management of debt and cash for central and state governments;
- management of foreign exchange reserves;
- foreign exchange management—current and capital account management;
- banker to banks;
- banker to the central and state governments;
- oversight of the payment and settlement systems;
- currency management;
- developmental role; and
- research and statistics.[1]

Institute of Agricultural Research Statistics

The institute has been engaged in research work in the field of agricultural statistics since its inception in 1931. It has introduced the method of random sampling in the official procedure for estimation of yield of crops and has evolved suitable designs for experimentation in cultivators' fields. It has developed itself into a centre for research and training in agriculture, animal husbandry, fishery, forestry and allied fields, as well as statistical genetics and computer applications. It conducts various courses for award of certificates, diplomas, and degrees in MSc and PhD in agricultural research statistics and related fields. It is responsible for developing techniques for analysis of survey data.

Besides the main statistical organizations described here, the various ministries and departments also have statistical cells. The list covering important units in various central ministries is given in MOSPI (2009).

International Statistical System

The statistical activities of the UN are carried out by the United Nations Statistics Division (UNSD), under the general guidance of the Statistical Commission (established in 1947), which is one of the functional commissions of the United Nations Economic and

[1] For further information, see the RBI website: https://www.rbi.org.in/ (last accessed on 23 March 2017).

Social Council. One of the main responsibilities of the commission is to advise the Council and the Secretary General of the UN in the development of statistical methodology.

The UNSD is the central agency for the collection, analysis, publication, standardization, and improvement of statistics serving the general purpose of the international organizations and the country governments. It functions in cooperation with the International Labour Organization (ILO); Food and Agricultural Organization of the United Nations (FAO); World Health Organization (WHO); International Monetary Fund (IMF); United Nations Educational, Scientific and Cultural Organization (UNESCO); United Nations Industrial Development Organization (UNIDO); as well as the Inter-American Statistical Institute (IASI). The Statistical Office is also assisted by a number of working groups and expert groups, which are set up by the secretary general in respective subject fields.

Some of these international organizations are briefly described next.

International Labour Organization

It is responsible for drawing up and overseeing international labour standards. It is the only 'tripartite' UN agency that brings together representatives of governments, employers, and workers to jointly shape policies and programmes promoting 'decent work for all'. This unique arrangement gives the ILO an edge in incorporating 'real-world' knowledge about employment and work. Since 1969, it has covered the official core labour statistics and estimates for over 200 countries. Further, the organization provides methodological descriptions of main national statistical sources.

Some of the major publications of the ILO are as follows:[2]

(1) *Global Employment Trends*: The annual Global Employment Trends (GET) reports provide the latest global and regional estimates of employment and unemployment, employment by sector, vulnerable employment, labour productivity, and working poverty, while also analysing country-level issues and trends

[2] For more information, see http://www.ilo.org/global/research/global-reports/global-wage-report/2012/WCMS_194843/lang--en/index.htm (last accessed on 23 March 2017).

in the labour market. The report for the year 2014–15 also gives projections for key indicators of the labour market.

(2) *Yearbook of Labour Statistics*: Since its first edition in 1935–6, the yearbook has established itself as the world's foremost work of statistical reference on labour questions. It brings together in a systematic form a mass of data from a vast network of authoritative sources in some 190 countries. Each yearly edition contains 31 tables corresponding to 9 major substantive chapters on the following: economically active population, employment, unemployment, hours of work, wages, labour cost, consumer prices, occupational injuries, and strikes and lockouts.

(3) *Bulletin of Labour Statistics*: Published quarterly, with supplements in the intervening months, the publication complements the annual data given in the *Yearbook of Labour Statistics* with monthly, quarterly, or six-monthly series for the last 4 years.

(4) *ILO October Inquiry*: This publication presents the latest results of the *ILO October Inquiry*, a worldwide survey of wages and hours of work by occupations and industry groups, and of retail prices of food items, conducted with reference to the month of October each year.

(5) *Sources and Methods in Labour Statistics*: It presents a detailed methodological information about the national sources of statistics disseminated by the Bureau of Statistics.

(6) *Wages and Equitable Growth: Global Wage Report*: It looks at differences in wages in countries around the globe and how they have been influenced by the economic crisis. It includes global and regional wage trends and statistics, as well as policy recommendations. The report for the year 2014–15 reviews the major trends in wages in developed, emerging, and developing countries. It also analyses inequality in the labour market and in household income. Further, it presents the evaluation of real wages around the world and relative purchasing power globally and by regions.

Food and Agriculture Organization of the United Nations

The FAO leads international efforts to defeat hunger. Serving both developed and developing countries, the FAO acts as a neutral forum where all nations meet as equals to negotiate agreements and debate policy formation and implementation. The FAO is also a source of knowledge and information. It helps developing countries and countries in transition to modernize and improve agriculture, forestry, and fisheries practices, and ensures good nutrition for all. Since its founding in 1945, it has focused special attention on developing rural areas, home to 70 per cent of the world's poor and hungry people.

Its publications are as follows.

(1) *The State of Food and Agriculture*: This is FAO's annual flagship publication. It aims at bringing to a wider audience the balanced science-based assessments of important issues. Each edition of the report contains a comprehensive, yet easily accessible, overview of a selected topic of major relevance for rural and agricultural development and for global food security.
(2) *The State of World Fisheries and Aquaculture*: This publication gives details about the status of fishing fleets, resources, production, utilization and processing, trade, and consumption, among others, and the issues involved with respect to these variables.
(3) *The State of Food Insecurity in the World*: This publication raises awareness about global hunger issues, discusses underlying causes of hunger and malnutrition, and monitors progress towards hunger-reduction targets established at the 1996 World Food Summit and the Millennium Summit. The publication is targeted at a wide audience, including policymakers, international organizations, academic institutions, and the general public with a general interest in linkages between food security and human and economic development.
(4) *FAO Statistical Yearbook: World Food and Agriculture*: It presents a visual synthesis of the major trends and factors shaping the global food and agricultural landscape and their interplay with broader environmental, social, and economic dimensions. It aims to be a unique reference point on the state of world food and agriculture for policymakers, donor agencies, researchers, analysts, as well as the general public. The four thematic parts of the yearbook are as follows:[3]
    - The state of the agricultural resource base: The setting measures the state of the agricultural resource base by assessing

[3] For more information, see http://www.fao.org/economic/ess/ess-publications/ess-yearbook/en/#.UlJhNdLI33 (last accessed on 23 March 2017).

the supply of land, labour, capital and inputs, and examining the pressure on the world food system stemming from demographic and macroeconomic change.

- Food insecurity and malnutrition: Hunger dimensions gauges the state of food insecurity and malnutrition, measuring the multitude of dimensions that give rise to hunger and shape undernourishment.
- Feeding the world: It evaluates the past and present productive capacity of world agriculture, together with the role of trade in meeting changing food, feed, and other demands.
- Sustainability of agriculture and the environment: Sustainability dimensions examines the sustainability of agriculture in the context of the pressure it exerts on the environment, including the interaction of agriculture with climate change, and how it can provide ecosystem services through the bio-based economy.

(5) *FAO Yearbook of Forest Products*: This is a compilation of statistical data on basic forest products for all countries and territories of the world. It contains a series of annual data on the volume of production and the volume and value of trade in forest products. It includes tables showing direction of trade and average unit values of trade for certain products. Statistical information in the yearbook is based primarily on data provided by the countries to the FAO Forestry Department through questionnaires or official publications. In the absence of official data, FAO makes an estimate based on the best information available.[4]

(6) *FAO Yearbook: Fishery and Aquaculture Statistics*: The yearbook contains global statistics on capture fishery/productivity by groups of species as well as by principal species, aquaculture production, commodities, and apparent fish consumption derived from food balance sheets as well as statistics on fleets and employment of major fish-producing countries.

(7) *Regional Yearbooks*: The regional statistical yearbooks provide statistics and indicators for a wide range of themes: agricultural

[4] For more information, see http://www.fao.org/forestry/statistics/80570/en/ (last accessed on 23 March 2017).

production; productivity and growth; investment; rural population and well-being; poverty; rural employment; gender; food security; food safety and nutrition; natural resource use in agricultural activities (for example, land, water, and forest); climate change; environmental pollution; and biodiversity. For example:

- *FAO Statistical Yearbook 2012: Africa Food and Agriculture*: This regional yearbook provides statistics and reliable indicators on food and agriculture that can be used for policy formulation, monitoring, and evaluation in the region.
- *FAO Statistical Yearbook 2012: Europe and Central Asia Food and Agriculture*: This first edition for Europe and Central Asia provides a set of statistics on food and agriculture related to the current themes and domains of interest in the region.[5]

World Health Organization

The WHO is the directing and coordinating authority for health within the UN system. It is responsible for providing leadership on global health matters, shaping the health research agenda, setting norms and standards, articulating evidence-based policy options, providing technical support to countries, and monitoring and assessing health trends.

In the twenty-first century, health is a shared responsibility, involving equitable access to essential care and collective defence against transnational threats.

The key WHO publications are as follows:

(1) *World Health Report*: First published in 1995, the report is WHO's leading publication. It combines an expert assessment of global health, including statistics, relating to all countries, with a focus on a specific subject. The main purpose of the report is to provide countries, donor agencies, international organizations, and others with the information they need to help them make policy and funding decisions. The report is also offered to a wider audience, from universities, teaching hospitals, and schools to

[5] For more information on regional statistical yearbooks, see http://www.fao.org/economic/ess/ess-publications/ess-yearbook/en/#.UlJhNdLI33E (last accessed on 23 March 2017).

journalists and the public at large—anyone, in fact, with a professional or personal interest in international health issues.

(2) *World Health Statistics*: The WHO's annual *World Health Statistics* reports present the most recent health statistics data for the 194 WHO member states. It may also include a summary of the progress made towards achieving health-related MDGs and associated targets. Also, it may include summaries on the topics of reducing the gaps between the world's most advantaged and least advantaged countries, and on current trends in official development assistance (ODA) for health.

(3) *Global and Regional Estimates of Violence against Women*: The report presents the first global systematic review of scientific data on the prevalence of two forms of violence against women: violence by an intimate partner (intimate partner violence); and sexual violence by someone other than a partner (non-partner sexual violence). It shows, for the first time, global and regional estimates of the prevalence of these two forms of violence, using data from around the world. Previous reporting on violence against women has not differentiated between partner and non-partner violence.

International Monetary Fund

The IMF is an organization of 188 countries, working to foster global monetary cooperation, secure financial stability, facilitate international trade, promote high employment and sustainable economic growth, and reduce poverty around the world. The IMF is responsible for doing the job for the BoP and banking statistics. The *Balance of Payments Statistics Yearbook* includes annual aggregate and detailed time series for BoP and international investment position for countries; provides world and regional tables of BoP components and aggregates; and descriptions of methodologies, compilation practices, and data sources used by individual countries.

It publishes a range of time series data on IMF lending, exchange rates, and other economic and financial indicators. Manuals, guides, and other material on statistical practices at the IMF, in member countries, and of the statistical community at large are also available.

Other key publications include the following:

(1) *International Financial Statistics*: The *International Financial Statistics* (*IFS*) is a standard source of statistics on all aspects of international and domestic finance. It publishes, for most countries of the world, current data on exchange rates, international liquidity, international banking, money and banking, interest rates, prices, production, international transactions (including BoP and international investment position), government finance, and national accounts.[6]

(2) *Government Finance Statistics*: It contains data on revenue, expenditure, and transactions in assets and liabilities for the state sector and sub-sectors, for 137 countries from 1990 to 2012. The related Historical Government Finance Statistics database covers the period from 1972 to 1989.[7]

(3) *World Economic Outlook* (WEO) Reports: A survey by the IMF staff, the *World Economic Outlook* (WEO) report is usually published twice a year. It presents IMF staff economists' analyses of global economic developments during the near and medium term. The chapters give an overview as well as a more detailed analysis of the world economy; consider issues affecting industrial countries, developing countries, and economies in transition to market; and address topics of pressing current interest. Annexes, boxes, charts, and an extensive statistical appendix supplement the text.[8]

(4) *Regional Economic Outlook* Reports: These reports discuss the recent economic developments and prospects for countries in various regions. They also address economic policy developments that have affected economic performance in the regions, and discuss the key challenges faced by policymakers. They address regional policy developments and challenges and provide

[6] For more information, see IMF (2013).

[7] For more information, see http://www.eui.eu/Research/Library/ResearchGuides/Economics/Statistics/DataPortal/IMFdata.aspx (last accessed on 23 March 2017).

[8] For more information, also see the WEO databases at http://www.imf.org/external/ns/cs.aspx?id=29 (last accessed on 23 March 2017).

country-specific data and analysis, including through analytical pieces on issues of interest to a particular region.[9]

(5) *World Economic Outlook* Databases: The WEO database are created during the biannual WEO exercise, which begins in January and June every year and presents its results in the April and September WEO publications. Selected series from the publications are available in a database format.

United Nations Educational, Scientific and Cultural Organization

The UNESCO works to create the conditions for dialogue among civilizations, cultures, and people, based upon respect for commonly shared values. It is through this dialogue that the world can achieve global visions of sustainable development encompassing observance of human rights, mutual respect, and the alleviation of poverty, all of which are at the heart of UNESCO's mission and activities. The UNESCO Institute for Statistics (UIS) gives the details of region-wise and country-wise statistics on: (i) education; (ii) science, technology, and innovation; (iii) culture; and (iv) communication and information. These statistics are available at the data centre of the organization. The UIS publishes a broad range of publications, including analytical reports, technical papers, and statistical frameworks. The aim is to disseminate timely and internationally comparable data relevant to evidence-based policymaking at the national, regional, and international levels.

The majority of publications focus on education issues, reflecting the breadth of related statistics and indicators in the database. There is also a growing number of titles featuring data and analysis in the fields of science and technology, culture, as well as communication. In addition, the institute regularly contributes data to publications produced by other UN organizations. A selection of these titles is available in the institute's online document library.

[9] See http://www.imf.org/external/pubs/ft/reo/reorepts.aspx (last accessed on 23 March 2017).

Following are some of the publications.

(1) *Education at a Glance 2014: OECD Indicators*: This report is an authoritative source on the state of education around the world. It provides data on the structure, finances, and performance of education systems in the Organisation for Economic Co-operation and Development's (OECD's) 34 member countries and partner countries.
(2) *The State of the World's Children 2014 in Numbers*: The 2014 edition focuses on the theme 'Every Child Counts: Revealing Disparities, Advancing Children's Rights'. It features UIS data on literacy and education with a specific focus on gender-related indicators.

United Nations Industrial Development Organization

The UNIDO, in collaboration with the OECD, assumes responsibility for the collection and dissemination of worldwide general industrial statistics, effective 1994.

The UNIDO has a number of publications, two of which are as follows.

(1) *International Yearbook of Industrial Statistics*: The 2015 yearbook pertains to the manufacturing sector only and is the 21st issue of UNIDO's annual publication, the *International Yearbook of Industrial Statistics*. The yearbook succeeded the *Handbook of Industrial Statistics*, which was published biennially by UNIDO up to 1992. At the same time, it replaced the UN's *Industrial Statistics Yearbook, Volume I* (General Industrial Statistics), which was discontinued after its 1991 edition was published in 1993. These changes were in accordance with the recommendations of the United Nations Statistical Commission (UNSC) at its 27th session.
(2) *World Statistics on Mining and Utilities*: UNIDO has also released a separate biennial publication, *World Statistics on Mining and Utilities*. The first publication was brought out in 2010.

In addition, UNIDO maintains a variety of databases comprising statistics of overall industrial growth, detailed data on business structure, and statistics on major indicators of industrial performance by country in the historical time series. The databases are updated regularly with the most recent data. Release of the new edition of the databases is announced every year in May. Data are available online on their UNIDO Statistics Data Portal and on CD-ROM.

The UNIDO industrial statistics database, at the four-digit level of International Standard Industrial Classification of All Economic Activities (ISIC) (INDSTAT4), contains highly disaggregated data on the manufacturing sector for the period 1990 onwards. Comparability of data over time and across the countries has been the main priority of developing and updating this database. INDSTAT4 offers a unique possibility of in-depth analysis of the structural transformation of economies over time. The database contains seven principle indicators of industrial statistics. The data are arranged at the three- and four-digit level of the ISIC Revision 3 and 4 pertaining to manufacturing, comprising more than 150 manufacturing sectors and sub-sectors.

The MINSTAT is a new and unique database on mining and quarrying and utilities sectors. In the past decades, a gradual depletion of natural resources worldwide has been observed. At the same time, demand for such resources as crude oil, natural gas, and water is soaring due to rapid industrial growth and the overall increase of the world population. In response to the increased interest from data users, UNIDO released its first biennial publication of the *World Statistics on Mining and Utilities* in 2010. Now users can obtain mining and utilities data in electronic form through online access to this website or by ordering the database on a CD-ROM. It contains time series data for more than 100 countries for the period 1995 onwards. Data are presented at two- and three-digit levels of ISIC Revision 3 and 4.

Inter-American Statistical Institute

The IASI is a professional organization whose purpose is to promote statistical development in the American region. The IASI is an affiliated member of the International Statistical Institute and has consultative status with the United Nations Economic and Social Council as a non-governmental organization.

United Nations Statistics Division

One of the chief functions of the UNSD is the collection and compilation of data obtained from member countries on a periodic as well as ad hoc basis. The data are obtained from official governmental agencies and cover the most significant economic and social subjects. The UNSD does not change or modify the basic data supplied by different governmental agencies. Some data are obtained from member countries by specialized agencies and are then supplied to the UNSD. The Statistics Division prepares general statistical compilations in special fields, including demographic and population statistics, international merchandise trade, national accounts, industrial commodities production, energy, environment, social statistics and indicators, gender statistics, and human settlements. The other functions of this division are:

- standardization of statistical methods, classifications, and definitions;
- technical cooperation programmes; and
- coordination of international statistical programmes and activities.

In addition, it facilitates the monitoring of progress towards the MDGs by leading the Inter-agency and Expert Group on MDG Indicators and maintains the global MDG indicator database. The UNSD supports the functioning of the UNSC. The UNSC is the highest body of the global statistical system. It brings together chief statisticians from member countries from around the world. It is the highest decision-making body for international statistical activities, especially the setting of statistical standards, the development of concepts and methods, and their implementation at the national and international level. It gets support for this purpose from UNSD.

The UNSD has a large number of publications.[10] Following are some of the important periodicals and ad hoc publications:

(1) *Monthly Bulletin of Statistics*: It presents the current economic and social statistics for more than 200 countries and territories of the world. It contains 55 tables, comprising over 100 indicators of monthly, quarterly, and annual data on a variety of

[10] See http://unstats.un.org/unsd/pubs/gesgrid.asp?sort=title (last accessed on 23 March 2017).

subjects, illustrating important economic trends and developments, including population, industrial production indices, price indices, employment and earnings, energy, manufacturing, transport, construction, international merchandise trade, finance, and national accounts.

(2) *Statistical Yearbook*: It is an annual compilation of a wide range of international economic, social, and environmental statistics of over 200 countries and areas, compiled from sources including UN agencies and other international, national, and specialized organizations. The 53rd issue contains data available to the Statistics Division as of 31 October 2009 and presents them in over 70 tables on topics such as agriculture, forestry, and fishing; BoP; communication; development assistance; education; energy; environment; finance; gender; industrial production; international merchandise trade; international tourism; labour force; manufacturing; national accounts; population; science and technology; transport; and wages and prices. The number of years of data shown in the tables varies from 1 to 10, with most tables covering 1996 to 2008. Accompanying the tables are technical notes providing brief descriptions of major statistical concepts, definitions, and classifications.

(3) *Demographic Yearbook*: The UN *Demographic Yearbook* collects, compiles, and disseminates official statistics on a wide range of topics. Data have been collected from national statistical authorities since 1948 through a set of questionnaires dispatched annually by the UNSD to over 230 national statistical offices.

The yearbook disseminates statistics on population size and composition, births, deaths, marriage, and divorce on an annual basis. Special issues of *Demographic Yearbook* cover a wide range of additional topics, including economic activity, educational attainment, household characteristics, housing, ethnicity, and language.

(4) *World Statistics Pocketbook*: The *World Statistics Pocketbook 2009* is the 29th in a series of annual compilations of key statistical indicators prepared by the UNSD of the Department of Economic and Social Affairs. Over 50 indicators have been collected from more than 20 international statistical sources and are presented in one-page profiles for 216 countries or areas of

the world. This issue covers various years from 2000 to 2010. For the economic indicators, in general, three years—2000, 2005, and 2008—are shown; and for the indicators in the social and environmental categories, data for one year are presented.

The topics covered include agriculture, BoP, education, energy, environment, food, gender, health, industrial production, information and communication, international finance, international tourism, international trade, labour, migration, national accounts, population, and prices. The technical notes contain brief descriptions of the concepts and methodologies used in the compilation of the indicators as well as information on the statistical sources for the indicators. Reference to primary sources of the data is provided for readers interested in longer time series data or more detailed descriptions of the concepts and methodologies.

(5) *Population and Vital Statistics Report*: This is a quarterly journal, released in English, and gives the estimates of world and regional populations as well as estimates for 218 countries. This publication updates population and vital statistics for each country of the world on a quarterly basis, and population aggregates for the world and each continent, annually. Included in each country are (i) results of the latest population census; (ii) latest official estimate of population irrespective of date; (iii) a midyear population estimate for a fixed (recent) year; and (iv) the latest birth, death, and infant mortality statistics. The reference data of the fixed-year population estimate for each country, as well as aggregate estimate for the world and each continent, are updated in the July issue.

(6) *National Accounts Statistics*: The first volume, *Main Aggregates and Detailed Tables*, contains a complete and consistent set of time series 1970 onwards, of main national accounts aggregates for more than 200 countries and areas in the world. It is maintained and updated on the basis of annual collections of the official annual national accounts statistics, supplemented by UNSD estimates of national accounts statistics for those years and countries for which the official statistics is incomplete or inconsistent. The national data for each country and area are presented in separate chapters using uniform table headings and classifications recommended in the UN

System of National Accounts 1993 (1993 SNA). Data collection is based on the UN National Accounts Questionnaire (NAQ) and contains the following sequence of tables. A summary of the conceptual framework of the 1993 SNA and definitions of important terms are also included.

- GDP by expenditures at current prices as well as at constant prices.
- Relations among product, income, savings, and net lending aggregates at current prices.
- Value added by industries at current prices as well as at constant prices (ISIC Revision 3 and 4).
- Output, GVA, and fixed assets by industries at current prices as well as at constant prices (ISIC Revision 3 and 4).
- Government final consumption expenditure by function at current prices.
- Individual consumption expenditure of households, non-profit institutions serving households (NPISHs), and general government at current prices.
- Total economy (S.1) at current prices.
- Rest of the world (S.2) at current prices.
- Non-financial corporations (S.11) at current prices.
- Financial corporations (S.12) at current prices.
- General government (S.13) at current prices.
- Households (S.14) at current prices.
- NPISHs (S.15) at current prices.
- Combined sectors: Non-financial and financial corporations (S.11 + S.12) at current prices.
- Combined sectors: Households and NPISH (S.14 + S.15) at current prices.
- Cross classification of GVA by industries and institutional sectors at current prices (ISIC Revision 3 and 4).[11]

Volume II of *National Accounts Statistics, Analysis of Main Aggregates*, in addition to the values of national accounts statistics,

[11] For more information, see http://unstats.un.org/unsd/nationalaccount/madt.asp#ts (last accessed on 24 March 2017).

contains analytical indicators and ratios derived from the main national accounts aggregates related to economic structure and development.[12]

In addition, an ad hoc publication is on SNA. The volumes are available on the website for the year 1993 and 2008. SNA 2008 contains the following details:

The 2008 SNA is the latest version of the international statistical standard for the national accounts, adopted by the UNSC. It is an update of the 1993 SNA. The update was entrusted to the Intersecretariat Working Group on National Accounts (ISWGNA) in 2003 to address issues brought about by changes in the economic environment, advances in methodological research, and the needs of users.

The first 17 chapters of the 2008 SNA, comprising the accounting rules, the accounts and tables, and their integration, were adopted by the UNSC in 2008; chapters 18–29, comprising the interpretations and extensions of the accounts and tables of the system, were adopted by the UNSC in 2009.

The 2008 SNA is the result of a process that was notable for its transparency and wide involvement of the international statistical community, both of which were made possible by the innovative use of the project's website 'Towards 2008, SNA' as a communication tool. In its adoption of the 2008 SNA, the UNSC encouraged member states and regional and subregional organizations to implement its recommendations and use it for national and international reporting of national accounts statistics.

Being a conceptual framework, the 2008 SNA does not attempt to provide comprehensive compilation guidance on how to make estimates; nor is it descriptive in setting priorities which accounts and tables should be implemented or expresses norms on the frequency and format of their presentation. For practical compilation guidance, international agencies have developed separate handbooks such as the *Handbook of National Accounting* prepared by the UNSD.

[12] For more information, see http://unstats.un.org/unsd/nationalaccount/ama.asp (last accessed on 23 March 2017).

A number of research issues emerged during the update of the 1993 SNA. However, they needed more extensive consideration than was possible in the course of the update process. These issues are listed in Annex 4 of the 2008 SNA. More information on these and emerging research issues and recommendations on the outcome of the research can be found under the 'Research' agenda.

(7) *International Trade Statistics Yearbook*: The yearbook is being issued in two volumes, which have been prepared at different points in time: *Volume I: Trade by Country* has been compiled to allow for an advanced release of an overview of international merchandise trade; and *Volume II: Trade by Commodity* contains detailed tables showing international trade for individual commodities (three-digit Standard International Trade Classification [SITC] groups) and 11 world trade tables covering trade values and indices with data.

(8) *Energy Statistics Yearbook*: The yearbook is a comprehensive collection of international energy statistics prepared annually by the UNSD. The 2010 edition is 54th in a series of annual compilations that commenced under the title, *World Energy Supplies in Selected Years, 1929–1950.*

(9) *Industrial Commodity Statistics Yearbook*: The 47th issue of the *Industrial Commodity Statistics Yearbook* annual compilation relates to the year 2012 and provides statistics on the production of about 600 industrial commodities for approximately 200 countries or areas for the years 2003–12. The present yearbook contains data in physical quantities, as well as in monetary value of production. Therefore, it is organized in two volumes, namely, *Volume I: Physical Quantity Data* and *Volume II: Monetary Value Data*. The selection of industrial commodities is based on their importance in world production and trade.

In addition to the aforementioned periodicals, special reports on various subjects appear from time to time, such as the survey of social statistics, world weights and measures, and retail price comparisons for international salary determination. Reports on sample surveys of current interest are issued from time to time to draw attention to sampling methods and techniques which are being used in various countries. The UNSD also publishes methodological studies, guides, and manuals. These studies and manuals give the methods and concepts to be used for different types of collection, compilation, and analysis of data. For example, the *National Accounts Statistics: Analysis of Main Aggregates 2008* is the 39th issue of this publication presenting a series of analytical national accounts tables for more than 200 countries and areas in the world. Some of the specialized agencies are also responsible for the development of statistics in their own special fields. The ILO is responsible for the collection and publication of labour statistics, for example, *Yearbook of Labour Statistics: Time Series, 2010*. Similarly, the FAO is responsible for the collection and publication of statistics on food and agriculture. The IMF is responsible for doing the job for the BoP and banking statistics. These specialized agencies have their regular publications.

Other World Agencies

Organisation for Economic Co-Operation and Development

The OECD provides a forum in which governments can work together to share experiences and seek solutions to common problems. It works with governments to understand what drives economic, social, and environmental change. It measures productivity and global flows of trade and investment. It analyses and compares data to predict future trends. It sets international standards on a wide range of things, from agriculture and tax to the safety of chemicals.

It also looks at issues that directly affect everyone's daily life, like how much people pay in taxes and social security, and how much leisure time they can take. It compares how different countries' school systems are readying their young people for modern life and how different countries' pension systems look after their citizens in old age.

Its key publications are as follows:

(1) *OECD Factbook*: The OECD's dynamic and comprehensive statistical annual shows a wide range of key statistics for its member countries and major additional countries. For each indicator presented, there is explanatory text including a definition, explanation of long-term trends, and bibliography; a table showing the indicator over a significant time span for all countries covered; and graphics showing the key messages contained in the data.

Under each table is a link to an excel spreadsheet, enabling the user to access the data. This publication is available in print form, as an iPhone application, and in Hypertext Markup Language (HTML) form.

Topics covered include population and migration; production and productivity; household income, wealth, and debt; globalization, trade, and foreign direct investment (FDI); prices, interest rates, and exchange rates; energy and transportation; labour, employment, and unemployment; science and technology, including research and development (R&D) and the information and communications technology (ICT) sector; environment, including natural resources, water, and air and climate; education resources and outcomes; government expenditures, debt, revenues, taxes, agricultural support, and foreign aid; and health status, risk, and resources.

(2) *At a Glance* Publications: These publications encompass a range of topics like environment, health, education, and national accounts.

(3) *OECD Outlooks*: One of its main publications is the *OECD Economic Outlook* which analyses the current economic situation and examines the economic policies required to foster a sustained recovery in member countries. Forecasts generally cover the next 18–24 months for both OECD countries and selected non-OECD economies. It is a unique tool to keep abreast of world economic developments.

Other *Outlook* publications cover a range of topics from agriculture, pensions, migration, communication, and energy to a host of countries.

(4) *Economic Surveys*: They provide information on different economic indicators of various countries.

Asian Development Bank (ADB)

The ADB aims for a poverty-free Asia and Pacific. Since its founding in 1966, ADB has been working to improve people's lives in Asia and the Pacific. Whether it is through investment in infrastructure, health care services, financial and public administration systems, or helping nations prepare for the impact of climate change or better manage their natural resources, ADB has been instrumental in helping its developing member countries evolve into thriving, modern economies that are well integrated with each other and the world. The main devices for assistance are loans, grants, policy dialogue, technical assistance, and equity investments.

Economic research and statistical work contributes to knowledge generation in ADB and helps strengthen its institutional priorities and effectiveness of country operations. By augmenting the stock of knowledge of developing member countries and the region and disseminating it, ADB's capability to provide informed policy advice and undertake capacity building is enhanced.

Its focus areas are: (i) agriculture and food security; (ii) education; (iii) energy; (iv) environment and climate change; (v) finance sector development; (vi) gender and development; (vii) governance and public management; (viii) health; (ix) ICT; (x) regional cooperation and integration; (xi) social development and poverty; (xii) transport; (xiii) urban development; and (xiv) water.

Some of its main publications are as follows:

(1) *Asian Economic Integration Monitor*: This is a semi-annual review of Asia's regional economic cooperation and integration. It covers 48 regional members of the ADB.
(2) *Asian Development Outlook*: The annual *Asian Development Outlook* provides a comprehensive analysis of economic performance in the past year and offers forecasts for the next two years for the 45 economies in Asia and the Pacific that make up developing Asia.
(3) *Technologies to Support Climate Change Adaptation in Developing Asia*: This publication showcases technologies that can be used to address impacts of climate change in Asia and the Pacific across six sectors: agriculture; coastal resources; human health; transportation; water resources; and disaster risk management.
(4) *Asia Bond Monitor*: The *Asia Bond Monitor* reviews recent developments in East Asian local currency bond markets, along with the outlook, risks, and policy options. This includes a special section on the *AsianBondsOnline* Bond Market Liquidity Survey.
(5) *Basic Statistics*: It is an annual publication providing updated data for 45 member economies of the ADB for indicators on MDGs and other key social and economic indicators, including land, population, national accounts, prices, money, BoP, reserves, external debt, and central government finance.

The World Bank[13]

Established in 1944, the World Bank Group is headquartered in Washington, DC. It has set two goals for the world to achieve by 2030:

- End extreme poverty by decreasing the percentage of people living on less than US$ 1.25 a day to no more than 3 per cent.
- Promote shared prosperity by fostering the income growth of the bottom 40 per cent for every country.

The World Bank is a vital source of financial and technical assistance to developing countries around the world. It is not a bank in the ordinary sense but a unique partnership to reduce poverty and support development. The World Bank Group comprises five institutions managed by their member countries.

The Bank provides low-interest loans, zero to low-interest credits, and grants to developing countries. It supports a wide array of investments in areas such as education, health, public administration, infrastructure, financial and private sector development, agriculture, and environmental and natural resource management. Some of the projects are co-financed with governments, other multilateral institutions, commercial banks, export credit agencies, and private sector investors.

The bank also provides or facilitates financing through trust fund partnerships with bilateral and multilateral donors. Many partners have asked the bank to help manage initiatives that address needs across a wide range of sectors and developing regions.

Publications by World Bank

There are about 200 publications that the World Bank comes out with, the particulars of which are given in the data catalogue on its website.[14] Among these, 122 are annual, six are quarterly, and five are monthly.

The topics covered include agriculture and rural development, aid effectiveness, climate change, economy and growth, education,

[13] Available at http://www.worldbank.org/.

[14] Available at http://datacatalog.worldbank.org/.

energy and mining, environment, external debt, financial sector, gender, health, infrastructure, poverty, private sector, public sector, science and technology, social development, social protection and labour, trade, and urban development.

The following are some of the important publications:

- World Development Indicators
- Millennium Development Goals
- Quarterly External Debt Statistics SDDS (New)
- Global Financial Development
- GDP ranking
- GDP ranking, purchasing power parity (PPP) based
- Gross national income (GNI) ranking, Atlas method
- GNI Per Capita Ranking, Atlas Method, and PPP Based
- International Debt Statistics
- World Development Report
- Poverty and Equity Data

Appendix 1A: Statistical Systems in Selected Foreign Countries

United States (US)

The statistical system is a decentralized one, with many government agencies concerned with the collection, compilation, and publication of data at the national level. These statistical agencies are located in different government departments. This structure basically keeps statistical work within close proximity to the various cabinet-level departments that use the information.

The US Office of Management and Budget (OMB) coordinates the federal statistical system. The OMB establishes and enforces statistical policies and standards. It ensures that resources are proposed for priority statistical programmes, and also approves statistical surveys conducted by the federal government under the Paperwork Reduction Act. Besides this, OMB—previously the Bureau of the Budget—acts as a coordinating agency to prevent duplication, adopt standards, and to develop procedures for an integrated system of statistics. This office has control over the data collection activities of various agencies. No statistics can be collected without examination and approval of OMB. This examination is done to prevent unnecessary duplication, reduce costs, and to improve the quality of general usefulness of statistics collected. This office is responsible for supplying data to international organizations and for preparing the consolidated budget of major statistical activities. There are three main types of statistical agencies:

(1) Agencies collecting data as a by-product of administrative work, such as Social Security Administration, International Revenue Services, Federal Communication Commission, Federal Power Commission, and Comptroller of the Currency.
(2) Agencies primarily responsible for the collection, compilation, and publication of statistics, such as Census Bureau, Bureau of Labor Statistics, National Office of Vital Statistics, and Bureau of Mines.
(3) Agencies responsible for analysing and interpreting the data collected by others, such as Council of Economic Advisers, Office of Business Economics, Board of Governors of the Federal Reserve System, and the Bureau of Foreign Commerce.

The states are independent in determining and carrying out their statistical programmes, although they may cooperate on certain data like vital statistics. The development of state and municipal statistics has been uneven in different states. Some states are quite advanced as far as the collection of statistics is concerned, while some others are far behind.

There are 13 principal statistical agencies, namely, Bureau of Labor Statistics, Census Bureau, Bureau of Economic Analysis, Energy Information Administration, Economic Research Service, National Agricultural Statistics Service, Bureau of Transportation Statistics, Bureau of Justice Statistics, National Center for Education Statistics, National Center for Health Statistics, Statistics of Income Division (Internal Revenue Service), National Center for Science and Engineering Statistics (National Science Foundation), and Office of Research, Evaluation, and Statistics (Social Security Administration). These agencies have statistical activities as their core mission and conduct much of the government's statistical work. For various purposes, like to streamline operations and reduce costs, several proposals have been made to consolidate the federal statistical system into fewer agencies, or even a single agency. In 2011, under the guidance of President Barack Obama, the US Department of Commerce reorganized several statistical agencies and placed them under one umbrella.[15]

United Kingdom (UK)

The UK Statistics Authority's responsibilities cover the whole of the UK statistical system, defined as all the organizations and persons responsible for producing official statistics in the UK. It was established on 1 April 2008 by the Statistics and Registration Service Act, 2007.

The key components of the UK system are as follows.

The UK Statistics Authority is responsible for promoting and safeguarding the production and publication of all UK official statistics, wherever produced, to ensure they serve the public good. The Office for National Statistics (ONS) was created in 1996. The ONS is the executive office of the UK Statistics Authority's, the largest producer of official statistics in the UK, and the UK's recognized national statistical institute (NSI).

Each UK government department and each of the devolved administrations retain operational responsibility for the collection and production of statistics which relate to their own areas of responsibility. The National Statistician is the Chief Executive of the UK Statistics Authority and the Head of the Government Statistical Service (GSS). The GSS consists of all the statistical staff working in the ONS, government departments, and the devolved administrations in Scotland and Wales. The GSS produces the vast majority of official statistics and the GSS staff is professionally accountable to the National Statistician through their own Departmental Head of Profession for Statistics, or in the case of the devolved administrations in Scotland and Wales, through their own chief statistician. Statistical staff in Northern Ireland maintains a close professional relationship with the GSS but are not members of the GSS. Many of

[15] Available at http://en.wikipedia.org/wiki/Federal_Statistical_System_of_the_United_States (accessed on 26 May 2017).

the official statistics produced by the GSS are designated as 'National Statistics'. Accreditation as National Statistics means that those statistics are deemed compliant with the *Code of Practice for Official Statistics*, published by the authority in January 2009.

The UK statistical system has five essential features that distinguish it from many others around the world.

(1) *Centralization*: The UK system has elements of both centralization and decentralization. The ONS is at the centre of the system as it is UK's largest statistical producer.

The GSS is an umbrella body. It binds together most of the distinct government organizations and employees in the UK who are responsible for producing official statistics. This community is managed by a network of Heads of Profession for Statistics in each department, who are professionally accountable to the National Statistician as the Head of the GSS. The ONS sets statistical policy and professional standards for the GSS, coordinates statistical production across the UK system, and itself produces many of the UK's key economic and social statistics.

(2) *Decentralization*: The UK system is also highly decentralized. More than 80 per cent of all professional statisticians in the GSS work beyond the ONS, often alongside policy colleagues, in the 38 government departments affiliated to the GSS. Further, about four-fifths of all official statistics that have been designated as 'National Statistics' are produced by statisticians working beyond ONS in government departments.

(3) *Devolution*: As per the devolution settlement, responsibility for the production of statistics relating to Scotland and Wales has passed to the respective devolved administration—but only for areas for which they have devolved policy responsibility. This requires additional governance mechanisms to ensure an appropriate balance between the delivery of coherent and comparable statistics across the UK, while simultaneously ensuring the availability of statistics which reflect local circumstances and meet local needs. The arrangements for ensuring coherence between statistics produced by the UK government and statistics produced by the three devolved administrations are set out in the 'Statistics Concordat', which was agreed between the UK government and the devolved administrations in 2001.

(4) *Globalization*: The UK joined the European Union (EU) in 1973 and, like other European NSIs, has been a major partner in the European Statistical System (ESS). As Britain is a leading member of the Commonwealth, the GSS is also a major player in the international statistical arena beyond Europe. The long-standing provision of technical assistance to the statistical offices of developing countries, and more recently to the EU's new member states, forms a major part in the work of the Department for International Development's statistical division.

(5) *Framework for National Statistics*: The *Framework for National Statistics*, published in June 2000, introduced the quality mark 'National Statistics'. The aim of the framework was to enhance public trust and confidence in official statistics by making the UK statistical system more independent. It launched a number of major innovations which, in one form or another, have largely been retained following the coming into force of the Statistics and Registration Service Act, 2007. These included the post of National Statistician and the adoption of a code of practice.[16]

Canada

In Canada, the statistical system is highly centralized. Before 1971, the Bureau of Statistics kept direct control of all the statistics except those which are available as by-products of departmental administration; however, post-1971, Statistics Canada replaced this organization.

Statistics Canada is required to 'collect, compile, analyse, abstract and publish statistical information relating to the commercial, industrial, financial, social, economic and general activities and conditions of the people of Canada', according to the Statistics Act of Canada. The two main objectives of Statistics Canada are:

- to provide statistical information and analysis about Canada's economic and social structure; and
- to promote sound statistical standards and practices.

[16] Available at http://statisticsauthority.gov.uk/about-the-authority/uk-statistical-system/index.html; http://statisticsauthority.gov.uk/about-the-authority/index.html (accessed on 26 May 2017).

At present, Statistics Canada conducts more than 380 surveys, covering 32 different subjects, as well as censuses of population and agriculture (every five years). The main topics covered are education, health and welfare, industry and international trade, labour and prices, transportation, national accounts and analytical studies, business and trade, and households surveys.[17]

Japan

The Statistics Bureau, the Director-General for Policy Planning of Japan, and the Statistical Research and Training Institute of the Ministry of Internal Affairs and Communications of the Government of Japan have been central to the official statistical system. They are responsible for the coordination of official statistical activities and the production and compilation of fundamental official statistics (including the population census). The statistical system of the Japanese government is decentralized, that is, while the Statistics Bureau conducts fundamental censuses and statistical surveys, other relevant ministries produce statistics for their own policy purposes. Under this decentralized system, it is generally difficult to maintain consistency in statistical activities among different ministries and to avoid duplication in the compilation of statistics. Therefore, the Director-General for Policy Planning is responsible for coordinating the statistical activities of different ministries.

The Statistics Bureau is responsible for fundamental censuses and statistical surveys. The main statistics produced by the Statistics Bureau are on population census, current population estimates, internal migration statistics, housing and land survey, labour force survey, employment status survey, economic census for business frame, economic census for business activity, unincorporated enterprise survey, survey of R&D, monthly survey on service industries, establishment and enterprise census (1947–2006), survey on service industries (1989–2004),[18] family income and expenditure survey,

[17] Available at http://www.statcan.gc.ca/about-apercu/mandate-mandat-eng.htm (accessed on 26 May 2017).

[18] The establishment and enterprise census and survey on service industries are integrated in the economic census.

national survey of family income and expenditure, survey of household economy, retail price survey, national survey of prices, CPI, and survey on time use and leisure activities.[19]

China

As is stipulated in the Statistical Law, the state has established a centralized and unified statistical system by instituting the statistical management system featuring unified leadership and decentralized administration. Government statistical agencies and personnel exercise their functions of statistical survey, reporting and supervision according to the law without any infringement. The official statistical system in China consists of the government statistical system and department statistical system.

Government Statistical System

The institution of statistical agencies and deployment of statisticians at all levels of the government constitute the government statistical system. The National Bureau of Statistics (NBS) is established under the State Council, while independent statistical agencies are set up in local people's governments at and above country level. The NBS is a main provider of national statistical data, and also acts as a coordinator of government department statistics and local statistics. It is, therefore, responsible for directing and coordinating the statistical work throughout the country, and also conducting national economic accounting.

At the township level, either statistical stations are instituted or full-time or part-time statisticians are employed. In addition, NBS has also established, under its direct leadership and administration, three survey-taking institutions, namely, Organization of Rural Socio-economic Surveys, Organization of Urban Socio-economic Surveys, and Organization of Enterprise Surveys, across the country.

Department Statistical System

The institution of statistical agencies and employment of statisticians by various departments both directly under the State Council and at

[19] Available at http://www.stat.go.jp/english/info/guide/2011ver/pdf/2011ver.pdf (accessed on 26 May 2017).

the local levels in light of the requirements of statistical tasks constitute the department statistical system.

According to the needs of the statistical work, the departments of the State Council and local governments establish statistical institutions at various levels. The main functions of departmental statistical system are to organize and coordinate the statistical work of various functional organs of such departments; execute the tasks of state and local statistical surveys; draw up and carry out statistical survey plans of such departments; collect, compile, and provide statistical data; and make statistical analysis of and exercise statistical supervision over the implementation of plans of the departments and of the enterprises and institutions under their jurisdiction.

As a main system of statistical work, the national statistical system has the power to direct and coordinate the departmental statistical system in statistical operation. Departmental statistics involves traffic, tourism, finance statistics, finance, import and export in customs, statistics of foreign capital utilization, culture, education, health, science and technology, registered permanent residence, and social development.

Local Bureau of Statistics

Independent statistical institutions are established in local governments at or above the country level. However, statistical stations are established in people's governments of townships and towns, or staffed with statisticians, who are responsible for carrying out their tasks of state statistical surveys and for organizing, guiding, and coordinating the statistical work in their respective administrative areas. The statistical institutions of local governments at various levels are subordinated to the dual leadership of the government at their level and the statistical institutions at higher level, in statistical work, under the leadership of the statistical institutions at higher level.[20]

[20] Available at http://www.stats.gov.cn/english/18round/others/200402/t20040220_44592.html; http://mospi.nic.in/mospi_new/upload/bricks_2012_24aug12/htm/annexture4.pdf (accessed on 26 May 2017).

Bibliography

Government of India (GoI). 2009. *Statistical System in India*. New Delhi: Ministry of Statistics and Programme Implementation, GoI.

Statistics Bureau of Japan. 2017. *Japan Statistical Yearbook*. Tokyo: Ministry of Internal Affairs and Communications.

Statistics Canada. 2012. *Canadian Yearbook, 2012*. Ontario: Statistica Canada.

UK Statistics Authority. 2000. Framework for National Statistics, June.

United Nations Statistics Division (UNSD). 2003. *Handbook of Statistical Organization*, Studies in Methods, Series F. No. 88. New York: Department of Economic and Social Welfare.

———. 2008. System of National Accounts. Available at https://unstats.un.org/unsd/nationalaccount/docs/SNA2008.pdf, last accessed on 24 July 2017.

US Office of Management and Budget. 2006. 'United States Federal Statistical System: Coordination, Cooperation, and Collaboration', Katherine K. Wallman, Chief Statistician. Washington, DC. US Office of Management and Budget.

2

Population Statistics

The basic source of information on population in India is the decennial census that was started in 1872. There was no permanent census organization prior to the 1951 census. Census Commissioners were appointed about 18 months before the actual day of the census. The Census Department and the census staff had a very short duration of service. The department would be disbanded soon after the census operations were over. In 1949, a Registrar General and Census Commissioner was appointed as the permanent single authority to conduct all the future censuses and to carry out the work of improvement of vital statistics. State Superintendents, now called Directors of Census Operation (until 1941 called Provincial Superintendents), are responsible for conducting the census in each state. States are further divided into districts, charges, and circles under district census officers, charge superintendents, and circle supervisors respectively. Circles are then divided into villages and blocks for rural and urban areas respectively. In rural areas, normally *patwaris* and elementary school teachers are appointed as the census enumerators and in urban areas school teachers and government clerks conduct the actual enumeration. A census supervisor is appointed over every five enumerators to supervise and guide their work.

Prior to 1941, a synchronous de facto system of population count was applied. Under this system, the census enumeration was taken on a particular night throughout the country and people were counted wherever they were found on that night. Elaborate arrangements had to be made to enumerate the moving population. In 1941, this system was dispensed in favour of the extended de facto (period) system. Under the period system people are counted on the basis of their normal residence and for this a period of reference is fixed and a person is counted at the place of normal residence if he had been there even for some time during the reference period, even though he is not present there on the day to which the census relates. On the other hand, if a person is not at his normal residence throughout the reference period, he is counted wherever he is found. The extended de facto system is supposed to be complete and less complicated than the single night de facto system. Under the single night de facto system, there is no method of verification about the number of persons in a house. The single night de facto system does not give a correct picture of the economic status and region-wise distribution of the population.

Certain items such as relationship to head, age, sex, marital status, religion, birth place, mother tongue, literacy, and occupation have always been included in the census schedules but some additional items have been included, at times. Changes were relatively few until 1941, but after Independence the scope of item coverage has been enlarged. The details of the changes implied specially with respect to economic categories are discussed in a later section.

Details of the Population Census

In the first stage of census, field operations consist of canvassing of the house listing schedules, about six to eight months before conducting the actual census. Census operations are carried out during February–March of the relevant year. Enumerators are supposed to visit every household or every human being on or before 28 February and fill the relevant schedules. They are required to visit the households again between 1 March and 3 March to enumerate any person found in a household either not enumerated elsewhere or changes due to birth or death after their earlier visit. The revisional round for the 2001 Census was between 1 March and 5 March. The reference date of all censuses up to 1991 was the sunrise of 1 March. For 2001, however, the time of the reference was changed from sunrise to 00.00 a.m. of the same day, that is, 1 March. The enumeration of the houseless population was carried out on the night of 28 February. From the census of 1961 to 1991, three schedules—namely, house list, household schedule, and individual slip—were canvassed. For the census of 2001, the household schedule and individual slip were merged into one and called Household Schedule (before the 1961 Census also only one questionnaire was circulated). Since the 1961 Census, along with the enumeration, all postgraduates and technically qualified persons were given a schedule to be filled up by them. The results of this schedule are so far available only up to the 1981 population census.

The 2011 Census was conducted in two phases: the first phase called the house listing and housing census, conducted in April to September 2010, depending upon local conditions of different states (actual conducting time 45 days), and the second phase being population enumerations between 9 February and 28 February 2011, with a revision round between 1 March and 5 March 2011. For the first time, it was decided to collect the details for the preparations of a National Population Register (NPR).

National Population Register in the Country

The government has decided to create an NPR in the country by collecting information on specific characteristics of each 'usual resident'. The NPR would also provide photographs, 10 fingerprints and 2 iris scans of all 'usual residents'[1] who are of age 5 years and above. The NPR database would be sent to the Unique Identification Authority of India (UIDAI) for deduplication and assigning of the Unique Identification (UID) numbers (known as Aadhaar). The objective of the NPR is to create a national register of Indian citizens. This register will be useful in improving security by checking illegal migration.

The fieldwork of biographic data collection for creation of NPR in the country has been completed in all the states/UTs. The scanning

[1] The person who resides or intends to stay for more than 6 months.

of these filled-in NPR schedules (approximately 27 crore) has also been completed.

The work of digitization and capture of biometry under NPR for the country has been entrusted to a consortium of central public sector undertakings (CPSUs) and the Department of Information Technology (DIT). According to an All-India Conference of State Coordinators, Collectors on NPR, Ministry of Home Affairs, held on 18 February 2016, it was stated that the NPR is expected to be finalized by 31 December 2016.

The list of usual residents along with their Aadhaar number, would be published in the local areas to invite claims and objections (if any) which would be dealt with as per the prescribed procedure. It is proposed to issue identity (smart) cards to all the usual residents (of age 18 years and above) in the country. The Office of the Registrar General of India (ORGI) will maintain and update the NPR database.

National Population Register in Coastal Areas

As one of the measures to strengthen coastal security, the creation of the NPR in 3,331 coastal villages in all the nine maritime states and four UTs has been undertaken ahead of the creation of the NPR for the country. In the Andaman and Nicobar Islands, all the towns have also been covered. In these areas, the method of direct data collection has been resorted to and photographs and fingerprints of all the usual residents of these villages (15 years of age and above) has also been undertaken. The direct data collection of more than 120 lakh persons and biometric details (for persons of age 15 years and above) and of more than 70 lakh persons have been completed. The Local Register of Usual Residents (LRUR) has been displayed in the local areas to invite correction and objections. After vetting by the Gram Sabha, the corrections in LRUR have been incorporated. The work of production and personalization of identity (smart) cards, has been completed with the issuance of more than 65 lakh resident's identity cards to usual residents of age 18 years and above in these areas.

Aadhaar

Aadhaar is a 12-digit individual identification number issued by the UIDAI. This is issued in the form of a card, which serves as a proof of identity and address anywhere in India. Up to April 2016, 101 crore cards have been issued.

Census Schedules

The House Listing and Housing Census is conducted once in a decade, by visiting the household and canvassing with the same questionnaire all over the country. The objective of the House Listing and Housing Census is to systematically list out all the structures, houses, and households throughout the country and number them. Censuses in India have been collecting information on housing stock as well as the various parameters concerning the population of the country since 1881. However, prior to Census 1961, different types of forms were in use in different regions of the country to collect data on the housing stock. Census 1961 started collecting data on housing by adopting a uniform and standardized House Listing Schedule throughout the country. The questions canvassed in the House Listing Schedule included the purpose for which the census houses are used, material of the wall and roof of the census house, number of the rooms occupied by the households, ownership status of households, and nature of activity carried out in industrial establishments. In Census 1971, a similar set of questions was canvassed except that the data on establishment was collected through a separate schedule. The information on the housing conditions and facilities was part of the House List Schedule of the Census 1971.

There was a major change in Census 1981 wherein only two questions—one pertaining to the use of the census house and other on the physically handicapped persons—were included in the house listing form, while information on the amenities available to the household was collected through a separate schedule canvassed at the time of Population Enumeration with the aim to produce household-level tables with cross-classification of amenities available, classified by the population characteristics of the household. Further, an enterprise list was canvassed along with the House List Schedule as part of the Economic Census organized by the Central Statistical Office (CSO).

In Census 1991, the scope of the House Listing Schedule was further expanded and data was collected for as many as 22 items along with the questions on amenities available to the households.

Questions on the type of fuel used for cooking by the households and availability of toilet facilities in rural households were also canvassed for the first time. In addition, a question on whether the head of the household belonged to a scheduled caste (SC) or scheduled tribe (ST) was asked enabling tabulation of various housing and amenities data items separately for SC and ST households.

The House Listing Operations of Census 2001 saw a major shift in approach to determine the quality of living of the households rather than just housing. Several new items were added in the House List Schedule besides improvements made in its format, resulting in increase in the number of questions from 22 in Census 1991 to 33 in Census 2001. The questions added in 2001 included the condition of residential or partly residential houses categorized as good, liveable, or dilapidated; number of married couples living in the household and number of married couples having independent rooms for sleeping; connection of waste water outlet to closed drainage, open drainage, or no drainage; possession of bathroom and kitchen facility within the house; availability of certain assets; and availing of banking services. One of the major changes was that almost all the questions in the House List Schedule had pre-coded numeric options which not only helped enumerators to record the response easily but also facilitated quick data processing.

In Census 2011, the questionnaire for House Listing and Housing Census was similar to that of Census 2001. Additional questions in Census 2011 included possession of 'Computer/Laptop with or without internet facility' and 'Mobile phone'. Apart from this, many of the questions were refined. One question, namely 'number of married couples having independent rooms for sleeping' was dropped.

Household Schedule and Individual Slips

The household schedule was introduced for the first time in the 1961 census. The purpose of this schedule was to collect information regarding agricultural households and household industries. The information collected was regarding the extent of land cultivated by the household on ownership or tenancy basis and the nature of the household industry if any, conducted by the household and the number of family workers and hired workers employed in these activities. In this schedule, the information was also collected on the various systems of land tenures existing in different states. At the back of the household schedule there was a census population record giving an abstract of information for each individual enumerated in the household as counted at the census, for example, name, sex, relation to head, age, marital status, and description of work in the case of workers. This information was taken down from the individual slips. There have been some changes in the information collected during different censuses, for example, some of the questions contained in the household schedule for 1981 census were transferred to the House List for the 1991 census and some questions like number of married couples living in a household were dropped. In fact, the question about married couples was added to the House List for the 2001 census with an additional question on the number of married couples having independent rooms to sleep. Also added to this list were questions regarding the possession of different consumer durables and whether the household was availing banking services. Otherwise questions of the 1991 and 2001 censuses were the same for the household schedule. The same continued for the 2011 census; in addition, the number under possession of consumer durables increased by adding items like mobiles, computers, and internet connections and dropping the question, number of married couples having independent rooms for sleeping.

Individual Slip

The individual slip was the main schedule of the census up to the 1991 census. In the individual slip essential demographic data such as relationship to the head of the household, sex, age, marital status and birthplace; social and cultural data such as nationality, religion, literacy, and mother tongue; and economic data such as occupation, industry, class of workers, and activity if not working were collected.

A number of questions of the household schedule were same as those of the individual slips. Due to this, as mentioned earlier, the two were merged and named as the Household Schedule for the 2001 Census. The House List and the Household Schedule for this census are given in Appendix 2A of this chapter. In the questionnaire for 2001, the question about physically/mentally disabled persons was introduced once again. In the Household Schedule for 2001 the questions on the travel to place of work, place of work from residence, and also the mode of transport to the place of work were also introduced. Questions on migration and fertility were about the same for the 1991 and 2001 Censuses. The Household Schedule had a new set of questions for households engaged in cultivation/plantation: (i) net area of land under cultivation/plantation; (ii) net area of land irrigated, and (iii) tenure status. This question was not canvassed in the 1991 Census but was canvassed in the 1981 Census in a slightly different form.

In the 2001 Census, for households engaged in cultivation some information regarding net area under cultivation/irrigation was collected in Part III, but in the 2011 Census this information was not collected. The questionnaires for the 2011 Census are given in Appendix 2B.

Comparison of the Questions Asked during Different Censuses

The concepts, definitions, and questionnaires varied from census to census. The questionnaire used for different censuses and the relevant instructions are published in General Economic Tables of the different censuses by the Registrar General of India (RGI). Data on literacy is available since the 1891 Census. From 1911 to 1961, all persons who could read and write a simple letter were treated as literate and those who could not as illiterate. Further, from 1921 to 1981 all children below five years of age were treated as illiterate. In the 1991 Census, all children below the age of seven years were treated as illiterate. In 1901, all persons who could read and write their names were treated as literate. In 1891 all persons who did not understand instructions and were also not able to read and write any language were treated as illiterate. Literacy rates for the 1951, 1961, and 1971 Censuses relate to the population aged five years and above. The rates for the 1981 to 2001 Censuses relate to the population aged seven years and above. The same definitions are also followed in the 2011 Census. The major changes that have taken place in the concepts and definitions relate to the economic activity. These are described as follows:

In 1872 and 1881 only the number of actual workers was recorded according to occupation. In 1891, the concept of the means of subsistence was introduced and the occupation or the means of subsistence was recorded in case of every individual. The population was divided into two groups: workers and dependents. The workers were those who worked for their living as well as those who lived on rent or income from investments or on pensions or annuities (the same definition was applied for the 1872 and 1881 Censuses). The dependents were the women, the children, and the old and the infirm who relied on others for support and whose occupation, if any, was not sufficiently important to increase the family income. In case of dependents the occupation of the person on whom they depended, was recorded. For the censuses of 1901, 1911, and 1921, the information was gathered under the three separate heads (i) the principal occupation or the means of livelihood of the actual worker; (ii) subsidiary occupations of the actual worker; and (iii) the means of subsistence of the dependents.

In the 1931 Census, the population was divided into earners, working dependents, and non-working dependents. The term earner was defined as wage receiver or subsistence obtained in a principal or subsidiary occupation (persons whose incomes were not sufficient for their individual maintenance were also shown as earners). The term 'working dependent' was applied only to those dependents who worked for their families without receiving any wages explicitly. The information collected in this census was about the principal occupation and the most important subsidiary occupation, if any, of the earner and the industry in which he was employed. The working dependent was not regarded as having any principal occupation but was to be recorded in the column for the subsidiary occupation as following any occupation which contributed to maintenance.

In 1941, the concepts of 'wholly', 'partly dependent', and 'wholly independent' persons were introduced. The wholly dependent were the persons in whose case there was no income in cash or kind; partly dependent were to represent those who contributed towards the support of households without being capable of fully supporting themselves. Independent workers were those who did not depend on any other persons. In the case of persons who were wholly or partly dependent, the means of livelihood of the persons who did not depend on anybody else, their own means of livelihood was recorded. In addition to these, there were questions on paid assistants employed, unemployment, and search for employment, seasonal employment, and industry. No detailed tabulation was done for this census because of the Second World War.

The concepts applied in the 1951 Census were the same as those of 1941 but the nomenclature was different. The information was obtained separately under three heads:

(1) self-supporting persons
(2) earning dependents
(3) non-earning dependents

The information regarding self-supporting persons was collected on their principal means of livelihood and secondary means of livelihood. For earning dependents, the principal means of livelihood was that of the persons on whom they depended and their own occupation was treated as a secondary one. In the case of non-earning dependents, the means of livelihood of the persons on whom they depended was recorded under principal means of livelihood.

Although the concepts and definitions applied in different censuses are different, some rough comparison can be made after making some adjustments in the data in various censuses. Some work in this respect has been done in the past by some research workers. The names of Alice Thorne and V.N. Kothari can be mentioned, who tried to compare the working force during the period 1881–1951. The RGI prepared two charts—'Comparable Chart of Concepts and Definitions Relating to Economic Questions 1901–1961' and 'Comparable Chart of Economic (Industrial) Classifications 1901–1961'. The first chart gives the concepts and definitions applied during different censuses. The second gives comparable major groups and sub-groups of economic classification of various censuses according to 1961 major groups and sub-groups. These charts have been published in the General Economic Tables, Part-IIB(I), *Volume I of Censuses of India*, 1961. Actually, in getting comparable figures, there are two main difficulties: one is due to the difference in concepts and definitions of workers in different censuses and the other is due to different industrial classifications in different censuses. A rough comparison of the figures of workers of the 1961 Census with that of previous censuses can be made as follows:

Workers of 1961 = (self-supporting persons + earning dependents + non-earning but working dependents - non-working self-supporting persons) of 1951
= (Independent workers + partly dependent workers + non-earning but working dependents - earning but non-working independent persons) of 1941
= (earners + working dependents - non-working earners) of 1931
= (workers - non-working earners) of 1901, 1911, and 1921

The comparison would have given good results if the information about non-earning but working and non-working but earning persons was separately available for various censuses. Since this information is not available from the censuses, the non-comparability from a concept point of view would continue. In 1961, economic data were collected on the basis of work. The population was divided into two classes—workers and non-workers. In the case of regular employment in any trade, profession, service, business, or commerce, the basis of work would be satisfied if the person had been employed during any of the 15 days preceding the day on which he was enumerated. In the case of seasonal work, such as cultivation, livestock, dairying, and household industry, if a person had some regular work of more than one hour a day throughout a greater part of the working season, he was to be registered as a worker.

Work included not only actual work but effective supervision and direction of work. Persons who were not engaged in any economic activity were treated as non-workers. However, in the 1971 Census, the main activity of a person was first ascertained as to how he spent his time as a worker, producing goods and services or as a non-worker. A person was regarded as a worker only if the main activity was participation in some economically productive work. Work included not only the actual one, but also its effective supervision and direction. For regular work in industry, trade, or service, the reference period was the week prior to the day of enumeration (it was a fortnight in 1961) and in the case of seasonal work such as agriculture, it was the preceding one year. In 1971, data on secondary work was also collected. Where a worker engaged in work other than his main activity and a non-worker such as a student or housewife, made some marginal contribution to work, that work was recorded as secondary work. Thus, workers together with non-workers who have secondary work in 1971 are expected to correspond to the workers of the 1961 Census.

The dichotomy of worker and non-worker of the 1961 and 1971 Censuses was improved in the 1981 Census and instead a trichotomy as main workers, marginal workers, and non-workers was adopted. For the main worker, the time criterion of engagement in work for the major part of the year, that is, at least 183 days, was adopted while those who worked for some time during the last year were treated as marginal workers. Those who had never worked during the last year were non-workers. This trichotomy partially permits a comparability of the 1981 Census economic data with that of 1971 as well as 1961. The main workers of the 1981 Census can be expected to correspond to the workers of 1971 and the main workers and marginal workers of 1981 together correspond to the workers and marginal workers of 1961. The same concept of work as in the 1981 Census was adopted for the 1991 as well as 2001 censuses.

(1) The economic questions were different in the 1981 Census. The work concept of 1961 and 1971 Censuses, as opposed to the 'income' or 'economic independence' concept of the earlier censuses was adopted for 1981 Census. But the criterion for classification of persons as workers has changed. In the 1961 and 1971 Censuses, two approaches—namely usual status and current status—were adopted. There was a reference period of one year for seasonal work in both the censuses, while for regular work it was a fortnight in 1961 and a week in 1971. In the 1961 and 1971 Censuses, classification as worker or non-worker was made through different criteria. In 1961, a person qualified as a worker if he had worked regularly during the last season or if he had worked at least for a day in regular (non-seasonal) work during the preceding fortnight. At the 1971 Census, a person was

treated as a worker only if he spent his time mainly in seasonal work or if he worked at least for a day in regular (non-seasonal) work during the preceding week.

A new item seeking/available for work was also added to the economic questions of the 1981 Census. These questions were asked from both marginal workers and non-workers. The economic questions in the 1991 Census were, more or less, the same as in the 1981 Census. It was apprehended in 1981 that many persons, especially women and children, engaged in unpaid work on farms or in family enterprises were not netted as workers. To net such persons at the 1991 Census, it was emphasized in question 14A and also in the relevant instructions that work included unpaid work on farms or in family enterprises. The instructions were also elaborated with repeated emphasis on probing enquiries and with various illustrations so as to net the women's work participation. The question on seeking/available for work has been asked from only non-workers at the 1991 Census unlike from both marginal workers and non-workers at the 1981 Census. Further, those seeking/available for work have been asked at the 1991 Census if they had worked before in order to know about the fresh entrants in the labour market.

(2) Industrial Classification: Occupational classification of the census economic data is available since 1981. In earlier censuses, no clear distinction was made between industry and occupation. All occupations were grouped under a few classes, sub-classes or orders/sub-orders, and groups. While several changes and modifications were made in the classification over the censuses, almost a similar classification was followed for 1881 to 1901 and another for 1911 to 1941. In 1951, the Indian Census Economic Classification was adopted which grouped all industries and services other than cultivation into 10 divisions, 88 sub-divisions and 217 groups on the lines of the International Standard Industrial Classification of all Economic Activities (ISIC) evolved by the International Labour Organization (ILO). In the 1961 Census, for the first time, economic data was classified separately by industry and occupation. The National Classification of Occupations (NCO) and the Standard Industrial Classification (SIC) of 1961 were adopted. For the 1971 and 1981 Censuses,

the revised version of NCO 1968 and the National Industrial Classification (NIC) 1970 were followed.

In the 1991 Census, the NCO 1968 was further modified so as to present data for certain occupations pursued by SCs and STs. The revised NIC 1987 was adopted for the 1991 Census. For the 2001 and 2011 Censuses, the 1998 and 2008 industrial classifications were used, respectively.

The pattern of broad industrial categories in the 1961 and 1971 Censuses are nearly the same except that from Category III of 1961, mining and quarrying has been separated and made as a separate Category IV in 1971; and Category IV of 1961, workers in household industry have been brought into sub-category V(a) in 1971. For other differences in the broad as well as the detailed industrial classification, refer to the Comparative Chart of Economic Classification 1901–71 vide *Census of India, 1971*, Part I-B(I), General Economic Tables, India (pp. xi to xviii). The following are the major categories of industrial activity for the 1991 as well as 2001 Censuses:

(1) Cultivators
(2) Agricultural labourers
(3) Livestock, forest and fishing, hunting, plantation, orchards, and allied activities
(4) Mining and quarrying
(5) Manufacturing, processing, servicing, and repairs (household and non-household)
(6) Construction
(7) Trade and commerce
(8) Transport, storage, and communications
(9) Other services

New Features of the 2001 Household Schedule

(1) Information regarding age at marriage was collected for males as well.
(2) For type of educational institutions being attended by a person: vocational, other institute, and literacy centre were added.
(3) A new question to collect information on total or partial disability was canvassed. In 1981, the question on disability was canvassed in the first phase and dropped in 1991.

(4) A question on seeking and available for work was also canvassed for marginal workers and the question on secondary work of main workers was dropped.
(5) A new question on distance travelled by a person to his/her work place and also mode of travel was canvassed for persons engaged in non-agriculture activities.
(6) Sex-wise information was collected for the children born alive during the last one year.
(7) Net area of land under cultivation/plantation and net area of irrigated land was also collected for those households who were engaged in cultivation/plantation in Part III of the Household Schedule.
(8) For the first time, provision was made in the Household Schedule for taking signature or thumb impression of the respondent.

A quantum leap was also made in the technology front for the 2001 Census. The schedules for the phases were scanned through high-speed scanners and handwritten data from the schedules were converted into digitized form through Intelligent Character Reading (ICR).

New Features in the Household Schedule of the 2011 Census

(1) Pre-printing of location particulars up to district: A highlight of Census 2011 was the pre-printing of location codes up to district level and the use of shorter location codes in the field. This reduced the burden on the enumerators to an extent and improved compliance in the writing of location codes on every schedule.
(2) Printing of barcodes/form number: The introduction of unique form number and barcodes in each schedule were a new feature. This greatly facilitated proper inventory management and tracking of schedules.
(3) Colour drop-out: The colours chosen for printing the schedule were such that they dropped out totally after scanning. This was designed to facilitate considerable improvement in ICR.
(4) Linking of House Listing with population enumeration: A procedure to link the housing census data of matched households

to the population enumeration data has been attempted for the first time.

(5) Tracking system in case of more than one form is used: A provision to record the number of the continuation forms used in the case of normal/institutional households where more than one schedule has been used, was made.

(6) Description of institutional households: A provision has been made for recording the description of institutional households.

(7) Gender: In a radical departure from the past, a provision has been made for the respondent to return a gender other than male or female. This is an option to be exercised by the respondent and not determined by the enumerator.

(8) Date of birth: A provision has been made to record age in completed years as well as date of birth. This is expected to improve reporting of age at least among a section of the population.

(9) Current marital status: Separate codes have been assigned for 'divorced' and 'separated'.

(10) Disability: The question on disability has been vastly enlarged in Census 2011. In comparison to the five codes in Census 2001, eight codes have been provided in the 2011 census.

The new codes are mental retardation, mental illness and any other, and multiple disability.

The questions and the instructions have been finalized after extensive deliberation with civil society organizations and the Ministry of Social Justice and Empowerment. Respondents with multiple disabilities would now be able to report up to three disabilities for the first time.

(11) Status of Current Attendance in Educational Institution: Separate codes have been given for persons who have never attended any educational institution and persons who have attended earlier. An additional code for recording persons attending special institution for the disabled has also been added.

(12) Worked any time during last year: The question on work status has been modified as follows:

- Main worker: If worked for six months or more
- Marginal worker: If worked for less than six months. These are further bifurcated into those who worked between three

and six months and those who worked for less than three months.

- Non-worker: If not worked at all

Such a classification would not only retain the older categorization of main, marginal, and non-worker, but would also offer richer data on the period of work.

(13) Non-economic activity: A category of 'others' has been included to account for commercial sex workers and persons involved in illegal activities. A new code for renter has also been introduced.

(14) Migration: While processing of the Census 2001 data, it was found that the non-response with respect to providing the district names was relatively more both in the question on place of birth and place of last residence. It was felt that as the names of the districts might have undergone a change, the respondent was unable to provide the correct names. Thus, in Census 2011, an added item, namely, the name of village/town, has been added in both these questions.

(15) Number of children born alive during last one year: Mention of the specific period '1st March, 2010 to 28th February, 2011' on the body of the schedule has been done.

Questions Dropped

Households engaged in cultivation/plantation: The questions pertaining to the following topics were canvassed in Census 2001: 'Total net area of land under cultivation/plantation'; 'Net area of irrigated land', and 'Tenure status of land under cultivation/plantation'. The question was canvassed but could not be tabulated on account of widespread non-response. There were also other technical problems, such as variation in the units of measurement, comparability with other sources of data—namely, the agricultural census and land holding survey of the NSS. Hence it was decided to drop these questions in Census 2011.

Census Publications

The results of the population census are given in the following publications. Series 1 presents all-India tables, while Series 2 gives the same for different states/UTs.

(1) General population tables
(2) General economic tables
(3) Social and cultural tables
(4) Migration tables
(5) Fertility tables
(6) Tables on houses and household amenities

In addition, special tables relating to scheduled castes and tribes are generated. In addition, a district census handbook is prepared for each district and a village directory is prepared for each village from the data collected separately from a number of sources. Also prepared are the life tables. The brief contents of these tables are given in the following paragraphs.

Population tables are given in the form of a few papers. Paper I issued immediately after completion of the census, gives the provisional population figures along with its distribution by sex. It also gives the literacy rates by sex and the decadal variation in the population. Paper II gives some more details separately for rural and urban population.

The *Primary Census Abstract* is the basic publication issued, which gives data on final population figure for number of houses and households, total population, scheduled castes and tribes, population in the age group 0–6 years, number of literates, number of workers classified by main industrial categories (nine at present), marginal workers, and those seeking and available for work. These data are available down to the village level for rural areas and ward level for cities and towns. Since the 1991 Census, these data are available on electronic media, on the RGI website.

The data on main workers and non-workers seeking work are given in the series of general economic tables. The data on workers are available by industrial and occupational classification, age, sex, and educational level; non-workers by main activity, age, sex, and educational level; and those seeking work by age, sex, educational level, and whether they have worked before. Data presented in these tables are based on a 20 per cent sample in bigger states and on full counts in respect of smaller states and UTs.

The series of social and cultural tables gives data on age, marital status, educational level, school attendance, mother tongue, religion, bilingualism, and trilingualism (1991 Census onwards). Data on marital status, educational level, and school attendance are available, cross-classified by age groups; while data on school attendance in the age group 5–19 years has also been classified by work participation. Like for economic tables, the data for these tables are based on the same size of sampling. The tables for scheduled castes and scheduled tribes giving data on educational level and school/college attendance cross-classified by sex and age are based on full count.

Data on migration characteristics, such as place of birth, place of last residence, reason for migration, and duration of residence at the place of enumeration are available by sex through migration tables. These are cross-classified by workers, marginal workers, and non-workers by educational level. Data on educational level, economic activity, and age distribution of the migrants are also available. Migrants who have reported employment as reason for migration have been further cross-classified by educational levels marital status, occupational divisions, age, sex, and duration of residence at state and city level. Some data on migration pertaining to the years before the 1981 Census are available in social and cultural tables.

The series of fertility tables provids data on female age at marriage, number of children ever born and number of children surviving to ever married women and birth to currently married women during last year. Data on age at marriage have been classified by duration of marriage while all other data are classified by age of the woman. These data are available at district level. At the state level, data are also available by religion, educational level, and work status of the women.

Housing tables give information on housing by categories, such as vacant houses, residence, shops and workshops-cum-residence including household industries, business houses, offices, factories, hotels, and places of worship. These detailed tables are available 1981 Census onwards and include household amenities like the type of material used for construction, tenure status, number of rooms, and household size, availability of electricity, drinking water supply (by source), and toilet facilities to the households and type of fuel used for cooking. These tables are available up to district, city, and town level and also in the electronic media.

The village directory gives information for each village on the availability of educational and medical facilities, drinking water, post and telegraph facilities, communication facilities, approach to village, nearest town and its distance, power supply, and land-use pattern, among others. In the town directory, seven statements containing the details and the data of each town have been presented, namely (i) status and growth history of towns; (ii) physical aspects and location of towns; (iii) civic and other amenities; (iv) medical facilities; (v) educational, recreational and cultural facilities; (vi) industry and banking; and (vii) civic and other amenities in slums. District census handbook gives details about census and non-census data given in the directory for each town and village of the district. In addition the details about civil finance, civic and other amenities, medical, educational, recreation and cultural facilities, trade, industry, banking facilities and population by religion including scheduled castes and tribes are given. Also given are the details of occupied residential houses and households, main workers by nine broad industrial classifications by sex, rural, and urban in the district census handbook.

A life table states the probabilities of survival of a hypothetical group or cohort at different ages, which gradually diminish due to deaths. In India, it has been the practice to construct life tables using age composition of the population from successive population censuses. With the introduction of the Sample Registration System (SRS), an alternative source of data has become available for construction of life tables. Based on SRS data, life tables have been prepared for the periods 1970–5, 1976–80, 1981–5, and 1986–90 at five-yearly intervals. Since the 1986–90 issue, life tables have been brought out annually on a five-yearly moving average basis so as to form a continuous series. The latest report[2] contains the abridged life tables for the period 2003–7, 2004–8, 2005–9, and 2006–10 by sex and residence for India and major states.

Disabled Population

Census on Disabled Population

The Census of India 2011, the largest administrative exercise in the whole world, was the 15th since 1872 and the 7th after Independence.

[2] RGI (2012).

Data on disability dates back to the very inception of the Indian census. However, disability became invisible on paper after 1931 as questions on disability were excluded until 1981, the year declared by the UN as the 'International Year of the Disabled'. Census 1981 included the question of disability but the practice was again discontinued in the 1991 Census because of the question on the reliability of information. It was by the sheer commitment and determination of some individuals and other prominent activists and organizations that disability in a more comprehensible form was listed in the 2001 Census.

The challenge to enumerate people with disability with near accuracy is not only on the enumerators who visit each household to gather census data, the challenge is also with the household/family with disabled persons to grasp the significance of census data and have their disabled sons/daughters/family members counted/made visible in the corridors of power and schemes of fund allocations for their development and empowerment as equal citizens of the country.

The questions on disability for the Census of India 2011 are given as follows. (The question numbers are same as given in the Census 2011 questionnaire.)

> (9) a) Is this person mentally/physically disabled? Yes-1/No-2
> (9) b) If yes in (9) a) give code in the box against (9) b) from the list below.
> (9) c) If multiple disability code 8 in (9) b), give maximum three codes in boxes against (9) c) from the list below:
> (1) In Seeing (2) In Hearing (3) In Speech (4) In Movement (5) Mental Retardation (6) Mental Illness (7) Any Other (8) Multiple Disability

National Sample Survey on Disabled Persons in India

The National Sample Survey Office (NSSO) conducts disability surveys at different intervals. The definitions are changed by NSSO in different surveys.

The National Sample Survey (NSS) made its first attempt to collect information on the number of physically handicapped in the 15th Round from July 1959 to June 1960. The enquiry was exploratory in nature and was confined to rural areas only. However, in the

16th Round (July 1960–June 1961), the geographical coverage was extended to urban areas. The subject was again taken up in the 24th (July 1969–June 1970) and in the 28th (October 1973–June 1974) Rounds of the NSS. The objective of these early enquiries was only to provide estimates of the number of persons in the country who suffered from certain specified physical handicaps. However, the types of physical handicap covered in all those rounds were not always the same. The results obtained from the 24th and 28th Rounds of the NSS are published in *Report No. 220*.

For reasons of economy, information on the physically handicapped was collected in the early rounds in the survey schedules meant for other subjects. There was, therefore, very little scope for collecting information on cause, specific nature, and other details of the physical handicap. The enquiries were also not comprehensive due to obvious limitations of the survey methodology of those rounds.

The NSSO undertook a comprehensive survey of disabled persons in its 36th Round during the second half of 1981, the International Year of Disabled Persons. After a gap of 10 years, a second survey on the disabled was carried out in the 47th Round during July–December 1991 at the request of the Ministry of Social Welfare, Government of India (GoI). In these surveys, the objective was to provide a database regarding the incidence and prevalence of disability in the country. The basic framework of these surveys—namely the concepts, definitions, and operational procedures—was kept the same. While the earlier surveys were restricted to only physically handicapped persons, in the surveys conducted during the 36th and 47th NSS Rounds, an extended definition was used to cover all physically disabled persons. Information was collected from all persons with one or more of the three physical disabilities—visual, communication (that is, hearing and/or speech), and locomotors. The particulars of disability of the disabled persons, such as, the type of disability, degree of disability, cause, age at onset of disability, type of aid/appliance used, among others, were collected along with some socio-economic characteristics. The results of the 36th Round survey were released in two mimeographed reports—*Report No. 305: Report on Survey of Disabled Persons* and *Report No. 337: Characteristics of Disabled Persons* and that for the

47th Round survey in *Report No. 393: A Report on Disabled Persons in India*.

Again, after a gap of 11 years, the third survey on the disabled was carried out in the 58th Round during July–December 2002 at the request of the Ministry of Social Justice and Empowerment (MSJE), GoI. In this round, the coverage was extended to include mental disability as well, keeping all other concepts, definitions, and procedures for physical disability same as those of the 47th Round. Along with the particulars of physical and mental disabilities, the socio-economic characteristics of the disabled persons, such as age, literacy, vocational training, employment, cause of disability, and age at onset of disability, among others, were collected.

It may be mentioned here that in the surveys conducted during the 36th and 47th Rounds, an attempt was made to collect information on developmental milestones reached by children at different age ranges. However, this was not attempted in the 58th Round survey.

The results presented in this report relate to mental disabilities as well as physical disabilities, such as (i) mental disability; (ii) visual disability; (iii) hearing disability; (iv) speech disability; and (v) locomotor disability. More specifically, the report gives the incidence and prevalence of different forms of disability and the distribution of the disability by cause of disability (as reported by the informant), marital status, educational level, living arrangements, and activity status, among others.

Survey Period

The fieldwork for the 58th Round survey was carried out during the second half of 2002 starting from July and continuing up to December—thus covering a period of six months.

Geographical Coverage

The survey covered the Union of India, except (i) Leh and Kargil districts of Jammu and Kashmir (J&K); (ii) interior villages of Nagaland located beyond 5 km from the bus routes; and (iii) villages in the Andaman and Nicobar Islands which were inaccessible throughout the year.

Work Programme

The survey period was divided into two sub-rounds of three-month duration each. An equal number of sample first-stage units were allocated to each of these sub-rounds with a view to ensuring uniform spread of the interviews over the entire survey period.

Sample Design

A stratified, multistage sample design was adopted for the 58th Round. The first stage units were in most cases 1991 Census villages in rural areas and urban blocks—demarcated by the Urban Frame Survey—in urban areas. The ultimate stage units were households—constituting a group of persons normally living together and taking food from a common kitchen. The details of stratification, allocation of samples to various states into stratum, and selection of sample, among others, are given in 'Appendix B: Sample Design and Estimation Procedure' of *Report No. 485*.

Sample Size

The number of sample villages and urban blocks surveyed in the central sample was 4,637 and 3,354, respectively. A total of 45,571 and 24,731 households were surveyed in rural and urban areas, respectively. Statement 1.1 provides the number of first stage units allocated and surveyed in different states/UTs. The state-wise sample number of disabled persons for each type of disability is given in the statement for rural and urban areas. It may be noted that while in Statements 1.1 and 1.2 sample persons with only a particular type of disability is given, while generating tables for any particular disability, all persons with that disability together with any other disability (multiple) have also been considered.

Contents of the Report

The results presented in this report relate to the data of only the central sample. The report contains three sections and three appendices. The second section provides the concepts and definitions used for the purpose of survey on disability. The summary of findings giving important features at the all-India level as revealed by the survey is given in the third section. The detailed tables for all-India cross-classified by age, sex, and other correlates are given for rural and urban India separately in Appendix A of the *Report No. 485* of the NSSO.

While the sample design and estimation procedure have been outlined in Appendix B of the report, the facsimile of the schedule is given in Appendix C of the report.

Table 2.1 gives the estimates of the number of disabled persons by types of disability.

Table 2.2 compares the estimates of disability from the NSSO survey of 2002 and the population census of 2001.

List of Publications of Census of India, CSO, and NSSO on Disability

(1) The publications of the Census of India (2001) on disability are as follows:

a. *Disabled Population by Type of Disability, Age, and Sex for General Category, for Scheduled Castes and for Scheduled Tribes*: It gives the data on type of disability in speech, in seeing, in hearing, in movement, and mental.

Table 2.1 Estimated Number of Persons Suffering from Different Types of Disabilities ('000)

Types of Disabilities	Rural	Urban	Male	Female	All persons
Mental Retardation	700	295	626	369	995
Mental Illness	840	261	665	437	1,101
Blindness	1,603	410	929	1,085	2,013
Low Vision	655	159	369	444	813
Hearing Disability	2,369	693	1,613	1,448	3,062
Speech Disability	1,603	552	1,291	863	2,155
Locomotor Disability	7,983	2,651	6,634	4,000	10,634
Any Disability*	14,085	4,406	10,891	7,600	18,491

Source: NSSO Survey on Disability, 2002.

Note: *At least one of mental, visual, hearing, speech, or locomotor disability.

Table 2.2 Estimates of Disability in India by Census and NSSO

S. No.	Types of Disabilities	Census 2001		NSSO 2002	
		Number	Percentage of Total Disabled	Number	Percentage of Total Disabled
1	Seeing	1,06,34,881	48.55	28,26,700	15.29
2	Speech	16,40,868	7.49	21,54,500	11.65
3	Hearing	12,61,722	5.76	30,61,700	16.56
4	Movement	61,05,477	27.87	1,06,34,000	57.51
4	Mental	22,63,821	10.33	20,97,500	11.34
4	Total	2,19,06,769	100.00	1,84,91,000	100.00

Source: *Census of India* (2001) and NSS 58th Round (2002).

b. *Disabled Population by Type of Disability, Marital Status, Age, and Sex*: Marital status, which is given by type of marriage–married, never married, widowed, divorced/separated, and unspecified.

c. *Disabled Population among Main Workers, Marginal Workers, Non-workers by Type of Disability, Age, and Sex*: Data by type of main worker, marginal worker and non-worker.

(2) *National Sample Survey Report (Report No. 485) on Disability*, NSSO.

(3) Data on Disability-2001 (India, state, districts), Census of India

(4) *Disability in India: A Statistical Profile*, MOSPI.

These publications are based on the findings of the population census and sample survey conducted by the NSSO on the subject of disability.

National Sample Survey on Migration

In addition to the migration tables on the basis of population census, various surveys conducted by the NSSO are also important sources of migration data. To assess the volume and structure of migration in India, NSSO, starting with the 9th Round (May–August 1955), conducted a number of surveys to collect data on migration as part of its employment and unemployment enquiries. In the 9th, 11th (August 1956 to January 1957), and 12th Rounds (March—August

1957) of survey, migration particulars were collected for the labour force population only. The 13th Round (September 1957 to May 1958) onwards, more detailed information on migration has been collected. In the 18th Round, a survey on migration was conducted on a much larger scale. In the NSS 28th Round (October 1973–June 1974) a survey on birth, death, morbidity, and disability, and migration particulars of the usual members of the sample households were also collected. In the 38th Round (January 1983–December 1983), the collection of migration data was integrated with the regular quinquennial survey on employment and unemployment. The same approach was followed during the 43rd Round (July 1987–June 1988) also. Data on migration was collected during the 49th Round (January–June, 1993) survey through Schedule 1.2 (details in *Report No. 430*) which had a comprehensive coverage including, inter alia, housing condition and migration in India. In the sixth quinquennial survey on employment and unemployment during NSS 55th Round (July 1999–June 2000) information on migration particulars was collected for each household member of the sample household through the employment–unemployment schedule.

An all-India survey on migration along with the situation of employment and unemployment in India was carried out during NSS 64th Round (July 2007 to June 2008), *Report No. 530*. The collection of information on the employment and unemployment part of the schedule particulars was as a part of the annual series of the NSSO which was started in the NSS 60th Round and repeated in the NSS 62nd Round. In this round, the scope of the survey on employment and unemployment was further widened with the collection of information on migration particulars of the households, of the household members, and of the outmigrants. In this survey, a nationwide enquiry was conducted in a moderately large sample of households to provide estimates on various characteristics pertaining to employment and unemployment and migration in India and some characteristics associated with them at the national and state levels. Based on the data collected during the survey period, estimates pertaining to migration in India along with various characteristics associated with these have been presented in *Report No. 530*.

Details on Migration of the 64th Round

The information relating to migration collected in this round can be broadly categorized into four groups. First, those relating to household migration, such as location of last residence, pattern of migration (temporary or permanent), and reason for migration. Second, information for the outmigrants, like present place of residence of the outmigrant, reason for migration, period elapsed since leaving the erstwhile household, whether engaged in economic activities, and frequency and amount of remittances sent during the last 365 days to the households by such former members who had migrated out. The information on the use of remittances received from the outmigrants by the households was also collected. Third, detailed information on the migrants relating to the nature of movement, period elapsed since leaving the last usual place of residence (UPR), location of last UPR, usual activity status at the time of leaving last UPR, reason for migration, and whether a return migrant. Finally, for those who had stayed away from the village/town for one month or more but less than six months during the last 365 days for employment or in search of employment (henceforth referred to as short-term migrants), destination during longest spell, and industry of work.

Vital Statistics

Data on births and deaths are available on the basis of registration done by the local registrars. On the occurrence of the vital event, each household is supposed to give the information to the local registrar. In rural areas, the data are collected at the village level by the village panchayats, while in urban areas the data are collected by the municipal committees of various towns. The registration of these vital events in India is well known to be incomplete and defective. There is lot of under-reporting of births and deaths. However, over a period of time there has been lot of improvement in the reporting of the events.

These data are published by the RGI in the *Vital Statistics of India based on CRS.*[3] This publication gives state-wise data regarding births and deaths and infant deaths and their rates by month,

[3] CRS refers to Civil Registration System. See RGI (2014).

by age, and by sex separately for rural and urban areas. Part II of this publication gives these data at the district level. Distribution of deaths by specific diseases based on ICD-10 (International Statistical Classification of Diseases and Related Health Problems; modified according to Indian conditions) are published under the *Report on Medical Certification of Cause of Death*. The data are based on the deaths occurring in hospitals (both public and private). The data are available by sex and broad age-groups.

In order to provide reliable estimates of birth and death rates, a sample registration scheme was started by the ORGI in 1964–5 on a pilot basis and on full scale from 1969–70. Under this scheme, vital statistics recorded continuously in selected sample villages/blocks by a special local enumerator (part-time) are matched and supplemented with the data collected independently in half-yearly surveys by the supervisors (full-time) in the selected sample units. Based on the two sets of data, the vital rates are calculated for each state, by the RGI. This scheme, in addition, provides information on a variety of other useful parameters like age-specific fertility and mortality rates, and type of medical attention at birth and death. These estimates are published in the *Sample Registration System Bulletin* on an annual basis. The estimates of birth rate, death rate, and infant mortality rate (IMR) at the state level are also available in this bulletin. The annual publication gives a detailed account of the SRS along with other aspects connecting with the implementation of the SRS. The revision of the SRS sampling frame is undertaken every 10 years on the basis of the results of the latest population census. The SRS sample has been revised based on the Census 2011 frame. The sample units have been increased to 8,861 from 7,597 based on Census 2001. The earlier sample was based on the reliability of the indicator at state level while the sample with the 2004 frame is taken to have the reliability up to national division levels for rural areas.

In 1965, the ORGI started a Model Registration Scheme (more appropriately known as the *Survey of Causes of Death*) which was being operated in rural areas through selected primary health centres. In this scheme, information is collected on the cause of death by ascertaining the broad symptoms and conditions, anatomical site, and duration of complaint by personnel enquiries from the family of the deceased. The results of the survey are published in the form of annual reports like *Survey of Causes of Death—Rural* (annual). This scheme has been merged with the SRS from January 1999. The results are now available separately for rural as well as urban areas. First, such a report was published relating to 2001–3.

Although SRS estimates are a substantial improvement over the Civil Registration System (CRS), the latter is the only source of data at district and lower levels and hence emphasis should be put on improving the data based on the CRS.

Indirect estimates of birth and death rates have been prepared, however, for a 10-year period, by analysing sex–age distribution of the population as enumerated in consecutive decennial censuses by applying three differential methods. In the first method, population enumerated aged less than 10 years at a census was used to estimate the number of births and, hence, deaths that occurred since the previous decennial census, by the reverse survival method based on relevant life tables. K. Davis (1968) used this method to work out the death rates and birth rates during different censuses. The ORGI later prepared the estimates using the difference method. The difference method, which is the second method, consists of taking the difference between the population of one census year and population above 10 years according to the next census (taken after a period of 10 years) which actually represents the deaths in the population of the earlier census. This difference along with plausible assumptions on infant and child mortality for the decade was utilized to arrive at deaths and, hence, births that occurred during the decade. The third method was based on the stable or quasi-stable population theory; it assumed no change in the age–sex distribution or its rate of increase over a long period of time.

Socio-Economic and Caste Census, 2011

The Socio-Economic and Caste Census (SECC), 2011 had been carried out for the first time for both rural and urban India by the GoI to generate information on a large number of social and economic indicators relating to households across the country. It will have three important outcomes or objectives:

(1) The SECC, 2011 will rank households based on their socio-economic status, so that the state/UT governments can

objectively prepare a list of families that are below the poverty line in both rural and urban areas.
(2) Authentic information on the caste-wise breakup of the population in the country will also be made available.
(3) The socio-economic profile of various castes will be provided as well.

The exercise will enable the government to better target the welfare schemes to the right beneficiaries, and ensure that all eligible beneficiaries are covered and all ineligible beneficiaries are excluded. Highly deprived households will have the highest inclusion priority under the government welfare schemes.

The Rural and the Urban Socio-Economic and Caste Census shall follow the common enumeration approach and shall be taken up across the entire state concurrently, with only the questionnaire in the rural and urban areas being different.

In the rural and urban areas, information is being collected at the level of the individual and household, including, occupation, education, disability, religion, SC/ST status, name of caste/tribe, employment, income and source of income, assets, housing, consumer durables and non-durables, and land.

The questionnaire for urban areas is almost the same as for rural areas except for additional information regarding the amenities, such as source of drinking water and source of lighting. In addition, for the urban areas the questionnaire does not include any information on land. As of 15 January 2015, the final results are available only for 140 out of 640 districts.[4]

Population Projections

Population projections involve projections of birth rates and death rates or alternatively the projections of the growth curve fitted to the population itself. In the past several projections of India's population have been made. Davis (1968) made population projections up to 2001 (starting with the year 1956), using three alternative

[4] For details, see http://www.secc.gov.in/stateFinalList (accessed on 26 May 2017).

assumptions—two regarding growth rate and the third regarding the growth curve. The Census Commissioner and the RGI for 1951, R.A. Gopalaswami made projections for the period 1950–80, assuming two alternative growth rates (Gopalaswami 1953). The two sets of aforementioned projections were published around 1951. Coale and Hoover (1958) made projections for the year 1971, 1976, and 1981 using three alternatives regarding fertility and two regarding infant mortality rates. They employed the component method and have given the projections by age and sex. They used stable population theory to estimate their own vital rates from the age-distribution of India's population for 1951. Agarwala (1960) made projections for the period 1956–81 on the basis of anticipated birth and death rates.

The need for population projections at different levels and by different components like age, sex, and rural–urban for use by the official agencies uniformly, both at the centre and the states was felt at the time of the formulation of the Third Five Year Plan. As a result, an Expert Committee was set up, under the chairmanship of the RGI, by the Planning Commission (now the NITI Aayog) in 1958 to provide a set of projections of population of India and the states. The projections were released to the Planning Commission up to the year 1971 pending the release of 1961 Census results. From that time, the Expert Committee has been reactivated from time to time to revise projections on the strength of latest available information from the census, the NSS and other sources, taking into consideration the progress of the family planning programmes in the country. A revision was made in 1961 soon after the release of the 1961 Census provisional totals, extending the projections up to 1976. Subsequently, with the release of the final population, totals of the 1961 Census as well as the Life Table 1951–60, the Expert Committee was once again reactivated in 1963 for affecting a further revision of the projections extending them up to 1981. This committee set up a working group in 1964 to consider the methodology of projections and to work out a set of quinquennial projections of population of all India and states up to 1981 by sex and age groups and by individual ages for the population of school-going ages 5–25. The working group worked out three sets of projections, namely, high, medium, and low, using the component method for all of India and one set of projections for the states.

Following the release of the 1971 Census provisional population totals, the Expert Committee was once again reconstituted to revise the existing official series of population projections. The Planning Commission again felt the need for another series of projections based on more recent data and subsequently constituted another Expert Committee in 1974, which submitted its report in 1978.

After the release of the 5 per cent sample data of the 1981 Census, the Planning Commission reconstituted the Expert Committee on Population Projections in 1984. Population projections for the period 1981–2001 were prepared under three assumptions on the basis of trends in fertility. This report was published in 1988 and the medium projections were recommended for official use.

In the light of the trends observed during 1980s in major demographic parameters, as revealed by the SRS, the Planning Commission apprehended that the future size of India's population might be higher than that projected by the Expert Committee. In order to have a fresh look at the projections, the Planning Commission set up a Standing Committee of Experts on Population Projections towards the end of October 1988. This Committee reviewed the medium projections made by the Expert Committee of 1984, in the light of the further data available on fertility, mortality, and contraceptive prevalence (family planning) and submitted its report in 1989.

With the availability of age–sex distribution of population from the 1991 Census, the latest data relating to family planning performances and recent levels and trends in fertility and mortality as emerging from the SRS, a need was felt by the Planning Commission for a new set of population projections. As such, the Planning Commission constituted a Technical Group on Population Projections in 1996 under the chairmanship of the RGI with the following objectives:

(1) To review the methodology of population projections adopted in the past
(2) To prepare fresh projections of mortality status and parameters of fertility conditions based on changed pattern of contraceptive use and proportion of married females (1991 Census) and other characteristics
(3) To make population projections afresh up to 2026

(4) To prepare projections of the possible period when net reproduction rate (NRR) = 1 will be achieved by the states/UT's and the country as a whole

The assumptions made to project the population of India up to 2016 are discussed as follows:

(1) The Technical Group considered the Total Fertility Rate (TFR) as the overall indicator of fertility. The earlier approach of taking NRR = 1 as the replacement level of fertility was changed to TFR = 2.1 the TFR estimates based on the SRS for India and major states were adopted. The lowest threshold of TFR was assumed to be 1.6. Two sets of TFR values from the SRS for India and major states for two time periods 1981–93 and 1985–93 were considered by the group. On careful examination, the group recommended the use of projected values of TFRs based on the period 1985–93 except for the states of Madhya Pradesh, Punjab, Rajasthan, and Uttar Pradesh. For these four states, the projected levels of TFR based on the period 1981–93 were adopted. The projected levels of TFRs assumed for India for the initial period 2001–5 and terminal period 2021–5 were 2.9 and 2, respectively.
(2) Although the SRS-based sex ratio at birth of 110 for the period 1981–90, was found to be much higher than the internationally accepted conventional sex ratio at birth of 105–6, the technical group recommended the use sex ratio at birth as obtained from the SRS in view of the overall broad consistency and reliability of the SRS data.
(3) For projecting the mortality levels, initially the group considered two sets of mortality projections: The first one was based on five-yearly abridged life table constructed from SRS Age Specific Death Rates (ASDR) for the period 1981–93. The second set of mortality projections were considered by utilizing the projected survival ratios based on the observed ASDR value from the SRS. After examining the merits of the two sets of mortality projections, the later one, that is, the survivorship ratio method, was recommended for undertaking the population projections. An upper limit of 70 years for the expectation of life for males and females was recommended for all India and major states except for Kerala and Tamil Nadu. The projected levels of expectation

of life at birth for males were 63.8 years for the period 2001–5 and 69.8 for the duration 2021–5. Similarly, for females, these figures were 66.1 years and 72.3, respectively.

(4) In addition to considering the increase in the expectation of life at birth, the group also considered the likely impact of acquired immune deficiency syndrome (AIDS) on death rate. After considering the effect of likely deaths due to AIDS, it was found that future levels of the expectation of life at birth would have no significant impact of AIDS in the next 25 years.

In Table 2.3, the mortality and fertility assumptions used for projecting India's population, projected values of expectation of life at birth, TFR, and the corresponding population projections for different periods are given.

Technical Group-2001

A technical group was constituted by the National Commission on Population (NCP) in 2001 under the chairmanship of the RGI to prepare population projections for the period 2001–26.

Table 2.3 Mortality and Fertility Assumptions

S. No.	Indices	Period					
		2001–5	2006–10	2011–15	2016–20	2021–5	2026–30
1	2	3	4	5	6	7	8
1	Projected values of expectation of life at birth:						
	Males	63.8	65.8	67.3	68.8	69.8	
	Females	66.1	68.1	69.6	71.1	72.3	
2	TFR	2.9	2.6	2.3	2.2	2	
3	Projected population (in millions)	1,028.6 (2001)	1,112.2 (2006)	1,192.5 (2011)	1,269.0 (2016)	1,339.7 (2016)	1,399.8 (2026)

Source: *Populations for India and States: 2001–2026*, 2006.

Note: Figures in parentheses indicate the end year for which the corresponding projections have been made.

The terms of reference of the group are as follows:

(1) The group will review the methodology of population projections adopted in the past.
(2) The group will prepare fresh projections of fertility rate.
(3) The group will prepare fresh projections of mortality rate.
(4) The group will prepare fresh population projections up to the year 2025 with age, sex, urban–rural and state–UT break-ups for five-year intervals.
(5) The group will prepare projections of the possible period when the population replacement level TFR 2.1 will be reached by states/UTs and the country as a whole.
(6) In undertaking the aforementioned exercise, the group may take into consideration data/information brought out by Census 2001, SRS, NSS, and National Family Health Surveys (NFHS), and other sources as may be needed.
(7) The group may give interim population projections under alternative assumptions pending availability of age, sex, and distribution data from Census 2001 and may revise the interim projections, if required, when such data would become available.
(8) The group may take into account factors like level and pattern of contraceptive use, proportion of married females, the impact of major diseases like AIDS, immigration, and migration, among others, while undertaking population projections.
(9) The group may constitute sub-groups to consider any specific issue and co-opt members as necessary.

The technical group submitted its report to the NCP in 2006.

Assumptions Regarding Fertility

The SRS and NFHS provide estimates of TFR for states of the country. The SRS data have been used as base-level estimates, these being available as a time series. The SRS data show that in most of the states, the level of total fertility has been falling since 1971.

Although annual estimates of TFR are available from SRS from 1971 to 2002 for all India and for major states of India, reliable estimates are available 1981 onwards. It may be seen from the SRS data that there has been consistent decline in fertility during the last two decades.

The trend analysis of TFR in terms of log linear, logistic, and Gompertz models for projecting the future levels of fertility were discussed at length by the technical group. It was decided by the group that the Gompertz model may be used for projecting the future levels of TFR in all the states as well as for the country as a whole. Following is the mathematical form of the Gompertz model.

$$\frac{TFR-L}{U-L}=(a)^{b^t}.$$

Alternatively,

$$L_n\left(-L_n\left(\frac{TFR-L}{U-L}\right)\right)=L_n(-L_n\cdot a)+t\cdot L_n\cdot b,$$

where U and L are the upper and lower limits of TFR, respectively, and a and b are constants. The lowest threshold of TFR was assumed to be 1.8. For all the states except Himachal Pradesh, the observed values of TFRs from 1981 to 2000 were considered for projecting the future levels of TFR as the reliable estimates from SRS are available 1981 onwards. For Himachal Pradesh, the same was considered for 1991–2000, as the same was not available for earlier years.

In fitting the Gompertz model, three types of upper asymptotes have been taken for the states depending upon whether the particular state is a high-, medium-, or low-TFR state. The upper asymptote (U) has been taken as 6 for southern states and 7 for the northern states. For western and eastern states, U has been taken as 6.5.

The projected values of TFR for India along with the weighted average of TFRs for the period 2001–25 at five-yearly intervals have been presented in Table 2.4. The weighted estimates of TFRs for India for these years are based on the TFRs of 21 states with weights being percentage share of country's females in the age group 15–49 for different quinquennial periods beginning 2001. The weighted estimates of TFR were recommended for the population projection for India.

Assumptions Regarding Mortality

For projecting the likely levels of expectation of life at birth (e_o), working models developed by the UN have been adopted. The UN

Table 2.4 Projected Levels of TFR, India, 2001–25

Period	Unweighted Estimates	Weighted Estimates
SRS 2000	3.2	–
2001–5	2.82	2.9
2006–10	2.48	2.6
2011–15	2.21	2.35
2016–20	2.01	2.17
2021–25	1.89	2.02

Source: *Report of the Expert Group, 2006.*

uses a standard pattern of improvement depending on whether the expectation is likely to improve slowly, moderately, or fast, based on historical patterns. It has been assumed that increase in the life expectancy becomes relatively slower as it reaches higher levels. The age-specific survival rates were calculated by assuming that the age pattern of mortality observed in the SRS for 1999–2001 would slowly converge to the West model life table pattern as levels of life expectancy increase.

Starting with the average SRS-based ASDR for 1999–2001 centred at 2000, which was taken as the base year, separate life tables for males and females, separately for each state have been constructed without taking into consideration the omission factor due to death reporting. Three years' average was chosen, since the year-wise mortality rates, particularly at the state level, would be subject to higher variability. With the help of the West model life table and the expectation of life at the base level, the values of *nLx* for each of the five-year age groups were projected up to 2021–5 by interpolation. The West model life tables were adopted as the standard life tables for this purpose.

To decide whether high, medium or low improvement should be assumed for each state, the levels of expectation of life at birth for the periods 1990–4 and 1995–9 obtained from SRS life table have been examined and pattern obtained through this for e_0 has been assumed to continue in future for India and all the states.

Assumptions Regarding Migration

Based on the migration data of Census of India 2001, interstate net migrants during the decade 1991–2001 have been assumed to remain constant throughout the projection periods for all the states (except Goa), where component method of projections were used. The component of international migration has been assumed to be negligible, so it has not been considered for projection exercise.

Table 2.5 gives the population projections for each of the four census years since 1971 by the various expert committees and absolute and percentage variations from the final or provisional totals at the country level. This allows us to know the confidence with which one can use the projected population figures for various planning purposes. In 1971, the projected population was higher than the actual population aggregates while in 1981 it was just the reverse. The final population total in 1991 was fairly close to the projected population as estimated by the Standing Committee for that census. For the Census 2001, the projected population fell short by over 16 million.

Table 2.5 Projected and Actual Population ('000) of India, 1971–2026

Year	Projected Population	Actual Population	Difference(9)	Percentage Difference(10)
1	2	3	4	5
1971	5,59,622(1)	5,48,160	–11,462	-2.05
1981	6,72,014(2)	6,85,185(6)	13,171	1.96
1991	8,37,249(3)	8,46,421(7)	9,172	1.10
2001	10,12,386(4)	10,28,737(8)	16,351	1.62
2011	11,92,506(5)	12,10,855	18,349	1.54

Source: RGI (2011).

Notes: (1) According to Planning Commission (1968).

(2) According to Planning Commission (1978).

(3) According to Planning Commission (1988).

(4) According to Planning Commission (1996).

(5) According to Planning Commission (2006).

(6) Including interpolated population of Assam for 1981.

(7) Includes interpolated population of Jammu and Kashmir for 1991.

(8) Includes estimate population of Paomata, Mao Maram, and Purul sub-divisions of Senapati District of Manipur for 2001.

(9) {Column (3) – Column (2)}.

(10) {Column (3) – Column (2)} × 100 / Column (2).

In 2011 also the census population was found to be higher than projected population by about 11 million. This possibly implies that either mortality has improved faster than expected or decline in fertility is a bit slower than assumed. Another possibility that exists is that the base population itself needed a revision. It is quite clear that more than one of these factors are operating simultaneously.

Appendix 2A: Census Schedules for 2001

House Listing Operations

Col. 1: *Line Number*
Col. 2: Building Number *(Municipal or local authority or census number)*
Col. 3: Census House Number
Col. 4: Predominant material of the Floor of the Census House Codes
Col. 5: Predominant material of the Wall of the Census House Codes
Col. 6: Predominant material of the Roof of the Census House Codes
Col. 7: Ascertain the use of Census House Codes
Col. 8: Condition of this Census House
Col. 9: Household Number
Cols 10–12: Total number of persons normally residing in this household (*persons, males, females*)

Information Relating to the Head of the Household

Col. 13: Name of the Head of the household
Col. 14: Sex Codes
Col. 15: If SC (scheduled castes) or ST (scheduled tribe) or other?

Only for Normal Households

Col. 16: Ownership status of this house?
Col. 17: Number of dwelling rooms with this Household (Record 0, 1, 2, 3...)
Col. 18: Number of married couple(s) living in this household (Record 0, 1, 2, 3...)
Col. 19: Number of married couple(s) having Independent room for sleeping (Record 0, 1, 2, 3...)

Col. 20: Drinking water source (*Type*)
Col. 21: Drinking water source (*Availability*)
Col. 22: Source of lighting

Col. 23:	Latrine within the house	Codes
Col. 24:	Waste water outlet connection	Codes
Col. 25:	Bathroom within the house	Codes
Col. 26:	Kitchen within the house	Codes
Col. 27:	Fuel used for cooking	Codes
Col. 28:	Radio/Transistor	Codes
Col. 29:	Television	Codes
Col. 30:	Telephone	Codes
Col. 31:	Bicycle	Codes
Col. 32:	Scooter/Motor Cycle/Moped	Codes
Col. 33:	Car/Jeep/Van	Codes
Col. 34:	Availing Banking Services	Codes

Household Schedule

Part I: Location Particulars

Name of State/UT
Name of District
Name of Tahsil/Taluk/Police Station
Name of Town/Village
Development Block/Circle/Mandal, among others
Enumeration Block Number
Serial number of household (*to be copied from column 7 of the abridged house list*)
Type of household (*appropriate code number*)

Part II: Individual Particulars

GENERAL AND SOCIO-CULTURAL CHARACTERISTICS

Q. 1: Name of the person
Q. 2: Relationship to head
Q. 3: Sex (*Male/Female*)
Q. 4: Age on last birthday (*in completed years*)

Q. 5: Current marital status
Q. 6: Age at marriage (*in completed years*)
Q. 7: Religion (*write name of the religion in full*)
Q. 8: If Scheduled Castes, write name of the Scheduled Castes from the list supplied
Q. 9: If Scheduled Tribe, write name of the Scheduled Tribe from the list supplied
Q. 10: Mother tongue
Q. 11: Other languages known (*enter up to two languages in order of proficiency*)
Q. 12: Literacy status (Literate/Illiterate)
Q. 13: Highest educational level attained (*for diploma or degree holder, also write the subject of specialisation*)
Q. 14: If attending educational institution
Q. 15: If the person is physically/mentally disabled, give appropriate code number

CHARACTERISTICS OF WORKERS AND NON-WORKERS

Q. 16: Did the person work any time last year? (*Includes even part time help or unpaid work on farm, family enterprise or in any other economic activity*)
(*Categories: Main worker: If worked for* 6 *months or more, Marginal Worker: If worked for less than* 6 *months, Non-Worker: If not Worked at all*)
Q. 17: Economic activity of Main or Marginal Worker:
Q. 17(i): Category of the economic activity of the Main or Marginal Worker
Q. 17(ii): For Workers in Household Industry and for other Workers only:
Occupation of the person
(Describe the actual work of the person)
Q. 17 (iii): Describe in detail the nature of industry, Trade or service where the person works/worked or of self-employment
Q. 17 (iv): Class of Worker
Q. 18: If Marginal Worker or Non-Worker, under Q. 16, record non-economic activity
Q. 19: If Marginal Worker or Non-Worker, is the person seeking/available for work?

Q. 20: Travel to place of work (for Other Workers Only):
Q. 20 (i): Distance from residence to place of work in Kilometres
Q. 20 (ii): Mode of travel to place of work

MIGRATION CHARACTERISTICS:

Q. 21: Birth Place: Is the person born in this village/town?
(*If 'Yes', put dash* [-] *against* Q. *21(i) and* Q. 21 *(ii) or, If 'No', enter particulars*)
Q. 21 (i) State/Country
(If birth place within India, write the present name of the state or if birth place outside India, write the present name of the country)
Q. 21 (ii) District
(If *birth place within India, write the present name of the district or if birth place outside India, put dash* [-])
Q. 22: Place of Last Residence: Has the person come to this village/ town from elsewhere?
(*If 'No', put dash* [-] *against Qs. 22(i) to* 22 *(v) or if 'Yes', give following particulars*):
Q. 22 (i) State/Country:
(*If place of last residence within India, Write the present name of the state or if place of last residence outside India, write the present name of the country*)
Q. 22 (ii) District:
(*If place of last residence within India, write the present name of the district or if place of last residence outside India, put dash* [-])
Q. 22 (iii) At the time of migration, was the place of last Codes Residence: Rural/Urban
Q. 22 (iv) Reason for migration of this person
Q. 22 (v) Duration of stay in this village or town since Migration (*in completed years*)

FERTILITY PARTICULARS:

Q. 23 Fertility For Ever Married Women only (*Currently Married, Widowed, Divorced or Separated*):
Q. 23 (i) Number of children surviving at present *(also include daughters and sons presently not staying in this household)[Separately for Daughter(s) and Son(s)]*

Q. 23 (ii) Total number of children ever born alive (*include both living and dead daughter(s) and son(s)*)
[Separately for Daughter(s) and Son(s)] For currently married women only:
Q. 23 (iii) Number of children born alive during last one year (*after 9th February 2000*)
[Separately for Daughter(s) and Son(s)]

PART III: For Household Engaged in Cultivation/Plantation

(i) Total net area of land under cultivation/plantation (*in Hectares*)
(ii) Net area of irrigated land (*in Hectares*)
(iii) Tenure status of land under cultivation/plantation

Appendix 2B: Census Schedules for 2011

House Listing Operations

Col. 1: *Line Number*
Col. 2: Building Number (*Municipal or local authority or census Number*)
Col. 3: Census House Number
Col. 4: Predominant material of the Floor of the Census House Codes
Col. 5: Predominant material of the Wall of the Census House Codes
Col. 6: Predominant material of the Roof of the Census House Codes
Col. 7: Ascertain the use of Census House Codes
Col. 8: Condition of this Census House
Col. 9: Household Number
Cols 10–12: Total number of persons normally residing in this household (*Persons, Males, Females*)

Information Relating to the Head of the Household:

Col. 13: Name of the Head of the household
Col. 14: Sex Codes
Col. 15: If SC (Scheduled Castes) or ST (Scheduled Tribe) or Other?

Only for Normal Households:

Col. 16: Ownership status of this house?
Col. 17: Number of dwelling rooms with this Household (*Record 0, 1, 2, 3...*)
Col. 18: Number of married couple(s) living in this household (*Record 0, 1, 2, 3...*)
Col. 19: Drinking water source (*Type*)
Col. 20: Drinking water source (*Availability*)
Col. 21: Source of lighting

Col. 22:	Latrine within the house	Codes
Col. 23:	if 1 in Col. 22 give code from 1 to 8 , if 2 in Col. 22 give code 9 or 0 from the list below	
Col. 24:	Waste water outlet connection	Codes
Col. 25:	Bathroom within the house	Codes
Col. 26:	Kitchen within the house	Codes
Col. 27:	Fuel used for cooking	Codes
Col. 28:	Radio/Transistor	Codes
Col. 29:	Television	Codes
Col. 30:	Computer/Laptop	
Col. 31:	Telephone/Mobile	Codes
Col. 32:	Bicycle	Codes
Col. 33:	Scooter/Motor Cycle/Moped	Codes
Col. 34:	Car/Jeep/Van	Codes
Col. 35:	Availing Banking Services	Codes

National Population Register

Side A

PART 1: LOCATION PARTICULARS

Name of State/UT
Name of District
Name of Tehsil/Taluk/Police Station
Name of Town and Village
Dev. Block/Circle/Mandal, etc.
House listing Block Number
Serial number of household

PART II: INDIVIDUAL PARTICULARS

Q. 1: Name of the person and resident status
Q. 2: Name of the person as should appear in the National Population Register
Q. 3: Relationship to Head
Q. 4: Sex
Q. 5: Date of Birth
Q. 6: Marital Status
Q. 7: Educational Qualification
Q. 8: Occupation/Activity
Q. 9: Names of Father, Mother and Spouse in full

Side B

Q. 10: Name of the Person
Q. 11: Place of Birth
Q. 12: Nationality as declared
Q. 13: Present address of usual residence
Q. 14: Duration stay at present address
Q. 15: Permanent residential address

Household Schedule

PART I: *LOCATION PARTICULARS:*

Name of State/UT
Name of District
Name of Tahsil/Taluk/PS/
Name of Town/Village
Dev. Block/Circle/Mandal etc.
Enumeration Block Number
Serial number of household (*to be copied from column 7 of the abridged house list*)
Type of household (*appropriate code number*)

PART II: *INDIVIDUAL PARTICULARS*

GENERAL AND SOCIO-CULTURAL CHARACTERISTICS

Q. 1: Name of the person
Q. 2: Relationship to head

Q. 3: Sex (Male/Female)
Q. 4: Age last birthday (*in completed years*)
Q. 5: Current marital status
Q. 6: Age at marriage (*in completed years*)
Q. 7: Religion (*write name of the religion in full*)
Q. 8: If Scheduled Castes or Schedule Tribe, write name of the Scheduled Castes or Schedule Tribe from the list supplied
Q. 9: If the person is physically/mentally disabled, give appropriate code number
Q. 10: Mother tongue
Q. 11: Other languages known (*enter up to two languages in order of proficiency*)
Q. 12: Literacy status (Literate/Illiterate)
Q. 13: Status of Attendance
Q. 14: Highest educational level attained (*for diploma or degree holder, also write the subject of specialisation*)

CHARACTERISTICS OF WORKERS AND NON-WORKERS:

Q. 15: Did the person work any time last year? (*Includes even part time help or unpaid work on farm, family enterprise or in any other economic activity*)
(Categories: Main worker: If worked for 6 months or more, Marginal Worker: If worked for less than 6 months, Non-Worker: If not Worked at all)
Q. 16: Economic activity of Main or Marginal Worker:
Q. 17: Category of the economic activity of the Main or Marginal Worker
Q. 18: Occupation of the person (*Describe the actual work of the person*)
Q. 19: Describe in detail the nature of industry, Trade or service where the person works/worked or of Self Employment
Q. 20: Class of Worker
Q. 21: non-economic activity
Q. 22: If Marginal Worker or Non-Worker, is the person seeking/available for work?
Q. 23 (i): Distance from residence to place of work in kilometres
Q. 23 (ii): Mode of travel to place of work

MIGRATION CHARACTERISTICS:

Q. 24: Birth Place: Is the person born in this village/town?
(If 'Yes', put dash (-) *against* Q. *21(i) and* Q. 21 *(ii) or, If 'No', enter particulars :)*
Q. 24 (i): State/Country (*If birth place within India, write the present name of the state or if birth place outside India, write the present name of the country*)
Q. 24 (ii): District [*If birth place within India, write the present name of the district or if birth place outside India, put dash (-)*]
Q. 25: Place of Last Residence: Has the person come to this village/town from elsewhere?
(If 'No', put dash (-) *against Qs. 22(i) to* 22 *(v) or if 'Yes', give following particulars :)*
Q. 25 (i): State/Country:
(*If place of last residence within India, Write the present name of the state or if place of last residence outside India, write the present name of the country*)
District:
[*If place of last residence within India, write the present name of the district or if place of last residence outside India, put dash (-)*]
Q. 25(ii): At the time of migration was the place of last Codes Residence: Rural/Urban
Q. 26: Reason for migration of this person Q. 26: Duration of stay in this village or town since Migration (*in completed years*)

FERTILITY PARTICULARS:

Q. 27: Fertility For Every Married Women only *(Currently Married, Widowed, Divorced or Separated):*
Q. 28: Number of children surviving at present *(also include daughters and sons presently not staying in this household) [Separately for Daughter(s) and Son(s)]*
Q. 29: Total number of children ever born alive *(include both living and dead daughter(s) and son(s))*
[Separately for Daughter(s) and Son(s)] For currently married women only:
Q. 30: Number of children born alive during last one year *(after 9th February 2000) [Separately for Daughter(s) and Son(s)]*

Comparison Part of Two Censuses:

The excluded questions from Census 2011 which were included in Census 2001:
Q. 1: For Household engaged in cultivation/plantation

(i) Total net area of land under cultivation/Plantation (in Hectares)
(ii) Net area of irrigated land (in Hectares)
(iii) Tenure status of land under cultivation/plantation

Q. 2: Number of married couple(s) having Independent room for sleeping

The included questions in Census 2011:
Q. 1: Condition of the Census House
Q. 2: Information relating to Computer/Laptop
Q. 3: National Population Register
Q. 4: Status of attendance

Bibliography

Agarwala, S.N. (ed.). 1960. *Some Projections of India's Population in Some Problems in Perspective Planning*. Bombay: Asia Publishing House.

Central Statistical Organization. 1999. *Guide to Official Statistics*. New Delhi: Ministry of Statistics and Programme Implementation.

Coale, A.J. and Edgar M. Hoover. 1958. *Population Growth and Economic Development in Low Income Countries*. Princeton: Office of Population Research.

Davis, Kingsley. 1968. *The Population of India and Pakistan*. Princeton: Princeton University Press, Office of Population Research.

Kothari, V.K. 1960. 'Long Term Trends in Employment Pattern in India', *Indian Economic Journal*, 7(April): 415.

Office of the Registrar General and Census Commissioner. 2011. *History of Census in India: Drop-in-Article: Census, No. 5*, Census of India 2011. New Delhi: Ministry of Home Affairs.

———. 2001. *Census and You, Census of India, 2001*. New Delhi: Ministry of Home Affairs.

———. 2011. *Overview of Census 2011*. New Delhi: Ministry of Home Affairs.

Planning Commission. 1978. *Report of the Expert Committee on Population Projections*, Paper 1 of 1979, October. New Delhi: Planning Commission of India.

———. 1988. *Report of the Expert Committee on Population Projections*, Occasional Paper 4 of 1988, January. New Delhi: Planning Commission of India.

———. 1996. *Population Projections for India and States, 1996–2016*, Report of the Technical Group on Population Projections constituted by the Planning Commission, August. New Delhi: Planning Commission of India.

———. 2006. *Population Projections for India and States, 2001–2026*, Report of the Technical Group on Population Projections constituted by the Planning Commission, May. New Delhi: Planning Commission of India.

Registrar General of India (RGI). 1952. *Census of India 1952*, Volume I, part IA. New Delhi: Office of the Registrar General of India.

———. 1999. *Survey of Causes of Death-Rural* (annual). New Delhi: Office of the Registrar General of India.

———. 2001. *Report of the Expert Committee on Population Projections, Paper 1 of Census of India 2001*. New Delhi: Office of the Registrar General of India.

———. 2014a. *Report on Medical Certification of Cause of Death*. New Delhi: Office of the Registrar General of India.

———. 2014b. *Sample Registration System—Statistical Report*. New Delhi: Office of the Registrar General of India.

———. 2014c. *Vital Statistics of India based on CRS*. New Delhi: Office of the Registrar General of India.

Thorner, Alice. 1962. 'The Secular Trends in the Indian Economy', *Economics Weekly*, 14(July): 28–30.

3

Agricultural Statistics

Agriculture plays a vital role in the Indian economy. Over 70 per cent of rural households depend on agriculture as their principal source of livelihood. Collection and maintenance of agricultural statistics are, therefore, of great importance.

Agricultural statistics refer to all statistics related to an agricultural economy, such as statistics of land utilization, area and production of crops, livestock, forests and fisheries, agricultural prices and wages, land holdings, and cost of cultivation. However, agricultural prices and wages will be dealt with in the chapter on prices and labour (Chapter 10), while the remaining topics are discussed here.

The collection of agricultural statistics is the responsibility of the states. The Directorate of Economics and Statistics (DES) in the Ministry of Agriculture (now the Ministry of Agriculture and Farmer's Welfare [MOAFW]), set up in 1947, is the central coordinating agency responsible for the collection, compilation, and publication of agricultural statistics at the state and all-India level.

Agricultural statistics are divided into the following six parts each of which will be discussed separately:

(1) Land utilization statistics
(2) Yield statistics
(3) Animal husbandry statistics
(4) Fishery statistics

(5) Forestry statistics
(6) Miscellaneous agricultural statistics

Land Utilization Statistics

Land utilization statistics give the area of land put to different uses, area irrigated and crops irrigated, and the area under different crops. These are continuously available since 1884. In 1884 forecasts on area and production of wheat were issued. By 1900, oilseeds, rice, cotton, jute, and sugarcane were added to the list. The scope and geographical coverage of these statistics have been gradually expanding. These statistics are available for 93 per cent of the total geographical area. The area for which statistics are available is called the reporting area and the remaining area is called the non-reporting area.

About 83 per cent of the non-reporting area is in Jammu and Kashmir (J&K) and most of it is under the occupation of Pakistan and China. The percentage of reporting area has been almost the same since 1970–1. The remaining non-reporting area consists of areas or pockets covered by forests and barren mountains, and hilly forests mostly in Himachal Pradesh and the northeastern states.

For estimation of land utilization as well as crop area estimates, the states and union territories (UTs) can be divided into three broad groups:

(1) States where the statistics are collected on a complete enumeration basis. In these states (referred to as temporarily settled states) an elaborate machinery called revenue agency collects the statistics as part of the land records. These statistics are collected on the basis of complete field-to-field enumeration by a *patwari* during the harvest inspection (18 states and 5 UTs). The work of the patwari is supervised by senior revenue officers.
(2) Kerala, Odisha, and West Bengal are known as permanently settled states, where there is no land revenue agency at the village level and land used and crop area statistics are collected through specially appointed field staff under a scheme known as the Establishment of an Agency for Reporting Agriculture Statistics (EARAS) of sample surveys. The sample surveys are conducted in a random sample of 20 per cent of the villages of the state that

are selected in such a way that during a period of five years, all the villages of the state are covered.

(3) Parts of Assam (the hill districts), Arunachal Pradesh, Manipur, Meghalaya, Mizoram, Nagaland, Sikkim and Tripura, and the UTs of Andaman and Nicobar Islands and Lakshadweep have only conventional estimates based on the personal assessment of a village *chowkidaar*.

The three categories of states account for 86, 9, and 5 per cent respectively of the total reporting area.

Even for those areas which are covered either by complete enumeration or sample surveys, the plots under mixed crops give rise to a special difficultly in deciding the cropping pattern of the cropped area. Sowing of mixed crops is common in Bihar, Uttar Pradesh, Madhya Pradesh, Rajasthan, and Punjab. A source of inaccuracy arises on account of different methods used for estimation of the area under mixed crops in different states. For some states, the gross area is apportioned between its constituents at the field level by the state village officials by eye-appraisal. For some other states, the entire area under mixed crops is recorded at the field level. The apportioning into constituents is done only at the district level by means of fixed ratios assumed to be representative of average crop conditions. Attempts are, however, being made to standardize the method for all the states. The area sown under each crop represents the area actually sown, irrespective of whether the crop reaches maturity or not except in cases where the land, after the failure of the first crop, is devoted to another crop. In that case, such area is shown under the latter crop and is excluded from the area of the original crop. If no other crops are sown, then the area is allowed to continue under the old crop. In addition, the temporary bunds lying within cropped fields are generally included in the area under the crop. The area of permanent bunds and uncultivated patches is generally excluded from the cropped area.

The area irrigated is available as part of land utilization statistics, both according to crops irrigated and according to sources of irrigation. Areas classified according to sources of irrigation is the net area. If two crops are irrigated from the same source on the same land in the same year, the area is counted only once. Gross area is given while classifying according to crops. No data is available regarding the quantity of irrigation.

Till 1949–50 the land area in the country was classified into five heads. A Technical Committee on the Coordination of Agricultural Statistics was set up in 1949 by the Ministry of Food and Agriculture which found that this classification did not give a clear and meaningful picture of the present state of exploitation of land and the potential uses to which it could be put. In addition, this classification was not sufficiently detailed to serve the needs of agricultural planning, nor were the definitions uniform all over the country. On the recommendations of the Technical Committee a ninefold land use classification replaced the old classification in 1950–1. This committee also laid down uniform concepts and standard definitions of the various classes in the new classification. The distribution of the total geographical area (all-India basis) into nine classes is given in Appendix Table 3A.1. The table in the appendix gives an idea about the variation over years in the different uses of land. The relationship between the old fivefold and the new ninefold land use classification and also the concepts and explanations of the new classification are given in Appendix Table 3A.2. Appendix Table 3A.3 gives an idea about the different sources from which the area is irrigated and the shifting pattern of the use of different sources over the years.

Land use statistics are also being collected through land use or cover mapping by the National Remote Sensing Agency (NRSA) according to a 22-fold classification (for a definition see Annex 4.6 of the *Report of the National Statistical Commission*).[1] This classification is very wide and provides useful information for land development programmes. However, these details are not yet available at the local block and panchayat levels. At a conference of central and state statistical organizations, there was a consensus on the addition of social forestry, marshy and water logged land, and land under still waters to the existing ninefold classification. However, so far this has not been done. Under land utilization statistics, irrigation statistics have special importance. Irrigation statistics relate to data on gross as well as net area irrigated by different sources (canals, tanks, and tube wells, among others) and under different crops. In addition to the data compiled by the DES as part of the land utilization statistics, the data on irrigation is available through the agricultural census conducted at

[1] *Report of the National Statistical Commission*, volume 2, page 501–3.

an interval of about 5 years. Data are also available in the publications of the Ministry of Water Resources. The Minor Irrigation Division (MID) of this ministry compiles information on minor irrigation at the national level on the basis of statistics furnished by the nodal offices designated for this purpose in individual states. Under the scheme of Rationalization of Minor Irrigation Statistics (RMIS), a periodical census of minor irrigation is conducted throughout the country. The primary field work of the census is entrusted to the patwari and the village-level worker (of a community development block) under the supervision of block-level officials, who also exercise a 5 per cent sample check in randomly selected villages. The results of the sample check are used to apply a correction factor to the main census results. So far four censuses relating to the years 1986–7, 1993–4, 2000–1, and 2006–7 have been conducted. The reports have been published for the censuses. Information System Organization (ISO) of the Central Water Commission (CWC) is responsible for statistics pertaining to major and medium irrigation projects. These statistics are published in Water and Related Statistics, brought out once in every two years. It covers a wide range of data on water and its related resources in the country. It deals with key indicators of water resources such as water availability, creation of storage, and ultimate irrigation potential, and data on utilization of water resources. Statistics supplied by the ISO on major and medium irrigation projects and those compiled by the MID are the alternative sources of estimation of area under irrigation. There is no substantial difference in the estimates of irrigated area for the agricultural census years given by the census and by the DES. This is because the basic data sources for both are the same. However, the estimates given by the Ministry of Water Resources are about 10 per cent higher than those of the DES. *Land Use Statistics at a Glance* is published by the DES and it gives the data on land utilization at state level.

Estimates of the Area and Yield of Different Crops

For the estimation of area and yield, crops can be divided into five broad categories, the details of which are given in Appendix Table 3A.4.

(1) Principal crops
(2) Minor crops

(3) Plantation crops
(4) Fruits and vegetables
(5) Miscellaneous and unspecified crops
(6) By-products

The method of estimation under these categories will be discussed in the following sections.

Principal Crops

Principal crops are called so because forecasts for those of acreage and production are issued. Since the final estimates of production based on the complete enumeration of area and yield through crop-cutting experiments (CCEs) become available much after the crops are harvested and since the government requires advance estimates of production for various policy purposes, forecasts giving advance estimates are issued in respect of principal food and non-food crops (food grains, oilseeds, sugarcane, and fibres, among others) to give the features of the crop at various stages of its growth. Four forecasts are issued: the first in the middle of September, the second in January, the third towards the end of March, and the fourth by the end of May. Final estimates of crop area and production are issued in December; those estimates are fully revised in the following December along with the final estimates for the next year.

The first forecast relating to the kharif crops is mostly based on reports prepared by the states, mainly guided by the visual observation of field officials. The second forecast covering both the kharif and rabi crops takes into account additional information obtained from various sources including agricultural inputs, incidence of pests and diseases, and weekly reports of state departments of agriculture regarding area coverage and conditions of standing crops, among others. Results of remote sensing data are also considered at this stage. In the third forecast, the earlier advance estimates of both the kharif and rabi seasons are firmed up, again taking into account information received from sources such as Market Intelligence Units, the Meteorological Department, and the Crop Weather Watch Group (CWWG). The fourth forecast is based on firm figures supplied by State Agricultural Statistics Authorities (SASAs) who are by then in a position to obtain fairly dependable estimates of yield rates through general crop estimation surveys (GCES). In addition to the four forecasts, the DES issues the 'Final Estimates' of crop area and production in December. As a few states continue to revise their data on delayed receipt of information, the all-India crop statistics are brought out as 'fully revised' in the next crop year in the following December. The four forecasts are issued for 27 principal crops. For 17 minor crops, only two estimates, namely the final and fully revised, are available in December that year and December next year. The estimates are published in *Agricultural Statistics at a Glance*.

The estimates given by the advance forecasts are based on the subjective appraisals at various levels and do not reflect the ground situation correctly.

Recently, the MOAFW has set up a National Crop Forecasting Centre (NCFC) with the object of examining the existing mechanism of building forecasts of principal crops and developing more objective techniques. The NCFC takes into account information on weather conditions, supply of agricultural inputs, pests, diseases, and related aspects, including the proceedings of CWWG in the formulation of scientific and objective forecasting methods to replace the present system. The work of the NCFC is still at a preliminary stage and it needs more statistical support to be able to develop appropriate models of forecasting.

Method of Yield Estimation

The state of data on crop yields per acre 50 years ago was much less satisfactory. The average yields were normally estimated as a product of 'normal' or 'standard yields' and the crop 'condition factor'. The standard yields were obtained through CCEs conducted in the fields, which were considered (subjectively) by the officials to be bearing an average crop. The standard yield was subject to revision once every few years. The condition factor was a subjective index of the condition of a crop in any particular season in relation to the 'normal condition' of the crop in a 'normal' year in the recent past. In other words, in the data on crop yields at the dawn of independence, subjective judgment played a far more dominant role than scientifically established facts.

The traditional method has been gradually getting replaced by the crop cutting method of yield estimation. The CCEs are conducted under scientifically designed GCES. The primary objective of GCES is to obtain fairly reliable estimates of average yield (yield rate) of principal food and non-food crops for states and UTs that are important from the point of view of crop production. The GCES consist of identification and marking of experimental plots of a specified size and shape in a selected field on the principle of random sampling, threshing, weighing, and recording of harvested produce from the plot. These weights form the basic data for yield estimation. The number of experiments and the distribution over the strata are made in a manner so as to be able to obtain the yield rate estimates with a fair degree of precision at the level of the state and each major crop-growing district.

The GCES (2010–11) covered 68 crops (52 foods and 16 non-foods) conducted in 20 land record states/UTs, three EARAS states and six other states/UTs. Around 9,00,000 experiments are conducted every year with the help of state revenue and agricultural staff of a rank higher than the primary field staff of the departments. The survey design adopted is that of a stratified three-stage random sampling with the *tehsil* or *taluka* as the stratum, a village as the first-stage unit, the field growing the crop as second-stage unit, and a plot of a specified shape and size (usually 5m × 5m) as the ultimate unit of sampling. In each selected village, generally two fields growing the crop are selected for conducting the CCE. In each stratum, a simple average of sample plots is obtained. The district average is obtained by weighing the stratum average in proportion to the net area under the crop in different strata of the district. The state average is similarly obtained as the weighted average of the district averages. The improvement of crop statistics (ICS) scheme carries out a quality check on the field operations of GCES under which around 30,000 experiments are supervised by the ICS staff at the harvesting stage.

The details of timely reporting scheme and the scheme for the implementation of crop statistics are given as follows.

Timely Reporting Scheme (TRS) and the Scheme for the Improvement of Crop Statistics

Under this component timely and reliable estimate of area under principal crops for each of the agricultural seasons are generated on the basis of complete enumeration of 20 per cent villages selected randomly, within a specific time frame. The TRS is implemented in 19 land record states. Implementing states provide a breakup of area under irrigated/un-irrigated and high yielding varieties (HYVs). The Agricultural Statistics division compiles the data.

In order to improve the timeliness and quality of area statistics the aforementioned two schemes are in operation since the early 70s.

The TRS has the principal objective of reducing the time lag in making available the area statistics of major crops in addition to providing the sampling frame for selection of crop-growing fields for CCEs. Under the TRS, the patwari is required to complete the *girdawari* on a priority basis in a 20 per cent random sample of villages and to submit the village crop statements to higher authorities by a stipulated date for the preparation of advance estimates of the area under major crops. These are used in the framing of crop forecasts. The TRS sample of villages is also selected in such a way that the entire temporarily settled parts of the country are covered over a period of five years.

Under the ICS scheme, an independent agency of supervisors carries out a physical verification of the patwari's girdawari in a sub-sample of the TRS sample villages (in four clusters of five survey numbers each); each makes an assessment of the extent of discrepancies between the supervisor's and patwari's crop area entries in the sample clusters. The supervisor also scrutinizes the village crop abstract prepared by the patwari and checks whether it is free from totalling errors and whether it has been dispatched to the higher authorities within the stipulated time. The ICS also covers the permanently settled states and the supervising agency in this case too carries out the check in a sub-sample of EARAS sample villages using the same methodology as followed in the temporarily settled states. In all, 10,000 sample villages are covered by the ICS, roughly 8,500 in the temporarily settled states and 1,500 in the permanently settled states. The National Sample Survey Office (NSSO) is responsible for the planning and operations of the ICS and employs full-time staff for field supervision. It shares the fieldwork with the designated state agencies, which carry out the field supervision in about half the number of sample villages. As mentioned earlier, the ICS is used for improvement in the crop output through supervision in CCEs.

More recently, since 1990, an attempt has been underway to use remote sensing (RS) technology for estimation of crop areas and land use through a centrally sponsored scheme, Crop Acreage and Production Estimation (CAPE). The objective of CAPE, among others, is to provide state-level crop area estimates, meeting a 90/90 accuracy goal using RS data covering mainly the crop growing parts of the states. Pre-harvest area estimates are reported to be generated on a regular basis for major crops like rice, wheat, *ragi*, *jowar*, groundnut, and cotton. The feasibility of RS in providing detailed and disaggregated area statistics at the local level (village or panchayat) has yet to be established.

As noted earlier, the main purpose of the ICS scheme is to monitor the performance of the primary reporting agency in the TRS and EARAS villages. The findings of the ICS over a number of years reveal a high degree of negligence in carrying out the girdawari, thereby casting doubt on the reliability of crop area statistics. For instance, a review of the ICS results for the four years ending 1998–9 (see Annexe 4.1 of *Report of the National Statistical Commission*, Volume 2, pp. 493–5) shows that the following:

(1) The patwaris submit crop statements to the processing centres without completing the girdawari in about 10 per cent of the villages.
(2) Village crop statements are received at the processing centre from only around 78 per cent of the sample villages (that is, a non-response of 22 per cent) and around 45 per cent only by due date.
(3) Crop entries of the patwari and the supervisor do not tally with each other in about one third of the survey numbers inspected.
(4) The net effect of discrepancies between the patwari's and supervisor's crop entries is quite large in respect of even some major crops.

It is significant that the aforementioned ratios are of the same order in a previous study of ICS results for the four-year period ending 1988–9.

This is the kind of performance in the TRS sample despite the patwari being aware that his work will be subjected to technical supervision; one cannot therefore expect a better performance in 80 per cent of the remaining villages.

These findings are a clear indication of the patwari's neglect of one of his major functions. It is a matter of concern that this has continued on for many years evidently with the knowledge and indulgence of the higher level officials of the state departments of revenue and land records.

The central problem is the deterioration of the system of maintaining village land use and crop records—the basic source of primary data. Village-level revenue staff is increasingly overburdened with multiple functions; maintenance of accurate and complete agricultural data is given low priority. Supervision of records relating to land agriculture is increasingly rare and far too perfunctory to ensure their completeness and accuracy. The trend to shift from the traditional system of appointing village officials into one where they are drawn from a transferable cadre adds greatly to the difficulties of collecting data based on first hand inspection of all plots. Over the years the priority attached by state revenue departments in ensuring maintenance of complete and reliable land use and crop data has declined to the point of indifference. Periodic inspection of these records by higher level officials has become increasingly rare and lax.

Another deficiency of crop area statistics needs to be mentioned. With the development and modernization of agriculture, several new short duration crops are grown. Although the patwari is required to undertake intermediate crop inspection between the two major kharif and rabi seasons, this does not appear to be done regularly. Even if short duration crops, such as vegetables, flowers, and mushrooms, are covered during the crop inspection, they are not listed separately in the final crop abstract but are clubbed together under 'other crops'.

The statistics thus collected are compiled and published by different states in their season and crop reports. These statistics are also sent to the DES, Department of Agriculture Cooperation and Farmers Welfare. The Directorate compiles the figures and used to publish these in the annual publication, *Indian Agricultural Statistics* Vol. 1 and Vol. 2. This publication was giving classification of area, area irrigated and crops irrigated, and area under different crops. There was a considerable time lag in the publication of these volumes. The time lag for volume one was about three years, and for volume two about six years. This publication has since been discontinued and replaced by state-wise and district-wise land utilization statistics at a glance. The Directorate also isues, in a mimeographed form, state-wise provisional figures of land utilization with a time lag of only about a year. Land utilization estimates are also given in *Agricultural Statistics at a Glance*.

There have been a number of problems in the estimates of various crop-wise area statistics. The regular village-level revenue agencies have been removed in the states of Andhra Pradesh,[2] Karnataka, and Tamil Nadu. During last 10–12 years the crop acreage statistics have been reduced to bad fiction (Minhas and Roy Choudhary 2002). There are problems in the estimation of crop area statistics in the states of Bihar, Odisha, and West Bengal. It is also mentioned by them that subjective elements are increasingly directing the choice of crop cuts. The TRS introduced to provide a scientific basis for selection of fields for crop cuts has totally failed in some states (Andhra Pradesh, Bihar, Karnataka, and Tamil Nadu) and worked unsatisfactorily in some others. According to Minhas and Roy Choudhary (2002), the reported figures relating to crop production in the late 1990s are based more on negotiations across the table than scientific procedures implemented earlier. According to a press release issued on 12 February 1999 by the Department of Statistics, it is pointed out that area enumeration in respect of about 40 per cent of land under major agricultural crops is unscientific. Productivity measurements in crops, based on CCEs, are in bad shape (see Economic and Political Weekly Research Foundation [EPWRF] 2004). From this statement, one can get an idea about the reliability of area and hence yield estimates.

If one goes through the value of output of crops as given in the detailed tables of the National Accounts Statistics (NAS), one can notice that the estimates given for a year are revised the next year and again revised after another year. This is after the quick estimates issued a year earlier than the first estimates are issued. In a number of crops, the difference between the estimates given for a year in three volumes of NAS is more than 20 per cent. These differences may be due to the revised data available regarding the quantity of production and prices. However, it may be noted that at the aggregate level gross domestic product (GDP) from the agriculture sector the difference due to revision is small.

Yield Estimates by More than One Agency

Apart from the estimates of production compiled and published by the DES, a separate series is prepared by the trade organizations in

[2] This volume refers to the unified state of Andhra Pradesh before the reorganization of 2014.

case of cotton and oilseeds. Estimates of cotton production are published by the Cotton Advisory Board (CAB) and those for oilseeds by Central Organization for Oil Industry and Trade (COOIT).The CAB estimates for cotton are based on the data on market arrivals, volume of cotton ginned and pressed in all ginning mills irrespective of the area sown, and the condition of the crop. However, these estimates are based on the reports from various agencies, such as the Cotton Corporation of India and Indian Cotton Mills Federation. The estimates from the two sources differ widely. The DES estimates are considerably less than the CAB.

There are differences in the estimates provided by the two sources for oilseeds as well. The COOIT estimates are based on the feedback from important markets about arrivals, trends of the crop, and the additional information provided by the members of the industry.

For official circles, the estimates by the DES are mainly used.

In addition, there are wide differences in the estimates of state agricultural statistical authorities and state cane commissioners (SCC) in the case of sugarcane.

Plantation Crops

The estimates of plantation crops are based on the returns received from the respective commodity boards.

Minor Crops

For minor crops the estimates of area are reliable only in temporarily settled states while the yield estimates are partly ad hoc in nature.

Fruits and Vegetables

For some of the items under this group, such as potatoes, onions, bananas, and papayas final and fully revised estimates are issued, while for the remaining, no reliable estimates are available. Recently there have been some improvements in the database of horticulture crops. The DES operates a centrally sponsored scheme 'Crop Estimation Survey on Fruits & Vegetables' in 11 states covering seven fruits and seven vegetables and spice crops (mangos, bananas, apples, citrus, grapes, pineapples, guavas, potatoes, onions, tomatoes, cabbages, cauliflower, ginger, and turmeric) for estimating area and production. The survey is still in a plot stage. The results of the DES pilot survey are published in its *Report and Database of Pilot Scheme on Major Fruits & Vegetables*.

On recommendations of the National Statistical Commission (NSC), the Indian Agricultural Statistical Research Institute (IASRI) has undertaken a study to develop an alternative methodology for estimating the production of horticultural crops with the financial support of the Central Statistics Office (CSO), Ministry of Statistics and Programme Implementation (MOSPI).

Under this study, an alternative sampling methodology has been developed for (i) the estimation of acreage under each major fruit and vegetable crop; and (ii) the estimation of yield rates and total production of major fruit and vegetable crops grown in the state. The survey procedures under the alternative methodology have been simplified which are cost effective and less time consuming. As the NSC has also recommended that the alternative methodology should be tried out on a pilot basis before actually implementing it on a large scale, IASRI has submitted a proposal to undertake a pilot study in five states to test the methodology to the MOSPI for financial support. A final decision in this regard is still awaited.

The National Horticultural Board (NHB) compiles and publishes estimates of area, production and prices of all important fruit and vegetable crops based on reports furnished by the state directorates of horticulture and agriculture. The methodology followed by NHB is not clearly spelt out. The estimates are apparently based on the informed assessment of local-level officials dealing with horticulture and the reports of market arrivals in major wholesale fruit and vegetable markets. The estimates are of doubtful reliability being based on subjective reports received from ground-level staff. The estimates are published in its annual publication, *Indian Horticulture Database*.

The survey by the DES, which is still in a 'pilot' stage, follows a stratified three-stage random sampling design in the case of fruit crops, with village, orchard, and fruit-bearing trees as the sampling units at the successive stages. The sample size is usually 150 to 200 sample villages in each major fruit-growing district, five orchards per sample village, and four fruit-bearing trees per orchard. The number and weight of fruits gathered from the sampled trees is observed and recorded, which form the basis for yield estimation. The survey approach in the case of vegetable crops is somewhat more complex due to special features of cultivation of these crops, especially the short duration of the crop and the number of pickings required to record the harvested produce.

The production estimates of fruits and vegetables available from the DES pilot survey are based on sound technical methodology. However, the survey procedures are complex, time consuming, and rather difficult to implement in practice. Further, the survey is limited to 11 states and its extension to the remaining states will take a long time due to the fact that many of them do not possess the necessary staff resources to carry out the fieldwork. Adoption of this methodology on a nation-wide scale is a remote possibility.

The estimates furnished by the NHB relate to the entire country but they are of doubtful reliability being essentially based on subjective reports received from the ground-level staff. There is, in fact, considerable divergence between the NHB and the DES estimates for the crops covered by both.

According to the NAS the value of output of fruits and vegetables for the year 1993–4 was Rs 24,181 crore according to National Accounts with 1980–1 as the base year while it was Rs 38,420 crore according to the series with 1993–4 as the base year. For the series with 1993–4 as the base, the data for other fruits and vegetables is based on the NHB, which according to them is a better source. However, according to *Report of the National Statistical Commission (2001)*, the estimates are not at all reliable. It may be that this source is used to show higher output from this component. The CSO should, therefore, deeply analyse this source before using it in the series to be revised again. However, there is no difference in the estimates based on the series with 1993–4, 1999–2000, and 2004–5 bases.

Miscellaneous and Unspecified Crops

For crops under this group, direct output estimates are not available. The estimates of output of these crop groups are obtained by applying an appropriate average value of yield per hectare to the estimated area under each of these crop groups (obtained as part of land use statistics).

The average value of yield per hectare under each unspecified crop group is obtained as the weighted average of value of yield per hectare of the crops contained in that group. These are used by the CSO for getting the GDP from agriculture. Estimates of output in terms of quantity are not available.

By-Products

Estimates of the output of by-products, such as straw and stalks, bagasse, cane trash and sticks of different crops, are also required for estimation of GDP. These are based on the results of CCEs. The estimates are not separately published anywhere, but are available in value terms from the NAS.

Forecasting Agricultural Output Using Space, Agro-Meteorology and Land-Based Observations (FASAL)

The FASAL scheme envisages forecasts of crop acreage and production at various stages of crop growth. Initial forecasts (at the time of sowing) are to be provided based on econometric models in the beginning of the season followed by mid-stage and pre-harvest forecasts based on agro-met parameters and through RS technology. The use of these new approaches is expected to enhance capabilities of the existing system of crop forecasts and crop estimation. The department visualized the adoption of emerging technologies such as RS and Geographic Information Systems (GIS) as early as 1987, when the project 'Crop Acreage and Production Estimation (CAPE)' was launched in collaboration with the Space Application Centre, Ahmedabad. The project successfully demonstrated national-level forecasts of wheat and kharif rice, in addition to making district-level pre-harvest production forecasting of cotton, rapeseed/mustard, and rabi sorghum in their major growing regions in the country. Besides RS, other important inputs such as weather data, land-based observations and economic parameters influencing farmers' decisions also serve as complementary and supplementary inputs for making crop forecasts. While crop forecasting with RS techniques is carried out when a crop has grown sufficiently, forecasting at the sowing stage is attempted through econometric and agro-met models using previous years' crop acreage and production data, market prices, and current season weather data. Thus, an approach which integrates inputs from these diverse sources was needed to make forecasts of desired coverage, accuracy and timeliness, and the concept of FASAL was devised. The scheme came into operation from August 2006.

In 2011, the implementation of the scheme was reviewed and it was decided to revise the implementation strategy by including drought assessment, horticulture crops, rain-fed area assessment and global monitoring in the scope of work of the FASAL scheme and operationalizing the methodology developed so far through the creation of a new centre in the department itself. The Standing Finance Committee in its meeting held on 23 March 2011 approved the revised implementation strategy of the FASAL scheme and a new centre namely the Mahalanobis National Crop Forecast Centre that has been set up in the Indian Agricultural Research Institute Campus, New Delhi. The centre was inaugurated on 23 April 2012 and has started providing crop forecasts to the department on a regular basis.

Vaidiyanathan Committee Report on Agricultural Statistics

The Committee of Experts on Agricultural Statistics has recommended a radical restructuring of farm statistics in a phased manner to ensure objective, reliable, and timely estimates of crop-wise areas and yields.

The Committee of Experts, headed by A. Vaidyanathan, was constituted in 2009 to study a system of agricultural statistics and recommend necessary improvements.

The report has brought out the deficiencies in the current system, of both area and yield estimation, arising from serious lacunae in institutional arrangements to collect, supervise, and validate basic data on large scale on diverse crops. The immediate focus, therefore, should be on putting in place an institutional arrangement that would provide reliable and timely data needed for monitoring agricultural trends and for policymaking at the state and national levels.

The committee recommended setting up of National Crop Statistics Centre (NCSC) as the nodal agency to undertake the work in collaboration with the Departments of Agriculture and Space. Its specific terms of reference are as follows.

- Review current methodology used in TRS, EARAS and ICS, and GCES for estimating land use, crop-wise area, irrigated area, yield, and production.
- Assess problems being faced in observing prescribed methodology, organization, and procedures for collection and validation of data.
- Suggest ways and means to ensure availability of estimates, which are reliable and collected timely.
- Suggest institutional framework for improvement of agricultural statistics.
- Review experience of RS technology for estimating area and yield of various crops.
- Suggest measures, techniques, and organizational arrangements needed to make satellite data more reliable by ground-truthing the same.
- Other relevant issues for improving reliability, accuracy, standards, and timely collection of agricultural statistics.

In reviewing the strengths and weaknesses of the existing system, the committee has studied available material in (i) detailed documentation of the methodology, organizational procedures used for collection of agricultural statistics generally, and of the specific schemes for estimation of area, yields, and production of crops; (ii) numerous critical reviews of the functioning of the system in scholarly publications, seminar proceedings, and reports of various official committees; (iii) discussion and recommendations on Agricultural Statistics in the NSC's report as well as other recent publications on the subject; (iv) the annual reports on the working of TRS/ICS/EARAS and their ability to provide complete, reliable, and timely data based on inspection of a sub-sample of TRS villages; and (v) the organization and functioning of FASAL, the scope of estimates generated by it and their use by the ministry for estimating area and yields.

Compared to the central sample, state-level inspectors consistently report a higher rate of on-time completion (and a much lower rate of non-completion) of girdawari both overall and in a large majority of states. Both show an increase in non-completion rates since 2000–1. The extent of timely completion difference varies across states and seasons.

In the central sample, the overall proportion of villages submitting TRS returns on time is smaller compared to the proportion which has completed girdawari on time.

To sum up, the inspection reports show that a large proportion of the sub-sample of central sample villages supposed to be supervised and inspected closely (i) have not completed girdawari at the time of inspection; (ii) do not submit TRS returns on time; (iii) submit returns after a delay and/or without completing girdawari, this often being a sizeable proportion; (iv) contain sizeable errors in recording of crop area by patwaris whose estimates are on the average below those of inspectors; and (v) contain large differences in all these respects across states and crops with state sample inspections presenting a more favourable picture than those emerging from the central sample.

Animal Husbandry Statistics

The Department of Animal Husbandry, Dairying and Fisheries (DADF) came into existence with effect from 1 February 1991, by converting two divisions of the Department of Agriculture Cooperation and Farmers Welfare—namely, Animal Husbandry and Dairy Development—into a separate combined department.

This department is responsible for matters relating to livestock production, preservation, protection from disease, and improvement of stocks and dairy development, and also for matters relating to the Delhi Milk Scheme and the National Dairy Development Board. It also looks after all matters pertaining to fishing and fisheries—inland and marine. The statistical activities of the department are carried in its two major divisions—namely, Animal Husbandry Statistics Division and Fisheries Division. The Animal Husbandry Statistics Division implements three schemes—Integrated Sample Surveys for Estimation of Major Livestock Products, Livestock Census, and Livestock Insurance. While the first two schemes are central sector schemes, the third scheme is a centrally sponsored scheme.

The Animal Husbandry Statistics Division of the department conducts integrated sample surveys to estimate productions of major livestock products, such as milk, eggs, meat, and wool. It also collects other livestock statistics through interaction with state governments and other central departments/organizations concerned with development of the livestock sector. Major livestock products are estimated on the basis of sample surveys being conducted throughout the year under the central scheme of Integrated Sample Survey for the Estimation of Major Livestock Products. All the states and UTs have been implementing the scheme. The survey covers 15 per cent of the villages of the country.

The Livestock Census, which gives the livestock population of different species—earlier conducted quinquennially by the DES of the MOAFW with the help of different agencies in states/UTs—has been transferred to the DADF of the MOAFW from the 17th Livestock Census conducted with reference to October 2003. The 18th Livestock Census was conducted with reference to 15 October 2007 and the 19th with 15 October 2012.

The statistical publications brought out by the department are:

(1) *All India Summary Reports of Livestock Census*; state reports; UT reports
(2) *Basic Animal Husbandry Statistics*

The details of these publications are given in the following paragraphs.

All India Summary Report of Livestock Census

In view of the importance of livestock sector to the national economy and considering the short span of reproductivity and life of domestic animals, the first census was organized during 1919–20 and since then it has been conducted quinquennially by all states/UTs in India. So far, 19 such censuses have been conducted and the latest one is the 19th Livestock Census in the series with 15 October 2012 as the date of reference. The 17th Livestock Census was due to be conducted in 2002 but due to the transfer of this work from the Department of Agriculture Cooperation and Farmers Welfare to the DADF in February 2002, it got delayed and was conducted with reference date 15 October 2003; but the 18th census was conducted on time, that is, with reference date 15 October 2007 and 19th with 15 October 2012.

The ultimate responsibility for conducting the livestock census rests with the state governments. The Department of Animal Husbandry in the respective states/UTs was responsible for managing the enumeration and computerization of data with Directors of the Animal Husbandry Services as the nodal officers. The central government has coordinated the work of the states and issued necessary guidelines to ensure uniformity in collection of census data and their processing.

The National Informatics Centre (NIC) imparted training to state officials on the software developed by them for computerizing the 18th and 19th Livestock Census data. The census data was computerized by the respective state governments or private agencies engaged by them, using the software developed by the NIC. The computerized data from states was processed at the NIC for validations and verifications before generation of tables as per an approved tabulation plan. In the 18th Livestock Census, for the very first time, digital data up to the household level was processed at the central level through the NIC. The All India Report (Provisional Results) on the 18th Livestock Census, processed by the NIC from the digital data–village level totals is available on the official website of the department. The same applies to the 19th Census.

Basic Animal Husbandry Statistics

The Animal Husbandry Statistics Division of the department conducts integrated sample surveys. Surveys are done throughout India around the year. A three-stage stratified random sampling is adopted to find the annual estimates of livestock production of major livestock products after building it on a seasonal basis. The survey design is that of multistage sampling with villages as the first stage, households as the second stage and animals from the selected households as the third and ultimate stage. The survey provides the estimates of the livestock numbers as well as major livestock products (milk, meat, wool, eggs, and the unit cost of production of milk and eggs). For other livestock products and by-products, the estimates of production are prepared by the CSO on the basis of yield rates obtained from different District Management Team reports. These are published in the consolidated annual report of the sample survey prepared by the states/UTs. At the national level, state-wise annual estimates are published in the biennial publication known as *Basic Animal Husbandry Statistics* or through the department's website.

Annual Report

This department also publishes an annual report. Ten topics and annexures are included in this annual report: (i) organization, (ii) approach and strategies, (iii) animal husbandry, (iv) dairy development, (v) fisheries, (vi) trade matters, (vii) special component plan and tribal sub-plan, (viii) empowerment of women, (ix) international cooperation (x) results framework document.

Fisheries Statistics

The Fisheries Statistics Division of the department deals with all matters concerning fisheries statistics, such as collection, compilation, analysis, and publication of fish production, and fish exports, among others. The division implements a central sector scheme, Strengthening of Database and Information Networking for the Fisheries Sector with the following objectives:

(1) To improve the database of inland and marine fisheries resources and catch of fish by adoption of standardized methodology of data collection through sample surveys for estimation of inland fisheries resources, such as ponds and tanks, lakes and reservoirs, rivers, lagoons, and estuaries, among others, and inland as well as marine fish catch in all the states/UTs.
(2) To improve Information Technology System in the states/UTs as well as National Level Fishery Institutes so that data collection and their analysis can be done efficiently and effectively.
(3) To conduct census of inland as well as marine fisheries.

Fisheries can be classified into marine and inland. The DADF of the MOAFW is in charge of compiling the data related to this sector from the Fisheries Departments of the state governments. To collect data regarding marine fish, a multistage stratified sample survey is used to estimate the fish production. The survey design consists of sampling of landing sets of the fishing craft as well as sampling over time of the landings. Data on deep-sea fishing are obtained through reports furnished by trawler and other deep-sea vessels (reports are essential). The sampling design is developed by the IASRI and the Central Marine Fisheries Research Institute (CMFRI). Data are obtained on total marine landing of species-wise fish by mechanized and non-mechanized boats, total efforts in terms of man hours spent on fishing and number of units operated. In case of landings by trawlers, the information is based on complete enumeration.

Regarding inland fishery, several attempts have been made to develop sampling techniques for estimating the production of inland fish, but they have remained inconclusive. The Central Inland Fisheries Research Institute (CIFRI) has recently devised a methodology for collection of data relating to some important still water areas. Various sampling and other techniques are adopted for different states and different kinds of water and different sources of water, such as rivers and canals. The estimates of output are much less reliable than those of the marine fish. It may be mentioned here that for estimation of GDP from fisheries, the production of deep-sea fishing was taken into account in the series with 1980–1 as the base year. The estimates of output of other products like pearls are obtained by multiplying the number of workers engaged in the trade with the output per worker (obtained for a few states).

The collected statistics are published in *Handbook on Fisheries Statistics*. This publication contains information on fish production by states/UTs, including marine and inland fish production, disposition of fish catch, preserved and processed fish, fish seed production, prawn production, and shrimp production.

Forestry

The principal forest statistics refer to the area under forests, volume of outstanding timber, outturn and value of timber and fuel wood, value of minor forest products, and employment in the sector. The data are collected by the state forest departments and supplied to the Forest Survey of India (FSI), created in 1981, for getting it published in the biennial *India State of Forest Reports* (*ISFR*). The latest report (2013) contains data on forest cover and recorded forest area, tree cover, mangroves cover, and growing stock both in forests and areas outside forests special thematic information on forest cover such as hill districts, tribal districts, and north-eastern regions is also separately given in this report. It also includes data on bamboo resources of the country, production and consumption of forest resources in India, carbon stock in India's forests, forest and tree resources in states and UT (that is, state- and district-wise distribution).

Also, since 1987, the FSI has been using RS to collect data on forest cover under five broad classes (very dense, moderately dense forests, open forests, scrub, and mangroves) on a countrywide scale through a biannual survey. The areas under forests are available separately for reserved forests, protected forests, and un-classed forests. Reserved forests are the ones where right of grazing and cultivation is seldom allowed. In protected forests, these rights are allowed subject to mild restrictions. Un-classed forest consists largely of forests not included under the reserved or protected forest category. These occur mostly in Madhya Pradesh, Assam, Bihar, and Maharashtra.

The FSI has been estimating the carbon stock in India's forests as per the methodology of Good Practices Guidance developed by the Intergovernmental Panel on Climate Change (IPCC).

Estimates of area under forests are also compiled and published by the DES as part of land utilization statistics. There is huge discrepancy between the areas published by the two sources. This is mainly due to the different concepts and definitions followed by them. Area shown by the DES is much higher than that shown by FSI.

Besides the FSI, the Indian Council of Forestry Research and Education (ICFRE) is collecting, collating, and compiling primary and secondary data generated by the State Forest Departments, FSI, and various other sources. The data on area under forests and forest products are published in *Forestry Statistics—India*. Also available are details about protected areas and wildlife: number and total area of protected areas in India; state-wise national parks, wildlife sanctuaries and zoos; and population estimates of tigers and elephants in

India; among others. These data are available at the state level and are published in *Forestry Statistics—India*, however, with a considerable time lag.

Though the statistics on major forest products are complete, those on minor forest products are far from satisfactory. A serious limitation of those data is that they represent only the authorized exploited forest resources and a substantial quantity of production goes unrecorded.

Due to the considerable time lag, the CSO has been directly getting the data on outturn of forest products and prices prevailing in the assembling centres from the state forest departments on a financial year basis. About 10 per cent of the value of recorded industrial wood and 10 times the value of recorded fuel wood were assumed to be unrecorded for the series with base 1980–1.

These ratios for unrecorded production were not based on any scientific methods and were thus not reliable. In the series of National Accounts with 1993–4 as base year and onwards, the method of valuation of industrial wood remains the same. For fuel wood, the estimates of output are based on the consumption approach. Total consumption by households plus total industrial consumption and consumption on funerals is taken to be equal to the value of output. For the series of National Accounts with base 2004–5, CSO has included industrial wood produced from trees outside forests. It is, however, mentioned in Sources and Methods 2007 that in the production of trees in village common fields, ridges, canal sides, road sides, and fruit trees, the production has been indirectly estimated. Due to this, the value of output has increased from Rs 2,292 crore to Rs 36,922 crore. In addition, the value of output of minor forest products has increased from Rs 2,595 crore to Rs 11,510 crore. This is stated to be due to the inclusions of fodder grown in the forests.

Miscellaneous Statistics

Cost of Cultivation of Principal Crops

Since 1954–5, the DES had been sponsoring farm management surveys in various regions of the country. The objective of these studies was to show input–output relationships and to ascertain the relative efficiencies of different combinations of inputs, to study the cost of production of field crops on per hectare and per unit of production basis, and to study the extent of employment of family labour and capital equipment of farms. These surveys were, however, of limited coverage and were not repeated often enough. The results of those studies were published in the reports entitled *Studies in the Economies of Farm Management*. Each report referred to a district. A two-stage random sampling design was adopted with a village as the first stage unit and operational holding as the ultimate unit. The number of villages selected varied from district to district while 10 operational holdings were usually taken in each village. These studies continued up to 1969.

A comprehensive survey of the cost of cultivation of principal crops was initiated in 1970–1.The survey is in operation in 19 states and covers 30 crops, the choice of crops in each state depending upon their importance in the state. The DES is in charge of these surveys, generally carried out by agricultural universities. Each state is divided into homogeneous agro-climatic zones. Three-stage sampling design is being done with tehsils as the first stage, a cluster of villages as the second stage, and an operational holding as the third stage units. Tehsils are allocated to different zones in proportion to the total area of all crops covered in the study. In each zone, the tehsils are selected with probability proportional to area under the selected crops and replacement villages are selected in a similar manner. Villages once selected are retained for three years. In each selected village all operational holding are classified according to five size classes. In each size class, two holdings are selected by simple random sampling without replacement. The fieldwork consists of collecting from each operational holding through the cost accounting method by considering all aspects of cost of cultivation (inputs and outputs), by keeping records on a day-to-day basis. Full-time staff are engaged by the universities for this purpose. The results of these studies are particularly useful for the Commission for Agricultural Costs and Prices for fixing procurement prices and by CSO for estimating GDP from the agriculture sector and for construction of input–output (I–O) tables.

Cost Items

Following are the items of cost of cultivation covered under paid-out and imputed costs.

Paid-Out Costs

(1) Hired labour (human, animal, and machinery)
(2) Maintenance labour on owned animals and machinery
(3) Expenses on material inputs, such as seeds, fertilizers, pesticides, manure, and irrigation
(4) Depreciation on implements and farm buildings
(5) Land revenue
(6) Rent paid for leased-in land

Imputed Costs

These are in terms of family labour, rent of own land, and interest on owned fixed capital. Different types of costs are defined and calculated. The types of costs defined and the method of estimation of different imputed costs are given in the *Cost of Cultivation of Principal Crops in India* (three volumes, one each for 1990, 1996, and 2000, have been published). From 2004–5, the annual issues are available on the DES website.[3]

Agricultural Census

An agricultural census forms part of a broader system of collection of agricultural statistics, which is a large-scale statistical operation for collecting and deriving quantitative information about important facets of agriculture in the country. Agricultural census in India is conducted at an interval of five years for which operational holding has been taken as the statistical unit at the micro-level for data collection, as this is the ultimate unit for taking agriculture-related decisions. The main objectives of the Agricultural Census are:

(1) To describe the structure and characteristics of agriculture, providing statistical data on operational holdings, operated area, land utilization, livestock, agricultural machinery and implements, use of fertilizers, and pattern of input use.
(2) To provide benchmark data needed for formulating new agricultural development programmes and evaluating their progress.

[3] Available at http://eands.dacnet.nic.in (accessed on 26 May 2017).

(3) To provide a basic framework of operational holdings and its characteristics for carrying out future agriculture surveys.
(4) To lay basis for developing integrated programme for current agricultural statistics.

Periodic Agricultural Censuses are the main sources of information on number and area of operational holdings, basic characteristics of holdings such as land use, cropping patterns, irrigation status, tenancy, terms of leasing, and dispersal of holdings, and is tabulated by different farm sizes and social groups. The agricultural census also provides data on input use patterns for different size classes of farmers. The agricultural census is implemented in three distinct phases with the reference year as the agricultural year (July–June).

The Agricultural Census data (phase-I/phase-II) is collected following two broad approaches; in states where comprehensive land records exist (Land Record states), data is collected and compiled through re-tabulation of information available in the Village Land Records. For other states (non-Land Record states), this data is collected on a sample basis. In phase-I of the census, data on primary characteristics like number of operational holdings and area operated by different size class (marginal, small, semi-medium, medium, and large), social groups (scheduled castes [SCs], scheduled tribes [STs], and others), gender (male/female), types of holding (individual, joint, and institutional), among others, is collected. This operation covers all villages in land record states and 20 per cent of the villages in non-land record states. During, phase-II, the holding schedule is canvassed in the selected 20 per cent villages in each tehsil for collecting detailed data on irrigation status, tenancy particulars, cropping pattern, and dispersal of holdings, etc. The estimates of agricultural characteristics of operational holdings are prepared at the tehsil/district/state/national levels.

Phase-III of the Agricultural Census (referred to as the Input Survey) is conducted as a follow-up survey to the Agricultural Census (reference year as the next agricultural year to that of the Agricultural Census) to collect data on input use pattern of operational holdings in the country. The Input Survey relates to the collection of data on pattern of input use (fertilizer, irrigation, seed, pest management), agriculture credit, size of the household, age and educational level of the holders, multiple cropping across various crops, states, and size group of holders. This survey is conducted in 7 per cent of villages selected in each tehsil and the estimate for input characteristics is prepared at district/state/national level. For the Input Survey, institutional holdings and holdings operated by persons not residing in the village are excluded in the purview of the survey. These surveys are conducted from the census of 1976–7.

The major objective of this survey is to generate data on consumption of various agricultural inputs according to major size groups of operational holdings, to get an insight into the consumption pattern of inputs by various categories of farmers. The inputs are inclusive of various capital items, such as agricultural implements and machinery as well as livestock and agricultural credit. A two-stage stratified sampling was adopted for the input survey 2010–11. Tehsils/community development blocks constituted the strata, villages within a stratum formed first stage units and 'operational holdings' in the selected villages constituted the second stage units.

It is important to note that the estimates of both the Agricultural Census and Input Survey are to be prepared for all tehsils/blocks in the country. For this it is necessary that the survey is conducted in at least one village in each tehsil/block.

Nine Agricultural Censuses since 1970–1 have been conducted in the country so far, the latest one being with reference year 2010–11. The report on the number and area of operational holdings in the country based on the data of the Agricultural Census 2010–11 (Phase-I) and Agricultural Census Phase II have been released. Results have also been released for Phase-III of the Census. The All India Report on the number and area of operational holdings by size classes and tenancy status, as well as by irrigation status has also been published. Estimated irrigated and un-irrigated area by size class under different crops is also given in the Report. The 10th Census with reference year 2015–6 has been launched on 3 February 2016.

Before 1970–1, the information on agricultural holdings was obtained from 1950–1 and 1960–1 through sample surveys carried out by the NSSO. These data were collected through the 17th Round of the NSSO. These data are also required for Decennial World Census of Agriculture sponsored by Food and Agriculture Organization of the United Nations (FAO). Before 1970–71, that is, 1950 and 1960, data were collected through sample surveys carried out by the NSSO.

Marketable Surplus and Post-Harvest Losses

Current Status

The Directorate of Marketing and Inspection (DMI), MOAFW has been conducting surveys on marketable surplus and post-harvest losses of foodgrains. The surveys provide information on marketable surplus ratios as well as on a variety of other important items like farm retention for family consumption, for seed, feed and wastage, among others. The present surveys collect information on these parameters using the methodology approved by a Technical Committee constituted for the purpose under the chairmanship of the Agricultural Marketing Advisor to the Government of India (GoI). The surveys cover the following crops: paddy, wheat, jowar, bajra, maize, ragi, barley, red gram, green gram, black gram, and lentils. The methodology used is that of stratified random sampling and consists in selecting 20 per cent of the districts in a state, 15 villages in each selected district and 10 cultivator households from each selected village with a maximum of 100 districts, 1,500 villages, and 15,000 households.

The fieldwork of the surveys is conducted by Designated State Agencies through field investigators employed by them under the overall supervision of the DMI. The data so collected are analysed with the support of IASRI and published by the directorate in reports. The information collected through these surveys is used in the NAS, and Ministry of Commerce and Industry in fixing the weights for certain agricultural commodities while compiling the all-India index number of wholesale prices in addition to its uses in planning procurement operations and market development programmes.

Index Numbers of Agricultural Production

Index numbers are required in order to study the trend over time in respect of area, yield, production, productivity, and for studying the comparative performance of the agriculture sector in relation to other sectors. Index numbers are constructed after taking into account the changes in coverage and method of estimation as the absolute figures of area; the production, for example, may not be exactly comparable over time. Index numbers are constructed by the DES. The base year of the current series is the triennium ending 2007–8. Until 1999–2000, the index numbers were compiled with triennium ending 1981–2 as base period and up to 2006–7 with base triennium ending 1993–4. In order to smoothen the fluctuations of area and production from one year to another, the average of area and production over the triennium is taken for determining the base level area and production. The weight of a commodity for the production index is taken as the average production of the commodity in the triennium of that period and the average national price of the commodity during 2007–8. Statewise and national level indices are available for the two groups, eight subgroups and 46 individual crops (list of crops given in Appendix Table 3A.5). At the base, the same item basket is taken for all the states and at all-India level. This, however, is not proper because of differing importance of crops in different states. The following is the methodology given in *Agricultural Statistics at a Glance*.

Methodology for Calculation of Index Numbers of Area, Production, and Yield

Let

a_{ijk} be the area under *i*th crop in the *j*th year in *k*th state
a_{iok} be the area under *i*th crop in base year period in *k*th state
P_{ijk} be the production of *i*th crop in the *j*th year in *k*th state
P_{iok} be the production of *i*th crop in base year period in *k*th state
w_{ik} be the weight of *i*th crop in *k*th state
P_{io} be the price per unit of the *i*th crop in the base period

For the state *k* and for the year j, individual crop indices are calculated as follows:

(a) Index number of area = $\left(\frac{\sum aijk}{\sum aiok}\right)\times 100$

(b) Index number of production = $\left(\frac{\sum pijk}{\sum piok}\right) \times 100$

(c) Index number of yield = $\left(\frac{\sum IPijk}{\sum IAijk}\right) \times 100$

For any sub-group G of commodities, the indices are for the year *j* and state *k* are as follows.

(a) Index number of area = $\left(\frac{\sum aijkPio}{\sum aiok}\right) \times 100 \, (\Sigma a_{ijk}/\Sigma a_{iok}) \times 100$

The state index is obtained by including all the items of the state in sub-group G where the summation is taken over items in G.

(b) Index number of production = $\left(\frac{\sum PijkPio}{\sum PiokPio}\right) \times 100$

(c) Index number of yield = (Index number of production/Index number of area) × 100

Weights have been mentioned here, though they have not been used anywhere earlier.

Appendix 3A

Table 3A.1 Classification of Area and Irrigated Area in India (Million Hectares)

Classification	2005–6	2006–7 (P)	2007–8 (P)	2008–9	2009–10	2010–11	2011–12	2012–13
Geographical Area	328.7	328.7	328.7	328.7	328.7	328.7	328.7	328.7
Reporting Area for Land Utilization Statistics (1 to 5)	305.4	305.65	305.65	305.8	305.8	305.9	305.8	305.9
1. Forest	69.99	70.02	69.96	70.0	70.0	70.0	70.0	70.0
2. Not Available for Cultivation (A+B)	42.32	42.73	42.90	43.1	43.3	43.6	43.5	43.7
(A) Area Under Non-agricultural Uses	24.99	25.44	25.88	26.2	26.2	26.4	26.3	26.5
(B) Barren and Un-culturable Land	17.33	17.28	17.02	16.9	17.2	17.2	17.2	17.3
3. Other Uncultivated land excluding Fallow Land (A+B+C)	27.06	27.04	26.80	26.4	26.5	26.2	26.1	26.0
(A) Permanent Pasture and Other Grazing Land	10.45	10.42	10.36	10.3	10.3	10.3	10.3	10.2
(B) Land under Miscellaneous Tree Crops and Groves Not Included in Net Area Sown	3.39	3.35	3.40	3.3	3.2	3.2	3.2	3.2
(C) Culturable Waste Land	13.22	13.27	13.04	12.7	12.9	12.6	12.6	12.6

4. Fallow Lands (A+B)	24.91	26.02	24.97	24.5	26.8	24.6	25.2	26.3
(A) Fallow Lands Other Than Current Fallows	10.69	10.51	10.33	10.3	10.8	10.3	10.7	11.0
(B) Current Fallows	14.21	15.51	14.65	14.2	16.0	14.3	14.5	15.3
5. Net Area Sown (6–7)	141.16	139.82	141.01	141.9	139.2	141.6	141.0	139.9
6. Total Cropped Area (Gross Cropped Area)	192.7	192.3	195.22	195.3	189.0	197.6	195.6	194.4
7. Area Sown More Than Once	51.58	52.55	54.20	53.4	49.8	56.0	54.7	54.5
8. Cropping Intensity*	136.4	137.6	138.4	137.7	135.8	139.6	138.8	138.9
Net Irrigated Area	60.83	62.74	63.19	63.6	61.9	63.7	65.7	66.1
Gross Irrigated Area	84.28	86.75	88.06	88.9	85.1	88.9	91.7	92.6

Source: *Land Use Statistics at a Glance*, DES, MOAFW.

Notes: 1. Provisional cropping intensity is percentage of the gross cropped area to the net area sown.

2. The decline in net area sown in 2002–3 reflects the impact of the severe drought of 2002–3 on agriculture operations.

Table 3A.2 Classification Adopted for Land-Utilization Statistics

Old Classification	New Classification	Definition
1. Forests	1. Forests	These include all actually forested area on the lands classed or administered as forests under any legal enactment dealing with forests, whether state-owned or private. If any portion of such land is not actually wooded but put to some agricultural use, that portion shall be included under the appropriate heading of cultivated or un-cultivated land.
2. Area not available for cultivation	2. Land put to non-agricultural use	All lands occupied by buildings, roads, and railways, or under water, for example, rivers and canals and other lands put to uses other than agricultural.
	3. Barren and unculturable land	All barren and unculturable land, such as mountains and deserts. Land which cannot be brought under cultivation, unless at a high cost, shall be classed as unculturable, whether this land is in an isolated block or within cultivated holdings.
3. Other cultivated land excluding current fallows	4. Permanent pastures and other grazing lands	All grazing lands, whether they are permanent pastures and meadows or not. Village common and grazing land shall be included under this head.
	5. Miscellaneous tree crops and groves not included in the net area sown	All cultivable land, which is not included under net area sown, but is put to some agricultural use. Lands under Casuarina trees, thatching grass, bamboo bushed, and other groves for fuel, among others, which are not included under orchards, shall be classed under this category.

	6. Culturable waste	All lands available for cultivation, whether not taken up for cultivation or abandoned after a few years for one reason or the other. Such lands may be either fallow or covered with shrubs and jungles which are not put to any use. They may be assessed or unassisted and may lie in isolated blocks or within cultivated holdings. Land once cultivated but not cultivated for five years in succession shall also be included in this category.
4. Current fallows	7. Current fallows	Cropped areas which are kept during the current year only.
	8. Other fallow lands	All lands which were taken up for cultivation but are temporarily out of cultivation for a period of not less than one year and not more than five years. The reasons for keeping such lands fallow may be of one of the following: 1. Poverty of the cultivations 2. Inadequate supply of water 3. Malarial climate 4. Silting of canals and rivers 5. Unremunerative nature of fanning
5. Net area sown	9. Net area sown	Consists of net area sown with crops and orchards; counting areas sown more than once in the same year only once.

Source: Study of Uniform Coding Scheme for Computerization of Land Records, Land Records Information Systems Division, National Informatics Centre, Department of Information Technology Ministry of Communications and Information Technology, Government of India, August 2008.

Table 3A.3 Net Area Under Irrigation by Sources ('000 Hectares)

Year	Canals			Tanks	Tube Wells	Other Wells	Other Sources	Total
	Government	Private	Total					
2003–4	14,251	206	14,458	1,916	26,691	9,693	4,299	57,057
2004–5	14,553	214	14,766	1,734	25,235	9,956	7,538	59,229
2005–6	16,490	227	16,718	2,083	26,026	10,044	5,966	60,837
2006–7	16,802	224	17,027	2,078	26,942	10,698	5,999	62,744
2007–8	16,531	217	16,748	1,973	28,497	9,864	6,107	63,189
2008–9 (P)	16,686	195	16,881	1,981	28,367	10,389	6,020	63,638
2009–10 (P)	14,789	188	14,978	1,587	28,371	9,992	7,008	61,936
2010–11 (P)	15,476	171	15,647	1,980	28,544	10,630	6,855	63,657
2011–12 (P)	15,838	172	16,010	1,918	29,942	10,595	7,228	65,693
2012–13 (P)	15,462	165	15,628	1,748	30,497	10,764	7,466	66,103

Source: *Land Use Statistics at a Glance*, 2014, DES, MOAFW.

Note: P means Provisional.

Table 3A.4 Crops Classified for Estimation of Yield

Crops	
Principal crops major crops cereals	Paddy, jowar, *bajra*, maize, ragi, small millets, wheat, and barley.
Pulses	Gram, *tur*, *moong*, *masoor*, *urad*, other kharif and rabi pulses.
Other crops	Sugarcane, potato, tobacco, turmeric, *guar* seed, coconuts, black pepper, dry ginger, dry chillies, coriander, cardamom.
Oilseeds	Groundnut, sesame, rape seed, soybean, sunflower, mustard, safflower, linseed, castor seed, Niger seed, and cottonseed.
Fibres	Cotton, jute, *mesta*, and *sann*-hemp.
2. Plantation crops	Tea, coffee, and rubber.
(b) Minor crops	Indigo, papaya, opium, and lac.
4. By-products	Bagasse, cotton sticks, sesame sticks, jute sticks, *arhar* sticks rice bran, rice husk, cane trash, stalks, and straw.
5. Miscellaneous and unspecified crops	Other cereals, other oil seeds, other sugars, other fibres, other dyes and tanning materials, other drugs and narcotics, other fruits and vegetables, other condiments and spices, fodder, grass, miscellaneous food and non-food crops.

Sources: (i) *National Accounts Statistics: Sources and Methods*, CSO, 2007.
(ii) *Agriculture Statistics at a Glance*, 2014, DES, MOAFW.

Table 3A.5 Crops Covered for Index Numbers

Foodgrains	Cereals	Rice, wheat, jowar, bajra, maize, ragi, barley and small millets. (Crops other than rice and wheat constitute the sub-group coarse cereals.)
	Pulses	Gram, tur, moong, urad, lentils, and other pulses.
Non-foodgrains	Oilseeds	Groundnut, sesame, rapeseed and mustard, linseed, castor seed, safflower, Niger seed, soyabean, sunflower, coconut, and cottonseed.
	Fibres	Cotton, jute, mesta, and sann-hemp (jute and mesta constitute a sub-group).
	Plantation crops	Tea, coffee, and rubber.
	Condiments and Spices	Pepper, ginger, garlic, chillies, turmeric, areca nut, coriander, and cardamom.
	Fruits and vegetables	Potato, onion, banana, cashew nut, tapioca, and sweet potato.
	Other crops	Sugarcane, tobacco, and guar seed.

Source: *Agriculture Statistics at a Glance*, 2014.

Bibliography

B.S. Minhas. 2002. *National Income Accounts and Data Systems. Agricultural and Industrial Production Statistics*. New Delhi: Oxford University Press.

Central Statistical Organization. Various years. *National Accounts Statistics*. New Delhi: Ministry of Statistics and Programme Implementation, Government of India.

Department of Animal Husbandry, Dairying and Fisheries (DADF). 2014. *Handbook on Fisheries Statistics*. New Delhi: DES Ministry of Agriculture.

Directorate of Economics and Statistics (DES). 1999. 'Comments on Press Reports Relating to Advance Estimates of National Income', 12 February. New Delhi: Ministry of Agriculture and Farmer's Welfare. *Report and Database of Pilot Scheme on Major Fruits and Vegetables*. New Delhi: Ministry of Agriculture, and Farmer's Welfare.

———. 2001.

———. 2009. *Vaidiyanathan Committee Report*. New Delhi: Ministry of Agriculture and Farmer's Welfare.

———. Various Issues. *Land Use Statistics at a Glance*, 2003–4 to 2012–13. New Delhi: Ministry of Agriculture and Farmer's Welfare.

Economic and Political Weekly Research Foundation (EPWRF). 2004. *National Accounts Statistics of India: 1950–51 to 2002–03—Linked Series with 1993–94 as the Base Year*, Fifth Edition. Mumbai: EPWRF.

Forest Survey of India (FSI). 2013. *India State of Forest Reports (IFSR)*. Dehradun: FSI.

Indian Council of Forestry Research and Education. 2011. *Forestry Statistics*. Dehradun: Indian Council of Forestry Research and Education.

Information System Organization (ISO). 2013. *Water and Related Statistics*. New Delhi: Central Water Commission.

Ministry of Agriculture and Farmer's Welfare. 2014. *Agricultural Statistics at a Glance*. New Delhi: Government of India

———. 2015. *Basic Animal Husbandry Statistics*. New Delhi: The Animal Husbandry Statistics Division, DES, Government of India.

———. 2013–14. *Cost of Cultivation of Principal Crops in India*. New Delhi: Government of India.

National Horticulture Board. 2014. *Indian Horticulture Database*. Gurgaon: Ministry of Agriculture and Farmer's Welfare, Government of India.

National Statistical Commission. 2001. *Report of National Statistical Commission*. New Delhi: Government of India.

Rathi, R.P., 'General Crop Estimation Survey 2008--09 (GCES)', NSSO (FOD). Available at http://www.iasri.res.in/ebook/TEFCPI_sampling/GENERAL%20CROP%20ESTIMATION%20SURVEY%20(GCES).pdf, last accessed on 24 July 2017.

Agricultural Statistics in India. Various years. New Delhi: Government of India.

4

Industrial Statistics

The compilation of industrial statistics assumes importance, considering the pivotal role of the industrial sector in the Indian economy, both for research and policymaking. The users should be conversant with the type of available data sets and the gaps therein. Besides this, of course, it is essential to know the quality of data. Therefore, an attempt has been made in this chapter to discuss different sources, their limitations, and the methods of filling up the data gaps on industrial statistics.

For the purpose of collection of data on manufacturing industries, the entire industrial activity is divided into factory and non-factory sectors based on the size of employment in different producing units under the activity. The factory sector covers units registered under Factories Act, 1948. The non-factory sector consists of the remaining manufacturing units. The factory sector is designated as the registered or organized sector and non-factory sector is called the unregistered or unorganized sector. Moreover, electricity and major minerals are also part of the organized industrial sector, while minor minerals belong to the unorganized sector. On the other hand, the manufacturing industries are divided into large and small-scale industries on the basis of the limit of capital employed in plant and machinery. Units below that limit are called small-scale industries (SSI), while the rest are called large- and medium-scale units.

The sources of data on industrial statistics regarding organized and unorganized and large and small sectors of manufacturing industries are the *Annual Survey of Industries* (*ASI*), the follow-up surveys of the economic census, Department of Industrial Policy and Promotion (DIPP), census-cum-surveys of the small-scale industries, and the index of industrial production (IIP) by the Central Statistics Office (CSO) and various other organizations (see in Appendix Table 4A.1) dealing with the industrial sector.

Organized Sector

The main source of data pertaining to the organized sector is the *ASI*. In most advanced countries, the censuses of manufacturing industries were started in the late nineteenth or early twentieth century. In India, the importance of these censuses was not realized until 1942, when the Government of India (GoI) was empowered to collect statistics from various industries under the Industrial Statistics Act, 1942. This act provided for the collection of statistics from establishments registered under the Indian Factories Act, 1934. In 1945, the Directorate of Industrial Statistics was set up to coordinate and supervise the census operations and to compile and publish its results. An annual census of 29 industry groups (the entire industrial activity was divided into 63 groups) was conducted first in 1946 under the provisions of the Industrial Statistics Act, 1942 and the Census of Manufacturing Industries (CMI) Rules, 1945 framed thereunder and extended only to 11 states. By 1958, the geographical coverage extended to 13 states and two union territories (UTs). As CMI covered only 29 industries, the Sample Survey of Manufacturing Industries (SSMI) was started in 1950 on the recommendations of the National Income Committee. The SSMI covered all the 63 industry groups on a sample basis. The Industrial Statistics Act, 1942 was replaced in 1956 by a more comprehensive collection of Statistics Act, 1953. The CMI continued on a voluntary basis for the years 1957 and 1958. The SSMI also continued up to 1958.

The CMI was confined only to factories employing 20 or more workers and using power in any manufacturing process. The data were published for each industry regarding the quantity and value of output of different products and by-products in the industry, different kinds of fuels and materials consumed in value terms and in quantity terms wherever feasible, details of employment along with wages and salaries, component-wise fixed and working capital employed, depreciation, value added, among others. The data were available state-wise and for all India. The SSMI covered factories employing 10 or more workers if using power and 20 or more if not using power. Only value estimates regarding capital employed, output, total of all inputs, value added, and emoluments to employees were published. Employment estimates were given in numbers.

Annual Survey of Industries

The *ASI* replaced both the CMI and the SSMI in 1959. Although the collection of Statistics Act, 1953 came into force on 10 November 1956, the collection of Statistics Rules, 1959 (given in Appendix I, Volume I of the *ASI* 1960) under this act were notified only in January 1960 providing for a comprehensive *ASI* in India for the reference year 1959. Since 1959, the survey has been conducted annually under the statutory provisions of the 1953 Act and 1959 Rules, except in Jammu and Kashmir (J&K), where it is conducted under the State Collection of Statistics Act, 1961 and the rules framed thereunder in 1964. From 2010–11, the *ASI* was conducted under the collection of Statistics Act, 2008 and the rules framed thereunder in 2011, except in J&K where it is conducted under the Jammu and Kashmir Collection of Statistics Act, 1961 and rules framed thereunder in 1964. The fieldwork of the survey is carried out by the Field Operations Division (FOD) of the National Sample Survey Office (NSSO). The director, FOD is the authority appointed under the act for the purpose of collection of data and for the successful execution of the survey programme. Framing the instructions, processing of data, and publication of reports are the responsibilities of the CSO. However, the overall guidance regarding the sampling design, sample size, types and techniques of data collection, processing, and tabulation is provided by the Standing Committee on Industrial Statistics constituted by the governing council of the NSSO.

Coverage

The *ASI* covers all factories under Sections 2m(i) and 2m(ii) of the Factories Act, 1948, that is, employing 10 or more workers and using power and those employing 20 or more workers if not using power on any day of the preceding 12 months. The survey also covers *bidi-* and cigar-manufacturing establishments registered under the Bidi and Cigar Workers Act, 1966, that is, employing 10 or more workers and using power and 20 or more if not using power. Up to 1997–8, all the electricity undertakings engaged in the generation, transmission, and distribution of electricity registered with the Central Electricity Authority (CEA) were covered under *ASI* irrespective of their employment size. From *ASI* 1998–9, the electricity units registered with the CEA and the departmental units such as railway workshops, Road Transport Corporation (RTC) workshops, government mints, sanitary, water supply, gas storage, among others, are not covered, as there are alternative sources of their data compilation for the GDP estimates by the National Accounts Division of CSO. Certain services and activities, such as cold storage, water supply, and repair services, are also covered under the survey.

ASI Frame and its Updation

The *ASI* frame is based on the lists of registered factory/units maintained by the chief inspector of factories in each state and those maintained by registration authorities in respect of bidi and cigar establishments and electricity undertakings. The frame is being revised and updated every year before selection of the units by the FOD of NSSO in consultation with the chief inspector of factories in the state. At the time of revision, the names of the de-registered factories are removed from the *ASI* frame and those of the newly registered factories are added. In updation, only new registrations are added to the existing frame. In case the state government also conducts the survey on the state sample, the FOD office concerned should also collect the feedback while updating the frame.

For the purposes of *ASI*, the factories in the frame are classified into two sectors, namely the census sector and the sample sector. While the factories employing 100 or more workers constitute the census sector, the remaining factories constitute the sample sector.

Once a factory is classified into census/sample sector, its status is not altered till the frame is revised though change in employment might warrant it. All the factories in the census sector together with all the electricity undertakings and all the factories located in relatively less industrialized states and UTs (12 up to 1997–8 and 5 from 1998–9) for the sample sector continue to be completely enumerated every year. Besides, factories falling under Category I as described as follows have also been completely enumerated since 1987–8.

Sampling Design

The sampling design adapted for *ASI* from 1987–8 to 1996–7 continued to be a stratified uni-stage one for the sample sector. The stratum was an industry group at the 3-digit level of National Industrial Classification (NIC) 1987 in a state or UT. The strata were divided into the following three categories for the purpose of sampling:

- Category I: Those industry groups (at 3-digit level) or strata where the number of factories/units is 20 or less were designated as a complete enumeration category.
- Category II: Those strata where the number of factories/units, within each stratum, is between 21 and 60 were said to form segment S1.
- Category III: Those strata where the number of factories/units, within each stratum, was 61 and more were said to be in segment S2.

All the factories/units in Category I were completely enumerated. A fixed sample of 20 units from each stratum belonging to segment S1 was drawn while a sampling of one in three was adopted from each stratum of segment S2. Selection of factories in categories II and III was done in a circular systematic design with a random start.

Also 12 states/UTs, namely Himachal Pradesh, J&K, Manipur, Meghalaya, Nagaland, Tripura and Puducherry, Andaman and Nicobar Islands, Chandigarh, Goa, Daman and Diu, and Dadra and Nagar Haveli, which were industrially backward, were covered under the census sector. Also all public sector units irrespective of their employment size were covered under the census sector.

This sampling design is more complex than the one adopted till *ASI* 1986–7. Up to 1986–7, the factories under the non-census sector were covered either on a complete enumeration basis or on a uniform 50 per cent sampling. The sampling fraction was one-sixth until 1967 and one-third until 1971.

Also, till 1986–7, all factories employing 50 or more workers and using power and those employing 100 and more if not using power were under the census sector. From 1987–8, the coverage of the census sector was reduced to cover only factories employing 100 or more workers irrespective of the use of power. For the year 1997–8, 1998–9, and 1999–2000, the census sector was limited only to factories employing 200 or more workers. From 2000–1, again the factories employing 100 or more workers were considered under the census sector. Due to these changes in the definition, there may be some problems of comparison of the estimates over time. The change in the sampling design in 1997–8 was done to reduce workload and cost. It was revised so that about 60,000 units being covered under the *ASI* up to 1996–7 are reduced to about 30,000 units while maintaining a fair level of degree of precision in the estimates at the state level. A consensus decision was taken not to attempt the estimation at the district level. The state-wise allocations were made proportional to the number of factories in a state. Sample allocations to the 4-digit industry group in a state were again a proportional allotment. From 1998–9, 4-digit level 1998 classification was used for making allotments. If the total number of factories in a state at the 4-digit level was less than or equal to eight then complete numeration was done otherwise a minimum value of four of sample size was maintained.[1]

From 2004–5, a new sampling design was adopted. The census sector for 2004–5 has been defined as all industrial units belonging to the five less industrially developed states/UTs, namely Manipur, Meghalaya, Nagaland, Tripura, and the Andaman and Nicobar Islands. For all other states/UTs, units having 100 and more workers and all factories covered under joint returns will come under the census sector. In the sample sector the units will be stratified at the 4-digit level of NIC 2004 in each state. A sampling fraction of 20 per cent in the sampling sector is taken for sampling with a minimum of six samples in each stratum in the form of two independent sub-samples with half in each of the two sub-samples. According to this design the samples are to be selected in such a manner so as

[1] For details see Volume 1 of *ASI* 1999–2000.

to cover the entire frame in five years. In states where the number of units is less than six, these will be covered on a census basis. It was mentioned in the sample design that the complete cycle will be covered in a period of five years. The sampling design was, however, revised again with reference to 2007–8; based on the decision taken by the Standing Committee on Industrial Statistics (SCIS), a new sampling design was adopted for 2007–8. Accordingly, for *ASI* 2007–8, the census sector was defined as follows.

(1) All industrial units belonging to the five less industrially developed states/UTs, namely Manipur, Meghalaya, Nagaland, Tripura, and the Andaman and Nicobar Islands.
(2) For the remaining 26 states/UTs, (i) units having 100 or more workers, and (ii) all factories covered under joint returns.
(3) Strata (state by 4-digit NIC 2004) having less than or equal to six units after selecting the census sector units as defined earlier are also selected as census sector.
(4) From the remaining merged frame (main frame 2004–5 *plus* supplementary frame 2005–6 *plus* supplementary frame 2006–7 *plus* supplementary frame 2007–8), samples were drawn considering higher allocation for states having a relatively higher percentage contribution in the sample sector in terms of gross value added (GVA) based on last two years' available data. Accordingly, state-wise census and sample sector contribution of GVA was calculated based on last two years' available data along with the relative standard error of GVA estimates in sample sector based on data of *ASI* 2005–6. In general, a sampling fraction of 12 per cent was considered for all the states within a State × Sector × 4-digit NIC with a minimum of six units evenly distributed in two subsamples, except (i) J&K, Himachal Pradesh, Chandigarh, Madhya Pradesh, Daman and Diu, Dadra and Nagar Haveli, and Goa with a 20 per cent sampling fraction, (ii) Delhi and Rajasthan with a 13 per cent sampling fraction, (iii) Bihar and Puducherry with a 15 per cent sampling fraction due to relatively higher contribution of sample sector to the total GVA and higher relative standard error.

For 2008–9 again, there have been minor changes compared with 2007–8. Strata (State × 4-digit of NIC 2008) having less than or equal to four units after selecting the census sector units are also selected as census sector. From the remaining frame considering uniform sampling fractions of 20 per cent for the states within a state 4-digit NIC with a minimum of four units evenly distributed in two sub-samples. For 2007–8, the number was six as against four for 2008–9. This reduction in numbers may be because of the constraints on the resources.

Accordingly, for *ASI* 2009–10, the census sector has been defined as follows.

(1) All industrial units belonging to the six less industrially developed states/UTs, namely Manipur, Meghalaya, Nagaland, Sikkim, Tripura, and Andaman and Nicobar Islands.
(2) For the remaining 26 states/UTs, (i) units having 100 or more workers, and (ii) all factories covered under joint returns.

Strata (State × 4-digit of NIC 2008), having less than or equal to four units after selecting the census sector units as defined earlier, are also selected as census sector.

From the remaining frame, samples are drawn considering a uniform sampling fraction of 19 per cent for the states within a State × 4-digit NIC with a minimum of four units evenly distributed in two sub-samples. There has been no change in the sampling design for the years 2010–11 and 2011–12.

From 2012–13 again, there have been changes in the design. The following design has been applied, accoding to which all the factories in the updated frame are divided into two sectors, namely census and sample.

Census Sector

Census sector is defined as follows:

(1) All industrial units belonging to the six less industrially developed states/UTs, namely Manipur, Meghalaya, Nagaland, Tripura, Sikkim, and Andaman and Nicobar Islands.
(2) For the remaining 29 states/UTs, (i) units having 100 or more employees, and (ii) all factories covered under Joint Returns (see paragraph 3.2.11 of *ASI* 2012–13 Vol-1 for definition).
(3) After excluding the census sector units as defined earlier, all units belonging to the strata (District × 4-digit of NIC 2008) having less than or equal to four units are also considered as census sector units.

Selection Procedure of Sample Sector Units

The remaining units, excluding those of the census sector, called the sample sector, are arranged in order of their number of employees and samples, then drawn circular systematically considering a sampling fraction, say 20 per cent, within each stratum (District × Sector × 4-digit NIC) in the form of four independent sub-samples.

This will be done for each district and thus, for each state/UT. An even number of units with a minimum of four are selected from each stratum and evenly distributed in four sub-samples. The sectors considered here are bidi, manufacturing, and electricity.

Allocation of Samples

All the units belonging to the census sector together with selected units of two sub-samples, say, of sub-samples 1 and 3, will form the central sample and information for these units will be collected and processed by the central agency (that is, NSSO and CSO [Industrial Statistics Wing]). After selecting the central sample in the way mentioned earlier, the units selected for the remaining two sub-samples, say, of sub-samples 2 and 4, will be allocated for each state/UT separately. Validated state-wise unit-level data of the central sample will also be sent to the states for pooling this data with their surveyed data to get a combined estimate at the sub-state level.

Selection of State Samples

After selecting the central sample in the way mentioned earlier, the remaining units in the sample sector are treated as residual frame for selection of sample units for the states/UTs. Note that for the purpose of selecting samples from the residual frame for the state/UTs, stratification is done afresh by grouping units belonging to District × 3-digit of NIC 2008 for each state to form the strata. The sample units are then drawn circular systematically from each stratum. The basic purpose of introducing the residual sample was to increase the sample size for the sample sector of the states so as to get more reliable estimates at the district level. Validated state-wise unit-levels of the central sample are also sent to the states to pool this data with their surveyed data to get a combined estimate at the sub-state level.

Unfortunately only 18 states participate in this exercise. Others have various types of difficulties in conducting the survey, the main being a capacity deficit. The number of states that actually process and tabulate the data is only seven, namely Andhra Pradesh, Gujarat, Kerala, Odisha, Tamil Nadu, Uttar Pradesh, and West Bengal.

Industrial Classification

For *ASI* 1973–4 to 1988–9, NIC 1970 was followed to classify factories. Previously, a standard industrial classification was adopted. From 1989–90 to 1997–8, NIC 1987 was employed. NIC 1998 was used from 1998–9 to 2003–4. From 2004–5 to 2007–8 NIC 2004 was used. From *ASI* 2008–9, NIC 2008 is being used.

ASI Schedule

The *ASI* schedule is the basic tool to collect required data for the factories registered under Sections 2(m)(i) and 2(m)(ii) of the Factories Act, 1948. The schedule for *ASI*, at present, has two parts. Part-I of the *ASI* schedule—processed at the CSO (Industrial Statistics Wing), Kolkata—aims to collect data on assets and liabilities, employment and labour cost, receipts, expenses, input items: indigenous and imported, products and by-products, distributive expenses, among others. Part-II of the *ASI* schedule is processed by the labour bureau. It aims to collect data on different aspects of labour statistics, namely working days, man-days worked, absenteeism, labour turnover, man-hours worked, among others.

National Product Classification for Manufacturing Sector (NPCMS 2011)

Central Product Classification (CPC) serves as the reference classification for all product classifications within the international system of economic classifications put in place by the UN. It is a complete product classification covering all goods and services that follows the definition of products within the System of National Accounts (SNA). Goods and services are understood as being the results of production. The scope of the CPC covers (i) physical goods (which include transportable and non-transportable physical goods); (ii) intangible goods; and (iii) services.

CPC, Ver. 2.0 has already been adopted for products of the service sector by the CSO. Now, NPCMS 2011 has been constructed by CSO, IS Wing, Kolkata, based on Sections 0 to 4 of CPC, Ver. 2.0 that relates to products of the manufacturing sector. NPCMS, 2011 is a 7-digit classification and the structure is 5-digit CPC Code + 2-digit Indian requirement; and will have 5 sections, 40 divisions, 190 groups, 785 classes and 1501 sub-classes with ultimate 7-digit products. From *ASI* 2010–11 onwards, the 7-digit code and its description as per NPCMS, 2011 are being used for collecting and recording of all input and output items in the *ASI* schedule and the earlier classification, known as the ASI Commodity Classification (ASICC), was discarded.

Presentation of the Results

The results of summary block of part I of the filled up schedules are presented by the CSO in the *Annual Survey of Industries Summary Results for Factory Sector*. This report presents summary results in respect of about 30 selected characteristics at various levels of aggregation, namely (i) all industries by states; (ii) all-India at 2-digit level of NIC with rural urban break-up; (iii) all-India at 3-digit level of NIC; and (iv) state-wise at 2-digit level. Information on employment in the non-responding units belonging to the factory sector, at all India 3-digit level of NIC and states at 2-digit level of NIC was also included up to 1996–7. The latest reports also contain, for the entire industrial activity, the results of principal characteristics by years of initial production and time series data from 1980–1. Summary reports also give principal characteristics by size of employment, size of capital, type of ownership, type of organization, size of output, and size of net value added (NVA) for the entire organized industrial sector. These reports also provide the explanatory notes on the scope, coverage, design of the survey, and concepts and definitions, among others.

Up to 1973–4 the detailed results for the census sector were published every year in 10 volumes. For sample sectors, separate summary reports were published. For 1959, only summary results were published for the census sector. For 1967 no volume was published, and for 1972 no survey was conducted because of lag in the work relating to earlier years. After that it was decided to publish the detailed results once in five years. The detailed results for 1978–9 are available in 10 volumes separately for the census and the factory sectors, while for 1983–4 the results are given only for the factory sector in 15 volumes. The data for 1989–90 and 1993–4 were published in 15 volumes for the factory sector only. In the detailed volumes, the data are available regarding quantity and value of different fuels, raw materials, packing material, materials consumed, and quantity and value of output of different products and by-products produced by each industry. Sex-wise details are available regarding employment and wages. Also available for each industry are the quantity and value of different imported items consumed. Volume I gives the summary tables along with explanatory notes on the scope coverage and concepts and definitions. It also contains tables on the value of additions to fixed capital and other transactions and the quantity of electricity produced, purchased, and sold. The other volumes provide detailed all-India, state-wise, as well as industry-wise data at 4-digit level of industrial classification.

From 1998–9, the results are tabulated at the 4-digit level classification for all India and at the 3-digit level for states/UT. Volume 1 contains data related to capital, employment, emoluments, and several economic parameters, such as number of factories, fixed/working capital and value added, fuels consumed, among others. Volume 2 contains details of materials consumed (quantity and value) and products and by-products produced (quantity and value). In addition to Volumes 1 and 2, summary results of factory sector are brought out as a separate publication. The publishing of data in two volumes is being done since 1995–6. Detailed volumes (15) were published only up to 1993–4. The input–output items are classified as per ASICC introduced in *ASI* 1995–6 and revised from time to time. The latest product classification for manufacturing sectors (NPCMS) is for 2011.

In addition to the volumes issued, the unit-level data as well as reports are sent on electronic media, to the computer centre, Ministry of Statistics and Programme Implementation (MOSPI), New Delhi, for the purpose of dissemination to users on request as per the pricing policy fixed by the ministry. From 1997–8 onwards, panel data is also available with the computer centre.

Economic and Political Weekly Research Foundation (EPWRF) compiled and presented at one place in Volume I the summary results from 1973–4 to 1997–8. In addition, it documented the different sources of data relating to industrial activity. Some of the inconsistencies in the *ASI* results were also given in this volume. In January 2008, EPWRF repeated this exercise and updated the data from 1973–4 to 2003–4 on CD-ROM. This volume also contained different sources of data relating to industrial activity and the limitations, particularly of the *ASI* data.

Limitations of ASI

The data collected through *ASI* are fairly reliable. There used to be a considerable time lag in the availability of data. For example summary results for the year 1993–4 were available only in January 1997. Up to the end of August 1997, the detailed results were available only for the year 1983–4. With the advent of structural reforms and openness of the economy and also the rapid structural changes in the industrial sector, the available data with such a time lag were not of much use. The input-output relation of even the latest input-output table (for 2007–8) are not relevant today as we are 8 years ahead of that table. Also the structure of production under each industry group has undergone a sea change over the period. For example, during 1983–4, the contribution of electronics was not as important as it is today. There has been a revolution in the communication equipment industry. Over time, however, there has been a considerable reduction in the time lag which is a welcome development.

Up to 1996–7, while presenting data, only the reporting factories were taken into account. The aggregates based on these data, therefore, needed adjustment because of non-reporting units. The CSO, while estimating GVA from the registered sector used to inflate the GVA given by the *ASI* by using the number of workers in the non-reporting units. The implicit assumption was that value added per worker in the reporting units is the same as that in the non-reporting units. This assumption was, however, not correct as one of the reasons cited in *ASI* reports regarding non-reporting units was that the factory remained closed for the major part of the year due to labour and management disputes. This fact was verifiable from the data regarding number of workers and gross output of non-reporting units given for the first time in *ASI* 1993–4 based on only 34 per cent of the non-reporting units. The value of output per worker in the non-reporting units of all industries are only Rs 73,625 while the same for the reporting units was as high as Rs 6,41,923. Hence, it is evident that some error will be there in the estimates of gross value added and other characteristics from the registered sector. From 1997–8, estimates of value added and other characteristics in the registered manufacturing industries as given by the *ASI* are inclusive of non-reporting units. The method of estimation of the characteristics of non-reporting units is, however, not given in the *ASI* reports.

Fixed capital represents the value of fixed assets owned by the factory as on the closing day of the accounting year. These values, for different components of fixed assets on the closing day of the accounting year are obtained by adding the values of additions during the year to the values as on the opening day of the year and subtracting depreciation from these values. Ratios like capital–labour and capital–output are worked out by making use of the book values of fixed capital for different industries and, therefore, have obvious limitations. Data on un-depreciated original values of plant and machinery are also being collected. These values again have a problem in cases where the factory purchased plant and machinery in phases (from 1998–9 the collection of this data has been discontinued).

The *ASI* covers factories employing 10 or more workers on any day of the year if using power and 20 or more if not using power. Tables 3A to 3L of *ASI* 1992–3 give the principal characteristics by employment size for different sizes of gross investment in plant and machinery. According to these tables, more than 26 per cent of the total factories employ less than 10 workers on an average. Further, these should not have been taken as factories as normally units will try to avoid becoming factories and would not show such employment if it is only for a few days in a year. For 1994–5 and 2000–1, this number was 29,619 and 29,185, respectively. However, employment in these factories employing less than 10 workers is only 2 per cent of total employment of all factories covered by the *ASI*. Besides, for the same reason factories employing 10 to 19 workers and not using power should have been outside the scope of factories. The reason for inclusion of smaller units as factories needs to be looked into.

For the year 2009–10 there were 58,150 factories in the employment range of 0–14 forming 36.6 per cent of the total. The percentage of employment, output, and GVA were 1.78 per cent, 2.17 per cent and 1.49 per cent, respectively. Based on unit-level data, it was found that there were 30,654 units employing 0–10 workers.

Also, according to the report of the National Statistical Commission (NSC), August 2001, in 1994–5, as estimated by the NSSO 51st Round, about 1.45 lakh eligible units (that is employing 10 or more workers and using power and 20 or more but not using power) were not included in the *ASI* frame. The GVA of the missing units was, however, only 4.1 per cent of the units covered under *ASI*. During 2000–1 the number of excluded units is 1.05 lakh. However, during this period value added rate increased from 4.0 to 12.7 (Bedi and Banerjee 2007). One explanation can be given for non-inclusion of such a large number of units in the *ASI*. A large number of units employ on a regular basis less than the number required to term the unit as a factory, but a large number of casual workers may be appointed for manufacturing work, and under the NSSO survey they report the total number as workers. This usually happens in the readymade garments industry. For the year 2010–11 the number of units employing more than 20 workers was 1,07,441 in the manufacturing sector.

There are problems with some of the items of inputs as well as output, such as other chemicals, other packing materials, work done by and for others, among others. Also for each industry only 10 individual items of inputs are given; the rest are put under others which, in some cases, forms a substantial portion of the total value of inputs. Sometimes, because of some classification problems, even important items are either not covered individually or are misclassified. As an example, Naptha (part of petroleum products) is an important input into fertilizers. The *ASI* data did not show it. In the 1998–9 input–output tables, the input of petroleum products into fertilizers was much less than what it should have been. For the 2003–4 I–O tables also this problem was there with the *ASI* data and the input of Naptha into fertilizers was based on Indian Petroleum and Gas Statistics.

The total number of persons engaged have been divided into three categories: (i) working proprietors and their family members, who are actively engaged in the work of the factory even without any direct pay; (ii) those workers who are employed directly or indirectly but do not include supervisory and managerial staff or persons employed in some specific departments, such as storekeeping, administrative office, watch and ward staff, among others; and (iii) persons holding supervisory and managerial duties and also all workers not covered by the specific departments mentioned in (ii). Generally, the wages and salaries of category (ii) employees and also that of specified departments are on the lower side. Therefore, it is natural that the workers of those specific departments should have been included under category (ii) and not in category (iii). Also the imputed values of benefits in kind as well as workmen and staff welfare expenses and old-age benefits are also not available separately for workers and for those other than workers. The suggested categorization is quite useful for research and policymaking.

From 1997–8, only the value of consumption of all petroleum products taken together is given. For previous years, the quantity and value of consumption of different petroleum products was given as part of a block on 'fuels consumed'. This block was very useful specially for energy modelling.

ASI Estimates and Estimates of National Accounts Statistics (NAS)

The GVA estimates for the organized (registered) manufacturing sector are normally estimated by making use of *ASI* data on the value of outputs and value of inputs. For the series with 1999–2000 as base, the estimates for the year 1999–2000 were based on the *ASI*, while for other years these were inflated by making use of the IIP and the wholesale price index (WPI) (both indices with very outdated base years). (For concepts about National Accounts, see Chapter 12.) The reason for not using *ASI* data was that the growth rates for the years 2000–1 and 2001–2 were not in line with the growth rates obtained from other sources.[2] For series with 2004–5 as base, again the *ASI* estimates are used. If the estimates for the year 2004–5 at the 2-digit level based on the 1999–2000 series are compared with

[2] See NAS Sources and Methods (2007).

those based on the 2004–5 series, there are huge differences between the two in a number of sectors. In some of the sectors, the GVA according to new series is one-third of that calculated according to the 1999–2000 series. When we compare the estimates based on the new series with that of the *ASI*, we find that the estimates from both the sources are the same for most of the sectors for the year 2004–5, while for many sectors there are substantial differences between the estimates from the two sources for the later years (2007–8 and 2008–9—see various volumes for comparison; also see Tables 4A.6 and 4A.7 in the appendix to this chapter).

This shows that there are some serious problems with the *ASI* data. The WPI and the IIP—both with 2004–5 as the base—are available. After that an exercise with the methodology of the series with 1999–2000 as base should be carried out and compared with the estimates based on the series with 2004–5 as the base. This may help in the valuation of *ASI* data.

Unorganized Sector

There is no periodical collection and publication of statistics for the unorganized sector as a whole and on an all-India basis. The NSSO surveyed the unregistered sector at the national level and collected data from household enterprises as part of their multipurpose surveys in some of their rounds. The first such survey was conducted during the 7th Round, covering the period from October 1953 to March 1954. It was regularly done up to the 10th Round and again taken up in the 14th Round (1958–9). The surveys were again conducted during the 23rd (1968–9) and 29th (1974–5) Rounds. During these two rounds, the data were collected on a sample basis from household as well as non-household units. The idea behind these two surveys was to get the data for the entire unregistered sector which could be aggregated with the data for the registered sector so as to cover the entire manufacturing industry. However, the results for the non-household sector were not encouraging because of incomplete coverage. For the 1970–1 series of national product, the data of the 29th Round only on the household unorganized sector (along with other sources) were used for estimating industry-wise GVA per worker. The same sources were used for the 1980–1 base series until the results of the 1984–5 follow-up survey were available.

Although a number of surveys were conducted by the NSSO and other organizations, no reliable estimates could be prepared for the entire unregistered manufacturing sector. To remove the data gaps in the unorganized sectors of the non-agricultural economy covering unregistered manufacturing, trade, transport, and services, the CSO took a major step in 1976 by launching the Central Plan Scheme on economic censuses and surveys.

The Economic Census

The first economic census was conducted in 1977 and follow-up surveys based on this census were conducted in 1978–9 (unorganized manufacturing) and 1979–80 (other unorganized sectors). So far, six economic censuses—one each in 1977, 1980, 1990, 1998, 2005, and January 2013–April 2014—have been conducted. The first census covered units with at least one hired worker, while all the subsequent censuses covered, in addition, own-account enterprises. Also, the first census covered only non-agricultural establishments. In the later censuses, all establishments engaged in agricultural and non-agricultural activities are covered except those agricultural establishments engaged in crop production and plantations. Seven series of follow-up surveys covering non-factory manufacturing, trade, hotels and restaurants, transport, storage and warehousing, mining and quarrying, and services sectors have been undertaken. The information collected during these censuses relates to location of the establishment, the description of the economic activity, number of persons usually working with its hired component and break-up of male and female workers, type of ownership, social group of owner, use of power/fuel (for details of coverage, see *All-India Report on Sixth Economic Census* [CSO 2014]).

Other than manufacturing, the recent surveys have been integrated ones, covering different components of services. It is, however, surprising that these surveys have not covered trade services; we therefore, do not have recent estimates of this very important sector of the economy. However, for the survey for the year 2010–11, trade is also covered.

Follow-Up Surveys

The economic census provides a framework for conducting follow-up sample surveys to collect detailed information on an enterprise basis. Initially the surveys on Directory Manufacturing Establishments (DME) employing six or more persons with at least one hired worker were conducted by the CSO while Non-Directory Manufacturing Establishments (NDME) employing less than six persons with at least one hired worker and Own-Account Manufacturing Enterprises (OAME) were surveyed by the NSSO. The surveys on non-factory manufacturing have been conducted for 1978–9, 1984–5, 1989–90, 1994–5, 2000–1, and 2005–6. During the 67th Round (July 2010 to June 2011), NSSO carried out an all-India enterprise survey on economic and operational characteristics of unincorporated non-agricultural enterprises in manufacturing, trade, and other service sectors (excluding construction).

These surveys were designed to collect detailed industry-wise information on the nature of activity, employment, emoluments, inputs, output, inventory of fixed assets, working capital, outstanding loans, among others. The results for DME were published by the CSO in the form of *Reports on Directory Manufacturing Establishments* and by NSSO for NDMEs and OAMEs and the integrated surveys in *Sarvekshana* and also in the form of individual reports. From 1994–5, the responsibility for collecting and analysing data and publishing the results for the entire unorganized sector lies with the NSSO.

Table 4A.2 in the Appendix gives the estimated number of enterprises and principal characteristics per enterprise separately for OAME, NDME, DME, and for rural and urban areas for the seven follow-up surveys which have been conducted so far. Table 4A.3 in the Appendix gives the estimates of GVA for 1984–5 ,1989–90, 1994–5, 2000–1, 2005–6, and 2010–11 at 2-digit level of industrial classification, based on the follow-up surveys and those given in the NAS. The following points regarding the reliability of the data emerge from these two tables:

Estimated number of manufacturing units in the OAME and NDME and also in the entire unorganized sector more than doubled between 1978–9 and 1984–5, while from 1984–5 to 1989–90 the absolute number of units decreased substantially for OAME and NDME for both rural as well as urban areas. In spite of the methodology of the surveys remaining almost the same, it is difficult to account for the difference of such magnitude. For DME there has been an annual growth of about 5 per cent between the first and second and the second and third surveys. This decrease in the number of units continued for most of the components for the year 1994–5 as well. There was, however, an increase of 17 per cent in the number of units for the entire unorganized manufacturing sector between 1994–5 and 2000–1. The number for 2000–1 was still less than the number in 1984–5 and only 4 per cent more than the number in 1989–90. The average employment per enterprise was almost the same for the three surveys but less for 1984–5 and more for 1994–5 for the entire unorganized manufacturing sector. For different components, however, there were differences in the average for different surveys.

There was no significant increase in the estimated number of enterprises for the entire unorganized manufacturing sector from 2000–1 to 2005–6. For urban areas the number in fact decreased in 2005–6. This decrease was in the OAME and NDME enterprises. Even the estimated employment decreased in 2005–6. For 2010–11, there was less than 1 per cent increase in the number of enterprises from 2005–6. In fact, the number decreased in case of own-account enterprises. Also, NDMC and DME estimates are not separately available for 2010–11.

For 1984–5, the difference between GVA for the entire unregistered sector based on the follow-up survey and that given by the NAS was only 12 per cent; this difference for 1989–90 increased to 55 per cent. It may be mentioned here that for 1989–90, the NAS used the GVA per worker based on the 1984–5 survey and the large difference may be due to other factors, such as the use of physical indicators and price indices. The differences, however, increased to 66 per cent and 78 per cent for the years 1994–5 and 2000–1, respectively. For 1994–5 and 2000–1, however, there was a change in the methodology of obtaining the GVA per worker. For 2005–6, the difference was 86.9 per cent and for 2010–11, the difference was 63.2 per cent.

For food products, the value added according to NAS (1980–1 series) was much less than the NSS for the year 1984–5 and 1989–90. For 1994–5 onwards, with a change in the series, the value added according to NAS was substantially higher than the corresponding NSS values. For 2005–6 value added for wood products according to

NSS was more (8.5 per cent) than the corresponding NAS value. In case of tobacco products and wearing apparel, the values added from both the sources were almost the same. In all other sectors the value added from NSS was much less than the same from NAS, sometimes the ratio being as low as 11 per cent.

Although, at the aggregate level, the difference between the estimates of GVA from the two sources for 1984–5 was not large, there were wide differences at the 2-digit level of industrial classification. For example, the GVA for food products according to the follow-up survey, was more than three times the GVA reported in the NAS. The same dimension of difference was there for 1989–90. For metals and machinery taken together, the estimates based on follow-up surveys were about half of those given in the NAS for 1984–5. For 1989–90, the corresponding estimates based on the follow-up survey were about one-fourth of those given in the NAS. For wood and wood products, the estimates based on the follow-up survey were substantially higher than those given in the NAS for 1984–5 (40 per cent) as well as 1989–90 (85 per cent). For 1994–5 and 2000–1, the estimates based on the survey were lower than those of the NAS. For 2005–6 again, the position was changed. According to series with 2004–5 as base, the position, however, remained the same, although at the aggregate level the GVA according to NAS for 2005–6 was more than double than that from the survey.

According to the NAS, the increase in the aggregate GVA from 1984–5 to 1989–90 was 107 per cent while the corresponding increase according to follow-up surveys was only 47 per cent; while for later periods the difference between the estimates of the growth rates from the two sources had substantially reduced. The difference in the growth rate between the two sources from 2000–1 and 2005–6 was only about 10 per cent, although there was a change in the methodology of estimation of GVA for these two years.

Comparing the first two follow-up surveys, it can be seen that, in the textile industry, there was only a 7 per cent increase in GVA in nominal terms. For leather and leather products and transport equipment, there had been a substantial decrease in GVA over the two survey periods. For beverages, wood and wood products, and non-metallic mineral products as well, the NAS estimates were less than the estimates of the follow-up surveys for the earlier two years, while the NAS estimates were higher for the later two periods. The value added in nominal terms more than doubled between 1994–5 and 2000–1 for food and beverages and tobacco products taken together and also for textiles (code 23 + 24 + 25). For textiles products and non-metallic mineral products the value added for 2000–1 was about three times the same for 1994–5. On the other hand the value added for transport equipment for 2000–1 was about one-fourth of the value for the 1994–5 survey while, according to the NAS, the value added for 2000–1 was more than double that of the same for 1994–5.

It may be mentioned here that for 2000–1, the 1998 classification was used while for 1994–5, the 1987 classification was taken. There might have been some differences because of different classifications but this cannot be significant up to this extent at the 2-digit level of classification. For metals and their products the value added given by the follow-up surveys are too much on the lower side compared with those given by the NAS in the case of old as well as new series. It may be noted that in the new series the value added estimates of all products of metals, except base metals, are much lower than the corresponding estimates in the series with 1980–1 as base. The growth rates (in nominal terms) obtained for these sectors do not seem to be reflective of the actual growth.

Besides this, a few more comments on the tables are in order. During all these surveys, about 84 to 87 per cent of the enterprises were reported as OAME, while 10 to 11 per cent as NDME. The DME as a percentage of total enterprises vary from 2.4 in 1984–5 to 4.5 in 1994–5. However, on the basis of value added, the share of OAME varied from 40 per cent to 47 per cent for these surveys, while the corresponding contribution of NDME varied from 20 per cent to 26 per cent and that of DME from 27 per cent to 40 per cent.

Another point worth noting is that the number of own-account enterprises in manufacturing industries according to the 1998 Economic Census[3] is 38 lakh while the number of establishments is

[3] The corresponding figures according to the 1980 Census are 46.6 and 13.2 lakh respectively, and according to the 1984–5 survey, the numbers are 171 lakh and 2.6 lakh respectively. For the 1990 census, the corresponding numbers are 38 lakh and 15.5 lakh. The detailed results of the census conducted for 2005 are not yet available.

17.1 lakh. While, according to the follow-up survey for 2000–1, the number of own-account enterprises is 146.6 lakh and the number of establishments in the unorganized sector is 23.6 lakh. The employment figures based on the economic census are 70 lakh for own-account enterprises and 155 lakh for establishments including 84 lakh in the organized sector. The corresponding figures of employment for the two categories based on the follow-up survey for 2000–1 are 251 and 120 lakh, respectively. For the 2005 economic census, the number of enterprises is 83.22 lakh and employment 254.81 lakh, while according to follow-up survey 2005–6, the number of enterprises is 170 lakh and the number of workers 364.43 lakh. The figures based on the two sources are wide apart. There seems to be some problem with the number of enterprises based on the economic census. For 2005–6, the number of enterprises according to the follow-up survey is more than double the number according to the previous economic census. The sixth Economic Census (2013–14) covered 58.5 million enterprises/establishments. The fieldwork of this census was done from January 2013 to April 2014. Provisional results are available in the all-India report.

The estimates for the unorganized manufacturing industries are available only once in five years. For other years, the CSO carries forward the estimates by making use of physical indicators which are not quite reliable. Even for the years for which the surveys are done, the results are not used to get macro aggregates. Only value added per worker, in different industry groups, is used. Even the estimates of value added per worker as obtained from the first follow-up survey (1978–9) were not considered reliable for estimation of GVA from the unorganized manufacturing sector. The results of the 1984–5 and 1989–90 surveys have, however, been found satisfactory and have been used for estimating the GVA per worker.

For the series with 1980–1 as base the estimates of GVA from the unregistered manufacturing sector were obtained as a product of workforce and GVA per worker estimated from the nearest follow-up survey of the economic census. However, in the series with base 1993–4, 1999–2000, and 2004–5, these estimates have been compiled separately for the units belonging to the SSI group and others. The unregistered manufacturing units have been divided into two separate groups. The estimates of GVA for the unregistered units belonging to the SSI group have been made using the estimates of GVA per worker based on the results of Second All-India Census on Small Scale Industrial Units, 1987–8 published by Development Commissioner, SSI (DC-SSI) and the corresponding workforce for the 1993–4 base series and the Third Census conducted with reference to 2000–1 for the series with 1999–2000 as base. This GVA per worker has been duly inflated for the base year 1993–4 using the WPI, and the corresponding workforce has been duly extrapolated using the inter-survey growth rate of the workforce of the 43rd (1987–8) and 50th (1993–4) rounds of NSS. The estimates of other unregistered manufacturing units, that is, the units other than the one belonging to SSI group mentioned earlier, have been compiled using information on GVA per worker from the follow-up surveys of the economic census for DMEs and from the results of NSSO 51st Round (1994–5) for NDMEs and OAMEs. The GVA per worker from the 51st Round of NSS that relates to the year 1994–5 is suitably deflated to 1993–4. The estimate of workforce for this portion of unregistered manufacturing, that is, for the units neither belonging to *ASI* nor to SSI, has been obtained from the total workforce, on manufacturing activities by subtracting the workforce relating to *ASI* and SSI (non-*ASI*) segments. For the series with 1999–2000 and 2004–5 as base, the same methodology with later data sets has been used. There is, however, one exception for the series with 1999–2000 as base. From the third economic census only the value of output could be estimated. The ratios of GVA to value of output based on the enterprise survey 2000–1 were used. The same methodology was repeated for the series with base 2004–5.

The reason for using two different sources for estimation of GVA is not clear specially when the sector-wise estimate of GVA per worker for the entire unregistered manufacturing is available and workforce can be easily calculated. It has been assumed in the CSO methodology that the productivity of 1987–8 per worker will be same as of 1993–4. Also, per worker GVA of the entire unorganized sector has been used for the remaining part (excluding SSIs). There is no justification for doing that.

Although because of the revisions from the old (1980–1 as base) to the new series (1993–4 as base) there is a difference of only 6 per cent in the GVA for the entire unregistered manufacturing for the year 1993–4, there are wide differences at the 2-digit level (see Table 4A.4 in the Appendix). In some of the sectors, like repair services and transport equipments, the value added according to the old series is 7 and 3.6 times more than the corresponding value added according to the new series. The value added in food products, beverages, and a number of other sectors is double or more than the corresponding value added estimates in the old series. One cannot, therefore, say that the estimates for the benchmark year are reliable according to the revised series.

During the previous revision, the difference in the total GVA from the unregistered sector for 1993–4 was only 6 per cent while the difference in the series with 1999–2000 as base year was 21.6 per cent. For the series with 1999–2000 as base, the GVA for the new series in case of food products increased substantially, although the increase was less than that in the previous series. In the previous series, the GVA, in case of beverages and tobacco products, more than doubled while the same in the current series was less than half of the previous series. The same was the case in wood and wood products, and paper and paper products, rubber, plastic, and petroleum products. On the other hand, in the previous series, GVA from textiles and metal products reduced substantially while it increased in the current series. For other sectors also one can compare the changes in GVA due to change in the base year (Table 4A.4 in the Appendix). The same strategy continues for the series with 2004–5 as base.

For such a vast unorganized sector it is not feasible to collect detailed data annually. The only improvement that could be affected is to make the framework more reliable and to conduct surveys up to that level of confidence with which the aggregates like total employment, wages, inputs, and value added could be estimated and used from the survey results at least at the 2-digit level of industrial classification and at the state level.

Also reliable physical indicators should be worked out for carrying forward the estimates to other years. For the series with 1980–1 as base, the CSO used the GVA per worker from these surveys and population census reports for workforce to arrive at the aggregates for the benchmark year. Using GVA per worker from one source and workforce from the other creates errors because of different concepts and definitions, especially when the industry-wise workforce in the unorganized sectors are obtained by the CSO as residuals, that is, after subtracting the workforce in the organized sector from the total workforce for each industry group. There are, however, more problems in the methodology used for the series with 1993–4 as base.

The physical indicators used by the CSO for carrying forward the base year estimates are mainly the IIPs. This is not justified as the indices relate mainly to the growth of large industries and the growth of large industries cannot be assumed as the growth for small industries. From April 1984, the IIP includes production relating to 18 items produced in the small-scale sector. For the NAS series, the indices of small-scale production should be used as physical indicators to carry forward the estimates to different years. An alternative is to use the growth in GVA in the sample sector part of *ASI* at the 2-digit level of NIC as indicators for the growth in the GVA of the corresponding industries in the unregistered manufacturing sector. Even CSO admits that the estimates of GVA for intervening years are not reliable because of non-availability of suitable physical indicators. For a few industry groups, the availability of main raw material in the group was used as an indicator up to the series with 1980–1 as base—for example, value of output of industrial wood and plywood for wood products duly adjusted for use in the construction industry, hides and skins for leather and leather products, and raw jute for jute products. For these industry groups, the indicators should have been used after netting the use of raw materials in the organized segments of the industry group. At present, however, for all industry groups, the IIP is being used.

The responsibility for improvement in data collection in some particular segments of the unorganized sector rests with All-India Handicrafts Board, Central Silk Board, Coir Board, and Khadi and Village Industries Commission. These organizations conduct industry and area surveys mainly to meet their data needs. For example All-India Handloom Board and Coir Board estimate production in these sectors by an indirect method. The production of handlooms is estimated on the basis of mill yarn supplied to weavers. For coir, the output is based on the actual exports and assessed internal consumption.

Modern Small Scale Industries

As pointed out earlier, the definitions of small- and large-scale industries are on the basis of capital employed in plant and machinery. The data are collected from time to time on sample/census basis regarding modern SSIs. The first such exercise carried out prior to 1960 was a field survey of 11 important industries conducted in 27 centres by Small Industries Development Organization (SIDO) to collect data on production and employment, among others, during 1958–9.

A system of voluntary registration of SSI units with states was introduced in 1960 with a view to build up a framework of small-scale units which would facilitate sample surveys for collection of statistical information. Also, at the time of registration, brief statistical information, such as employment, investment, and installed capacity, was proposed to be collected from the units. These units were expected to give quarterly production returns. However, the returns were not submitted regularly and no meaningful analysis of data was possible.

The SIDO collected production data from selected industries on a sample basis during the period 1970–2. Initially, a statistical survey of 20 industries—10 engineering and 10 non-engineering—was conducted. A brief report was brought out by SIDO for these 20 industries. This was followed by the second round of the survey covering four more industries and the results were tabulated and utilized for official purposes only.

The first major effort to provide realistic database in respect of small industries was made in 1973–4 through the All-India Census of Registered Small Industrial Units with 1972 as the reference year. The coverage of the census was restricted to units registered with state directorates of industries as unregistered units were not covered because of non-availability of frame of such units. Also, units under the purview of other specialized boards were excluded. The modern small-scale units were defined as those having capital investment of Rs 7.5 lakh or less in terms of original value in plant and machinery having Rs 10 lakh or less in the case of ancillary units. The frame for the survey included 2.58 lakh units which were reported to be registered up to 30 November 1973. Out of these registered units, data could be collected from only 1.4 lakh working units. The remaining were either closed, non-traceable, or outside the purview of SIDO.

A few did not respond. The motivation of the survey was to generate the benchmark estimates of employment, capital investment, capacity utilization, and production, both at the all-India and state level. The data were collected for three years—1970, 1971, and 1972. The results were published in the *Report on All-India Census of Small-Scale Industrial Units* brought out in 1976.

In order to have an idea of the trend in production in the small-scale sector at a broad industry group level, it was decided to collect production data from a small sample in 1976, that is, 2 per cent of the total working small-scale units and to compute an index of production with 1970 as the base year. A sample of 2,400 units covering 356 important products was thus drawn from the frame of working small-scale registered units. The effective sampling fraction over the years, got reduced due to a significant increase in the total number of registered SSI units, and was thus much lower than 2 per cent. Therefore, the index thus computed may not give a realistic picture of the trends in production in this sector.

The need for updating this data was felt and, as a result, the second census of small-scale industrial units under the purview of SIDO was undertaken by the office of DC-SSI in association with state/UT governments and the NIC during the period 1989–91. The reference year of the census was 1987–8. The primary objectives of the census were to update the frame of the working units, to assess the contribution of the working small-scale units (among the registered units) and to estimate the mortality rate for SSI units in different industry groups. The data were collected on employment, investment, working capital, capacity, production, exports, raw materials, and energy consumption, among others.

The report on the 1987–8 Census gives data at the 2-digit level of industrial classification regarding employment, wages, capital employed, energy consumption, production, and capacity utilization at the state level. The report also provides the distribution of closed units by reasons of closure. Some important characteristics, such as output, investment in fixed assets, GVA and NVA, and employment, are given for 100 leading industries classified at the 4-digit level of NIC. Similar reports giving data at the district level are published for different states and union territories. Table 4A.5 in the Appendix reports a comparative picture of some important characteristics for the first and the second census. It also gives the data about some of the characteristics for a sample survey conducted with reference to the year 1999–2000 and the third census conducted with reference to the year 2001–2 and the fourth with reference to 2006–7.

According to this table the average annual growth rate between 1972–3 and 1987–8 was 9.4 per cent for the number of units in the frame as well as net value added, while the growth in the number of working units tabulated was 10 per cent. There was a remarkable increase in the share of working units in backward areas, that is, from 35 per cent to 62 per cent. Production (at 1972–3 prices[4]) during this period increased by 11.6 per cent, that is, by 2.2 per cent more than the increase in NVA. Investment in fixed assets increased by 9.1 per cent while the growth in plant and machinery was slightly less at 8.2 per cent. On the other hand, the employment increased by 5.5 per cent only. The employment per unit, during 1987–8, was about half of that in 1972–3.

These results showed an impressive growth in the performance of the SSI sector during a span of 15 years. These results should, however, be used with caution as there are problems in comparing the two censuses because of changes in the definitions of small-scale units in the two censuses. As a matter of fact, there will be some shift over time of units from medium-scale units to SSI units because of an increase in the minimum limit on investment in plant and machinery. It may be added here that according to NAS, the growth rates in the net value added from registered and unregistered manufacturing industries were 5.8 per cent and 5.0 per cent, respectively, which were much lower than those reported in the two censuses.

In addition, data on the 18 selected items are being collected from a sample of about 4,800 units, located in areas of concentration of these products through field offices of SIDO, to work out the estimate of production and these estimates are being supplied to CSO with effect from July 1984. This is being done for the purpose of including these items in the IIP.

[4] The absolute values at 1972–3 prices are given in the *Report on the Second Census* (1988).

The following points should be kept in mind while using the data on small-scale industrial units: (i) The DC-SSI publishes annual data about key parameters, such number of units, production, and employment at the all-India level This data may not be realistic because it is based on a mere 2 per cent sample of the working units (over time this percentage has gone down). This fact is acknowledged by the DC-SSI itself. (ii) The definition of small-scale units has undergone changes over time. Investment ceilings in plant and machinery for a unit to be a small-scale one were Rs 7.5, 10, 20, 35, 60, and 100 lakh, in 1966, 1975, 1980, 1985, 1991, and 1997, respectively. Over time, a number of units got shifted from medium-scale to small-scale units. The rate of growth of the sector shown in a number of documents is thus overestimated. This fact is verifiable from the data given in the aforementioned table. iii) The total number of registered units under SSI during the first and the second censuses were 2.5 and 10.8 lakh, respectively. The data could be collected only from 1.4 lakh and 5.8 lakh units, respectively, from these two censuses. Most of the remaining units were found to be closed. With this background of the high mortality rate of SSI units, the data thrown by these censuses cannot be taken as reliable. Also, there are a sizeable number of unregistered units for which no data were available up to the conduct of the third census. A rough estimate of unregistered units, based on the data supplied by the DC-SSI was being published in various issues of the *Economic Survey*, by the Ministry of Finance. According to the *Economic Survey 1992–93* the number of small units in 1991–2 was 20.8 lakh consisting of 14.96 lakh units registered with State Industries Departments and 5.84 lakh unregistered units. The *Economic Survey* also mentions that according to 1987–8 censuses, about 30 to 40 per cent of these units may not be functional. These data should therefore be used with caution.

After a gap of another 15 years, the third census was conducted during 2002–3 with 2001–2 as the reference year. All units registered up to 31 March 2001 were surveyed on complete enumeration basis. The NIC 1998 was used in this census as against the 1970 classification for the second census. The third census, for the first time, apart from covering the registered sector, on census basis, has attempted to cover the unregistered SSI sector by way of a two-stage stratified sample survey.[5] The first stage units were the census villages in rural and blocks in urban sector. The second stage units were enterprises falling in the unregistered SSI sector. A sample size of 2.16 lakh units was fixed for the sample, but actually 1,67,655 enterprises were surveyed.

In between, however, sample surveys were conducted with reference to the years 1992–3 and 1999–2000. The information collected during this census was similar to that collected during the previous censuses. The results for the third census have already been published. The report gives the estimates of the parameters for the registered as well as unregistered sector. The available results for the third census as well for the 1999–2000 survey are given in Table 4A.5 in the Appendix. According to these results, the increase in the number of tabulated units was 131 per cent between the second and the third census, while the employment increased only by 68 per cent. Also, the employment per enterprise decreased during this period. The reason for non-registration of the units is also analysed. Of these, 53 per cent of the units informed that they were not aware of the provision for registration, while 40 per cent indicated that they were not interested in registration. The details about sickness of the units are also given in the report of this census.

Regarding the third census, two points need special mention.

(1) No estimates have been or can be obtained for net or gross value added.

(2) According to *Economic Survey 2002–03*, the total number of units in the SSI sector was 33.12 lakh consisting of 26.14 lakh registered and 6.98 lakh unregistered units. According to the third census, the numbers are 22.6 lakh and 91.5 lakh, respectively. There are wide differences in the numbers from the two sources. Employment according to the third census (249.32 lakh) is more than that given in the *Economic Survey* (185.64 lakh) only by 34 per cent. On the other hand the production as given in the *Economic Survey* (Rs 6,39,024 crore) is more than double the production according to the third census (Rs 2,82,270 crore). This sounds astonishing.

[5] For detailed sample design see *Report on the Third All-India Census of Small Scale Industrial Units (2004).*

According to later economic surveys, however, the estimates have been corrected. Also in place of SSI, since 2 October 2006, the name given is Micro, Small and Medium Enterprises (MSME) (under the Micro, Small and Medium Enterprises Development Act, 2006, or the MSMED Act).[6] To update the data accordingly, the fourth census was conducted during 2008–9, with 2006–7 as the reference year, and was completed during 2011–12. In this census a number of additional services like trade have been added and medium enterprises have been included. Quick results were tabulated in the Census of Micro, Small and Medium Enterprises 2006–7 and released as a draft report. Final reports separately for the registered and unregistered sector and for both sectors taken together have also been released. Some summary results for this census have also been given in Table 4A.5 in the Appendix.

The reports give the estimates of values of output, fixed assets, assets in plant and machinery, net imports and exports, number of enterprises, and employment at the 2-digit level of 2004 industrial classifications. The details regarding number of enterprises and employment are available at the 4-digit level of industrial classifications and at the state levels. Also for the unregistered part, the activities—trade, legal, educational and social services, hotels and restaurants, transport and storage, and warehousing (except cold storage)—were excluded from the coverage of the survey.

Subsequent to the implementation of the MSMED Act, with effect from October 2006, registered MSME had to file entrepreneur memorandum with the district industries centres. From this memorandum, the growth of the number of registered units can be estimated. This memorandum is, however, discretionary in nature.

Large-Scale Industries (Non-SSI)

The Directorate General of Technical Development (DGTD, originally known as the Development Wing) was set up in 1951, to cover

[6] The enterprises have been categorized as micro, small and medium based on the following criteria:

Micro Enterprises: investment in plant and machinery service and manufacturing units up to Rs 25 lakh.

Small Enterprises: investment above Rs 25 lakh and up to Rs 5 crore.

Medium Enterprises: investment above Rs 5 crore and up to Rs 10 crore.

units licensed or registered with its directorates in all the industries except iron and steel, sugar, tea, coffee, *vanaspati*, cotton textiles, jute textiles, petroleum products, among others. As against the entire factory sector covered by the *ASI*, the coverage of the DGTD was restricted to large- and medium-scale units having a certain minimum investment in plant and machinery. The units covered by the DGTD are also called non-SSI units. The minimum investment limit changed from time to time. The monthly data were being collected regarding installed capacity and quantity and value of output of different industries (products). While the data on capacity and production of different products were being supplied to the CSO which was using these for the compilation of the IIP, it also used to publish these in *Monthly Statistics of Production of Selected Industries of India*. Now the publication has been discontinued; besides, the DGTD was publishing these data in its annual report. The DGTD was disbanded in 1995. The work on collection of data has been taken over by the DIPP. Only production data on the items of the index are regularly being collected and supplied to the CSO in addition to being published in *SIA Statistics* (Secretariat for Industrial Assistance [Various years]) on a monthly basis.

Regarding specific items mentioned in the previous paragraph (those not covered by the DGTD), the data are being collected and published by different official as well as non-official agencies, such as the Indian Sugar Mills Association, Indian Cotton Mills Federation, Textile Commissioner, Ministry of Petroleum, Ministry of Chemicals and Fertilisers, Steel Authority of India, among others, pertaining to their own fields. Some of the agencies along with their publications are mentioned Table 4A.1 of the Appendix.

Index of Industrial Production

The monthly IIP is published by the CSO since 1950. The index has been revised from time to time by shifting the comparison base to a relatively recent period, by enlarging the coverage of items, and by taking into account the changing structure of industries. The base years of the indices along with the item coverage are given in Table 4.1.

The IIPs are published by the CSO. The latest index with base 2004–5 is confined to mining, manufacturing, and electricity. Items

Table 4.1 Base Years and Number of Items for Different Indices

Base Year	Number of Items Covered
1946	35
1951	88
1956	201
1960	312
1970	352
1980–1	352
1993–4	538 (clubbed into 283 item groups)
2004–5	682 items (clubbed in 399 item groups)

Source: 'Index of Industrial Production—Revision of Base Year to 2004–5 and Overview', CSO, MOSPI.

of this index are grouped according to NIC 2004 as against 1987 for the series with 1993–4 as base. The index with 1993–4 and 2004–5 as base included production relating to 18 items produced by the small-scale sector.[7]

For the index with 2004–5 as base, weights for the entire industrial sector have been divided into its three components on the basis of their GVA in the base year as available from the NAS 2010. For the first time, the weighting diagram of IIP had taken into account the contribution of the unorganized manufacturing sector.

The weight of the manufacturing sector has been allocated amongst the industry groups, that is, NIC 2-digit codes in proportion to the total GVA by the respective industry groups based on the total contribution of both the registered and unregistered sectors. The GVA of registered manufacturing sector has been taken from *ASI* (2004–5) and the unregistered manufacturing sector from the 62nd Round of NSS (2005–6) on unregistered manufacturing enterprises. The 2-digit weights were further assigned in stages to 3-/4-digit level of NIC 2004 in proportion to their respective GVA at the all-India level from *ASI* (2004–5). Finally the 4-digit level weights were distributed to selected items in proportion to their gross value of output (GVO).

[7] The index has been revised on 12 May 2017. For details see http://pib.nic.in/newsite/PrintRelease.aspx?relid=161745, last accessed on 24 July 2017.

For the index, the CSO gets monthly production data from a number of official sources, the largest being the DIPP which provides the monthly production data on 213 out of 285 groups of items included in the manufacturing sector. It may be noted that the returns received by the DIPP are on a voluntary basis and there may be substantial non-reporting. For mining and quarrying, data are provided by the Indian Bureau of Mines (IBM) and for electricity by the CEA.

The index is a quantitative one, based on the production in physical quantities. However, in case of 26 items belonging to the manufacturing sector, the production figures are available in value terms only. These values are first deflated by the indices of wholesale prices and then used for the compilation of IIP.

The weights obtained as mentioned earlier have been used to estimate the IIP by using the formula:

$$I = \frac{\sum R_i W_i}{\sum W_i},$$

where, I is the index, R_i is the production relative of the ith item for the month concerned, and W_i is the production-weight of the item.

The indices are also available by use-based categories: basic goods, capital goods, intermediate goods, consumer durables, and non-durables.

It may be noted that for getting the production relatives, all these IIPs represent only large-scale industries (except for 18 items which are from SSI) and the coverage is not complete. These indices do not reflect the real growth rate of the total industrial activity even in the organized sector as it covers only the medium and large units in these sectors.

Table 4A.6 in the Appendix gives the GVA for the organized manufacturing industries based on the *ASI* results as well as those obtained by applying IIPs and index numbers of wholesale prices to the estimates of the previous year based on *ASI*, for 1998–9 and 1999–2000. For 1998–9, the difference between these two set of estimates is more than 30 per cent for two industry groups, between 20 per cent to 30 per cent for four industry groups and between 10 and 20 per cent for another four industry groups. For 1999–2000, the corresponding numbers are 3, 4, and 4, respectively. These differences are due to the use of IIPs for increase in production and wholesale prices. It may be noted that for the entire registered sector, the difference between the two sets of estimates is 3 per cent for 1998–9 and 2 per cent for 1999–2000. For 1992–3, there was no difference, and the difference was 6 per cent for 1993–4 (see Pradhan and Saluja 1998). However, the fact remains that IIPs are not representative of the increase of output even in the organized sector.

As the base of this index was very old, a committee under the chairmanship of B.N. Golder was set up to change the base year to a recent one and suggest the changes in the methodology and weighting diagram. In spite of the base year being very old, NAS since 2000–1 was using IIP and WPI to estimate the value added for the registered manufacturing sector in place of the estimates based on *ASI* data. This was being done for the series with 1999–2000 as base. For 1999–2000, the estimates are based on *ASI* data. The reason for using IIP as a source for estimating value added, given in *Sources and Methods 2012*, is that growth rates according to *ASI* data are different from the growth rates obtained by using IIP and WPI. This logic is surprising. In fact from the previous paragraph we can see that even for 1999–2000, the values based on *ASI* and the index are quite different. Using this method for growth rates assumes that the growth remains the same for the value added and value of output and also for the registered and unregistered parts at the 2-digit level of industrial classification.

The growth rate of GVA for all registered manufacturing industries is higher according to NAS than according to *ASI*. The maximum difference is 22 per cent for 2001–2 and the minimum 4.5 per cent for 2005–6. For some sectors the growth of GVA according to NAS is higher than the corresponding growth rate according to *ASI*, for all the years. For a couple of sectors it is the other way. For the remaining sectors there is year-to-year variation in the growth rates from the two sources (see Table 4A.7 in the Appendix).

This method, however, cannot be applied for estimating gross state domestic product (GSDP) for the manufacturing sector at the state level, as relevant indices of growth are not available for all the states. The states are also using *ASI* GVA estimates for the years 2000–1 onwards.

Also, since 1993–4 there have been significant structural changes in the Indian industry and 1993–4 weights do not represent the present structure. The quality of the index will, however, improve significantly only when reliable estimates of production of the small scale part are available. The DC-SSI has to make special efforts to collect data through regular sample surveys, so that this problem can be rectified. With the conduct of the third census, it was expected that there would be improvement in the quality of the indices. Even today, that is, after conducting the third census, only 18 items of SSI are covered in the index. However, DC-SSI is compiling and issuing quarterly indices with 2001–2 base. This is being done since April 2002. The data are mainly for internal use.

Previously these indices were being issued with 1970–1 as base. The index with base 2001–2 has 465 items grouped into 29 major industry groups as against 356 items in the series with 1970–1 as base. The weighting diagram as well as number of units is based on the third census conducted with 2001–2 as the reference year. The items are arranged in descending order of the value of production. A 75 per cent cut-off criterion in total production was adopted to select the number of items for the index and the same values were used for the weighting diagram. A sample of about 2 per cent of the total number of registered working units as per the third census was selected for getting monthly data on production. The growth rates of SSI sector with 2001–2 as base are as in Table 4.2.

The NAS has revised the series and has 2004–5 as base year. The growth rates based on the series with 2004–5 as base and the growth rates in the IIP are given in Table 4A.8 in the Appendix.

Mines

Up to 1955, data on quantity and value of production of minerals were being published by the Geological Survey of India (GSI). From

Table 4.2 Growth Rates of SSI Sector with 2001–2 as Base

Year	Growth Rates
2002–3	8.68
2003–4	9.64
2004–5	10.88
2005–6	12.32
2006–7*	12.60

Source: DC-SSI (2009).

Note: * Based on the first three quarters. Since then the index has been discontinued.

1955, IBM has been entrusted with the task of collecting data on mining under the Mineral Conservation and Development Rules (MCDR), 1955. The rules were revised in 1958 and again in 1987. The rules apply to all minerals except (i) petroleum and natural gas; (ii) coal and lignite; (iii) minor minerals; and (iv) any mineral declared as a prescribed substance for the purpose of the Atomic Energy Act, 1962.

The mineral statistics division of IBM maintains statistics on the following aspects of mining: (i) mining leases; (ii) mining inventory; (iii) number of reporting mines; (iv) mineral production—quantity and value at pithead prices; (v) mineral stocks; (vi) mineral dispatches; (vii) employment in mining; (viii) inputs in mining; (ix) capital investment; (x) foreign trade in minerals and metals; (xi) metal production; and (xii) world mineral production and trade.

Under the MCDR, monthly and annual returns of all major minerals, except coal and petroleum and natural gas, are submitted by the mine owners to the IBM. In respect of petroleum and natural gas, the data are collected by the Economics and Statistics Division of the Department of Petroleum. Monthly data on coal are collected by the IBM from the Coal Controller.

Statistics regarding minor minerals are collected by the state geological departments under the Minor Minerals Concession Rules framed by the respective state governments for regulating the extraction of such minerals and relate to value only as quantities are not uniformly available for all states. The Director General of Mines Safety collects and maintains data on employment in all mines by district and by state.

A number of publications with different periods and contents are being published by the IBM, the most exhaustive among these being the *Indian Minerals Year Book* (*IMYB*). The data published in *IMYB* constitutes the quantity and pithead value of ores, prices of ores, trade in minerals and metals, industry-wise use of ores during the reference year, mineral contribution to national income, and variety of other data relating to mining. The production figures for ferrous and non-ferrous metals are also available. Figures for non-ferrous metals are obtained from individual producers while figures for ferrous metals are obtained from the iron and steel controller. The data on consumption of ores are received from industrial units consuming these minerals on a non-statutory basis and are thus incomplete. In most of the cases state-wise figures are available.

The data regarding different characteristics of all major minerals are fairly reliable. As far as the minor minerals arc concerned, the reliability of the estimates is not of the same order as that of major minerals which is even admitted by NAS. One point may be kept in mind. According to NAS in the latest series of GDP, the values of output of coal have been revised by using different prices than used in the previous series. But still the value of output for 2000–1 given in the Statistical Abstract (issued by the same organization) is 27 per cent less than the value given in the NAS. Similar differences are there in the values of production of crude oil and natural gas. The same story is carried forward to other years.

Electricity

The CEA, Ministry of Power, is the agency for collection and dissemination of data regarding the generation, transmission, trading, distribution, and utilization of electricity. These data are published in *All-India Electricity Statistics, General Review*. This publication carries out important statistics on installed capacity, electric energy generation, and utilization of electric energy. Data are also given regarding transmission and distribution losses and per capita consumption. Electricity consumption is given by various types of users like domestic, commercial, agriculture, industries, public lighting, traction, and public sector works, among others. Data are given state-wise, sector-wise, category-wise, or mode-wise. In addition, detailed data are given regarding installed capacity and generation by captive plants in industries. The contents of this publication are: review of growth of Indian electricity sector; organisational structure of electricity supply industry in India; installed electrical energy generation capacity; description; electricity generation; electrical energy generation in captive power plants in industries having demand of 1 MW and above non-utilities; electric power supply and system losses; operating data (utilities); electricity transmission and distribution system; electricity utilization; electricity consumers and connected load; urban and rural electrification; and power trading.

In addition, the CEA publishes the details of different modes of electricity in their publications *Review of Performance of Thermal Power Stations* and *Hydro Performance Review*.

Appendix 4A

Table 4A.1 Agencies Providing Data for Different Industries

S. No.	Source Agency
1	Department of Industrial Policy and Promotion
2	Indian Bureau of Mines, Ministry of Mines
3	Ministry of Textiles, Textile Commissioner
4	Joint Plant Committee Iron and Steel, Ministry of Steel
5	Department of Chemicals and Petrochemicals
6	Ministry of Petroleum and Natural Gas
7	Department of Food and Public Distribution, Directorate of Vanaspati, Ministry of Consumer Affairs, Food and Public Distribution
8	Jute Commissioner of India, Ministry of Textiles
9	Railway Board
10	Coal Controller of India
11	Central Electricity Authority, Ministry of Power
12	Directorate of Sugar, Ministry of Consumer Affairs, Food and Public Distribution
13	Salt Commissioner, Government of India
14	Tea Board
15	Coffee Board
16	Department of Fertilizers

Source: Quick Estimates of IIP and Use-Based Index for the Month of December 2016 (Base 2004–05 = 100), CSO, MOSPI.

Table 4A.2 Selected Characteristics per Enterprise by Type of Enterprise and Rural–Urban

	1978–9					
	OAME			NDME		
	Rural	Urban	Total	Rural	Urban	Total
Estimated number of enterprises (lakh)	57.25	14.53	71.78	5.03	4.53	9.56
Total gross value added (Rs crore)	787	412	1,199	235	381	616
Estimated employment per enterprise	1.61	1.65	3.26	2.79	3.05	5.84
Value added per enterprise (Rs)	1,375	2,832	4,207	4,679	8,413	13,092
Output per enterprise (Rs)	2,490	4,942	7,432	9,499	10,173	19,672
Value added per worker (Rs)	854	1,716	2,570	1,677	2,758	4,435
Value added as proportion of output	0.55	0.57	1.12	0.49	0.83	1.32

	1984–5					
	OAME			NDME		
	Rural	Urban	Total	Rural	Urban	Total
Estimated number of enterprises (lakh)	134.39	36.48	170.87	10.25	11.34	21.59
Total gross value added (Rs crore)	4,001	1,961	5,962	896	2,369	3,265
Estimated employment per enterprise	1.63	1.46	3.09	2.3	2.24	4.54
Value added per enterprise (Rs)	2,877	5,374	8,251	8,736	20,897	29,633
Output per enterprise (Rs)	5,267	9,970	15,237	17,844	13,248	31,092
Value added per worker (Rs)	1,826	3,688	5,514	3,791	9,338	13,129
Value added as proportion of output	0.57	0.54	1.11	0.49	0.48	0.97

DME			Total		
Rural	Urban	Total	Rural	Urban	Total
1.4	1.95	3.35	63.68	21.01	84.69
332	883	1,215	1,354	1,676	3,030
13.44	9.92	23.36	1.96	2.72	4.68
23,675	45,277	68,952	2,126	7,975	10,101
88,796	2,04,320	2,93,116	4,941	24,575	29,516
1,761	4,565	6,326	1,083	2,933	4,016
0.27	0.22	0.49	0.43	0.32	0.75

DME			Total		
Rural	Urban	Total	Rural	Urban	Total
1.79	2.96	4.75	146.43	50.78	197.21
665	2,790	3,455	5,561	7,120	12,681
11.14	9.14	20.28	1.79	2.08	3.87
35,151	94,257	129,408	3,798	14,020	17,818
1,12,626	3,22,905	4,35,531	7,460	35,640	43,100
3,335	10,316	13,651	2,117	6,744	8,861
0.33	0.29	0.62	0.51	0.39	0.90

(Cont'd)

Table 4A.2 *(Cont'd)*

	1989–90					
	OAME			NDME		
	Rural	Urban	Total	Rural	Urban	Total
Estimated number of enterprises (lakh)	112.82	28.22	141.04	7.38	8.89	16.27
Total gross value added (Rs crore)	5,588	2,685	8,273	1,292	3,534	4,826
Estimated employment per enterprise	1.73	1.77	3.50	2.95	3.3	6.25
Value added per enterprise (Rs)	4,953	9,514	14,467	17,518	39,622	57,140
Output per enterprise (Rs)	9,588	6,915	16,503	39,925	96,902	1,36,827
Value added per worker (Rs)	2,861	5,386	8,247	5,943	11,997	17,940
Value added as proportion of output	0.52	0.56	1.08	0.44	0.41	0.85

	1994–5					
	OAME			NDME		
	Rural	Urban	Total	Rural	Urban	Total
Estimated number of enterprises (lakh)	95.4	27.2	122.6	6.7	9.3	16.0
Total gross value added (Rs crore)	8,448	5,334	13,782	1,954	5,705	7,659
Estimated employment per enterprise	1.87	1.77	3.64	2.73	3.29	6.02
Value added per enterprise (Rs)	8,860	19,648	28,508	29,252	61,214	90,466
Output per enterprise (Rs)	17,126	35,813	52,939	68,683	1,43,807	2,12,490
Value added per worker (Rs)	4,743	11,073	15,816	10,683	18,662	29,345
Value added as proportion of output	0.517	0.548	1.065	0.425	0.427	0.852

DME			Total		
Rural	Urban	Total	Rural	Urban	Total
2.24	3.43	5.67	122.44	40.54	162.98
1,597	4,243	5,840	8,474	10,452	18,926
12.29	9.02	21.31	2	2.71	4.71
71,307	1,23,663	1,94,970	6,924	25,781	32,705
2,88,006	6,03,579	8,91,585	16,509	84,113	1,00,622
5,804	13,711	19,515	3,466	9,510	12,976
0.25	0.21	0.46	0.42	0.31	0.73

DME			Total		
Rural	Urban	Total	Rural	Urban	Total
2.9	3.6	6.5	105	40.1	145.1
2,482	7,993	10,475	12,884	19,032	31,916
8.46	8.9	17.36	2.11	2.76	4.87
96,571	2,21,881	3,18,452	12,270	47,461	59,731
2,84,672	7,66,017	10,50,689	27,805	1,26,413	1,54,218
11,586	24,958	36,544	5,823	17,182	23,005
0.344	0.29	0.634	0.441	0.375	0.816

(Cont'd)

Table 4A.2 *(Cont'd)*

	2000–1					
	OAME			NDME		
	Rural	Urban	Total	Rural	Urban	Total
Estimated number of enterprises	110.58	36.07	146.65	6.3	10.82	17.12
Total gross value added (Rs crore)	16,817	8,632	25,449	3,692	11,368	15,060
Estimated employment per enterprise	1.73	1.64	3.37	3.07	3.35	6.42
Value added per enterprise (Rs)	15,208	23,929	39,137	58,656	1,05,045	1,63,701
Output per enterprise (Rs)	30,146	49,408	79,554	1,45,073	2,72,338	4,17,411
Value added per worker (Rs)	8,783	14,595	23,378	19,103	31,328	50,431
Estimated employment ('000)	19,147.15	5,914.10	25,061.25	1,932.89	3,628.75	5,561.64
Value added as proportion of output	0.504	0.484	0.988	0.404	0.386	0.79

	2005–6					
	OAME			NDME		
	Rural	Urban	Total	Rural	Urban	Total
Estimated number of enterprises	1,11,08,720	35,04,186	1,46,12,906	7,45,269	10,25,013	17,70,282
Total gross value added (Rs crore)	18,825	9,236	28,061	6,415	14,705	21,120
Value added per enterprise (Rs)	16,946	26,356	43,302	86,076	143,460	2,29,536
Value added per worker (Rs)	10,446	16,300	26,746	26,909	43,308	70,217
Output per enterprises	32,446	54,230	86,676	2,37,579	4,55,735	6,93,314
Estimated employment per enterprise	1.62	1.62	3.24	3.2	3.31	6.51
Estimated employment ('000)	1,8021.31	5,665.99	23,687.30	2,383.98	3,395.43	5,779.41
Value added as proportion of output	0.522	0.486	1.01	0.362	0.351	0.71

DME			Total		
Rural	Urban	Total	Rural	Urban	Total
2.47	4	6.47	119.35	50.9	170.25
6,163	13,521	19,684	26,672	33,521	60,193
11.77	8.88	20.65	2.01	2.57	4.58
2,49,615	3,37,858	5,87,473	22,349	65,863	88,212
8,78,214	18,92,320	27,72,534	53,752	2,41,724	2,95,476
21,210	38,064	59,274	11,120	25,598	36,718
2905.66	3,552.25	6,457.91	23,985.70	13,095.09	37,080.79
0.284	0.179	0.463	0.416	0.272	0.688

DME			Total		
Rural	Urban	Total	Rural	Urban	Total
2,74,277	4,13,355	6,87,632	1,21,28,266	49,42,554	1,70,70,820
12,788	25,617	38,405	38,028	49,558	87,586
4,66,247	6,19,734	10,85,981	31,355	1,00,267	1,31,622
41,887	65,298	1,07,185	16,211	38,167	54,378
18,87,791	56,64,321	75,52,112	87,009	6,06,679	6,93,688
11.13	9.49	20.62	1.93	2.63	4.56
3,053	3,923.09	6,976.09	23,458.29	12,984.51	36,442.80
0.247	0.109	0.356	0.36	0.165	0.525

(Cont'd)

Table 4A.2 *(Cont'd)*

	2010–11					
	OAME			NDME		
	Rural	Urban	Total	Rural	Urban	Total
Estimated number of enterprises	91,38,228	52,91,761	1,44,29,989	9,76,854	18,03,426	27,80,280
Total gross value added (Rs crore)	29,289	27,323	56,612	27,295	70,813	98,108
Value added per enterprise (Rs)	32,051	51,633	83,684	2,79,418	3,92,660	6,72,078
Value added per worker (Rs)	29,873	56,286	86,159	63,999	1,01,877	1,65,876
Output per enterprises	1,62,833	3,22,782	4,85,615	13,59,316	21,57,227	35,16,543
Estimated employment per enterprise	0.0014459	0.0014422	0.0028881	0.0054235	0.0048497	0.00102732
Estimated workers' ('000)	1,3213	7,632	20,845	5,298	8,746	14,044
Value added as proportion of output	0.1798714	0.0846485	0.2645199	0.02008	0.0328259	0.0529059

Source: Different reports of NSSO on unorganized sectors.

*: We give the figures for 'establishment', since the same for NDME and DME were not separately available.

DME			Total		
Rural	Urban	Total	Rural	Urban	Total
			1,01,15,082	70,95,188	1,72,10,270
			56,585	98,136	1,54,721
			55,941	1,38,314	1,94,225
			37,241	78,527	1,15,768
			2,65,283	7,48,666	10,13,949
			0.0018299	0.0023083	0.0041382
			18,510	16,378	34,888
			0.2133005	0.1310811	0.3443816

Table 4A.3 Estimated Value Added in Unorganized Manufacturing Based on Field Surveys and NAS (Rs Crore)

Industry		1984–5		1989–90		1994–5	
		FS	NAS	FS	NAS	NAS	FS
20–21	Food products	2,201	702	3,230	1,210	6,078	4,948
22	Beverages, tobacco and tobacco products	465	440	915	738	3,123	1,367
23	Cotton textiles					5726	1759
24	Wool-silk, synthetic textiles	3,263	4,042	3,494	6,435	903	1,336
25	Jute textiles					327	122
26	Textile products					2,391	2,519
27	Wood and wood products	1,493	1,064	2,255	1,221	5,257	4,082
28	Paper, paper products and printing, etc.	285	409	717	772	1,985	904
29	Leather and leather products	421	293	314	500	1,279	673
30	Rubber, plastic, petroleum, and coal products	172	260	436	583	2,911	386
31	Chemicals and chemical products	189	285	423	376	1,407	787
32	Non-metallic mineral products	609	523	1,003	862	2,525	1,813
33	Basic metals and alloys	139	213	259	507	1,979	310
34	Metal products	823	1,405	1,099	3,389	3,971	2,081
35–36	Electrical and non-electrical machinery	420	1,095	616	3,054	3,905	1,427
37	Transport equipment	525	851	245	1,879	1,013	2,982
38	Miscellaneous industries	515	626	1,433	1,979	5,115	1,092

39	Repair services	1,162	2,002	449	2,951	986	3,657
97	Other services	0	0	1,793	2,944	2,796	30
	All industries	12,682	14,210	18,681	29,400	53,677	32,275

		2000–1		2005–06		NAS (2005–6	2010–1	
		NAS	FS	NAS	FS	2004–5 Series)	NAS	FS
20–21	Food products	10,797	10,765*	24,161	15,406	20,818+838	30,968	20,797
22	Beverages, tobacco and tobacco products	9,234	2,404**	3,877	2,863	4,641	9,758	5,326
23–25	Textiles	11,198	8,704***	17,822	12,234	29,131	46,350	22,445
26	Textile products	5,005	7,653	10,329	9,331	14,113	19,412	25,092
27	Wood and wood products	4,673	2,192	5,035	5,463	8,549	38,016	17,450
28	Paper, paper products and printing, etc.	3,022	951	5,667	2,766	6,150	9,305	6,290
29	Leather and leather products	8,963	5,547	4,504	1,358	6,026	8,543	1,579
30	Coke, Refined Petroleum products	6,884	970	10,929	1,495	4,721	8,401	3,652
31	Chemicals and chemical products	3,282	1,387	7,000	1,632	9,128	12,701	2,265
32	Other Non-Metallic Mineral products	6,143	5,039	11,261	6,610	14,028	25,798	12,298
33	Basic Metals	3,388	618	10,455	1,168	6,554	13,418	1,012

(Cont'd)

Table 4A.3 *(Cont'd)*

		2000–1		2005-06		NAS (2005–6 2004–5 Series)	2010–1	
		NAS	FS	NAS	FS		NAS	FS
34	Metal products	7,057	3,832	23,188	13,053	6,554		14,254
35	Non-electrical machinery	4,182	1,859				45,571	3,318
36	Electrical machinery	3,598	1,215	7,604	1,551	21,463	10,864	1,679
37	Transport equipment	9,464	6,798	3,514	55,250	5,673	15,304	1,555
38	Miscellaneous industries	2,280	780	16,981	32,533	7,174	25,385	11,893
39	Repair services	2,446		325	57	14,632		3,754
97	Other services	6,937	82			331		
	All industries	1,08,553	60,796	1,62,652	87,585	1,80,068	2,52,441	1,54,720

Source: Different Reports of NSSO on Unorganized Sectors and Various Issues of NAS.

Notes: * Including beverages.

** Only tobacco products.

***Jute textile.

Table 4A.4 GDP from Unregistered Manufacturing—Old and New Series of NAS (Rs crore)

		1993–4			1999–2000			2004–5		
		Old Series 1980–1 (as base)	New Series 1993–4 (as base)	%	Old Series 1993–4 (as base)	New Series 1999–2000 (as base)	%	Old Series 1999–2000 (as base)	New Series 2004–5 (as base)	%
20–21	Food products	1,983	4491	44.15	9,993	13,247	75.44	20,932	21,447	97.59
22	Beverages, tobacco and tobacco products	1,190	2,563	46.43	8,571	4,081	210.02	4,819	4,008	120.23
23	Cotton textiles	12,635*	7,988*	158.17	15,342*	17,978*	85.34	17,291	28,581	60.49
24	Wool-silk, synthetic textiles									
25	Jute textile									
26	Textile products									
27	Wood and wood products	2,703	4,774	56.62	9,386	7,217	130.05	4,924	8,360	58.89
28	Paper, paper products and printing, etc.	1,505	1,723	87.35	4,642	3,743	124.02	5,592	6,402	87.34
29	Leather and leather products	906	1,346	67.31	2,821	3,763	74.97	4,368	5,654	77.25
30	Rubber, plastic, petroleum, and coal products	1,162	2,371	49.01	6,058	3,702	163.64	9,300	4,078	228.05

(Cont'd)

Table 4A.4 *(Cont'd)*

		1993–4			1999–2000			2004–5		
		Old Series	New Series		Old Series	New Series		Old Series	New Series	
		1980–1 (as base)	1993–4 (as base)	%	1993–4 (as base)	1999–2000 (as base)	%	1999–2000 (as base)	2004–5 (as base)	%
31	Chemicals and chemical products	545	1,230	44.31	2,375	3,677	64.59	6,237	8,610	72.43
32	Non-metallic mineral products	1,522	2,102	72.41	5,914	6,872	86.06	9,410	11,735	80.18
33	Basic metals and alloys	1,001	1,614	62.02	3,201	4,101	78.05	8,403	5,226	160.79
34	Metal products	4,289	3,582	119.74	5,947	12,475	47.67	20,158	17,728	113.70
35	Non-electrical machinery	2,329	1,501	155.16	3,739					
36	Electrical machinery	2,264	1,672	135.41	3,118	3,177	98.14	6,517	4,938	131.97
37	Transport equipment	2,981	835	357.01	2,196	1,806	121.59	3,009	6,204	48.50
38	Miscellaneous industries	2,154	4,198	51.31	8,207	6,225	131.84	11,716	12,076	97.01
39	Repair services	5,880	827	711	2,202	127	1733.86			
97	Other services	2,877	2,345	122.69	6,246					
	All industries	47,926	45,162	106.12	99,958	82,203	121.6	1,44,062	1,63,984	87.85

Source: Various issues of NAS.

Note: *The figures are the total of sectors 23–26.

Table 4A.5 Comparison of Selected Characteristics of First, Second, Third and Fourth (All-India) Census and 1999–2000 Survey of SSI Units

	First Census (1972–3)	Second Census (1987–8)	Third Census (2001–2)		Survey 1999–2000	Fourth Census (2006–7)	
			Reg.	Unreg.		Reg.	Unreg.
Number of units in the frame	2,57,797	9,86,861	22,62,401		19,63,000	22,48,000	
Number of working units	1,59,321	5,93,769	13,74,974	91,46,216	13,98,000	15,64,000	1,9874 lakh
Production (Rs lakh)	2,60,274	42,97,205	2,03,25,462	79,01,536	1,86,11,830	7,07,510	3,69,70,259
Employment ('000 nos)	1,653	3,666	61,63,479	1,87,69,284	5,040	9,309	40,834
Net value added (Rs lakh)	84,100	10,26,105	–	–	60,95,637	–	–
Investment in fixed assets (Rs lakh)	79,674	9,29,603	91,79,207	62,55,660	38,64,661	4,49,138	2,40,81,646
Investment in plant and machinery (Rs lakh)	53,696	5,54,258	30,32,868	24,56,492	22,58,922	1,05,025	94,63,960

Source: Reports of Censuses and Surveys.

Table 4A.6 Sectoral GVA Based on ASI, IIP, and WPI (Rs Crore)

	1998–9			1999–2000		
	ASI	IIP	ASI/IIP	ASI	IIP	ASI/IIP
20–21	16,773	16,504	1.02	16,314	17,643	0.92
22	5,540	5,486	1.01	7,081	6,226	1.14
23	8,917	7,518	1.19	8,545	9,455	0.90
24	3,663	6,289	0.58	4,169	4,067	1.03
25	1,321	1,317	1.00	1,374	1,396	0.98
26	4,433	3,513	1.26	5,725	4,472	1.28
27	1,028	494	2.08	1,124	839	1.34
28	4,925	5,673	0.87	5,642	5,978	0.94
29	1,457	1,453	1.00	1,650	1,963	0.84
30	39,189	34,692	1.13	41,462	45,654	0.91
31	13,600	15,372	0.88	13,750	14,296	0.96
32	6,972	8,709	0.80	9,740	8,442	1.15
33	21,438	24,239	0.88	23,304	23,012	1.01
34	4,251	4,613	0.92	5,493	4,229	1.30
35	10,963	9,905	1.11	10,376	13,202	0.79
36	13,224	11,570	1.14	12,516	15,416	0.81
37	10,535	14,681	0.72	14,027	11,397	1.23
38	6,646	6,412	1.04	8,294	6,253	1.33
39	3,395	4,371	0.78	3,841	3,859	1.00
97	223	912	0.24	66	257	0.26
Total GDP unadjusted for FISIM	1,78,492	1,83,723	0.97	1,94,493	1,98,056	0.98

Source: *ASI* 1997–8 to 2007–8, CSO, and NAS.

Note: FISIM: Financial Intermediation Services Indirectly Measured.

Table 4A.7 Index of Growth in GVA from ASI and NAS

		1999–2000	2000–1	2001–2	2002–3	2003–4	2004–5
15	Food Products and Beverages						
	ASI	100	95.81	100.38	101.94	100.63	112.95
	NAS	100	106.93	109.60	134.80	152.21	166.94
16	Tobacco and Related Products						
	ASI	100	108.16	103.88	127.74	128.15	133.44
	NAS	100	96.67	85.09	80.89	74.01	83.97
17	Textiles Products						
	ASI	100	109.25	94.81	106.01	112.32	124.89
	NAS	100	108.34	108.56	115.38	123.43	139.71
18	Wearing Apparel, Dressing and Dyeing of Fur						
	ASI	100	99.93	90.17	107.70	103.78	138.21
	NAS	100	128.39*	105.76*	130.35*	135.14*	166.04*
19	Leather and Related Products						
	ASI	100	88.83	100.29	94.38	104.50	105.54
	NAS	100	104.78**	105.61**	93.38**	100.45**	116.05**
20	Wood and Wood Products						
	ASI	100	85.30	100.94	112.24	116.89	112.07
	NAS	100	95.51	82.25	69.66	74.61	68.31
21 + 22	Paper and printing, etc.						
	ASI	100	127.02	108.51	131.80	134.94	137.49

(Cont'd)

Table 4A.7 *(Cont'd)*

		1999–2000	2000–1	2001–2	2002–3	2003–4	2004–5
	NAS	100	100.64	108.33	116.52	134.52	149.43
23 + 25	Rubber, petroleum products, etc.						
	ASI	100	108.14	134.99	216.02	270.03	322.02
	NAS	100	149.29	174.15	195.06	217.62	251.23
24	Chemicals and chemical products, etc.						
	ASI		88.00	85.56	94.81	102.19	117.80
	NAS		113.65	122.40	130.59	143.90	169.63
26	Non-Metallic Mineral Products						
	ASI	100	101.98	106.14	102.56	110.40	155.69
	NAS	100	103.86	112.99	118.27	126.78	136.94
27	Basic Metals						
	ASI	100	78.85	74.54	108.22	148.78	247.52
	NAS	100	105.85	110.81	125.15	159.34	204.90
28 + 29 + 30	Metal products and machinery						
	ASI	100	102.42	103.44	104.60	124.56	145.96
	NAS	100	107.77	102.94	117.54	129.94	154.92
31 + 32	Electrical machinery						
	ASI	100	95.06	101.73	115.44	117.61	130.77
	NAS	100	124.79	147.51	130.26	156.31	205.14

34 + 35	Other manufacturing						
	ASI	100	80.69	95.41	112.93	152.48	202.19
	NAS	100	110.17	116.76	129.36	142.04	161.10
33 + 36	Transport equipment						
	ASI	100	76.48	101.86	89.49	109.34	139.90
	NAS	100	103.86	113.56	130.74	152.79	166.63
	All Industries						
	ASI	100	94.58	97.17	113.68	131.40	164.19
	NAS	100	112.10	118.39	129.58	146.47	171.63

Source: *ASI* and NAS.

Notes: * Only wearing apparels.

** Including fur products.

Table 4A.8 IIP—2-Digit Level

(Base 2004–5 = 100)

Industry code	Description	Weight
15	Food products and beverages	72.76
16	Tobacco products	15.70
17	Textiles	61.64
18	Wearing apparel, dressing and dyeing of fur	27.82
19	Leather products	5.82
20	Wood and products of wood	10.51
21	Paper and paper products	9.99
22	Publishing, printing, and reproduction of recorded media	10.78
23	Coke, refined petroleum products, and nuclear fuel	67.15
24	Chemicals and chemical products	100.59
25	Rubber and plastic products	20.25
26	Other non-metallic mineral products	43.14
27	Basic metals	113.35
28	Fabricated metal products	30.85
29	Machinery and equipment	37.63
30	Office, accounting, and computing machinery	3.05
31	Electrical machinery and apparatus	19.80
32	Radio, TV, and communication equipment and apparatus	9.89
33	Medical, precision, and optical instruments, watches and clocks	5.67
34	Motor vehicles, trailers, and semi-trailers	40.64
35	Other transport equipment	18.25
36	Furniture; manufacturing	29.97
10	Mining and quarrying	141.57
15–36	Manufacturing	755.27
40	Electricity	103.16
	General Index	1,000.00

Source: IIP, Revision of Base Year to 2004–05; Overview, CSO, MOSPI.

Bibliography

Bedi, J.S., and P.K. Banerjee. 2007. 'Discrepancies and Validation of Indian Manufacturing Data', *Economic and Political Weekly*, XLII(10): 874–881.

Central Electricity Authority. *All India Electricity Statistics (2013–14) General Review*. New Delhi: Ministry of Power, Government of India.

Central Statistics Office. *National Accounts Statistics Sources and Methods 2012*. New Delhi: Government of India.

———. *National Product Classification for Manufacturing Sector 2011*. Kolkata: IS Wing, Government of India.

———. 1999. *New Series on National Accounts Statistics (Base year 1993–94)*. New Delhi: Government of India.

———. 2001. *Economic Census 1998—All India Report*. New Delhi: Government of India.

———. 2011. *Index of Industrial Production, Revision of Base Year to 2004–05. An Overview*. New Delhi: Ministry of Statistics and Programme Implementation, Government of India.

———. 2014. *All-India Report of Sixth Economic Census, 2013–14*. New Delhi: Ministry of Statistics and Programme Implementation.

———. 2000. *Guide to Official Statistics 1999*. New Delhi: Government of India.

———. July 1982; April 1989; September–October 1995 *Monthly Abstract of Statistics*. New Delhi: Government of India.

———. 1989. *National Accounts Statistics—Sources and Methods 1989*. New Delhi: Government of India.

———. 1993–94 *Summary Results for Factory Sector 1993–94, Annual Survey of Industries*. New Delhi: Government of India.

———. 1995–96 to 2007–08. *Time Series Data ASI*, Vol. 1. New Delhi: Ministry of Statistics and Programme Implementation, Government of India.

Development Commissioner. 1988. *Report on the Second-All India Census of Small Scale Industrial Units*. New Delhi: Ministry of Small Scale Industries, Government of India.

———. 2011. *Final Report—Registered Sector, Unregistered Sector: Fourth All India Census of Micro, Medium and Small Industries 2006–07*. New Delhi: Ministry of Micro, Small and Medium Enterprises. New Delhi: Government of India.

Development Commissioner-Small Scale Industries (DC-SSI). 2009. *Annual Report 2008–9*. New Delhi: Ministry of Small and Medium Enterprises.

Economic and Political Weekly Research Foundation. *Annual Survey of Industries 1973–74 to 1997–98—A Database on Industrial Sector in India*. Maharashtra.

Government of India. 2002. *Report on Sample Survey of Registered SSI Units 2000–01*, February. New Delhi.

Indian Bureau of Mines. *Indian Minerals Year Book, 2011*. Maharashtra: Ministry of Mines, Government of India.

Manna, G.C. 2010. 'Current Status of Industrial Statistics in India: Strengths and Weakness', *Economic and Political Weekly*, XLV(46): 3108–15.

Ministry of Finance. 2003–4. *Economic Survey 2002–03*. New Delhi: Government of India.

Ministry of Micro, Small & Medium Enterprises. 1976. *Report on First All India Census of Small-Scale Industrial Units*. Government of India.

———. *All India Census of Small-Scale Industrial Units, 2001–2002*. New Delhi: Government of India.

———. 2012. *Annual Report 2011–12*. New Delhi: Government of India.

———. Various years. *An Overview of Revision of Base Year of All-India Index of Industrial Production (IIP) for SSI Sector*. New Delhi: Government of India.

Ministry of Small Scale Industries. 1992. *Census of Small Industrial Units*, August. New Delhi: Government of India.

———. 2004. *Third All India Census of Small Scale Industries, 2001–2002*. New Delhi: Government of India.

Ministry of Statistics and Programme Implementation. 2008. *Handbook on Collection of Statistics Act, 2008*. New Delhi: Government of India.

———. August 2011. *Instructions to Field Officials on Annual Survey of Industries*. New Delhi: Government of India.

National Statistical Commission. 2001. *Report of National Statistical Commission August*, Vol. I, II. New Delhi: Government of India.

Pradhan, B.K., and M.R. Saluja. 1998. 'Industrial Statistics in India Sources, Limitations and Data Gaps', *Economic and Political Weekly*, XXXIII(21): 1263–70.

Secretariat for Industrial Assistance. Various years. *SIA Statistics*. Department of Industrial Policy and Promotion, Ministry of Industry, Government of India, SIA Statistics.

5

Labour Statistics

Labour force is the totality of the gainfully employed and the unemployed persons. Employment and unemployment as well as wages and earnings statistics of different categories of gainfully employed persons are essentially part of labour statistics. Besides these, the statistics relating to trade unions, industrial injuries, industrial disputes, absenteeism, and social security also come under the scope of labour statistics.

The major sources of labour statistics are the Labour Bureau, decennial population census, National Sample Survey Office (NSSO), as well as the Employment Market Information (EMI) Programme and the National Employment Service (NES), both of Directorate General of Employment and Training (DGE&T). Various other organizations such as the Central Statistical Office (CSO), the Directorate of Economics and Statistics (DES) of the Ministry of Agriculture and Farmer's Welfare (MOAFW), Commodity Boards, and Directorate General of Mines Safety also collect and publish employment data on specific sectors of the economy. The details of the different sources of data on labour are discussed in the following sections.

Employment

Factories

Labour Bureau

The Labour Bureau is the central agency collecting and disseminating data on various aspects of labour since its inception in 1946. It collects statistics through statuary and voluntary returns under different labour acts. It disseminates and publishes these statistics in its various publications.

The details of the collected statistics regarding labour are given as follows:

The statistics regarding daily employment in registered factories and the number of factories are collected by the State Chief Inspector of Factories (on a half-yearly and yearly basis) under the statutory provision of the Factories Act, 1948. This act covers factories employing 10 or more workers if using power and 20 or more if not using power and factories specially brought under the purview of the act under Section 85, by the state governments. These statistics are consolidated and furnished to the Labour Bureau. The data, after processing, are published by the Labour Bureau in the annual publication *Indian Labour Statistics* (*ILS*). The average daily employment (as published) during a year for each factory is obtained by dividing the total man-days worked during the year by the total number of days worked by the factory. There are some non-reporting factories for which the estimates are prepared by the Labour Bureau on the basis of recent factory inspection reports and previous year's employment data, among others. The employment figures are available for different industries at the 3-digit level as well as for different states. Both reported and estimated figures of average daily employment for all the factories belonging to an industry or a state are added up to obtain the total average daily employment for the industry or the state. The *ILS* also gives the total employment and employment of women, by age group, for major industry groups based on the factories submitting returns only and do not include the estimated employment in factories not submitting returns. A worker is defined as a person employed directly or through any agency, whether for wages or not, in any manufacturing process or in cleaning any part of the machinery or premises used for manufacturing process or in any kind of work incidental to or connected with the manufacturing process. Thus the definition of a worker as laid down in the act does not cover manual workers alone but some clerical and supervisory personnel as well. Here it may be noted that the statistics do not cover the total persons employed. The data are also published in *Statistics of Factories*. This publication covers the following chapters: Salient Features of the Factories Act, 1948; Distribution of Factories; Average Daily Employment; Hours of Work; Leave and Holidays; Industrial Injuries; Safety Measures; Health; Welfare; and Inspections and Convictions.

Average daily employment separately for men, women, and children is also covered by the *Annual Survey of Industries* (*ASI*) which tabulates the figures at the 4-digit level of industrial classification at an all-India level and a 3-digit at the state level. The concepts and definitions applied by the two sources are different and the coverage is also not the same.

The *ASI* gives the number of workers excluding supervisory and managerial employees and employees of a number of special departments and it also gives the total number of employees including the aforementioned categories. The concepts used by the *ASI* are given in Appendix 5B. There is wide difference in the number of factories and the number of workers given by the two sources (Table 5.1 gives the number of factories and the average daily employment covered by the two sources.)

Mining

The Directorate General of Mines Safety collects information regarding the number of persons employed in and around mines and quarries (except those specially exempted by the central government) covering wage earners, salaried employees, foremen, and apprentices. The method of computation of average daily employment is the same as for factories. The data are published in the *Statistics of Mines in India*, issued in two volumes. One volume gives data regarding coal mines, while the other covers non-coal mines. Figures are available separately for all the important mines covered by the Mines Act, 1952 (with amendment in 1959). The employment figures are available by sex also. These statistics are also published by the Labour Bureau

Table 5.1 Total Number of Working Factories and Estimated Average Daily Employment

Year	Labour Bureau		ASI	
	Total Number of Working Factories	Estimated Average Daily Employment ('000)	Total Number of Working Factories	Estimated Average Daily Employment ('000)
2001	1,44,800	5,733	1,31,268	7,687
2002	1,41,085	6,330	1,28,549	7,871
2003	1,11,895	4,927	1,27,957	7,804
2004	1,58,991	6,802	1,36,353	8,383
2005	1,75,341	7,180	1,40,160	9,039
2006	1,96,097	8,269	1,44,710	10,252
2007	1,63,299	8,015	1,46,385	10,452
2008	1,37,808	7,421	1,55,247	11,327
2009	1,43,389	6,488	1,58,877	11,792
2010	2,28,259	10,855	1,72,177	12,695
2011	2,40,824	11,578	1,75,710	13,430

Sources: *ILS* (2012 and 2013), *ASI* (various issues).

in the *ILS* and the *Labour Year Book*. Prior to 1965, these data were published in the *Annual Report of the Chief Inspector of Mines*.

Plantations

Statistics of the average daily employment in coffee and rubber are compiled by the DES while for tea the data are maintained by the Tea Board. All workers in the gardens and outside are covered. The average daily employment is taken as the total attendance during the year divided by 300. Consolidated statistics are published in the *ILS*. The data relate only to the estates submitting returns. The Tea Board publishes the employment statistics at the district level and by sex in the annual publication *Tea Statistics*. In the case of small estates of the size of 20 hectare and below, the employment is estimated by conducting sample surveys, which are not covered by the Labour Bureau. Employment given in the Statistical Abstract is inclusive of the estimated employment. The employment figures given in *ILS* for coffee and rubber estates are less than 10 per cent of those given in the Statistical Abstract. For tea as well, the employment estimates given in the *ILS* are substantially lower than those given by the Statistical Abstract. In other words, the number of estates submitting returns is very small.

Transport and Communications

Statistics of employment (as on 31 March every year) in the Posts and Telegraphs Department are directly obtained from the Directorate General of Posts and Telegraphs and published by the Labour Bureau in the *ILS*. Statistics relating to the number of persons employed as on 31 March of every year in open-line and in construction in the railways and in the office of the Railway Board (including gazetted officers) are given in the *Annual Report of the Railway Board*. Women employment is given separately. Employment in production units and other railway offices and metropolitan transport projects (railways) are included. Casual and contract labour, however, is not covered by these figures.

The Dock Worker's (Regulation of Employment) Scheme framed under the Dock Worker's (Regulation of Employment) Act, 1948 is at present in operation in the major ports of Mumbai, Kolkata, Kochi, Kandla, Chennai, Visakhapatnam, and Mormugao. This scheme, inter alia, provides for the regulation of recruitment of dock workers and their registration. In the ports of Mumbai, Kandla, Chennai, and Visakhapatnam, the decasualization schemes are supplemented by the 'listing schemes' called the Unregistered Dock Workers' (Regulation of Employment) Schemes and the 'listing schemes' are called 'Registered' and 'Listed' workers, respectively. The total number of workers (registered and listed) under each of the boards as on 1 January each year is given in the *ILS*.

The data on employment in insurance have been obtained from the Life Insurance Corporation (LIC) of India and General Insurance Corporation of India.

The data on employment given for banks is on a calendar-year basis and is supplied by the Reserve Bank of India (RBI). These relate to the total number of persons employed in the scheduled and non-scheduled banks and the RBI. Recently, however, private insurance companies have started business, which are still not covered.

Motor Transport Undertakings

Under the Motor Transport Workers Act, 1961, data are collected from all transport companies which employ five or more workers. However, the state governments are empowered to extend the scope and collect data from any company employing less than five workers. State-wise data were published for the first time in *ILS* 1971 and related to the period 1968. In the case of non-responding undertakings, the employment figures are estimated on the basis of recent inspection reports, previous year's employment data, and employment figures reprinted in the application of registration and/or grant of renewal of licence.

Employment in the Public Sector

Statistics of employment in the central government, state governments, quasi-government, and local bodies are regularly collected on a quarterly basis by the DGE&T. The figures relate to the employment on the last day of each quarter. They exclude employment in the defence forces. These figures are published by the DGE&T in the *Employment Review.*

Agricultural Employment

There are no periodical statistics of employment in India. However, there have been quinquennial rural labour enquires which have collected data on various socio-economic aspects, namely employment and unemployment, consumption expenditure, wages and earnings, and indebtedness of rural and agricultural labours. These enquiries are also aimed at making available data on household consumption expenditure of agricultural/rural households to draw weighting diagrams for price index numbers of agricultural/rural labourers.

The first Agricultural Labour Enquiry (ALE) was conducted in 1950–1 and the second in 1956–7. The scope of the subsequent enquires were expanded to cover all rural labour households. Hence the third enquiry in the series conducted in 1963–5 was known as the first Rural Labour Enquiry (RLE) followed by the second in 1974–5 and the third in 1977–8. From 1977–8, RLE was integrated with the general Employment and Unemployment Survey of the NSSO. The latest enquiry relates to the year 2004–5.

The data collected during these enquires have been published on different aspects of rural/agricultural labour households, namely (i) indebtedness; (ii) wages and earnings; (iii) employment and unemployment; and (iv) household consumption expenditure. In addition, a report is given on the general characteristics of rural/agricultural labour households. The report on general characteristics of households deals with demographic structure of labour households, size of households, and land-holding pattern of rural agricultural households, and occupational pattern of agricultural and non-agricultural labourers. All these data are available at the state level and by classes—scheduled castes, scheduled tribes, other backward classes, and others. Other aspects of the enquires, such as wages and employment, are covered under relevant topics. The comparative picture of the main features of different rural labour enquires is given in tables in Appendix 5B.

Commercial Establishments

Some of the states furnish data to the Labour Bureau about employment in shops and commercial establishments. The data is very partial, representing only certain selected urban areas of some of the states (wherein the Shops and Commercial Establishment Act is applicable). These data are published in the *ILS*.

Scheme of Market Employment by the DGE&T

The DGE&T collects data regarding employment at quarterly intervals regarding organized sectors of the economy. Since 1961, these data are regularly published in the *Quarterly Employment Review* and the *Annual Employment Review*. The DGE&T collects data regarding all establishments in the public sector and all employing 10 or more workers in the private organized sector. While data regarding all the establishments in the public sector and those employing 25 or more in the private sector are being collected under the Employment

Exchanges (Compulsory Notification of Vacancies) Act, 1959,[1] information in respect of private establishments employing 10–24 workers is collected on a voluntary basis from March 1966. The data collected exclude employment in agriculture, self-employed persons, household establishments, and establishments in the private sector employing less than 10 workers. These data are supplied by different establishments to the employment exchanges. The data comes to the DGET via state departments.

The data given in the *Employment Review* refer mainly to: (i) total employment, zone-wise and state-wise; and (ii) public sector employment classified by different branches. The branches are (a) central governments; (b) state governments; (c) quasi-governments; (d) local bodies; (e) employment in selected industries for the public and the private sectors separately; and (f) work-seekers by age and by educational level.

All the aforementioned details are separately available for women employees and women work-seekers.

Occupational Patterns in India

Employment exchanges have been collecting information on the employment market patterns/trends in the country from different industries and occupations in a systematic manner. This system of collection of information is known as the EMI Programme which covers the organized sector of the economy, that is, all establishments in the public sector and non-agricultural establishments in private sector employing 10 or more persons. Insofar as occupational–educational profile enquiries are concerned, data/information is collected from public and private sectors in alternate years for the purpose of studying the occupational pattern of employees. With the expansion of education, the need for data on the educational pattern of employees has grown. Therefore, the DGE&T under the Ministry of Labour and Employment has been bringing out, at the national level, reports on the occupational and educational pattern of employees based on occupational details

[1] With effect from 1 September 1971, Jammu and Kashmir (J&K) was brought under the purview of the Employment Exchanges Act, 1959.

collected under the EMI programme. The present report relates to the private sector enquiry ending September 2003 and the report published in 2008. The information contained in this report is likely to prove useful to manpower planners, educational authorities, employment services, vocational guidance officers, career counsellors, training institutes, job-seekers, trade unions, and employers of various industrial establishments.

The first study in the series related to the year 1958–9 in which all establishments in the public sector were covered. This was followed by a study on the occupational pattern of the employees in the private sector during 1961. Since then the surveys are being conducted for the public sector and private sector in alternate years. To make the studies on occupational patterns more useful, 1966 onwards, the data on the educational profile of employees are also being collected. The data on the occupational distribution of employees is available up to the 3-digit level of the National Occupational Classification (NOC). The separate publications on this topic are not available in the list of publications of DGE&T. It may be because the publications have been discontinued. However the data is now available in Employment Review (2011–12).

Census of Central Government Employees

The DGE&T, Ministry of Labour and Employment, Government of India (GoI), has been conducting the Census of Central Government Employees, since 1960, with 31 March as its reference date. The main purpose of the census is to provide employment details on aspects such as pay ranges of employees, sex, structure, status, tenure of services, group of posts, and location by states and class of cities, among others.

The latest census of central government employees was conducted in 2011. The total number of central government employees was 31.16 lakh in the 2011 Census.

Employment, Unemployment, and Underemployment

There is no reliable time series statistics available regarding unemployment. However, some statistics are available through employment exchanges and some estimates of employment, unemployment, and underemployment are being prepared by the NSSO. (In addition to these sources some information on unemployment is collected during different censuses of population.) The details of these sources are given in the following paragraphs.

Employment Exchanges

There are about 947 employment exchanges, mostly located in the urban areas of the country. The employment exchange figures relate to the number of persons seeking work at the end of each month classified according to different occupational groups, number of applicants placed in employment, number of vacancies notified, and the number of persons registered. These are published every month in the *Indian Labour Journal.* The consolidated annual figures are published in *ILS.*

These statistics cannot reflect the actual position of urban unemployment due to certain limitations. Some of the limitations are:

(1) The employment exchanges do not cover the whole of urban area, only those items were taken for which the information could be available from the establishments themselves.
(2) All unemployed persons do not register themselves with the employment exchanges.
(3) Some employed people also register their names for better employment.

National Sample Survey on Employment and Unemployment

The NSSO has been conducting surveys on employment and unemployment since its 9th Round (May–November 1955). During different initial rounds, different concepts and definitions were tried. Following the recommendations of the expert committee (the Dantwala Committee) on unemployment estimates set up in 1970, the first comprehensive survey on employment and unemployment was carried out during 1972–3 (27th Round). Since then the quinquennial surveys are conducted by following a more or less identical approach in the measurement of employment and unemployment parameters. Nine such surveys have already been conducted (the latest being for the year 2011–12).The workers are classified according to three approaches, namely usual status, current weekly status, and current daily status; and further by demographic, social, economic, and spatial characteristics.

Data on unemployment are also available according to three approaches (definitions of these approaches are given in Appendix 5C) and the aforementioned characteristics. Limited data are also available from annual surveys based on thin samples and based on usual and current weekly status (collected as part of the Schedule 1.0 on household consumption expenditure). Estimates of employment as well as unemployment and also underemployment at the state level are available in the various reports of the NSSO and also in various issues of *Sarvekshna*.

The reports give the labour force as well as workforce participation rates. Labour force includes employed as well as unemployed, while workforce includes only the employed ones. The unemployment as well as proportions of unemployed have also been calculated and given in the reports. Unemployment rate is defined as the number of persons unemployed per thousand persons in the labour force, that is, the unutilized portion of the labour force. Proportion unemployed is merely the number of unemployed per thousand persons in the population as a whole.

At the aggregate level the number of persons employed per thousand persons according to the different classifications for all the quinquennial surveys are given in Tables 5A.1 and 5A.2, separately for rural and urban areas and by sex. It can be seen from the tables that as expected, the proportions of employed is highest for usual status and lowest for the current daily status (CDS). Table 5A.3 gives the unemployment rates for all these surveys.

Underemployment is commonly defined as the underutilization of labour time of the workers. Some of the persons categorized as usually employed do not have work throughout the year due to seasonality in work or otherwise and their labour time is not fully utilized. They are, therefore, underemployed. Their underemployment is defined as the visible underemployment, if they report themselves to be available for work in respect to a short reference period, for instance, a week or each day of the week. This measure of underemployment is obtained by cross classifying persons by their usual and CDS; one can have the idea about this kind of underemployment from Table 5A.4.

On the other hand, some employed persons may appear to work throughout the year. But in terms of productivity or income, the work they are pursuing may not be sufficient for them. They may, therefore, want additional and or alternative work for this purpose. Such underemployment is termed as invisible underemployment and therefore not directly measurable. Some details have, however, been collected from usually employed persons by asking them a set of probing questions on them regarding availability for additional work and the reasons for searching such additional work. Table 5A.5 gives some idea about the invisible underemployment, however, at the aggregate level only, and for the year 2011–12 Also, some of the usually employed had shown their availability for alternative work. Their details are shown in 5A.6.

For all quinquennial surveys up to 1993–4, the data on consumption expenditure, employment, and unemployment were collected from the same households. For 1999–2000 and later surveys, however, different households were selected for the two topics. For the survey, a stratified multistage sample design is used both for rural and urban areas with villages and blocks respectively as the first stage and households as the second (ultimate) stage units.

Data are collected regarding economic as well as non-economic activities from all individuals of the sample households. For economic activities, the NOC 1968 is being used since the first quinquennial survey, while the National Classification of Industries (NIC) has changed over time. For 1999–2000, NIC 1998 was used; for 2004–5, NIC 2004 was used while for 2009–10, NIC 2008 was used. For 2011–12, NOC 2004 was used.

Data are also obtained regarding status of the workers, such as self-employed, casual workers, and regular employed. In the case of workers with current weekly status, the data on their earnings are also collected. The data on average daily earnings are tabulated for regular workers by broad industry groups and by education level (see Tables 5A.7 and 5A.8 for rural and urban employees for 2011–12). The data for casual workers are also given by only industry for urban areas and by only operations for rural areas (Tables 5A.9 and 5A.10 for 2009–10). For 1999–2000, the tabulated data are available in seven reports. The first report, namely *Report No. 455*, presents the key results on employment and unemployment in India 1999–2000; the second report (*Report*

No. 458) deals, in some detail, with the employment–unemployment estimates measured in terms of the three basic approaches of usual status, current weekly status and current daily status and their pattern along with their correlates. It also covers some aspects of underemployment. The report also gave the results generated at the all-India level and some important results for different states/union territories. The third report, namely *Report No. 460*, dealt with non-agricultural workers by their various attributes with special emphasis on workers in the informal sector, that is, those working in proprietary or partnership type of enterprises. The fourth report (*Report No. 462*) discussed some features of employment and unemployment in cities and towns of India. The fifth report (*Report No. 465*) dealt with participation of women in household work and other specified household activities. The sixth report (*Report No. 468*) discussed certain aspects of the persons in different religions with reference to their employment–unemployment situation. among other factors. The seventh one (*Report No. 469*) discussed some aspects of employment and unemployment and some other features pertaining to people belonging to different social groups in India. The estimates of workers relate to age-specific labour-force participation rates according to usual status based on the primary status and by primary and secondary status taken together, by education level, and by sex separately for rural and urban areas. Estimates are also available according to current weekly and current daily status by education level and by sex. Data on unemployed are tabulated according to education level and also according to age groups, separately, by sex and rural–urban. *Report No. 515* to *Report No. 521* give similar data for 2004–5.

The quinquennial survey on employment and unemployment by NSSO was conducted in 2009–10. The five reports released so far are *Report No. 537, Report No. 539, Report No. 543, Report No. 552*, and *Report No. 553*. In addition three more reports, *Report No. 563, Report No. 568*, and *Report No. 564* have been released. In all, eight detailed reports were released in addition to *Key Indicators of Employment and Unemployment in India 2009–10*.

In this connection the following points may be noted:

(1) Compared to census population or the projections thereof, population estimates from NSSO surveys are, in general, on the lower side. This difference arises mainly due to the differences in the methods and coverage adopted by the NSSO in comparison to the census operation. On the other hand the estimates of workforce based on population census do not capture the female workers adequately especially in rural areas. To estimate an absolute number in any category (say workforce), it is advisable to use the survey estimates of ratios (of employment and unemployment) to the census population or the projections thereof, for that category. For the series on National Accounts with 1993–4 as base, the CSO has estimated the industry-wise workforce for 1993–4 by using the estimates of worker-to-population ratios as obtained from the NSSO survey (1993–4) to the population based on the census. The estimates of workforce have been apportioned to different economic activities at the 1-digit level of the NIC also by using the NSSO workforce participation rates. However, at the 2- and 3-digit level, the estimates have been apportioned by using the proportions given by the population census (1991). Similarly the 2001 Census has been used for series with base 2004–5.

(2) Approaches for classification of activity status:
   (a) The estimate is based on the weekly status and gives the average weekly picture during the survey year. It includes both chronic unemployment caused by seasonal fluctuations in the labour market of those considered as usually employed.
   (b) The estimate based on daily status concept gives average volume of unemployment on a day during the year. It is the most inclusive rate of unemployment capturing three aspects, namely:
      (i) The unemployment days of the chronically unemployed.
      (ii) The unemployed days of the usually employed who become intermittently unemployed during the reference week.
      (iii) The unemployed days of those classified as employed according to the priority of current weekly status.

The difference between the CDS rates and usual status or current weekly status (CWS) rates is a reflection of the extent of underemployment.

Decennial Census

The decennial census of population constitutes the main source of information on the economically active population of the country. A large volume of socio-economic data, such as age, sex, composition of workers, rural–urban distribution of workers, and industrial and occupational classification, also flow from the census. Although, the censuses are being conducted on an all-India basis since 1872, it has not been possible to compare these data with the data made available from other sources and that of successive censuses because of the differences in the concepts and definitions used. This lack of comparability has been particularly conspicuous in the economic data collected in the censuses conducted since 1951. In order to resolve this difficulty, the Registrar General of India (RGI) carried out a sample re-survey in which information relating to 'workers' and 'non-workers' according to the concepts and definitions used for the 1961 and 1971 Censuses was collected and analysed with a view to providing the basis for comparison between the 1961 and 1971 Censuses. Details of the concepts and definitions used in various censuses to decide the economic activity are given in a chapter on population statistics.

Economic Census of Enterprises

An economic census provides data on the total number of enterprises and the total number of persons usually working and hired workers with a break-up in male/female and adult/child categories by broad industrial classification separately for Own Account Enterprises (OAE), Non-directory Establishments (NDE), and Directory Enterprises (DEs). An economic census covers all agricultural (except crop production and plantation) and non-agricultural activities. The data have been tabulated at the state level, in the all-India reports, but are available at *tehsil* and district levels with the DES of each state. The data given by the economic census on employment includes workers as well as supervisors, managers, and proprietors (for details of the economic census see the chapter on industrial statistics). In the 5th Economic Census (2005) the number of workers by type of enterprises and by major activity groups is given in Table 5A.11. The 6th Economic Census was conducted from October 2012 to June 2013.

Report of Labour Bureau on Quarterly Surveys on Employment

The Labour Bureau conducted quarterly surveys on employment to access the effect of the economic slowdown on employment in India. The first survey related to the period October to December 2008. So far, 20 such surveys have been conducted. The last one related to the period October to December 2013. The report on the surveys comes one month after the conduct of the survey, the survey being conducted during the month after the reference period.

These surveys are conducted in selected sectors of the economy likely to be badly affected by the global economic slowdown.

The first survey was conducted in seven important sectors of the economy, namely textiles, metals, automobiles, gems and jewellery, transport, IT/BPO, and mining.

In these surveys, a two-stage stratified sampling technique was adopted. The first-stage units (FSUs)—districts/centres—are selected using purposive sampling and the second-stage units (SSUs)—the establishments—are selected using circular systematic sampling. The sample is apportioned among different sectors in proportion to the units in the frame in these sectors at the all-India level.

The reduction in employment was only in the first and the third quarterly surveys.

Annual Survey on Employment and Unemployment

In order to fill the data gap for ascertaining the employment–unemployment scenario in the country, the Labour Bureau has been entrusted, by the ministry, the task of conducting Annual Employment–Unemployment Surveys (EUS). So far four such surveys have been conducted by the Labour Bureau and reports for all these have been released.

The Labour Bureau launched its first Nation-wide EUS in April 2010 to assess the employment scenario in the country. The survey was conducted in 300 districts spread across 28 states and UTs. About 46,000 households were covered during the survey. The report was released by the ministry in November 2010.

The Second EUS was launched in July 2011. In this survey all the 35 states/UTs of the country were covered. The sample size was more than 1.25 lakh household schedules. The report was released in the month of July 2012.

The Third EUS was launched in October 2012. In the third survey all the districts in all the states/UTs of the country were covered. The sample size in the third EUS was about 1.33 lakh households. The report was released in the month of September 2013.

A brief of the third survey and its results are as follows:

(1) Survey was conducted in all districts across 35 states/UTs of the country.
(2) A total of 1,33,354 household schedules were covered during the survey, out of which 82,624 were in rural areas and 50,730 were in urban areas.
(3) A moving reference period of the last 12 months from the date of survey was used to derive the estimates based on the usual status approach. For CWS and CDS approach, the week comprising seven days preceding the date of the survey was taken as the reference period.
(4) All the labour-force–related tables were generated state-wise/gender-wise/sector-wise/social-group–wise.
(5) Based on the survey results, 51.2 per cent or a majority of the households were found to have self-employment as the major source of income under agricultural and non-agricultural activities.
(6) The Worker–Population Ratio (WPR) was estimated to be 48.5 per cent at the all-India level under the usual principal status (UPS) approach.
(7) The female WPR was estimated to be 20.9 per cent at the all-India level under the UPS approach as compared to the male WPR of 73.5 per cent.
(8) The unemployment rate was estimated to be 4.7 per cent at the all-India level under the UPS approach.
(9) In rural areas, the unemployment rate was 4.4 per cent whereas in urban areas the same was 5.7 per cent under the UPS approach.

The Fourth EUS was conducted during the period January to July 2014 in all the states by covering all the districts in the country. The following five volumes have been published:

(1) *Employment–Unemployment Scenario 2013–14*
(2) *Youth Employment–Unemployment Scenario 2013–14*
(3) *Education, Skill Development and Labour Force 2013–14*
(4) *Employment in Informal Sector and Conditions of Informal Employment 2013–14*
(5) *Employment–Unemployment Scenario among Different Social Groups 2013–14*

A brief of the fourth survey and its results are as follows:

(1) A total sample of 1,36,395 households was covered with a break up of 83,385 households in the rural sector and 53,010 households in the urban sector.
(2) From the households covered, 6,80,392 members were surveyed, out of which 4,20,239 respondents resided in rural households and the remaining 2,60,153 in urban households.
(3) Labour force estimates were derived for two approaches, namely UPS approach and Usual Principal and Subsidiary Status (UPSS) approach.
(4) All the Labour Force Estimates were derived for persons aged 15 years and above only.
(5) Labour Force Participation Rate (LFPR) was estimated to be 52.5 per cent under the UPS approach at the all-India level or in other words 52.5 per cent of the persons aged 15 years and above was either working or seeking work during the reference period.
(6) In the rural sector, the LFPR was estimated to be 54.7 per cent whereas in the urban sector, the LFPR was 47.2 per cent under the UPS approach.
(7) Female LFPR was significantly lower as compared to LFPR among males. At the all-India level, female LFPR was estimated to be 25.8 per cent as compared to 74.4 per cent for males.
(8) The WPR was estimated to be 49.9 per cent at the all-India level under the UPS approach or in other words about 50 per cent of the persons aged 15 years and above were employed.

(9) The female WPR was estimated to be 23.8 per cent at the all-India level under the UPS approach as compared to the male WPR of 71.4 per cent.
(10) The unemployment rate was estimated to be 4.9 per cent at the all-India level under the UPS approach or about 5 per cent of the persons aged 15 years and above who were available for work could not get work during the reference period.
(11) In rural areas, the unemployment rate was 4.7 per cent, whereas in urban areas, the unemployment rate was 5.5 per cent under the UPS approach.
(12) At the all-India level, 49.5 per cent persons were estimated to be self-employed under the UPS approach.

Observations on the Surveys

The Second, Third, and Fourth annual EUS provide robust and precise estimates at the state/UT/all-India level. The sample size of the second, third, and fourth surveys has increased considerably from the first survey. As compared to about 46,000 households covered in the first survey, in the later three surveys, information was collected from more than 1.25 lakh households. In terms of persons, the information was collected from more than 6 lakh members residing in these sampled households. Unlike in the First EUS, where only UPS approach-based results were disseminated, in the later surveys, the employment–unemployment estimates were generated by the UPS approach, the UPSS approach, the CDS approach, and the CWS approach. Employment, unemployment, and its derivatives were also analysed by industry, skill, sex, social group, among others. Demographic particulars of the sample household members were also presented in the reports. The results of the second survey were presented in two volumes. (For further details, refer to the Foreword by the DG, Sept. 2013 in Vol. I.)[2] For the third survey, an additional volume giving details of youth employment and unemployment was

[2] *Report on Second Employment-Unemployment Survey*, Volume 1, Labour Bureau, May 2012.

published. The volumes published for the fourth survey have already been listed earlier.

Comparison of NSSO and Labour Bureau on Employment and Unemployment Survey

The Second EUS, 2010–11 by the Labour Bureau shows an improvement in the employment situation while attributing the positive trend to a change in methodology, sample size, and to some extent, an improved labour situation in the country.

The new survey reflects the post-economic slowdown scenario, and hence, reports a lower unemployment rate. The earlier survey reported joblessness of 9.4 per cent and the year was next to 2008–9, when the global financial crisis deepened.

However, the two surveys are not comparable as the methodology and the sample size were totally different. Yet, there is no denying a positive trend.

The new survey also paints a brighter rural scenario against urban areas in terms of employment generation. The improvement in rural areas could be attributed to government schemes such as the Mahatma Gandhi National Rural Employment Guarantee Scheme (MGNREGS).

The NSSO revealed that the unemployment rate fell to 2.5 per cent in 2009–10 (July 2009 to June 2010) from 3.1 per cent in 2004–5. This was much less (2.2) compared to the 2009–10 survey.

The labour survey for 2010–11 showed a higher unemployment rate compared to the NSSO survey.

The later surveys have followed the NSSO pattern and have covered all districts and taken a sample size of more than 1,25,000 households, compared to 46,000 households in the first survey.

Wages and Earnings

Agricultural Wages

There are a number of sources collecting data on wages for different agricultural occupations. The Labour Bureau collects and compiles data on wages for 11 agricultural and 7 non-agricultural occupations entailing manual work. The wage rates are collected along with rural retail prices from 600 sample villages spread over 20 states within the country since July 1986. However, due to certain reasons, the data could not be tabulated for some period. From the 1995–6 agricultural year onwards, the monthly data are published in the *Indian Labour Journal.* These data are also released by the Labour Bureau in *Wage Rates in Rural India.* Monthly as well as annual average daily wage rates by occupation are available by sex and at the state level.

As against the wage rate data collected for 11 agricultural and 7 non-agricultural occupations, following the recommendations of the working group constituted by CSO on advice of the National Statistical Commission (NSC), the Labour Bureau has started collecting wage rate data for 25 occupations (12 agricultural and 13 non-agricultural), November 2013 onwards.

The work of collection has been entrusted to Field Operations division of the NSSO. Collection of data from 600 sample villages is staggered over four weeks of a month with one-fourth of them being covered every week. The days of canvassing of the schedule are fixed. The data on normal working hours and the prevailing wage rates in cash and kind for reported working hours are collected sex-wise for each of the selected occupations. Wages in kind are evaluated at local retail prices. The wage rate data are first normalized for an eight-hour working day. The simple average of the normalized wage rate is taken as the normal average wage rates for the state. Similarly, the wage rates at the all-India level are obtained as a simple average of the state-level average daily wage rates. State-wise averages have to be restricted only to those occupations where the number of quotations is five or more in order to avoid inconsistency in wages paid to different categories of workers on account of difference in the number of quotations. However, for working of the all-India averages all those neglected quotations have been taken into account to arrive at the total number of quotations at the all-India level. At the all-India level also, the number of quotations for working out occupation-wise averages have been restricted to five or more. Average daily wages during a month are published in the *Indian Labour Journal.*

Wage Rate Based on Rural Labour Enquiry

Average daily earnings based on the rural labour enquiries have been published by the Labour Bureau for all the enquiries conducted so far. These are available state-wise and for men, women, and children; for all classes, scheduled castes, scheduled tribes and other backward classes; and for different operations. The wages/salaries may be in cash as well as in kind. The wages in kind are evaluated at current market prices. Amount paid as overtime was included for the first time in 1999–2000. The normal working day in case of casual workers constitutes eight hours. The wages are based on the CWS of the employment and the number of days to which earnings related are recorded in terms of defined intensities (half day, full day).

The wage rate data based on rural enquires are for all 35 states and UTs, while the annual data collected along with retail prices relate only to 20 important states. Also, for non-agricultural operations the operation-wise data are not given in rural enquiries reports.

Wage Rates Collected by the DES

Data on agricultural wages prevailing in the selected villages/ centres, spread over the entire country is collected by the DES on a monthly basis since 1948. The returns are received by the DES from the state governments. The data is collected on a monthly basis. The primary reporting agencies are required to send the returns pertaining to the particular month, by the 2nd of the succeeding month, to the concerned district headquarters. The district headquarters, after scrutiny and consolidation, send them to the state headquarters, which in turn send them to the DES immediately.

The wages paid could be either in cash or in kind or both. Wages paid in kind are evaluated at the local retail prices. Simple arithmetic averages (monthly and annual) at various levels of aggregations (district, state, all India) are worked out on the basis of returns received from different villages/centres. The wages are available for different operations of field labour (ploughman, sowers, reapers and harvesters, weeders and transplanters, among others) except for the states of Andhra Pradhesh, Karnataka, and Maharashtra which do not give operation-wise details, and also separately for men, women, and children. The data are also available for the skilled labour (carpenter, blacksmith, and cobbler, among others). Statistics are published in *Agricultural Wages in India*.

Wages in Manufacturing Industries

Statistics of per capita average annual earnings of persons employed in factories are available on the basis of the data secured, under the Payment of Wages Act, 1936 from various states and UTs. Under this act, the authorities in each state collect annual returns from individual factories as defined in the Factories Act, 1948 and furnish these to the Labour Bureau after consolidation. The statistics are collected on average daily employment and the total wage bill and per capita annual earnings are obtained by dividing the total wage bill by the average daily employment. The Labour Bureau compiles, consolidates, and publishes in the *ILS*, the per capita annual income of workers classified according to states, industries, and components of wages. Up to 1957, the aforementioned act applied to employees earning less than Rs 200 per month. In 1958, the act was amended to bring within its scope employees earning Rs 200 or more but less than Rs 400 per month. Up to 1964, the returns were called for in two groups, namely (i) persons earning less than Rs 200 per month and (ii) persons earning less than Rs 400 per month.

In 1976, the coverage was extended to persons earning up to Rs 1,000 per month and was again extended in 1982 to cover earnings up to Rs 1,600 per month.

While computing the average annual earnings, industries producing food products, tobacco, and cotton ginning and pressing have been excluded as these groups include only seasonal factories where the annual earnings of workers rarely relate to the whole year and, therefore, would not be comparable with the data on earnings of the other industries. Railway workshops are also excluded. The Payment of Wages Act was amended in 2005. Accordingly, the wage ceiling limit has been enhanced to Rs 10,000 from August 2007.

The wages data are also available from the *ASI*. The data available give industry-wise wages and salaries separately for men, women, and children and for different states. The data are also available for total emoluments and other benefits on social security. Different concepts for which data are available are given in Appendix 5D. From *ASI* data, one could work out the entire cost of labour input while the data based on payment of wages act do not cover the entire expenditure of the industries. It does not cover even the wages of all the employees, that is, persons earning more than Rs 10,000 per month.

Mining

The Directorate General of Mines Safety collects and compiles the statistics of earnings of employees in different mines. In case of coal, the information regarding the total payments made to workers for the work done during the first complete working week of each month is collected. The per capita weekly cash earnings are then computed by dividing the total payments by the average daily employment during the week. These statistics are available for each month of the year. For mines other than coal, up to 1960, the annual statistics related to the average daily earnings in December each year. Since 1961 the data on average daily earnings relate to the whole year and not to December only. These data are published in the *ILS* and *Statistics of Mines in India*.

Railways

Statistics of average annual earnings of staff under selected categories in the government railways are published in the *Annual Report of the Railway Board*. The average annual earnings are obtained by dividing the total remuneration by the average number of staff employed. The average number of staff is the total arithmetic average of the number of staff actually working on the last day of each of 12 months of the financial year.

Dock Labour

The Calcutta Dock Labour Board, Kolkata Port Trust gives the rates of wages of the reserve pool workers (daily rated) on the

Calcutta Dock. In the case of Mumbai and Chennai, similar boards give the required data in their annual reports. Some data regarding wages are also available for Visakhapatnam, Kochi, Kandla, and Mormugao ports. The data is consolidated by the Labour Bureau and published in the *Labour Year Book*.

Plantations Statistics

Statistics relating to the tea estates in Assam are collected by the Controller of Emigrant Labour and published in the Annual Report on the Working of Tea District Emigrant Labour Act, 1932. For the purpose of these statistics a labourer is defined as a person working on wages, excluding clerks, domestic servants, mechanics, carpenters, masons, bricklayers, or other artisans. Figures are based on the return submitted by the tea estates. The data for other estates for plantations coming within the purview of the Payment of Wage Act are available from reports under the Payments of Wages Act. For West Bengal tea estates, the figures are taken from the Labour Commissioner, West Bengal. The figures relate to persons having per capita annual earnings less than Rs 1,600. These statistics are reproduced in the *ILS*. The Tea Board and Coffee Board publish sex-wise and district-wise wage rates in their publications.

Occupational Wage Surveys

The enumeration of the occupational wage rates in India was done from time to time by various committees and commissions. The Royal Commission on Labour in 1929 and the Labour Investigation Committee in 1944, among others, did some surveys on this topic. These surveys were of very limited scope and no uniform concepts were applied for the surveys.

The First round Occupational Wage Survey (OWS) was conducted by the Labour Bureau during the year 1958–9. In all, 44 major industries in the manufacturing, mining, and plantation sectors were selected for the purpose of the survey. The aims of the survey were to obtain basic data for building up industry-wise index numbers of wage rates and to obtain data on wage components of workers in different occupations in an industry so as to enable proper study of wage differentials and the distribution of workers by wage levels. The aims of the latest two rounds were extended to examine the implementation of the Equal Remuneration Act, 1976 (for men and women); the concepts and definitions applied were uniform. The term 'worker' was defined as in the Factories, Mines or Plantations Acts. The survey was conducted on sample basis. Data were collected regarding (i) occupational wage rates and (ii) payroll earnings by components of industrial workers for each occupation for a particular pay period. Apart from these, the information relating to overtime earnings and incentive bonus schemes was also collected. The results were published by the Labour Bureau in the form of one *General Report* covering 44 industries and various special industry reports covering details of individual industries. Important data presented in the *General Report* related to industry-wise distribution of workers by employment status (permanent or temporary), by methods of wage payments (time and piece rate), by wage periods and by sex, wage rates (minimum and maximum), average daily earnings by components, average daily earnings of time-rated and piece-rated workers and of men, women, and children and distribution of workers by levels of earnings. Information relating to the proportion of workers doing overtime and wages earned thereby and similar information in respect of incentive bonus schemes was also given.

A Second OWS was conducted in 1963–5, more or less, on the same lines and with the same objective and coverage. However, instead of collecting data in respect of all occupations in the various industries, a study was made of important occupations which accounted for the bulk of employment in the selected industries and the remaining occupations were clubbed together to form the residual group. Thus, statistics relating to important occupations are available which are comparable to similar statistics collected during the First survey. The *Summary Report* was issued by the Labour Bureau. This report gave a summarized form on an all-India basis the figures relating to the following:

(1) employment
(2) average range of wage rates
(3) employment status of workers
(4) mode of wage payments
(5) payroll earnings
(6) incentive schemes

Comparable figures obtained during the First Survey were also presented in this report. This *Summary Report* was followed by more comprehensive reports containing data relating to the aforementioned items in greater details and also furnishing a breakdown up to the level of region of concentration of different industries. The third and the Fourth Round surveys were conducted in 1974–9 (81 industries) and 1985–92 (53 industries), respectively. The Fifth Round was undertaken in 1993 and has been completed. This round covered 57 industries (45 manufacturing, 5 mining, 3 plantation, and 4 service sectors). The industry-wise details about these surveys have been given in a number of reports.

The Sixth Round OWS (2006) has also been conducted. This survey covered 56 industries.

The reports in respect of four service sector industries, three plantations industries, one tea-processing industry, four mining industries, five textile industries and textile garments industry, and ten engineering industries under the Sixth Round OWS have been released. The report on nine engineering industries has also been released.

Survey of Labour Conditions

During the Second Five Year Plan, the Labour Bureau was entrusted to survey the labour conditions in 46 major industries (38 in manufacturing, 5 in mining, and 3 in plantations). For different industries the data were collected on a sample basis regarding employment, absenteeism, labour turnover, length of service, system of training and apprenticeship, wages and earnings, working conditions, leave and holidays with pay, welfare and other amenities, social security, and industrial relations, among others. Stratified systematic random sampling was adopted with industries, with regions of concentration as strata. The decision regarding the number of regional strata for each industry was taken after a study of dispersion of its establishments. The latest available frames were utilized for different industries. The survey was covered in different phases, each phase covering a group or groups of industries, over the period from 1959 to 1965. The establishment approach was followed and the subjects like housing and living conditions had to be excluded. The results were published by the Labour Bureau in the individual industry reports. This programme has since been continued and at present three or four industries are being covered every year. For some industries the surveys are being repeated to get a comparable picture.

In all, 62 surveys (including two repeat surveys) in 60 industries have been conducted so far and reports thereon have been released.

Contract Labour Surveys

These surveys aim to collect information to assess the working conditions of contract labour under the Contract Labour Act, 1970. Under the contract labour surveys, information is collected on employment, wages and earnings, working conditions, labour welfare, social security, and industrial relations.

The Labour Bureau has been conducting all-India, industry-specific contract labour surveys since 1956–7. So far, 45 surveys have been conducted in 39 industries, including repeat surveys conducted in six industries, namely iron ore mines, rice milling, petroleum refineries and oil fields, building and construction, iron and steel industry, and mica mines. Reports on all these surveys have been released.

Socio-Economic Conditions of Women Workers in Industry

These surveys aim at collecting socio-economic data to study the conditions of women industrial workers and the problems faced by them. So far 21 such surveys have been conducted and all the reports thereon released. The last survey was conducted in the plantation industry in October 2008, for which the report has already been released.

The first enquiry to study socio-economic conditions of women workers was undertaken by the Labour Bureau in the year 1953 and a report titled *The Economic and Social Status of Women Workers in India* was brought out. The enquiry was conducted through the mail questionnaire method and was confined to important industries in the country employing women in large numbers, namely cotton and jute textiles, coal mines, and plantations. Later on, the Labour Bureau and Planning Commission jointly prepared a study in

1958 titled *Women in Employment 1901–1956*. Thereafter, the Labour Bureau brought out a few reports on the basis of available published/unpublished data. One such report, *Women in Employment*, was brought out in the year 1964 and another publication, *Women in Industry*, in the International Women's Year (1975) presented an objective assessment of the trend of women's employment, their wages and earnings, and laws and regulations governing their employment and working conditions.

In the year 1975, a full-fledged scheme, namely Socio-economic Conditions of Women Workers, was entrusted to the Labour Bureau with the objective of assessing the working and living conditions of women workers employed in organized industries where they were significantly employed. In the earlier years, the scope of the survey was restricted to organized industries only where predominantly women workers were employed. However, in view of the importance of the labour force and also the dominant existence of the unorganized sector in the Indian economy, where more than 90 per cent of the labour force is engaged in the unorganized sector/employment, the scope of the survey was extended to unorganized sector also. The first survey under the scheme was conducted in the mines sector in the year 1976–7.

Evaluation Studies on the Implementation of the Minimum Wages Act, 1948

The Ministry of Labour and Employment entrusted the Labour Bureau, in May 1981, to conduct evaluation studies on the implementation of the Minimum Wages Act, 1948. The scheme aims at evaluating the extent to which the Minimum Wages Act, 1948 has been implemented in various scheduled employment in different parts of the country. Initially, these evaluation studies were conducted in the scheduled employment of agriculture in different states in a planned manner. The first study was done in the agriculture sector in Gujarat during the year 1982 and subsequently, similar studies were conducted in Rajasthan, Bihar, and Karnataka, among others.

Keeping in view of the utility of the data so collected, the scope and coverage of the study was extended to organized employment, such as bauxite mines, building construction industry, and bidi-making establishments. The Labour Bureau has so far conducted 27 such evaluation studies, with all the reports released.

Report on the Working of the Minimum Wage Act, 1948

The Labour Bureau also brings out an annual report on the working of the Minimum Wages Act, 1948. The report presents information on employments added, employments in which the minimum wages were fixed for the first time, the minimum wages in different scheduled employments prevalent during the year, the range of minimum wages, comparative minimum wage rates prevailing in scheduled employments, and number of inspections. Information contained in this volume is based on the annual reports/returns received from the Chief Labour Commissioner (Central) as well as the concerned authorities of the state governments and UTs.

Working and Living Conditions of Workers in the Unorganized Sector of Industries

The aim of the survey is to collect data on working and living conditions of workers engaged in the unorganized sector of industries/employments for amelioration of their lot. So far, 31 surveys have been conducted and all the reports have been released.

In pursuance of the recommendations of the National Commission on Labour, the Labour Bureau has been conducting comprehensive surveys on the working and living conditions of workers engaged in the unorganized sector of industries, who comprise more than 90 per cent of the total employment in the economy. Data on working and living conditions of workers are collected under this scheme with a view to bridge the gaps in the much-needed labour statistics in respect of this hitherto neglected lot. Initially, due to resource constraints, the coverage of the survey was restricted only to pockets of concentration. Fifteen centre-specific surveys were conducted between 1977 and 1982. Keeping in view the utility of these surveys, their coverage was subsequently extended to all of India. So far all-India–level surveys have been conducted for 12 industries and reports thereon have been released.

Working and Living Conditions of Labour Belonging to Scheduled Castes/Tribes

The Labour Bureau conducts the following two types of enquiries under the segment:

(1) Working and living conditions of the scheduled castes (SCs) workers engaged in the following four unclean occupations in urban areas:
   - sweeping and scavenging
   - tanning and flaying
   - bone-crushing
   - shoe-making

   The scope of the survey has, however, extended to clean occupations in factories and the adjoining rural areas as well.

(2) Working and living conditions of scheduled tribe (STs) workers in industrial centres/industrial belts.

So far, the Labour Bureau has conducted nine surveys for both SC and ST workers. The ST survey was conducted in the ST belt of Kalahandi, Bolangir, and Koraput districts of Odisha in the month of September 2009. The reports of the same have been released.

Trade Unions and Other Miscellaneous Statistics

Trade Union Statistics

Under the Indian Trade Union Act, 1926 the registered trade unions submit annual returns relating to the membership and finances to the Labour Bureau. The data received are compiled and published in *Trade Unions in India.* The information is available in these reports regarding (i) number of trade unions in India; (ii) their membership according to states, industrial classification, size, and funds; and (iii) items of income and expenditure.

These data are available separately for workers' trade unions and employers' trade unions. These statistics are also published in the *ILS.* No data are available regarding unregistered trade unions. Even among registered unions the coverage of data is not complete as some of the unions fail to submit returns. In fact, the response of the unions submitting results is generally less than 50 per cent.

Industrial Disputes

The statistics are collected on a voluntary basis by the state labour departments and regional labour commissioners. The collected statistics relate to (i) number of disputes by state, by industry, and by causes of disputes; (ii) workers' involved in the disputes; (iii) man-days lost; and (iv) severity ratio (ratio of man-days lost to the total number of man-days available for work).

Figures are computed only in respect of those disputes which result in the stoppage of work and involve at least 10 workers. The scope of these statistics extends to those strikes and lockouts which are the result of the disputes between the employers and the employees. The statistics do not cover political and other such strikes. These statistics are published by the Labour Bureau in the *ILS*.

Absenteeism

The Labour Bureau series regarding absenteeism are based on the voluntary returns furnished by a few selected large units. The statistics relate to manufacturing mining and plantation industries and are published in the *ILS*. Absenteeism in the case of mining is compiled and published by the Director General of Mines Safety (except for gold where it is given by the Labour Commissioner, Mysuru), Plantations cover only tea in Assam compiled by the Controller of Emigrant Labour, Assam.

Industrial Injuries

Statistics are available for (i) factories, (ii) mines, and (iii) railways and dock workers.

In the case of factories, statistics of injuries are available, classified as fatal and non-fatal injuries. These are collected by the Labour Bureau directly from factory owners. Industry-wise statistics are published by the bureau in the *ILS*. For mines, the statistics are recorded according to fatal and serious injuries. Minor injuries are not recorded by the Director General of Mines Safety. For railways, these are published in the annual reports by the Railway Board. Injuries are classified as (i) fatal and (ii) non-fatal.

Non-fatal injuries are further divided into serious and minor injuries. Regarding dock workers, details of fatal and non-fatal injuries are available in the report on the working of the Indian Labour Act, 1934.

Social Security

Nowadays, many forms of social security benefits are given to the labour. The following statistics are collected and published by the Labour Bureau in *ILS*:

Workmen's Compensation Act, 1923

Data on the number of compensated injuries and the amount of compensation paid, classified according to injury resulting in death, permanent disablement, and temporary disablement, are published annually for factories, plantations, docks, posts and telegraphs, and railways, among others.

Maternity Benefit Act, 1961

Data relating to the average number of women employed, number of women who claimed maternity benefits, number of women who are given maternity benefits, and total amount paid are available for factories, plantations, and mines on an annual basis.

Employee State Insurance Act, 1948

Data regarding the number of persons taking benefit and the amount of cash and other benefits are published on an annual basis, classified by (i) sickness benefits, (ii) maternity benefits, (iii) disablement benefits, (iv) dependents benefits, and (v) medical benefits.

A person who is entitled to benefits under this scheme is not entitled to get the benefits under the Workman's Compensation Act and the Maternity Benefit Act. These benefits are given by the factories employing 20 or more persons and using power.

Employee's Provident Fund Act, 1952

Data regarding the number of establishments covered under the act, number of subscribers, and the amount of provident fund contribution collected from the establishments are published for each industry and for each state.

Scientific and Technical Manpower

Scientific and technical manpower constitutes one of the major input resources to scientific and technological activities. It is, therefore, necessary to study the total numerical strength of the qualified human resources, namely the total stock and the outturn of scientific and technological personnel. Due to the importance of these data, a scheme, National Register of Scientific and Technical Personnel, was introduced in 1948. This register was maintained by the Directorate of Scientific and Technical Personnel (DSTP) of the Council of Scientific and Industrial Research (CSIR). It enrolled personnel holding degrees or diplomas in science, engineering, technology, and medicine. Both employed and unemployed persons could get themselves enrolled. Emolument was, however, not compulsory.

Up to 1955, the information collected was published in eight parts, as given in Table 5.2.

Publication of further volumes was discontinued. However, arrangements were made to maintain up-to-date information regarding the old registrants by sending periodic revision forms to them. The new registrants are maintained on a card index in the DSTP of the CSIR.

The National Register is incomplete. It is affected by the omissions in registration as well as in deletions. On the one hand, the registration is not compulsory but only optional and on the other hand, there are unrecorded out-flows of trained personnel, not only by death but also by emigration.

Table 5.2 Information Published By National Register of Scientific and Technical Personnel

		Year of Publication	Total Number of Persons Included
I) Engineering	Part I	1949	3,600
	Part II	1950	4,600
	Part III	1951	3,776
II) Medical personnel	Part I	1950	4,072
	Part II	1951	4,728
	Part III	1954	5,650
III) Scientist and technologist	Part I	1955	4,691
	Part II	1955	9,221

Source: Saluja (1972).

Since January 1959, the information on the enrolment, stock, out-turn, age composition, sector of employment, nature of activities, salaries, mobility, unemployment, and other characteristics of different categories of technical and scientific manpower was being published by the DSTP of the CSIR in its monthly journal *Technical Manpower*. In this journal, other information was also given, such as occupational bibliography, qualifications, and experience of those scientific and technical personnel who were abroad but were willing to return to India. The stock of personnel in different fields and at different levels was worked out by the use of data on the out-turn, after adjusting for attenuations. The out-turn figures were based on the data collected from various universities and institutions. This journal has since been discontinued.

Regarding medical personnel, another source of data are the state medical registers published by the state medical councils. The registration in the case of medical personnel is compulsory. Based on the information from the state medical councils, the Medical Council of India, for the first time, published the Indian Medical Register in 1965. The details regarding all medical personnel enrolled up to 31 December 1960 were given. According to the register, there were 75,828 registrants constituting 42,276 graduates, 32,220 licentiates, and 1,332 postgraduate medical personnel. Since then, the medical registers are published every year.

For dentists, nurses, and pharmacists also, there are similar councils giving details about these categories of personnel.

Since the information based on the register of scientific and technical personal was not reliable, it was decided to take up this activity along with the population census from 1961.

During the Census of India 1961, a special questionnaire was distributed to scientific and technical personnel. The returns were received back from about 60 per cent of the personnel. On the basis of the returns received, the RGI published data regarding technical and scientific manpower in the *Census of India*, Vol. I, Part II (i) 'Social and Cultural Tables'. The data published relate to the (i) distribution of scientific and technical personnel by age composition for each branch and sub-branch of science and technology (58 branches and 12 sub-branches) and (ii) year of obtaining postgraduate degrees in physical science and graduates and doctorates in engineering and technology and selected bases of medicine.

The nature and sector of employment, and total monthly income of persons in employment in each branch is also published. In the case of unemployed persons, the distribution by age and period of unemployment is also available. This special questionnaire was also circulated during the 1971 Census. During the 1961 Census, graduates in science, engineering, technology, or medicine were covered, while for the 1971 Census, the graduates in commerce, arts, and humanities were also covered.

During the 1971 Census, the filled-in cards were received from about 70 per cent of the total graduates. For the 1961 and 1971 Censuses, the data were obtained on complete enumeration basis. For the 1981 Census, the data were collected on 20 per cent sample basis from 12 states, while a complete enumeration was done in other states and UTs. The results for the 1971 and 1981 Censuses have been published by the RGI. During 1991, a postgraduate degree holder and technical personnel survey was conducted along with the census. The results have not been yet made available.

Data regarding technical and scientific personnel have been collected and published on the basis of the general economic questions in the individual slip for the 1961 Census. Such data are available in *Census of India*, Vol. I, Part IIB (ii), 'General Economic Tables'.

The Institute of Applied Manpower Research (IAMR, now the National Institute of Labour Economics Research and Development [NILERD]) is actively engaged in the research regarding scientific and technical manpower. The Institute was established in 1962 under the control of the Directorate of Manpower, Ministry of Home Affairs. This institute has made a number of supply and demand studies, wastage studies, and utilization patterns of different categories of manpower, such as engineers, doctors, and agricultural personnel The institute has estimated the stock of different categories of engineers and other technical personnel. In addition, it has collected manpower data from various sources and published a *Fact Book on Manpower* in three volumes. The book was first published in 1963. The fact book was revised, enlarged, and again published in three volumes. The first volume was published in 1968, the second in 1969, and the third in 1970.

The first volume deals with data on various categories, such as population; labour force; employment according to occupational, industrial, educational, organizational, and other categories; unemployment; and underemployment. The data given in this volume are based on the various reports of the RGI, the *ILS* and other publications of the Labour Bureau, different publications of the DGET, and the NSS reports. The second volume covers education and training. The data given in this volume refer to different stages and branches of education, namely, general school stage education; vocational and technical school education; university education such as arts and science, commerce and science, commerce and management, and engineering and technology; agriculture; and teacher training. The data for this volume are based on the various reports of the RGI, different publications of the Ministry of Education, and the NSS reports, among others. The third volume deals with the scientific and technical personnel. This volume is divided into these seven sections: (i) engineering and technology personnel; (ii) scientific personnel; (iii) health and medical personnel; (iv) agricultural personnel; (v) teaching personnel; (vi) managers, administrators, and social scientists; and (vii) scientific and technical personnel (aggregate of topics i to vi).

The IAMR continued publishing this type of data at regular intervals. Since 1993, it has been regularly providing details of the various characteristics of manpower in its annual publication *Manpower Profile India Year Book*. The statistics and information are based on the aforementioned sources.

The profile contains time series data on current aspects such as human resource planning and development and labour market analysis including utilizations, magnitude, and nature of unemployment. Educational and training statistics in terms of enrolment, out-turn, and teacher–pupil ratio is also given. Estimates of stocks of technical personnel of different categories including medical and nursing personnel, average monthly emoluments received by fresh engineers, number of unemployed engineers (of different categories), and percentage of fresh engineers absolute in gainful activities are prepared by the IAMR itself. The estimate of stock of technical personnel is based on the 1981 Census figures and the out-turn figures available from various official and non-official sources.

Manpower Journal is a referred journal published quarterly from IAMR since 1965. This journal provides a forum for the dissemination of information and research findings on different aspects of manpower, employment, and related issues. The *Manpower Journal* also publishes special issues from time to time.

Department of Science and Technology (DST)

The Department of Science and Technology (DST) was set up in 1971, and by virtue of its responsibility in Science and Technology (S&T) policies, implementation, and funding involving multi-agencies/ministries, the department has been acting as the nodal agency to establish an S&T statistical system and collect national science statistics at regular intervals in the country.

The National Science and Technology Management Information System (NSTMIS) Division formerly known as Science and Technology Statistics, a division of DST, has been entrusted with the responsibility of carrying out studies relating to resources devoted to S&T activities at regular intervals. The division published the first report *Research and Development Statistics* in the year 1973–4.

Publications

The publications brought out by NSTMIS are acclaimed both nationally and internationally and are widely referred by S&T policymakers, planners, scholars, and academicians. These are as follows:

REGULAR PUBLICATIONS

- *Research and Development Statistics* (Biennial)
- *Directory of R&D Institutions* (Biennial)
- *S&T Statistics Data Book* (Biennial)

OCCASIONAL PUBLICATIONS

- *Analysis of Outcomes of Extramural R&D Projects*
- *Funding Pattern Analysis of Sponsored Research by Scientific Agencies*
- *General Information Booklet on R&D Funding Schemes of Central Government*

Details of the Publications

RESEARCH AND DEVELOPMENT STATISTICS

Financial and human resources directed towards research and development (R&D) represent principal 'inputs' to R&D and are used as indicators of the status of R&D effort in any country. The DST has been undertaking biennial National Surveys since 1973–4 to collect valuable statistics on these resources deployed on R&D activities in India. Based on the data thus collected, a number of analytical reports are being published by the department. While collecting the data, the UNESCO recommendations on science and technology are adopted so that the data are comparable with other countries.

The available report is for the year 2010–11. The DST has strived to gather data from a large number of scientific agencies, research laboratories, socio-economic ministries/departments, and public- and private-sector industries, including multinational companies. The report presents analysis on a number of parameters based on data drawn both from primary and secondary sources. It includes several cross-tabulations on financial and manpower resources deployed for R&D by sector, objectives, fields of science, industry groups, qualification, nature of activity, gender, and emoluments, among others. Data mining and data reduction have considerable challenges. There are some inescapable situations in which data estimations are unavoidable. Under such circumstances, proven statistical methods of estimations have been used to bridge the gap.

Nine chapters and statistical tables are contained in this publication. The chapters are as follows:

(1) National resources for research and development
(2) Scientific and technical manpower
(3) Research and development in the central sector
(4) Research and development in the state sector
(5) Research and development in industrial sector
(6) Higher education and scientific research
(7) Research and development output indicators
(8) International comparison of research and development
(9) Extramural support for research and development projects by central government

The statistical tables are as follows:

- Table 1–Table 3: National expenditure on research and development by sector, in relation to GNP/GDP, major scientific agencies, and state governments
- Table 4–Table 8: Expenditure on R&D by major scientific agencies, type of work by central and state governments and by co-operative research associations

- Table 9: Research and development expenditure, advertising expenditure, new plant and machinery expenditure versus sales turnover in public and private sector industry
- Table 10–Table 14: Expenditure on R&D by industry groups for public and private sector Expenditure on R&D by objectives, field of science, by public/joint sector undertakings, by industry groups for public sector and private sector, by objectives, by field of science
- Table 15–Table 16: Manpower employed in research and development establishments by sex
- Table 17–Table 18: Sex-wise R&D manpower by qualifications
- Table 19: Annual gross emoluments of R&D personnel employed in different sectors
- Table 20: Estimated stock of S&T personnel
- Table 21–Table 24: Faculty-wise enrolment in higher education by sex
- Table 25: Out-turn of scientific and technical personnel from universities in India
- Table 26: Estimated stock of engineering degree holders in the working age-group by selected disciplines
- Table 27: Doctorate degrees awarded faculty-wise
- Table 28–Table 30: Sector-wise expenditure on education by central and state governments
- Table 31: Number of job seekers on the live registers of employment exchanges
- Table 32–Table 35: Applications for patents from persons in India and abroad

The latest available report refers to the year 2011–12. The chapters of this report are the same as for the earlier report. The statistical tables are also on the same lines.

DIRECTORY OF R&D INSTITUTIONS

The DST has been compiling information on the addresses of R&D institutions in the country since 1978 to conduct national level surveys on resources (both financial and human) deployed on R&D activities. The present directory contains information on the 4,288 R&D organizations in the form of phone number, fax number, email, and website.

The term R&D institution, used in this directory, refers to either a national laboratory, research institute, research station, private or public sector in-house R&D unit, not-for-profit Scientific and Industrial Research Organization (SIRO), or an academic institution. The organizations under various aforementioned sectors are not homogeneous and are of varied sizes in terms of infrastructure, facilities, and research inputs, such as manpower and expenditure, deployed in S&T activities.

S&T STATISTICS DATA BOOK

This data book, the tenth in the series, is an attempt to put together such data which are directly or indirectly related to S&T activities. It covers time series data in variety and form on resources deployed on S&T, S&T personnel, international comparison of resources, input for S&T activities, and some selected economic parameters of relevance. The data are depicted as graphs/charts.

In the present series, an attempt has been made to incorporate a new dimension under the title Information and Communication Technology (ICT) Indicators, realizing the potential of the ICT revolution in development and application of S&T for the welfare of the society.

The data book is aimed primarily for policymakers, planners, researchers, scientists, and technologists requiring pocket-size editions giving a quantitative overview of national S&T activities. The primary data for it was collected as a part of national surveys conducted by the DST on resources devoted to S&T activities and further supplemented by the various relevant national and international secondary sources. However, the latest available report is for the year 2007.

ANALYSIS OF OUTCOMES OF EXTRAMURAL R&D PROJECTS

There has been a significant increase in government support for S&T from the early 1970s. Today, India has a wide base of infrastructure for R&D. There are a number of agencies and organizations involved directly by conducting R&D work and indirectly through funding to extramural R&D projects in the field of S&T. During the period 1995–2000, a total amount of Rs 1,342 crore was approved for funding of 9,134 projects sanctioned by 21 central government departments and agencies. There was a need felt by stakeholders and policymakers to analyse the outcomes of these R&D projects.

The NSTMIS division of the DST has been bringing out directories on extramural R&D projects approved by various agencies on an annual basis since 1990–1. The division has also been analysing the outcome of these research projects and decided to undertake this exercise for the projects approved during the period 1995–2000.

The analysis was conducted on a number of parameters, such as new processes, products developed, instruments and theories developed, patents granted, research papers published, and manpower generated. The findings of the study would be useful to understand the outcome of extramural R&D projects and provide appropriate information to policymakers and funding agencies/organizations to design a future course of action.

FUNDING PATTERN ANALYSIS OF SPONSORED RESEARCH BY SCIENTIFIC AGENCIES

This document presents an analysis of funding patterns of sponsored (extramural) research supported by 23 central government departments and agencies.

The projects are classified into eight major subject areas, namely, agricultural sciences, biological sciences, chemical sciences, earth sciences, engineering and technology, mathematics, medical sciences, and physical sciences.

The institutions have been classified into 11 categories—universities, deemed universities, science colleges, engineering colleges, medical/pharmacy colleges/hospitals, institutes of national importance, national laboratories, government departments/state S&T councils, SIROs, corporate sector companies/research institutions, and voluntary organizations.

GENERAL INFORMATION BOOKLET ON R&D FUNDING SCHEMES OF CENTRAL GOVERNMENT DEPARTMENTS AND AGENCIES

A need for a general information booklet providing details of the various R&D funding schemes was expressed by an Inter-ministerial Committee in 1984 and the responsibility was assigned to the DST to bring out such a compendium. The DST has been bringing out such publications for the last one and a half decades. Seven editions of this publication have been brought out in the past.

The present compendium is an English edition which provides updated and revised information on various R&D funding schemes operated by 22 central government departments/agencies. It is hoped that this compendium would be useful to all those who are interested in extramural funding. This will also help the scientific community in approaching the appropriate department/agency to submit project proposals in their areas of interest. For each funding scheme, relevant particulars that are of interest to scientists for submitting proposals are provided.

The R&D is also supported by various state governments. In order to facilitate the scientific community, the addresses of the contact persons of the state councils for S&T are given in Annexure 1 of this publication. The latest government orders on some issues related to R&D are also given as annexures.

Appendix 5A

Table 5A.1 Number of Persons Employed per 1,000 Persons According to UPSS from 1972–3 to 2011–12 in Different NSS Rounds, All India

Round (Year)	Rural			Urban		
	Male	Female	Person	Male	Female	Person
(1)	(2)	(3)	(4)	(5)	(6)	(7)
68 (2011–12)	543	248	399	546	147	355
66 (2009–10)	556	265	414	559	146	362
61 (2004–5)	546	327	439	549	166	365
55 (1999–2000)	531	299	417	518	139	337
50 (1993–4)	553	328	444	520	154	347
43 (1987–8)	539	323	434	506	152	337
38 (1983)	547	340	445	512	151	340
32 (1977–8)	552	331	444	508	156	341
27 (1972–3)	545	318	*	501	134	*

Source: NSSO *Report No. 554*.
Note: *= Not Available.

Table 5A.2 Number of Persons Employed per 1,000 Persons According to CWS and CDS from 1972–3 to 2011–12 in Different NSS Rounds, All India

Round (Year)	CWS Employed				CDS Employed			
	Rural		Urban		Rural		Urban	
	Male	Female	Male	Female	Male	Female	Male	Female
(1)	(2)	(3)	(4)	(5)	(6)	(7)	(8)	(9)
68 (2011–12)	526	207	539	138	504	169	528	125
66 (2009–10)	548	231	556	141	536	197	550	129
61 (2004–5)	524	275	537	152	488	216	519	133
55 (1999–2000)	510	253	509	128	478	204	490	111
50 (1993–4)	530	267	511	139	504	220	498	120
43 (1987–8)	504	220	492	119	501	207	477	110
38 (1983)	511	227	492	118	482	198	473	106
32 (1977–8)	519	232	490	125	488	194	472	109
27 (1972–3)	530	277	491	123	503	231	477	108

Source: NSS Report No. 554: Employment and Unemployment Situation in India, 2011–12.

Table 5A.3 Unemployment Rates from 1972–3 to 2011–12 in Different NSS Rounds, All India

Round (Year)	Male				Female			
	UPS	US	CWS	CDS	UPS	US	CWS	CDS
(1)	(2)	(3)	(4)	(5)	(6)	(7)	(8)	(9)
				Rural				
68 (2011–12)	21	17	33	54	29	17	35	62
66 (2009–10)	19	16	32	64	24	16	37	80
61 (2004–5)	21	16	38	80	31	18	42	87
55 (1999–2000)	21	17	39	72	15	10	37	70
50 (1993–4)	20	14	31	56	13	9	29	56
43 (1987–8)	28	18	42	46	35	24	44	67
38 (1983)	21	14	37	75	14	7	43	90
32 (1977–8)	22	13	36	71	55	20	41	92
27 (1972–3)	–	12	30	68	–	5	55	112

			Urban					
68 (2011–12)	32	30	38	49	66	52	67	80
66 (2009–10)	30	28	36	51	70	57	72	91
61 (2004–5)	44	38	52	75	91	69	90	116
55 (1999–2000)	48	45	56	73	71	57	73	94
50 (1993–4)	54	41	52	67	83	61	79	104
43 (1987–8)	61	52	66	88	85	62	92	120
38 (1983)	59	51	67	92	69	49	75	110
32 (1977–8)	65	54	71	94	178	124	109	145
27 (1972–3)	–	48	60	80	–	60	92	137

Source: NSS Report No. 554: Employment and Unemployment Situation in India, 2011–12.

Table 5A.4 Per 1,000 Distribution of Person-Days of UPSS by Their Broad Current Daily Status for Various Survey Periods

All India	Rural								Urban							
Current Daily Status	Male				Female				Male				Female			
	2011–12	2009–10	2004–5	1999–2000	2011–12	2009–10	2004–5	1999–2000	2011–12	2009–10	2004–5	1999–2000	2011–12	2009–10	2004–5	1999–2000
1	2	3	4	5	6	7	8	9	10	11	12	13	14	15	16	17
Employed	927	916	893	897	677	692	657	676	966	961	945	942	852	846	798	791
Unemployed	36	47	61	53	28	43	47	41	18	23	37	27	17	24	31	22
Not in Labour Force	36	38	46	51	25	265	296	283	16	16	19	31	131	131	171	187

Source: *NSS Report No. 554: Employment and Unemployment Situation in India, 2011–12.*

Table 5A.5 Number of Persons Who Sought or Were Available for Additional Work per 1,000 Persons of Age 15 Years and above Employed in the Usual Status (PS) and Their per 1,000 Distribution by Reason for Seeking or Availability for Additional Work, All India

Category of Persons	No. per 1,000 Workers Who Sought or Were Available for Additional Work	Per 1,000 Distribution of Workers Who Sought or Were Available for Additional Work by Reason				
		To Supplement Income	Not Enough Work	Not Enough Work and to Supplement Income	Others	All (including not reported)
1	2	3	4	5	6	7
			Rural			
Male	78	584	144	235	33	1,000
Female	52	652	170	146	25	1,000
Person	72	596	148	220	32	1,000
			Urban			
Male	40	630	112	203	48	1,000
Female	34	582	128	232	51	1,000
Person	39	622	115	208	49	1,000

Source: *NSS Report No. 554: Employment and Unemployment Situation in India, 2011–12.*

Table 5A.6 Number of Usually Working Persons of Age 15 Years and Above, Who Sought or Were Available for Alternative Work per 1,000 Usually Employed Persons (PS) (15 years and above) and Their per 1,000 Distribution by Reason for Seeking or Availability for Alternative Work for 2011–12

Category of Persons	Workers Who Sought or Were Available for Alternative Work	Present Work Not Remunerative Enough	No Job Satisfaction	Lack of Job Security	Workplace Too Far	Wants Wage/ Salary Job	Others
Rural: Male	67	561	145	65	17	104	92
Rural: Female	38	679	108	36	21	56	96
Urban: Male	40	587	131	115	11	99	54
Urban: Female	41	628	146	82	14	54	59

Source: NSS Report No. 554: Employment and Unemployment Situation in India, 2011–12.

Table 5A.7 Average Wage/Salary Earnings per Day Received by Regular Wage/Salaried Employees (31, 71, and 72) of Age 15–59 Years by Industry of Work and Broad Education Category (Rupee), All India (Rural)

Sector of Work Industry Division	Level of General Education									
	Not Literate		Literate up to Middle		Secondary and Higher Secondary Above		Graduate and Above		All	
	Male	Female	Male	Female	Male	Female	Male	Female	Male	Female
Agriculture	128.52	88.20	143.14	107.48	274.51	351.02	466.72	242.76	168.83	101.24
Mining and Quarrying	535.36	483.50	475.5	433.29	657.87	95.15	984.17	120.47	648.63	286.17
Manufacturing-1	141.06	94.52	149.38	118.23	210.23	125.99	329.90	262.20	182.64	121.36
Manufacturing-2	170.33	86.65	200.57	114.41	225.14	145.91	543.97	162.24	265.65	131.33
Electricity, Gas and Water	246.78	336.72	350.28	87.83	543.74	551.43	649.65	483.79	462.71	248.06
Construction	243.55	153.32	224.74	176.56	295.29	280.10	524.82	82.80	279.15	322.43
Trade	128.20	55.15	150.04	90.25	183.02	115.13	270.56	341.02	175.15	140.27
Transport and Storage	197.30	282.20	196.97	264.62	271.61	312.87	415.48	161.11	235.55	295.87
Services	219.55	83.54	266.80	98.46	439.94	192.23	577.90	388.28	471.51	248.67
Private Households with Employed Persons	146.14	57.55	241.13	88.34	119.68	39.59	100.52	–	169.32	64.79
Others	–	–	195.52	–	–	–	–	–	195.52	–
All	174.37	89.31	202.48	104.27	319.46	179.98	550.23	377.85	322.28	201.56

Source: *NSS Report No. 554: Employment and Unemployment Situation in India, 2011–12.*

Table 5A.8 Average Wage/Salary Earnings per Day Received by Regular Wage/Salaried Employees (31, 71, and 72) of Age 15–59 Years by Industry of Work and Broad Education Category, All India (Urban)

Sector of Work Industry Division		Education Category						Person-Days	
		Not Literate	Literate and up to Middle	Secondary and Higher Secondary	Diploma/ Certificate	Graduate and Above	All (Including Estimated, not Reported, '00)		Sample
(1)		(2)	(3)	(4)	(5)	(6)	(7)	(8)	(9)
				Male					
Agriculture	(01–03)	156.64	156.37	352.92	605.33	962.87	438.14	17,180	1,236
Mining and Quarrying	(05–09)	630.78	557.53	601.90	1,192.97	1,457.71	946.25	38,211	2,031
Manufacturing-1	(10–18)	182.15	196.78	268.41	329.55	507.48	258.90	3,08,553	10,803
Manufacturing-2	(19–33)	182.18	242.22	335.39	502.04	934.95	451.64	4,20,627	14,946
Electricity, Gas, and Water	(35–39)	291.34	280.78	570.85	704.10	1,029.54	524.55	74,874	3,591
Construction	(41–43)	238.07	268.39	269.80	545.59	748.11	403.30	83,637	3,642
Trade	(45, 46, 47, 55, 56)	158.65	175.36	229.87	389.20	514.51	254.59	4,01,699	19,452
Transport & Storage etc.	(49–53)	216.71	269.69	415.10	614.07	902.45	443.76	2,49,393	12,397
Services	(58–96)	256.90	304.57	443.81	543.41	809.79	631.96	9,94,477	60,600
Private Households with Employed Persons	(97)	153.69	229.05	209.39	175.7	199.35	211.82	44,522	1,881
Others	(99)	–	–	–	–	–	–	0	0

All		207.65	237.24	358.51	524.33	805.52	469.87	26,33,174	1,30,578
Estimated Person-Days ('00)		1,64,460	7,39,006	7,38,856	1,26,027	8,64,475	2,63,3174	–	–
Sample Person-Days		6,797	34,664	38,444	6,146	44,506	1,30,578	–	–
				Female					
Agriculture	(01–03)	107.18	132.22	161.33	–	497.45	160.35	4,713	294
Mining and Quarrying	(05–09)	534.52	258.71	301.49	–	472.26	467.78	2,341	130
Manufacturing-1	(10–18)	126.77	125.84	151.81	236.36	299.08	149.03	51,630	1,869
Manufacturing-2	(19–33)	113.65	115.05	182.41	254.23	652.62	276.09	29,057	1,190
Electricity, Gas and Water (35–39)		177.78	374.26	400.64	427.52	1,014.62	531.96	9,822	518
Construction	(41–43)	106.96	311.26	806.92	280.26	543.40	270.29	7,535	294
Trade	(45, 46, 47, 55, 56)	147.93	158.83	203.65	582.89	335.66	231.33	32,950	1,908
Transport and Storage	(49—53)	123.61	306.39	389.76	1,133.29	690.68	455.01	8,928	462
Services	(58–96)	145.69	151.1	381.33	401.46	623.82	480.74	3,87,488	23,660
Private Households with Employed Persons (97)		93.65	102.73	159.86	50	101.22	102.93	1,03,158	4,157
Others	(99)	–	–	–	–	600	600	161	7
All		123.43	132.81	306.96	391.43	609.69	366.15	6,37,783	34,489
Estimated Person-Days ('00)		1,00,248	1,46,727	1,00,003	29,036	2,61,676	6,37,783	–	–
Sample Person-Days		4,725	6,916	6,482	1,827	14,532	34,489	–	–

Source: *NSS Report No. 554: Employment and Unemployment Situation in India, 2011–12.*

Table 5A.9 Average Wage Received by Casual Labourers in Urban India per Day by Industry (Rupees)

Industry Division	2009–10	
	Male	Female
(0) Agriculture, Hunting, Forestry, and Fishing	105.20	71.21
(1) Mining and Quarrying	142.89	98.45
(2) Manufacturing	112.82	63.70
(3) Manufacturing	131.57	76.19
(4) Electricity, Gas, and Water	89.96	77.94
(5) Construction	145.98	103.06
(6) Wholesale and Retail Trade, and Restaurants and Hotels	112.95	79.46
(7) Transport, Storage, and Communication	129.53	92.66
(8) Financial, Insurance, Real Estate, and Business Services	150.62	109.57
(9) Community, Social, and Personal Services	111.67	61.29
(1–9) Total Non-Agricultural	133.72	77.24
All India	130.66	75.53

Source: NSSO, *Employment and Unemployment in India, July 2009–June 2010.*

Table 5A.10 Average Wage Received by Casual Labourers per Day by Type of Operation in Rural India, 2009–10 (Rupees)

Category	Status Broad	Type of Operation	2009–10	
	Industry		Male	Female
Casual Labourers in Public Works	–41		95	80
Casual labourers in Other Types of Works (a)	(51) 01–05 (a)	Manual work in		
		Cultivation	71.67	55.29
		Ploughing	90.06	70.00
		Sowing	118.73	80.00
		Transplanting	67.03	49.44
		Weeding	80.86	47.25
		Harvesting	74.82	60.49
		Other cultivation	–	–
		Activities	56.97	53.89

(b)	Manual work in		
(c)	Other agricultural Activities	70.98	69.10
	Forestry	–	–
	Plantation	50.00	70.00
	Animal husbandry	71.84	30.00
(d)	Cultivation	–	50.00
	Cultivation	72.30	73.06
	All	72.77	61.09

Source: NSSO, *Employment and Unemployment in India, July 2009–June 2010.*

Table 5A.11 Number of Enterprises and Employment per Enterprise, 2005

Industry	Number of Enterprises ('000)			Employment per Enterprise		
	Own Account Enterprise	Establishment	Total	Own Account Enterprise	Establishment	
					All	Hired
Agriculture	51,322	9,478	60,800	1.5	1.8	3.2
Mining and Quarrying	423	425	848	1.6	6.9	12.1
Manufacturing	50,930	32,292	83,222	1.5	3.1	5.6
Electricity, Gas, and Water	140	512	652	1.2	6.7	8.2
Construction	2,049	1,154	3,203	1.1	2.3	4.5
Wholesale and Retail Trade	1,10,359	47,659	1,58,054	2.4	4.2	6.8
Hotels and Restaurants	8,321	6,598	14,918	1.3	2.5	3.8
Transport and Storage, and Warehousing	10,875	4,250	15,125	1.1	1.9	4.1
Communications	4,289	2,685	6,974	1.1	2.1	3.8
Financing, Insurance, Real Estate, and Business Services	5,390	4,760	10,150	1.2	2.7	4.5
Community, Social, and Personal Services	15,541	10,721	26,262	2.1	1.9	1.8
Other Sectors (Unspecified)	9	9	18	2.0	3.1	3.9
Total	2,69,400	1,48,870	4,18,270	1.3	2.4	4.3

Source: CSO, *Economic Census*, 2005.

Note: Agricultural Enterprise has been defined as one involving livestock production, agricultural services, trapping and game propagation, forestry and logging and fishing.

Appendix 5B: Definition of the Number of Workers and Total Persons Engaged According to ASI

Workers are defined to include all persons employed directly or through any agency, whether for wages or not, and engaged in any manufacturing process, cleaning any part of the machinery or premise used for manufacturing process, or in any other kind of work incidental to or connected with the manufacturing process or the subject of the manufacturing process. Labour engaged in the repair and maintenance or production of fixed assets for the factory's own use or labour employed for generating electricity or producing coal and gas are included. However, persons holding positions of supervision or management, or employed in an administrative office, storekeeping section and welfare section, or sales department as also those engaged in the purchase of raw materials and in production of the fixed assets for the factory and watch and ward staff, are excluded.

Total persons engaged refers to all persons engaged by the factory whether for wages or not, in work connected directly or indirectly with the manufacturing process and include all administrative, technical, and clerical staff as also labour engaged in production of capital assets for the factory's own use. This is inclusive of persons holding supervisory or managerial positions or engaged in administrative office, storekeeping section and welfare section, sales department as also those engaged in the purchase of raw materials, and the production of fixed assets for the factory and watch and ward staff. It also includes all working proprietors and their family members who are actively engaged in the work of the factory even without any pay and the unpaid members of the co-operative societies who worked in or for the factory in any direct and productive capacity.

The number of workers or employees is an average number, obtained by dividing man-days worked defined later by the number of days the factory had worked during the reference year. In case of factories where only repair, maintenance, or construction activities are carried out, the average is calculated by dividing the man-days worked by the number of days the repair and maintenance/construction work was carried on.

Main Findings of the Rural Labour Enquiries

Table 5B.1 General Characteristics, All India

Items	1st RLE 1963–5	2nd RLE 1974–5	3rd RLE 1977–8	4th RLE 1983	5th RLE 1987–8	6th RLE 1993–4	7th RLE 1999–2000	8th RLE 2004–5
1	2	3	4	5	6	7	8	9
1 Estimated number of Rural Households (in millions)	70.4	82.1	95.7	100.5	108.4	119.5	137.1	150.2
2 Percentage of RLH to Rural Households	25.4	30.3	36.8	37.3	39.7	38.3	40.2	36.7
3 Percentage of ALH to Rural Households	21.8	25.3	29.9	30.7	30.7	30.3	32.2	25.8
4 Average size of the household ALH	4.5	4.8	4.7	4.6	4.6	4.4	4.6	4.5 (P)
RLH	4.5	4.8	4.7	4.6	4.6	4.5	4.7	4.6 (P)
5 Average number of wage earners ALH	2.0	2.2	1.8	1.9	1.4	1.7	1.8	1.8 (P)
RLH	2.0	2.2	1.7	1.8	1.3	1.6	1.7	1.7 (P)

Source: *Rural Labour Enquiry: Report on General Characteristics of Rural Labor Households 1999–2000 and 2004–5.*

Notes: ALH = Agricultural Labour Households; RLH = Rural Labour Households.

Table 5B.2 Indebtedness—Agricultural Labour Households

Items	1st RLE 1963–5	2nd RLE 1974–5	3rd RLE 1977–8	4th RLE 1983	5th RLE 1987–8	6th RLE 1993–4	7th RLE 1999–2000	8th RLE 2004–5
1	2	3	4	5	6	7	8	9
A. Indebtedness:								
(i) Percentage of Indebted Households	60.6	66.4	52.3	51.1	39.4	35.5	25.1	48.4
(ii) Average Debt per Household (Rs)	148	387	345	774	769	1,031	1,312	3,946
(iii) Average Debt per Indebted Household (Rs)	244	584	660	1,516	1,952	2,901	5,230	8,145
B. Percentage of Debt by Source:								
(i) Government	–	–	–	2.9	3.6	8.2	4.1	3.7
(ii) Co-operative Societies	4.9	5.3	8.6	7.9	10	7	10.3	8.9
(iii) Employers	19.7	10.1	7	13.9	13	12.2	7.9	7.3
(iv) Moneylenders	30.7	47.8	37.3	18.6	22	29.4	34	44.5
(v) Shopkeepers	7.4	6.7	6.7	4.6	7.7	6.9	6.9	6.5
(vi) Banks	–	3.6	6	33.3	21	20.7	16.6	14

(Cont'd)

Table 5B.2 *(Cont'd)*

Items	1st RLE 1963–5	2nd RLE 1974–5	3rd RLE 1977–8	4th RLE 1983	5th RLE 1987–8	6th RLE 1993–4	7th RLE 1999–2000	8th RLE 2004–5
1	2	3	4	5	6	7	8	9
(vii) Relatives and Friends	–	–	–	10.8	13.7	12.9	16.1	12.9
(viii) Others	37.3	26.5	34.4	8	9	2.8	4	2.2
C. Percentage of Debt by Purpose:								
(i) Household Consumption	53.3	48.1	44.4	30.4	34.3	32.3	31	33.1
(ii) Marriage and Other Ceremonials	24.2	18.8	22.3	14.7	13.8	17.1	24.1	22.9
(iii)Productive Purposes	11.9	12.7	20.9	41.4	29.1	28.3	21.5	20.8
(iv) Purchase of Land and Constr. of Building	–	–	–	6.3	8.5	10	14.6	15
(v) Repayment of Debt	–	–	–	–	1.2	1.7	1	2.5
(vi) Others (More than one purpose)	10.6	20.4	12.4	7.2	13.1	10.6	7.8	5.7

Source: Rural Labour Enquiry: Report on General Characteristics of Rural Labour Households 1999–2000 and 2004–05.

Table 5B.3 Indebtedness—Rural Labour Households

Items	1st RLE 1963–5	2nd RLE 1974–5	3rd RLE 1977–8	4th RLE 1983	5th RLE 1987–8	6th RLE 1993–4	7th RLE 1999–2000	8th RLE 2004–5
1	10	11	12	13	14	15	16	17
A. Indebtedness:								
(i) Percentage of Indebted Households	59.2	65.4	50.5	50.4	39.1	35.1	25	47.3
(ii) Average Debt per Household (Rs)	148	395	348	806	787	1,113	1,515	4,852
(iii) Average Debt per Indebted Household (Rs)	251	605	690	1,598	2,014	3,169	6,049	10,259
B. Percentage of Debt by Source:								
(i) Government	–	–	–	4.1	3.6	8.3	5.4	3.2
(ii) Cooperative Societies	5.6	5.6	9.4	10.2	9.4	7.9	13.1	9.3
(iii) Employers	17.9	9.6	6.7	12.2	12.2	11.4	6.9	5.3

(Cont'd)

Table 5B.3 *(Cont'd)*

Items	1st RLE 1963–5	2nd RLE 1974–5	3rd RLE 1977–8	4th RLE 1983	5th RLE 1987–8	6th RLE 1993–4	7th RLE 1999–2000	8th RLE 2004–5
1	10	11	12	13	14	15	16	17
(iv) Moneylenders	31.9	46.4	36.7	21.3	21.7	27.6	31.7	44.2
(v) Shopkeepers	8.4	7.3	6.8	5.3	9.2	7.3	7.1	6.0
(vi) Banks	–	4	6.5	28	20.8	18.9	17.2	16.5
(vii) Relatives and Friends	–	–	–	11.6	14.4	12.4	15.1	12.8
(viii) Others	36.2	27.1	33.9	7.3	8.7	6.2	3.5	2.7
C. Percentage of Debt by Purpose								
(i) Household Consumption	51.8	47	42.9	32	33.6	29.9	27.6	29.4
(ii) Marriage and Other Ceremonials	24.7	19.3	22.9	15.5	15.4	17.8	24	21.6
(iii) Productive Purposes	12	12.7	20.4	38.2	26.9	25.3	18.5	22
(iv) Purchase of Land and Construction of Buildings	–	–	–	7.6	11.1	15	21	18.4
(v) Repayment of Debt	–	–	–	–	1.1	1.8	1	2.8
(vi) Others (More Than One Purpose)	11.5	21	13.8	6.7	11.9	10.2	7.9	5.8

Table 5B.4 Wages and Earnings, All India

Items	1st RLE 1963–5	2nd RLE 1974–5	3rd RLE 1977–8	4th RLE 1983	5th RLE 1987–8	6th RLE 1993–4	7th RLE 1999–2000	8th RLE (P) 2004–5
1	2	3	4	5	6	7	8	9
Average Earning Strength								
RLH	2.1	2.3	2.1	2	2	2	2	2
ALH	2.1	2.3	2.1	2.1	2	2	2	2
Average number of wage-earners								
RLH	2	2.2	1.7	1.8	1.3	1.6	1.7	1.7
ALH	2	2.2	1.8	1.9	1.4	1.7	1.8	1.8
Average Daily Earnings of Workers in Agricultural Operations (Rs)								
Rural Labour Household								
Men	1.41	3.26	3.79	4.63	9.46	21.53	40.58	48.07
Women	0.89	2.28	2.67	3.46	7.05	15.33	28.57	33.77
Children	0.76	1.82	2.17	2.2	6.01	12.32	24.32	29.93
Agricultural Labour Household								
Men	1.43	3.24	3.74	4.72	9.42	21.35	40.14	47.53
Women	0.95	2.22	2.62	3.56	7	15.18	28.38	33.41
Children	0.72	1.82	2.16	2.32	6.01	12.45	24.23	29.55

(Cont'd)

Table 5B.4 *(Cont'd)*

Items	1st RLE 1963–5	2nd RLE 1974–5	3rd RLE 1977–8	4th RLE 1983	5th RLE 1987–8	6th RLE 1993–4	7th RLE 1999–2000	8th RLE (P) 2004–5
1	2	3	4	5	6	7	8	9
Average Daily Earnings of Workers in Non-agricultural Occupations (Rs)								
Rural Labour Household								
Men	–	–	–	7.27	11	32.49	64.92	74.88
Women	–	–	–	3.78	7.99	17.45	56.13	42.59
Children	–	–	–	3.18	6.55	15.13	28.65	29.93
Agricultural Labour Household								
Men	–	–	–	5.12	10.23	26.95	54.09	55.62
Women		–	–	2.98	7.92	16.21	34.08	35.5
Children	–	–	–	2.83	6.3	15	24.14	25.24

Source: *Rural Labor Enquiry – Report on General Characteristics of Rural Labor Households 1999–2000 and 2004–05*. These Enquiries Donot Give the Reason for these Date.

Table 5B.5 Employment and Unemployment—Average Number of Days Worked/Not Worked by Usually Occupied Workers Belonging to Rural Labour Households (in Estimated Number of Full Days in a Year)

Category of Employment	1st RLE 1963–5	2nd RLE 1974–5	3rd RLE 1977–8	4th RLE 1983	5th RLE 1987–8	6th RLE 1993–4	7th RLE 1999–2000	8th RLE 2004–5
1	2	3	4	5	6	7	7	8
A. Number of Days Worked On								
1. Wage Employment								
Men	–	212	227	225	223	235	222	215
Women	–	147	182	187	186	203	192	177
Children	–	179	183	166	173	178	185	164
2. Self-employment								
Men	–	33	59	53	56	55	52	51
Women	–	37	48	42	59	55	55	64
Children	–	78	115	118	116	120	93	104
3. Salary Basis								
Men	–	5	7	8	17	15	24	25
Women	–	1	2	4	9	7	9	9
Children	–	5	6	3	13	8	12	18

(Cont'd)

Table 5B.5 *(Cont'd)*

Category of Employment	1st RLE 1963–5	2nd 1974–5	3rd RLE 1977–8	4th RLE 1983	5th RLE 1987–8	6th RLE 1993–4	7th RLE 1999–2000	8th RLE 2004–5
1	2	3	4	5	6	7	7	8
B. Number of Days Not Worked								
1. Due to Sickness								
Men	–	28	27	33	30	30	31	28
Women	–	45	87	86	82	75	77	75
Children	–	20	28	53	36	38	43	38
2. Due to want of work								
Men	–	71	45	46	39	30	36	46
Women	–	115	46	46	29	25	32	40
Children	–	72	33	24	27	21	32	41

Table 5B.6 Consumption Expenditure–Average Annual Expenditure per Household on Different Item Groups (Rupees)

Groups		1st RLE 1963–5	2nd RLE 1974–5	3rd RLE 1977–8	4th RLE 1983	5th RLE 1987–8	6th RLE 1993–4	7th RLE 1999–2000	8th RLE 2004–5
1	2	3	4	5	6	7	8	9	10
(a) Rural Labour Households									
1	Food	771	1,971	2,048	34,255	4,674	8,135	14,218	14,450
		(73.3)	(78.4)	(67.7)	(68.2)	(66.2)	(65.3)	(61.4)	(57.7)
2	Clothing, Bedding, and Footwear	72	105	241	365	439	622	1,751	1,090
		(6.8)	(4.2)	(8.0)	(7.3)	(6.2)	(5.0)	(7.6)	(4.3)
3	Fuel and Light	79	168	217	403	604	1,006	1,868	2,793
		(7.5)	(6.7)	(7.2)	(8.0)	(8.6)	(8.1)	(8.1)	(11.2)
4	Stimulants and Intoxicants	42	78	112	191	293	494	838	875
		(4.1)	(3.1)	(3.7)	(3.8)	(4.2)	(4.0)	(3.6)	(3.5)
5	House Rent	–	2	–	–	15	33	79	96
		–	(0.1)	–	–	(0.2)	(0.3)	(0.3)	(0.4)
6	Services and Miscellaneous	87	190	405	640	1,030	2,158	4,398	5,728
		(8.3)	(7.5)	(13.4)	(12.7)	(14.6)	(17.3)	(19.0)	(22.9)
7	Total Consumption Expenditure	1,051	2,514	3,023	5,024	7,055	12,448	23,152	25,032
		(100)	(100)	(100)	(100)	(100)	(100)	(100)	(100)

(Cont'd)

Table 5B.6 *(Cont'd)*

Groups		1st RLE 1963–5	2nd RLE 1974–5	3rd RLE 1977–8	4th RLE 1983	5th RLE 1987–8	6th RLE 1993–4	7th RLE 1999–2000	8th RLE 2004–5
1	2	3	4	5	6	7	8	9	10
(b) Agriculture Labour Households									
1	Food	760	1,926	1,944	3,295	4,483	7,788	13,668	13,601
		(73.9)	(78.8)	(68.6)	(68.7)	(67.1)	(66.3)	(62.3)	(59.1)
2	Clothing, Bedding, and Footwear	69	99	215	347	402	578	1667	962
		(6.7)	(4.1)	(7.6)	(7.2)	(6.0)	(4.9)	(7.6)	(4.2)
3	Fuel and Light	78	164	206	392	590	976	1783	2638
		(7.6)	(6.7)	(7.3)	(8.2)	(8.8)	(8.3)	(8.1)	(11.5)
4	Stimulants and Intoxicants	41	74	105	179	274	461	790	805
		(4.0)	(3.1)	(3.7)	(3.7)	(4.1)	(3.9)	(3.6)	(3.5)
5	House Rent	–	1	–	–	7	15	34	36
		–	(0.0)	–	–	(0.1)	(0.1)	(0.2)	(0.2)
6	Services and Miscellaneous	80	179	363	587	925	1,941	3,986	4,953
		(7.8)	(7.3)	(12.8)	(12.2)	(13.9)	(16.5)	(18.2)	(21.5)
7	Total Consumption Expenditure	1,028	2,443	2,833	4,800	6,681	11,759	21,928	22,995
		(100)	(100)	(100)	(100)	(100)	(100)	(100)	(100)

Source: Rural Labour Enquiry: Report on General Characteristics of Rural Labor Households 1999–2000 and 2004–5.

Appendix 5C: Classification According to Different Approaches

(a) *Classification according to usual status approach*: This approach is based on a reference period of one year. The status of activity on which a person spent relatively longer time of the preceding 365 days from the date of survey is considered as the principal usual status activity of the person. Accordingly, a person is considered 'working' (or 'employed') if the person was engaged for a relatively longer time during the past year in any one or more work-related activities (economic activities). The person is considered as 'seeking or available' for work (or 'unemployed') if the person was not working but was either seeking or was available for work for a relatively longer time during the past year. If the person was engaged in any non-economic activity for a relatively longer time of the reference year s/he is considered as 'out of labour force'. The specific activity category is determined on the basis of time spent criterion, that is, the activity on which major time was spent being assigned as the usual status activity. A person categorized as 'worker' (or 'employed') on the basis of the principal status is called a 'principal status worker' or 'principal status employed'. A person categorized as a non-worker (that is, unemployed or out of the labour force) who pursued some economic activity in a subsidiary capacity is called a 'subsidiary status worker' (or subsidiary status employed). These two groups, namely principal workers and subsidiary status workers, together constitute 'all workers' according to the usual status classification.

(b) *Classification according to CWS approach*: This period is based on a reference period of one week. For classification, people are assigned a unique activity status with reference to a period of seven days preceding the date of survey. This is easily done in the case of persons having only one status during the week. But for persons pursuing more than one activity a priority-cum-major time rule is applied to obtain a unique status. Under the priority rule, the status of working gets priority over the status of not working but seeking/available for work. Further the status of not working but seeking/available for work gets priority over the status of not working and not seeking/available for work. Within the broad category of working and not working, the detailed activity category is assigned by the major time spent criterion. A person is considered working or employed if the person was engaged for at least one hour during the week is considered 'seeking/available for work'. Others are considered 'not available for work' (or as 'out of labour force').

(c) *Classification according to CDS approach*: The activity pattern of people particularly in the unorganized sector is such that a person might be pursuing more than one activity during a week and sometimes even during a day. In the CDS approach, up to two activity statuses were assigned to a person each day of the reference week. The unit of classification was thus 'half day' in the CDS. In assigning the activity status on a day, a person was considered working for the entire day if he had worked four hours or more during the day. If he had worked one hour or more but less than four hours, he was considered working(employed) for half day and seeking/available for work (unemployed) or not available for work (not in the labour force) for the other half day depending on whether he was seeking/available for work or not. On the other hand, if a person was not engaged in any work even for one hour but was seeking or available for work for less than four hours only, he was considered unemployed for half day. A person who neither had any work nor was available for work even for 'half' of the day was considered not in the labour force for the entire day.

(d) *Employment market information*: The EMI programme, first taken up on a pilot basis during the Second Five Year Plan, and strengthened by the provisions of the Employment Exchanges (Compulsory Notification of Vacancies) Act, 1959, makes available data in respect of the organized sectors of the economy. The programme covers all establishments in the public sector (except the defence establishments and armed forces) and those establishments in the private sector which employ 25 or more persons on the last day of the quarter under reference. Apart from this, since 1966, the establishments employing 10 to 24 persons are also covered on a voluntary.

Appendix 5D: Concept of Wages and Total Emoluments

Wages are defined to include all remunerations capable of being expressed in monetary terms and also payable more or less regularly in each pay period to workers, defined earlier as compensation for work done during the accounting year. It includes:

(i) Direct wages and salary (that is, basic wages/salaries, payment of overtime, dearness, compensatory, house rent and other allowances);
(ii) Remuneration for the period not worked (that is, basic wages, salaries, and allowances payable for leave period, paid holiday, lay-off payments and compensation for unemployment, if not paid from sources other than employers);
(iii) Bonuses and ex gratia payments paid both at regular and at less frequent intervals (that is, incentives, bonuses, good attendance bonuses, productive bonuses, profit sharing bonuses, festival, or year-end bonuses). It excludes lay-off payments which are made from trust or other social funds set up expressly for this purpose, that is, payments not made by the employer. It also excludes input value of the benefits in kind, employer's contribution to the old-age benefits and other social security charges, direct expenditure on maternity benefits and crèches, and other group benefits. Travelling and other expenditure incurred for the business purposes and reimbursed by the employer are excluded. The wages are expressed in terms of gross value, that is, before deduction for fines, damages, taxes, provident funds, and employee's state insurance contribution, among others.

Total emoluments are defined in the same way as wages defined earlier but paid to all employees plus imputed value of benefits in kind, that is, the net cost to the employer on those goods and services provided to employees free of charge or at markedly reduced cost which are clearly and primarily of benefit to the employees as consumers.

Contribution to provident fund and other funds includes old-age benefits, such as provident fund, pension, and gratuity, as well as employers' contribution towards other social security charges, such as employee's state insurance, compensation for work injuries, occupational diseases, provident-fund-linked insurance, retirement, and lay-off benefits. Workmen and staff-welfare expenses include group benefits, such as direct expenditure on maternity, crèches, canteen facilities, educational, cultural and recreational facilities, and grants to trade unions, and cooperative stores, among others, meant for employees.

Bibliography

Central Statistical Organization. Various Issues *Annual Survey of Industries*. New Delhi: Ministry of Statistics and Programme Implementation, Government of India.

Directorate of Economics and Statistics. 2014. *Agricultural Wages in India 2013–14*. New Delhi: Ministry of Agriculture and Farmer's Welfare.

Directorate General of Employment and Training.

———. 2008a. *Employment Review*. Ministry of Labour, Employment and Rehabilitation. New Delhi: Government of India.

———.2008b. Occupation–Educational Pattern in India (Public Sector). Ministry of Labour, Employment and Rehabilitation. New Delhi: Government of India.

———. 2003. Occupational–Educational Pattern of Employees in India (Private Sector), 2003. New Delhi: Ministry of Labour, Employment and Rehabilitation, Government of India.

Directorate General of Mines Safety. Various years. *Statistics of Mines in India*. Maharashtra: Ministry of Mines.

Division of Scientific and Technical Personnel, CSIR. Various years. *Technical Manpower*, monthly journal of the Division of Scientific and Technical Personnel, CSIR, Ministry of Science and Technology.

Institute of Applied Man-Power Research. 1968–70 *Fact Book on Manpower*, Vol. I, II & III. New Delhi.

Labour Bureau 2011. *Industrial Injuries Statistics*.

———.2015. *Wage Rates in Rural India*, 2014–15. New Delhi: Ministry of Labour, Employment and Rehabilitation, Government of India.

———.1959. *Occupational Wage Survey (General Report), 1958–59*. New Delhi: Ministry of Labour, Employment and Rehabilitation, Government of India.

———. 1965. *Second Occupational Wage Survey—Summary Report 1963–65*. New Delhi: Ministry of Labour, Employment and Rehabilitation.

———. 2009. *Statistics of Factories*. New Delhi: Ministry of Labour, Employment and Rehabilitation.

———. 2011. *The Indian Labour Year Book*. New Delhi: Ministry of Labour, Employment and Rehabilitation.

Labour Bureau. Various years. *Rural Labour Enquiry—General Characteristics*. New Delhi: Ministry of Labour, Employment and Rehabilitation.

———. *The Indian Labour Statistics* (Annual), 2012–13. New Delhi: Ministry of Labour, Employment and Rehabilitation.

———. 2004–05. *Rural Labour Enquiry—Wages and Earnings of Rural Labour Households*. New Delhi: Ministry of Labour, Employment and Rehabilitation.

———. 2005. *Rural Labour Households, 2004–05*. New Delhi: Ministry of Labour, Employment and Rehabilitation.

Ministry of Labour and Employment. 2011. *Census of Central Government Employees*. New Delhi: Ministry of Labour, Employment and Rehabilitation, Government of India.

Ministry of Railways. *Annual Report of the Railway Board, 2014–15*. New Delhi: Government of India.

Ministry of Statistics and Programme Implementation. 2013–14. *Sixth Economic Census—All India Report*. New Delhi: Government of India.

———. Various Years. *Statistical Abstract*. New Delhi: Government of India.

———. 2009. *Indian Official Statistical Systems*. New Delhi: Government of India.

Saluja, M.R. 1972. *Indian Official Statistical Systems*. New Delhi: Statistical Publishing Society and Indian Econometric Society.

6

Trade Statistics

Foreign Trade

Statistics relating to foreign trade are regularly published in the *Monthly Statistics of the Foreign Trade of India* (*MSFTI*) by the Directorate General of Commercial Intelligence and Statistics (DGCI&S). This covers foreign trade registered by the custom authorities at the Indian seaports, airports, and land customs' stations. Airborne trade with Nepal has been included from January 1957 and land trade from April 1964. Separate information was earlier available for re-exports. However, presently it is not available separately and is included in the exports. Similarly, re-imports are also included in the imports. Trans-shipment trade covering imported goods transferred under bond for reshipment from one vessel to another at the same or different Indian ports is not taken into account. Goods consigned by the government to its armed forces and diplomatic representatives abroad and those sent by the governments of foreign countries to their diplomatic personnel stationed in India are not taken into account. While purchase and sale of ships and aircrafts are included as imports and exports respectively, those purchase and sale of ships and aircraft for defence purposes as well as combatant items of defence equipment are not recorded. Personal baggage is excluded from the export trade. In the case of imports, only dutiable articles of personal baggage that are identifiable during processing are taken into account. All dutiable personal articles imported from foreign countries by parcel or letter post are included, while in the case of exports only articles of parcel post are included. Transactions in treasure, that is, gold, coins, and currency notes and coins not yet in circulations, or withdrawn from circulation, are included.

The figures of quantities are based on the declarations made by importers on the bills of entry and those made by exporters on shipping bills, as subsequently checked by the customs authorities. The quantity figures represent the net weights and are reported in the declared (by the exporters/importers) units or in terms of the units specified in the Indian trade classification for each item.

The value of goods represents the wholesale cash price less trade discount for which goods of the like kind and quality are sold or are capable of being sold at the time of import or export as the case may be, without any abatement or deductions whatever, except in the case of goods imported, of the amount of duties payable on the importation thereof, or where such price is not available, the cost at which the goods of the like quantity could be delivered at such place without any abatement or deduction except as aforesaid.

In the case of goods which are not in the nature of commercial transactions, the transaction values are imputed—for example, imports of foodgrains and capital goods—under foreign aid programmes. The import valuation in practice corresponds to cost, insurance, and freight (CIF), and the export value corresponds to free on board (FOB). A certain percentage of unloading charges is also included in the imported value, but import duties, internal taxes, and similar charges imposed at the time of import are excluded.

Method of Reporting

The Daily Trade Returns (DTRs) in the prescribed format are prepared by the customs authorities on the basis of shipping bills (for exports) and bills of entry (for imports), in which certain specific information is given. Some of the specific information that constitute the DTRs are commodity codes based on Indian Trade Classification (Harmonized System) (ITC HS), commodity description, shipping bill/bills of entry number and date, value and quantity of the item traded (gross as well as net), country of origin (for imports)/destination (for exports), name of the exporter/importer, and importer/exporter code, among others.

The shipping bill is passed by the customs authorities after some preliminary check about valuation. The actual export takes place after the shipping bill is passed. The original shipping bill is retained by the custom officials while the duplicate is sent to the shipping agents for the preparation of the manifest. The manifest along with the shipping bill is sent by the agent to the Manifest Clearing Department for checking, about a week after the shipment has actually taken place. Any short shipment (if only a part of the declared cargo is exported) is recorded on the duplicate bill but the correction is in terms of the number of packages shipped and the pro rata valuation.

Up to October 1965, the DTRs were being prepared on the basis of the original copy of the shipping bill. From November 1965, the customs authorities switched over to the duplicate copy.

Before 1965, when the returns were filled on the basis of the original copy, the adjustments were being done in the months in which the advices were received and not for the month to which the data related. After October 1970, the customs authorities, again, switched over to the original copy as there was considerable delay in reporting of the DTR. It was argued that for long-term trends and overall level figures, the shutout and short shipments do not have any material difference. This shifting from the original to the duplicate and back continued for a number of times and at present the duplicate copy of the bill is used. The DTR prepared by the customs officials is sent to the DGCI&S for compilation and publication of trade statistics.

Regarding imports, the returns submitted to the DGCI&S are based on the bill of entry submitted by the importers in quadruplicate. The bill of entry contains the import license code, the description, and quantity and value of imports, among others. The bill of entry is checked by the customs authorities regarding valuation before handing these over to the Statistics Section for compilation of the DTR.

About the Directorate

The directorate, a subordinate office under Department of Commerce, Ministry of Commerce and Industry, Government of India (GoI) is the pioneer official organization for collection, compilation, and dissemination of India's trade statistics and commercial information. Set up in the year 1862 as a statistical branch in the then Finance Department of the GoI with the aim of compilation of official statistics for the entire country, it has also engaged in commercial intelligence activities since 1905. It is thus one of the oldest serving organizations of this country.

The merchandise trade data, both for exports and imports, are processed centrally in this directorate using state-of-the-art technology and expertise. The directorate also compiles and publishes, on a regular basis, inland trade statistics inter alia *Inter-state Movements of Goods by Rail, River and Air*, *Inland Coastal Trade Statistics*, *Statistics of India's Customs and Excise Revenue Collection* according to tariff heads, shipping statistics, and *Selected Statistics of Foreign Trade of India* on an annual basis. Since 1906, DGCI&S has been publishing the *Indian Trade Journal*, a weekly publication which is a repository of material of commercial interest as well as a major channel for flow of information on tenders at the national and international level.

Organizational Setup and Functions

The directorate has following five main divisions

(1) Foreign Trade Data Processing and Dissemination Division: The directorate has been compiling foreign trade statistics right from its inception. However, its scope and coverage has enlarged with the passage of time and presently, the directorate brings out the monthly statistics of imports and exports of about 11,000 commodities, traded with more than 200 countries. The common ITC (HS) classification developed by the Central Board of Excise and Customs (CBEC) in consultation with the DGCI&S extending the 6-digit international classification to the 8-digit item level provides an opportunity to capture trade statistics in a detailed fashion. This division processes the data, manually as well as online, for exports and imports separately.

(2) Ancillary and Derived Statistics Division: This division mainly deals with the inland trade data, shipping data, coasting trade data, air borne data, revenue data, and compilation of indices.

(3) Commercial Intelligence Division and Commercial Library: This division mainly provides commercial information to the trading community. The information includes the whereabouts of foreign and Indian exporters and importers along with their choice of commodities, and information on various schemes and policies relating to foreign trade. This division is at present headed by a director from the Indian Economic Service.
(4) Computer Division and Administrative Division: The duties of these two divisions are self-explanatory.

In addition to this setup in Kolkata, DGCI&S has its officers posted in different customs houses in Mumbai, Chennai, Kolkata, and Kochi to monitor the flow of data from customs to DGCI&S.

Comments on the Data Sources for India's Foreign Trade

(1) *Foreign Trade Statistics* covers only commercial transactions of the merchandise trade. Items on defence goods are not covered in *Foreign Trade Statistics* as a matter of principle. This apart, non-commercial transactions—such as, personal baggage and effects, exhibition goods, and samples—are not covered in *Foreign Trade Statistics*. The direct transit trade, that is, goods of other countries passing and transit goods warehoused not for the purpose of disposal, are excluded completely. Although the exports and imports of crude oil and petroleum products are included in the *Foreign Trade Statistics*, the detailed commodity-wise or country-wise breakups are not published by the DGCI&S due to non-availability of detailed information.
(2) The DGCI&S receives trade data from about 40–50 major ports and some small ports in three different modes, namely Electronic Data Interchange (EDI), non-EDI, and manual. The data transcribed manually from shipping bills and bills of entry into DTR formats has about a 15 per cent share in the total merchandise trade, the remaining 85 per cent share being accounted for by EDI and non-EDI modes. In the EDI mode, customs clearance of shipping bills and bills of entry are given through the computer itself and the relevant information as required in the DTRs is furnished to the DGCI&S. The major ports are covered by the EDI system. The non-EDI mode relates to manual clearance

of shipping bills and bills of entry, but the DTRs are prepared with the help of computers and the data is transmitted to the DGCI&S in compact disks.

At present, in export, EDI constitutes around 85 per cent of the total transactions whereas non-EDI constitutes around 8 per cent, and the remaining 7 per cent is received as manual DTRs. In rupee value terms, EDI constitutes around 65 per cent, non-EDI constitutes around 20 per cent, and manual constitutes around 15 per cent of the total value of the export from India.

The scenario of import data is a bit different. The EDI's share in records is around 95 per cent whereas non-EDI covers around 2 per cent. The share of manual DTRs is very low and it is around 3 per cent. However, in value terms, EDI covers 70 per cent, non-EDI covers 5 per cent, and manual DTR covers around 24 per cent of the total imports.

(3) Before validating the data contained in the DTRs, the DGCI&S prepares the aggregated data of exports and imports within about 25 days from the close of the month in the form of a draft press note. As per the existing system, the draft press note is sent to the Ministry of Commerce and Industry for approval before its release. Quick estimates of exports and imports by principal commodities are prepared at the same time with a view to make a broad assessment of the performance of India's foreign trade and to study the impact of various trade policies, enabling the government to initiate suitable corrective measures, if necessary, in attaining the desired objective in the sphere of external trade. A monthly brochure entitled *Foreign Trade Statistics of India* (Principal Commodities and Countries) is then brought out in about two months' time from the reference month. At the final stage, detailed data of India's foreign trade are released in two publications, namely, *MSFTI* containing commodity by country details and *Statistics of Foreign Trade of India by Countries* (*SFTIC*) containing country by commodity details. The former is a monthly publication while the latter is a quarterly one, though the two publications are based on the same data set with varying presentation. The data reported in these publications are

according to the 8-digit ITC (HS) and are available with a time lag of about three to four months from the reference month.

Classification of Commodities

Before 1957, the total trade was given under the following five heads:

(1) Food, drink, and tobacco
(2) Raw materials and products and articles, partially manufactured
(3) Articles wholly manufactured
(4) Living animals
(5) Postal articles and packages not specified

In all, 1,717 items were separately specified—1,047 for imports, 460 for exports, and 210 for re-exports. In 1957, the classification was revised and Standard International Trade Classification (SITC) was adopted. The items were classified into the following 10 groups:

(1) Food
(2) Beverages and tobacco
(3) Crude materials, inedible oils except fuel oils
(4) Mineral fuels, lubricants, and related materials
(5) Animal and vegetable oils and fats
(6) Chemicals
(7) Manufactured goods classified by material
(8) Machinery and transport equipment
(9) Miscellaneous manufactured articles
(10) Miscellaneous transactions and commodities not elsewhere classified

The list of items became common for imports, exports, and re-exports. In April 1965, the trade classification was again revised and the commodities were classified according to the Revised Indian Trade Classification. From April 1987 and up to March 2007, trade was recorded as per Indian Trade Classification (Harmonised System) (ITC HS). This classification has been revised with effect from April 2008.

From April 2010 onwards, the values of exports, and from April 2011 onwards, the values of imports, are given in both Indian rupee and US dollar. In addition, the data-suppression policy approved by the Department of Commerce has been incorporated April 2010 onwards. All suppressed commodities have been coded as 99999999 for which only a value figure is published at the end of the detailed table of Chapter 99. In the classification adopted from April 2008, there are 98 chapters followed by Chapter 99 to record information on sample goods and returned goods, among others.

The 8-digit ITC HS Codes filled up in the shipping bills and bills of entry forms the basic input for generation of export and import data at the disaggregated level. It has been experienced that the exporters or importers or their agents do not report these codes properly. To improve the situation, the Directorate General of Foreign Trade (DGFT) issued a notification on 11 September 2000 making it mandatory to mention 8-digit ITC HS codes prepared by the DGCI&S against each export product that figures in the shipping bill. It has been mentioned in the notification that no benefit under the policy will be disbursed to the exporters unless the code appears on the shipping bill and this measure has been made effective from 1 October 2000. The DGCI&S has reported that after the issue of this notification, though the exporters are reporting valid codes in the shipping bills, it has been noticed that the problem of mismatching—that is, codes vis-à-vis description of the items—still persists. As regards imports, no such notification has been issued.

The status of the various publications brought out by the Office of DGCI&S on Foreign Trade is given in the following paragraphs.[1]

Monthly Publications

MONTHLY STATISTICS OF THE FOREIGN TRADE OF INDIA

The monthly publication is issued in two volumes. Volume 1 covers exports and re-exports and Volume 2 covers imports.

The detailed tables of exports, re-exports, and imports show the quantity and value for all the trade commodities. Separate figures for each commodity are available at the country level. Besides these

[1] For a reference of the publications, see http://www.dgciskol.nic.in/pub_list.asp (accessed 4 May 2017).

detailed tables, it contains a summary table by chapters and sections of ITC HS along with:

(1) the value figures for different groups, divisions, and sections of the ITC; and
(2) the total trade with each country.

The summary table shows only the value figures for the current month of and cumulative values from the April of the year up to current month. Comparative figures for the previous year are also shown. The March volumes give the values for the entire financial year.

FOREIGN TRADE STATISTICS IN INDIA (PRINCIPAL COMMODITIES AND COUNTRIES)

This is another monthly publication of the DGCI&S. This publication is intended to provide provisional current information on trade and is published regularly by DGCI&S since April 1981, after issue of a monthly press note. The contents of the publication were, however, widened from the April 1988 issue. From the April 1990 issue, principal port by commodities and principal commodities by ports for both exports and imports are being shown and from the April 1992 issue of the publication, the data in comparable baskets are also given for the previous year.

Presently the following information is furnished:

(1) India's import/export of principal commodities;
(2) India's import/export of principal commodities by country;
(3) India's import by/export from countries;
(4) India's import from/export to countries by principal commodities;
(5) India's import/export by principal ports;
(6) India's import/export (principal port by principal commodities); and
(7) India's import/export of principal commodities by principal ports.

Data reported in this publication are quantum and value figures (in Rs lakh) for the current month, cumulative month—that is, April to current month—as well as corresponding figures for the previous year for comparison. Data reported for the previous year are final whereas the same for the current year are provisional and are subject to change during compilation of foreign trade data at the 8-digit commodity code. The March issue gives the estimates for the entire financial year.

Quarterly Publication

STATISTICS OF THE FOREIGN TRADE OF INDIA BY COUNTRIES

This quarterly publication of DGCI&S appears in two volumes in CD form. Volume 1 contains details for exports and re-exports and Volume 2 gives similar information in respect of imports. Details of foreign trade are shown in the country commodity order. The statistics are presented in one table giving details of country-wise exports/imports by commodities.

Annual Publications

STATISTICS OF THE CUSTOMS AND EXCISE REVENUE COLLECTIONS OF THE INDIAN UNION

An annual publication entitled *Statistics of the Customs & Excise Revenue Collections of the Indian Union* is published by this directorate every year. This publication includes data on (i) customs revenue collections duties (import, export, cesses on export, and other receipts) by sea, air, and land; (ii) union excise revenue collections from central excise, coal cess, rubber cess, and salt cess; (iii) customs revenue collections from imports by detailed tariff heading numbers (by sea and air); and (iv) customs revenue collections from exports (by sea and air).

The data are based on the monthly/quarterly returns received from 94 customs/central excise commissionerates and 93 central excise commissionerates; coal cess from Office of the Coal Controller, Kolkata; Rubber Cess from the Rubber Board, Kottayam, Kerala; and Salt Cess from the Office of the Salt Commissioner, Jaipur.

The publication is compiled annually on a financial-year basis. The basic documents for compilation of statistics of customs and revenue collections are received from customs and central excise commissionerates.

The information presented in tabular form pertains to: (i) collections under custom duties in respect of imports and exports, cesses on exports with integrated figures for sea, air, and land according to commodities (budgetary heads); (ii) gross import customs revenue collections of commodities (budgetary heads)—commissionerates-wise; (iii) net customs revenue collections, refunds, drawbacks, and gross customs revenue, collections by customs/central excise commissionerates; (iv) collections in respect of articles liable to union excise duties as in the first schedule to the Central Excise and Salt Act, 1944 with subsequent amendments by the Finance Bill, 1979 and other changes made; (v) excise revenue collections, refunds, and gross excise revenue collections by central excise commissionerates; (vi) total import duty collections with some of additional duty against each heading of harmonized commodity descriptions and coding system (collections of land customs have been excluded); (vii) net import duty collections, refunds and drawbacks, and gross import duty collections by customs/central excise commissionerates; (viii) custom revenue collection from exports; (ix) net export duty collections and refunds and gross export duty collection by customs/central excise commissionerates.

STATISTICS OF THE INLAND COASTING TRADE CONSIGNMENT OF INDIA

The title of this publication has undergone changes from time to time. From the very beginning up to the March 1957 issue, the name of the publication was *Accounts Relating to the Coasting Trade and Navigation in India*. Later the tables relating to navigation in coasting trade were dropped and the said publication was renamed *Statistics of Inland Coasting Trade Consignments of India*.

The basic documents for compilation of *Statistics of Inland Coasting Trade* are received from customs authorities in the form of coastal trade returns. The classification followed for recording coastal trade consists of 450 items for presentation. For the purpose of compilation, the total coastal area has been divided into 12 maritime blocks, namely (i) Andaman and Nicobar Islands; (ii) Andhra Pradesh; (iii) Goa; (iv) Gujarat; (v) Karnataka; (vi) Kerala; (vii) Laccadiv, Minicoy and Amindives Island; (viii) Maharashtra; (ix) Odisha; (x) Puducherry; (xi) Tamil Nadu; and (xii) West Bengal, corresponding to the 12 maritime states of India.

The value of both inward and outward movements separately for each maritime block are shown in a 12 × 12 matrix form with subtotals (row/column) and grand totals at the beginning of the publication. All commodity-wise breakups with quantity and value in prescribed unit traded between the blocks are presented subsequently. In addition, the maritime block-wise trade flow of different commodities alongside internal movements amongst the ports within a block, if any, is also presented in a separate table.

INTERSTATE MOVEMENTS/FLOWS OF GOODS BY RAIL, RIVER, AND AIR

This directorate has been entrusted with the responsibility of compilation and publication of *Inland Trade Statistics by Rail and River* since 1917. From the year 1991–2, compilation of data on inland trade by air has also been added. The primary sources of the statistics are the returns received from the different railway zones, Central Inland Water Corporation (CIWTC), Kolkata and Air India at present. The data published in this volume relate to quantity of figures of 78 selected commodities/commodity groups moving by inland rail and river amongst 37 different trade blocks. Each of the states (provinces) of India is basically treated as an individual trade block; whereas, with a view to trace the foreign imports to their places of consumption and exports from their places of production, some of the important sea-port towns are segregated from the maritime states and identified as additional and independent trade blocks resulting in a total of 37 trade blocks.

The rail-borne trade data is represented in two different forms. The first is a 37 × 37 matrix representation of individual commodity-wise quantity in prescribed unit (in quintals) moved between the 37 trade blocks. The second is the presentation of state-wise inward and outward consignments of 78 selected commodities/commodity groups moved. This publication also contains cargo moving by air from airport to airport and also state to state within the country through domestic airlines, such as Air India, Jet Airways, and JetLite. The summary of river-borne trade is represented separately in an identical method akin to the rail.

STATISTICS OF FOREIGN AND COSTAL CARGO MOVEMENTS OF INDIA

This publication in its present form came into being in April 1965. It contains data on shipping in foreign and coasting trade of India relating to the entry and clearance of ships with cargo or in ballast at different ports and customs zones and the number and tonnage of vessels built and registered at different ports in India during a financial year. The primary sources of the statistics on cargo movements as well as shipping are the authorities at the customs zone in India, namely Kolkata, Chennai, Kochi, Ahmedabad, Mumbai, and Goa. In case of coasting trade, the data are compiled on the basis of returns received from the concerned customs authorities of 12 maritime blocks.

The data on cargo movements and shipping are presented in 12 tables. Tables 1 and 3 show the total number and net registered tonnage of vessels entered and cleared with cargoes/in ballast in foreign trade according to customs zones whereas Tables 2 and 4 show their breakup nationality-wise. Tables 5 and 6 show the number and net registered tonnage of Indian and non-Indian vessels entered and cleared with cargoes/in ballast in each port/state in foreign trade whereas Tables 9 and 10 show a similar picture on coasting trade. Tables 7 and 8 show the total number and nationality-wise breakup with net registered tonnage of vessels which entered and cleared with cargoes and in ballast in coasting trade, respectively. Tables 11 to 12 show data about number and net registered tonnage of vessels built and initially registered at each port in India.

SELECTED STATISTICS OF FOREIGN TRADE OF INDIA

This annual publication is being brought out by the DGCI&S since 1973. The latest in the series relates to the year 2010–11.

The publication contains the following information:

(1) India's foreign trade in treasure (including currency notes)
(2) Custom zone-wise data (value only) on Indian foreign trade both in merchandise and treasure
(3) Index of foreign trade (both quantum and value index)
(4) Export through foreign post offices (principal commodity-wise)
(5) Record of stock in bonded warehouses on 31 March every year: customs zone-wise
(6) Direct transit trade of neighbouring Nepal and Bhutan reported by Kolkata custom as passing through customs frontier of India.

The primary source of data is the concerned customs authority.

ASSESSMENT REPORT IN RESPECT OF INDIA'S FOREIGN TRADE BY AIR

The assessment report is an analytical report on the export/import performance airport-wise showing the trends in the share of air-borne trade, brought out/prepared annually. An analysis has been made to highlight the changing pattern of airborne export trade in relation to import trade by air through the construction of an index termed as export performance index. Besides, an account of the relative importance of the airports in India's international trade has also been presented. Further, principal commodity-wise exports and imports of different airports and vice-versa are also shown separately in the report.

VAANIJYA

Six-monthly analytical trade journal *Vaanijya* is also published to provide value added analysis and review of trade data.

INDIAN TRADE JOURNAL

The *Indian Trade Journal* (*ITJ*) is edited and issued by DGCI&S, Kolkata and is published by the Controller of Publications, Ministry of Urban Affairs and Employment, GoI. It is a weekly publication and is due on every Wednesday.

The *ITJ* has completed 100 years of its existence. With a view to keeping the Indian trading community informed about the latest business opportunities in India and abroad, the DGCI&S has been publishing *ITJ*, a weekly publication, since 1906. Since its inception on 5 April 1906, it has undergone many changes in the British period and also thereafter. Throughout its history, publication of the journal has never been interrupted even for a single week.

The *ITJ* publishes mainly domestic as well as foreign/global tenders floated by different organizations (government and private). In fact, it is provided in the general financial rules of the GoI that the *ITJ* is the standard medium for any government department/organization/office or public sector undertakings (PSUs) for publication of notifications relating to tenders that are floated for public purchases. These include foreign and global tenders floated by foreign private and government organizations as well. Another main objective of *ITJ* is to boost and promote exports efforts of India. It contains a section on exports opportunities providing enquiries from overseas firms expressing interest in Indian goods and services which are received from the Indian embassies abroad. At present, we are receiving trade enquiries from around 35 countries. In addition to these, there are many time-barred tender notices that cannot be published due to lack of proper time-gap between the probable date of publication of the tender notice and the date of opening of the said tender. The magnitude of the problem in this regard can be gauged from the fact that during the period from April 2008 to December 2008 alone, the number of such time-barred notices stands at 2066.

As an integral part of the export promotion efforts undertaken by the GoI, *ITJ* publishes various sections every week. The 'Focus on International Trade' is one such section that gives a brief overview of a particular country's economic and historical scenario, especially from the point of view of the Indian trading community. In another section entitled 'From Our Embassies Abroad', important information (regarding market trends of various commodities traded internationally, policy changes announced in foreign countries, and economic and financial conditions in foreign countries, among others) received from Indian embassies abroad are published in the backdrop of the information needs of the Indian exporters and importers. The 'Commodity Exim Update', another section of *ITJ*, gives a brief analysis of the statistics related to Indian imports and exports of various commodities. Except for these weekly sections, some sections/items are published occasionally. Notifications regarding 'Initiation on Anti-Dumping Investigation' concerning various commodities is also published in *ITJ*.

Other Publications

DIRECTORY OF INDIAN EXPORTERS

This contained particulars of 3,369 firms in export business and more than 10,000 exports and exportable items, classified as per the ITC-HS codes at the 6-digit level, wherever possible. This is a triennial edition of the *Directory of Exporters* containing details of Indian exporters including address, telephone/fax, e-mail, website, product/s manufactured/services rendered, quality standards, value, and destination of export, among others. The 26th edition consisting of 4,770 units has been published in CD form. Now work is in progress to bring out the next edition based on the live data received from customs houses in the form of DTR.

DIRECTORY OF INDIAN IMPORTERS

This contains the particulars of 1,507 firms in import business and records of approximately 6,500 imports made by them, classified as per the ITC HS chapters. This directory is a triennial edition containing details of Indian importers including address, telephone/fax, e-mail, website, product/s manufactured/services rendered, quality standards, value, and country of import. The third edition of the directory is now available. Now work is in progress for the next edition of the directory based on the live data received from different customs houses through DTR.

SOFTWARE FOR PUBLISHING FOREIGN TRADE IN E-MEDIA

From April 2003, all the foreign trade publications, namely *FTSI*, *MSFTI*, and *SFTIC* are made in CD form. All the master CDs of foreign trade publications are prepared in-house at this division before sending them for CD copies. From March 2005, the main 8-digit level publication of foreign trade statistics, namely *MSFTI*, is provided with additional software with a menu-driven report-generation facility on Windows platform. In this publication, the user has the choice to select his desired commodities and countries with multi-select options and generate reports based on queries for country, commodity, and both commodity and country. Further, the commodity-level data aggregation/generation can be done at the 2-digit, 4-digit, 6-digit, and 8-digit level of ITC HS. The user is also provided with the facility to save his query options prepared as a document view for future use. All printing facilities, such as print setup, print preview, and printing the generated report on all types of printers, are supported by the new application including onscreen view and saving the report as a text file.

DGCI&S Portal

The website of the directorate was developed and launched successfully in April 2003.[2] The website has two parts, namely static

[2] Available at www.dgciskol.gov.in (accessed on 26 May 2017).

pages and dynamic pages. The static pages of the website mainly consist of the history of DGCI&S and its various activities in brief. A new chapter on RTI (Right to Information Act, 2005) has also been introduced on the site as per government directives. These pages also contain summary data on principal commodities, chapters, sections, economic regions and country-wise final foreign trade data, and is updated regularly. This site also has free access to the revised Custom Tariff Code Classification implemented in DGCI&S with effect from April 2003 with section-wise and chapter-wise navigation facilities. The dynamic pages of the website are mainly for on-line data dissemination and provide access on both free and payment basis. This member section contains the latest 24 months final foreign trade data at the 8-digit commodity and principal commodity level along with a directory of exporters and importers and is updated regularly. As DGCI&S disseminates trade data under the Priced Information Service System, a small payment module is also incorporated in the website where one can become a member after registering through the website and making an advance payment of Rs 1,000. The advance payment is adjusted online as and when user extracts the data through web. The cost of data is kept nominal to facilitate users. At present, the cost of data is Re 1 per output record and no other charges are involved. Copies of the reports generated are also e-mailed to the users.

Compilation of Exports and Imports Statistics by the Reserve Bank of India

The statistics regarding exports and imports are collected by the Reserve Bank of India (RBI) on the basis of exchange control data for balance of payments (BoP) purposes. The basis for recording is the receipts and payments of foreign exchange for goods exported and imported.

Regarding export receipts the main document is the guaranteed remittance (GR) form submitted in triplicate to the customs authorities by the exporter. The customs authorities send the first copy to the RBI after adjusting for valuation changes, if any. The other two copies are given back to the exporter. The exporter gives these two copies to the authorized dealer to be given to the RBI as soon as the value is negotiated. This copy gives the value adjusted for short and shut-out shipments, if any. This copy is the main source for the RBI statistics and gives the likely realization value of exports. The third copy is sent to the RBI after the actual realization of receipts. As the actual realization, sometimes, takes a lot of time, the third copy is not used for compiling statistics.

In the case of imports, the documents for payment information are the A and the S forms. Importers are required to submit returns to the authorized dealers in the A form. The S forms have to be submitted by the importers when they deposit rupees with the government account in payment for aid financed imports under the direct settlement procedure. Payments for the government imports are made by the official agencies abroad and these agencies send the details directly to the RBI. It should be noted here that not all payments are made at the time when the imports arrive. Sometimes the payments are made in advance; sometimes the goods are received on deferred payments. The exchange control data are compiled not on the arrival of imports but when exchange is sold or transferred. These data are published occasionally by the RBI.

Differences between the Custom Data and the Exchange Control Data

The trade statistics compiled by the DGCI&S differ considerably from those compiled by the RBI. The following are the main reasons for the differences.

DIFFERENCES IN COVERAGE

The coverage has all along been different in the two series. For instance, in the case of Nepal, airborne trade (since January 1957) as well as land trade (since April 1964) is now included in the DGCI&S data. As there are no exchange restrictions, Indo-Nepal trade is not included in the RBI data. The commodity coverage is also different. The customs authorities cover all the commodities which enter or leave the country. The RBI data cover only those merchandise transactions which result in the receipt or payment of foreign exchange. Again, the customs authorities cover only non-combatant items of defence equipment, while the RBI data include all defence imports except those received by way of grants from friendly countries.

DIFFERENCE IN VALUATION

In the case of exports the values according to the custom authorities are at FOB. The export value as given in the GR form is the actual recorded invoice value and may be on FOB, CIF, and CF basis. An overall adjustment is, however, made to get the value at FOB. The basis of adjustment is a simple survey conducted several years ago.

DIFFERENCE IN TIMINGS

Imports and exports are entered in the customs records on the basis of arrival in and departure from India. In the exchange control records, exports are entered after the goods have been shipped and imports when the payments are made to the supplier.

REPAIRS AND IMPROVEMENTS

In the case of repairs and improvements the customs record the full value on arrival and on dispatch from the country. The RBI data takes into account only the value added by repairs and improvements.

Import and Export Licensing Statistics

The DGFT is responsible for licensing statistics. Formerly (till 1991), the DGFT was known as the Chief Controller of Imports and Exports (CCI&E).

Annual Report for Director General of Foreign Trade

An annual report is published by DGFT. The report contains statistical data for the current year and that of the previous year on the following aspects: (i) number and value of import licences issued; (ii) category-wise value of import licences according to office of issue; (iii) agency-wise breakup of release orders issued by the various offices; (iv) value of export licences issued for selected commodities; (v) imports, exports (including re-exports) and balance of trade; and (vi) imports and exports of items class-wise and percentage distribution of exports, receipts, disposal and pendency of export, import licences, and cash compensatory support under normal and special performance system (SPS), applications and other receipts and number of interviews granted at various offices.

Balance of Payments

The BoP is a record of economic transactions of the residents of a country with the rest of the world on account of goods exported and imported, services rendered and received, and transfers of capital. Residents cover nationals as well as non-nationals residing in the country. Foreign students, tourists, foreign officers, and international institutions are not considered to be residents, but diplomatic officers and armed forces of the country stationed abroad, are treated as residents notwithstanding their physical location. Balance of payment statistics are derived for the most part from exchange control records and are compiled by the RBI. They are given separately for the current account and the capital account, the current account given according to different currency areas. The following items are covered under the current account:

(1) Merchandise: This would include the import and export of goods.
(2) Travel account: The receipts are the expenditure in India by foreigners, who may come for sightseeing, education, and conferences. The payments are the similar expenses by Indians' abroad (unless financed by the government of the country where the foreigner visits).
(3) Transportation services: The freight charges received by Indian vessels against services rendered to foreign parties as well as charges met by foreign ships in India are treated as receipts, and payments are earnings by foreign shipping companies as well as the payments as operating expenses abroad of Indian steamship companies.
(4) Investment income: Apart from investment income of private parties—Indian and foreign—from each other, this includes the interest and discount on the investment of the RBI and reciprocally of the foreign credits to India effected at the state level.
(5) Insurance: The receipts and payments on life and general insurance are covered here.
(6) Government services not included elsewhere: This account is for the disbursement by the government of such sums as necessitated for the upkeep of its offices abroad.

(7) Miscellaneous: This account, in the main, is for receipts and payments for services such as those for agency services and film rentals and maintenance of estates.
(8) Transfer payments:
  (a) Official: Cover imports financed by aid under different aid programmes and cash grants. In addition, the receipts and payments of pensions on government account and contribution to international organizations are also covered.
  (b) Private: These are generally transfers such as gifts, maintenance, and remittances.

Errors and Omissions

This difference is due to the difference in timings between the two arms of a transaction or their coverage.

Capital account covers the following items:

(1) Private: Private long-term capital and private short-term capital movements.
(2) Banking: The changes in the assets and liabilities of the banking sector are shown separately under banking.
(3) Official:
  (a) Loans: Loans raised abroad by the GoI, including drawings on the International Monetary Fund (IMF), constitute receipts under loans while loans extended to foreign governments constitute the payments.
  (b) Amortization: Foreign payments under this account are the repayments of loans secured by the Government of India, while the receipts are the repayments of loans by foreign governments to India.
  (c) Miscellaneous: All other residual capital transactions come under this head, for example, changes in PL-480 rupee balances held by the US Government.
  (d) Reserves: Changes in the foreign exchange reserves of a country as a result of the rest of the transactions.

Distributive Trade

This trade arises because of the transactions from the producers to the ultimate consumers. No regular statistics are available regarding distributive trade. The National Sample Survey Office (NSSO) has conducted some surveys in various rounds on trading activities in the household sector. The following paragraphs describe the details about these surveys.

Some general information on household trade was given in the NSSO *Report No. 1*. The information was based on the data collected during the first round and related to rural areas only. The first separate report giving some broad information about household trade was *Report No. 24* covering the 7th, 8th, and 9th rounds (October 1953–November 1955). The surveys were also done during the 10th, 15th, 20th, and 24th Rounds and the latest rounds are 41st, 46th, 53rd. Household trading was defined as trading by individual households or jointly by two or more households as distinct from operations by non-household organizations, such as joint stock companies, cooperative societies, and other public limited companies. The NSSO covered only own account and non-directory establishments. Directory establishments for the same content and almost the same rounds were covered by the CSO. However, 51st Round onwards, all components were covered by the NSS. From the integrated survey on unorganized service sector for the 57th and 62nd Rounds, trade was excluded. It is heartening to note that for the year 2010–11, trade is included under the integrated survey on Non-agricultural Enterprises during the 67th Round for different services; however, we will be able to get the details about the estimates of revenue and expenditure of the trading units.

Bibliography

Directorate General of Commercial Intelligence and Statistics. Various Years. *Foreign Trade Statistics of India*. Ministry of Commerce and Industry. Available at http://www.dgciskol.nic.in/pub_brochure.asp (accessed on 3 August 2017).

———. Various Years. *Monthly Statistics of the Foreign Trade of India*. Ministry of Commerce and Industry. Available at http://www.dgciskol.nic.in (accessed on 3 August 2017).

———. Various Years. *Selected Statistics of Foreign Trade of India*. Ministry of Commerce and Industry. Available at http://www.dgciskol.nic.in/pub_selected_statistics.asp (accessed on 3 August 2017).

———. Various Years. *Statistics of Foreign and Costal Cargo Movements of India*. Ministry of Commerce and Industry. Available at http://www.dgciskol.nic.in/pub_cargo.asp (accessed on 3 August 2017).

Directorate General of Commercial Intelligence and Statistics. Various Years. *Statistics of India's Customs and Excise Revenue Collections of the Indian Union*. Ministry of Commerce and Industry. Available at http://www.dgciskol.nic.in/pub_revenue.asp (accessed on 3 August 2017).

———. Various Years. *Statistics of the Inland Coasting Trade Consignment of India*. Ministry of Commerce and Industry. Available at http://www.dgciskol.nic.in/pub_coastal.asp (accessed on 3 August 2017).

Director General of Foreign Trade of India. Various Years. *Import and Export Licensing Statistics*. New Delhi: Ministry of Commerce and Industry, Government of India.

National Sample Survey Organization. Various Years. *National Sample Survey Report (Report No. 443 and 444)*. Ministry of Statistics and Programme Implementation. Available at http://mospi.nic.in/Mospi_New/site/home.aspx (accessed on 3 August 2017).

Reserve Bank of India. Various Years. *Exports and Imports Statistics*. Available at http://www.rbi.org.in/(accessed on 3 August 2017).

7

Transport and Communication Statistics

From the statistical point of view, the transport sector can be divided into three parts, namely the state sector, the organized private sector, and the unorganized private sector. The state sector is thoroughly covered by regular statistics, the organized private sector only partly, and the unorganized private sector not at all. Different modes of transport are rail, road transport, inland water transport, shipping, major ports and development of minor ports. The details about the statistics available for these modes are given in the following sections.

Railways

The most important transport organization in the public sector is the railways. The Department of Statistics and Economics of the Indian Railway Board publishes the *Annual Year Book of Indian Railways*, *Annual Report*, and *Statistical Statement*. These refer to all aspects of the railway movements, namely rolling stock, route mileage, number of stations, gross receipts and gross expenses, net gain or loss to the government after meeting all charges, passengers and goods carried, the rates charged for their employment, and so on. Much of the information is supplied separately for passenger trains and goods trains; for steam, electric, and diesel locomotives; and for broad gauge, meter gauge, and narrow gauge lines. Details of the publications are described as follows.

Indian Railways Annual Report and Accounts

The report brought out yearly by the Railway Board since 1972–3 reviews the activities of the Indian Railways in different spheres and presents the relevant statistics and annual accounts. The latest issue relates to the year 2014–15. Some of the important topics regarding statistical data covered by this report are as follows:

(1) Finance: Provides financial results on traffic receipts and working expenses, in comparison to the previous year.
(2) Freight operation: Provides information on commodity-wise loading of revenue-earning traffic in comparison to the previous year. Commodities covered include coal, iron ore, cement, foodgrains, and fertilizers.
(3) Passenger business: Here, the profile of passenger traffic is compared against that of the previous year. Items covered include passengers originating (in millions), passenger kilometres (in millions), average lead (in kilometres), earnings (in rupees crore), and average rate per passenger kilometre (in paise).
(4) Engineering: Gives information on gauge conversion, doubling, new lines, track renewal, track upgrade, long-welded rails, higher axle load, concrete sleepers, track modernization, track machines, eliminating the use of wooden sleepers, bridges, level crossings, road over/under bridges, and land management.
(5) Electrification: Covers topics such as executive summary of railway electrification, plan period-wise progress of railway electrification, sections opened for electric traction after inspection by the Commissioner of Railway Safety in 2014–15, completion of electrification from Vellore to Villupuram to connect two trunk routes, that is, Chennai Beach–Villupuram–Tiruchchirappalli–Madurai–Nagercoil and Chennai–Katpadi–Jolarpettai–Thiruvananthapurum–Nagercoil on electric traction, direct current (DC) to alternate current (AC) conversion in the Mumbai area of the Western and Central Railways, and major new electrification works sanctioned in 2014–15, under Plan Head-Railway Electrification.

(6) Signal and telecom: This aspect is divided into two major components—signalling and telecommunication. Signalling provides information on topics such as complete track circuiting, block proving axle counter, automatic block signalling, train protection and warning systems, train collision avoidance systems, train management systems, and accidents at level crossings. Growth of signalling telecommunication provides information on topics such as train information display boards.
(7) Safety: It gives information on category-wise and cause-wise analysis of consequential train accidents during the last two years.
(8) Rolling stock: This gives information on rolling stock placed on line during the year and stock condemned during the year.
(9) Materials management: Covers topics like stocking depots, disposal of unserviceable items, expenditure on purchases, procurement of iron and steel material, modernization, agency of procurement, indigenous vendor development, and inventories.

Indian Railways Year Book

The year book has been published by the Railway Board since 1973–4. The contents of *Indian Railways Year Book* are given as follows:

Key Statistics and Other Statistics

It gives information of some major economic indicators such as gross domestic product (GDP), inflation, wholesale price indices (WPIs), external trade, economic review on agriculture, industry, and infrastructure.

Electrification

The advent of electric traction on Indian Railways dates back to 1925. Starting with the DC traction system, Indian Railways introduced electrification on single-phase 25 KV system and subsequently adopted the latest 2 × 25 KV Auto Transformer system on a limited scale. The report gives the extent of electrification of route kilometres up to the end of March of the year.

Signal and Telecom

Signalling

Advanced signalling systems, namely complete track circuiting, Multiple Aspect Colour Light Signalling (MACLS), panel/route relay/electronic interlocking, and last vehicle check by axle counter are deployed on IR for safe and efficient train control and optimum utilization of line capacity. A major thrust has been given for provision of LED-based signals, track circuiting, and replacement of signalling gears at block stations. On-board train protection system and train management system have also been introduced on Indian Railways. The report for the year 2014–15 gives the progress of various signalling devices as on March 2015 and also for the previous year.

Telecommunication

Telecommunication plays an important role in train control, operation, and safety. With the rapid growth in telecommunication technology, Indian Railways has decided to go for the state-of-the-art nationwide telecom network to meet its communication needs and earning revenue by exploiting surplus capacity commercially. With this objective, RailTel—a Railways' Public Sector Undertaking—was formed in September 2000.

As on 31 March 2015, 48,293 route kilometres of optical fibre cable was commissioned to carry gigabits of traffic. RailTel is significantly contributing in building National Knowledge Network. It is also planning to provide broadband connectivity to the panchayats.

Traction

The Indian Railways uses a mix of electric and diesel traction. The share of traffic in terms of train kilometres and gross tonne kilometres (GTKMs) for passenger and freight services is hauled under different traction types over the years. Energy consumption by types is given as follows.

- *Rolling Stock*: This gives the number of locomotives by type, number of coaches, and wagons by type.
- *Passenger Business*: This gives the number of passengers originating, passenger kilometres, and average load for suburban (all classes) and non-suburban (class-wise) with annual rate of growth and

passenger revenue earned by classes. The passenger services measured in terms of train kilometres and vehicle kilometres, and the density of train services as also the number and average speed of trains and passenger amenities are available.

- *Personnel*: The strength of railway employees under various groups, together with total expenditure on them, is given.
- *Social Service Obligation*: The Indian Railways carries out certain activities which are essentially uneconomic in nature in the larger interest of the economically disadvantaged sections of the society. Losses incurred on this account fall under the social service obligation of Indian Railways.
- *Freight Operations*: This includes revenue earning freight traffic trends (tonnes, tonne–kilometre, and lead); share of bulk commodities and other commodities in total tonnes and tonne–km, and commodity-wise breakup of the bulk traffic and earning thereof, freight services and loss and damage claims.
- *Asset Classification*: This includes the following: (a) Engine kilometres per day per engine in use: Engine kilometre, per day per engine in use by type of engine and by gauge; average speed of goods trains separately for broad gauge (BG) and metre gauge (MG); average train load for net and gross; net tonne-kilometre (NTKM) per engine hour and per goods train hour; (b) Coach utilization: In 2010–11 the vehicle kilometre per vehicle day was 532 on BG and 204 on MG; (c) Wagon utilization: On an average, a wagon moved 262.1 km per day on BG and 31.6 km on MG in 2010–11. The NTKM per wagon per day on BG was 9,247. NTKM per annum per tonne of wagon capacity on BG and MG were 57,953 and 7,369 respectively.
- *Tracks and Bridges*: This includes route/running track/total track kilometre increase in line capacity and track utilization standards of track for selected high-density routes, trunk and other main lines, and branch lines; and number of bridges and level crossings. Data on route kilometres are given gauge-wise and state-wise and also separately for single line and double/multiple lines, which are further divided into electrified and others. Information on management of railway land is also given.
- *Safety*: Included here are the number and incidence of accidents per million train kilometre, casualties and compensation paid, and damage to railway property.

- *Finance*: Railway financial position, balance sheet, cash flow, and accumulated borrowings on current accounts can be put under this head.
- *Security*: Value of property stolen, number of cases registered, and persons convicted, preserving the heritage of Indian Railways.

Annual Statistical Statement

This is the 26th (2014–15) issue of *Indian Railways Annual Statistical Statements* which have been brought out in bilingual form in pursuance of the GoI's policy. In this publication, the data format of the railways are provided at the zonal level. The Indian Railways has been divided into 17 zones. These zones publish their own reports as well.

The data on gross earnings by zonal railways and capital outlay during the financial year from funds provided by the government are given in this publication.

This annual statistical statement presents a total of 44 tables; some of the important tables are on: (i) aggregated financial results; (ii) gross earnings and working expenses of each railway system; (iii) rolling stock in service and net additions to or reduction in rolling stock; (iv) passenger and goods revenue statistics; (v) fuel consumption by classes of fuel and by classes of services; (vi) principal commodities carried by government railways and earnings therefrom; (vii) analysis of operating expenses; (viii) total number of employees by class and gender; and (ix) statistics of accidents and unusual occurrences.

The *Monthly Evaluation Report*

The *Monthly Evaluation Report* (previously known as *Monthly Railway Statistics*) gives zone-wise details about the following: (i) highlights—achievements and shortfalls for the month; (ii) loading (in million tonnes); (iii) number of passengers; (iv) approximate earnings/working expenses; (v) parcel and luggage earnings; (vi) ticket checking performance; (vii) position of compensation claims; (viii) accidents; (ix) equipment failure; (x) performance of production units; and (xi) selected operating indices of BG/MG like: (a) train engine kilometre; (b) NTKMs/wagon day; (c) wagon kilometre/wagon day; (d) wagon turnaround; (e) average load per wagon; (f) average net load of goods trains; (g) fuel consumption; (h) engine utilization; and (i) ineffective percentage of rolling stock.

Other publications regarding railway statistics, given in infrastructure statistics, are as follows:

- *Periodical*: Tri-monthly statement of approximate gross earnings of IR for every 10-/11-day period (for circulation in board's office only).
- *Monthly/Quarterly/Half Yearly*: (i) Monthly statement of revenue earning goods traffic on Indian Railways; (ii) Monthly railway statistics presenting the principal statistical results of Indian Railways relating to earnings and traffic, commercial statistics, operating statistics, and rolling stock performance; (iii) Supplement to *Monthly Railway Statistics* containing residual information of the railway performance; (iv) Monthly statistics of passenger and freight traffic; (v) Monthly digest of current trends in economic conditions and rail transport;(vi) Quarterly review of accident statistics; (vii) Half-yearly operating statistics of marshalling yards, terminal goods stations and break-of-gauge transhipment points.

Roads and Road Transport: Ministry of Road Transport and Highways

Statistics under this section relates to those for roads, road transport, and road accidents in the country, the details of which are discussed as follows.

Road Statistics

The statistics regarding different types of roads are given in the publication *The Basic Road Statistics of India* of the Ministry of Road Transport and Highways (MRTH), and are as follows:

The detailed data are spread over different sections comprising a section each on all-India and state-wise road length (total and surfaced), national highways (NHs), state highways (SHs), other Public Works Department (PWD) roads, zilla parishad roads, village panchayat roads, community development/panchayat samiti roads, urban roads, project roads, plan outlay and expenditure on roads and miscellaneous information on NHs and Pradhan Mantri Gram Sadak Yojana (PMGSY).

For analysis purposes the data compiled on road network has been broadly classified into five broad categories: (i) NHs; (ii) SHs; (iii) other PWD roads; (iv) rural roads; and (v) project roads. The NHs comprise less than 2 per cent of the road network, but carry a high volume of the road-based traffic. The SHs and major district roads (MDRs) constitute the secondary system of road transportation in the country. The SHs connect NHs, district headquarters, important towns, tourist locations, and minor ports.

Road Transport Statistics

Motor transport in India is basically a state subject. For the sake of uniformity among the states, the central government enacted the Motor Vehicles Act, 1939. The state governments, keeping in view the local needs and circumstances, have framed their own rules for the administration of this act. This act was replaced by the Motor Vehicles Act, 1988.

Data on road transport can broadly be classified into three main classes: (i) general motor vehicle statistics; (ii) passenger transport statistics; and (iii) goods transport statistics.

The general road transport statistics flow from the administration of the Motor Vehicles Act, 1988, which is applicable to all the states/UTs and the State Motor Tax Act on passengers and goods. The data collected cover registrations of various types of motor vehicles, number of vehicles taxed and tax exempted by various types, number of permits issued and valid drivers'/conductors' licenses issued and in force, taxes and fees realized, and number of motor vehicle accidents. The details are given in the *Road Transport Year Book*.

Road Transport Year Book

The Transport Research Wing (TRW) of the MRTH has traditionally been providing inputs by way of data, research, and analysis pertaining to roads, road transport and road accidents in India to the different divisions of the MRTH.

In respect of the road transport sector, the TRW used to bring out *Motor Transport Statistics*, which was a compilation of motor transport data. The last issue of this publication was brought out in 2005. It was felt that there was need for a more comprehensive and analytical publication relating to the road transport sector, in view of its importance in economic and social development of the country. It is with this objective in view that a new publication titled *Road Transport Year Book* was launched in 2005. The *Road Transport Year Book* focuses on the registered motor vehicle population and motor vehicle taxation structure in various states/UTs in the country.

There are six parts in this publication (for 2011–12): (i) Road transport sector at a glance: It gives data on total number of registered motor vehicles in India, number of buses owned by the public and private sectors in India, total bus fleet and buses in public sector (State Road Transport Undertakings [SRTUs]), production and sales of motor vehicles in India, and revenue realized from road transport; (ii) Profile of motor vehicles registration (state/UTs); (iii) Profile of motor vehicles registration (cities); (iv) Profile of permits and licenses issued; (v) Motor vehicle taxation gives data on (a) state-wise rates of motor vehicle taxes on personalized vehicles, taxis, and auto-rickshaws; and (b) state-wise rates of motor vehicle taxes on passengers and goods transport; and (vi) miscellaneous.

The details regarding the size of the fleet, their gross revenue, cost of operation (with breakdown), consumption of fuel and lubricants (miles per gallon), and staff employed are available only for the public sector transport. No data are available on a regular basis regarding private sector passenger transport and goods transport. At the instance of the Planning Commission, the Rail India Technical and Economic Services Ltd (RITES) conducted origin–destination surveys of goods traffic through check-posts spread over throughout the country for the year 1985–6. Information on various items including commodity description, quantity, and value were collected during the surveys. The survey by RITES has been repeated with the reference year 2007–8. The results of these surveys have been published. These surveys, however, have limited use.

Review of the performance of State Road Transport Undertakings

This is an annual publication of the TRW of the MRTH. The details are given regarding physical performance like fleet strength and utilization, its age profile, staff strength, productivity and staff–bus ratio, revenue earning barometers and vehicle productivity, fuel efficiency, passengers carried and occupancy ratio, and road accidents and financial performances such as total revenue, cost, and profit/loss. State-/UT-wise spread of SRTUs and their performance in metropolitan cities, and cross-country comparison of buses for 100 persons is also done.

Road Accidents in India

The TRW of the MRTH, being the nodal agency for providing information/data on various facets of roads and road transport, brings out an annual publication *Road Accidents in India*. The publication presents information on various aspects of road accidents in the country during the calendar year. The information is collected from states/UTs in the 19-item format devised under Asia Pacific Road Accident Data (APRAD)/Indian Road Accident Data (IRAD) project of United Nations' Economic and Social Commission for the Asia and the Pacific (ESCAP).

In the publication, the details are listed under the following headings:

(1) Introduction
(2) Trends in road accidents, injuries, and fatalities: Trends in number of accidents, injuries, and fatalities; profile of road accidents
(3) Normalized indicators of road accidents, injuries, and fatalities: All India averages
(4) Road accidents: Interstate comparisons—incidence of road accidents, injuries and deaths: states and UTs, per lakh of population; per ten thousand vehicles; and severity of road accidents across states/UTs
(5) Select cities: Road accidents, injuries, deaths, and severity
(6) Accidents in terms of classification of roads
(7) Spatial distribution of road accidents (urban vis-à-vis rural)

(8) Accidents in terms of involvement by vehicle type
(9) Time of occurrence of road accidents
(10) Age profile of accident victims (other than drivers)
(11) Causes of road accidents
(12) International comparison of road traffic injury accidents and deaths
(13) Recent road safety initiatives by the GoI

Air Transport

The Statistical Division of the Directorate General of Civil Aviation (DGCA) is responsible for maintaining civil aviation traffic statistics. This division collects data pertaining to civil aviation from various sources, namely Air India, private operators, foreign airlines and various airports managed by the Airports Authority of India (AAI). The data thus collected are compiled and published in *India Air Transport Statistics*.

The main objective of this publication is to provide a clear picture of the performance of air traffic in India and to study trends thereof. The publication includes traffic statistics in respect of scheduled and non-scheduled air services of domestic as well as foreign carriers; detailed information on fleet strength, aircraft utilization, staff strength, financial results, and operating statistics of Air India and other carriers; and airport statistics for both international and domestic airports. Further, it includes statistics in respect of international traffic to/from India to various countries, domestic traffic carried by scheduled, non-scheduled, and air taxi operators, and traffic carried on tourist charter flights, and flights operated under the Open Sky Policy for all-cargo services. The data on passengers, freight, and mail in this publication relates to revenue traffic only. The details of *India Air Transport Statistics* are as follows:

In 1964, when the publication was brought out for the first time, it was entitled *Basic Statistics of Air Transport in India*. In 1970, the scope and coverage of the publication was expanded and it was renamed as mentioned here.

At present the volume is divided into seven parts:

Part 1 has four sub-divisions (A–D). These four contain data on Indian Airlines and Air India, monthly figures for the current year, annual tables containing past ten years' data as well as comparative figures for the last three years showing percentage variation over the previous years, and the actual performance of the two carriers.

Part 2 gives data on private scheduled domestic airlines other than Air India and Indian Airlines.

Part 3 gives data on total traffic statistics of scheduled Indian carriers. Traffic and operating statistics of all Indian carriers on scheduled domestic services deal with data on aircraft flown, passengers, available seat kilometres, passenger load factor (PLF), cargo carried (in tonnes), tonne-kilometres performed (in million), available tonne-kilometres, and weight load factor.

Parts 4, 5, and 6 give data on non-scheduled traffic carried by private operators and scheduled operators, tourist charter operations, cargo statistics under the Open Sky Policy, and scheduled international operations.

Part 7 deals with data on airport statistics.

Monthly statistics of different airways are available on the internet for the following items: aircraft flown, passengers carried, kilometres performed, available seat kilometres, PLF, cargo carried, tonne-kilometres performed, available tonne kilometres, weight load factor, and market share of different airlines, among others.[1] The details regarding aircraft by class and type are available in the *Report on Aircraft Statistics*. Performance of domestic airlines is available on the website of DGCA.[2] Monthly details are available regarding passengers carried, PLF, cancellation passenger complaints, compilation en route dispersal guidelines, and on time performance.

Annual Report of Air India

The report is available since 1953–4. It gives detailed information regarding Air India and a brief account of the activities of its subsidiaries, namely Hotel Corporation of India and Air India Charters. Besides the balance sheet and profit and loss account, details of

[1] Available at http://dgca.nic.in/reports/stat-ind.htm (accessed on 25 May 2017).

[2] Available at http://dgca.nic.in/reports/stat-ind.htm (accessed on 25 May 2017).

operating expenses are given in the annual report. Ten years' comparative data are given on finance, revenue, hours flown, available seat kilometres, available tonne kilometres, revenue, passengers carried, mail carried, cargo, load factor, aircraft utilization, number of staff, and available tonne-kilometres per employee.

Airports Authority of India

Airports Authority of India (AAI) was constituted by an Act of Parliament and came into being on 1 April 1995 by merging the erstwhile National Airports Authority and International Airports Authority of India. The merger brought into existence a single organization entrusted with the responsibility of creating, upgrading, maintaining, and managing civil aviation infrastructure both on the ground and air space in the country.

The financial division of the AAI publishes an annual report, the details of which are as under:

Financial Highlights

Financial highlights on particulars of capital, reserve and surplus, loans and current liabilities and provisions, fixed assets (net), work in progress, investments, deferred tax asset (net), and current assets as on 31 March.

Performance at a Glance

It presents the performance, at a glance, on particulars of sources of funds, application of funds, income and profit, appropriation, net worth, capital employed, current assets, current liabilities and provisions, working capital, and other highlights.

Balance Sheet

It gives data of assets and liabilities. Under liabilities, the data on capital account, reserves and surplus, capital grants, borrowings, current liabilities, and provisions are given and under assets, data are available on fixed assets, investments, and deferred tax assets (net), and current assets.

Profit and Loss Account

It gives information of the sources of income and expenses. The sources of income are traffic revenue, non-traffic revenue, cargo revenue, income from leasing of airports and other miscellaneous income. On the other hand the types of expenses are pay and allowances, other staff cost, operating expenses, other administrative and miscellaneous expenses, depreciation, financing charges, provisions, extraordinary items, prior period adjustments (net), net profit carried over to profit and loss appropriation account.

Port Transport and Shipping

Port statistics regarding major ports are maintained by the respective port trusts. In respect of major and non-major ports, the data are available from the State Port Advisers of the respective maritime states. The port trusts issue the data in their respective administration reports. The data given refer to the movement of shipping, cargo loaded and discharged, passenger traffic, tonnage of principal exports and imports, and details of revenue and expenditure. Basic port data is published by the TRW, Ministry of Shipping in *Basic Port Statistics of India (BPSI)*.

The following are the important statistics covered in this publication (see the 2012–13 report):

(1) Traffic handled port-wise and principal commodity-wise
(2) Container traffic handled type-wise
(3) Commodity-wise breakup of container and general cargo and level of containerization at major ports—port-wise
(4) Overseas cargo of principal commodities loaded and unloaded by country and by major ports
(5) Inland container movement by major ports
(6) Availability and utilization of cargo handling equipment—major ports
(7) Employment, capital employed, and operating expenditure under major heads
(8) Commodity-wise coastal as well as overseas cargo traffic handled at selected non-major ports
(9) Manpower employed and physical performance of non-major ports

Shipping Statistics

The TRW is the nodal agency for both the Ministry of Shipping and the MRTH to provide information/data on various facets of road and water-borne transport. The annual issue *Indian Shipping Statistics* gives information on the current status of the Indian shipping sector in terms of tonnage by different dimensions, such ass age, size, and type. This publication also includes a section on the world maritime fleet. The main source agencies for this publication are the Directorate General of Shipping, Shipping Corporation of India, different shipping companies in the private sector, and World Fleet Statistics—Lloyd's Register Fairplay.

Another publication regarding shipping statistics of India is *Statistics of India's Ship Building and Ship Repair Industry*. This publication provides an overview of the current status of the shipbuilding industry and ship repairing industry under five sections. Section I gives a brief account of India's shipbuilding capacity. Section II contains information on ship repair capacity of the companies and major ports and the earnings on repairs carried out in respect of India and foreign ships. This also contains tables on ship repair facilities available at major ports. Section III provides data on the employment in shipbuilding/ship repairing sector. Section IV gives company-wise financial statistics. Section V provides a global perspective on the shipbuilding industry followed by a glossary and terminology of shipbuilding and ship repairing given in an appendix.

Inland Water Transport in India

The TRW is the nodal agency for providing data on various facts of waterborne transport. The data are published in *Statistics of Inland Water Transport in India*.

The publication as at present gives an overview of the current status of inland water transport (IWT). It consists of eight sections covering navigable waterways and infrastructure, cargo movement on waterways, commodity-/route-wise cargo movement, freight earned and source-wise income and expenditure, IWT activities undertaken state-wise, and type of vessels regarding number of passengers and cargo carried by vessels by private and public sector undertakings, plan outlays/expenditure for the IWT sector, accidents related to inland waterways in select countries.

National Sample Survey on Transport

The NSSO carried out surveys on transport in the 67th Round (2010–11) in unincorporated enterprises in India, in the 63rd Round (2006–7) in the service sector in India, in the 57th Round (2001–2) in the unorganized transport land and water, and in the previous rounds surveys on transport are covered under the 3rd to 10th Rounds, and in 15th, 29th, and 34th Rounds. The following are the details on which estimates are available:

Transport was defined as an activity that carried passengers and/or goods from one place to another as a business proposition. Supporting services incidental to transport, such as packing, freighting, and travel agencies, were included under transport enterprises.

Mechanized road transport, classified under National Industrial Classification class 6021 and sub-classes 60221 and 60231, meant passenger transport by bus (including tramways), passenger transport by other motor vehicles, freight transport by motor vehicles, or any other road transport by mechanized vehicle to qualify the activity as mechanized road transport.

Other transport and related activities mean transport of passengers and/or goods inland, other than by mechanized road transport. Activities of travel agencies and tour operators, activities of other transport agencies, and supporting services incidental to transport, such as packing, freighting, travel agencies, were also covered under other transport. The following activities were also covered: (i) hackney carriages, carriage by bullock carts/*ekka*/*tonga*, etc.; (ii) transport by animals like horses, elephants, mules, camels, etc.; (iii) transport by men including rickshaw-pullers and cart-operators; (iv) all kinds of water transport; (v) supporting services to land transport like operation of highway bridges, toll roads, and parking lots; and (vi) supporting services to water transport like operation and maintenance of piers, docks, lighthouses, and loading and discharging vessels. A household renting out transport vehicles to others and not operating directly with hired or household labour to render service to others was not considered as being a transport enterprise. Transport via pipeline and air transport were beyond the coverage of this survey. Thus, the activities covered in this survey fall under National Industrial Classification codes 601, 60222, 60232, 61, 6301, 6303, 6304, and 6309. The 67th Round integrated survey gives data on the estimated number of enterprises and workers, value of key characteristics, the workers emoluments, gross value added, and value of output. Similar results for the 63rd Round are available in *Report Nos 528* and *529*. The survey done in the 67th Round is being repeated in the 73rd Round.

Communication Statistics

The statistics were released by the Department of Posts and Telegraphs, which is now bifurcated into the Department of Posts and Department of the Telecommunications (from 31 December 1984). The details of the statistics compiled and published by both these departments are mentioned as follows.

Department of Posts

The Department of Posts under the Ministry of Communication and Information Technology is mainly responsible for providing universal access to basic postal services in the country.

Annual Report

The first annual report of the Department of Posts was published for the year 1984–5.

Since then the annual reports are issued. The present report describes the current Indian postal system. The Indian postal system currently provides a number of services which can be broadly classified into four categories: (i) communication services (letters, postcards, etc.), (ii) transportation services (parcels, logistics posts), (iii) financial services (savings bank accounts, money orders, international money transfer services, public private partnerships to extend financial service outreach through the post office network, postal life insurance) and (iv) premium value added services (like SpeedPost, business post, retail post). The Post Office Savings Bank is the largest bank in India in terms of network, accounts, and annual deposits.

The items on which the statistical information is available are as under:

(1) Financial Services: It contains data on number of accounts under different schemes. It covers data on the Mahatma Gandhi National Rural Employment Guarantee Scheme (MGNREGS) and collection of data for computing rural consumer price indices. The consumer price index was not being computed earlier as it was not found possible to collect relevant data from rural areas for the Ministry of Statistics and Programme Implementation (MOSPI), the ministry responsible for such work. A memorandum of understanding (MoU) was signed between MOSPI and Department of Posts to collect data on the prices being paid by the consumers in rural areas for selected consumer goods. Due to the engagement of Department of Posts, it was possible for the ministry to bring out Rural Consumer Price Index (CPI) and All-India CPI in February 2011, for the first time. Since then the CPI is regularly computed and issued by MOSPI, each month. Data for rural CPI is collected for 1,181 villages across the country every month. The Branch Post Masters concerned collect prices of 185 to 292 commodities from the local market on the weeks fixed for each village.
(2) Insurance: This is all about Postal Life Insurance. It gives information of performance of the insurance, name of plan, and name of policy procured.
(3) Postal operations.
(4) Technology: Computerization and networking of post offices.
(5) Financial Management.
(6) Gender Issues.

The details about this report are given on the site of Department of Posts.[3]

Department of Telecommunication

The Department of Telecommunication of the Ministry of Communication and Information Technology has been formulating developmental policies for the accelerated growth of the

[3] Available at https://www.indiapost.gov.in/vas/Pages/IndiaPostHome.aspx (accessed on 26 May 2017).

telecommunication services. The department is responsible for grant of licenses for various telecom services like Unified Access Service Internet and Very Small Aperture Terminal (VSAT) services and also for frequency management in the field of radio communication in close coordination with the international bodies. It also enforces wireless regulatory measures by monitoring wireless transmission of all users in the country.

Annual Report

The first annual report of the Department of Telecommunication was published for the year 1984–5.

A statistical supplement is appended at the end of the report depicting various tables to contain the following information:

(1) Relative Performance: Relative performance of wired line, wireless, public, and private phones during one year
(2) Telephone per 100 Population–Urban/Rural (tele-density): This is state-level data
(3) Number of Telephones (Wired Line and Wireless): License area-wise state-level data on number of telephones
(4) Number of Villages with Direct Access to Telecom Facilities: The data on villages covered with village public telephones as on March and December during the year
(5) Number of Employees—Total, scheduled caste/tribe, ex-servicemen (abled and disabled), and women
(6) Number of disabled employees

The annual report also contains graphs and charts on growth of the telecom network, tele-density, and diagram on wired line and wireless phone.

Department of Electronics and Information Technology

The Department of Electronics and Information Technology is mainly responsible for facilitating and catalysing adoption of e-governance packages in the central and state governments, as the nodal agency for the implementation of the National E-Governance Action Plan; evolving and implementing policy packages to propel the growth of electronics and hardware manufacturing; increasing PC penetration in the country; growth of the domestic software market; development of local languages in information technology (IT); encouraging the use of IT to increase productivity; and exploring use of IT as a means of generating employment. The department is also responsible for matters related to cyber laws, administration of the Information Technology Act, 2000 and other IT-related laws. Its publications are as follows.

Annual Report

The annual report brings information on the following.

(1) *Industry profile*: This includes industry profile on electronics hardware manufacturing, major policy initiatives on industry, production profile, and software and service sectors profile, among others.
(2) *Initiatives in the IT sector*: This is all about the e-governance plan.
(3) *Human Resource Development*: Information about e-learning, schemes for manpower development for the software export industry, and gender empowerment.
(4) *Infrastructure*: Brings information on e-infrastructure and the report on societies and the National Informatics Centre (NIC).

E-Readiness Assessment Report

The *E-Readiness Assessment Report* is published by the Department of IT since 2003.

The report has been referred to most top-level decision-makers in matters of resource allocation and policy formulation. Over the years, the publication of these rankings has led to direct policy competition between the states for a higher ranking.

National Informatics Centre

The NIC of the Department of Information Technology provides a network backbone and e-governance support to central government, state governments, UT administrations, districts, and other government bodies. It offers a wide range of Information and Communication Technology (ICT) services including a nationwide communication network for decentralized planning, improvement in government services, and wider transparency of national and local governments. The NIC assists in implementing IT projects, in close collaboration with central and state governments, in the areas of

(i) centrally sponsored schemes and central sector schemes; (ii) state sector and state sponsored projects; and (iii) district administration sponsored projects. The NIC endeavours to ensure that the latest technology in all areas of IT is available to its users.

Annual Report

The NIC, an attached office of the department, is at the forefront for active promotion and implementation of ICT solutions in the government. The NIC has spearheaded the e-governance drive in the country for the last few decades. As a major step in ushering e-governance, NIC has been involved in supporting the government in areas of internet/intranet infrastructure and IT empowerment of officers at all levels, preparing IT plans for sectoral development and developing IT-based services including government-to-government (G2G), government-to-business (G2B), government-to-customer (G2C), and government-to-employee (G2E) portals.

The NICNET, the pan-India computer communication network of NIC, has been the backbone for e-governance applications. The network operations incorporate cyber security, data centres, disaster recovery centres, network operations facilities, certifying authority, video conferencing, and capacity building setups across the country. The ICT support in terms of planning, software design, development, and roll-out is provided to all central government ministries, departments, state governments, and district administrations. The NIC has also been designated as the implementing agency for the National Knowledge Network (NKN) which aims at connecting institutions/organizations in science and technology, higher education, research and development, and governance with speed of the order of multiple gigabits per second.

A number of major initiatives have been undertaken for strengthening backend automation and implementation of citizen-centric services. E-payment for various government services, SMS service for sending alerts and updates, e-tendering, e-office, and web-based counselling for admission into professional courses are some such activities.

Ministry of Information and Broadcasting

The Ministry of Information and Broadcasting have four autonomous bodies, namely Prasar Bharati, Press Council of India, Film and Television Institute of India, Satyajit Ray Television Institute, Indian Institute of Mass Communication, and Children Film Society; and two public sector undertakings (PSUs), the National Film Development Corporation, and Broadcasting Engineering Consultants India Limited (BECIL).

The Audience Research Unit of the ministry, which is the main statistical unit, provides research support to programme planners, producers, sponsors, advertisers, and marketers by preparing audience profiles and assessing programme impact and effectiveness through audience measurement in the form of qualitative and quantitative research. It conducts regular in-house surveys (Doordarshan Audience Research Team) as well as customizes the data of the survey done by an outside agency (television audience measurement) for rating programmes telecast by Doordarshan to suit our requirement; conducts in-depth interviews; general viewership surveys, and monitors voluntary feedback (letters and e-mail) received from viewers.

Annual Report

The Ministry of Information and Broadcasting, through the mass communication media consisting of radio, television, films, press and print publications, advertising, and traditional modes of communication, such as dance and drama, plays an effective role in helping people to have access to a free flow of information. The ministry is involved in catering to the entertainment needs of various age groups and focusing attention of the people on issues of national integration, environmental protection, healthcare and family welfare, eradication of illiteracy, and issues relating to women, children, minorities, and other disadvantaged sections of the society. The ministry is divided into four wings, that is, the information wing, the broadcasting wing, the films wing, and the integrated finance wing. The ministry functions through its 21 media units/attached and subordinate offices, autonomous bodies, and PSUs. The main secretariat of the ministry is headed by a secretary, who is assisted by one additional secretary, additional secretary and financial advisor (AS&FA), three joint secretaries, an economic advisor, and a chief controller of accounts. There are 16 posts of the level of director/deputy secretary, 23 of under-secretary level, 3 of senior personal private secretary, 52 of other gazetted officers, and 293 non-gazetted posts in the different wings of the main secretariat.

Office of the Registrar of Newspapers for India

The Office of the Registrar of Newspapers for India came into being in July 1956. The office performs both statutory as well as some non-statutory functions. Under the statutory functions, it is responsible for compilation and maintenance of a register of newspapers containing particulars about all the newspapers published; issue of certificates of registration to the newspapers published under valid declaration; scrutiny and analysis of annual statements sent by the publishers of newspapers every year; ensuring that newspapers are published in accordance with the provisions of the Press and Registration of Books Act, 1867 and the rules made thereunder; and preparation and submission to the government on or before 31 December each year, a report containing all available information and statistics about the press in India with particular reference to the emerging trends in circulation and in the direction of common ownership units. Under the non-statutory functions, it is responsible for formulation of a Newsprint Allocation Policy, and assessing and certifying the essential need and requirement of newspaper establishments to import printing and composing machinery and allied materials.

There is no statistical setup as such in the organization. However, the Report Cell in the Office of the Registrar is responsible to bring out the *Annual Report of Press in India*. The data is compiled on the basis of annual statements submitted by publishers of the newspapers giving the details of their circulation.

National Sample Survey on Communication

The NSSO carried out surveys on communication in the 63rd Round (2006–7) in the service sector in India and in the 57th Round (2001–2) in the unorganized service sector.

The following are the details on which estimates are available:

All enterprises that provided communication services were communication enterprises. This included courier services, ISD/STD/PCO booths, voice mail services through computer networking, video/fax services, phone plus services, voiced and non-voiced leased circuits, telex/fax/data services through computer networks, radio paging, audio services, and activity of cable operators.

Communication, falling under National Industrial Classification group 64, not owned by government, public sector undertakings, and local bodies were covered in this survey. However, activities of the cellular service operators were outside the coverage of this survey, although their agencies were covered. The results of the 63rd Round survey are given in NSS *Report Numbers 528* and *529* while the results for the 57th round are available in *Report Numbers 482* and *483*. This sector has been covered as part of the survey on non-agricultural enterprises. During 2010–11 also this was covered as part of un-incorporated enterprises.

Ministry of Statistics and Programme Implementation

The MOSPI also publishes data on telecommunication and postal communication. In the section on communication infrastructure, the ministry gives information on the telecom network as the total number of exchanges, switching capacity, and microwave system, among others. Besides these it also gives data on telecom connections, such as wired lines and wireless connections, tele-density, and internet and broadband connections. Similarly in the postal communication section, it gives data on the important indicators, such as post offices, letter boxes, postboxes and bags rented by the public, inland Speed Post service centres, international Speed Post service merchandise and documents, number of postal employees, number of post offices computerized, revenue earned, and net expenditure. The data are supplied by the websites of the departments of Posts, Telecommunications, IT, as well as the Telecom Regulatory Authority.

Detailed information is given in the chapters on communication infrastructure in the publication of MOSPI.

Bibliography

Air India. 2014. *Annual Report of Air India, 2013–14*. Available at http://www.airindia.in/AnnualReport.htm? 16 (accessed on 3 August 2017).

Airports Authority of India (AAI). *Annual Report, 2013–14*. Available at http://www.aai.aero/public_notices/aaisite_test/annual_reports.jsp (accessed on 3 August 2017).

Department of Electronics and Information Technology. Various Years. *Annual Report and E-Readiness Assessment Report*. New Delhi: Ministry of Communication and Information Technology, Government of India.

Department of Posts. 2015. *Annual Report, 2014–15*. New Delhi: Ministry of Communication and Information Technology, Government of India.

Department of Telecommunication. 2015. *Annual Report, 2014–15*. New Delhi: Ministry of Communication and Information Technology, Government of India.

Director General of Civil Aviation (DGCA). 2015. *India Air Transport Statistics, 2014–15*. New Delhi: Ministry of Civil Aviation, Government of India.

Ministry of Information and Broadcasting. 2015. *Annual Report*, 2014–15. New Delhi: Government of India.

Ministry of Road Transport and Highways. 2013. *Basic Road Statistics in India, 2012–13*. New Delhi: Government of India.

———. 2014. *Review of the Performance of State Road Transport Undertakings, 2013–14*. New Delhi: Government of India.

———. 2012. *Road Transport Year Book*, 2011–12. New Delhi: Government of India.

Ministry of Road Transport and Highways, Transport Research Wing. 2011. *Road Accidents in India, 2011*. New Delhi: Government of India.

Ministry of Shipping. 2012–13. *Basic Port Statistics*. New Delhi: Government of India.

———. 2015. *Indian Shipping Statistics*. New Delhi: Government of India.

———. 2012–13. *Statistics of Inland Water Transport*. New Delhi: Government of India.

———. 2014–15. *Statistics of India's Ship Building and Ship Repairing Industry*. New Delhi: Government of India.

———. 2015. *Statistics of Inland Water Transport, 2014–15*. New Delhi: Government of India.

Ministry of Statistics and Programme Implementation. 2010.*Communication Infrastructure-Part-III, Infrastructure Statistics*. New Delhi: Government of India.

National Informatics Center. 2015. *Annual Report*, 2014–15. New Delhi: Government of India.

National Sample Survey Organization. Various Years. *Survey Reports on Communication*. New Delhi: Ministry of Statistics and Programme Implementation, Government of India.

Railway Board. 2015. *Annual Statistical Statement, 2014–15*. New Delhi: Ministry of Railways, Government of India.

———. 2015. *Indian Railways Annual Report and Accounts, 2014–15*. New Delhi: Ministry of Railways, Government of India.

———. Various Years. *Indian Railways Year Book*. New Delhi: Ministry of Railways, Government of India.

———. Various Years. *Monthly Evaluation Report*. New Delhi: Ministry of Railways , Government of India.

8

Tourism Statistics

The Ministry of Tourism is the nodal agency for the formulation of national policies and programmes and for the coordination of activities of various central government agencies, state governments/ union territories (UTs), and the private sector for the development and promotion of tourism in the country. This ministry is responsible for collection of data on tourism in India. It publishes *India Tourism Statistics*, presenting tourism-related data on a regular basis. The publication contains data on Foreign Tourist Arrivals (FTAs) nationality-wise and region-wise, mode of travel, port of entry, gender distribution, age-wise distribution, purpose of visit, source countries, Foreign Exchange Earnings (FEE) from tourism, world tourism scenario, Indian nationals' departure from India, domestic tourism, hotels and medical tourism, travel, trade, human resource development, and training institutions in the field of travel and tourism. The publication also gives domestic and foreign tourist visits to different states. The publication also includes guidelines of various schemes of Ministry of Tourism for wider dissemination of the same. Guidelines on the Market Development Assistance scheme have also been included in the publication. In addition, a small brochure called *India Tourism Statistics at a Glance* is brought out, giving updated and latest key statistical data.

These publications have been prepared by the Market Research Division of the Ministry of Tourism on the basis of information received from the Bureau of Immigration, states/UTs, Archaeological Survey of India, and United Nations World Tourism Organization (UNWTO). The Ministry of Tourism also estimates FTA and FEE data from tourism with a time lag of just four to five days every month.

National Sample Survey on Tourism

An all-India household survey on domestic tourism (the domestic tourism survey [DTS]) was carried out by the National Sample Survey Office (NSSO), Ministry of Statistics and Programme Implementation (MOSPI), Government of India (GoI), as part of the 65th Round of the National Sample Survey (NSS). The data were collected through a schedule of enquiry. The aim, inter alia, was to provide estimates of the volume of domestic tourism in terms of number of visitors (that is, persons performing trips), number of households undertaking domestic tourism, and number of trips that contributed to domestic tourism in India. It was also intended to study domestic tourism by different population categories, such as age, economic level, activity status, and occupation and industry of work; characteristics of trips such as purpose and main destination; and the expenditure incurred by the households in domestic tourism activity.

Based on the data collected during the survey period (July 2008 to June 2009), estimates pertaining to domestic tourism in India along with various characteristics associated with these have been generated and presented in *Report No. 536*.

Domestic tourism has not been covered comprehensively in any earlier NSS rounds. In the 54th Round (January–June 1998) of NSS, one of the subjects covered was tours involving overnight stay. The main household schedule of that round recorded details of journeys on tours involving an overnight stay undertaken by household members during a specified period.

The results of the 54th Round enquiry on travel (which included commuting to work or for education as well as tours involving an overnight stay) were published in NSS *Report No. 450*. The report, in its chapter on tours involving an overnight stay, gave state–sector-wise estimates of rate of occurrence of such journeys per 100 households and per 1,000 population in 60 days, distribution of journeys by mode of journey, distance travelled and purpose, and average number of travellers, average duration of a journey, and average expenditure on a journey for each mode and purpose. Due to differences in the coverage of 'tours involving overnight stay' as studied in the 54th Round survey from the 'overnight trips' of the 65th Round survey, it is not possible to compare the estimates from the two surveys in this report. Some of the important findings of the surveys of the 65th Round are given as follows.

Some Key Findings of Domestic Tourism Survey (DTS) 2008–9

- As many as 783.5 million people undertook at least one domestic overnight trip during the reference year 2008–9. These people might have undertaken more than one trip during this period. On the other hand, 939.1 million trips were undertaken by one or more household members during the same period.
- In all, there were 2,117.4 million tourist trips, taking into account all the trips undertaken by all the tourists in the reference period.
- In a one-year period, 418 overnight trips were made per 100 households. With increase in age, the number of overnight trips per person rose gradually.
- The leading purpose for which maximum trips were taken was social. These trips accounted for 75 per cent of overnight trips of the rural population and 71 per cent of the urban population.
- At the all-India level, the average expenditure per overnight trip was Rs 821 for the rural population and Rs 1,636 for the urban population.

Another such survey was done during the 72nd Round of the NSSO during the year 2014–15.

Survey on Domestic Tourism

Generation of statistics related to tourism has traditionally not received the attention it deserves given the perceived size and pervasive presence of the sector. With the recent adoption by the United Nations Statistical Commission (UNSC) of the Tourism Satellite Accounts (TSA), a well-developed methodological framework is in place to develop credible magnitudes related to economic phenomena stemming from tourism. Several countries around the world have now implemented their TSAs, while numerous others are in the process of developing them, including India.

Within this context, the National Council of Applied Economic Research (NCAER) had undertaken a feasibility study in 2001 for the Ministry of Tourism, GoI, on developing India's TSA. The Ministry of Tourism requested NCAER to undertake a national survey of domestic tourism with a view to both help move forward the process of TSA development, as well as to generate a better understanding of domestic tourism in India. The survey of domestic tourism in India marked the first national household survey in the country dedicated to tourism. Among its key findings, the survey documents the large size of domestic tourism, with almost 549 million domestic tourists estimated in the country in 2002. Altogether, these tourists generated 229 million tourist trips in India in the same period. Some categories of domestic tourism, such as those related to travel for social purposes, are relatively uniformly spread across the country, across social groups, and also across income classes. Others, such as for leisure and holiday travel, show more heterogeneity across different parts of the country. This comprehensive survey of domestic tourism provides several details of tourism behaviour, including expenditure on different types of trips in different sectors by varying groups of travellers and by different expenditure heads.

Objectives of the Survey

The two broad objectives of the survey were to estimate (i) the total number of domestic tourists by different purposes of travel; and (ii) the total magnitude and patterns of tourist expenditures.

Sample Selection and Sample Size

Selection of Rural Sample

Over 70 per cent of India's population lives in about 6,00,000 villages spread over 550 districts in 32 states. To provide adequate geographical coverage of sample tourist households within a state, the districts were cross-classified by rural population and income from agriculture to form homogeneous strata. The number of such strata in a state was determined on considerations of the range of the stratification variables and the resulting frequency in each stratum. From each of the effective strata a pre-assigned number of districts, depending on the size of the stratum, were randomly selected. A total number of 221 districts were selected as the first stage and the distribution of number of sample districts among various states was done in the proportion of rural population of the state in 2001 (Census 2001).

Selection of Urban Sample

The process of selection of tourist households in the urban areas was more or less similar to that in rural areas. According to the 2001 Census, there are about 4,850 cities/towns in the states/UTs of India (excluding Jammu and Kashmir [J&K]). The population of cities/towns in India varies from less than 5,000 to over a crore. There are 64 cities with population exceeding 10 lakh. All the cities were selected with a probability one. The remaining cities/towns were grouped into seven strata on the basis of their population size and from each stratum a sample of towns was selected independently. Sample size and its distribution is given in Table 8.1.

Table 8.1 Sample Size and Its Distribution

	First Round	Second Round
	Rural Sample	
States	24	33
Districts	221	222
Villages	858	837
Households:		
Listed	96,000	96,000
Selected	8,580	8,370
	Urban Sample	
States	24	33
Towns/cities	666	358
UFS blocks	3,100	1,663
Households:		
Listed	3,20,000	3,20,000
Selected	31,000	16,630

Source: DTS, Ministry of Tourism, GoI. Domestic Tourism Study, NCAER, 2002–3.

Survey Methodology

The survey methodology and sampling design adopted is quite similar to that used by the NSSO in its Household Budget Surveys, but also distinguished by the need to incorporate important aspects of tourism activities. At the all-India level as much as 40 per cent of tourist households are engaged in agriculture-related activities (cultivators and agricultural wage earners) as their primary occupation. While, over half of the rural tourist households depend on agricultural income (cultivators and agricultural wage earners), 63 per cent of urban tourist households depend on salaried jobs and businesses. To avoid the problem of seasonality, it was decided to divide the survey period into two rounds. The first round was from January to June 2002 and the second from July to December 2002. The number for each period is given in Table 8.1.

Expenditure Characteristics

This comprehensive survey of domestic tourism provides several details of tourism behaviour, including expenditures on different types of trips by varying groups of travellers. The average expenditure per trip and the distribution of tourist households by income are given in Tables 8.2 and 8.3.

International Passenger Survey

The International Passenger Survey (IPS), commissioned by Ministry of Tourism, was conducted by Horizon Industrial Consultancy Services during 2003. While the DTC was a household survey, this survey targeted the tourists visiting India and these were interviewed at the exit points. A pilot survey was carried out at the Indira Gandhi International Airport from 13 December 2002 to 31 December 2002. A regular survey was conducted at various international airports from January 2003 to December 2003. The survey covered four international airports: Chennai, Delhi, Kolkata, and Mumbai; 10 other airports: Ahmedabad, Amritsar, Bengaluru, Goa, Hyderabad, Kochi, Kozhikode, Thiruvananthapuram, Trichy, and Varanasi; and three land posts Raxaul, Sounali, and Haridaspur.

Table 8.2 Average Expenditure Per Trip (Rupees)

Items	Urban	Rural	All India
Transport	574	261	339
Accommodation	148	50	82
Food	230	124	150
Clothes	374	217	256
Processed food	59	42	46
Intoxicants	21	16	18
Durable goods	72	41	48
Footwear	41	28	31
Toiletries	33	25	27
Gems and jewellery	55	36	41
Books and magazines	14	8	10
Medicines	59	99	89
Others	363	214	251
Total	2,043	1,160	1,389

Source: DTS, Ministry of Tourism and Culture, GoI. Domestic Tourism Study, NCAER, 2002–3.

Table 8.3 Distribution of Tourist Households by Income (at 2002 Prices, Percentage)

Income Class	Urban	Rural	All India
Least income	7.1	23.2	19.2
Low income	19.9	32.1	29.1
Middle income	63	41.5	46.7
High income	10	3.2	4.9
Total	100	100	100
Average household income (Rs/annum)	89,191	55,780	64,199
Average per capita income (Rs/annum)	16,828	9,786	11,363

Source: DTS, Ministry of Tourism and Culture, GoI. Domestic Tourism Study, NCAER, 2002–3.

Survey Description

The principal objectives of the survey were to:

- estimate the total number of tourist arrivals in India—the tourists were to be identified as foreign tourists or non-resident Indians (NRIs);

- assess the demand profiles of the foreign tourists visiting the country, that included a demand for tourist places, tourism goods and services including transport and accommodation, food and beverages, travel agencies, tour operators, cultural services, recreational, and other entertainment services;
- assess the detailed expenditure pattern of foreign tourists visiting India, and estimates of expenditure on specific tourism products such as accommodation, food and beverage services, passenger transport, travel agency, tour operators and tourist guide services, transport equipment on rental, cultural services, recreation and other entertainment services, and other tourism-related products and services;
- evaluate the performance of existing tourist facilities in India;
- assess the number of outbound tourists to various countries;
- estimate the average duration of stay of foreign tourists in India including country-wise details; and
- obtain demographic, economic, and social profiles of foreign tourists visiting India and the motivational factors responsible for attracting them to India.

Sample Selection

A stratified two-stage sampling was adopted for the selection of passengers for the survey. Each of the selected exit points was treated as a stratum and the first level of sampling was time sampling. All the flights departing from the selected airports during the selected survey period was covered in the survey, and the passengers were selected at random on the basis of their entry into the respective lounges. In the case of land check posts, passengers were selected at random on the basis of their arrival at the check post (see Table 8.4).

Table 8.4 Sample Size of IPS and Its Distribution

	Delhi	Mumbai	Chennai	Kolkata	Total
Foreign	4,650	4,425	1,724	675	11,474
Indian	1,650	2,850	1,050	300	5,850
Transit	750	600	75	75	1,500
Total	7,050	7,875	2,849	1,050	18,824

Source: IPS, Ministry of Tourism.

Survey Findings

The total number of foreign tourists departing from the exit points during the period January to December 2003 was estimated at 2.62 million. Of these, 0.18 million were package tourists and the remaining 2.44 million were non-package tourists. The total number of NRIs visiting India was estimated at 2.5 million. For the maximum number of tourists—foreign tourists and NRIs—that visit India, the main purpose of visit was 'leisure and recreation', followed by 'business and professional' in case of foreign tourists and 'religion and pilgrimage' in case of NRIs. Table 8.5 gives the percentage distribution of tourists visiting India across purpose of visits.

Based on these two surveys, the TSA were prepared by the NCAER and submitted to the Ministry of Tourism.

International Passenger Survey 2010–11

The second such survey was conducted by the Indian Statistical Institute (ISI), Kolkata for the year February 2010–January 2011.

The survey targeted the following three categories of international tourists, namely: (i) foreign nationals visiting India; (ii) NRIs visiting India; and (iii) Indian residents travelling abroad.

For the purpose of the survey, separate questionnaires were prepared for foreign residents/NRIs and outbound Indian residents.

Table 8.5 Inbound Tourists Across Purpose of Visit (Percentage Distribution)

	Foreign Tourists	NRIs
Leisure, recreational, and holiday	45.45	29.32
Visiting friends, and relatives	12.01	13.91
Business and professional	23.00	19.71
Health and treatment	2.20	9.73
Religion and pilgrimage	12.24	25.23
Transit	0.41	0.78
Employment	0.10	1.33
Others	4.59	0.00
Number of tourists	26,16,355	16,64,817

Source: IPS, Ministry of Tourism.

While the DTS was a household survey, IPS targeted the tourists visiting India and the Indian tourists visiting abroad. These tourists were interviewed at the exit points.

Sampling Design

The sampling methodology used was stratified sampling with the 15 port points, selected initially, being divided into two sets of ports. No survey was conducted at Goa airport (permission was not granted) and also at Raxual (passenger size was very scanty as seen in the pilot/initial survey). The 13 identified airports and land check posts are given in Table 8.6.

The outbound Indian residents survey was conducted for 11 ports out of which four are international airports: Chennai, Delhi, Kolkata, and Mumbai; 4 other airports: Ahmedabad, Bengaluru, Kochi, Hyderabad; and three land check posts: Haridaspur, Ghojadanga, and Munabao.

Stratified random sampling was adopted for the selection of passengers for the survey. Each of the selected exit points was treated as a stratum and the passengers were selected at random on the basis of their entry into the port. In the case of land check posts passengers were selected at random on the basis of their arrival at the check post. The main advantage of this method is that at the time of exit the foreign visitor has completed his journey through India and is therefore able to give a complete account of his experience. Also, the complete population can be covered at exit points. The port-wise breakup of the IPS sample is given in Table 8.7.

The number of Indian nationals' departures during 2010–11 was 139.05 lakh of which 108.42 lakh were outbound tourists (falling

Table 8.6 IPS Entry Points

Strata	Category	Ports
I	Major international ports	Chennai, Delhi, Kolkata and Mumbai
II	Minor international ports land check posts	Ahmedabad, Bengaluru, Kochi, Hyderabad, Attari, Haridaspur, Ghojdanga, Munabao, and Sonauli

Source: IPS (2010–11).

Table 8.7 Sample Number of International Tourists by Port of Exit

Port of Exit	NRI	Foreigner PIO	Foreigner others	Total
Chennai	665	246	1,004	1,915
Delhi	794	1,336	4,668	6,798
Kolkata	154	219	6,741	7,114
Mumbai	297	474	14,903	15,674
Ahmedabad	39	129	413	581
Bengaluru	493	476	3,670	4,639
Kochi	133	34	160	327
Hyderabad	553	89	917	1,559
Attari land post	0	21	75	96
Haridaspur land post	9	91	1,550	1,650
Ghojadanga land post	0	3	29	32
Munabao land post	0	0	79	79
Sonauli land post	0	1	207	208
Total sample	3,137	3,119	34,416	40,672
Total estimated number	11,48,234	9,17,277	45,38,387	66,03,897

Source: IPS (2010–11).
Note: PIO refers to a person of Indian origin.

under the definition of outbound tourist) which excluded tourists who went abroad on deputation. The port-wise breakup of the outbound resident sample is shown in Table 8.8.

Scope of Survey

Since one of the principal objectives of the survey was to collect relevant data on inbound tourism to prepare TSA for India, suitably designed questionnaires in line with UNWTO guidelines were administered amongst respondents to obtain the required expenditure data. Questionnaires were designed separately for foreign nationals and outbound Indian residents. The questionnaires comprised of both close-ended, as well as open-ended questions.

Data were collected on following broad topics:

- demographics
- travel pattern

Table 8.8 Sample and Estimated Number of Outbound Tourists by Port of Exit

Port of Exit	Sample	Estimated
Delhi	1,586	27,26,617
Mumbai	3,874	29,72,553
Chennai	1,247	13,06,233
Bengaluru	599	6,57,052
Kolkata	957	4,06,863
Hyderabad	286	24,72,291
Ahmedabad	54	5,31,319
Kochi	401	26,15,336
Haridaspur land check post	78	49,433
Ghojadanga land check post	5	52,765
Munabao land check post	52	1,14,545
Total	9,139	1,39,05,007

Source: IPS (2010–2011).

- purpose and motivation of visit
- tour planning
- expenditure pattern
- experience evaluation and satisfaction

A demographic, economic, and social profile of foreign visitors was obtained from the survey. Data were collected for each foreign visitor on nationality, age, gender, marital status, educational level, family size, and occupation. Various trip characteristic data were also collected. These included major purpose of the trip, main destination, number of places visited, mode of travel, type of stay, place of night halt, number of nights spent outside usual place of residence, and so on.

Finally, for the latest trip, detailed data were collected on particulars of expenditure on different items under the heads of accommodation, food and drink, transport, shopping, recreation, religious, cultural, sporting and health-related activities, and other expenditures along with information of reimbursement/direct payment by any institution for such trips. To evaluate the performance of existing tourist facilities, data on expectation and satisfaction level for accommodation has also been collected.

Objectives of the Survey

The principal objectives of the survey were to:

- estimate the total number of tourist arrivals in India; the tourists were to be identified as foreign tourists (persons of Indian origin [PIO] and others) and non-resident Indians;
- assess the detailed expenditure pattern of the foreign tourists visiting the country, which included expenditure incurred on tourism goods and services including transport and accommodation, food and beverages, travel agencies, tour operators, cultural services, and recreational and other entertainment services;
- assess the number of outbound tourists to various countries;
- evaluate the performance of existing tourist facilities in India;
- estimate the average duration of stay of foreign tourists in India including country-wise details; and
- obtain demographic, economic, and social profiles of foreign tourists visiting India and the motivational factors responsible for attracting them to India.

The IPS 2010–11 collected the information of expenditure on the last trip ending during the last 30 days. These included all expenditure in connection with the trip except those to be used or intended to be used for resale or for productive purposes. Expenditure made before, during, and after the trip and which is related to that trip was recorded. The payment may be made through cash, cheque, credit card, debit card, in instalments, etc. The total expenditure in all such cases irrespective of mode of payment was recorded. The approach to be followed was a payable approach, that is, it included the expenditure which was already paid or was payable in the future. Expenditure related to the trip, whether directly paid or reimbursed by some institution like the government or other agencies on behalf of the selected household, was also included. It included expenditures made not just by the visitor but also those that might be made on his or her behalf. It also included expenditures incurred not just during the trip but also those incurred before and after (as long as they are related to the trip).

The expenditures were recorded under five major heads (which are explained in the same way as in DTS): (i) accommodation; (ii) food and drink; (iii) transport; (iv) shopping; (v) recreation, religious, cultural and sporting activities; and (vi) all other expenditure under a separate item 'others'.

Key Findings

Table 8.9 gives a region-wise distribution of foreign visitors to India in the year 2010–11. The percentage share in foreign tourists in India was the highest for Asia (57.2 per cent) followed by Europe (19.6 per cent), North America (15.3 per cent), Australia (4.4 per cent), Africa (2.5 per cent), and South America (0.8 per cent) accounted for less than 10 per cent of the foreign tourists coming to India. Table 8.10 gives the distribution of foreign tourists by purpose of visit.

The following are some other findings:

1. The percentage share of foreign tourists visiting India was the highest from Asia (57.2 per cent) followed by Europe (19.6 per cent), and North America (15.3 per cent), Australia (4.4 per cent), Africa (2.5 per cent), and South America (0.8 per cent) together accounted for less than 10 per cent of the foreign tourists coming to India.
2. Gender analysis of foreign tourists reveals a predominance of males with a share of nearly 69 per cent of all tourists visiting India.

Table 8.9 Estimated Number of International Tourists by Regions and Category

Continent of Residence	NRIs	Foreigner PIOs	Foreigner Others	Total
Asia	8,23,169	5,47,456	24,06,636	37,77,262
Europe	38,064	1,73,035	10,85,061	12,96,160
Africa	17,683	5,156	1,44,888	1,67,727
North America	2,46,849	1,24,769	6,38,557	10,10,175
South America	3,212	3,029	49,435	55,676
Australia	18,206	62,721	2,08,199	2,89,126
Other continents	1,050	1,110	5,610	7,770
Estimated Numbers	11,48,234	9,17,277	45,38,387	66,03,897

Source: IPS (2010–11).

Table 8.10 Number of Foreign Tourists by Purpose of Visit

Purpose of Visit	Number of Foreign Visitors
Business	16,76,291
Leisure	24,29,325
Social	11,83,578
Religious	2,26,855
Education and Training	3,14,163
Health and Medical	3,19,367
Shopping	12,244
Games/Sports	24,254
Jobs in foreign deputation	91,835
Invited by India on specific assignment	2,45,449
Others	80,536
Total	66,03,897

Source: IPS (2010–11).

3. Air travel has been the predominant mode for foreign visitors over the years, accounting for more than 91 per cent in 2010–11. The share of arrivals through land check-posts has been around 8.4 per cent. Arrivals through sea routes remain about 0.1 per cent.
4. Mumbai and Delhi airports accounted for about 41 per cent share of the outbound Indian tourists' departures. The top four ports—Mumbai, Delhi, Kochi, and Hyderabad—accounted for more than 77 per cent of the total departures. The individual shares of Chennai, Kolkata, Bengaluru, Ahmadabad airports are less than 10 per cent.
5. Over 60 per cent of the visits made abroad by Indian nationals were due to business (31.6 per cent) and holidays (28.5 per cent). Social visits accounted for 21.3 per cent, followed by education and training at 7.8 per cent.

Another survey on International Passengers was done during the year 2014–15 with almost the same objectives and methodology. The results are yet to be published.

Tourism Satellite Accounts

The TSAs consist of analysing in detail all the aspects of demand for goods and services which might be associated with tourism, in establishing the actual interface with the supply of such goods and services within the economy of reference or outside, and in describing how this supply (from domestic or imported origin) interacts with other economic activities, using the sustainable urban tourism (SUT) as a reference.

The TSA provides the conceptual framework and the organizational structure for the reconciliation of most tourism statistics within the broader framework of national economic statistics.

The complete TSA provides:

1. Macroeconomic aggregates that describe the size and the economic contribution of tourism, such as tourism direct gross value added (TDGVA) and tourism direct gross domestic product (TDGDP), consistent with similar aggregates for the total economy and for other productive economic activities and functional areas of interest.
2. Detailed data on tourism consumption, a more extended concept associated with the activity of visitors as consumers, and a description of how this demand is met by domestic supply and imports, integrated within tables derived from supply and use tables which can be compiled both at current and constant prices.
3. Detailed production accounts of the tourism industries, including data on employment, linkages with other productive economic activities and gross fixed capital formation.
4. Link between economic data and non-monetary information on tourism, such as number of trips (or visits), duration of stay, purpose of trip, and modes of transport, which is required to specify the characteristics of the economic variables.

Indirect Effects

Tourism primarily relates to movement of people to places outside their usual place of residence. Tourism induces economic activity either directly or indirectly, sometimes in places beyond those visited. This could be in terms of economic output or in terms of employment, besides other social and infrastructural dimensions. Therefore, for a holistic approach to tourism development, it is necessary that reliable statistics on tourism sector and analysis based on tourism statistics are available to the policymakers for decision-making. It is, therefore, important to measure both direct and indirect impacts of increased social and economic activity due to tourism and identify these data separately in the official statistics.

According to TSAs, it is possible to estimate the direct and indirect effects of tourism consumption through the application of input–output (I–O) models. The direct effects only take into account the immediate effects of the additional demand (tourism internal consumption) on production processes in terms of additional supply of goods and services, and additional value added and its components. However, the suppliers of this additional demand require additional inputs from other producers due to inter-industry linkages and those producers in turn would need additional inputs from their input suppliers. Thus, the additional demand (which generates direct effect on production process) induces a chain of activities for different factors of production, that is, inputs, labour, and capital, a phenomenon that continues through several rounds until exhausted. This chain of effects enables the producers directly serving the additional demand to do so, is called the indirect effects of additional demand.

Through TSA, it is only possible to measure the direct effects of tourism consumption on output and value added of tourism industries and other industries serving them (and it is what indicates the term 'direct' in the terminology used in TDGVA and TDGDP). However, by using an I–O table and I–O models, it is possible to estimate the indirect contribution of tourism consumption and tourism aggregates to the economy. The estimates of direct and indirect shares of tourism aggregates in the total economy facilitate a more realistic impact of tourism activity on the economy. Several producers, such as farmers or freight transporters, do not serve the tourists directly, but they provide goods and services indirectly to tourists through tourism industries. It is, therefore, important to understand and estimate these indirect contributions of other industries to tourism industries.

Tourism Satellite Account India

In India, so far two TSAs have been completed. The first TSA was computed for the year 2002–3. As per this TSA, the contribution of tourism in the GDP was 2.2 per cent direct and 5.8 per cent total. Total jobs in the country were 4.6 per cent direct and 8.3 per cent total. According to second TSA, the contribution of tourism to total GDP was 6.8 per cent (3.7 per cent direct and 3.1 per cent indirect) and to employment was 10.2 per cent (direct 4.4 per cent and indirect 5.8 per cent). In addition to this TSA, the TSAs are supposed to be estimated for all the states. So far the estimates are ready for 12 states.

Surveys/Studies

The market research division of Ministry of Tourism also conducts surveys, studies, and evaluation of plan schemes. For details of these surveys and other studies, see market research professional resources on the website of the Ministry of Tourism.[1]

Bibliography

Indian Statistical Institute. 2012. *International Passenger Survey Feb. 2010–Jan. 2011*. Kolkata, August.

Ministry of Tourism. 2014. *Indian Tourism Statistics at a Glance*. New Delhi: Government of India.

Ministry of Tourism and Horizon Industrial Consultancy Services. 2012. *International Passenger Survey*, Feb 2010–Jan. 2011, Indian Statistical Institute, Kolkata, August.

Ministry of Tourism and National Council of Applied Economic Research. 2002–03. *Survey on Domestic Tourism, 2002–03*. New Delhi: Government of India.

National Sample Survey Organization. 2010. *National Sample Survey Tourism*, Report No. 536. Ministry of Statistics and Programme Implementation. Available at http://mospiold.nic.in/Mospi_New/site/inner.aspx?status=3&menu_id=31 (accessed on 3 August 2017).

[1] Available at http://tourism.gov.in/ (last accessed on 16 May 2017).

9

Corporate Sector Statistics

The growing importance of the corporate sector calls for greater transparency and availability of data. Furthermore, the withdrawal of direct regulatory functions by the government such as industrial licensing, import licensing, capital issues, and exchange control means that a number of avenues of collection of data have ceased to exist while the need for them has grown for indicative planning, forecasting, and research purposes. Finally, the onset of the knowledge-based sectors or the new economy requires better reporting standards of certain attributes to help monitor the national economic performance and to assess its future prospects.[1] Corporate sector statistics are collected and disseminated by the Ministry of Corporate Affairs (MCA) and the Centre for Monitoring Indian Economy (CMIE).

Ministry of Corporate Affairs

The corporate sector statistics are released by the MCA. The details of the statistics compiled and published by the ministry, are mentioned as follows.

[1] Available at http://mospi.nic.in/nscr/css.htm (accessed on 16 May 2017).

The ministry is primarily concerned with administration of the Companies Act, 1956 and 2013, other allied acts, and rules and regulations framed thereunder mainly for regulating the functioning of the corporate sector in accordance with the law. The ministry is also responsible for administering the Competition Act, 2002 and other acts.

There are two divisions, namely the Statistical Division and Research and Analysis Division, in the MCA which perform the statistical activities.

The Statistics Division is responsible for corporate statistics and dissemination of information to various organizations. It looks after issues relating to improvements of corporate statistics generated from the MCA21 Portal (including in the eXtensible Business Reporting Language [XBRL] mode); shares statistical information on the corporate sector with central ministries and organizations such as the Central Statistics Office (CSO), the Reserve Bank of India (RBI), the Securities and Exchange Board of India (SEBI), and others, as and when necessary. The Statistics Division publishes the *Monthly Information Bulletin* containing statistical information and analysis of developments in the corporate sector.

The Research and Analysis Division is responsible for compiling, editing, and publishing (i) the *Annual Report* of the ministry, (ii) the *Annual Report on the Working and Administration of the Companies Act*, and (iii) *Monthly Newsletter* on the activities of the ministry. The division provides economic input on issues relating to corporate performance, capital market reforms, disinvestment, and foreign direct investment (FDI) at the macro level.

This division is responsible for carrying out research and analysis pertaining to growth in the corporate sector; analysis of the balance sheets of companies with paid-up capital of Rs 50 lakh and above; work pertaining to capital markets; and policy issues and manuals.

Data Dissemination

The Companies Act, 1956 ('the act') provides for, and casts an obligation on companies incorporated under the act, filing of various forms, returns, and documents with the Registrar of Companies (ROC), a field office under the MCA.

The forms, returns, and documents to be filed include various applications, documents, returns, balance sheets, prospectus, memorandums of agreement, articles of association, and particulars of charges. These are required to be maintained by the ROC. Further, these are open to be inspected by any member of the public on payment of the prescribed fees.

Prior to 2006, the forms, returns, and documents of the companies were received and stored in physical paper form in record rooms at the office of the ROC concerned. Filing of documents, their registration, and consequential placing in the respective file of the company, being done only through human interface, was a cumbersome and time-consuming activity, which was also prone to error.

In 2006, keeping in tune with the e-governance initiatives the world over, the MCA initiated an e-governance project called MCA21.[2]

[2] This is named as MCA21 as it aims at repositioning MCA as an organization capable of fulfilling the aspirations of its stakeholders in the 21st century. The 21-digit (alphanumeric characters) unique corporate identification number (CIN) allocated to each company in MCA21 is built upon certain defining characteristics of the company. The construction of the CIN number is given in Table 9.1.

Table 9.1 CIN and its Construction

Position of characters	Description	Remarks
1	Listed (L)/Unlisted (U)	Listing Status
2 to 6	5-digit industry code as per NIC 2004	Specific economic activity in which the company is engaged in.
7 to 8	State	Name of state in which registered office of the company is located.
9 to 12	Year	Year of incorporation
13 to 15	Ownership Status	Public Limited Company/Private Limited Company/Government of India/State Government Company
16 to 21	6-digit Registration number	Specific to ROC

Source: MCA (2013).

The project was aimed at enabling an easy and secure access of MCA services to the corporate entities, professionals, and the public. MCA21 is designed to fully automate all processes relating to the proactive enforcement and compliance of the legal requirements under the act.

Under MCA21, each Indian company is provided with a unique corporate identification number (CIN) and each foreign company a unique foreign company registration number (FCRN). Using these identification numbers, companies are enabled to file detailed financial and other information, including annual balance sheets and profit and loss accounts, using the specified e-forms online.

In order to maintain data integrity, important fields are made mandatory and an extensive help menu is made available subject-wise. Once the e-form is filed online using the MCA21 portal, it gets automatically saved into a central repository. Data security is built in the system through advanced technology like digital signatures and the data is easily retrievable into pre-defined formats.

Since September 2006, it is mandatory for companies to make all filings with the ROC online using specially designed e-forms under MCA21 system. The information contained in these filings provides a large repository of corporate sector data. The major source of corporate sector data lying with the MCA21 repository comes from all the e-filings made by companies with ROCs/the central government. Some offline filings, which include complaints, inspections, investigations, and prosecutions, are also updated into the MCA21 database.

Under Sections 159 and 160 of the act, every company has to file Annual Returns within 60 days of its Annual General Meeting (AGM). In compliance with the Section 159 of the act, Form 20B is filed by companies having a share capital, which contain details about (i) the company registered office; (ii) its shares and debentures holders; (iii) its indebtedness; and (iv) its directors and managing directors. In compliance with Section 160 of the act, Form 21A is filed by companies not having a share capital, which contains details about address of the registered office of the company, directors of the company, and attached particulars of the total amount of the indebtedness and charges.

Under Section 220 of the act, each company has to file its balance sheet and profit and loss account within 30 days of AGM. The MCA21 system provides for electronic filing of the same by using e-forms 23AC and 23ACA respectively.

The normal filings, accompanied by annexures/appendices in portable document format (PDF) have certain limitations with regard to their amenability to further data analysis. To overcome some of these issues, the ministry has adopted a new technology, namely, XBRL, to obtain the annual statutory filings from a select class of companies. The XBRL brings in a better financial reporting discipline on companies through: (i) standardization of financial information and (ii) compliance of mandatory disclosure requirements. The XBRL-based reporting format not only ensures adaptation of better financial reporting but also assures that the filings are validated and thus assists the ministry in better corporate governance.

The financial statements of a select class of companies are mandated, by rules under the Companies Act, to be filed in XBRL mode since FY 2010–11. The classes of companies required to file their financial statements in XBRL include: (i) all listed companies and their Indian subsidiaries; (ii) companies having paid-up capital more than Rs 5 crore; or (iii) companies having turnover of more than Rs 100 crore.

Companies belonging to banking, non-banking financial, power, and insurance categories, even if falling under either of the aforementioned points (i), (ii), or (iii) are exempted from XBRL filings of their financial statements till the finalization of their respective applicable taxonomy.

Since FY 2011–12, the cost audit and compliance reports have also been mandated to be filed using XBRL.

This system also monitors performance of MCA officials in terms of disposal and pendency of applications received from companies as well as their progress in matters related to inspection, prosecutions, complaints, and technical scrutiny. The detailed description about these Management Information Systems (MIS) reports is presented in Annexures 2.2 and 2.3 of the *Report of the Committee for Formulation of Data Dissemination Policy of Ministry of Corporate Affairs.*

Other kinds of MIS reports are generated using customized queries primarily for monitoring the status of various compliances, approvals, and inspections, pending with MCA officials. The detailed descriptions about these query reports and their search parameter is presented at Annexure 2.4 of the aforementioned report.

This system also provides the facility to access 'monitoring reports' based on a standardized/customized format, categorized as 'myviewreports' through back-office access. These reports are automatically generated in the system at regular intervals. These reports are grouped under 13 different groups as under:

(1) company details report
(2) user business process mapping report
(3) filing statistics
(4) work item related reports
(5) disposals reports
(6) pendency statistics
(7) dealing hand statistics
(8) citizen charter statistics
(9) non e-form reports
(10) statistical reports
(11) daily statistics reports
(12) monthly statistics reports
(13) CCM reports

The detailed list of reports and their description available under each group is provided at Annexure 2.5 of the aforementioned report.

A consolidated list of all the newly registered companies in the year with their names, addresses, industrial activities, and authorized capital is available month-wise. The distribution of companies by various categories such as government and non-government, public, and private, state of registration, and industrial activity is available. The capital raised by the existing companies is available on a quarterly basis. This set of data along with that available in the balance sheets of large-sized companies is used as an input for estimating the total paid-up capital of the private corporate sector at the end of each financial year and to identify large-sized companies.

Fact sheets containing selected financial parameters culled out from the balance sheets and profit and loss accounts filed by the companies in the respective ROC offices are generated for: (i) large-sized non-government companies; (ii) government companies; and (iii) Indian subsidiaries of foreign companies. Besides, certain basic information is maintained on the branches of foreign companies, which have established their places of business in India.

Data are available on companies liquidated and/or struck off under Section 560 of the Companies Act detailing the names, paid-up capital, industrial activity, state of registration, and date of liquidation, among other details. Similarly, data on companies amalgamated or transferred from one state to another, and companies, which have changed their names, are also available on a monthly basis, and can be utilized in a suitable fashion.

Section 60 of the Companies Act, 1956, requires that the prospectuses issued by or on behalf of companies or in relation to companies inviting offers from the public and subscription or purchase of any share or debenture be delivered to the ROC for registration. The prospectuses so registered in different ROC offices by non-government, non-financial public limited companies are analysed and a company-wise database is created annually indicating the number of equity shares and preferential shares or debentures set aside for the public, existing shareholders, promoters, directors and associates, NRIs, foreign collaborators, financial institutions, banks, employees, mutual funds, underwriters, and proprietors. Further, these prospectuses are analysed with reference to the cost of the project and its means of finance through public equity share capital, reserves and surpluses of the company, subsidies, debentures and bonds, deferred payment, and loans from various financial institutions such as the Industrial Development Bank of India (IDBI), Industrial Financial Corporation of India (IFCI), Industrial Credit and Investment Corporation of India (ICICI), Unit Trust of India (UTI), Life Insurance Corporation (LIC), State Financial Corporations (SFCs) and State Industrial Development Corporations (SIDCs), banks, General Insurance Corporation (GIC) and insurance companies, promoters, directors, and friends, among others. This database created from the prospectuses is used by the RBI for further analyses and studies.

Since 2006, corporate sector statistics are generated through the MCA21 portal. The *Monthly Information Bulletin* on the corporate sector gives information regarding state-wise totals as well as active number of companies, along with authorized capital by capital range and economic activity.

The *Monthly Information Bulletin on Corporate Sector* is brought out by the MCA, GoI, starting September 2013. Its latest issue was out in February 2016.

(1) It provides information on registered companies, namely the total number of companies registered in the country; state-/UT-wise distribution of registered companies; economic-activity-wise classification of active companies; and sector-wise active companies, among others.
(2) It also throws light on the total number and sector-wise one person companies (OPCs).
(3) It gives the trend of registration of new companies and limited liability partnerships (LLPs).
(4) It talks about the economic-activity-wise classification of new companies registered.
(5) In its discussion of LLPs and foreign companies, it discusses the obligation of contribution-wise distribution of LLPs and sector-wise LLPs, among others.
(6) The various tables that are detailed in the bulletin include:
    (a) summary statement on companies in India as on 29 February 2016;
    (b) active companies limited by shares as on 29 February 2016;
    (c) authorized capital-wise active companies as on 29 February 2016;
    (d) state-/UT-wise status of companies registered as on 29 February 2016;
    (e) economic activity-wise active companies as on 29 February 2016;
    (f) economic activity-wise OPCs;
    (g) number of companies and LLPs registered during the months;
    (h) registration of new companies during February 2016;
    (i) activity-wise new companies registered during February 2016;
    (j) state-/UT-wise registration of companies during February 2016;
    (k) obligation of contribution-wise active LLPs as on 29 February 2016;
    (l) economic activity-wise active LLPs as on 29 February 2016;

(m) economic activity-wise LLPs registered during February 2016; and
(n) state-/UT-wise registration of OPCs, LLPs, and foreign companies during February 2016.

Annual Report

The ministry is concerned with the administration of a wide range of statutes for the regulation of the corporate sector including the Companies Act, 1956.

The following chapters are included in the annual report: (i) overview; (ii) organizational structure and functions; (iii) The Companies Act, 1956 and its administration; (iv) The Limited Liability Partnership (LLP) Act, 2008; (v) The Competition Act, 2002 and other legislations; (vi) Towards Interactive and Responsive Administration and in the Annexure, the topics are (a) key features of the Companies Act, 2013; (b) senior functionaries of the Ministry of Corporate Affairs; (c) citizens'/clients' charter; (d) 'Performance Evaluation Report of Results Framework Document, 2012–13'; and (e) 'Results Framework Document, 2013–14'.

Centre of Monitoring Indian Economy Private Limited

Prowess is a service that can be availed by subscribing to the CMIE. According to CMIE, it is the largest database of the financial performance of Indian companies. It covers both listed and unlisted companies and is updated continuously. Its major source of data is the annual reports of individual companies. The database for listed companies additionally includes data from the stock exchanges. It provides time-series data from 1998–9, consisting of various analytical tabulations, such as ratio analysis, funds-flow analysis, benchmarks, and peer comparisons. Through the specially developed software that Prowess is accessed by, one can query the database according to one's need. It covers profit and loss statements and balance sheets. Furthermore, it provides a charting toolkit.

It is a database of 'active business entities' for which some 'structured information' related to their financial performance is available. Active business entities are those entities that are not mere registrations without any activity. By business entities, it implies that we are not restricted to only registered companies. They cover other forms of business entities as well. Structured information is a conventional presentation format such as an annual report or a similar filing and not merely a press release of stray numbers or an unofficial estimate. However, all the active business entities are not covered. Availability of structured information is of vital importance.

The number of indicators covered is more than 2,000 (for details, refer to prowess.cmie.com [accessed on 16 May 2017]).

Bibliography

Centre for Monitoring Indian Economy Pvt. Ltd. *Prowess*, Database of Financial Performance. Available at https://prowess.cmie.com/ (accessed on 16 May 2017).

Ministry of Corporate Affairs. Various Years. *Annual Report*. New Delhi: Government of India.

———. 2013. *Report of the Committee for Formulation of Data Dissemination Policy of Ministry of Corporate Affairs, June 2013*. New Delhi: Government of India.

10

Price Statistics

The three types of prices that generally prevail in different kinds of markets are wholesale prices, retail prices, and farm harvest prices.

Wholesale price is the rate at which a relatively large transaction is done (usually for further sale). Retail price is the price paid by the ultimate consumer, especially for small transactions. Farm harvest price is the average wholesale price at which the commodity is disposed of by the farmer at the village site during the specified harvesting period.

The sources and methods of collection of these prices are described in this chapter.

Wholesale Prices

Agricultural Commodities

A continuous series of wholesale and retail prices of agricultural commodities has been available in India for a long time. At present, the collection of data on agricultural commodities is done from different marketing centres under the supervision of the Directorate of Economics and Statistics (DES), Ministry of Agriculture and Farmer's Welfare (MOAFW), Government of India (GoI). The data on prices are collected mainly through various primary agencies specially set up under the Marketing Intelligence Scheme of the directorate. In a few cases, the Revenue and Civil Supplies staff collects and maintains records of prices as part of their normal duties. The work of the primary agencies is supervised by the supervisory officers of the state governments as well as those of the DES.

There are price reporters in all the markets, collecting model prices at the peak hours of the day. Where markets are held daily, the prices are collected on every Friday. In cases where markets are held on specified days of the week, the prices reported relate to the nearest market day preceding Friday. These prices are sent to the Office of the Economic Advisor (OEA) for their use in the construction of wholesale price index numbers and other uses. The variety and quality of the commodity to which the price should relate is specified for each market. The primary reporter collects the prices in terms of local measures and then converts them into standard measures. In cases when there is some change in the variety, the price of the new variety is also collected during the previous one or two weeks. At the time of the new crops coming to the markets, the price of both the old and the new crops are collected for about four-to-six weeks. All the information collected is supplied to different states as well as to the DES. Most of the states after processing these figures, issue a weekly bulletin of prices. The states also give monthly prices as well as average annual prices in their monthly and the annual publications, respectively. The DES has got a record of these prices for the entire price collecting centres. The *Agricultural Prices in India*, an annual publication of the DES, publishes the monthly as well as average annual wholesale prices of 92 commodities for different centres collecting prices from the state governments. Month-end wholesale prices of certain agricultural commodities and animal husbandry produce at selected centres in India are published in *Agricultural Situation in India*.

The Agricultural Market Information Network collects daily prices of a number of agricultural commodities. These prices are available on their networks.

Non-agricultural Commodities

The prices are required by the OEA for the publication of the *Weekly Wholesale Price Index*. This office does not collect the prices but gets the returns from various official and non-official agencies. The prices of agricultural commodities are received from the DES. (For a few agricultural commodities, the prices are received through other non-official agencies.) In the case of non-agricultural commodities, the collection of prices is not a serious problem. It is easy to recognize a particular specification or variety of a commodity. The following are the main agencies supplying the information regarding prices:

- Indian Chambers of Commerce and Industry
- Tea Board
- Coffee Board
- Coal Controller Organization
- Delhi Milk Scheme
- Rubber Board
- Directorate of Sugar and Vanaspati
- Office of the Textile Commissioner
- Steel Authority of India Limited
- Directly from the factories in some cases
- Indian Bureau of Mines
- Central Electricity Authority
- Central Silk Board
- Gas Authority of India
- Indian Oil Corporation
- National Horticulture Board
- Spices Board

The weekly prices are received by the OEA. In most of the cases, these are the closing prices on every Thursday of the week. Often, the prices of non-agricultural commodities are supplied by the Chambers of Commerce. These prices are collected from their member firms, and returns, after processing, are supplied to the OEA. Prices received are the basic prices along with excise and trade discounts. Recently there was a change in the policy of compilation of the wholesale price index numbers and therefore in the publication of prices. Since only monthly indices are compiled, hence there are only monthly prices.

Retail and wholesale prices of 22 commodities from 59 centres are received by the Price Monitoring Cell of the Department of Consumer Affairs daily from the State Civil Supplies Departments of the respective state governments online or by fax or email. As of now, prices for 45 centres are received online, five by e-mail and the remaining nine centres send daily prices by fax. Attempts are being made to encourage 100 per cent online data feeding by the states/centres.

Spot and future prices of eight essential commodities are collected daily from the National Commodity Derivatives Exchange (NCDEX) by e-mail and monitored.

Weekly mandi prices of 20 essential commodities, monitored since 2009, are collected from newswire by e-mail.

The daily price report consists of the following:

(1) Retail and wholesale prices of the selected 22 essential commodities in Delhi and the variations in prices over different time periods, that is, one week ago, one month ago, three months ago, six months ago, one year ago, and two years ago.
(2) Daily retail and wholesale prices of the 22 commodities from 59 centres.
(3) Variation in retail and wholesale prices of 17 select commodities from 59 centres over a fortnight.
(4) Spot and future prices of 8 select essential food items which are traded in the National Commodity Exchange.
(5) Comparative mandi and retail prices of 20 essential commodities and their variations over different time periods, that is, one week, one month, three months, six months, and one year as reported by the NCDEX.

Retail Prices

The prices are compiled by the DES, Labour Bureau, economic and statistics or labour departments of various states and the National Sample Survey Office (NSSO). The DES collects prices of cereals and products; pulses and products; edible oils; meat, eggs, fish, and food; milk and milk products; condiments and spices; vegetables and fruits; and other food. These prices relate to certain important consuming centres. The weekly prices are available on the website of the DES. The monthly prices of the following non-food groups of items—light, cloth and footwear, miscellaneous (medicines), personal care and effects, stationary items, transport and cement—for selected centres are available in the *Month End Retail Prices of*

Non-Food Items. Annually *Agricultural Prices in India* publish average retail prices of 46 commodities. Monthly prices are also published. The prices are collected on every Friday from that locality of the centre where middle class/lower class population is concentrated. One representative locality and some particular shops from that locality are selected and the prices are noted down. These prices are sent to the DES as well as the different states. Some of the states publish these prices in their weekly as well as monthly bulletins. The *Weekly Bulletin on Retail Prices of Essential Commodities* gives details of 45 food items group-wise and the *Monthly Bulletin on Non-Food Items* gives details of 43 non-food items. Data is received from 87 centres all over India. Data from 2000–1 are available on the website. From some markets, the daily prices are collected.

The retail prices are also collected by the Labour Bureau for the construction of consumer price index numbers. The retail prices of different commodities are published in the *Indian Labour Journal*. The prices are published for 24 commodities[1] for 78 centres selected for compilation of the consumer price index numbers for industrial workers. The prices used by the bureau are collected by the part-time staff belonging to the Department of Labour, or statistical departments of the states. Important markets are selected from each centre for the collection of prices. Two representative shops from each market are selected to get the prices. The prices are those actually paid by the consumers and include all taxes. These are taken for specified varieties of commodities and also collected by personal visit on every selected price collection day of the week from the selected shopkeepers. The price collection day and the time for the price collection are fixed from the point of view of popularity among the population group concerned. The prices quoted by the selected shopkeepers are verified from actual purchasers and other shopkeepers. The work of price collection is locally supervised by the price supervisors appointed by the state governments. The commodities for which prices are collected come under the groups cereals, pulses, other food articles, fuel and light and clothes, and miscellaneous.

[1] The data are collected for about 100 items but published only for 24 items.

The retail prices are also compiled by the states to get the consumer price index numbers (the number of centres is more in this case than that used by the Labour Bureau). The data are collected at intervals of a week, fortnight, or month. The time reference specified for price collection varies from state to state. The weekly prices relate to a particular day of the week while the last day of the fortnight in the case of fortnightly prices. The monthly prices are the averages of the weekly prices. These data are published in the *Monthly Bulletin of Statistics, Season and Crop Report* or state gazettes of different states.

National Sample Survey on Rural Retail Prices

The NSSO has been collecting rural retail prices mainly from village markets since its 5th Round. A continuous series of commodity prices starting with the 11th Round of the survey and up to the 13th Round for rural and urban areas was presented in the Weekly Price Bulletins by the Indian Statistical Institute (ISI). The rural retail prices collected in the 14th, 15th and 16th Rounds of the surveys were presented in the draft Report Numbers 49 (1, 2, 3), 119, and 123, respectively. A set of 419 villages was selected in the 16th round of the survey for conducting the price enquiry, and since then these villages, named price villages, were kept fixed till the 41st Round (1984–5). The collection of price data for the new commodity basket is now being done every month from a fixed set of 603 villages–markets spread over 21 states using schedule 3.01(R). At present the number of states has increased to 24 including 3 newly created states, although the number of markets and items remain the same.

Along with the price data, the daily wage rates of 18 major agricultural and non-agricultural occupations are also being collected in Schedule 3.01(R). This provides an alternative series of wage–rate data, as compared to that being brought out by the DES, MOAFW. The NSSO data has advantage over the DES data because of its uniform method of data collection, reporting, and classification which enables inter-state comparison and comparison over time.

The Data Processing Division (DPD) is now using a fully computerized system, developed by the software group of DPD (HQ), for processing the price data, 3.01(R) of the new series.

The processed data of the price schedule are disseminated through the quarterly publication *Prices and Wages in Rural India* (new series). The bulletin provides price data only at the national level and wage data at the national and state levels for 14 major states. The monthly averages are not provided for the items for which less than ten quotations are received. However, for all the items, quarterly averages are given in the bulletin.

In addition to the rural retail prices, the NSSO was collecting prices from 59 urban centres. These prices were utilized by the Central Statistical Office (CSO) for the compilation of consumer price index numbers for non-manual workers. These prices were collected every month from a fixed sample of outlets. Selection of markets and shops in different centres and the method of collection of prices are similar to that of rural areas. Now it is discontinued.

With the introduction of price index numbers for rural and urban areas, the field operation division of the NSSO is collecting prices from selected towns and department of posts from selected villages (for details see the chapter on index numbers).

The retail prices, like the wholesale prices, are collected by the Department of Consumer Affairs by the same method across the same centres.

Farm Harvest Prices

(1) Farm harvest price of a commodity is defined as the average wholesale price at which the commodity is disposed of by the producer to the trader at the village site during the specified marketing period after the commencement of harvest.

(2) The following procedure is followed for systematizing the collection and compilation of these statistics:

   (a) A certain number of representative villages are selected in each district at the rate of one, two, or three villages from each tehsil, depending upon the extent to which the crop is grown in the tehsil. The total number of villages to be selected in each district should, however, not be less than 10.

   (b) In each selected village, the price at which the commodity is sold by the producer is recorded in the specified form by the price reporter on every Friday during the peak period of marketing after the commencement of the harvesting season. If no sales take place on that Friday, the price at which the commodity was sold last during the week is recorded instead.

(c) In cases where village site transactions do not take place, the price reported relates to what the farmer receives for his produce, and is obtained by subtracting transport and other marketing charges from the wholesale prices quoted at the mandi where produce is disposed of.

(d) The price recorded is the wholesale price of the specified variety of the commodity and is expressed in terms of rupees and paisa per quintal (net weight) exclusive of gunny bags/container.

(3) The existence of different varieties and qualities of commodities with a wide variation in prices makes the task of giving a single harvest price for a commodity for the state as a whole difficult. In each district, however, it may be possible to determine a particular variety which is grown to the largest extent, and that variety is specified for the purpose of noting the farm harvest prices. In some cases, it may be necessary to give the farm harvest prices of two varieties separately if the difference in price is large, as for instance, in the case of prices of American and indigenous cotton.

(4) It is also necessary to fix the reference period of harvest and the subsequent peak period of marketing for each crop, as these tend to vary widely depending upon the variety of the crop and the nature of cultivation. In some cases, it is even difficult to define strictly the harvesting period, as for instance, in the case of cotton where there are more than four pickings in a year. These periods, however, are fixed in respect of each crop and each state by the state governments having due regard to the local conditions. Usually, in case of most commodities, six-to-eight weeks during the peak period of marketing after the commencement of the harvest season is taken to be the period during which farmers are generally expected to dispose of their produce.

(5) The method of arriving at the average price of a commodity for the state as a whole is the method of weighted average, with the district production figures for the concerned year as weights. However, the average price for the district for each week may be obtained as a simple arithmetic average of the tehsil prices which in turn, are the simple arithmetic average of village prices.

The average price for the season is the simple arithmetic average of the district prices for each commodity. The computation of the district average price is done at the district headquarters while the prices for the state as a whole are worked out at state headquarters.

(6) The farm harvest prices are required to be collected in respect of all the important crops and, in any case, they are required to be submitted for all the forecast crops. As the final estimate of every crop is published at least one month after the completion of harvesting, it may be feasible to get the farm harvest prices ready by the time of the final estimate.

These prices are published in the *Farm Harvest Prices of Principal Crops in India* for 34 commodities. These are based on the information sent by all states and five UTs. Minimum support prices of selected crops announced by the GoI for the corresponding years are also given in this publication.

Bibliography

Directorate of Economics and Statistics. *Weekly Bulletin of Food Items, Retail Price*. New Delhi: Ministry of Agriculture, Government of India. Available at http://rpms.dacnet.nic.in/Reports.aspx (accessed on 16 May 2017).

———. *Monthly Bulletin of Non-food Items, Retail Price*. New Delhi: Ministry of Agriculture, Government of India. Available at http://rpms.dacnet.nic.in/Reports.aspx (accessed on 16 May 2017).

———. Various Years. *Retail Price Information System*. Available at http://rpms.dacnet.nic.in/Reports.aspx (accessed on 16 May 2017).

Ministry of Agriculture. 2013. *Agricultural Prices in India* New Delhi: Government of India

———. Various months. *Agricultural Situation in India*. New Delhi: Government of India.

———. 2013–14. *Farm Harvest Prices of Principal Crops in India* New Delhi: Government of India.

Ministry of Statistics and Programme Implementation. 2013. *Prices and Wages in Rural India* (Quarterly, March 2013). New Delhi: Government of India.

Price Monitoring Cell of the Department of Consumers Affairs. Various Years. Available at http://consumeraffairs.nic.in/forms/contentpage.aspx?lid=610 (accessed on 16 May 2017).

11

Index Numbers

An index number may be defined as a device for measuring the magnitude of relative changes in a group of distinct but related variables. The changes may be in prices of different commodities or in the physical quantities of the good produced. The comparisons may be done between different time periods, between different places or between similar categories. The most common indices are, however, prepared to compare the different time periods.

Uses of Index Numbers

The construction of index numbers facilitates in knowing the average changes with regard to a wide range of economic activities. The price index can be used for deflating a value series in order to know the real changes in the series, for example, a national income series at current prices may be deflated by using the relevant price indices to find out the real growth of the economy. These indices can also be used for analysing the price situation in the country. The cause of the price changes and their effect can also be studied. Consumer price index numbers are used in some cases for the wage adjustments. The quantity indices like those of industrial production, volume of employment, and physical volume of trade are useful for forecasting purposes. These can also be used to study the trends, seasonal variations, and business cycles in the series.

Construction of Index Numbers

The following steps are involved in the construction of index numbers: (i) defining the purpose of constructing the index numbers; (ii) items to be selected and collection of relevant data; (iii) the choice of the base period; and (iv) methods of combining data and choice of weights. These steps are discussed, briefly, in the following sections.

Purpose for which an Index Number is Constructed

In the beginning, the purpose of constructing the index number should be clearly and explicitly stated. The selection of items, the collection of data and the selection of formula will depend on the purpose. If the purpose is the construction of the cost of living index, the retail prices of the commodities constituting the major part of the family budget should be collected. Moreover the cost of living of different classes of people differs. If it is intended to compute the index for agricultural labourers, the retail prices should be collected from the markets popular among the agricultural class (that is, from the rural areas). Again if we are interested in knowing the index of the cost of construction of private buildings, the prices of heavy structural steel (which is not used for the purpose) should not be collected.

Selection of Items and Collection of Data

The next question is about the selection of items to be included in the index. All the component items cannot be included—there are numerous items of consumption—while constructing the cost of living index. The items to be included should be representative of the taste, customs, and habits of the people and should cover a major portion of the total expenditure.

The problem of the selection of items should be solved in stages. First, the whole group of commodities should be divided into a number of homogeneous sub-groups and then from each sub-group an adequate number of items should be selected.

For collection of data we may either depend on the published sources or obtain periodic reports from leading dealers, manufacturers, or others who have with them the required information.

Irrespective of the source, it must be seen that the data should strictly relate to the thing being measured, for example, for the construction of the general purpose wholesale price index (WPI), the wholesale prices should be collected. The data collected should be accurate, homogeneous, adequate, and the sample representative. The different places and the sources from which the quotations are collected must be comparable.

Choice of the Base Period

To make index numbers comparable, a base period has to be selected. Generally a period of one year is taken as the base. A period less than that is generally not considered appropriate because seasonal and other similar variations may be present in that period. Sometimes even a period of several years is taken as the base. The base period should be of economic stability, a period which is called a normal period and is not far away from the given period. If the base period is not normal the prices in that period may be low or high or the production may be less or more due to certain abnormal conditions. The comparisons of such a base with other periods may not be valid. Again if the base period is far away from the given period, the pattern of consumption or production may change considerably. New types of commodities may enter the markets, which are not comparable with the similar types used during the base period. Therefore, the base period should not be too distant from the given period. In case a continuous long series of index numbers is maintained the revision and shifting of the period to a more recent base should be considered from time to time.

Methods of Combining Data and Choice of Weights

There are two methods of constructing index numbers: by computing aggregate values and by averaging relatives. The two methods are described in the following paragraphs.

Aggregate Index Numbers

The aggregative values may be simple aggregates or the weighted aggregates. In the simple aggregative method (one of the least satisfactory methods) the prices of all commodities in any given year are merely added together and expressed as the percentage of the corresponding total of the base year prices to get the index number for that year. If p is the price index in period n as compared to the base, then $p = \Sigma p_{ni} / \Sigma p_{oi}$, where p_{ni} refers to the price of the ith commodity in the period n and p_{oi} to the price of the ith commodity in the base period (summation being over the number of commodities).

In non-weighted aggregate it is assumed that all commodities are equally important. In practice this is not so. A large price change in an unimportant commodity may be of less significance than a small change in an important one. It is, therefore, advisable to use weighted rather than simple aggregates of prices.

To construct an index number by the weighted aggregative method, definite quantities of commodities, included in the index are taken and valuations are done to find out the worth of this aggregate of commodities at the base as well as at the given period prices.

To construct an index number by the weighted aggregative method, definite quantities of commodities, included the index are taken and valuations are done to find out the worth of this aggregate of commodities at the base as well as at the given period prices as percentage of the corresponding value at the base period prices. In other words the weighted aggregative price index measures the changing cost of a fixed basket of goods. While the component quantities remain the same, the total cost or value changes. The changes in values must reflect the changes in prices. The formula for the weighted aggregative index p is given by:

$$P = \Sigma p_n q / \Sigma p_0 q,$$

where q refers to the set of quantities of the specified commodities and p_n and p_0 refer to the set of prices of those commodities in the period n and the base period respectively.

The problem arises regarding the period the quantities of which should be taken as weights. The quantities of the base period or the given period or any combination of the quantities of different periods can be taken for the purpose. If the proportionate change in the quantities of different commodities is same from period to period, the quantities of any period can be used. But in practice this is not so. The relative importance of commodities changes over time. This creates a difficulty for which no satisfactory solution exists. A number of formulas have been suggested to overcome this difficulty. Some of these are given as follows.

USE BASE-PERIOD QUANTITIES AS WEIGHTS

This method is known as Laspayre's method is defined as:

$$P = \Sigma p_n q_0 \,/\, \Sigma p_0 q_0,$$

where q_0 refers to the base period quantities. This method has an upward bias and gives the upper limit of the price change.

USE GIVEN-PERIOD QUANTITIES AS WEIGHTS

This method is known as Paasche's method and is defined as:

$$P = \Sigma p_n q_n \,/\, \Sigma p_0 q_n,$$

where q_0 refers to the quantities of the period for which the index number is computed. This method has a downward bias and gives the lower limit of the price change. In this method we have to select a new set of weights for every period. The construction of index numbers becomes a cumbersome process. Also, the comparison of different periods is not valid among themselves, because the aggregate of goods differs from period to period.

USE THE AVERAGE OF QUANTITIES OF THE BASE AND THE CURRENT PERIOD

This method is called the Marshal Edgeworth method and is defined as:

$$P = \Sigma p_n \,(q_0 + q_n) \,/\, \Sigma p_0 \,(q_0 + q_n).$$

It is a compromise formula, although in this case the direction of the bias cannot be ascertained like Paasche's method, but here also the weights have to be selected afresh for every period and the comparison between different periods is not valid.

AVERAGE OF QUANTITIES FOR ALL THE PERIODS WHICH THE INDEX NUMBER INCLUDES

This formula for this type of index number is:

$$P = \Sigma p_n \,(q_0 + q_1 + \ldots + q_n) \,/\, \Sigma p_0 \,(q_0 + q_1 + \ldots. + q_n).$$

This index is good for historical studies but difficult to use if a continuous series of index numbers is to be maintained.

AVERAGE THE QUANTITIES OF SEVERAL PERIODS WHICH ARE CONSIDERED TYPICAL

This is again a compromise formula. This is a practicable and is adopted in some cases. After some time the list of quantities used will, however, become obsolete. When that is the case, a new index can be constructed and the old can be discarded.

KEYNES METHOD

Keynes suggested that the quantities common either to the base and the given period or to all the periods under comparison should be taken as weights. The formula can be written as:

$$P = \Sigma p_n q \text{ H.C.F.} / \Sigma p_0 q \text{ H.C.F.}.$$

IDEAL INDEX NUMBERS

This formula was suggested by I. Fisher and is defined as:

$$P = \sqrt{(\Sigma p_n q_o / p_0 q_0) \times (\Sigma p_n q_n / \Sigma p_0 q_n)}.$$

This index is called an ideal index. This index is the geometric mean of the Laspayre's ad the purchase's indices. This index confirms to certain mathematical tests (described in the later paragraphs). But it is difficult to find out what such an index number measures.

AVERAGE OF PRICE RELATIVES

In this method the price of each commodity of a given period is first expressed as a ratio of the corresponding price in the base period (called price relative). The index number is obtained by taking the average of the price relatives. The averages can be either simple or weighted. In case of weighted averages, the weights are the values (as against quantities in the case of aggregative method).

It can be shown that the weighted index prepared by the method of price relatives with the values of the base period as weights is the same as the weighted index prepared by the aggregative method with base period quantities as weightsin

$$P = \Sigma[(p_n / p_0)\ (p_0 q_0)] / \Sigma p_0 q_0 = \Sigma p_n q_0 / \Sigma p_0 q_0.$$

Similarly it can be shown that the weighted arithmetic average of the price relatives, with the product of the given period quantities and the base period prices as the weights, is equal to weighted index obtained by the aggregative method, with the given period quantities as weights.

Under various situations it is necessary to calculate index numbers by averaging price relatives, for example, when a general index is to be prepared from the price relatives (or index numbers) of different groups, the price relative for each group is weighted by the value of that group. It is difficult to work out such an index by the method of aggregating values. Also, when we want to substitute a commodity for the one formerly used, the relative for the old commodity may be replaced by the relative for the new commodity, using the old value weights.

QUANTITY INDEX NUMBERS

A quantity index is the counterpart of the corresponding price index. It measures the changing value of a varying aggregate of goods at fixed prices. The construction of a simple aggregative quantity index is not feasible unless all the quantities can be expressed in the same unit. The weighted quantity indices can be worked out by applying various methods of weighting discussed under the price indices. The weights used for these indices are prices and values in case of aggregative method and the averages of relative method respectively.

CHAIN INDEX

Over a number of years, various changes take place; old commodities disappear and new ones enter the market. Under such circumstances it becomes desirable to calculate the index numbers by the chain base method. Under this method, the index number of each period is obtained with the preceding period as the base. These indices are then chained together by successive multiplication to get the chain index. Thus if I_{rs} represents the index with r as the base period and s

as the given period, then the index number I_{0n} is calculated by using the relation:

$$I_{0n} = I_{01} \times I_{12} \times I_{23} \ldots I_{n-1} \times I_n.$$

The main advantage of this index is that the old commodities can be readily dropped and the new ones introduced. The weights can also be easily changed. The main disadvantage of this index is that while period to period comparisons are accurate, the long-term comparisons may not be strictly valid.

Mathematical Tests of Index Numbers

TIME REVERSAL TEST

This test is based on the logic that an index number should work both backwards and forwards. If P_{0n} is the index in the period *n* with period zero as the base and P_{n0} is the index in the period zero with period *n* as the base then:

$$P_{0n} \times P_{n0} = 1.$$

One index should be the reciprocal of the other. This test is satisfied by the Marshall Edgeworth's and Fisher's indices.

FACTOR REVERSAL TEST

A price index when multiplied by an index of quantity with the same base and the given period and by using the same formula should be equal to the value index. If P_{0n} is the price index for the *n*th period with base as period zero, Q_{0n} is the corresponding quantity index and $V_{0n} = \Sigma p_n q_n / \Sigma p_0 q_0$ is the corresponding value index. Then $V_{0n} / Q_{0n} P_{0n}$ should be equal to one.

Only the Fisher's index satisfies this test. This index is called an ideal index because both the aforementioned tests are satisfied.

PURCHASING POWER INDEX

Generally the reciprocal of a price index is taken to be the index of the purchasing power of money. But this is not correct. As for constructing a price index, the price changes of specific commodities are averaged; similarly, for constructing an index of purchasing power, the changes in the purchasing power of the rupee for specific commodities should be taken. For example:

$$P_{0n} = \Sigma(U_n / U_0) \times (p_0 q_0) / \Sigma p_0 q_0,$$

where U_n and U_0 are the purchasing power per rupee in the current and the base periods respectively and the summation is over commodities. Since $U = 1 / p\ P_{0n}$ can be written as:

$$P_{0n} = \Sigma(P_0 / P_n) \times (P_0 Q_0) / \Sigma p_0 q_0.$$

This is reciprocal of the harmonic mean of the price relatives weighted by the base year values. This can be shown as follows:

$$1 / \Sigma(1 / p_n / p_0)(p_0 q_0) / \Sigma p_0 q_0 = 1 / \Sigma p_0 / p_n p_0 q_0 / \Sigma p_0 q_0 = \Sigma p_0 q_0 / \Sigma p_0 / p_0 (p_0 q_0).$$

That shows that Ferger's formula is still the reciprocal of a price index, though not the usual price index based on the arithmetic average.

In the earlier paragraphs, different general problems regarding construction of index numbers have been discussed and different formulas have been listed. Among these formulas, Laspayer's formula is widely used, because this involves the calculation of weights for different commodities for the base year only. These weights can be used to get the index numbers for different years. By using any other formula the weights have to be calculated for all the years for which the index numbers are to be constructed. Some of the important index numbers compiled in India along with the method and sources of compilation are discussed in the following sections.

Price Indices

Wholesale Prices Index Numbers

The index numbers are compiled by the Office of the Economic Adviser (OEA), Ministry of Commerce and Industry. The first all-India WPI numbers were compiled with the week ending 19 August 1939 as the base. These index numbers are available with effect from the week ending 19 September 1931, although on a weekly basis, they were published by the OEA from the week commencing from 10 January 1942. The index was based on 23 commodities and 46 quotations divided into the following four groups: (i) food and tobacco; (ii) agricultural commodities; (iii) raw materials; and (iv) manufactured articles.

The non-weighted geometric average of the price relatives of 23 commodities was used for the compilation of this index. The compilation of this index was discontinued in December 1947. The OEA started compilation of a new index for food articles in 1945 with the last week of August 1939 as base. The index was compiled as a weighted geometric mean of the price relatives, the weights being proportional to the value of the marketable surplus of the various commodities during the year 1938–9. This series was subsequently expanded to replace the earlier index of wholesale prices and in 1947 another weekly general purpose index with the year ending August 1939 as the base was started. The index covered 78 commodities having 215 quotations. The weights were assigned on the basis of the marketed value of each commodity in 1938–9. The simple geometric average of the price relatives of different quotations of a commodity gave the commodity index. The group indices as well as the overall index were compiled by using the weighted geometric average. The monthly and annual indices were compiled from weekly and monthly indices respectively by using geometric averages. The weekly publication *Index Numbers of Wholesale Prices in India* contained information regarding price relatives and also the prices of the various commodities at different centres of the country.

After the Partition, the need was felt to revise the index in the light of major changes in the economic structure. The revised index was started from April 1956. This weekly index covered 112 commodities having 555 quotations. The base year of this index was 1952–3. The weighted arithmetic average was introduced for the compilation of the index. The weights assigned to different commodities were based on the estimates of the marketed value of domestic produce and value of imports inclusive of duties. In the case of manufactures, the weights were the gross value of products taken from the Census of Indian Manufactures, 1948 added by the imports during that year.

With regard to intermediate products, only the portion produced for sale was taken into account. For the food group, only marketed surplus and imports were taken. The base year for weights and prices were different for these indices. The general index and the indices for the following groups were compiled: (i) food articles; (ii) liquor and tobacco; (iii) fuel power, light, and lubricants; (iv) industrial raw materials; and (v) manufactured articles classified into intermediate products and finished products.

Monthly and annual indices were compiled as averages of weekly and monthly indices respectively and were published in the monthly and annual *Statistical Abstract of India* respectively.

This series was replaced by a series of index numbers with base 1961–2. This series covered 139 commodities having 774 quotations divided into seven groups. The two extra groups were those of chemicals and machinery and transport equipment which were separated from manufactures. The other four groups were not changed. As in the series with 1952–3 as base, the weights assigned to the new series were also based on the estimates of the marketed value of domestic produce added by the value of imports inclusive of duties. In the case of manufactured articles the gross value of products was taken from the *Annual Survey of Industries* (*ASI*), 1961. In cases where the production was not available from the *ASI*, it was taken from the Annual report of the Directorate General of Technical Development (DGTD). For intermediate goods, the portion produced for sale was taken. For agricultural items, the value of output was obtained on the basis of the quantity and price data available with the Directorate of Economic and Statistics (DES) of the Ministry of Agriculture and Farmer's Welfare (MOAFW). To arrive at the marketed surplus, the retention rates were supplied by the office of Agricultural Marketing Adviser. In the case of cotton, sugarcane, and cotton yarn, the quantities used by the mills only were taken into account. The weight for electricity was based on the energy sold by electricity undertakings and valued at the average all-India rate. Weights in the case of petroleum products were based on consumption figures. The method used for the compilation of commodity indices, group indices, and the general index was the same as that for the series with 1952–3 as base.

The base years of the index numbers were changed again to 1970–1, 1981–82, 1993–4, and the present base is 2004–5.[1] There has been a significant increase in number of items and price quotations for each item, particularly in the manufacturing segment to not only better reflect the structural shifts but also to make the WPI more broad based.

A comparison of the number of items and price quotations at the level of the groups in the series with base 1970–1 onwards are presented in Table 11.1.

The following points may be noted:

(1) **Concept of wholesale price:** The concept of wholesale price has hitherto covered the general idea of capturing all transactions carried out in the domestic market. The weights of the WPI do not correspond to contribution of the goods concerned either to value added or final use. In order to give this idea a more precise definition, it is decided to define the universe of the wholesale price index in the latest series as comprising as far as possible all transactions at first point of bulk sale in the domestic market.

(2) **Treatment of export and import:** In the 1993–4 series, the traded value (used for derivation of weighting diagram) was computed by subtracting exports from the domestic production and adding imports to the domestic production (production + import – export). This method of computing the traded value had an inherent bias since all exports are not necessarily direct exports without getting traded in the economy. The working group on the series with base 2004–5, therefore, decided that while computing the domestically traded value, only the direct export from the factories should be excluded. Similarly, import of goods which reach the factory directly (without being traded in the economy) should not be added to domestic production.

(3) **Method of selection of products in the manufactured group:** The manufactured product basket in the 1993–4 series included all such products with traded value of Rs 120 crore or above. This led to poor representation of products in some of the

[1] This index was revised to base year 2011–12 in May 2017.

Table 11.1 Comparative Statement of Commodities and Price Quotations

Major group/group	Number of Commodities				Number of Price Quotations			
	1970–1	1981–2	1993–4	2004–5	1970–1	1981–2	1993–4	2004–5
All commodities	360	447	435	676	1,295	2,371	1,918	5,482
Primary articles	80	93	98	102	411	519	455	579
Food articles	39	44	54	55	264	320	340	431
Non-food articles	26	28	25	29	115	132	96	108
Minerals	15	21	19	18	32	67	19	40
Fuel and power	10	20	19	19	30	73	72	72
Manufactured products	270	334	318	555	854	1,779	1,391	4,831
Food products	37	35	41	57	117	231	168	406
Beverages, tobacco, and tobacco products	8	7	11	15	19	39	49	102
Textiles	12	27	29	55	99	120	100	457
Wood and wood products	4	2	2	10	13	14	9	64
Paper and paper products	4	11	11	18	16	74	67	138
Leather and leather products	4	3	1	13	18	26	9	91
Rubber and plastic products	7	13	15	45	42	73	55	351
Chemicals and chemical products	67	77	69	107	182	428	276	1,111
Non-metallic mineral products	21	22	9	26	63	125	42	225
Basic metals, alloys, and metal products	42	57	53	69	125	235	203	696
Machinery and machine tools	35	44	56	107	104	266	312	903
Transport equipments and parts	21	22	21	33	39	118	101	287

Source: Department of Industrial Policy and Promotion (DIPP) (2008).

product groups. In order to remove the anomaly in a selection method based on a uniform cut-off criterion and make the method of selection more representative, the working group decided to adopt a method in which each product group in the manufactured basket gets represented by such number of items which together cover at least 80 per cent of the traded value at the group level.

(4) **Treatment of crude oil:** In the 1981–2 series, crude petroleum was included as an independent item in the mineral group of the major group primary articles. However, in the 1993–4 series, the crude petroleum was taken away from the mineral group as an independent item and its value was apportioned parametrically among the items in the mineral fuel group of the major group fuel and power. The analytical sub-group of the working group for the new series observed that the prices of crude petroleum could now be collected from the open market which is interlinked with international market. Further, the existing practice of imputing crude oil weight to petroleum products leads to an upward bias in fuel and power group index apart from the fact that the movement of crude oil prices and the prices of petroleum products may not be similar due to 'pass-on' lag.

(5) **Weighting diagram:** The weighting diagram for the new WPI series has been derived on the basis of gross value of output (GVO). The output values at current prices, wherever available at appropriate disaggregation level, have been obtained from the National Accounts Statistics (NAS) (2007) published by the Central Statistical Office (CSO), Ministry of Statistics and Programme Implementation (MOSPI). The same have been reallocated and aggregated to conform to the structure of WPI basket. A detailed methodology of assigning weights was also included in the report of the working group. The specific group-wise approach for allocation of weights has been as follows:

   (a) **Primary Articles:** In the case of agricultural and related commodities, the average value of output for the triennium ending 2005–6 (that is, 2003–4, 2004–5, and 2005–6) has been derived by using the value of output at current prices for the relevant years obtained from the *National Accounts Statistics 2012* (Statements 55 and 56).

The Marketed Surplus Ratios (MSRs) were supplied by the Sub-group on Agricultural Commodities, which computed the MSRs for the agricultural and related commodities for the base year 2000–1, initially considered by the working group. The MSRs have been used for deriving the value of marketed output for the agricultural and related commodities for the base year 2004–5, as it was felt that the MSRs are unlikely to undergo any significant change within a short span of three to four years.

(b) **Minerals:** Minerals is a group under the major group primary articles. The value of output of minerals other than crude petroleum has been taken from the *National Accounts Statistics 2012* (Statement 59). Crude petroleum has also been now been shifted to 'minerals' in the revised series. The output value of domestically produced crude petroleum has been taken from the Indian Bureau of Mines (IBM) and has been added to the value of output of minerals other than crude to arrive at the total value of output of minerals in the new WPI basket. The value of imported crude has not been taken into account while deriving the weighting diagram for the crude petroleum on the ground that crude is not traded as such in the domestic market and its derivatives are already included in the basket as independent items in the major group fuel and power.

(c) **Fuel minerals:** The value of output for fuel minerals—that is, coal, coke, and lignite—has been taken from *National Accounts Statistics 2012* (Statement 59). The export and import figures for fuel minerals have been taken from the Office of the Coal Controller, Kolkata, West Bengal. As in case of minerals (except crude petroleum), the imported fuel minerals are taken as traded in the domestic market and the export of such minerals are taken as direct exports from the mines for estimation of traded value figures for the fuel minerals.

(d) **Mineral oils**: The value of mineral oils as a group as well as item-wise values of important mineral oils—such as petrol, diesel, naphtha, liquefied petroleum gas (LPG), kerosene, and lubricants—are not available in *National Accounts Statistics 2012*. The Ministry of Petroleum has made available the sales figures of the mineral oils by different oil companies for the year 2004–5. The ministry has also provided the import and export figures for 2004–5 for such items. While computing the traded value of the items in the mineral oils group, the value of imports have not been included as the import figures are already included in the sales figures. It has been taken that the imported mineral oils are traded in the domestic market. The export of mineral oils has been treated as direct export for estimation of traded value figures for mineral oils and therefore subtracted from the sales value of the mineral oils to arrive at the traded value for mineral oils.

(e) **Electricity:** The quantum and value of output of electricity generated and as used by different sectors—that is, agriculture, industry, domestic, commercial, and railways traction—in the year 2004–5 was supplied by Central Electricity Authority (CEA) to the OEA. The value of generation of electricity has been used for derivation of weight for the electricity group and the item level weights have been derived by distributing parametrically the group level weight amongst different sectors of use as per the quantum of generated electricity used by these sectors.

(f) **Manufactured Products:** The *National Accounts Statistics 2012* provides the National Industrial Classification (NIC) 2-digit group-wise output figures for 2004–5 both for the registered (Statement 61) and unregistered (Statement 62-a) manufacturing sector. Necessary adjustments have been done in NIC group level output figures to arrive at the group level output figures for the 12 product groups of the manufactured products major group of the WPI basket. Adjustments were required in the NAS group level output figures for a few groups to harmonize it with the WPI manufactured product grouping.

The group-wise combined registered and unregistered manufacturing figures have been adjusted for import and direct export figures to arrive at the traded value figures in respect of each of the 12 groups. The group-level weights, derived on the basis of respective traded value figures, have been distributed pro-rata amongst the items covered in the respective groups, as per the output figures of such items obtained from *ASI* data/Office of the Development Commissioner, Small Scale Industries (DC-SSI).

(6) **Assignment of Weights:** The weights have been assigned on the basis of entire wholesale transactions in the economy. Table 11.2 presents a comparative picture of weights.

(7) **Seasonal Items:** There are a number of agricultural commodities, especially, some fruits and vegetables which are seasonal in their availability and whose prices are quoted only during a particular period of the year. Such seasonal items are handled in the index in a special manner. When a particular seasonal item disappears from the market and its prices cease to get quoted, the index for such an item ceases to be compiled and its weight is distributed over the remaining items within the concerned subgroup on a pro-rata basis. This system has been in practice in all the previous series and will be continued in the revised series also with a clear delineation of the specific period during which the index of a particular seasonal item will be compiled.

(8) **Other Methodological Changes:** The series of WPI with base year 1993–4 had included the public distribution system (PDS) price quotations for wheat and rice. The working group was of the opinion that since they did not represent the first point of sale, these may not be included. In view of this it was decided to include the procurement prices of paddy and wheat, which in a way represent the first point of sale in the price quotations for wheat and rice.

Since October 2009, release of WPI has been changed from weekly to monthly as per decision taken by Cabinet Committee on Economic Affairs (CCEA). However, WPI for primary articles and fuel and power continues to be released on a weekly basis.

In a bid to narrow the gap between provisional and final data, the DIPP has revised the base year for computing the WPI, the key inflation gauge for the country. The base year was changed to 2011–12 from 2004–5 in May 2017.

The DIPP has also replaced conventional manual collection and sourcing of data to improve the response rate and time lag in the

Table 11.2 Comparative Statement of Weights Assigned to Product Groups

Major Group/Group	1970–1	1981–2	1993–4	2004–5
All commodities	**100**	**100**	**100**	**100**
Primary articles	**41.667**	**32.295**	**22.025**	**20.118**
Food articles	29.799	17.386	15.402	14.337
Non-food articles	10.621	10.081	6.138	4.258
Minerals	1.247	4.823	0.485	1.521
Fuel and power	**8.459**	**10.663**	**14.226**	**14.91**
Coal		1.256	1.753	2.094
Mineral oils		6.666	6.987	9.364
Electricity		2.741	5.484	3.452
Manufactured products	**49.874**	**57.042**	**63.749**	**64.972**
Food products	13.322	10.143	11.538	9.974
Beverages, tobacco	2.708	2.149	1.339	1.762
Textiles	11.026	11.545	9.8	7.326
Wood and wood products	0.174	1.198	0.173	0.587
Paper and paper products	0.851	1.988	2.044	2.034
Leather and leather products	0.385	1.018	1.019	0.835
Rubber and plastic products	1.207	1.592	2.388	2.987
Chemicals and chemical products	5.548	7.355	11.931	12.018
Non-metallic mineral products	1.415	2.477	2.516	2.556
Basic metals, alloys, and metal products	5.974	7.632	8.342	10.748
Machinery and machine tools	5.045	6.268	8.363	8.931
Transport equipments and parts	1.673	2.705	4.295	5.213
Other industries	0.546	0.972	0	0

Source: DIPP (2008).

WPI. After mandating online data reporting for the WPI, the CSO found that the response rate jumped to 80 per cent, a 30 per cent growth. It is now trying to implement a similar system for the index of industrial production (IIP), which measures industrial activity in the country.

Consumer Price Index Numbers

The following different series of consumer price index (CPI) numbers are compiled at the all-India level: (i) CPI numbers for industrial workers; (ii) CPI numbers for non-manual workers; (iii) CPI numbers for agricultural labourers; and (iv) CPI numbers for rural and urban areas and for all India (rural + urban).

Consumer Price Index Number for Industrial Workers

The Labour Bureau started compiling an interim series of all-India working class CPI numbers, with 1949 as base. The all-India index was obtained as a weighted arithmetic average of consumer price indices for 27 centres out of which the indices for 15 centres were compiled by the Labour Bureau and for 12 by different state governments. These indices were being compiled with different base periods. For the construction of all-India index these were first shifted to 1949 as the base by the mathematical conversion. The weights used for the construction of all-India index were in proportion to the factory employment in different centres in 1949.

During 1958–9 fresh family living surveys (FLS) were conducted among working class population at 50 important factories, mining and plantations centres. These surveys were meant to provide the weights for different commodities consumed in a centre for the compilation of the index for the centre. The data collected during the surveys related to income, expenditure and demographic particulars, education, working conditions, and housing conditions, among others. Only manual workers employed in factories, mines, and plantations were covered. The surveys covered 23,400 families in 50 centres. On the basis of the results of these family surveys, the Labour Bureau started compiling 50 new series of CPI of the working class. For each centre about 100 items divided into six groups were taken for the compilation of the index. The year 1960 was, uniformly, the base year for all the centres. The indices were based on the weighted arithmetic average of the price relatives of different items, with the expenditure on different commodities during the year 1958–9 as weights. For these indices the base for weights and prices were different. The index numbers for different centres were published regularly since December 1962 by the Labour Bureau in the monthly publication *Indian Labour Journal*. An all-India general index and group indices were issued since October 1968. Previous to that only the interim all-India index used to be compiled. The all-India index for a particular group is the weighted arithmetic average of centre indices for the group, the weights being the consumption expenditure of the industrial workers, on that group during 1958–9. The general all-India index is the weighted arithmetic average of the general centre indices with the weights being the aggregate consumption expenditure of industrial workers of different centres.

Working-class family income and expenditure surveys were again conducted during the year 1971 in 60 centres. However, the results of these surveys were not utilized for constructing CPI.

These surveys were again conducted during 1981–2 in 76 centres for calculation of the all-India CPI numbers. Only 70 centres were taken, which formed the basis for construction of CPI with base 1982 = 100.

Under the 1960 series of CPI numbers for industrial workers, the coverage of industrial workers was limited to three sectors, that is, factories, mines, and plantations. The coverage of the industrial workers for the 1982 series for the conduct of FLS was extended to seven sectors by including four more sectors, namely, (i) railways; (ii) public motor transport undertakings; (iii) electricity generation and distribution establishments; and (iv) ports and docks.

WEIGHTING DIAGRAM

The total expenditure on consumption items was divided into six main groups, namely (i) food; (ii) *pan*, *supari*, tobacco, and intoxicants; (iii) fuel and light; (iv) housing; (v) clothing, bedding, and footwear; and (vi) miscellaneous. In the first and the last group, a few well-defined sub-groups were also formed.

For compiling housing index, the rent paid for rented, self-owned, and rent-free houses were taken into account. For compiling the housing group index, three separate indices were compiled for rent-free, rented, and self-owned houses and these indices were combined by using their respective weights, which were the proportion of families residing in these three categories of houses, to work out the weighted housing index for the centre. Housing index was compiled by following the chain base method, once in every six months—namely January and July—and kept constant for the subsequent five months. Rental data, utilized in the compilation of housing index, are collected by the field officials of the Labour Bureau, twice a year, from a sample of dwellings through a half-yearly Repeat House Rent Survey.

The series (1982 = 100) had replaced the old (1960 = 100) series in December 1988 with the release of the October 1988 index. This series was for 70 centres.

The series with 1982 = 100 has again been replaced by a series with 2000–1 = 100. Under the 2001 = 100 series, the Labour Bureau has been compiling CPI numbers for industrial workers for 78 selected centres and all-India index on the basis of 78 constituent centres as against 70 centres in the 1982 series. These 78 centres were selected on the basis of their industrial importance in the country and distributed among different states in proportion to the industrial employment in the state subject to a maximum allotment of five centres in a state in a sector.

The weighting diagram for the current series and series with base 1982 = 100 are given in Table 11.3.

The food group is divided into eight sub-groups, namely cereals and cereal products; pulses and pulse products; oils and fats; meat, fish, and eggs; milk and milk products; condiments and spices; vegetables and fruits; and other food. The miscellaneous group, which is used as a proxy for obtaining service price inflation, is divided

Table 11.3 Comparative Weighting Diagram at the Group Level for the All-India Index

S.No.	Group	Base 1982	Base 2001
1	Food	57	46.19
2	Pan, supari, tobacco, and intoxicants	3.15	2.27
3	Fuel and light	6.28	6.43
4	Housing	8.67	15.27
5	Clothing, bedding, and footwear	8.54	6.58
6	Miscellaneous	16.36	23.26
	Grand Total	100	100

Source: Ministry of Labour and Employment (2011).

into five sub-groups, namely medical care, education, recreation and amusement, transport and communication, personal care and effects, and others. The number of items directly retained in the index has increased to 392 items as against 280 items in the 1982 series.

The centre weights are determined as the ratio of product of average consumption expenditure per family and the number of working class families in a centre to sum of such products over all the centres. Each centre is assumed to have an equal share of the number of working-class families within the state, if the actual working class population for a particular centre exceeds the proportionate share accruing to the centre, the actual population of the centre is taken to determine its share and reminder of the working class population in the state as a whole is distributed equally amongst remaining centres in the state.

Non-Manual Workers

Since 1961, the CSO had been regularly compiling CPI numbers for urban non-manual employees for 45 selected urban centres in the country, as also for all of India, with a view to depicting changes in the level of average retail prices of goods and services consumed by this segment of population. The weights for calculation of the index were based on the data thrown up by FLS, designated as Middle Class Family Living Survey conducted in 1958–9, in each of the 45 selected urban centres covering about 36,000 families deriving the major portion of their income from non-manual occupations in the non-agricultural sector. Only the general indices are published for different centres and on all-India basis in the *Monthly Abstract of Statistics* published by the CSO.

The retail prices for selected items of goods and services collected by the National Statistical Survey Office (NSSO) from selected markets/outlets patronized by this segment of population had been utilized for compiling the index.

The index was later revised to base 1984–5. Some details of the index are given as follows.

WEIGHTING DIAGRAM

The source of weights for this series was an FLS conducted during 1982–3 in 59 selected urban centres in the country. The survey covered

45,000 families of urban non-manual employees in 59 selected urban centres, which derived 50 per cent or more of their income from gainful non-manual employment on occupations of one or more of its members in the non-agriculture sector. The average monthly consumer expenditure data obtained from the FLS were utilized in deriving the weighting diagrams, which indicate the percentage share of expenditure of an average family on each of the items in the consumption basket. For preparation of the weighting diagram, all the goods and services featuring in the budget of an average family have been classified and arranged into different sub-groups and groups on the basis of the proportion of expenditure.

In case of certain sub-groups like fruits and vegetables, further disaggregation into sections was made and the corresponding weights were computed. The classification of items into sub-groups and groups corresponds to the one followed in the 1960 base CPI for urban non-manual employee (UNME). The groups are as follows:

- Group 1: Food, beverages, and tobacco: (i) cereals and products; (ii) pulses and products; (iii) oils and fats; (iv) meat, fish, and eggs; (v) milk and products; (vi) condiments and spices; (vii) vegetables; (viii) fruits; (ix) sugar, honey, and others; (x) non-alcoholic beverages; (xi) prepared meals and refreshments; and (xii) pan, supari, tobacco, and others.
- Group 2: Fuel and light;
- Group 3: Housing;
- Group 4: Clothing, bedding, and footwear: (i) clothing and bedding; (ii) footwear;
- Group 5: Miscellaneous: (i) medical care; (ii) education; (iii) recreation and amusement; (iv) transport and communication; (v) personal care and effects; (vi) household requisites; (vii) others.

RELEASE OF INDEX

The index for UNMEs (referred to as CPI [UNME]) is released every month on the 15th or the next working day. As per the standard data dissemination system (SDDS) of the International Monetary Fund (IMF), the index for a month is released on the first working day on or after 15th of the following month. A six-monthly brochure giving CPI (UNME) at group and sub-group levels for all the

59 urban centres and for all India is also brought out in a consolidated form. The brochure relates to the period January to June and July to December.

The National Statistical Commission (NSC) in its meeting held on 15 February 2008 decided the following:

(1) It decided to (i) discontinue the CPI (UNME); (ii) adopt a link index, based on the ratio method after aggregating the sub-group level indices of the Labour Bureau's CPI (industrial workers) using CPI (UNME) weights at group/sub-group level for all India; and (iii) compile linked CPI (UNME) numbers till new series of CPI (urban) is brought out.
(2) Based on the methodology given by the NSC, the ratio of CPI (UNME) numbers to CPI (Industrial Workers) numbers for each of the 24 months for the two-year period from January 2006 to December 2007 at the sub-group level have been worked out. The average ratio at each level based on the 24-month figure is taken as the linking factor at the respective level. The CPI (UNME) weights have been used to get the indices at the group and all group levels.
(3) Price collection for CPI (UNME) has been discontinued with effect from April 2008. As decided by the NSC, linked all-India CPI (UNME) numbers of the month of April 2010 are given in Table 11.4 to meet the requirement of users.

Consumer Price Index Numbers for Agricultural and Rural Labourers

This section looks at the CPI numbers for (i) agricultural labourers; and (ii) rural labourers on base 1986–7 = 100.

INTRODUCTION

The Labour Bureau has been compiling CPI numbers for agricultural labourers since September 1964. The existing series of CPI Numbers for (i) agricultural; and (ii) rural labourers (base 1986–7 = 100) replaced the earlier series on base 1960–1 = 100 with effect from November 1995. For compilation of these index numbers, the field operations division (FOD) of the NSSO collects the data every month on prices from 600 sample villages selected from 20 states.

Table 11.4 Linked All-India CPI (UNME) on Base 1984–5 = 100 for April 2010

Group	UNME Weight	Linked Index for April 2010	Index for April 2009	Percentage Change
I. Food, beverages, tobacco	47.13	691	602	14.8
II. Fuel and light	5.48	655	625	4.8
III. Housing	16.41	775	582	33.2
IV. Cloth, bedding and footwear	7.03	494	471	4.9
V. Miscellaneous	23.95	599	568	5.5
General index (all groups)	100.00	667	583	14.4

Source: Release of linked CPI (UNME) for September 2008. Data available at http://mospi.nic.in/sites/default/files/press_release/Release_of_linked_CPI_html.pdf (accessed on 17 May 2017).

Consumer expenditure data collected by the NSSO during the 38th Round of NSS (1983) formed the basis of the state-wise weighting diagrams for the series.

SCOPE AND COVERAGE

The CPI numbers for agricultural labour cover the households of agricultural labourers and the CPI numbers for rural labour cover the households of rural labourers (including agricultural labourers). The rural retail prices utilized in these two series of index numbers are the same, but the weighting diagrams used for compiling these indices are different. As regards coverage of states, a Technical Working Group on Rural Retail Prices was constituted in 1974 under the chairmanship of the Director General, CSO which recommended 20 states, for which a separate series of CPI numbers were to be maintained. For union territories (UTs), the group felt that an attempt to compile separate series would increase the fieldwork considerably without commensurate increase in utility. Therefore, the group recommended that the UTs could use the index series of the adjoining states.

The state-wise sample sizes were decided by studying the variations in village-wise prices in the old series of index numbers and keeping in view the need for constructing state-wise CPI numbers for agricultural and rural labourers. The sample size for a state was allocated to the regions within it in proportion to their rural population and in multiples of three. A number of regions were formed within a state, according to similarity of agro-climatic conditions and density of population. Within each region, strata were formed by treating each district as a separate stratum. However, the smaller districts, within a particular NSS region, were merged to form a separate stratum. The allocation to a stratum was generally three villages, except in case of 13 strata (one each in Assam, Karnataka, Manipur, and Meghalaya; two each in Jammu and Kashmir (J&K), Kerala, and West Bengal; and three in Odisha) which had six villages each.

WEIGHTING DIAGRAM

The consumer expenditure data collected by the NSSO, in its 38th Round in 1983, was used for deriving weighing diagrams for all the 20 states and all India, separately for agricultural labourers and rural labourers. The average budget derived from the household consumer expenditure survey recorded expenditure on a large number of goods and services. These items of expenditure were divided into two categories: (i) non-consumption out-go including untraceable items; and (ii) consumption expenditure. Only consumption expenditure was taken into account for derivation of weighting diagrams. Expenditure on items like rent and repair of residential buildings or land, direct taxes, priest services (including ceremonial expenditure), and precious jewels or ornaments, such as gold, silver, and pearl) was treated as non-consumption expenditure and thus excluded from the average budget. The expenditure on rest of the items (including the durable goods) in the average budget was considered as consumption expenditure.

METHOD OF COMPILATION

Agricultural Labourers: The compilation work of this index was done by the Ministry of Labour and Employment up to 15 September 1958. This responsibility was then transferred to the Labour Bureau. The interim series of index numbers was constructed with March 1950 to February 1951 as the base year. The weights and the base year prices were based on the results of the first all-India agricultural labour enquiries. The base period prices were collected during the enquiry for the period of 12 months from 800 villages spread over 75 zones.

COLLECTION OF RURAL RETAIL PRICES

The FOD of the NSSO has been assigned the job and responsibility of collection of rural retail prices every month from shops and markets catering to 600 representative sample villages spread over 66 NSS regions in 20 states. Price collection from these sample villages is staggered over the four weeks of a month, with one-fourth of the sample being covered every week. These prices are collected on the fixed price collection day which may be a *haat* day for non-daily markets and any market day for daily markets. The price returns are scrutinized and processed in the Labour Bureau and the discrepancies, if any, are sorted out through correspondence and field inspections by the staff of the bureau. Thus, verified and accurate rural retail prices are utilized for index compilation.

Consumer Price Index Numbers for Rural and Urban Areas and for All India (Rural + Urban)

The CPI numbers presently compiled and released at the national level reflect the fluctuations in retail prices pertaining to specific segments of population in the country, namely industrial workers, agricultural labourers, and rural labourers. These indices do not encompass all the segments of the population in the country and as such do not reflect the true picture of the price behaviour in the country. To overcome this, the CSO of the MOSPI compiles a new series of CPI for the entire urban population, namely CPI (urban) and CPI (rural) to reflect the changes in the price levels of various goods and services consumed by the urban and rural population respectively. These new indices are compiled at the state/UT and all-India levels.

For construction of CPI numbers, two requisite components are weighting diagrams (consumption patterns) and price data collected at regular intervals.

The weighting diagrams for the new CPI series have been derived on the basis of average monthly consumer expenditure of an urban/rural household obtained from the NSS 61st Round Consumer Expenditure Survey (2004–5).

The consumption items are classified into the following groups (Table 11.5).

CRITERIA OF SELECTION OF ITEMS

Multiple norms were adopted for selecting the items depending on their importance, popularity, and suitability for pricing on a continuing basis.

Accordingly, the following four-fold criteria was adopted: (i) to include all PDS items; (ii) to include all items accounting for 1 per cent or more of total expenditure at the sub-group level; (iii) to include all items accounting for more than specified percentage

Table 11.5 Classification of Consumption Items

Gr. 1: Food, beverages, and tobacco		
1.1 Cereals and products	1.2 Pulses and products	1.3 Milk and milk products
1.5 Egg, fish, and meat	1.6 Condiments and spices	1.7 Vegetables
1.8 Fruits	1.9 Sugar, honey, among others	1.10 Non-alcoholic beverages
1.11 Prepared meals	1.12 Pan, tobacco, and intoxicants	
Gr. 2: Fuel and light		
Gr. 3: Housing		
Gr. 4: Clothing, bedding, and footwear		
4.1 Clothing and bedding	4.2 Footwear	
Gr. 5 Miscellaneous		
5.1 Education	5.2 Medical care	5.3 Recreation and amusement
5.4 Transport and communication	5.5 Personal care and effects	5.6 Household requisites
5.7 Others		

Source: CPI, Changes in the Revised Series (base year 2012 = 100), MOSPI.

of total expenditure of all consumption items: food, housing, and miscellaneous > 0.04 per cent; fuel > 0.03 per cent; and clothing > 0.02 per cent; and (iv) to include all items for which more than 75 per cent households have reported consumption.

All items satisfying any of these four conditions were retained. These are termed as weighted items. Expenditure on certain items was imputed considering its insignificant share and/or difficulties involved in pricing to the item(s) retained on the basis of mainly same or similar price movements. All-India weights of CPI (rural), CPI (urban), and CPI (combined) are as shown in Table 11.6.

PRICE COLLECTION IN URBAN AREAS

Number of price schedules (quotations) that could be canvassed by the field investigators available was fixed around 1,100. These quotations were distributed to states/UTs on the basis of urban population (Population Census 2001). For regular price collection by NSSO (FOD)/specified state governments, all cities/towns having a population (Population Census 2001) more than 9 lakh and all state/UT capitals not covered therein were selected purposively. Quotations were allotted to these cities/towns as per the criteria as given in Table 11.7.

After selecting the towns/cities purposively (as stated earlier), each state/UT was divided into following four strata:

- Stratum I: remaining class I towns (population more than 1 lakh but less than 9 lakh)
- Stratum II: all class II towns (population 50,000–1 lakh)
- Stratum III: all class III towns (population 20,000–50,000)
- Stratum IV: all class IV towns (population less than 20,000)

After allocating quotations to the towns selected purposively, the remaining quotations allocated to a state/UT were further allocated to different strata in proportion to total urban population of the towns falling in different strata.

The number of towns to be selected from Strata I and II was decided on the basis of the number of quotations allotted to those strata taking four quotations per town. For Strata III and IV, the number of towns to be selected was decided on the basis of the number of quotations allotted to those strata taking two quotations per town. Towns were selected from each stratum in a circular manner, ensuring regional

Table 11.6 New Series of CPI—All-India Weights

Sub-Group/Group	Rural	Urban	Combined (Rural + Urban)
Cereals and products	19.08	8.73	14.59
Pulses and products	3.25	1.87	2.65
Milk and milk products	8.59	6.61	7.73
Oils and fats	4.67	2.89	3.90
Egg, fish, and meat	3.38	2.26	2.89
Vegetables	6.57	3.96	5.44
Fruits	1.90	1.88	1.89
Sugar and honey	2.41	1.26	1.91
Condiments and spices	2.13	1.16	1.71
Non-alcoholic beverages	2.04	2.02	2.03
Prepared meals	2.57	3.17	2.83
Pan, tobacco, and intoxicants	2.73	1.35	2.13
Food, beverages, and tobacco	**59.31**	**37.15**	**49.71**
Fuel and light	**10.42**	**8.40**	**9.49**
Clothing and bedding	4.60	3.34	4.05
Footwear	0.77	0.57	0.68
Clothing, bedding, and footwear	**5.36**	**3.91**	4.73
Housing		**22.53**	**9.77**
Education	2.71	4.18	3.35
Medical care	6.72	4.34	5.69
Recreation and amusement	1.00	1.99	1.43
Transport and communication	5.83	9.84	7.57
Personal care and effects	3.05	2.74	2.92
Household requisites	4.48	3.92	4.30
Others	1.12	0.99	1.06
Miscellaneous	**24.91**	**28.00**	**26.31**
All Groups	**100.00**	**100.00**	**100.00**

Source: CPI, Changes in the Revised Series (base year 2012 = 100), MOSPI.

representation. In all 310 towns have been selected covering all the states and UTs from which 1,114 price quotations (schedules) are canvassed every month. Quotations allocated to a particular town have been distributed by ensuring both the geographical coverage of

Table 11.7 Criteria for Allotting Quotations to Cities/Towns

Town Population	Number of Quotations Allotted
9–25 lakh	8
25 lakh–1 crore	12
More than 1 crore	24
Remaining state/UT capitals	4

Source: CPI, Changes in the Revised Series (base year 2012 = 100), MOSPI.

the selected town and the different segments of population living in the town (poor, middle, and affluent). Further, quotations allotted for the town have been distributed over the four weeks of a month to take into account week-to-week variation in the prices.

In the selected towns, a market survey was undertaken by NSSO (FOD) for (i) identification of popular markets; (ii) selection of shops/outlets for different commodities in the selected markets; and (iii) determination of specifications of commodities to be priced. Rented dwellings, from which house rent data are to be collected, were also identified in all the selected towns during the market survey. Prices are collected by the NSSO (FOD) every month.

HOUSE RENT DATA COLLECTION

For compilation of the house rent index which is a component in the housing group of CPI (urban), rent data are also collected from sample rented dwellings in each of the selected towns. For each quotation, six rented dwelling units have been selected. These are selected in such a way that they represent various categories of dwellings with a different number of living rooms. Dwellings are visited once in six months to canvass for the house rent schedule.

PDS PRICE DATA COLLECTION

The PDS prices, also known as fair price shop prices, are also collected in respect of four items, namely Rice–PDS, Wheat/wheat flour –PDS, Sugar–PDS and Kerosene–PDS. These are collected in respect of two groups of beneficiaries, namely above poverty line (APL) and below poverty line (BPL) households.

PRICE COLLECTION IN RURAL AREAS

With a view to have a workload within manageable limits and considering the fact that the CPI (rural) would provide the price changes for the entire rural population of the country, a total of 1,181 villages have been selected at the all-India level. The broad criterion of selection of villages is indicated as follows. These villages have been distributed more or less equally among the four weeks to take in to account weekly variations in the prices.

(1) Within each state/UT, the top 50 villages (if villages in a district are more than 50; all villages if it is less than 50) are arranged in the descending order on the basis of the 2001 population for each district.
(2) A total of 50 villages selected here have been divided into two sets—Set 1 and Set 2 (Set 1 consists of the top 25 villages and Set 2 the remaining 25 villages).
(3) Within a district two villages (one each from Set 1 and Set 2) have been selected randomly from different *tehsils*. In case of only one tehsil available in a district, both the villages have been selected from the same tehsil.
(4) In case of some UTs, where number of districts are less than three, minimum five villages were selected within the UT.
(5) Sample size in some states/UTs, wherever required, was adjusted on the basis of rural population of the state/UT.

As the field investigators of NSSO (FOD) are not available for price collection in the rural areas, this work has been entrusted to the Department of Posts. India Post is helping the CSO under the MOSPI to collect data for the consumer price index since 2010. It uses an online portal system to collect uploaded data, a system that could be used to collect data to compile the IIP. Through the online portal, every postman collecting price data across the country uploads his findings in a standardized format directly into a central data server of the CSO. This has proved to be a simple replacement of conventional collection procedures in which the district data collectors pass information to state level officers, who collate it and send it to the CSO, who work the final figures out. The excessive mediation at two to three levels results in low response rates, delayed reporting, and increased errors due to lack of standardized format of collection and collation—problems which all important Indian statistics including the IIP are currently facing.[2] Postal officials are trained by NSSO (FOD) and CSO at selected centres in the country for price data collection in the rural areas. Data from different locations are uploaded through a web portal developed by the Department of Posts and NIC. This web portal has all the features needed for monitoring of fieldwork and scrutiny/editing of price data, as explained in the case of uploading of urban price data.

SELECTION OF BASE YEAR

Considering the availability of reliable data, especially rural price data from January 2010 and also the necessity of bringing all these CPI numbers at the earliest, the Technical Advisory Committee on Statistics of Prices and Cost of Living (TAC on SPCL) in its 49th meeting decided to have 2010 (January–December) as the base year.

COMPILATION OF INDICES

All the new series of CPI numbers are compiled at the Computer Centre of the MOSPI.

Compilation of CPI numbers generally consists of two stages: (i) calculation of price indices for elementary aggregates (item level indices); and (ii) the aggregation of these elementary price indices to higher level indices using the weights associated with each level. Laspeyre's formula is used for aggregation of indices. Specifications of items have been selected on the basis of popularity in the respective areas. These specifications are different in terms of units and quality for different price schedules. Price relative of each product specification (current month price/base year average price) is worked out. Average of these price relatives under the respective item multiplied with 100 gives the index for that item.

[2] Available at http://articles.economictimes.indiatimes.com/2012-04-24/news/31392791_1_iip-data-data-systems-index-of-industrial-production (accessed on 17 May 2017).

In case of seasonal items of vegetables and fruits, whenever prices of these items are not reported in a particular month, weights of such items are imputed on pro-rata basis to the items in the respective section (root vegetables, fresh vegetables, fresh fruits, and dry fruits).

House rent index is compiled in a different way. Two categories of dwellings—namely, rented dwellings and self-owned dwellings—are considered in the compilation of the house rent index. The rental equivalence approach is adopted in respect of self-owned dwellings. For each state/UT, six months data (January to June or July to December) are used to compile rent relatives. Rent relative is calculated as current month rent/rent six months ago and then simple average relative is worked out by classifying the dwellings by number of living rooms (one room, two rooms, three rooms, and four or more rooms). These rent relatives are weighted to get a combined rent relative using the estimated proportions of dwellings under each group, obtained from the NSS 58th Round survey on housing conditions (July–December 2002). The chain base method is adopted in the compilation of house rent index and these indices are repeated for the subsequent six months period. That is, indices compiled using the data of January to June are repeated for the period July to December. For the period January–June 2011, house rent is taken as 100, as the previous six-month period is a part of the base year 2010.

For PDS items, price relatives are worked out separately for APL and BPL categories. These price relatives are combined with the respective share of expenditure as obtained from the Consumer Expenditure Survey (2004–5).

The all-India index at the sub-group level is compiled by taking the respective expenditure of the state/UT (average household expenditure × total estimated households) as weights. State-/UT–wise shares in all-India CPI (rural) and all-India CPI (urban) are indicated in Annexure V and Annexure VI respectively of the *Report on Consumer Price Index Numbers* separately for rural and urban and combined (rural plus urban). Rural and urban indices are also combined by taking expenditure as weight so as to get state/UT and national indices (Annexure VII of the report).

DISSEMINATION OF INDICES

The CSO, MOSPI, releases CPI on base 2010 = 100 for all India and states/UTs separately for rural, urban, and combined every month with effect from January 2011. The CPIs (rural/urban/combined) are released on the 12th of the following month, if it is a working day or on the next working day. Indices for states/UTs are released, if prices for more than 80 per cent of the allocated villages/markets in the states/UTs are received.

REVISION OF THE BASE YEAR

The base year has been revised to 2012. The item basket and weighting diagram for the new index are based on consumer expenditure survey conducted by the NSSO for the year 2011–12. The number of villages and towns remains the same. The sample size in case of rented housing has been doubled, for calculation of house rent index. There are six groups in the new index as against five with earlier base. Pan, tobacco, and intoxicants have been made a separate group. Also egg is a separate item under sub-groups. The item indices are compiled by using geometric mean in place of arithmetic mean. The number of priced items has been increased from 437 to 448 in the rural and from 450 to 460 in the urban index. Prices of Antyodaya Anna Yojana have been included under the PDS.

Index Numbers of Share Prices

Index numbers of share prices are compiled by stock exchanges. The BSE Sensitive Index with base 1978–9 = 100, NSE Nifty Index of Ordinary Share Prices with base 3 November 1995 = 1000, and BSE-100 with base 1983–4 = 100 are constructed, which are available online.

BSE SENSITIVE INDEX

The BSE SENSEX is one of the famous indicators in the world of stock market. BSE SENSEX stands for Bombay Stock Exchange sensitive index. This includes the top 30 companies listed in the BSE. These 30 companies are selected from different sectors of the industry. The SENSEX indicator is one of the main indicators which tells us where the overall stock market in India is heading.

METHODOLOGY

The SENSEX is calculated using a Market Capitalization-Weighted methodology. As per this methodology, the level of index at any point of time reflects the total market value of 30 component stocks relative to a base period (the market capitalization of a company is determined by multiplying the price of its stock by the number of shares issued by the company). An index of a set of a combined variable (such as price and number of shares) is commonly referred as Composite Index by statisticians. A single indexed number is used to represent the results of this calculation in order to make the value easier to work with and track over time. It is much easier to graph a chart based on indexed values than one based on actual values.

The base period of SENSEX is 1978–9. The actual total market value of the stocks in the index during the base period has been set equal to an indexed value of 100. This is often indicated by the notation 1978–9 = 100. The formula used to calculate the index is fairly straightforward. However, the calculation of the adjustments to the index (commonly called index maintenance) is more complex.

The calculation of SENSEX involves dividing the total market capitalization of 30 companies in the index by a number called the index divisor. The divisor is the only link to the original base period value of the SENSEX. It keeps the index comparable over time and is the adjustment point for all index maintenance adjustments. During market hours, prices of the index scrips, at which latest trades are executed, are used by the trading system to calculate SENSEX every 15 seconds and disseminated in real time.

NSE S&P CNX Nifty

As with the BSE SENSEX, other indices also are constructed worldwide in a similar way, with some variations in their computation.

For instance, the National Stock Exchange (NSE)—the larger of the two stock exchanges in the country—uses its own index called the NSE S&P CNX Nifty. The S&P CNX Nifty is the headline index on the NSE of India Ltd. This index is a well-diversified 50-stock index accounting for 24 sectors of the economy. It is used for a variety of purposes such as benchmarking fund portfolios, index-based derivatives, and index funds.

Standard & Poor's (S&P) is a leading company in the world in offering indexing services. The CNX in its name stands for Credit Rating Information Services of India Limited [CRISIL] NSE Indices. The X in CNX represents the 'x' in the word 'index' or 'exchange'. Nifty represents the 'NSE fifty' stocks.

METHODOLOGY

The S&P CNX Nifty is computed using a market capitalization weighted methodology, wherein the level of the index reflects the total market value of all the stocks in the index relative to a particular base period. The methodology also takes into account constituent changes in the index and corporate actions, such as stock splits and rights issuance, without affecting the index value. The base is defined as 1000 at the price level of 3 November 1995.

BSE National Index

For the premier stock exchange that pioneered the securities transaction business in India, over a century of experience is a proud achievement. A lot has changed since 1875 when 318 persons by paying a then princely amount of Re 1, became members of what today is called the BSE Limited.

Over the decades, the stock market in the country has passed through good and bad periods. The journey in the twentieth century has not been an easy one. Till the decade of 1980s, there was no measure or scale that could precisely measure the various ups and downs in the Indian stock market. The BSE, in 1986, came out with a Stock Index—SENSEX—that subsequently became the barometer of the Indian stock market.

The launch of SENSEX in 1986 was later followed up in January 1989 by the introduction of the BSE National Index (base: 1983–4 = 100). It comprised 100 stocks listed at five major stock exchanges in India—Mumbai, Kolkata, Delhi, Ahmedabad, and Chennai. The BSE National Index was renamed BSE-100 Index from 14 October 1996 and since then, it is being calculated taking into consideration only the prices of stocks listed at the BSE. The BSE launched the dollar-linked version of the BSE-100 index on 22 May 2006.

Production Indices

Index numbers of agricultural and industrial production have been described in the chapters on agriculture and industrial statistics respectively.

Index Numbers of Agriculture's Terms of Trade

Raw price data, when properly processed, can yield index numbers. Index numbers of prices received by farmers, studied over time, indicate the extent to which changes in the value of output or farm disposals are attributable to changes in prices. Similarly, index numbers of prices paid by farmers throw light on the contribution of prices to changes in the total expenses incurred by farmers. The ratio of the two indices gives agriculture's terms of trade with the rest of the economy, and can be useful in explaining the variations in farmers' prosperity from time to time. This index number is constructed by DES, published in the *Agricultural Statistics at a Glance*. The index is constructed with 1990–1 as base.

INDEX NUMBERS OF MINERAL PRODUCTION

This index is compiled by the IBM, Ministry of Steel Mines and Fuels. Before 1962, the base year was 1951 and 30 minerals, classified into five groups, were included in the index. The weights utilized for the index were the value of production in the base year 1951. The chain base method was used to get the index. In 1962, the base year was changed to 1960. The index covered 37 minerals divided into four broad groups: (i) coal mining; (ii) metal mining; (iii) stone quarry clay and sand pits; and (iv) other non-metallic mining and quarrying (in the previous series iron ore was a separate group, while it has been merged with metal mining for the current series).

The fixed-base method is employed. The weights were in proportion to the net value of production (value added) of different minerals in 1960. The indices for sub-groups, groups, and the general index were obtained as the weighted arithmetic average of relevant components. Indices are published in the quarterly publication mineral statistics of India, by the Indian Bureau of Mines and also in the *Annual Indian Minerals Year Book*. The base years were revised to 1970, 1981–2, 1993–4, and the present base, that is, 2004–5. The latest index includes 70 items. To get the weighting diagram, gross value added (GVA) is taken as against net value added in all the previous series.

Earnings Indices

Index Numbers of Earnings of Factory Workers

The indices are published in *Indian Labour Statistics* by the Labour Bureau since 1953. The base year for the first series was 1939. In 1951 the base year was changed to 1951. All factories registered under sections 2m(i) and 2m(ii) of the Factories Act, 1948 which refer to the establishments using power and employing 10 or more workers and those not using power and employing 20 or more workers on any day of the preceding 12 months. The indices were prepared for all industries for each state, for each industry for all states and all industries and all the states combined. The formula used for the calculation of the index was $I = (n_0\ e\ /\ n_0e_0) \times 100$ where e_0 and e stand for the average earnings in the base and the current periods respectively, n_0 the numbers of workers for each industry in the base period. The series continued up to 1964. The base year was revised a number of times to a present base 2001. The method of compilation is the same as for the previous series. The index of money earnings for states is a weighted arithmetic average of the ratio of the current earnings to the earnings in the base period, the weights being the base period wage bills in the respective industries within each state.

INDEX NUMBERS OF EARNINGS FOR MINING WORKERS

The base year of the index is 2001. The index is prepared by the Director General of Mines Safety. The formula used for the compilation of the index is $I = (\Sigma n_0 e_1 / \Sigma n_0 e_0) \times 100$ is the average daily employment in 2001; e_0 and e_1 are the average daily earnings during the base and current years, respectively. The wage data used are the average daily earnings in December in the case of non-coal mines and average weekly earnings for coal mines. The general index is the weighted index of coal and non-coal indices, the weights being proportional to the estimated wage bills of coal and non-coal groups during the base year. These indices are provided to CSO for being included in the IIP.

Index Numbers of Foreign Trade

The indices are compiled by the Department of Commercial Intelligence and Statistics. The first series was compiled with the year ending March 1923 as base. The base was revised in 1949–50 and indices with the base were compiled up to 1952–3. This series was again revised to have 1952–3 as base. The index numbers with the base were compiled form 1953–4 to 1957–8. Then the base year was revised for a number of times. Like the year 1968–9 as base and included 489 items for exports and 511 items for imports. Then 1978–9 as base included 728 for exports and 623 for imports. The base year was again revised for the present series as 1999–2000.

METHODOLOGY

The fixed base method is adopted for the index. The unit values of indices as well as quantity indices are compiled. The unit value index p_n is defined as:

$$p_n = \Sigma p_n q_n \;/\; \Sigma p_0 q_0,$$

where p_n and p_o denote the value of an article during the base and the current periods respectively; q_o and q_n are the respective quantities in the base and the current periods.

The quantity index is given by $Qn = (Vn \;/\; Vo) \times (100 \;/\; Pn)$, where Vo and Vn are the total values of trade during the base and current years respectively. In determining group indices Vo and Vn represent the value of trade in the group. The quantum index Qn can also be written as $Qn = (\Sigma p_0 q_n \;/\; \Sigma p_0 q_0) \times 100$, where p_0, q_0, and p_n have the usual meanings.

Bibliography

Central Statistics Office. 2009. *Monthly Abstract of Statistics*, No. 62 November–December. New Dlehi Ministry of Statistics and Programme Implementation.

———. 2012. *National Account Statistics*. New Delhi: Ministry of Statistics and Programme Implementation, Central Statistics Office.

Croxton, Frederick E., Dudley J. Cowden, and Sidney Klein. 1973. *Applied General Statistics*. New Delhi: Prentice-Hall of India.

Department of Industrial Policy and Promotion (DIPP). 2008. *Technical Report of the Working Group of Wholesale Price Index Numbers, Base Year (1993–94 to 2004–05)*, Revision of index numbers of wholesale prices in

India 2004–05 as 100, office of economic advisor, Ministry of Commerce & Industry, http://eaindustry.nic.in/wpi_2004_05/Report.pdf.

Department of Industrial Policy and Promotion (DIPP). 2008. *WPI Compilation Manual.* Office of the Economic Adviser, Government of India. Available at http://eaindustry.nic.in/WPI_Manual.pdf (accessed 24 March 2017).

Directorate of Economics and Statistics. 2014. *Agricultural Statistics at a Glance.* New Delhi: Ministry of Agriculture and Farmer's Welfare.

———. 2013. *Farm Harvest Prices of Principal Crops in India.* New Delhi: Ministry of Agriculture and Farmer's Welfare.

Gupta, K.R. 2007. *Studies in Indian Economy,* Vol. 3. New Delhi: Atlantic Publishers Limited.

Indian Bureau of Mines. Various years. *Indian Mineral Industry at a Glance.* New Delhi: Department of Mines, Ministry of Mines.

———. 2011. *Indian Minerals Year Book.* New Delhi: Department of Mines, Ministry of Mines, 2011.

———. Various issues. *Monthly Statistics of Mineral Production.* New Delhi: Department of Mines, Ministry of Mines.

Labour Bureau. 2012, 2013. *Indian Labour Journal.* New Delhi: Ministry of Labour and Employment.

———. Various years. *Indian Labour Statistics.* New Delhi: Ministry of Labour and Employment.

Ministry of Labour and Employment. 2011. 'Consumer Price Index Numbers for Industrial Workers', *Annual Report* 2011. New Delhi: Ministry of Labour and Employment.

Ministry of Statistics and Programme Implementation (MOSPI). 2011. *Consumer Price Index numbers separately for Rural and Urban and also combined (Rural plus urban).* New Delhi: MOSPI.

National Sample Survey Office (NSSO). 2005. Agricultural/Rural Labour Enquiry: 2004–05. New Delhi: MOSPI.

Reserve Bank of India (RBI). 2011. *Weekly Statistical Supplement.* Mumbai: RBI.

12

National Accounts

National accounts are the accounts of the economy as a whole in respect of the various value flows between different modes of generation and utilization of value as well as the flows between different institutional sectors of the economy. National accounts play an important role in planning. In order to prepare these accounts, the details regarding the estimates of national income, savings, capital formation, and consumers' expenditure are required. The details regarding the estimates of national income and other related topics are given as follows.

Concepts and Different Methods of Estimation of National Income

National income may be defined as the value of commodities and services produced by the nationals of a country during a particular period, counted without duplication. It consists of the net domestic product and the net income earned from abroad. The net domestic product is the unduplicated output originating within the geographical boundary of a country. This can be obtained in three ways. The first is to sum the value of gross output of all producers and to deduct from this total, the purchases of these producers from other producers, that is, the value of intermediate products and the depreciation of equipment used up in the process of production. A net figure of this kind can be obtained from each producer separately and represents the value added by him to the value of the intermediate products with which he starts and hence his contribution to the total value of unduplicated production. The second is the sum of wages, profits, and other forms of income that accrue in productive activity and hence the sum total can be obtained by summing up various incomes paid and accrued. The third method is to segregate all final products available for consumption or for investment and to add the corresponding values leading again to the same total. These three approaches for the estimation of national income are respectively called the product approach, the income approach, and the expenditure approach. Any one of these approaches or a combination of these can be applied for estimating the national income.

National Income Estimates for India

Dadabhai Naoroji estimated the national income of India for the year 1867–8, using the available official statistics. Since then various estimates have been prepared (see Mukherjee 1969). These estimates relate to different time periods; their methods of estimation as well as the geographical coverage are also different. The estimates are, therefore, not comparable and do not give any idea of the economic progress of the country over time. Among the estimates prepared, those of Dr V.K.R.V. Rao were more authoritative and the approach of estimation was scientific. He estimated the national income for India for the period 1925–9, 1931–2, and 1942–3 using a combination of the product approach and the income approach.

Although various attempts were made to estimate the national income, no regular official series was available before 1948–9.[1] In August 1949, the Government of India (GoI) appointed the National Income Committee under the chairmanship of P.C. Mahalanobis to prepare a report on the national income and related aggregates,

[1] The Ministry of Commerce and Industry issued the estimates of national income for the years 1945–6, 1946–7, and 1948–9. The estimates for the year 1945–6 and 1946–7 related to the Union Provinces, while the same for 1948–9 related to the Indian Union.

to suggest measures for improving the quality of available data and for further collection of essential data, and to recommend ways and means of promoting research in the field of national income. The committee submitted the first report in April 1951 and the final report in February 1954.

The estimates by industrial origins for the year 1948–9 were given in the first report of the committee. The final report gave the estimates for the years 1948–9,[2] 1949–50, and 1950–1, both at current as well as at 1948–9 prices. The sector break-down according to which the estimates were available is shown in Appendix 12A. Following the procedure adopted by the committee, the CSO issued for the first time, in September 1954, the *Estimates of National Income* (*ENI*) giving the estimates for the years 1948–9 to 1951–2.[3] Since then the *ENI*[4] continued as an annual publication and a series of estimates of national income were issued up to 1964–5.[5]

The CSO combined in its estimation procedure two approaches, the product approach and the income approach. The sectors for which annual production data were available, namely agriculture, fisheries, forestry, animal husbandry, mining, and large-scale manufacturing industries, were treated by the product approach. The value added for each of the aforementioned sectors was worked out by subtracting the material inputs and provision for capital consumption from their gross output at factor cost. The gross output at factor cost for each

[2] The estimates given in the *Final Report of the Committee* (1954) were worked out afresh for the year 1948–9 and made comparable with estimates for 1949–0 and 1950–1. These estimates are, therefore, different from those given in the *First Report of the Committee* (1951).

[3] The estimates for the years 1948–9 to 1950–1 are the same as those given in the *Final Report of the Committee* (1954).

[4] The publication also gives some related aggregates like national product at market prices, transfer payments, private income, etc. In addition the publication gives some other accounts: (i) share of public sector in domestic product; (ii) income and outlay account of public authorities, administration; (iii) operating accounts of public authorities, departmental enterprises; (iv) capital finance account of public authorities, administration, and enterprises combined; and (v) external transactions account amongst others.

[5] This was then replaced by a revised series of estimates, the details of which are given in a subsequent paragraph.

of these sectors was worked out by evaluating their quantities at factor cost prices. The estimates of income from small enterprises, other commerce and transport, professionals and liberal arts, and domestic services were worked out on the basis of the number of persons working in each sector and the corresponding average earnings per person. The method of estimating work force for the latest series is given in a later paragraph. The income from banks and insurance comprises of wages and salaries, directors' fees, rent, and other surpluses. These were estimated by analysing the balance sheets and profit and loss accounts of all banks and the annual reports and accounts of the Life Insurance Corporation (LIC) of India.[6] The contribution to the national income from railways and communications consisted of all factor payments and the operating surplus. The operating surplus is the excess of gross receipts over working expenses and provisions for capital consumption. The income from government administration was taken to be the total wages and salaries paid by the administration departments of public authorities to their employees. Pensions and gratuities were considered as part of wages and salaries. The contribution from house property was taken as the net rental income originating in the ownership of residential dwellings. The net rental income figures were obtained by using the available data on the average rental per person and the estimated population for rural and urban areas separately.

Revised Estimates

Subsequent to the publication of *Final Report of the Committee* in 1954, various studies were conducted regarding the reliability of the sources of data and the suitability of the methods adopted in the compilation of national income. There were also some improvements in the availability of primary statistical data. On this basis, the CSO prepared a study in 1961 *Proposals for a Revised Series of National Income Estimates* for 1955–6 to 1959–60. These proposals elicited a number of valuable comments and suggestions. A number of other studies were subsequently undertaken which made it possible to compile the revised series of national income at current and

[6] Before nationalization of life insurance, the reports of individual insurance companies were being analysed.

constant (1960–1) prices. The revised series was presented for the first time for the years 1960–1[7] to 1964–5 in the form of an official publication entitled *Brochure on Revised Series of National Product for 1960–1 to 1964–5*. The brochure describes the methodology used for the revised series along with that used for the series which started in the year 1948–9 (now called the conventional series). The brochure also compared sector-wise estimates for the conventional and the revised series and pointed out the reasons for the differences in the estimates. The first issue of the annual publication of the CSO the *Estimates of National Product* (*ENP*) giving the estimates according to the revised series for the years 1960–1 to 1966–7 at current as well as 1960–1 prices was issued in October 1967. Up to 1968–9, the conventional series were being compiled and published both at the current and the 1948–9 prices in the form of appendices in the *ENP*. From the year 1969–70, the compilation and publication of the conventional series was discontinued.

The sector break-downs according to which the estimates for the revised series were available went through a change. The sector 'other commerce and transport' in the conventional series was divided into two sectors:

(i) trade, storage, and hotels and restaurants
(ii) transport other than railways

Professions, liberal arts, and domestic services of the conventional series were put as one sector 'other services'. The scope of house property was extended in the revised series to cover real estate (previously included under 'other commerce and transport'). Construction, electricity, gas, and water supply were shown separately in the revised series while, according to the conventional series, electricity was put under large-scale manufacturing, private construction under small-scale enterprises, and government construction under public administration. The revision was done because of the availability of fresh data from different government and non-government agencies. For this series also the production approach was applied in the

[7] Although the revised series started with the year 1960–1, the estimates according to revised series were also worked out for the year 1954–5 to 1959–60 at 1960–1 prices (see *ENP* 1960–1 to 1969–70).

case of agriculture, animal husbandry, forestry and logging, fishery, mining and quarrying, and large-scale manufacturing. For construction, the estimates were prepared by following the commodity flow approach and the expenditure approach. The income approach was applied for all other sectors. The coverage of this publication was extended gradually from time to time to incorporate the estimates of private consumption expenditure, saving, capital formation, factor incomes, consolidated accounts of the nation, and detailed accounts of the public sector. The title of the publication was again changed to the present title—*National Accounts Statistics* with effect from January 1975. Further, to meet the demand of the users, a special supplement—*National Accounts Statistics 1960–61 to 1972–73—Disaggregated Tables* (1975)—was brought out in March 1975. This publication included disaggregated tables on output, input, and value added. From the subsequent issue, that is, *National Accounts Statistics* 1976, all the tables presented in the supplement became regular features of the *National Accounts Statistics*.

The base year of the series has been revised periodically, from 1960–1 to 1970–1 to 1980–1 to 1993–4 to 1999–2000 and 2004–5[8] (present base). The changes in the base year were necessary because of the passing of time and the availability of new data from various sources and improvements in the methodology, whenever changes were made; the detailed methodology was published in the special publications known as *National Accounts Statistics—Sources and Methods* (1980, 1989, 2007, and 2012). For the current series the changes in methodology over the 1999–2000 series were published in *New Series on National Accounts Statistics* base year 2004–5 issued in March 2010. With each revision in the base year, the back series 1950–1 onwards is changed to the series with new base. For each base year, the estimates are prepared separately for rural and urban areas by broad sectors of the economy. At present the NAS is divided into five parts. Part I presents the summary statements of macroeconomic aggregates and their relationship, growth rates, implicit price

[8] With effect from the issue of Press Release of the new series of National Accounts on 30 January 2015, the base year has been revised to 2011–12. The details about the major changes due to this revision are given at the end of this chapter.

deflators, consolidated accounts of the nation and performance of the public sector. Part II presents statements on gross and net domestic product by kind of economic activity. Part III gives estimates of Private Final Consumption Expenditure (PFCE), domestic saving, and capital formation. The estimates of PFCE are presented for broad items of consumption although the estimates are available with the CSO at a fairly detailed level. Estimates of saving are presented in current prices only, and are presented by type of institutions and by type of saving instruments. The estimates of capital formation are presented by assets, by type of institutions, and by industry of use. Estimates of capital formation are also issued by broad sectors of the economy and by type of institution. Estimates of net capital stock are available by type of institution and by industry of use. Part IV deals with the public sector transactions, such as details of aggregates like GDP, net domestic product (NDP), government final consumption expenditure, savings, capital formation, capital stock, and economic accounts separately for administrative department's discounted cumulated utility and normalized discounted cumulated utility. Part V presents disaggregated statements giving values of output, input, and value added for each type of economic activity at a fairly detailed level. This part also includes detailed external transactions accounts and factor incomes, property incomes, and financial intermediary services indirectly measured separately for organized and unorganized parts by broad economic activity. After Part V, special statements consisting of quarterly estimates of GDP and that of expenditure of GDP at market prices and GDP at factor cost by broad sectors of economic activity. Also given in this section is the value of output and domestic product from livestock sector and a number of other tables like rural–urban break-up for the base year, advance estimates of national product for the year just ended are given. In addition some special statements not of regular nature are provided in this part. At the end are given notes on methodology and revisions in estimates. The following sections give some specific points about the methodology and data sources used for estimating national product, consumption expenditure, saving, capital formation, and other major accounts given in the NAS. It may be mentioned here that the concepts of different variables under national product and the methodology of their estimation is based on System of National

Accounts (SNA) issued by the United Nations (UN). The SNAs have been issued by the UN for the years 1953, 1968, 1993, and 2008. So far CSO broadly follows SNA 1993. Efforts have been made to implement SNA 2008, which is an updated version of SNA 1993; to the extent data is available. However, presentation of accounts in NAS generally conforms to SNA 1968.

Estimation of National Product

Different available estimates of national product relate to gross and net, national, and domestic product at factor cost and market prices. The difference between factor cost and market price is indirect taxes net of subsidies between gross and net as consumption of fixed capital and between national and domestic being net factor income earned from abroad. Net national product at factor cost is equivalent to national income. The other macro concepts relating to income are private income, personal income, and personal disposable income. Private income is equal to net domestic product at factor cost less income from entrepreneurship and property accruing to government administrative departments and saving of non-departmental enterprises plus interest on public debt, current transfers from government administrative departments, and other current transfers from rest of the world and net factor income from abroad. Personal income is obtained by subtracting savings of private, corporate sector net of retained earnings of foreign companies, and corporate tax from private income. Personal disposable income is obtained by subtracting direct taxes paid by households and miscellaneous receipts of government administrative departments from personal income. The sector breakdown, according to which the series with 2004–5 as base year is available, is given in Appendix 12B. Still the production approach is used for agriculture, animal husbandry, forestry, fishery, mining, and registered manufacturing. For construction the estimates are prepared by following commodity flow approach and the expenditure approach. For all other sectors, the income approach is applied. In this regards the following points may be noted:

(1) For estimation of domestic product, the agriculture sector includes livestock and operations of the irrigation system. The estimates of domestic product from these activities are obtained

by using the product approach except in the case of operation of irrigation systems which is obtained from the government records through the income approach. The production approach requires the estimation of GVO and value of inputs. The methodology of getting these values for agriculture and also for other sectors is described in the discussion on relevant sectors. As the inputs are generally common to both the livestock and agriculture sub-sectors, the gross value added (GVA) is estimated for livestock and agriculture taken together. However, in an appendix in the NAS, the GVA is separately estimated for the animal husbandry sector.

(2) In the case of some of the crops the estimates are still not reliable, for example, for fruits and vegetables the value of output in the revised series (1993–4 as base) changed by a staggering amount of Rs 8,747 crore in 1993–4 when the information source was changed (National Horticulture Board). According to board sources the data are not based on any scientific methodology. Also by making use of a different source for prices, the value of outputs increased by Rs 5,158 crore, which is also huge. However there is no significant difference in the values of output between the series at 1993–4 and 1999–2000 and between 1999–2000 and 2004–5. Also for some of the crops like grass and fodder the estimates are based on the yield rates of the 1950s. Similarly the estimates of quantities of different components of concentrates consumed per cattle were based on the 1975–6 survey of the NSSO. For the series with 1999–2000 and 2004–5 bases the estimates of concentrates are based on cost of cultivation studies. There has been increase in the cost of feed in the series with 1999–2000 as well as 2004–5 bases. The increase according to the 1999–2000 series is because of change in the output by using different norms based on type studies, while for 2004–5, the increase is because of including for the first time the output of fodder produced in forests.

(3) A total of 10 per cent of the value of output was taken to be equal to the value of inputs in the forestry sector. This percentage was constant for at least the last three decades. For the series with 2004–5 as base, the percentage has been increased to 15.6. The value of output of industrial wood for 2004–5, according to the series with base 2004–5, is 16 times more than the value according

to series with 1999–2000 as base. Although this increase seems to be because of the inclusion of estimates of social forestry, still this seems amusing. For all these years we were ignoring such a huge figure. Also there is an increase in the value of minor forest products of the magnitude of Rs 8,906 crore. This is due to inclusion of the output of fodder in the forests. On the other hand the cost of feed has gone up by Rs 27,039 crore because of change in the source of input of concentrates as cost of cultivation studies and other changes like consumption of fodder by the cattle grazing from the forest areas. Similarly the input percentages for inland and marine fish have been constant for a long time.

(4) In the case of unregistered manufacturing the benchmark estimates are prepared by using the income approach, that is, by multiplying the value added per worker with the workforce for different industries. These are carried forward mainly by making use of the index of industrial production (IIP) at the 2-digit level. This index, however, represents the movements of large industrial establishments and is not a proper indicator for this purpose. Even for registered manufacturing the estimates for the latest year are prepared by using the IIP to the estimates of the previous years. These estimates are revised when the data becomes available from the *Annual Survey of Industries* (*ASI*). In fact for estimating GVA from unregistered manufactures, for the base year for the series with 1999–2000 and 2004–05 as base, this sector is divided into two parts, that is, those units coming under the small-scale sector and other unregistered manufacturing. The GVA is separately calculated for the two parts and then added (see the chapter on industrial statistics), also for registered manufacturing for the estimates for the years 2000–1 and onwards. The *ASI* data since the year 2000–1 could not be used as the growth rates for the years 2000–1 and 2001–2 were not in line with the growth rates indicated by the IIP, excise revenue collections, or the corporate sector (manufacturing segment) data. The *ASI* data has again been used to get the values of output and GVA estimates for the series with base 2004–5. Recently the compilation of the IIP has been criticized by a number of experts and National Statistical Commission (NSC) has already decided about having a committee to enquire about the problems with this index. If we compare

the estimates for 2004–5 with 1999–2000 and 2004–5 as base at the 2-digit levels, we see that in some sectors the GVA according to new series is about one-third of the GVA according to series with base 1999–2000. In many other sectors the differences are more than 20 per cent. There is a similar magnitude of variations in the unregistered sector (see CSO March 2010).

(5) The estimates of value added in construction (*pucca*) are based on the commodity flow approach. This approach envisages estimation of the values of the main inputs like cement, steel, wood, and bricks and tiles by making use of values of output, imports, exports, and use in other industries and a constant percentage is used for other inputs and factor incomes.

(6) Various norms used in the estimation of output and material inputs on construction are old and need revision. For labour-intensive *kutcha* construction, the expenditure approach is used. For public sector annual budget, documents and annual reports are used while for private sector, the RBI-based surveys are used. For the household sector, the estimates are based on the All-India Debt and Investment Survey (AIDIS). Different types of constructions should be classified into homogenous groups and the input and output should be separately estimated for each type and then combined for the sector as a whole.

(7) For trade and also the hotels and restaurant sector, the estimates of value added per worker under the unorganized sectors are based on the data available from the enterprise surveys. The estimates of value added per worker, particularly for the trade sector, are not very reliable especially for non-directory establishments and own-account trading enterprises which form an overwhelming proportion of the trading activity. The benchmark estimates of trade are carried forward to other years by making use of the index of gross trading activity; which is based on a number of very old coefficients regarding marketable surplus and are not reliable. For other sectors, the estimates for the public sector are fairly reliable and are based on the annual reports of different units. For the organized private sector, the estimates are based on sample surveys done by the RBI and for the unorganized part the value added is obtained for the benchmark year by using the workforce estimates based on the population census and employment and

unemployment surveys conducted by the NSSO and value added per worker based on the follow-up surveys of the Economic Census. The estimates are carried forward to other years at constant prices by making use of relevant physical indicators and for current prices by making use of additional data about relevant indices of prices. The trade has been excluded from the survey of the services in the unorganized sector. The position regarding trade estimates for the benchmark year has worsened. The estimates for the series with 2004–5 base are the same as for the series with 1999–2000 as base. It is heartening to note that trade is included in the 2010–11 survey on unincorporated non-agricultural enterprises.

(8) The estimates in the case of ownership of dwellings are based on the number of dwellings as per the population census and gross rental per dwelling available from the surveys conducted by the NSSO. Constant price estimates for other years are worked out by moving forward the base year estimates with growth rates of houses based on the data for the two population censuses (1981 and 1991 in case of series with 1993–4 as base year) and the estimates have been converted to current prices by using the index of house rent separately for rural and urban areas. The indices used are not having stability with the actual increase in rent. Due to this fluctuation, the gross domestic product (GDP) from this sector for 1993–4 has gone up from Rs 21,981 crore according to the 1980–1 series to Rs 44,140 crore according to the series with base 1993–4. The same methodology is used for the series with 2004–5 for urban dwellings, while for rural residential houses, the user cost approach is used. The user cost estimates the cost of repair and maintenance, consumption of fixed capital, and net operating surplus of owner-occupied households (for details, see *Sources and Methods* 2012).

(9) The GVA obtained either from the production approach or income approach is in most of the cases inclusive of the financial intermediation services indirectly measured (FISIM; in the 1980–1 series these were called imputed bank charges). Imputed value of services in case of banks and similar financial institutions is equal to interest and dividend received minus interest paid to the depositors. It is entered as a receipt item in the output of financial institutions. The output thus includes

the interest paid by producing industries. This interest paid by the industries is already accounted for in the GDP of the respective industries, its inclusion in the GDP of bank industry amount to duplication. To avoid this duplication FISIM is allocated to the user industries as intermediate input. The CSO has done a special study for allocating these to various consumers. Allocations are done by broad sectors like for the entire registered manufacturing sector taken together, entire mining, and entire unregistered manufacturing sector, among others.

(10) The estimates of fuel wood for the revised series with 1993–4, 1999–2000, and 2004–5 as base are based on the consumption expenditure surveys of the NSSO for household expenditure after adjusting for the use of fuel wood in production sectors and also taking into account the fuel wood used for cremation purposes.

The National Accounts Division (NAD) of the Ministry of Statistics and Programme Implementation (MOSPI) in addition is releasing advance estimates of net national product (NNP), gross national product (GNP), GDP, and net domestic product (NDP), about two months before the close of the year. These estimates are based on the anticipated production in agriculture and industry, and performance of other key sectors. These estimates are subsequently revised and released with a lag of three months, as updates of advance estimates. Again quick estimates of NAS and revised estimates of the earlier years are released by the CSO, utilizing the available data of various sectors in the month of January or February of the following year (10-month lag). The annual estimates undergo revisions for about two to three years after the release of quick estimates.

The CSO introduced the quarterly estimates of GDP with effect from the estimates relating to January–March 1999, both at constant (1993–4) and current prices, on 30 June 1999. The estimates have been compiled from the first quarter of 1996–7 onwards and are separately available for eight broad sectors of the economy. The estimates take into account the quarterly performance of various sectors of the economy. The methodology involves the following three steps:

(1) Preparing quarterly estimates for the benchmark year at constant prices (the benchmark year is dynamic and refers to the latest

year for which fully revised estimates and quarterly data on the indicators are available).

(2) Preparing quarterly estimates for the reference quarter at constant prices.

(3) Implicit price deflators to get the estimates at current prices. The indicators used for different sectors are given in Appendix 12C (for detailed methodology see NAS 2012).

Rural–Urban Breakup

Since 1970–1 CSO has been compiling rural and urban estimates of income for the base year of each revised series. This is done by allocating the NDP of each industry group on the basis of the product of the number of workers with the value added/earnings/wages per worker separately for rural and urban areas, except for forestry, fishery, and registered manufacturing where the production approach is used. The data on value added/earnings/wages per worker is gathered from the latest results of various enterprise surveys conducted by the NSSO and other relevant material.

The estimates of rural and urban income have generally been prepared by allocating the NDP except in the case of registered manufacturing where the GDP estimates for rural and urban areas are directly available and consumption of fixed capital (CFC) has been allocated in proportion to the fixed assets in rural and urban areas to arrive at the corresponding NDP.

For the purpose of estimation of rural–urban distribution of income, different sectors of the economy have been grouped into the following four categories:

(1) Group A (product approach): Forestry and logging, fishery, and manufacturing (registered).

(2) Group B (working force × wage rate): agriculture, mining and quarrying, and construction.

(3) Group C (working force × different rural–urban earnings per worker): Electricity, gas and water supply, railways, communication, public administration and defence, banking and insurance, recognized education services, medical and health services (public sector), research and scientific services, and TV and radio broadcasting.

(4) Group D (working force × value added or earnings per worker): Manufacturing (unregistered), transport by other means and

storage, trade, hotel and restaurant, real estate and business services, and other services excluding those covered under Group C.

Private Final Consumption Expenditure

The PFCE includes consumption expenditure of households and non-profit institutions serving households (NPISH).

The final consumption expenditure of households relates to outlays on new durable as well as non-durable commodities and on services. The consumption expenditure includes the imputed gross rent of owner-occupied dwellings, consumption of own-account production evaluated at producers prices and payment in kind of wages and salaries valued at cost, for example, provision of food and clothing to employees.

The estimates are obtained by following the commodity flow approach. This approach implies working of commodity balances relating to various items of consumption, taking into account (i) production; (ii) consumption by other producing units; (iii) net imports; (iv) stock variations; and (v) consumption on government account and private final consumption.

To obtain PFCE, the expenditure incurred on all other categories is subtracted from the total availability. The quantity of final consumption obtained from commodity balances is generally evaluated at market prices. For some products and almost all services the expenditure in terms of money are directly obtained. The basic data on output and prices are mostly the same as used for the preparation of GDP estimates (for details of the sources, see NSC, pp. 393–8).[9] The estimates at current and constant prices (1993–4) are published for 38 items and sub-groups, covering the entire consumption expenditure and are available since 1960–1. The same methodology is used for the series with 1999–2000 and 2004–5 as base.

Expenditure Surveys by the NSSO

The NSSO is conducting household surveys on consumption expenditure (CES) since its inception. The data is collected on sample basis

[9] Available at http://mospi.nic.in/national-statistical-commission-0 (accessed on 25 May 2017).

in different rounds conducted by the organization. Since 1972–3, quinquennial surveys have replaced the annual surveys conducted earlier and the surveys are being conducted along with employment and unemployment surveys. Up to 1993–4, the schedules for both the subjects were canvassed on the same set of sample households. For 1999–2000 and onwards, however, the households sampled are different for the consumption expenditure and employment and unemployment survey. Starting from the 46th round (1986–7), the sample surveys on these subjects are being conducted for the intervening period between successive quinquennial rounds on annual base using, however, a much smaller sample. Also, for 1999–2000, there were two reference periods for food items, pan, tobacco, and intoxicants—last 7 days and last 30 days—and last 30 days for fuel and light, miscellaneous goods and services including non-institutional medical, rents, and taxes. The reference period for educational, medical (institutional), clothing, bedding, footwear, and durable goods were the last 365 days. The 30-day reference period means the consumption during the last 30 days. Also the surveys carried out by the NSSO generally correspond to an agricultural year, that is, the beginning of July of one calendar year to the end of June of the next.

The results of these surveys are published in separate reports as well as in different issues of *Sarvekshana* in the form of per capita expenditure for a period of 30 days by broad groups of items of food and non-food separately for rural and urban areas and by states, and also by occupation for some of the years. *Report No. 481* for the first time gives the detailed item-wise, state-wise expenditure for 1999–2000, separately for rural and urban areas. For 2004–5, the detailed results are given in *Report numbers 509* to *514*, for 2009–10 in *Report numbers 538*, *541*, and *554*, and *555* for 2011–12.

Comparison of the NSS and NAS Estimates

The two data sets are not strictly comparable and disagreement between the estimates is expected, because of the following reasons:

(1) Inclusion of consumption of NPISHs in the PFCE and out of the purview of CES.
(2) Exclusion of the houseless and institutional population like inhabitants of orphanages, hospitals, and prisons from CES.

(3) Inclusion of imputed rentals of owner-occupied dwellings in PFCE but not in CES.
(4) Differences in the reference periods. The PFCE relates to a fiscal year while CES generally relates to an agricultural year.

However, the gap between the two sets of estimates has been widening progressively over time (Kulshreshtha and Kar 2005). In some of the items the difference between the two estimates is very wide, for example, the expenditure on the sugar and *gur* and fruits and vegetables according to NAS is more than double the expenditure according to the NSSO for the year 1993–4. In the non-food group, the expenditure on furniture and furnishing as well as transport equipment according to NAS is about three times that of NSSO. For communication and transport services, the NAS expenditure is four times that of NAS; a similar magnitude of difference is noted for the years 1999–2000 and 2004–5. The magnitude of these differences is such that it cannot be because of the difference in concepts and coverage; this is a reflection on the reliability of the estimates.

The difference between the total NSS and NAS estimates for the year 1972–3 was only 5 per cent. The difference has been increasing over time. It was about 43 per cent in 1999–2000 and 50 per cent in 2004–5. The difference between the two sources of expenditure is more for non-foodgrains than for foodgrains. Fuel and lights is the only sector where the expenditure based on NSSO is more than that from the NAS.

From time to time, a number of studies have been conducted, centring on the coverage and measurements procedure of these estimates. These studies have analysed the reasons for the difference between the two sets of estimates. In the study conducted during the year 2007, the detailed sector-wise comparisons of the estimates on food and non-food items was taken up to identify the components mainly responsible for the differences (CSO January 2008).

Even the estimates of private consumption expenditure given in the NAS are very different from the estimates given in the input–output (I–O) table for 1998–9 and also for earlier years. For example, the expenditure on hotels and restaurants given in the NAS for 1998–9 is Rs 14,406 crore while according to I–O table the figure is Rs 34,075 crore. Similar is the difference for the years 2003–4 and

2007–8. Also with the change in the base year of the GDP series the estimates of PFCE change. Since they are based on the output and with the change in the values of outputs, the estimates of the consumptions also change. There are wide differences in other sectors also like sugar and gur and clothing between those given in the NAS and the I–O table.

Saving and Capital Formation

Saving

Saving represents the excess of current income over current expenditure and is the balancing item on the income and outlay account of producing enterprises and households, government administration, and other final consumers. For preparation of the accounts, the economy has been divided into three broad institutional sectors: (i) the public sector; (ii) the private corporate sector; and (iii) the household sector.

The estimates are presently prepared at current prices only. The Reserve Bank of India (RBI) published the first series of saving estimates in the *RBI Bulletin*, March 1960. Covering the period 1950–1 to 1957–8. From 1965, the RBI continued compiling and publishing regularly the estimates of saving until the acceptance of the Raj Working Group on saving when the responsibilities for the compilation of the estimates of different components of saving were divided between RBI and CSO. It may be mentioned here that from 1965, RBI stopped publishing the estimates of household saving in the form of physical assets. Instead it continued publishing regular saving estimates of government, the private corporate sector, and only estimates of financial assets relating to households.

The CSO brought out a mimeographed paper entitled 'Financing of Gross Capital Formation in India' for the first time in 1962. In this paper the estimates of gross saving were obtained as a residual by deducting net capital inflow from abroad from the gross capital formation. The saving of the government and private corporate sector were obtained independently and the household saving were obtained as residual. Another paper entitled 'Estimates of Savings in India' was published in 1969 giving the estimates for the years 1960–1 to 1965–6 at current prices. The estimates were prepared separately for the public sector, private corporate sector, and household sector and added to get the estimates for the economy as a whole.

In pursuance of the recommendations of the Raj Working Group, the CSO and RBI agreed on a uniform methodology and database. It was also decided that each agency would be responsible for compilation of estimates of specified sectors and supply the data (estimates) to the other agency. Accordingly, the CSO now prepares the estimates of public sector and household saving in the form of physical assets, life funds, provident and pension funds, while the responsibility of estimating the saving of private corporate sector and that of the household sector in other instruments of financial saving has been entrusted to RBI. Thus, the estimates released by the organizations are based on the uniform methodology and same data sources. However, the two sets of estimates may differ slightly due to difference in timings of their release. In 1995, another working group on saving and capital formation was appointed under the chairmanship of Raja Chelliah, according to which a number of improvements were done in the series with 1993–4 as base. In recent years after 1997–8, RBI has been releasing only the household saving in the form of financial assets on its own; otherwise it has been reproducing CSO estimates in its publications. The following paragraphs give a brief account of the methodology and data sources used for different components of saving.

Public Sector

The public sector covers government administration, departmental enterprises, and non-departmental enterprises. The non-departmental enterprises comprise government companies, statutory corporations, and port trusts. The gross saving of the government administration and departmental enterprises is obtained as the difference between current receipts and current expenditure and are based on the budget documents of the central and state governments and local bodies. The gross savings of the non-departmental organizations is obtained from their profit and loss accounts. In the current series, the saving of public sector has been revised to include the R&D expenditure as capital expenditure as against current expenditure in the old series. The savings of public authorities have also been revised due to the inclusion of construction and machinery (which has been included in commodity flow estimates) component of capital account head 4076 from Defence Service Budget estimates as capital expenditure instead of current expenditure as was treated in the old series.

Private Corporate Sector (PCS)

Estimates of PCS savings, except private commercial banks, is based on the analysis of the annual accounts of sample companies duly inflated for full coverage on the basis of data on paid-up capital of sample companies and all companies. The gross saving has been taken as equivalent to the retained profits gross of depreciation provision. The saving of private commercial banks is estimated as addition to the reserve fund. These include net amount carried to reserves, depreciation provisions, amount allocated for other special purposes and amount carried forward to next year's account net of surplus/deficit of the previous year brought forward as available from the earnings and expenses of commercial banks published in RBI publication, *Statistical Tables Relating to Banks in India*.

In case of cooperative societies data on statutory reserves/funds, bad debt reserves, and other reserves are prepared from the data supplied by the National Bank for Agriculture and Rural Development (NABARD).

Households

The estimates of financial saving in respect of households including non-profit institutions and unincorporated private business are estimated by changes in net financial assets held by them in the form of currency, deposits with financial institutions, shares and debentures, claim on government, net equity in the life funds, provident, and pension funds net of changes in financial liabilities. Since annual data on household savings as excess of income over current expenditure are not directly available, the saving of the household sector in various financial instruments are arrived at as a residual after duly accounting for these instruments in public and private corporate sectors.

Net addition to physical assets of the households comprising fixed investment in fixed assets of construction and machinery and equipment and changes in stocks is taken to constitute households' saving in physical assets. Estimates of fixed investment for the economy as a whole are worked out independently in connection with the estimates of capital formation. The estimates for the household sector are derived as a residual by deducting the corresponding estimates of public and private corporate sector from the total.

Net Domestic Saving

The estimates of net domestic saving for different institutional sectors are obtained by subtracting the corresponding estimates of CFC from the estimates of gross domestic saving of each of the institutional sectors. The method of estimation of CFC is discussed along with the estimates of capital stocks. The estimates of net saving provided by the CSO for the corporate saving sector would be different from those provided by the RBI because the RBI uses the CFC as the depreciation provided in the books of accounts of enterprises. The estimates of saving suffer from a number of limitations mainly because of deficiency of data. This refers mainly to the estimates for the private corporate sector and the household sector, especially for the latter, and the estimates for a number of components are obtained as residuals and no direct estimates are available.

The National Council for Applied Economic Research (NCAER) has conducted a number of household surveys on income, expenditure, and saving starting from as early as 1961–2 (for different surveys see the bibliography at the end of this chapter).

It may be mentioned here that the estimates of saving obtained from the surveys refer to households only and do not include institutions serving households. However, it may include own-account business enterprises which made no difference between business income and household income, and corresponding expenditure and savings as well as saving disposition into financial and physical assets. An important survey in this regards relates to the year 1994–5 (for details, see NCAER 2003).

Another survey was done by NCAER: the National Survey on Household Income and Expenditure (2004–5), primarily aimed to generate more robust and reliable estimate of household income besides other sets of information such as demographic profile of households (religion, caste, education, and occupation), estimates of market size and penetration of manufactured consumer goods (consumables and durables), and ownership patterns. The target population of the survey was the total population in the country, with states and urban/rural categories as sub-populations or target groups, for whom representative estimates were also sought. Still another survey has been conducted by the NCAER for the year 2011. The results of this survey are not yet available in the public domain.

Capital Formation

Gross capital formation (GCF) refers to the aggregate of gross addition to fixed assets and increase in inventories and valuables. Fixed assets comprise new construction, machinery, and equipment (including transport equipment and breeding stock, drought animals, dairy cattle and the like). Construction for military purposes, defence equipment, and increase in the stock of defence materials and durable goods in the hands of households are excluded from the scope of capital formation. However capital outlays of defence enterprises on ordnances and clothing factories are included.

Construction activity covers all new construction; alterations and repairs of buildings, highways, streets, bridges, culverts, railroad beds, railroads, subways, airports, parking areas, dams, drainage, wells and other irrigation sources; water and power projects; communication systems such as telephone and telegraph lines; land reclamations; *bunding* and other land improvements; planting and cultivating new orchards, tea, coffee, and rubber plantations; afforestation projects; and all other types of heavy construction. Activities of the special trade contractors such as carpenters, plumbers, plasterers, and electricians relating to construction projects, and assembly and installation at site of prefabricated integral parts into bridges, storage, and warehousing facilities are also included.

Machinery and equipment comprises all types of machinery like agricultural machinery, power generating machinery, manufacturing, transport equipment, and furniture and furnishings. Also included are increments in livestock in respect of breeding stock, drought animals, dairy cattle, and other animals raised for wool clippings. Addition to livestock other than these is accounted for under change in stock.

The estimates of GCF for the economy as a whole include all relevant items of new capital goods which are produced domestically (exclusive of exports) and new and second-hand imported goods. According to SNA, imports should include the outlays in foreign countries of the embassies, consulates, and other extra-territorial establishments of the government of the given country on new fixed assets reduced by the net sales of their second-hand and scrapped assets. Similarly, the net outlays of foreign embassies, consulates, and other diplomatic bodies located in a country, on fixed assets produced within the country, are to be recorded in the exports and not in the gross fixed capital formation (GFCF) of the given country. The fixed capital outlays of international agencies located in the country are to be treated in an identical manner. Due to want of data, it has not been possible to account for these. The estimation, therefore, follows the domestic concept, whereby, the geographical boundary of the county has been taken into account. Accordingly, the GCF refers to gross domestic capital formation (GDCF).

Additions to non-reproducible tangible assets, such as land, mineral deposits, and the natural growth of standing timber or crops, have not been included in GCF. However, outlays on improvement of land and development or extension of mining piles, outlays on timber tracts, and plantation are part of capital formation. The outlays on uncompleted construction works incurred during the period are included in the estimates of fixed assets. Inventories consist of materials and supplies, work-in-progress, and finished products and goods in the possession of producers and dealers. Stocks of strategic materials, grains, and other commodities of special importance to the nation in the possession of government are also included in the estimates of change in stocks. From the series with 1999–2000 onward as base, valuables are taken as part of the GCF and are shown separately in the capital formations by assets and by industry of origin.

The estimates of capital formation were released for the first time by the CSO in 1961 in the *Estimates of Capital Formation in India 1948–49 to 1960–61*. A paper with the same title gave the estimates for the year 1960–1 to 1965–6. The estimates were published for the first time in the *ENP 1960–61 to 1968–69* for the years 1960–1 to 1965–6. Since then the estimates are regularly published by the CSO in the publication now called *National Account Statistics*. The estimates are separately compiled for the public, private corporate, and the household sectors. For the public sector, the estimates are based on the budget documents and annual reports of departmental and non-departmental undertakings. For the private corporate sector the estimates are based on the results of sample companies published by RBI duly adjusted for data on paid-up capital of all companies. For household sector the estimates are based on AIDIS and in a number of financial instruments as residuals. The estimates of capital formation are prepared separately by three methods, that is, from the financing side as the sum of saving and net capital inflow from abroad, by assets, and by industry of use. The estimate obtained by the first method, that is, by adding net capital inflow to the saving is considered to be firmer than the estimates obtained by the other two methods. The estimates based on this method are, therefore, taken to be the control total for capital formation. The difference between the control total and those obtained by the other two methods are shown as the errors and omissions.

Domestic Capital Formation by Assets

For estimates based on the assets, for the construction sector, the estimates of capital formation are prepared by following the commodity flow approach for pucca construction supplemented by the expenditure approach for kutcha construction. Data on expenditure on kutcha construction works are available from various budget documents in respect of public sector and reports of various plantation boards. Such estimates for the private corporate sector are based on the sample studies of the RBI on joint stock companies and for cooperatives based on the data from NABARD. For the household sector the estimates are based on the decennial survey AIDIS, for the benchmark year and carried forward with the help of suitable indicators. The estimates in machinery and equipment are prepared by commodity flow approach. Various items of machinery and equipment domestically produced, imported and exported are classified into (i) capital goods; (ii) parts of capital goods; (iii) partly capital goods; and (iv) parts of partly capital goods. The total availability of the items under (i) is taken for capital formation. For the other three categories, some ratios based on the data from *ASI* and AIDIS have been applied for getting their share under capital formation.

Domestic Capital Formation by Type of Institutions

The estimates of gross capital formation for the public sector and private corporate sector are also prepared by expenditure approach on the basis of analysis of budget documents and annual reports of enterprises. These estimates of public sector plus private corporate sector including cooperatives by type of assets (construction and machinery and equipment) are subtracted from the corresponding estimates of commodity flow to arrive at the estimates for household sector as a residual.

Gross Capital Formation by Industry of Use

An independent set of estimates of GFCF and change in stock (CIS) for each of the industrial categories is prepared primarily following the expenditure approach. The GCF estimates have been prepared for each industry group by aggregating the GFCF and CIS estimates, which are prepared separately. Broadly, for each industry, institution-wise estimates of GFCF are prepared wherever possible and aggregated to arrive at the industry-level estimate. The estimates of GFCF have been prepared separately for each of the three institutional sectors, namely, the public sector, the private corporate sector, and the household sector. While the estimates for the public sector are from the budget documents, those of private corporate sector are on the basis of data provided by the RBI from a sample of joint stock companies and also the data provided by NABARD on cooperatives. However, for the household sector for some specified items, benchmark results obtained from various NSSO surveys (especially the capital output ratios) and growth rates in the GVO and GVA are used to obtain the GFCF estimates (by extrapolating the benchmark capital stock data with the growth observed in GVO/GVA and taking the difference between two years' capital stock data).

Gross Fixed Capital Formation

PUBLIC SECTOR

Under the public sector, all the three institutional sub-sectors, namely Government Administration, Departmental Commercial Undertakings (DCUs) and Non-departmental Commercial Undertakings

(NDCUs) are covered for compiling the GFCF estimates. Using the information collected on the actual expenditures incurred on the new construction of roads, buildings, and other construction, and expenditures made on acquisition of the machinery, transport vehicles and equipment, software, research and development, and other capital outlays on livestock, the estimates of the GFCF at current prices for the current year are prepared for administration and DCUs. Here net purchase of second-hand assets is also included. In case of the NDCUs, the information obtained from the books of accounts is used. The expenditure incurred on usual/routine repair and maintenance is not covered for compilation of capital formation.

PRIVATE CORPORATE SECTOR

In respect of the joint-stock companies of the private corporate sector, the estimates of GFCF and CIS for each industrial category are made available directly by the RBI on the basis of their sample studies of joint stock companies. The results of the sample studies are published in their publication entitled *Finances of Public and Private Limited Companies*. Generally, the RBI gives data every year on GFCF and CIS for a set of three years based on the analysis of sample of companies for the Indian economy. The estimates of GFCF of private commercial banks and private insurance companies are estimated separately as given in para 25.40 of *Sources and Methods* (CSO 2012).

COOPERATIVES

Mostly, the cooperative societies are involved in the activities of registered manufacturing, trade (non-credit societies), and banking (credit societies). For compilation of GFCF estimates, all three activity groups are covered. Data in respect of this sector is obtained from the publication *Statistical Statements Relating to Co-operatives Movement in India* published by NABARD. The latest data available is for the year 2003–4 in the form of various tables for credit and non-credit societies. For other years, the 2003–4 estimates of credit and non-credit societies GFCF are prepared on the basis of growth observed in GVA of credit societies and GVA of trade respectively. The methodology of estimation of GVA of trade and GVA of credit societies is explained in chapter 16 ('Trade') and chapter 18 ('Banks and Insurance') respectively.

HOUSEHOLD SECTOR

For most of the industries, the GFCF estimates of the household sector for the current year at current prices are derived from the benchmark surveys using appropriate indicators, ratios, or norms, or by capital–output ratio. The wholesale price index (WPI) for the appropriate industry group is used to convert current price estimates to constant price estimates, and vice versa in a specific industry. Wherever, an appropriate WPI is not available, the WPI of all commodities is used.

CHANGE IN STOCKS

The estimates of CIS at current price (CP) and constant price (KP) and estimates of inventory at CP and KP are compiled for all three institutional sectors (public sector, private corporate sector, and household sector) and for each industry category. These are estimated through the expenditure method. They are compiled first for each of the three institutional sectors or sub sectors wherever data is adequately available separately and thereafter, the industry level estimates are obtained by combining them.

The estimates of inventories are prepared by industry of origin only and the estimates of gross fixed capital formation are prepared by industry of origin and by assets also. Whereas the public and private cooperate sector estimates are made on the basis of the analysis of budget documents and annual reports of the DCUs/NDCUs and the RBI study of company finances, those for the household sector are made initially for the benchmark year and for subsequent years through appropriate indicators. The sources of data are the enterprise surveys for a number of sectors and the AIDIS (for details, see *Sources and Methods* 2012). However, for registered manufacturing the annual data available from *ASI* are used. The estimates of the values of the valuables available is obtained in a manner obtained for machinery. Since these valuables have industrial use, norms of 40 per cent and 90 per cent respectively for gold and silver, 30 per cent for gold and silver ornaments and gems, and 40 per cent for diamond and platinum, have been used to arrive at the estimates on acquisition of these items as a store of value.

Capital Stock and Consumption of Fixed Capital

Capital stock of a country is broadly referred to as that part of national wealth which is reproducible. It consists of all resources which contribute to the production of goods and services. Consumption of fixed capital (CFC) may be defined as that part of gross product which is required to replace fixed capital used up in the process of production during the period of account. This flow is based on the concept of economic lifetime of the individual assets. Estimates of capital stock for each of the years are built up on the basis of perpetual inventory method (PIM) with the help of independent data on the average age structure of assets by type of assets in different sectors and sub-sectors. The PIM means the building up of annual series of net fixed capital stock based on a benchmark estimate of the stock, annual addition to the stock in the form of investment, assumed life profile of assets, and estimated depletion of assets based on the life profile. The CSO has provided a list of assumed average life for each type of asset (CSO 1988). The rate of consumption of fixed capital is arrived at as a proportion of the value of the stock of fixed capital. Net fixed capital stock estimates are available separately for public, private corporate and household sectors and also by industry of origin. (For a detailed methodology and also latest assumed assets of life see *Sources and Methods* 2012).

The sources of estimating capital stock are about the same as used for estimating capital formation. For the estimates in the case of the public and private corporate sector, the start is with the year as far back as 1949–50. Also for the household sector the All India Rural Credit Survey 1951–2 has been used for the purpose. For the public sector, the estimates have been separately prepared for the administrative departments, departmental enterprises, and non-departmental enterprises. Private corporate sector comprises joint stock companies and cooperative societies. For estimation of inventories, the sources used for the public and private corporate sector are the same as used for estimating net fixed assets. For households for a number of sectors like manufacturing, the estimates are obtained as residual. The official estimates of capital stock as on 31 March 1981 by industry of use and by type of institutions were for the first line published in a special publication *Estimates of Capital Stock of Indian Economy, 1988* and then in a regular annual publication. It may be mentioned here that before publication of official estimates, a number of individual researchers had prepared the estimates of net capital stock by making use of benchmark estimates of capital stock and carrying forward these estimates by using the estimates of net capital formation prepared by CSO.

Regional Accounts

The most important aggregate of the state's accounts is the state domestic product (SDP). To get the SDP (gross as well as net) conceptually two approaches, namely the income accruing and income originating approach can be used. The income accruing concept relates to the income accruing to the normal residents of a state. The income originating concept relates to the income originating to the factors of production located in the state and presents the value of goods and services produced within the state.

Due to non-availability of reliable data on interstate flows of goods and services, compilation of estimates of income according to income accruing concept is not feasible, although it is a better measure of the welfare of the residents of the state. Therefore, all the states and union territories prepare estimates of gross SDP (GSDP) and net SDP (NSDP) at current and constant prices based on the income originating concept.

In fact, for goods-producing sectors and also for a number of tertiary sectors the all-India estimates are aggregates of the estimates at the state level. The estimates for commodity producing sectors are prepared using the production approach, while for service sectors the estimates are prepared by the income approach. Different states issue the disaggregated tables on GVA corresponding to Section V of the NAS. For super-regional sectors, such as railways, banks and insurance, and communication, the CSO allocates the GVA among states on the basis of certain indicators. Some of the states prepare estimates of GFCF by type of assets as well as by industry of origin, by following the expenditure approach. State Directorates of Economics and

Statistics have the responsibility of compiling the estimates of SDP and other aggregates. At the state level, the only data available regarding consumption expenditure of households is through household surveys being conducted by the NSSO.

Most of the states prepare estimates of Domestic Product by districts (DDP) and by sectors. To estimate DDP, the economy is divided into various economic activities, such as agriculture, forestry, fishing, mining, manufacturing, construction, electricity, transport, communication, and trade. In the commodity-producing sectors, such as agriculture, forestry, fishing, mining, and manufacturing (registered), the estimates of DDP are prepared using the production approach, that is, GVA = value of output – value of inputs used in the process of production. In the services sectors, such as trade, transport, and hotels and restaurants, the estimates for the public sector are prepared by the income approach, that is, gross domestic income = compensation of employees + gross operating surplus. For unorganized sectors like manufacturing, unregistered and the unorganized segments of the remaining sectors of the economy, that is, unorganized trade, unorganized hotels and restaurants, unorganized road transport, unrecognized educational institutions, and unorganized medical and health services, the estimates of GVA are compiled as a product of workforce and GVA per worker. While the GVA per worker is derived from the follow-up surveys of economic censuses carried out by the NSSO, the workforce is estimated from the quinquennial surveys of employment and unemployment of the NSSO and the population censuses.

For supra-regional sectors the state-wise value added estimates are again, divided into DDP on the basis of relevant indicators.

Public Sector Accounts

Public sector comprises (i) government administrative departments; (ii) departmental enterprises like railways, road, water transport, and communication; and (iii) non-departmental enterprises—financial and non-financial. Financial enterprises consist of (i) nationalized banks and the banking department of the RBI; (ii) financial corporations; (iii) the LIC, the General Insurance Corporation, and its subsidiaries and employees of state insurance corporations. The non-financial enterprises consist of all other undertakings under different industry groups.

For government administration and departmental enterprises, the sources of data are the budget documents of the central and state government and of local bodies. For non-departmental enterprises, the annual reports giving the profit and loss accounts and balance sheets obtained from the individual undertakings are the data sources for getting all the details.

The estimates for many components are available in current prices. These are deflated by using the corresponding price index numbers on the current price estimates. In some cases, however, the estimates are first prepared at constant prices by making use of relevant physical indicators (for example, in the case of value added for trade, hotels, and restaurants) to the base year estimates and then are obtained at current prices by making use of relevant price indices.

Consolidated Accounts of the Nation

For a comprehensive picture of the macroeconomic behaviour of the country it is essential that the different estimates are put together in the form of a set of national accounts for presentation of the overall picture of the economy. For this purpose consolidated accounts recommended by the SNA have been adopted. The new system provides a comprehensive and detailed framework for the systematic recording of the flows and stocks of the economy. The accounts of the system are: (i) production; (ii) consumption; (iii) income and outlay; (iv) capital formation; (v) capital finance; and (vi) external transactions of the nation.

These accounts are based on the national product and other related aggregates.

The CSO has started preparing four of these six accounts. These are: (i) GDP and expenditure; (ii) national disposable income and its appropriation; (iii) capital finance; and (iv) external transactions.

These accounts are prepared at current prices. These were published for the first time in *ENP* 1960–61 to 1968–69 and the consolidated account related to the years 1960–1 to 1965–6. In the next issue (for 1960–1 to 1969–70) these accounts were extended to the year 1967–8. The entries in these accounts are obtained from different aggregates otherwise presented in the NAS and also from the Balance of Payments (BoP) statements (RBI) and foreign trade statistics from the DGCI&S (for external accounts).

Estimates at Constant Prices

The estimates of national product in the case of agriculture, forestry, fishery, and mining are prepared mainly by valuing different items of output and input at the base year prices. For items where only value terms are available, the constant price values are obtained by making use of some price indicators. For registered manufacturing, the estimates at the 2-digit level of industrial classification are obtained at constant prices by making use of relevant WPIs for the years for which *ASI* data are available. For the years for which *ASI* data are not available, the industry wise constant price estimates are first prepared by making use of the IIP and then getting the price by making use of WPIs.

For unregistered manufacturing the estimates are first prepared at constant prices by carrying forward the benchmark year estimates by so-called physical indicators. These are then converted to the estimates at current price by making use of indices of wholesale prices. For construction, the current price estimates are deflated by the weighted wage rate index of different types of workers. This index is specially constructed by the CSO. For most of the tertiary sectors the estimates are first prepared at constant prices by carrying forward the base year estimates by using physical indicators and then converting these to current price estimates by making use of relevant price indices.

Estimates of PFCE at constant prices in the case of all food items, for which the output estimates are available in quantity terms, are prepared by evaluating the quantities at the base year prices. In cases where the estimates are available in value terms, the current prices estimates are deflated by suitable price indices of wholesale prices to get the estimates at current prices. Estimates of saving are available only at current prices. Estimates of capital formation are obtained by deflating the current price estimates by making use of relevant wholesale price indices.

Input–Output Transactions Tables

The SNA includes an integrated set of supply use tables as well as input-output tables. These tables provide a detailed analysis of the process of production and use of the goods and services products and the income generated in that production.

The first Input–Output Transactions Table (IOTT), consistent with the NAS related to the year 1968–9, was published by the CSO in the publication *National Accounts Statistics 1978* This table was prepared jointly by the CSO and the Planning Commission. Subsequent to its completion, the CSO undertook the preparation of IOTT for the year 1973–4 on its own and decided to continue the work relating to the preparation of IOTT on a regular basis and publishing them once in every five years. The IOTT 1973–4, in the aggregated 60-sector form, was included in *National Accounts Statistics*, 1981. A detailed report entitled *Input–Output Transactions Table 1973–74* was published by the CSO in September 1981. Thereafter, the reports on IOTT for the reference years 1978–9, 1983–4, 1989–90, 1993–4, 1998–9, 2003–4 and 2007–8 in June 1989, September 1990, November 1997, July 2000, March 2005, 2008, and 2012 respectively were brought out.

IOTT Structure

The I–O table gives the inter-industry transactions in value terms at factor cost presented in the form of commodity × industry matrix, also called absorption as well as use matrix, where the columns represent the industries and the rows as group of commodities, which are the principal products of the corresponding industries. Each row of the matrix shows in the relevant columns the deliveries of the total output of the commodities to the different industries for intermediate consumption and final use. The entries read down the industry columns giving the commodity inputs of raw materials and services, which are used to produce outputs of particular industries. The column entries at the bottom of the table give net indirect taxes (indirect taxes – subsidies) on the inputs and the primary inputs (income from use of labour and capital), that is, GVA.

As the IOTT is in the form of commodity × industry matrix, the row totals do not tally with the column totals. The difference between each column and the corresponding row totals is due to the inclusion of secondary products, which appear particularly in the case of manufacturing industries. This is so because secondary and by-products are also manufactured by industries in addition to their main products. Thus, while determining the entries in the rows, a secondary or by-product of an industry is transferred to the sector (commodity row), whose principal product is the same as the by-product under reference. The columns, however, show the total of principal products and secondary or by-products of each industry.

To get a symmetrical IOTT, a make (supply) matrix is constructed. In the make matrix each row gives the distribution of the output of the different commodities produced by the industry of that row. Each column of this matrix gives the values of output of that commodity produced by different industries.

The construction of pure tables, namely commodity × commodity or industry × industry table involves transfers of inputs and outputs between sectors and such transfers are in fact possible by suitably combining the make matrix and the absorption matrix by making use of mathematical models and making certain technology assumptions about the input structure of commodities.

Sources of Construction of the Table

The input structure in respect of different sectors together with commodity-wise details of final demand vectors and indirect taxes are compiled from the details available in the relevant worksheets made for the preparation of national income and related aggregates released annually by the CSO through NAS and other official and non-official sources. The details of sources of information and methodology in this respect have been discussed in the *Input-Output Transaction Tables-2007–08* published by MOSPI.

System of National Accounts

The CSO of MOSPI brings out the publication *National Accounts Statistics* annually. This publication presents the estimates of national product and its utilization in the form of current consumption and capital formation; accounts of the public sector; and consolidated accounts of the nation.

Presently, the NAS incorporates the estimates of GDP compiled through all the three approaches, namely, the production approach, the expenditure approach, and the income approach. While the level of GDP estimated through the production and income approaches are the same, the discrepancy between the production-approach GDP and the expenditure approach GDP is recorded separately under the GDP expenditure components. The NAS also incorporates the consolidated accounts of the nation along with the accounts of the public sector.

The compilation practices of NAS broadly follow the SNA, which was brought out jointly by the five international organizations—the UN, the World Bank, the IMF, the Organisation for Economic Co-operation and Development (OECD)—and the European Union. In the NAS, the production boundary and the asset boundary adopted is similar to that recommended in the SNA.

Although SNA 1993 recommends compilation of a sequence of accounts (current accounts, accumulation accounts, and balance sheet) for all institutional sectors (non-financial corporations, financial corporations, general government, households, and NPISHs), it has been possible to construct only the following accounts and aggregates on the basis of data available and publish them in SNA. This publication has been issued since 2010:

(1) For the total economy, the sequence of accounts (current accounts; and of the accumulation accounts only the capital account and finance account, and the rest of the world account).
(2) For the total economy, the social accounting matrix which depicts all accounts in a single matrix.
(3) For the institutional sectors (general government, households, and NPISHs combined into one sector, financial corporations, and non-financial corporations) only the production and generation of income accounts (of the current accounts).
(4) For the general government and household (including NPISHs) sectors, the sequence of accounts up to finance accounts.
(5) GDP at basic prices.
(6) Cross-classification of output and value added by industry.
(7) Classification of the functions of the government.
(8) Classification of individual consumption according to purpose.

Features of SNA Implemented in NAS

The CSO has implemented some of the recommendations of the SNA, to the extent available data permits. These relate to the following:

(1) Valuation of non-market agricultural crops on the basis of prices of similar products made by market producers and their inclusion in the production boundary.
(2) Inclusion of own-account production of housing services by owner–occupiers and of domestic and personal services produced by employing paid domestic staff.
(3) Inclusion of premium supplements in respect of life and non-life insurance output estimates.
(4) Inclusion of reinvested earnings of foreign direct investors in the rest of the world account. This treatment affects gross national product, saving, and capital formation.
(5) Imputed value of own-account labour treated as mixed income of self-employed.
(6) Expenditures on mineral exploration treated as capital expenditure.
(7) Allocation of FISIM to the users of these services, as intermediate consumption to industries and as final consumption to final users.
(8) Inclusion of expenditures on valuables, which are held as stores of value, and are treated as GCF.
(9) Treatment of expenditures on software as GCF.
(10) Inclusion of natural growth of livestock as GCF.
(11) Inclusion of expenditures made on few tree crops during the gestation period as GCF.
(12) Addition of capital expenditure incurred on installing the wind energy systems in the GFCF.
(13) Estimation of consumption of fixed capital of all fixed assets, including government buildings, roads, and dams, as PIM.
(14) R&D expenditures in public sector has been treated as capital expenditures.
(15) User-cost approach is used for estimating the services of owner-occupied dwellings in rural areas as against the practice of imputing these services on the basis of rent per dwelling.

(16) Construction component and machinery/transport outlay of defence capital account is being treated as capital formation, which was earlier being treated as intermediate consumption in the Indian national accounts.

In the NAS, the CSO presently provides, among others, estimates of (i) GDP; (ii) NDP; and (iii) factor incomes by industry of origin and also by organized and unorganized sectors of the economy. The data available from these three aggregates, and their sources, methodology, and coverage have been used to prepare the institutional sector accounts. In the NAS, the total economy has been broadly divided into organized and unorganized segments. Corresponding to these, in the institutional sector accounts being presented, the unorganized sector has been treated as the household (including the NPISHs) sector and the organized sector has been sub-divided into financial corporations, non-financial corporations, and general government.

Household (Including NPISHs) Sector

For the purpose of compilation of accounts the SNA institutional sectors of households and NPISHs have been combined into one institutional sector, namely the household (including NPISHs) sector. This sector corresponds to the unorganized sector in the NAS. The details of the coverage of the unorganized sector in the NAS is given in the CSO's publication, *Sources and Methods 2007*.

Gross Domestic Product at Basic Prices

With the adoption of the SNAs by the United Nations Statistical Commission, member countries are expected to prepare and present their national accounts statistics following the accounting structure and framework recommended in it. One of the recommendations relate to presentation of GDP at basic or at producers price instead of at factor cost.

In the present NAS (India), GDP estimated at factor cost is equated to estimates of expenditure on final uses of GDP (government final consumption, private final consumption, capital formation, and net exports) by adding indirect tax less subsidies. The GDP so estimated is called GDP at market price.

The concept of GDP at basic price/producer's price is a concept in between GDP at factor cost and at market price. This concept includes some of the taxes/subsidies on production and products as part of the value added at establishment/enterprise/institutional level and some other taxes (such as value added tax [VAT]) at total economy level to get the value added at basic/producers price by industry of origin and to value the goods and services for the supply and use table at purchasers price.

To implement the SNA, CSO also compiles industry-wise GDP estimates at basic price.

Changes Due to Base Year Revision to 2011–12

In case of base year revision, apart from a shift in the reference year for measuring the real growth, conceptual changes as recommended by the international guidelines (SNA 2008) are incorporated. Also, statistical changes, like revisions in the methodology of compilation, adoption of latest classification systems, and inclusion of new and recent data sources, are made. Changes other than conceptual, relate to the changes in the institutional sectors, changes in the GVA estimates by industry, and changes in the expenditure aggregates and saving. These are briefly given in the following sections. For details of the changes, see MOSPI (June 2015).

Changes in the Concepts

In place of GDP at factor cost, as used in the series with 2004–5 as base, the basic price concept will be used in the new series. Also the term GVA will be used in place of GDP for industry wise estimates. GVA at factor cost (earlier called GDP at factor cost) can be compiled from the estimates of GVA at basic prices by subtracting production taxes less subsidies. Taxes and subsidies have been divided into production and product taxes and subsidies. Production taxes and subsidies are valid in relation to production and are independent of the actual volume of production, while product taxes and subsidies are valid as per unit of production.

Changes in the Institutional Sectors

In the new series, the institutional sectors are: (i) public non-financial corporations (departmental and non-departmental undertakings); (ii) private non-financial corporations (the private corporate sector also includes quasi-corporations); (iii) public financial corporations (departmental and non-departmental undertakings); (iv) private financial corporations; (v) general government (government administrative departments); and (vi) the household sector including NPISHs.

Improvements in Coverage

(1) Comprehensive coverage of the corporate sector through use of MCA21 database.

(2) Financial corporations:

  (a) 2004–5 series: Financial corporations in the private sector, other than banking and insurance, limited to a few mutual funds and estimates for the non-government non-banking finance companies as compiled by the RBI.

  (b) 2011–12 series: Inclusion of stock brokers, stock exchanges, asset management companies, mutual funds, and pension funds, as well as the regulatory bodies: the Securities and Exchange Board of India (SEBI), the Pension Fund Regulatory and Development Authority (PFRDA) and the Insurance Regulatory and Development Authority (IRDA).

  (c) Further, the financial corporations have been sub-sectored as recommended by SNA 2008. The sub-sectors are: (i) the Central Bank; (ii) deposit-taking corporations except the Central Bank; (iii) money market funds (MMF); (iv) non-MMF investment funds; (v) other financial intermediaries except insurance corporations and pension funds (ICPF); (vi) financial auxiliaries; (vii) captive financial institutions and money lenders; (viii) insurance corporations (IC); and (ix) pension funds (PF).

(3) Private Non-financial Corporate Sector: In addition to MCA21 data (contributing 74 per cent of GVA of non-financial private corporate sector in 2011–12).

  (a) Estimates derived from data on Limited Liability Partnerships (LLPs) from Ministry of Corporate Affairs (MCA) (contributing less than 1 per cent of GVA of non-financial private corporate sector in 2011–12).

(b) Estimates for the quasi-private corporate sector from NSSO's sample survey results (Enterprise Survey).

GVA of Unorganized Financial Enterprises

In the 2004–5 series, the GVA of this sector was estimated as one-third of the GVA of government financial companies and the non-government, non-banking financial companies (NGNBFCs, including Housing Development Finance Corporation [HDFC]). This sector included private moneylenders and the remaining unorganized financial services, which in the new series, had been estimated separately as under:

(1) For the private moneylenders, the following steps are followed to compute the GVA –
   (a) The quantum of loan advanced by the moneylenders to the households has been estimated using the data from the NSS 70th Round, AIDIS 2013 and RBI's annual publication—*Basic Statistical Returns of Scheduled Commercial Banks in India*—which gives the loans advanced to households.
   (b) Interest rates charged by private moneylenders have been taken from RBI's *Report of the Technical Group to Review Legislations on Moneylenders, 2007*.
   (c) FISIM calculated by the reference rate (RR) method has been taken to be equivalent to the output.
   (d) The ratio of intermediate consumption to the total interest receipts, as estimated from the NSS 67th Round *Survey on Unincorporated Enterprises, 2010–11*, has been used to estimate intermediate consumption, and hence, GVA.

(2) For the remaining unorganized segment, the estimate of GVA has been prepared from the NSS 67th Round *Survey on Unincorporated Enterprises, 2010–11*.

Public Financial and Non-financial Corporations

There have been no major changes in the methodology. Only the additional and updated data have been used, except for GVA from

Post Office Savings Bank (POSB). In the series with 2004–5, GVA was taken to be a fixed percentage of receipts. In the new series, actual data of POSB, which is available in the Demand for Grants of Department of Posts have been used to estimate GVA.

General Government

There has been no change in the methodology adopted for compilation of estimates of general government. However, a change in the sector is that the RBI's Issue Department, which was earlier included in the government, is now treated as part of financial corporations.

Output and GVA of RBI

In the Indian context, disaggregated accounts are not available for RBI separately for the three services—monetary policy services, intermediary services, and supervisory services. Therefore, in the new series, the entire operation of the RBI has been considered as non-market and the value of its output has been computed using the cost approach.

FISIM

In the previous base, the FISIM component of the output of financial intermediaries was based on the difference between total property receipts (dividend + interest + net profit on sale of investments) and total interest payments by the banking sector. In the present base, the FISIM has been computed only on loans and deposits, using the RR approach, as recommended in the SNA 2008. In short, it is (LR – RR) × average stock of loans + (RR – DR) × average stock of deposits (where LR refers to Lending Rate and DR refers to Deposit Rate). The RR = harmonic mean of LR and DR for the banking sector.

Changes in Allocation of FISIM

The FISIM produced by the domestic financial intermediaries is either consumed by producing units or households or exported. Utilizing the sector-wise loan and/or deposit for each of the financial institutions as indicator, total FISIM is allocated to different users (intermediate use or final use).

Changes in the GVA Estimates by Industry

Agriculture and Allied

In the new series, the GVA of the crop sector and livestock sector has been compiled separately by bifurcating the common inputs. Bifurcation is based on a number of studies conducted in this regard and the more recent available data. Also, there have been other changes because of new data and direct availability of the values of output for more crops. Except for changes because of availability of more and recent data, the methodology remains almost the same.

Mining and Quarrying

The revision in the estimates is because of change in the data source, from Indian Bureau of Mines (IBM) to annual financial statements of the companies for non-departmental enterprises and private corporate sector enterprises (based on the MCA21 database).

In the old series, the estimates of production and input costs were taken from IBM, while for the new series, the GVAs have been directly compiled from the financial statements of companies given by MCA21 database.

For minor minerals, the change is only in the case of sand. An indirect estimate of value of output of 'extraction of sand' is derived through the value of sand used for construction. This is based on the study conducted by the Central Building Research Institute.

Manufacturing (Organized and Unorganized)

There have been changes in the estimation due to adoption of the 2008 classification, the enterprise approach for organized manufacturing, and the effective labour input method for unincorporated manufacturing enterprises. Also the names have been changed from registered and unregistered to organized and unorganized sectors.

CLASSIFICATION CHANGES

One of the major changes due to classification is that 'recycling' and 'publishing' of books, periodicals, and other publishing activities were included in the manufacturing sector, which in the new series would be the part of 'remediation activities' in 'other utility services' and 'services related to broadcasting'.

ORGANIZED MANUFACTURING

Till recently, the *ASI* was the only comprehensive data for registered manufacturing. The *ASI*, however, provides estimates for the manufacturing establishments only and does not cover the services provided by other components of enterprises like head offices. The head office has been, in most cases, allocated to the non-financial corporate sector. In the revised series, the enterprise approach is used in manufacturing also. The estimates for the corporate sector are based on the MCA21 database, available from the MCA. Estimates from departmental enterprises, railway workshops, the GoI printing press, and ordinance factories are available from the annual reports. The methodology is the same as for the old series. For non-departmental enterprises (NDE), annual accounts are taken into account.

The *ASI* captures the data by type of organization such as private and public limited companies, NDEs, proprietary and partnership factories, Hindu undivided family, and the Khadi and Village Industries Commission (KVIC). Annual accounts of DEs, NDEs, and the private corporate sector being already available, the estimates relating to the non-government unincorporated enterprises, which include partnership and proprietorship enterprises in *ASI* have been estimated and are classified as quasi-corporations. These enterprises being small in size, their coverage from *ASI* has been treated as of enterprise even if the data is collected through establishment approach. In addition, in accordance with the recommendation of SNA 2008, unincorporated manufacturing enterprises maintaining accounts are quasi-corporations and therefore, their estimates have been included in organized manufacturing. For obtaining estimates of GVO/GVA by compilation category in the case of private corporate sector, the estimates as obtained as the sum of all enterprises have been apportioned using the corresponding share in *ASI*.

UNORGANIZED MANUFACTURING

In the old series, the base year estimate of unregistered manufacturing was estimated as a combination of GVA from the micro, small, and medium enterprise (MSME) sector and residual unregistered sector using the labour input method. The MSME estimate of GVA was obtained by applying the GVA/GVO Ratio of directory establishments (as derived from the NSS 62nd Round Survey on Manufacturing Enterprises) to the GVO obtained from MSME Census of 2006–7. The GVA of the residual unregistered sector was obtained by multiplying the GVA per worker (from the 62nd Round) and labour input from the 61st Round Employment–Unemployment Survey (EUS) after making suitable adjustments for the labour input in MSME.

In the new series, the effective labour input method has been used for compilation category-wise estimation of GVA of unincorporated manufacturing enterprises from the NSS 67th Round Survey on Unincorporated Enterprises, 2010–11 and NSS 68th Round EUS, 2011–12.

In the labour input method (LI method), as was being used in the earlier series, while compiling GVA per worker from the enterprise survey, it is assumed that there is an equal contribution from all categories of workers engaged in an economic activity, that is, the productivity of an employer, a casual wage worker, or a family worker is equal. The new method addresses differential labour productivity issue by assigning weights to the different categories of workers engaged in an economic activity based on their productivity. The weights were compiled using the data on establishments covered in the NSS 67th Round Survey on Unincorporated Enterprises, 2010–11. A nested Cobb-Douglas function has been used for computing the weights of different categories of workers (for details, see MOSPI June 2015).

The estimates for organized manufacturing are compiled by summing up the estimates from DEs, NDEs, private corporate sector enterprises, non-corporate manufacturing establishments covered under *ASI*, and the quasi-corporations of the unincorporated enterprises. The unorganized manufacturing consists of the household enterprises.

Electricity, Gas, Water Supply, and Other Utility Services

In the new series, the major changes in estimates are due to (i) changes in NIC classification; (ii) the enterprise approach; and (iii) the use of annual accounts of private corporate sector from MCA21 database. Remediations and other utility services form a part of this group, the details of which are given in the following paragraph.

The estimates for this sector have been compiled by aggregating the estimates for recycling, remediation, sewerage, and other waste management services. The estimates for recycling in the organized sector have been obtained from *ASI*, while those for the remaining services have been estimated by aggregating the estimates of DEs and enterprises of the private corporate sector. Estimates for the unincorporated enterprises have been estimated using the NSS 67th Round Survey on Unincorporated Enterprises, 2010–11 and NSS 68th Round EUS, 2011–12. As in the case of unincorporated manufacturing, unincorporated enterprises are classified as quasi-corporations if they maintain accounts and otherwise as household enterprises.

Construction

The GVA from construction comprises the following components: (i) dwellings, other buildings, and structures (DOBS); (ii) construction in plantations; and (iii) mineral explorations.

The GVA of DOBS further consists of two components, namely (i) pucca; and (ii) kutcha. The former continues to be measured through the commodity flow approach, and the latter through the expenditure approach. However, in addition to these estimates, expenditure on construction activity in plantations and mineral explorations is separately estimated and included in GVA from construction.

The broad methodology adopted in the new series for estimating the total GVO and GVA from construction is broadly the same as the one used in earlier series except for some modifications and different data sources and 'bitumen and bitumen mixtures', and 'glass and glass products' added to the list of specified materials used (see MOSPI June 2015).

The capital expenditure incurred on cultivation of plantation crops during the gestation period is treated as output of the construction industry for that year. The coverage of capital expenditure in cultivation of plantation crops now includes cardamom based on data available from National Housing Bank and NABARD for the year 2014–15. Using information on the asset 'tree, crop and plant resources yielding repeat products' available from the MCA21 database for private corporations and from budgets and annual reports for public corporations, the capital expenditure for the households sector is worked out as a residual.

As regards expenditure in mineral exploration, this is the expenditure incurred on mineral exploration asset by all institutional sectors. This information is separately available in accounts of public corporations and private corporations. This is added separately to the commodity flow estimates of construction.

The estimate of GVA from construction is compiled as the sum of (i) factor payments in pucca DOBS; (ii) 75 per cent of output in kutcha DOBS; (iii) 75 per cent of expenditure incurred on plantations; and (iv) a fixed proportion of expenditure on mineral exploration based on information available from annual accounts of public and private corporations.

Trade and Repair Services

In the new series, the estimates of GVA for trade and repair services have been prepared separately for the following categories, as per NIC 2008 classification:

(1) trade and repair of motor vehicles (including motorcycles) and retail sale of automotive fuel.
(2) wholesale trade except of motor vehicles and motorcycles + wholesale of lottery tickets.
(3) retail trade except of motor vehicles and motorcycles + retail sale of lottery tickets.
(4) repair of computers and personal and household goods.

The revision in GVA estimates of public, private, and unorganized components in 2011–12 in the new series has been due to the availability of latest data from different source agencies. For public sector trading units, that is, DEs and NDEs, GVA estimates have been compiled by analysing the budget documents and the annual accounts of public trading enterprises, respectively. There is no change in the sources and methods of estimating the GVA of these enterprises. Estimates for 2011–12 of private organized part comprising private corporate sector, quasi-corporations, and cooperative societies engaged in trade and repair services have been prepared as follows:

(1) Private Corporate: Estimates of private incorporated enterprises have been derived using the MCA21 database.
(2) Quasi-corporations: Estimates for the quasi-corporations have been derived using the labour input method.
(3) Cooperatives: No changes are made in the methodology adopted for compilation of estimates of the cooperatives, since cooperatives were not covered in the NSS 67th Round Survey on Unincorporated Enterprises, 2010–11 and updated information on trading cooperatives is not available from NABARD.

The estimates of the unincorporated segment (quasi-corporations and household enterprises) have been compiled using the labour input method.

Hotels and Restaurants

The methodology followed for estimating GVA of public, private organized, and households in the new series is same as that of trade and repair services.

Transport and Storage

There are no changes in compilation procedure for estimation of GVA of railway transport services. However, in the new series, estimates of 'railways' operated by private companies, has been included using their accounts as available in the MCA21 database.

For other transport and storage, there is no change in the methodology for public sector enterprises, while for the private corporate sector, MCA21 database is used. For the unorganized sector in some cases the effective weighted labour input method is used while for others the simple labour input method is used. In case of services incidental to transport, the activities of travel agencies and tour operators are no longer a part of this category as per NIC 2008. This will form part of a new category in the real estate ownership of dwellings and professional services group. In the communication sector, a new category—recording, publishing, and broadcasting services—has been included.

Real estate, Ownership of Dwellings, and Professional Services

REAL ESTATE AND PROFESSIONAL SERVICES

The economic activities covered in this sector in the new series are (i) real estate activities; (ii) computer and information related services; (iii) professional, scientific, and technical activities including R&D; and (iv) administrative and support service activities and other professional activities.

In the new series, for all these services other than 'ownership of dwellings' in this category, the MCA21 database has been used for the private corporate sector, while the effective labour input method has been used for compiling the estimates of the unincorporated sector.

Owing to the modifications in this categorization of services based on NIC 2008 (other than 'real estate'), the estimates of the old series and new series are not comparable. The major changes are given in the following paragraphs.

(1) Computer and Information-Related Services: 'Repair of computers' and 'software publishing' are no longer parts of this category and have been moved to 'trade and repair services' and 'communication and services related to broadcasting' respectively.
(2) Professional, Scientific and Technical Activities Including R&D: The category 'research & development etc.' in the old series has been modified with inclusion of 'veterinary activities' and appropriately renamed.
(3) Administrative and Support Service Activities and Other Professional Activities: This is a new category culled out from certain activities of the previous category—'research & development etc.' and includes all administrative and support service activities. It also includes legal and accounting activities.

OWNERSHIP OF DWELLINGS

The same methodology has been continued except for the changes because of availability of new data.

Other Services

The economic activities covered under this sector are (i) education services; (ii) human health and care services; (iii) recreation, cultural, and sporting activities; (iv) activities of membership organizations; (v) personal services including washing, hair dressing, custom tailoring, and other personal service activities; and (vii) private households with employed person/s. The activities of extra-territorial organizations and bodies are not a part of GDP and have hence been excluded from this group. The categories 'sewerage and refuse disposal' and 'veterinary services' have been removed from this group and classified as a part of utility services in 'electricity, gas, water supply and utility services' group and 'professional services' respectively.

In the new series, there is no change in the estimation of the public part. There is a deviation in the case of private corporate sector, which has now been covered using the MCA21 database. For the private unincorporated enterprises (quasi-corporations and household enterprises), the estimates of all categories except 'private households employing persons' have been compiled using effective labour input method.

CLASSIFICATION CHANGES

In a few categories of the industry group, there have been changes in classification due to the adoption of NIC 2008. 'Social work with and without accommodation' which was part of 'activities of membership organisations' is now a part of 'human health and care services'. Further, 'broadcasting' which was earlier a part of 'recreation' is now covered in the group 'communication and services related to broadcasting'.

PRIVATE HOUSEHOLDS WITH EMPLOYED PERSONS

Data on private households with employed persons is usually not collected in the Survey on Unincorporated Enterprises, as it is not feasible to identify such households as enterprises. The value added generated by this activity relates to wages paid to 'employed persons' by the households. Therefore, the wages related information was estimated from the NSS 68th Round EUS, 2011–12.

Expenditure Aggregates and Saving

Private Final Consumption Expenditure

The PFCE in most cases is estimated by making use of commodity flow approach. For some of the items, such as education and health, PFCE is based on the *CES Survey 2011–12*, supplemented by the expenditure incurred by NPISH on these items. In some cases the data sources have been changed and in some other new ratios and norms have been worked (for details, see MOSPI June 2015).

Savings

The estimates of savings are prepared separately for each of the six institutional sectors namely, general government, public financial corporations, public non-financial corporations, private financial corporations, private non-financial corporations, and households. In the new series, the major revisions that have taken place are: (i) physical assets of quasi-corporations have been excluded from households and included in the private corporations; (ii) savings estimates for non-government non-financial companies, previously taken from RBI, have now been derived from the MCA21 database; (iii) savings estimates for non-government financial companies, life and non-life private insurance companies, and non-nationalized banks have been taken from analysis of annual accounts of companies and banks; (iv) expenditure of households on valuables has been included along with the physical assets of households; (v) addition of organizations for providing provident and pension fund data of households; (vi) savings of the household sector in mutual funds has been taken from analysis of annual accounts of mutual fund companies. Estimates of financial savings of households are compiled by the RBI. Separate information on financial savings of quasi-corporations is not available. Therefore, household savings in the form of financial assets continues to include financial savings of quasi-corporations.

Gross Capital Formation

The GCF refers to the aggregate of gross additions less deductions of fixed assets (GFCF), CIS, and valuables.

The GFCF estimates in the new series are compiled for four broad categories of assets as per System of National Accounts, 2008. These asset categories are: (i) DOBS; (ii) machinery and equipment; (iii) cultivated biological resources; and (iv) intellectual property products.

Table 12.1 gives the comparison between categories of fixed assets in the new and old series.

In the new series, the GFCF estimates have undergone revisions mainly due to (i) use of information on financial parameters of non-government companies from the MCA21 database provided by the MCA instead of results from sample studies of non-government companies by RBI; (ii) use of *ASI* 2011–12 detailed results; (iii) estimation of GFCF for four broad categories of assets as per SNA 2008, namely DOBS; machinery and equipment; cultivated biological resources; and intellectual property products as against only two asset categories 'construction' and 'machinery and equipment' in the previous series; (iv) separating out estimates for quasi-corporations from households and inclusion in private corporations based on recommendations of SNA 2008; and (v) use of NSS 70th Round, AIDIS 2013, and NSS 67th Round Survey on Unincorporated Enterprises, 2010–11 for updating ratios for preparing benchmark estimates in the household sector.

Table 12.1 Comparison between Fixed Asset Categories in 2011–12 Series vs 2004–5 Series

Fixed assets in new (2011–12) series	Corresponding fixed assets in old (2004–05) series
Dwellings, others buildings & structures	Construction assets of 2004–05 series excluding plantation
Machinery & equipment	Machinery & equipment of 2004–05 series excluding increment in livestock, software, expenditure on R&D
Cultivated biological resources (CBR)	Increment in livestock
	Plantation
Intellectual property products (IPP)	Expenditure on R&D
	Software

Source: MOSPI June 2015.

Following are the new categories:

(1) Cultivated biological resources: Capital expenditure on plantations and increment in livestock used as capital asset (breeding, dairying, and as draught animals) comprises of the 'cultivated biological resources' in the new series, for which the estimation methodology at the broad level remains unchanged.
(2) Intellectual property products: The IPP consist of expenditure on research and development, mineral exploration, computer software, and other intellectual property products. The data for IPP is separately available from the MCA21 database as well as analysis of annual reports of government companies and autonomous bodies. For the households sector, IPP information pertains only to software for which information has been obtained from the NSS 67th Round Survey on Unincorporated Enterprises, 2010–11. Further, from the total estimate of software estimated using data from NASSCOM and imports, the residual obtained after netting out the corresponding expenditure by corporations and households is added to the private corporations.

CHANGE IN STOCKS

For estimation of CIS of inventories, the book values of change in stocks for the corporations are now revalued in the new series. Expenditure of households on valuables has been included as savings in the form of physical assets of households.

(1) GFCF by Industry of Use: The estimates for the general government and public corporations are obtained from the budget documents and annual accounts of public corporations. The estimates for private corporations are mainly prepared using information on financial parameters of non-government companies from MCA21 database provided by MCA instead of results from the RBI sample study of companies. Estimates for LLPs, cooperatives, insurance companies and banks have been obtained from MCA, NABARD, and annual reports of IRDA and banks, respectively and included in the private corporate sector. As regards the 'households' sector, benchmark results

obtained from various NSS surveys (especially the capital stock to output/GVA ratios) and growth rates in GVO and GVA, are used to obtain the GFCF estimates (by extrapolating the benchmark capital stock data with the growth observed in GVO (or GVA) and taking the difference between two years' capital stock data). The estimates have been prepared for the disaggregated level of assets, as per SNA 2008, based on the information available.

(2) CIS by Industry: The estimates of CIS at current price (CP) and constant price (KP), and of inventory at CP and KP are being compiled for all the institutional sectors and for each industry, separately. The WPI for the appropriate industry group is used to convert CP estimates to KP estimates and vice versa for the specific industry.

For individual industry groups, the details are available in the brochure.

(3) Valuables: Data on expenditures made on net acquisition of valuables on precious items, such as gold, gems, ornaments, and precious stones, has been included under GCF, as a separate category (separately from the GFCF and change in stocks) as in the old series. The coverage is broadly the same as in the old series. However, the ratios of inter-industry use of the output have been updated from *ASI* 2011–12 and NSS 67th Round Survey on Unincorporated Enterprises, 2010–11 to account for use of these imported products in manufacturing activity.

Features of the Revised NAS (2015)

The NAS up to 2014 was based on the series with 2004–5 as base. There were five chapters in the publication, as against eight in the revised NAS. In the previous series, values of output were given only for agriculture and allied, mining, and registered and unregistered manufacturing. The revised NAS, in addition, contains the values of output of construction, electricity, and most of the service sectors. The contents of the revised NAS are as in Table 12.2.

With the publication of NAS 2015, most of the items of the SNA publication have been covered in NAS. Hence the publication of SNA 2015 has been discontinued.

Table 12.2 Contents of the Revised NAS

	Statements
	Economic Overview
	Chapter 1: Macro-economic Aggregates Including Sectoral Analysis
1.	Statement 1.1—Key aggregates of national accounts at current and constant prices
2.	Statement 1.2—Per capita income, product and final consumption
3.	Statement 1.3—Relationship of national income and other aggregates
4.	Statement 1.4—Price and quantum indices
5.	Statement 1.5—Output by economic activity and capital formation by industry of use at current and constant prices
6.	Statement 1.6—Gross value added by economic activity at current and constant prices
7.	Statement 1.6A—Percentage share of GVA by economic activity at current and constant prices
8.	Statement 1.6B—Percentage change in GVA by economic activity at current and constant prices
9.	Statement 1.7—Net value added by economic activity at current and constant prices
10.	Statement 1.8—Consumption of fixed capital by economic activity at current and constant prices
11.	Statement 1.9—Finances for gross capital formation
12.	Statement 1.10—Gross capital formation by industry of use
13.	Statement 1.11—Gross fixed capital formation by asset and institutional sector at current and constant prices
14.	Statement 1.12—Private final consumption expenditure at current and constant prices
15.	Statement 1.13—FISIM by uses—intermediate consumption and expenditure at current prices
16.	Statement 1.14—Institutional sectoral accounts—key economic indicators at current prices
17.	Statement 1.15—Sequence of accounts for total economy
	Accounts by Institutional Sector
	Chapter 2: Non-financial Corporations
18.	Statement 2.0 SOA—Non-financial corporations
19.	Statement 2.1 SOA—Public non-financial corporations

(Cont'd)

Table 12.2 *(Cont'd)*

20.	Statement 2.1A SOA—Public non-financial corporations—DE
21.	Statement 2.1B SOA—Public non-financial corporations—NDE
22.	Statement 2.2 SOA—Private non-financial corporations
	Chapter 3: Financial Corporations
23.	Statement 3.0 SOA—Financial corporations
24.	Statement 3.1 SOA—Public financial corporations
25.	Statement 3.2 SOA—Private financial corporations
	Chapter 4: General Government
26.	Statement 4.0 SOA—General government
27.	Statement 4.1—Value added by central and state governments
28.	Statement 4.2—Expenditure of general government classified by function, COFOG
	Chapter 5: Households
29.	Statement 5.0 SOA—Households
30.	Statement 5.1—Private final consumption expenditure classified by item
31.	Statement 5.2—Individual consumption expenditure by households and general government
32.	Statement 5.3—Financial assets and liabilities of the household sector
	Chapter 6: Rest of the World
33.	Statement 6.0 SOA—Rest of the world
34.	Statement 6.1—Detailed external transactions accounts
35.	Statement 6.2—Selected aggregates of external transactions at constant (2011–12) prices
	Industry-wise Analysis
	Chapter 7: Aggregates by Economic Activity
36.	Statement 7.1—Output, value added, CE, OS/MI, by industry
	Statement 7.1 A—Output, value added, CE, OS/MI, by industry—public sector
	Statement 7.1 B—Output, value added, CE, OS/MI, by industry—private corporations
	Statement 7.1 C—Output, value added, CE, OS/MI, by industry—households
37.	Statement 7.2—GCF, GFCF, CIS, CFC by industry
	Statement 7.2 A—GCF, GFCF, CIS, CFC by industry—Public sector
	Statement 7.2 B—GCF, GFCF, CIS, CFC by industry—Private corporations
	Statement 7.2 C—GCF, GFCF, CIS, CFC by industry—Households

38. Statement 7.3—GFCF by type of asset, by industry
Statement 7.3 A—GFCF by type of asset, by industry—public sector
Statement 7.3 B—GFCF by type of asset, by industry—private corporations
Statement 7.3 C—GFCF by type of asset, by industry—households
39. Statement 7.4—Net capital stock by industry
Statement 7.4 A—Net capital stock by industry—public sector
Statement 7.4 B—Net capital stock by industry—private corporations
Statement 7.4 C—Net capital stock by industry—households
Derived Statistics
Chapter 8: Disaggregated Statements
40. Statement 8.1.1—Output and value added from crop sector
41. Statement 8.1.2—Crop-wise value of output
42. Statement 8.2—Output and value added from livestock
43. Statement 8.3—Output and value added from forestry and logging
44. Statement 8.4—Output and value added from fishing and aquaculture
45. Statement 8.5—Output and value added from mining and quarrying
46. Statement 8.6.1 Part-1—Output from manufacturing in corporate sector
Statement 8.6.1 Part-2—Value added from manufacturing in corporate Sector
47. Statement 8.6.2 Part-1—Output from manufacturing in household sector
Statement 8.6.2 Part-2—Value added from manufacturing in household sector
48. Statement 8.7—Output and value added from electricity, gas, water supply, and other utility services
49. Statement 8.8—Output and value added from construction
50. Statement 8.9—Outputs and value added from trade, repair services, hotels, and restaurants
51. Statement 8.10—Output and value added from transport services
52. Statement 8.11—Output and value added from storage, communication, and services related to broadcasting
53. Statement 8.12—Value added from financial services
54. Statement 8.13—Outputs and value added from real estate, ownership of dwelling and professional services

(Cont'd)

Table 12.2 *(Cont'd)*

55.	Statement 8.14—Outputs and value added from other services
56.	Statement 8.15.1—Output, value added, CE, OS/MI, by industry—general government
	Statement 8.15.2—Output, value added, CE, OS/MI, by industry—DE
	Statement 8.15.3—Output, value added, CE, OS/MI, by industry—NDE
57.	Statement 8.16—Depreciation as provided in book of accounts
58.	Statement 8.17.1—Provisional Estimates of national income and other aggregates, 2014–15
	Statement 8.17.2—Provisional Estimates of GVA by economic activity, 2014–15
59.	Statement 8.18.1—Quarterly estimates of GVA by economic activity
	Statement 8.18.2—Quarterly estimates of GDP-expenditure components
60.	Statement 8.19—Net value added by economic activity by rural and urban sectors
	Notes on methodology on estimation of NVA by rural and urban sectors

Source: NAS (2015).

Appendix 12A

Sector Breakdowns in which National Income Estimates were Published (Conventional Series)

(1) *At Current Prices*

(i) Agriculture, animal husbandry, and ancillary activities; (ii) Forestry; (iii) Fishery; (iv) Total of agriculture; (v) Mining; (vi) Factory establishments; (vii) Small enterprises; (viii) Total of mining, manufacturing, and small enterprises; (ix) Communications; (x) Railways; (xi) Organized banking and insurance; (xii) Other commerce and transport; (xiii) Total of commerce, transport, and communications.

Other Services

(xiv) Professions and liberal arts; (xv) Government services (administration); (xvi) Domestic services; (xvii) House property; (xviii) Total of other services.

(2) *At Constant Prices*

(i) Agriculture, animal husbandry, and ancillary activities; (ii) Mining, manufacturing, and small enterprises; (iii) Commerce, transport, and communications; (iv) Other services.

Appendix 12B

Sector Breakdowns in which National Income Estimates are Published

At Current Prices

(1) Agriculture, Forestry, and Fishery: (i) Agriculture; (ii) Forestry and logging; (iii) Fishery
(2) Mining and quarrying
(3) Manufacturing: (i) Registered; (ii) Unregistered
(4) Electricity, gas, and water supply
(5) Construction
(6) Trade, hotels and restaurants: (i) Trade; (ii) Hotels and restaurants
(7) Transportation, storage, and communication: (i) Railways; (ii) Transport by other means; (iii) Storage; (iv) Communication
(8) Financing, insurance, real estate, and business services: (i) Banking and insurance; (ii) Real estate, ownership of dwellings, and business services
(9) Community, social, and personal services: (i) Public administration and defence; (ii) Other services
(10) GDP at factor cost (1 to 9)

Appendix 12C

Table 12C.1 Indicators used for Quarterly Estimates of GDP

Sector	Indicators used for Quarterly Estimates
1. Agriculture	Quarterly agriculture production estimates of forecast crops
2. Livestock	Quarterly production of milk, eggs, and wool
3. Forestry	Apportioning equally in all the four quarters.

(Cont'd)

Table 12C.1 *(Cont'd)*

4. Fishery	Quarterly production of inland and marine fish
5. Mining and quarrying	Production of coal, crude petroleum, and IIP (Mining)
6. Manufacturing	IIP (Manufacturing).
7. Electricity, gas, and water supply	IIP (Electricity) and IIP (Group 31—relating to petroleum products), central government revenue expenditure, CPI (industrial workers)
8. Construction	Production of cement, steel, coal, and IIP (Group 27)
9. Trade, hotels, and restaurants	Gross Trading Index, which is computed using the value of output of commodity producing sectors and imports
10. Railways	Net tonne km and Net passenger km
11. Transport by other means	Number of commercial vehicles for the road sub-sector, cargo handled at major ports for the water sub-sector and passenger kilometres flown and freight tonne kilometres flown for the air sub-sector.
12. Communication	Postal and telecommunication revenues, WPI
13. Banking and insurance	Aggregate deposits, bank credits, and the WPI for the banking sub-setor, life insurance (sum assured) and life fund and WPI for the life insurance part of the insurance sub-sector and non-life fund (gross less claims) and the WPI for the non-life insurance part of the insurance sub-sectorc
14. Public administration	Central government revenue expenditure and CPI (industrial workers)
15. Other services	For the public component, central government revenue expenditure and CPI (industrial workers) and for the private part, apportioning equally in all the four quarters

Source: CSO June 2015.

Bibliography

Central Statistical Organisation. 1961. *Proposals for a Revised Series of National Income Estimates for 1955–56 to 1959–60*. New Delhi: Ministry of Statistics and Programme Implementation.

———. 1967. *Brochure on Revised Series of National Product, for 1960–61 to 1964–65*. New Delhi: Ministry of Statistics and Programme Implementation.

———. 1969a. *Estimates of Saving in India, 1960–61 to 1965–66*. New Delhi: Ministry of Statistics and Programme Implementation.

———. 1969b. *Estimates of Capital Formation in India 1960–61 to 1965–66*. New Delhi: Ministry of Statistics and Programme Implementation.

———. 1975. *National Accounts Statistics 1960–61 to 1972–73—Disaggregated Tables*. New Delhi: Ministry of Statistics and Programme Implementation.

———. December 1988a. *Estimates of Capital Stock of Indian Economy as on March 31, 1981*. New Delhi: Ministry of Statistics and Programme Implementation.

———. 1988b. *Estimates of Capital Stock of Indian Economy as on 31st March, 1981*. New Delhi: Ministry of Statistics and Programme Implementation.

———. July 2002. *National Accounts Statistics of India 1950–51 to 2000–01*. New Delhi: Ministry of Statistics and Programme Implementation.

———. January 2008 and March 2010. *New Series of National Account Statistics (base year 2004–05 = 100)*. New Delhi: Ministry of Statistics and Programme Implementation.

———. January 2008. *Report of the Group for Examining Discrepancy in PFCE Estimated from NSSO Consumer Expenditure Data and Estimates compiled by National Accounts Division*. New Delhi: Ministry of Statistics and Programme Implementation.

———. *Estimates of National Income* (annual publication). New Delhi: Ministry of Statistics and Programme Implementation.

———. *Estimates of National Product* (annual publication). New Delhi: Ministry of Statistics and Programme Implementation.

———. *Input–output Transaction Table 2003–04*. New Delhi: Ministry of Statistics and Programme Implementation.

———. *National Accounts Statistics, 2015*. New Delhi: Ministry of Statistics and Programme Implementation.

———. *National Accounts Statistics, Sources and Methods, 1980, 1989, 2007, and 2012*. New Delhi: Ministry of Statistics and Programme Implementation.

Central Statistical Organisation. *National Sample Survey Reports on Consumption Expenditure*. New Delhi: Ministry of Statistics and Programme Implementation.

Central Statistics Office. *System of National Accounts*. New Delhi: Ministry of Statistics and Programme Implementation.

Department of Economic Affairs. 1951. *First Report of the National Income Committee*. New Delhi: Ministry of Finance.

———. 1954. *Final Report of the National Income Committee*. New Delhi: Ministry of Finance.

Directorate General of Supplies and Disposals. *Directory of Government Purchases*. New Delhi: Ministry of Commerce and Industry.

Kulshreshtha, A.C., and A. Kar. 2005. *Estimates of Food Consumption Expenditure from Household Surveys and National Accounts: The Great Indian Poverty Debate*. New Delhi: Macmillan.

Ministry of Statistics and Programme Implementation. March 2015. *Changes in Methodology and Data Sources in The New Series of National Accounts, Base Year 2011–12*.

Mukherjee, M. 1969. *National Income of India: Trends and Structure*. Calcutta.

National Council of Applied Economics Research. 1965. *All-India Rural Household Survey for the year 1961–62*. New Delhi: National Council of Applied Economics Research.

———. 1972. *All India Household Survey of Income, Saving and Consumption Expenditure for 1967–68*. New Delhi: National Council of Applied Economics Research.

———. 1980. *All India Survey on Household Survey on Income and Its Disposition*. New Delhi: National Council of Applied Economics Research.

National Statistical Commission. *Report of National Statistical Commission August, 2001*.

National Council of Applied Economics Research. 1965. *Saving in India (1950–51–1961–62)*. New Delhi: National Council of Applied Economics Research.

———. 'Saving in India during the Plan Periods', Occasional Paper No. 16.

Pradhan, Basanta K. and P.K. Roy. 2003. The well being of Indian Households: MIMAP – India Survey Report. New Delhi: Tata McGraw-Hill.

———. 2005. *National Survey on Household Income and Expenditure*.

Rao, C. R. (ed.). 1972. *Data Base of Indian Economy*, Vol. I. Calcutta: Statistical Publishing Society.

Reserve Bank of India. 1960. RBI Bulletin March 1960. Monthly Bulletin of the Reserve Bank of India, Mumbai.

———. March 1965. Estimates of Saving and Investment in the Indian Economy, 1950–51 to 1962–63. Monthly Bulletin of the Reserve Bank of India, Mumbai.

13

Financial Statistics

Financial statistics can be divided into three classes: (i) statistics relating to banking; (ii) insurance; and (iii) statistics relating to public finance—the finances of the government of India, state governments, and local bodies and finances of the railways. A detailed description of these three types of financial statistics is given in the following sections.

Banking Statistics

Banking statistics are compiled and published mostly by the Reserve Bank of India (RBI). The RBI was established in April 1935 as the central bank of the country. The RBI is the note-issuing authority and controls the country's exchange. It is the bank of the bankers. To discharge these duties, the bank collects and compiles a large amount of data. Commercial banks in the country are required to submit a number of returns to the RBI. From these returns a large amount of information is available. These data along with other economic data are published by the RBI, in the following main publications. In addition, the RBI publishes a number of occasional papers, analysing the data and giving details about concepts and rules.[1] It also publishes

[1] See RBI's website https://www.rbi.org.in/Scripts/Publications.aspx?publication=Occasional (accessed on 18 May 2017).

annual reports giving the details about the review and prospects of the economy and the details about the working and operations of the RBI.

Branch Banking Statistics

This publication on 'Branch Banking Statistics' presents detailed information on branches/offices of commercial banks (CBs) in India.

The detailed information on bank branches/offices is regularly collected by the RBI from the banks in Proformae I and II to allot uniform code numbers to them. Details of new branches/offices opened in banked/unbanked centres such as date of opening of branch/office, name and address of branch/office, other locational details, population of centre, nature of business activities pursued, and also some auxiliary information covering authorized dealer (AD) category, currency chest details, and status of computerization are also reported through Proforma I. The information of relocation/closure/merger/conversion of a bank branch/change of branch name/AD category/change of any auxiliary information is collected through Proforma II. The latest available report, fourth in the series, pertains to the year 2009.

Handbook of Monetary Statistics of India

The RBI has been publishing the *Handbook of Statistics on the Indian Economy* since 1998, with a view to improving data dissemination by providing a storehouse of statistical information at one place. The handbook provides time series data at annual, quarterly, monthly, and higher frequencies in respect of real, monetary, fiscal, banking, financial, and external sectors of the Indian economy.

In addition to the *Handbook of Statistics on the Indian Economy*, the RBI has taken the initiative to bring out sectoral handbooks to provide time series of disaggregated data relating to a particular sector in one place. As a part of this initiative, the *Handbook of Statistics on State Government Finances* was published in 2004.

This process is being carried forward with the publication of the present volume titled *Handbook of Monetary Statistics of India*. This volume provides disaggregated data on monetary, banking, prices and select financial market statistics at annual as well as monthly/fortnightly/weekly frequencies. Data are provided in most cases from 1950–1 onwards and in the case of the RBI's balance sheet and profit and loss account from the inception of the bank, that is, 1935 onwards. This publication is expected to be useful for researchers, policy makers, financial market participants, and analysts interested in monetary economics. This handbook is being released in three versions, namely in printed form, as a CD-ROM, and as a web-based source.[2] The latest report was published in the year 2006.

Handbook of Statistics on Indian Economy

The dissemination of macroeconomic and financial data through the *Handbook of Statistics on the Indian Economy* is increasingly becoming user friendly. The first handbook publication was brought out by the bank in 1998, the CD-ROM version started in 1999 and subsequently, since December 2000, it is being released on the bank's website.

The *Handbook of Statistics on the Indian Economy* covers time series statistics on a wide range of economic and financial indicators pertaining to national income aggregates, output, prices, money, banking, financial markets, public finances, foreign trade, balance of payments, and select socio-economic indicators, which are released at various frequencies. The publication for the year 2014–15 contains 248 statistical tables. This publication in print/CD-ROM form is now being brought out from the bank's data warehouse by the Data Management and Dissemination Division (DMDD), Department of Statistics and Information Management (DSIM).

State Finances: A Study of Budgets

This is an annual publication of the RBI. The latest report for the year 2015–16 contains four chapters: (i) overview; (ii) quality of sub-national public expenditure; (iii) fiscal position of state governments; (iv) issues and perspectives. From 2005–6, the report also incorporates a special theme based on a specific issue of relevance. Continuing this

[2] Available at www.rbi.org.in (accessed on 26 May 2017).

practice, the special theme covered in the report for 2015–16 relates to 'quality of sub-national public expenditure' (Chapter 3).

The results are based on the receipts and expenditure data presented in the budget documents of the state governments. The data are published for accounts of the previous year, revised estimates of the present year, and budget estimates of the next year. Some materials received from the Planning Commission relating to state-wise plan outlays are also incorporated. Some details of the revenue and capital receipts and expenditure are as follows.

Revenue Receipts

Items
Total Revenues (1 + 2)

(1) Tax Revenues (a + b)
    (a) State's own tax revenue
        (i) Taxes on income
        (ii) Taxes on property and capital transactions
        (iii) Taxes on commodities and services
    (b) Share in central taxes
(2) Non-tax Revenue (c + d)
    (c) State's own non-tax revenue
        (i) Interest receipts
        (ii) Dividends and profits
        (iii) General services
        (iv) Social services
        (v) Fiscal services
        (vi) Economic services
    (d) Grants from the centre
        (i) State plan schemes
        (ii) Central plan schemes
        (iii) Centrally sponsored schemes
        (iv) NEC/special plan schemes
        (v) Non-plan grants

Revenue Expenditure

Items
Total expenditure (1 + 2 + 3 + 4 + 5)

(1) Developmental Expenditure (a + b)
  (a) Social services
  (b) Economic services
    (i) Agriculture and allied activities
    (ii) Rural development
    (iii) Special area programmes
    (iv) Irrigation and flood control
    (v) Energy
    (vi) Industry and minerals
    (vii) Transport and communications
    (viii) Science, technology and environment
    (ix) General economic services
(2) Non-developmental expenditure(general services) (a to f)
  (a) Organs of state
  (b) Fiscal services
  (c) Interest payments and servicing of debt (i + ii)
    (i) Appropriation for reduction or avoidance of debt
    (ii) Interest payments
  (d) Administrative services
  (e) Pensions
  (f) Miscellaneous general services
(3) Grants-in-aid and contributions
(4) Compensation and assignments to local bodies and panchayati raj institutions
(5) Reserve with finance department.

Capital Receipts

Items
Total receipts (1 to 13)

(1) External debt
(2) Internal debt
(3) Loans and advances from the centre
(4) Recovery of loans and advances
(5) Inter-state settlement (net)
(6) Contingency fund (net)
(7) Small savings and provident funds (net)
(8) Reserve funds (net)

(9) Deposits and advances (net)
(10) Suspense and miscellaneous (net)
(11) Appropriation to contingency fund (net)
(12) Miscellaneous capital receipts
(13) Remittances (net)

Capital Expenditure

Items
Total disbursements (1 + 2 + 3 + 4)

- (1) Total capital outlay (a + b)
  - (a) Developmental (i + ii)
    - (i) Social services
    - (ii) Economic services
      - Agriculture and allied activities
      - Rural development
      - Special area programmes
      - Major and medium irrigation and flood control
      - Energy
      - Industry and minerals
      - Transport
      - Communications
      - Science, technology and environment
      - General economic services
  - (b) Non-developmental (general services)
- (2) Discharge of internal debt
- (3) Repayment of loans to the centre
- (4) Loans and advances by state governments (a + b)
  - (a) Developmental purposes (i + ii)
    - (i) Social services
    - (ii) Economic services
  - (b) Non-developmental purposes

Report on Currency and Finance

This is an annual report started in this form in 1937. This report reviews the economic and financial developments during the financial year and is divided into two parts since 1975–6. Part I gives an overall review of the developments in the economy during the year; Part II deals with the developments in various sectors of the country's economy in detail with a separate chapter for each of these, namely output and price trends, money and banking, capital markets, budget and public debt, trade and tariff developments, and currency and coinage. Part II also contains a few appendices which give a summary in tabular form of the details of the union and the state government budget proposals for the year, important export and import policy announcements, the tariff commissioner's recommendations, and India's trade agreements with foreign countries. From 1998–9, the *Report on Currency and Finance* has become theme based. So far the following ten reports have been published (Table 13.1).

Table 13.1 Details of Reports Published

Number	Year	Theme
1.	1998–9	The structural transformation of the Indian economy
2.	1999–2000	Financial sector and market integration
3.	2000–1	Revitalizing growth
4.	2001–2	Stock taking of the reform process and its outcomes
5.	2002–3	Management of the external sector in an open economy framework
6.	2003–4	The evolution of monetary policy
7.	2004–5	The evolution of central banking in India
8.	2005–6	Development of financial markets and role of the central bank
9.	2006–7 and 2007–8	The banking sector in India: Emerging issues and challenges
10.	2008–9	Global financial crisis and the Indian economy
11.	2009–12	Fiscal monetary co-ordination

Source: *Report on Currency and Finance*, various issues.

Statistical Tables Relating to Banks in India

This annual publication, being brought out by the RBI since 1941, provides comprehensive data on the working of commercial banks in India. It covers banks functioning in India, whether registered in India or abroad. It is divided into three parts. The first part consists of summary tables which present the serial data for the Indian banking system as well as its component units in respect of assets and liabilities, offices, and profits. The first table 'Statistics at a Glance' shows the progress of banking in India since 1951. The liabilities and assets are given for different classes of commercial banks (the classes are State Bank of India, subsidiaries of the State Bank of India, other Indian scheduled banks, foreign banks, and non-scheduled banks). Liabilities and assets are also given by size of deposits of banks. Data regarding earnings and expenses of banks are also available separately for Indian and foreign scheduled banks and non-scheduled banks. Data on the analysis of investments by the banks, purpose-wise distribution of advances, ownership of deposits, deposits of various rates of interest, advances of scheduled commercial banks at various rates, and liabilities and assets of Indian scheduled banks in foreign countries is also available in great detail in this publication.

The second part consists of detailed tables which give data in respect of individual scheduled and non-scheduled commercial banks.

The third part has certain appendices which contain information on the location of the offices of different banks and the centre-wise details of bank deposits and bank credit in India, members and sub-members of clearing houses, and also the location of offices and names of agents and correspondents of Indian banks in foreign countries.

The detailed information given in this publication is not available in any other report.

Trend and Progress of Banking in India

This is also an annual publication giving a review of important events in the field of banking during the year. The effects of these events on the nation's economy are also discussed. It also contains a table giving the trends and progress of banking in India, at a glance. The statistics given here are also available in other publications of the RBI.

Besides this there is an *Annual Report of Central Board of Directors*. The report deals with the review of important events during the year and other such problems which are also discussed in the *Trend and Progress of Banking in India*. Since there was some duplication of data, these two publications have been merged under the name *Annual Report on the Working of the Reserve Bank of India and Trends and Progress of Banking in India*.

Basic Statistical Returns of Scheduled Commercial Banks in India

This annual publication provides granular data on a number of key parameters of banks. The information is collected from bank branches through Basic Statistical Returns 1 and 2 (BSR 1&2). Under BSR 1, account-level data for loan accounts with credit limit more than Rs 2 lakh and occupation-wise consolidated data for loan accounts with credit limit up to Rs 2 lakh are collected branch-wise. Under BSR 2, branch-wise data related to parameters such as staff, type of deposits, and maturity pattern of term deposits are collected. The data through BSR 1&2 are being collected since 1972.

The volume, in the series, provides detailed data on credit and deposits of scheduled commercial banks as on 31 March of the year. The volume ending March 2016 covers nearly 1 lakh branches with more than 131 million credit accounts and 903 million deposit accounts spread across more than 36 thousand centres. This publication provides detailed occupation-wise credit data on different dimensions, namely, type of account, organization, interest rate range, and size of credit limit. It also provides information on population group, bank group, state-wise credit data, and district-wise credit data according to type of occupation. One unique feature of this publication is that it covers spatial distribution of both, credit sanctioned and credit utilized. The publication is also made available on CD-ROM and through the RBI website.

Reserve Bank of India Bulletin (Monthly)

The *RBI Bulletin* has two sections. The first section contains various articles regarding banking, money, and credit. It deals with monetary and credit trends, money rates, credit policy, industrial securities, bullion, general prices, commodity markets, and trade developments.

These articles appear in all issues of the bulletin. The other articles are different for different issues and some of them are the results of various surveys and studies carried out by the RBI. The second part gives statistical tables regarding currency and banking, public finance, and other economic statistics. Important monthly statistics on banking and currency relate to the following:

(1) Liabilities and assets:
    (a) Reserve Bank of India
        (i) Issue department
        (ii) Banking department
    (b) All scheduled banks
    (c) All scheduled commercial banks
    (d) Indian scheduled commercial banks
    (e) Foreign banks
    (f) State cooperative banks (SCBs) maintaining accounts with the Reserve Bank
    (g) Non-scheduled commercial banks
    (h) Industrial Financial Corporation of India
    (i) State financial corporations
    (j) Industrial Development Bank of India
    (k) Industrial Credit and Investment Corporation of India.
(2) Advances of scheduled commercial banks according to classes of security.
(3) Reserves of scheduled commercial banks and state cooperative banks with the RBI (separately available for Indian scheduled commercial banks and foreign banks).
(4) Savings deposits with scheduled commercial banks (separately available for Indian banks and foreign banks).
(5) Borrowings by scheduled commercial banks from the RBI at various rates of interest.
(6) Advances of the RBI to scheduled commercial banks and state cooperative banks (separately available for these two categories of banks and under different sections).
(7) Cheque clearances.
(8) Money supply with the public along with factors affecting money supply. It is available according to the following classes:
    (a) Currency with the public
        (i) Notes in circulation

(ii) Circulation of rupee coins
(iii) Circulation of small coins
(iv) Cash on hand or with banks
(b) Deposit money with the public
(i) Net demand deposits of banks
(ii) Other deposits with the Reserve Bank
(9) Foreign exchange rates
(10) Money rates
(11) India's foreign exchange reserves
(12) Sterling's transactions of the RBI

Other statistics given in the bulletin refer to public finance and general economic statistics, the primary sources for the collection of which are agencies other than the RBI. That is the reason the details of those statistics are not given here.

Reserve Bank of India—Weekly Statistical Supplement

This is a weekly statistical supplement issued by the RBI. The data is as at the close of every Friday. The statement gives the liabilities and assets of the banking and issue departments separately.

Liabilities and Assets (RBI)

The liabilities of the banking department consist of the deposits with (i) the central government; (ii) state governments; (iii) scheduled commercial banks; (iv) scheduled cooperative banks; (v) non-scheduled state cooperative banks; (vi) other banks; and (vii) other deposits and other liabilities including paid-up capital and reserve funds.

The assets of this department consist of (i) notes and coins; (ii) balances held abroad; (iii) loans and advances to the central and state governments; (iv) loans and advances to the scheduled commercial banks, state cooperative banks, and other loans and advances; (v) bills purchased and discounted; (vi) investments; and (vii) other assets.

The liabilities of the issue department are classified into (i) notes in circulation; and (ii) notes held in the banking department.

The assets are classified into (i) gold coins and bullion; (ii) foreign securities; (iii) rupee coins; and (iv) rupee securities of the government of India.

Scheduled Commercial Banks

This supplement gives comprehensive data regarding all the scheduled banks. This statement is issued every week by the RBI and relates to the position as at the close of every Friday. The RBI receives weekly returns from all the scheduled banks. The data relates to the assets and liabilities of the scheduled banks.

These are given according to the following classifications (Table 13.2).

Table 13.2 Assets and Liabilities of Scheduled Banks

Liabilities	Assets
(1) Demand liabilities: Reserve Bank (a) Deposits: (i) inter-bank; (ii) others (b) Borrowings from banks	(1) Cash in hand and balances with Reserve Bank (a) Cash in hand (b) Balances with Reserve Bank
(2) Times liabilities (breakdown is same account as for demand liabilities)	(2) Balances with other banks in account as for demand liabilities) current
(3) Borrowings from Reserve Bank: (a) Against usance bills and/or promissory notes (b) Others	(3) Investments in government securities
(4) Borrowings from State Bank (and/or a notified bank and state governments): (a) Demand (b) Time	(4) Money at call and short notice
	(5) Bank credit: (a) advances: (i) loans, cash credits, and overdrafts; (ii) due from banks (b) bills purchased and discounted: (i) inland; (ii) foreign

Source: Weekly Statistical Supplement, RBI.[3]

[3] Available at https://rbi.org.in/Scripts/Publications.aspx?Publication=weekly (accessed on 25 May 2017).

The following half-yearly publications are issued:

(1) Half-yearly Financial Stability Reports
(2) Macro-Economic and Monetary Developments
(3) Report on Foreign Exchange Reserves
(4) Monetary Policy Report

For occasional papers and other reports see on the website of the RBI.

Statistical Statements Relating to the Cooperative Movement in India

The information published by National Bank for Agriculture and Rural Development (NABARD), since its inception in 1982, relates to state and central cooperative banks (CCBs) and credit societies, land mortgage banks, and non-credit societies. Since 1963–4 this publication has been available in two parts. Part I gives details regarding credit societies (SCBs, CCBs, Industrial Cooperative Banks [ICBs], Primary Agricultural Credit Societies [PACS], Grain Banks (GBs), Primary Cooperative Banks [PCBs], Primary Non-Agricultural Credit Societies [PNACS], State Cooperative Agricultural and Rural Development Banks [SCARDBs] and Primary Cooperative Agricultural and Rural Development Banks [PCARDBs]). Part II covers non-credit societies (marketing societies, processing societies, farming, fisheries, weavers, housing, consumer cooperatives, forest labourers, and other industrial societies, among others). The contents of the publication include statistical data on number, membership, liabilities, assets, and operations in respect of both credit and non-credit societies based on audited balance sheets and profit and loss accounts for the particular year pertaining to the respective cooperative societies.

Insurance Statistics

The main publications on insurance statistics are

(1) *Annual Report of the Life Insurance Corporation of India.*
(2) *Annual Report of General Insurance Corporation of India and its Subsidiaries.*

Annual Report of the Life Insurance Corporation of India

Life insurance was nationalized in 1956. Since then the business regarding insurance on life is done by the LIC only. In addition to this general insurance is also done by the LIC along with other private companies. The annual report of the corporation gives details of its business done during the year. The statistics are available for the following main aspects:

(1) New business and business in force, number of policies and sum assured, zone-wise, division-wise, and month-wise progress in India for individual insurance.
(2) Distribution according to plans of insurance of new business for individual policies only.
(3) Classified statements of life insurance policies, ordinary policies, annuity contracts, etc., group insurance policies, group annuity contracts, etc.
(4) Additions and deductions from policies separately for business transacted in India and outside India.
(5) Particulars of policies forfeited, surrendered, and lapsed after acquiring paid-up value and without acquiring paid-up value.
(6) Details of income and outgo and working results of life insurance.
(7) State-wise, zone-wise, and sector-wise distribution of investments in India.
(8) Country-wise distribution of investments outside India including loans.
(9) Distribution of investments in shares and debentures among various industries etc.
(10) Financial statements of accounts in respect of life insurance business and capital redemption (including annuity contracts) and general balance sheet.
(11) Number of staff and salaries.
(12) Other related statistics.

It is a statutory report under Section 27 of the Life Insurance Corporation Act, 1956. Recently a number of private companies have entered in the field of life insurance.

Annual Report of General Insurance Corporation of India and its Subsidiaries

The annual report provides details of the corporation and its four subsidiaries, namely National Insurance Co. Ltd., The New India Assurance Co. Ltd., The Oriental Insurance Co. Ltd., and The United India Insurance Co. Ltd.

The statistics are available separately for fire, marine, and miscellaneous insurance balances on the following items:

(1) Gross and net premium income relating to business in India and outside India.
(2) Net claims payable.
(3) Commission on direct business and on reinsurance business.
(4) Expenses of management and other charges.
(5) Reserve for unexpired risks.
(6) Underwriting profit.
(7) Summary of profit and loss accounts.
(8) Distribution of assets under various classes as well as investments in public sector, joint sector, and private sector. Information is also available on proposed dividends, capital and funds, investments, large general insurance claims, and number of employees.

The report also gives following information in respect of four subsidiary companies:

(1) Organizational setup, that is, number of regional offices, divisional offices, and branch offices.
(2) Class-wise gross direct premium income and net premium income.
(3) Underwriting results.
(4) Investment income.
(5) Profit before tax and after tax.
(6) Dividends declared.
(7) Paid-up capital and the holding of General Insurance Corporation of India in share capital.
(8) Number of claims instituted, settled, and outstanding.
(9) Countries in which they are transacting general insurance business through branch offices or agencies or associated companies.

Annual reports of the subsidiary companies are also available. These provide detailed data on their performance during the year.

Recently a number of private companies have entered this field, but no consolidated data are available regarding these companies.

The list of public and private general insurance companies is given as follows:

(1) Public Sector
  (a) New India Assurance Company Limited
  (b) National Insurance Company Limited
  (c) The Oriental Insurance Co. Ltd.
  (d) United India Insurance Co. Ltd.
  (e) Export Credit Guarantee Corporation
  (f) Agriculture Insurance Company of India Ltd.
(2) Private Players
  (a) Bajaj Allianz General Insurance Co. Ltd.
  (b) ICICI Lombard General Insurance Co. Ltd.
  (c) IFFCO-Tokyo General Insurance Co. Ltd.
  (d) Reliance General Insurance Co. Ltd.
  (e) Royal Sundaram Alliance Insurance Co. Ltd
  (f) TATA AIG General Insurance Co. Ltd.
  (g) Cholamandalam General Insurance Co. Ltd.
  (h) HDFC Chubb General Insurance Co. Ltd.
  (i) Star Health Allied Insurance Co. Ltd.
  (j) Apollo DKV Insurance Co. Ltd.
  (k) Future Generali India Insurance Co. Ltd.
  (l) Universal Sompo General Insurance Co. Ltd.
  (m) Bharti AXA General Insurance Co. Ltd.
  (n) Raheja QBE General Insurance Company Ltd.

Public Finance Statistics

Public finance statistics are available in the budgets of the central and state governments. The budgets give a complete account of the revenue and expenditure of the governments. Statistics are separately available for the railway budget. The budgets for different states are presented in their state assemblies while the budget for the central government and the railway budget are presented before Parliament.[4]

[4] From 2017–18, the railway budget is a part of the Central general budget.

For different states and the Indian union these budgets are printed in the form of different reports, called Budget Papers. Statistics presented in these papers relate to revenue receipts and expenditure on revenue account and receipts and expenditure on capital account.

Statistics relating to public finance are mainly available in the following publications:

(1) Budget of the Central Government (annual).
(2) Explanatory Memorandum—Expenditure Budget, Volume 1 and 2 and Receipt Budget.
(3) An Economic and Functional Classification of the Central Government Budget (annual).
(4) Economic Survey (annual).
(5) Combined Finance and Revenue Accounts of the Union and State Governments in India.
(6) Indian Public Finance Statistics.

Central Budget

The following are the main papers presented before Parliament regarding the central government budget.

Budget of the Central Government

The 'annual financial statement' laid before both Houses of Parliament, in accordance with the provisions of the constitution, is the budget of the central government. This statement as provided under Article 112 covers all the transactions of the central government during the current and the ensuing year. This statement shows estimated receipts and expenditure of the Government of India (GoI) for the ensuing year in relation to revised estimates for the current year as also expenditure for the previous year. The budget of the Indian Railways is separately presented to Parliament and dealt with by it, but as the receipts and expenditure of the railways is, nevertheless, the receipts and expenditure of the GoI, the figures relating to these are also included in lump in the general budget.

The annual financial statement is prepared by major heads of account, prescribed in consultation with the Comptroller and Auditor General (CAG). These heads fall either under the Consolidated Fund of India flows from Art. 266 of the Constitution or in the Public Account of the government. In addition, the GoI also maintains a Contingency Fund, set up under Article 267(1) of the Constitution, with a corpus of Rs 500 crore (at present), for making advances for urgent unforeseen expenditure, which are recouped to the fund by debit to the Consolidated Fund of India, after obtaining Parliamentary sanction for such expenditure. The receipts and expenditure of the government fall under one or other of the major heads either in the Consolidated Fund or the Public Account in accordance with the prescribed rules of classification.

All revenues received by the GoI, all loans raised by the government by the issue of treasury bills, loans or ways and means advances, and all monies received by government in repayment of loans are credited to the Consolidated Fund and monies can be appreciated from that fund only in accordance with law and for the purposes and in the manner provided in the Constitution. All other public monies received by or on behalf of the government of India credited to the Public Account. Government expenditure including expenditure on loans and advances by the government, the repayment of loans, treasury bills, and ways and means advances is met out of the Consolidated Fund. The estimates of expenditure have to show separately the sums required to meet other expenditure which the Constitution has charged upon the Consolidated Fund and the sums required to meet other expenditure. The latter covers expenditure on the repayment of loans, treasury bills, and ways and means advances.

Under the Constitution, the budget has to distinguish expenditure on revenue account from other expenditure. The government budget, therefore, comprises (i) revenue budget; and (ii) capital budget.

REVENUE BUDGET

Revenue budget consists of the revenue receipts of government (tax revenues and other revenues) and the expenditure met from these revenues. Tax revenues comprise proceeds of taxes and other duties levied by the union. The estimates of revenue receipts shown in the Annual Financial Statement take into account the effect of various taxation proposals made in the Finance Bill. Other receipts of government mainly consist of interest and dividend on investments made by the government, fees, and other receipts for services rendered by the government. Revenue expenditure is for the normal running of government departments and various services, interest payments on debt, and subsidies. Broadly, the expenditure which does not result in creation of assets for the GoI is treated as revenue expenditure. All grants given to state governments/UTs and other parties are also treated as revenue expenditure even though some of the grants may be used for creation of assets.

CAPITAL BUDGET

Capital budget consists capital receipts and capital payments. The capital receipts are loans raised by the government from the public, called market loans, borrowings by the government from the Reserve Bank and other parties through sale of Treasury Bills, loans received from foreign governments and bodies, disinvestment receipts, and recoveries of loans from state and UT governments and other parties. Capital payments consist of capital expenditure on acquisition of assets like land, buildings, machinery, equipment, as also investments in shares, and loans and advances granted by the central government to state and UT governments, government companies, corporations, and other parties.

DEMAND FOR GRANTS

Article 113 of the Constitution mandates that the estimates of expenditure to be met from the Consolidated Fund are presented to the Lok Sabha in the form of Demands for Grants, are shown according to the accounting classification prescribed under Article 150 of the Constitution, except to the extent to which such expenditure is charged on the Consolidated Fund and, in consequence, does not require a vote of the Lok Sabha. These demands generally cover the requirements of each individual administrative service. For example, a ministry has a demand for its own expenditure and one for the expenditure of each one of the various departments under its administrative control. Except in special circumstances, a demand does not cover more than one department or more than one head of account. The main exception to this is that all revenue expenditure controlled by the head of each UT without legislature is brought together in a single demand. Similarly all capital expenditure in the UTs without legislature under the control of the heads of these territories has been provided in a single demand. Each ministry has also generally a demand for its miscellaneous expenditure which may cover more than one head of account. The loan requirements, whether for payment to states or others of all ministries and UTs without legislature are included in a composite demand, presented on behalf of the Ministry of Finance. Likewise the provision for payment of grants-in-aid to states and UTs with legislature, by all ministries, is included in a composite demand. Distinct demands are presented for expenditure met from revenue and for capital expenditure. The charged expenditure under any head for which there is a voted demand, is included is that demand, not presented for vote. Where expenditure is wholly charged, a separate appropriation is included for it in the Book of Demands.

In budget 2016–17 there are 98 Demands for Grants. Within each demand the estimates are arranged by suitable sub-heads, which indicate the categories and nature of expenditure included in the demand. So long as the total demand is not exceeded, government (and authorities subordinate to them to whom powers may be delegated) can meet excesses in charged expenditure.

One qualification must be remembered in considering the demands for grants. Although they are generally by major heads, the total of all the demands relating to a major head and the charged expenditure provided under that head may not agree with the total shown in the annual financial statement. This is because certain recoveries are taken in the accounts in reduction of expenditure while in the demands, which when passed; provide the authority for incurring the particular item of expenditure, these recoveries are not taken into account. The recoveries mostly relate to inter departmental adjustments or recoveries from other governments and ad hoc funds, among others. Thus, if the Union Excise Department does some work for customs the gross expenditure will appear in the demand under Union Excise while the accounts will show only the net expenditure (that is, gross expenditure less recovery from customs) under the major head 'Union Excise Duties'.

After the demands have been voted by the Lok Sabha, the monies required to meet the grants so voted and the expenditure charged on the Consolidated Fund and included in the annual financial statement presented to parliament are withdrawn from the Consolidated Fund under the authority of an Appropriation Act passed by Parliament.

For payments out of the Public Account, no demand is required to be presented to Parliament and the requirements are met from time as they arise. These payments are largely of the nature of banking transactions. State Provident Funds, depreciation and other reserve funds of government departments Post Office Savings Bank (POSB), Post Office Cash and other Savings Certificates, Postal Life Insurance Funds, and ad hoc funds created by the government by appropriation from revenue or otherwise. Miscellaneous deposits and remittances are included in the Public Account. It is broadly correct to say that none of the monies lying in the Public Account belongs to the government. They have to be paid back sometime or the other to the public as in the case of the State Provident Funds, Postal Savings Bank, Postal Cash Certificates, and Postal Life Insurance funds, or to be utilized by the government in an agreed manner as in the case of ad hoc funds set up for special purposes. It may be mentioned that to complete the picture that the approval of parliament is necessary to any appropriation from revenue to create a fund and unless the monies thus funded are made over to corporate bodies with separate legal status of their own, similar approval is required for incurring subsequent expenditure from such funds. When an amount is transferred to any such fund, it is shown as expenditure in the estimates of the year, in which the transfer is made. Expenditure met from these funds is similarly shown in the estimates of the year in which it is incurred but an equivalent amount is transferred from the fund to meet this expenditure. Parliamentary control is thus secured on both the creation of such funds and the utilization of the monies held in them.

APPROPRIATION BILL

Under Article 114(3) of the Constitution, no amount can be withdrawn from the Consolidated Fund without the enactment of such a law by Parliament. After the Demands for Grants are voted by the Lok Sabha, Parliament's approval to the withdrawal from the Consolidated Fund of the amounts so voted and of the amount required to meet the expenditure charged on the Consolidated Fund is sought through the Appropriation Bill. The whole process beginning with the presentation of the Budget and ending with discussions and voting on the Demands for Grants requires sufficiently long time. The Lok Sabha is, therefore, empowered by the Constitution to make any grant in advance in respect of the estimated expenditure for a part of the financial year pending completion of procedure for the voting of the Demands. The purpose of the 'Vote on Account' is to keep the government functioning, pending voting of 'final supply'. The Vote on Account is obtained from parliament through an Appropriation (Vote on Account) Bill.

FINANCE BILL

At the time of presentation of the Annual Financial Statement before Parliament, a finance bill is also presented in fulfilment of the requirement of Article 110(1)(a) of the Constitution, detailing the imposition, abolition, remission, alteration, or regulation of taxes proposed in the budget. A finance bill is a money bill as defined in Article 110 of the Constitution. It is accompanied by a Memorandum explaining the provisions included in it.

MEMORANDUM EXPLAINING THE PROVISIONS IN THE FINANCE BILL

To facilitate understanding of the taxation proposals contained in the finance bill, the provisions and their implications are explained in the document titled *Memorandum Explaining the Provisions in the Finance Bill.*

MACRO-ECONOMIC FRAMEWORK STATEMENT

The Macro-economic Framework Statement, presented to the parliament under Section 3(5) of the Fiscal Responsibility and Budget Management (FRBM) Act, 2003 and the rules made there under contains an assessment of the growth prospects of the economy with specific underlying assumptions. It contains assessment regarding the GDP growth rate, fiscal balance of the central government, and the external sector balance of the economy.

FISCAL POLICY STRATEGY STATEMENT

The *Fiscal Policy Strategy Statement,* presented to the parliament under Section 3(4) of the FRBM Act, 2003, outlines the strategic priorities of the government in the fiscal area for the ensuing financial year relating to taxation, expenditure, lending and investments, administered pricing, borrowings, and guarantees. The statement explains how the current policies are in conformity with sound fiscal management principles and gives the rationale for any major deviation in key fiscal measures.

MEDIUM-TERM FISCAL POLICY STATEMENT

The *Medium-Term Fiscal Policy Statement*, presented to the parliament under Section 3(2) of the Fiscal Responsibility and Budget Management Act, 2003, sets out three-year rolling targets for four specific fiscal indicators in relation to GDP at market prices, namely (i) revenue deficit; (ii) fiscal deficit; (iii) tax to GDP ratio; and (iv) total outstanding debt at the end of the year. The statement includes the underlying assumptions, an assessment of sustainability relating to balance between revenue receipts and revenue expenditure and the use of capital receipts including market borrowings for generation of productive assets.

To facilitate a more comprehensive understanding of the major features of the budget, certain other explanatory documents are presented. These are briefly summarized as follows.

MEDIUM-TERM EXPENDITURE FRAMEWORK STATEMENT

The *Medium-Term Expenditure Framework Statement* (MTEF), presented to the parliament under Section 3 of the Fiscal Responsibility and Budget Management Act, 2003, sets forth a three-year rolling target for the expenditure indicators with specification of underlying assumptions and risks involved. The objective of the MTEF is to provide a closer integration between budget and the FRBM Act, 2003 statements.

This statement is presented separately in the session next to the session in which the budget is presented, that is, normally in the monsoon session.

EXPENDITURE BUDGET VOLUME 1

(1) This document deals with revenue and capital disbursements of various ministries/departments and gives the estimates in respect

of each under 'plan' and 'non-plan'. It also gives analysis of various types of expenditure and broad reasons for the variations in estimates.

(2) Under the present accounting and budgetary procedures, certain classes of receipts, like payments made by one department to another and receipts of capital projects or schemes, are taken in reduction of the expenditure of the receiving department. While the estimates of expenditure included in the Demands for Grants are for the gross amounts, the estimates of expenditure included in the Annual Financial Statement are for the net expenditure, after taking into account the recoveries. The document, *Expenditure Budget*, makes certain other refinements like netting expenditure of related receipts so that inflation of receipts and expenditure figures is avoided and there can be better appreciation of the magnitudes of various expenditure. Contributions to international bodies and estimated strength of establishment of various government departments and provision therefore are shown in separate annexes. A statement each, showing (i) plan grants and loans released by ministries/departments directly to state and district level autonomous bodies, under various central and centrally sponsored plan schemes; (ii) gender budgeting; (iii) schemes for development of scheduled castes and scheduled tribes; and (iv) schemes for welfare of children are also included in this document.

(3) Plan expenditure forms a sizeable proportion of the total expenditure of the central government. The Demands for Grants of the various ministries show the Plan expenditure under each head separately from the Non-Plan expenditure. *Expenditure Budget Vol. 1* also gives the total plan provisions for each of the ministries arranged under the various heads of development and highlights the budget provisions for the more important Plan programmes and schemes. A description of important schemes included in the plan along with the objectives, targets, and achievements is given in the outcome budget of the respective ministry. Variations in the estimates of plan expenditure are also explained.

(4) A large part of the plan expenditure incurred by the central government is through public sector enterprises. Budgetary support

for financing outlays of these enterprises is provided by government either through investment in share capital or through loans. *Expenditure Budget Vol. 1* shows the estimates of capital and loan disbursements to public sector enterprises for plan and non-plan purposes and also the extra budgetary resources available for financing their plans. A detailed report on the working of public sector enterprises is given in a document titled, *Public Enterprises Survey* brought out separately by the Department of Public Enterprises. A report on the working of the enterprises under the control of various administrative ministries is also given in the annual reports of the various ministries circulated to Members of Parliament separately. The annual reports along with the audited accounts of each of the government companies are also separately laid before parliament. Besides, the reports of the CAG on the working of various public sector enterprises are also laid before the Parliament.

(5) Regarding commercial departments, the railways is the principal departmentally run commercial undertaking of the government. The budget of the Ministry of Railways and the Demands for Grants relating to railway expenditure are presented to the parliament separately. The total receipts and expenditure of the railways are, however, incorporated in the Annual Financial Statement of the GoI. To portray the actual working and not inflate receipts or expenditure, the expenditure as reflected in the receipts budget, and *Expenditure Budget Vol. 1* and *Vol. 2* have been taken net of receipts of the departmental commercial undertakings.

(6) The receipts and expenditure of the defence demands shown in the Annual Financial Statement are explained in greater detail in the document defence services estimates presented along with the Detailed Demands for Grants of the Ministry of Defence.

(7) The details of grants given to bodies other than state and UT governments are given in the statements of grants-in-aid paid to non-government bodies appended to Detailed Demands for Grants of the various ministries. Annexure 5 to *Expenditure Budget Vol. 1* shows details of grants-in-aid exceeding Rs 5 lakh (recurring) or Rs 10 lakh (non-recurring) to private institutions, organizations, and individuals.

EXPENDITURE BUDGET VOLUME 2

The provisions made for a scheme or a programme may spread over a number of major heads in the revenue and capital sections in a Demand for Grants. In *Expenditure Budget Vol. 2*, the estimates made for a scheme/programme are brought together and shown on a net basis at one place, by major heads. To understand the objectives underlying the expenditure proposed for various schemes and programmes in the Demands for Grants, suitable explanatory notes are included in this volume in which, wherever necessary, brief reasons for variations between the budget estimates and revised estimates for the current year and requirements for the ensuing budget year are also given.

RECEIPTS BUDGET

Estimates of receipts included in the Annual Financial Statement are further analysed in the document *Receipts Budget*. The document provides details of tax and non-tax revenue receipts and capital receipts and explains the estimates. The document also provides the arrears of tax revenues and non-tax revenues, as mandated under the Fiscal Responsibility and Budget Management Rules, 2004. Trends of receipts and expenditure along with deficit indicators, statement pertaining to the National Small Savings Fund (NSSF), statement of revenues foregone, statement of liabilities, statement of guarantees given by the government, statements of assets, and details of external assistance are also included in receipts budget.

STATEMENT OF REVENUE IMPACT OF TAX INCENTIVES UNDER THE CENTRAL TAX SYSTEM

The statement seeks to list the revenue impact of tax incentives that are a part of the central government. The document was earlier called *Statement of Revenue Foregone*.

AN ECONOMIC AND FUNCTIONAL CLASSIFICATION OF THE CENTRAL GOVERNMENT BUDGET

The budget presented to Parliament is rearranged according to economically significant categories (consumption, capital formation, and financial investment) with the object of understanding the economic impact of the budgetary operations of the central government. Economic classification is prepared by the Economic Division of the Ministry of Finance since 1957–8. Under economic classification, the following details of the accounts are given:

(1) Transaction in commodities and services and transfers:
   (a) Current account of the government administration.
   (b) Current account of departmental commercial undertakings.
   (c) Capital account of the government administration and departmental commercial undertakings.
(2) Capital account of the government administration and departmental commercial undertakings
   (a) Changes in financial assets.
   (b) Changes in financial liabilities.
(3) Cash and capital reconciliation account of the government administration and departmental commercial undertakings.

The system of accounts given here analyses the various aspects of central government's transactions vis-à-vis the rest of the economy. A set of six accounts containing the reclassified data from the central government budget is placed at the end of this section. Some significant magnitudes emerging from this system of accounts are:

(1) The central government's total expenditure.
(2) The central government's final outlays.
(3) Capital formation out of the budgetary resources of the central government.
(4) Net capital formation and savings of the central government.
(5) The various measures of deficit in the central government's budgetary transactions.
(6) Income generation by the central government.

Beginning with 1967–8, an attempt was made to present an economic-cum-functional classification of the budget. The functional classification groups the governments' expenditure according to particular purposes to be served by such expenditures, these being administration, defence, education, and health and economic services. This classification was done because the classification in terms of the economic categories alone often leads to misleading impressions. Consumption expenditure is a case in point. Such expenditure includes not only normal administration expenditures but also provision for education, health, and other social services; the later contribute to development and cannot be ranked as capital expenditure. A cross-classification of the government expenditure by both economic and functional categories brings together at one place all the relevant information by showing under each economic category the broad purpose to which the government spending is directed and under each functional head the economic character of the expenditure. Therefore an attempt is made to present economic-cum-functional classification with a view to have greater understanding of the budgetary operations of the central government.

BUDGET AT A GLANCE

(1) This document shows in brief, receipts and disbursements along with broad details of tax revenues and other receipts. This document also exhibits a broad breakup of expenditure—plan and non-plan, allocation of plan outlays by sectors as well as by ministries/departments, and details of resources transferred by the central government to state and UT governments. This document also shows the revenue deficit, the gross primary deficit, and the gross fiscal deficit of the central government. The excess of government's revenue expenditure over revenue receipts constitutes revenue deficit of the government. The difference between the total expenditure of the government by way of revenue, capital, and loans net of repayments on the one hand and revenue receipts of government and capital receipts which are not in the nature of borrowing but which finally accrue to government on the other, constitutes gross fiscal deficit. Gross primary deficit is measured by gross fiscal deficit reduced by gross interest payments. In the budget documents 'gross fiscal deficit' and 'gross primary deficit' have been referred to in abbreviated form 'fiscal deficit' and 'primary deficit', respectively. This document also shows liabilities of the government on account of securities (bonds) issued in lieu of oil and fertilizer subsidies.

(2) The document also includes a statement indicating the quantum and nature (share in central taxes, grants/loan) of the total resources transferred to state and UT governments. Details of these transfers by way of share of taxes, grants-in-aid and loans

are given in *Expenditure Budget Volume 1*. The bulk of grants and loans are disbursed by the Ministry of Finance and are included in 'Demand Transfers to State and Union Territory Governments'. The grants and loans released to states and UTs by other ministries/departments are provided for in their respective demands.

HIGHLIGHTS OF BUDGET

This document explains the key features of the Budget 2015–16, inter alia, indicating the prominent achievements in various sectors of the economy. It also explains, in brief, the budget proposals for allocation of funds to be made in important areas. The summary of tax proposals is also reflected in the document.

DETAILED DEMANDS FOR GRANTS

The *Detailed Demands for Grants* are laid on the table of the Lok Sabha sometime after the presentation of the budget, but before the discussion on demands for grants commences. *Detailed Demands for Grants* further elaborate the provisions included in the demands for grants as also actual expenditure during the previous year. A break-up of the estimates relating to each programme/organization, wherever the amount involved is not less than Rs 10 lakh, is given under a number of object heads which indicate the categories and nature of expenditure incurred on that programme, such as salaries, wages, travel expenses, machinery and equipment, and grants-in-aid. At the end of these detailed demands are shown the details of recoveries taken in reduction of expenditure in the accounts.

OUTCOME BUDGET

(1) With effect from financial year 2007–8, the performance budget and the outcome budget hitherto presented to parliament separately by ministries/departments, have been merged and presented as a single document titled *Outcome Budget* by each ministry/department in respect of all demands/appropriations controlled by them, except those exempted from this requirement. *Outcome Budget* broadly indicates physical dimensions of the financial budget of a ministry/department, indicating actual

physical performance during the year 2012–13, performance during the year 2013–14 and the targeted performance during the year 2014–15.

(2) *Outcome Budget* contains a brief introductory note on the organization and function of the ministry/department, list of major programmes/schemes implemented by the ministry/department, its mandate, goal, and policy framework, budget estimates, scheme-wise analysis of physical performance and linkage between financial outlays and outcome, review covering overall trends in expenditure vis-à-vis budget estimates in recent years, review of performance of statutory and autonomous bodies under the administrative control of the ministry/department, reform measures, targets and achievements, and plan for future refinements.

(3) As far as feasible, coverage of women and SC/ST beneficiaries under various developmental schemes and schemes for the benefit of the northeastern region are also separately indicated.

ANNUAL REPORTS

A descriptive account of the activities of each ministry/department is given in the annual report which is brought out separately by each ministry/department and circulated to Members of Parliament at the time of discussion on the Demands for Grants.

ECONOMIC SURVEY

Along with the central budget, the *Economic Survey* is presented before the parliament. This report reviews the position of the economy during the current year. The report in particular reviews the position regarding the state of the Indian economy, agricultural and industrial production, energy, infrastructure and communications, human development, climate change, fiscal development, monetary development, situation of prices, and position regarding balance of payments and foreign aid. The report also gives the prospects and tasks for the year to which the budget relates. This analysis is contained in the Economic and Functional Classification of the Central Government Budget which is brought out by the Ministry of Finance separately.

Railway Budget

Like the general budget, the Railway Budget gives the details of the revenue and expenditure of the Indian Railways. The details are given for the previous year, the current year, and the ensuing year. The revenue sides of the railways are from passenger earnings, goods earnings, and other miscellaneous earnings. The expenditure side consists of working expenses, net miscellaneous expenditure, appropriation to depreciation reserve fund, and payment to worked lines. Net railway revenue is divided into two parts (i) dividend to general revenue; and (ii) net surplus.

State Budgets

The budgets of different states are prepared on the lines of the budget of the central government. Now almost all states prepare economic classification of the budget. Some of the states have started preparing even the functional classification.

Indian Public Finance Statistics

Indian Public Finance Statistics is an annual publication prepared by the Economic Division of the Department of Economic Affairs, Ministry of Finance. This provides a comprehensive overview of the budgetary transactions of the central and state governments. In addition, this publication contains information relating to annual plan outlays and pattern of their financing, trends in domestic savings and investment, trends in net domestic product of states, tax revenue as proportion of gross domestic product, and more.

Combined Finance and Revenue Accounts of Union and State Governments CAG

The CAG issues a document giving in one place comparable information relating to the accounts of the Union and all the states for a year, together with their balances and outstanding liabilities and other information relating to their financial health. These accounts were being given in the part under the Audit and Control Order, 1936, and adopted by the GoI in 1947. From 1971, it is not the statuary responsibility of the CAG to issue this document. The document is, however, prepared continuously as the compilation is considered useful.

The document is at present being issued in three volumes. The first volume contains a major head-wise summary of receipts and disbursements of various governments from the consolidated fund, contingency fund, and the public account. The second volume contains subsidiary accounts relating to economic services. The third volume gives subsidiary accounts relating to the central services and social services, among others. The subsidiary accounts give details generally by minor heads of the figures shown in the general accounts in Volume I.

An overview on government accounts has been added in Volume I which is further supplemented by a study wherein receipts, expenditure, debt, and deficits have been expressed as percentages of GDP/GSDP.

Most of the information in this document comes from the basic budgetary accounts maintained at different layers of government and associated economic and statistical data collected and compiled at the centre or lower levels of organization.

Income Tax Statistics

In 2016, the Income Tax Department brought out time series data ranging from 2000–1 to 2014–15. The details are given for corporate tax, income tax, and other direct tax. State-wise breakup for 2008–9 to 2014–15 is given. The contribution of direct taxes to total tax revenue is also given. Number of effective assesses are given for 2011–12 to 2014–15. For 2012–13, the details available are that of number of returns, sum of salary income, house property income, business income, capital gains, long term and short term, interest income, and other sources—all by income classes. Total income tax payable by range is available for individuals, household undivided families, firms, and companies. Corporate and non-corporate taxpayers by industry are also given.

Bibliography

Annual Report of the General Insurance Corporation of India, 2014–15.
Annual Report of the Life Insurance Corporation of India, 2014–15.

Comptroller and Auditor General of India. *Combined Finance and Revenue Accounts of Union and State Governments*, 2013–14.

Economic Division of the Department of Economic Affairs. 2015. *Indian Public Finance Statistics*. New Delhi: Ministry of Finance.

Ministry of Finance. 2016. *Economic and Functional Classification of the Central Government*, 2015–16. New Delhi: Ministry of Finance.

———. 2016. *Economic Survey, Indian Budget*, 2015–16. New Delhi: Ministry of Finance.

National Bank of Agriculture and Rural Development (NABARD). *Statistical Statements Relating to the Cooperative Movement in India*, 2003–04. Mumbai: NABARD.

———. 1972–2002 (various issues). *Banking Statistics*, 1972–2002. Mumbai: Reserve Bank of India.

———. Various issues. *Bulletin* (Monthly). Mumbai: Reserve Bank of India.

———. Various issues. *Bulletin Weekly Statistical Supplement* Mumbai: Reserve Bank of India.

———. 2006. *Handbook of Monetary Statistics of India*, 2006. Mumbai: Reserve Bank of India.

———. 2009. *Branch Banking Statistics*, 2009. Mumbai: Reserve Bank of India.

———. 2009–12. *Report on Currency and Finance*, 2009–12. Mumbai: Reserve Bank of India.

Reserve Bank of India. 2015. *Annual Report of the Central Board of Directors*, 2014–15. Mumbai: Reserve Bank of India.

———. 2015. *Handbook of Statistics on Indian Economy*, 2014–15. Mumbai: Reserve Bank of India.

———. 2015. *State Finances: A Study of Budgets: Annual Publication*, 2014–15. Mumbai: Reserve Bank of India.

———. 2016. *Budget of the Central Government*, Indian Budget, 2015–16. Mumbai: Reserve Bank of India.

14

Environment Statistics

The Ministry of Environment, Forests, and Climate Change (MoEFCC) is the nodal agency in the central government for overseeing the implementation of India's environment and forest policies and programmes relating to conservation of the country's natural resources including lakes and rivers, its biodiversity, forests and wildlife, ensuring the welfare of animals, and prevention and abatement of pollution. While implementing these policies and programmes, the ministry is guided by the principle of sustainable development.

Environment statistics can be divided into the following components: (i) biodiversity, flora, forests, fauna; and (ii) abatement and control of pollution (energy, industry, agriculture, land use, land use change and forestry, waste). The details about these two components are given as follows.

Biodiversity

The term 'biodiversity' encompasses the variety of life on earth. It is defined as the variability among living organisms and the ecological complexes of which they are part, including diversity within and between species and ecosystems. Biodiversity manifests at species genetic and ecosystem levels. Biodiversity has direct consumptive value in food, agriculture, medicine, and industry, among others. It also has aesthetic and recreational value.

Plant biodiversity is a national and global resource. The details about plant species, rare and threatened species, and also the same of animal species are discussed in *The Compendium of Environment Statistics*. The main source for plants is the Botanical Survey of India (BSI) and for animals, it is Zoological Survey of India (ZSI). Some idea about their functions is given as follows.

The BSI is the apex research organization under the MoEFCC for carrying out taxonomic and floristic studies on wild plant resources of the country. It was established on 13 February 1890, with the basic objective of exploring the plant resources of the country and to identify the plants species with economic virtues.

Main Objectives of BSI

- Exploration, inventorying, and documentation of phytodiversity in general and protected areas, hotspots, and fragile ecosystems in particular; publication of national, state, and district floras, and also flora of protected areas. About 300 publications of BSI, consisting of books, periodicals, and occasional papers, are available on the website of the BSI.[1]
- Identification of threatened/red-list species and species-rich areas needing conservation; ex-situ conservation of critically threatened species in botanical gardens.
- Survey and documentation of traditional knowledge (ethnobotany) associated with plants.
- Develop a national database of Indian plants, including herbarium and live specimens, and botanical paintings/illustrations.
- Preparation of a seed, pollen, and spore atlas of Indian plants.

The ZSI, established in 1916, is a prominent research institution under the MoEFCC. It has 16 regional centres. This institution is tasked with the survey and exploration of faunal resources of the country. The ultimate goal is the taxonomic identification and documentation of the country's biodiversity. The primary objectives of ZSI are as follows.

[1] Available at http://bsi.gov.in/ (accessed on 18 May 2017).

The current mandate of ZSI is survey, collection, documentation (including the traditional knowledge associated with animals) and ex-situ conservation of wild animal diversity of the country.

High priority areas include:

(1) Digitization of present collections, preparation of fine scale distribution maps based on primary occurrence data and making it available in a searchable format.
(2) Publication of national and state faunas. The details about publications is available in the annual report of the MoEFCC.
(3) Taxonomic studies, revisionary/monographic studies on selected animal groups.
(4) Identification of red-list species and species-rich areas needing conservation and focus on data-deficient species to collect more information on populations.
(5) Development of a national database of Indian animals, including museum specimens, live specimens, paintings, and illustrations, and maintenance of already existing collections with modern facilities and as per international standards of collection management.
(6) Developing and maintaining museums and using such facilities for conservation education for people, especially students.
(7) Ex-situ conservation of critically threatened taxa.
(8) Capacity building in taxonomy, nomenclature, specimen collection, preservation, and maintenance through training programmes.

The ZSI in recent years reoriented its plan of work by grouping the survey and studies under the following six major programmes:

(1) Fauna of States
(2) Fauna of Conservation Areas
(3) Fauna of Important Ecosystems
(4) Status Survey of Endangered Species
(5) Ecological Studies/Environment Impact Assessment Survey
(6) Computerization and Dissemination of Data

The details about forestry have been given in the chapter on agricultural statistics.

More details about the data on these two subjects are given in the annual report by the MoEFCC and also in *The Compendium of*

Environment Statistics of India. The contents of these publications are given in a later section.

Abatement and Control of Pollution

The concern for environmental quality has become the top-most issue in the present scenario of rising population, increasing urbanization, industrial, and vehicular pollution as well as pollution of water due to discharge of effluents without conforming to the environmental norms and standards. The ministry earlier adopted a Policy for Abatement of Pollution in 1992, which provides multi-pronged strategies in the form of regulations, legislation, agreements, fiscal incentives, and other measures to prevent and abate pollution. To give effect to various measures and policies for pollution control, various steps have been initiated which include stringent regulations, development of environmental standards and periodical revision therein, control of vehicular pollution, control of air and water pollution, abatement and prevention of noise pollution, spatial environmental planning, and identification of critically polluted areas and improvement plans therein. The government also adopted the National Conservation Strategy and Policy Statement on Environment and Development, 1992. Afterwards, the government adopted the National Environment Policy (NEP; 2006) which seeks to extend the coverage, and fill in gaps that still exist, in light of present knowledge and accumulated experience. This policy does not displace, but builds on the earlier policies of the government. It lays emphasis on many new issues. The details of these are discussed as follows.

The Major Sources of Pollution

Environment Pollution due to Energy Use

A considerable amount of air pollution results from burning of fossil fuels. Fuels are primarily derived from fossilized plant material and consist mainly of carbon and/or its compounds. The household sector is the largest consumer of energy in India (See Compendium 2013). Burning of traditional fuels introduces large quantities of carbon dioxide (CO_2) when the combustion is complete, but if there is incomplete combustion and oxidation then carbon monoxide (CO) is produced, in addition to hydrocarbons. Incomplete combustion of coal produces smoke consisting of particles of soot or carbon, tarry droplets of unburnt hydrocarbons (HCs), and CO. Fossil fuels also contain 0.5–4.0 per cent of sulphur which is oxidized to sulphur dioxide (SO_2) during combustion.

The environmental effects of various fuels, such as coal, oil, and nuclear, are of growing concern owing to increasing consumption levels. The combustion of these fuels in industries and vehicles has been a major source of pollution. Coal production through opencast mining, its supply to and consumption in power stations, and industrial boilers leads to particulate and gaseous pollution. Another major impact of coal mining is land degradation, especially of forest areas.

The consumption of petroleum products in vehicles, industries, and domestic cooking activities results in the emission of pollutants in large quantities. Radioactive emissions from nuclear power plants are of grave concern as they can cause serious impact both in terms of spatial and intergenerational concerns. In addition, two key problems are long-term waste disposal and the eventual decommissioning of plants.

Industrial Emissions

Airborne emissions emitted from various industries are a cause of major concern. These emissions are of two forms—suspended particulate matter (SPM) and gaseous emissions, such as SO_2, nitrogen dioxide [NO_2], and CO. Liquid effluents, generated from certain industries, containing organic and toxic pollutants, are also a cause of concern. Heavily polluting industries were identified which are included under the 17 categories for the purpose of monitoring and regulating pollution from them. The MoEFCC has developed standards for regulating emissions from various industries and emission standards for all the polluting industries including thermal power stations, iron and steel plants, cement plants, fertilizer plants, oil refineries, pulp and paper, petrochemicals, sugar, distilleries, and tanneries. The maximum permissible levels for industrial effluent discharges are given in the *Compendium of Environment Statistics*. The basic source in this case is, however, Central Pollution Control Board (CPCB) (a summary of the functions of the board is given in a later section). The details regarding measures taken to control pollution in industries, vehicles, and other areas are given in the *Compendium*. Some idea about the sectors causing pollution is given as follows.

Road Transport

Road vehicles are the second major source of pollution. They emit CO, HCs, NO_2, SO_2, and other toxic substances such as total suspended particles (TSP) and lead. Diesel engines are much less polluting than petrol engines. The major pollutant is CO, amounting to 91 per cent by weight of all vehicle emissions. The primary pollutants produced in vehicle emissions undergo a series of complex interrelated chemical reactions in the troposphere and lower stratosphere to form secondary products.

Acidifying Emissions

SO_2 and nitrogen oxide (N_2O) emitted into the air are converted into acids. At their deposition, they have an acidifying effect on soil and water. The emission of ammonia also contributes to acidification. Main sources of emission of SO_2 in the air are due to burning of sulphur-containing fuel like coal mines, power plants, oil by vehicles, and also due to refining of oils in refineries.

Land and Soil

LAND DEGRADATION

Land is degraded when it suffers a loss of intrinsic qualities, decline in its capabilities, or loss in its productive capacity. Land degradation may be due to natural causes, human causes, or a combination of both. Soil erosion is the major cause of land degradation.

SOIL EROSION

Soil is the non-renewable natural resource which supports life on earth. It is estimated that one-sixth of the world's soils have already been degraded by water and wind erosion. This has two important consequences: the reduced ability of society to produce sufficient food due to loss of quality and depth of soils and the resultant off-site pollution associated with erosion. These include siltation of dams, pollution of water courses by agricultural chemicals and damage to property by soil-laden runoff. On-site issues of declining soil quality tend to be spatially dispersed, occurring on many different soil types whereas off-site pollution issues tend to be locally concentrated.

Among fertilizers, the conversion of fertilizer-N to gaseous forms—ammonia (NH_3) and various oxides of Nitrogen lead to atmospheric pollution. Escape of fertilizer-N as ammonia gas is called ammonia volatilization. The presence of ammonia and sulphur dioxide may lead to acid rains which ultimately degrade the soil. Atmospheric ammonia contaminates water bodies, impairs visibility, and causes corrosion. N_2O also contributes to global warming.

Water Pollution

The types and sources of water contamination include 'point' sources of pollution which usually refer to wastes being discharged from a pipe; and 'non-point' sources, which means all other sources such as storm water run-off (which picks up oils and other contaminants from various areas), irrigation (which carries fertilizers and pesticides into groundwater), leaks from storage tanks, and leakage from disposal sites. The non-point sources are technically the most difficult to regulate in India. Water pollution comes from three main sources: domestic sewage, industrial effluents, and run-off from activities such as agriculture. Water pollution from domestic and human wastewater causes many severe water-borne diseases. The problem of water pollution due to industries is because of the inadequate measures adopted for effluent treatment than to the intensity of industrial activities. The 13 major water-polluting industries have been identified and are closely monitored by the CPCB.

Urban Wastewater (Sewage)

The predominant cause of water pollution in India is the presence of Fecal Coliform, mainly due to large amount of untreated sewage discharged into water bodies. Many a times, even if treated sewage is discharged into a water body, high Coliform levels still remain as a significant pollution issue.

The CPCB initiated a study to evaluate performance of the existing sewage treatment plants in the country with the help of two reputed institutes in the subject.

Efficiencies of primary and secondary sewage treatment process in Coliform removal are stated in the manual on sewage and sewage treatment published by the Ministry of Urban Development.

Wind Erosion

Wind erosion is created from phosphogypsum stacks. Phosphogypsum generated from phosphoric acid plants are presently stacked and some quantity of the same is sold to other industries for beneficial use especially as raw material in cement manufacturing as a substitute for mineral gypsum as well as for alkali soil amendments or re-conditioning. The handling of phosphogypsum through trucks or railways involves loading, unloading, and temporary storage at yards/depots and is likely to cause environmental impacts especially during the rainy season. In order to have minimal impacts on the environment, there is a need for evolving guidelines for safe handling and disposal of phosphogypsum.

The details for the estimates of the Emissions of the Greenhouse gases (GHGs) are available for the following sectors in the report on Greenhouse Gas Emissions for the year 2007 by the MoEFCC. The methodology for estimation of emissions due to various sources as given in the report is given as follows.

The methodology for these estimates is given for energy, industry, agriculture, land use, land use change and forestry, and waste.

Under the aegis of the Indian Network for Climate Change Assessment, the report on 'India's Greenhouse Gas Emission' contains updated information on India's greenhouse gas emissions. India is the first developing country to publish such updated numbers. The assessment has been prepared by 83 experts belonging to 19 institutions country-wide (for details see the report).

This assessment provides information on India's emissions of GHGs (such as carbon dioxide, methane and nitrous oxide, water, vapour, ozone) emitted from anthropogenic activities at the national level from energy, industry, agriculture, waste, and land use, land-use change and forestry (LULUCF). By increasing the concentrations of natural GHGs and by adding new GHGs like chloro-flouro carbons, the global average and the annual mean surface-air temperature (referred to as the global temperature) can be raised.

Methodology for Estimating Emissions

The estimates presented in this report have been calculated using standard methodologies contained in the Intergovernmental Panel on Climate Change (IPCC) Revised 1996 Guidelines for National Greenhouse Gas Inventories (IPCC 1997), the IPCC Good Practice Guidance and Uncertainty Management in National Greenhouse Gas Inventories (IPCC 2000), and the IPCC Good Practice Guidance for Land Use, Land-Use Change, and Forestry (IPCC 2003).

The simplest representation of the methodology used for estimating particular GHG emission from each source category is when activity data for a source category is multiplied by respective emission factor to obtain emissions from that source category for a specific gas. To calculate the total emissions of a gas from all its source categories, the emissions are summed over all source categories.

$$\textit{Emissions Gas} = \sum \text{Category } A \times EF.$$

Here, emissions gas is the emissions of a given gas from all its source categories, *A* is the amount of individual source category utilized that generates emissions of the gas under consideration, and *EF* is the emission factor of a given gas by type of source category (emissions per unit of activity data utilized). These are explained as follows:

- **Activity Data**: Activity data have been primarily derived from the published documents of the various ministries and organizations of the Government of India (GoI), from industry associations (such as the Cement Manufacturers' Association [CMA] of India) and from reputed data organizations such as the Centre for Monitoring Indian Economy (CMIE). See Annexure 1 of the report for a comprehensive list of activity data sources.
- **Emission Factors**: The emission factors used in this report are a mix of default emission factors available in IPCC publications (1997, 2000, 2003, and 2006) and country-specific emission

factors. Default emission factors have been used for gases and categories where country-specific factors are not available. Some of the country-specific emission factors used is given in the sources mentioned in this report (GHG Emissions 2007).

Sectoral Description of the Emissions

Energy

The energy systems of most economies are largely driven by the combustion of fossil fuels, namely, coal, oil, and natural gas, and are the major sources of emissions amongst all other sectors. Fossil fuel combustion oxidizes the carbon in the fuel and it is emitted as CO_2. Some carbon is also released in the form of CO, methane (CH_4), and non-methane hydrocarbons which is oxidized to CO_2 in 10–11 years.

Also emitted are N_2O, SO_2, and black carbon. Under energy document includes CO_2, CH_4, and N_2O emitted from fossil fuel combustion in electricity generation; transportation including road, rail, aviation, and navigation; commercial, institutional, residential, agriculture, and fisheries; and fugitive emissions from coal mining and handling, and from exploration of oil and natural gas and their transport and storage are also accounted for in this sector.

METHODOLOGY AND CHOICE OF EMISSION FACTORS

The IPCC 1996 revised guidelines (IPCC 1997) methodology has been used for estimating the GHG emission from various types of fossil fuel combusted in the energy sector. The emission factors of the fossil fuels, such as coal, oil, and natural gas, are the most important considerations in estimating the GHG emissions from combustion of these fuels. In India, coal as a fuel constitutes more than 50 per cent of the total fossil fuel mix of the country used for energy related activities. This document uses the country-specific CO_2 emission factors derived on the basis of net calorific values (NCVs) of different types of coal produced in the country, namely, coking, non-coking, and lignite. The non-CO_2 emissions have been estimated using non-CO_2 default emission factors for different fuel types published in IPCC 1997 and 2006.

The general equation representing the emissions is as follows:

Carbon emissions = Σ fuel consumption expressed in energy units for electricity generation (fuel type) $\times$ carbon emission factor – carbon stored $\times$ fraction oxidized.

Non-CO_2 emissions = Σ fuel consumption $\times$ net calorific value of fuel $\times$ gas-specific emission factors (fuel type).

The details about estimates of emissions for electricity generation are also available with the Central Electricity Authority (CEA). The emissions factors for various fuels and the estimates of emissions of gases for the energy sector are given in tables 5.2 and 5.3 of the report of GHG emissions 2007.

Industry

The industry sector includes emissions from fossil fuel combustion and the emissions related to various processes to manufacture industrial goods. The categories covered under this sector are: (i) mineral-based industries—cement, glass production, ceramics; (ii) chemicals—ammonia, nitric acid, carbides, titanium oxide, methanol, ethylene, ethylene dichloride and vinyl chloride monomer production, carbon black, and caprolactam, etc.; (iii) metals—iron and steel, ferro alloys, aluminium, lead, zinc and copper; (iv) other industries—textiles, leather, food and beverages, food processing paper and pulp, non-specified industries, and mining and quarrying; (v) non-energy product uses of lubricants and paraffin wax.

METHODOLOGY AND CHOICE OF EMISSION FACTORS

For estimating the GHG emissions from the industry sector, the IPCC 1996 revised guidelines (IPCC 1997) have been used for each of the categories. The activity data for the various industries are sourced from national statistical organizations, listed companies, annual reports of ministries of the GoI, research organizations, trade magazines, and other publications of the sector associations (see Annexure 1 of the report of GHG emissions 2007).

The energy conversion units and the emission factors used for fossil fuel combustion related to fossil and biomass are same as used in the energy sector. For cement and nitric acid production, the CO_2 and N_2O are based on country-specific circumstances. The industry emissions factors used for estimating process emissions are given in the report of GHG emissions 2007.

Agriculture

The GHG emissions from the agriculture sector are emitted mainly in the form of CH_4. These are due to enteric fermentation and from rice paddy cultivation.

N_2O is also emitted from this sector and is mainly from the agricultural fields due to application of fertilizers.

The sources of emissions included in the agriculture sector are (i) livestock; (ii) enteric fermentation; (iii) animal manure; (iv) rice cultivation; (v) upland; (vi) irrigation—continuously flooded, singular aeration, multiple aeration; (vii) rainfed—drought prone, flood prone; (viii) deep water; (ix) agriculture soils; (x) direct emissions; (xi) indirect emissions; and (xii) field burning of agriculture crop residue.

METHODOLOGY AND CHOICE OF EMISSION FACTORS

LIVESTOCK

- **Enteric Fermentation:** In order to estimate the CH_4 emission from livestock, at a higher tier, the cattle population has been divided into dairy and non-dairy categories, with sub-classification into indigenous and cross-bred types for different age groups (Ministry of Agriculture and Farmer's Welfare [MOAFW] 2005), using the emission factors provided in the report (NATCOM 2004).
- **Manure Management:** Not much systematic management of manure from livestock is done in India. It is mainly converted into dung cakes and is used for energy purposes in rural areas. It is estimated that about 0.115 million tons of CH_4 and 0.07 thousand tons of N_2O are emitted from this source.

The dung management practices vary in different regions depending upon the need of the fuel and manure as well as the available fuel resources and climatic conditions of the regions (details not available).

RICE CULTIVATION

The annual amount of CH_4 emitted from a given area of rice is a function of the crop duration, water regimes, and organic soil amendments. The CH_4 emissions from rice cultivation have been estimated by multiplying the seasonal emission factors by the annual harvested areas.

The total annual emissions are equal to the sum of emissions from each sub-unit of harvested area using the following equation.

$$CH_4\ Rice = \sum_{i,j,k} (EF_{i,j,k} \times A_{i,j,k} \times 10^{-6})$$

where,

CH_4 *Rice* = annual methane emissions from rice cultivation, Gg CH_4/yr;

$EF_{i,j,k}$ = a seasonal integrated emission factor for *i*, *j*, and *k* conditions, kg CH_4/ha;

$A_{i,j,k}$ = annual harvested area of rice for *i*, *j*, and *k* conditions, ha/yr;

i, *j*, and *k* = represent different ecosystems, water regimes, type, and amount of organic amendments, under which CH_4 emissions from rice may vary.

Separate calculations were undertaken for each rice ecosystem (that is, irrigated, rain-fed, and deep-water rice production).

AGRICULTURE SOILS

This entails estimates of N_2O emissions using human-induced net nitrogen (N) additions to soils (for example, synthetic or organic fertilizers, deposited manure, crop residues, sewage sludge), or of mineralization of N in soil organic matter following drainage/management of organic soils, or cultivation/land-use change on mineral soils (for example, forest land/grassland/settlements converted to cropland).

The emissions of N_2O that result from anthropogenic N inputs or N mineralization occur through both a direct pathway (that is, directly from the soils to which the N is added/released), and through two indirect pathways: (i) following volatilization of NH_3 and NO_x from managed soils and from fossil fuel combustion and biomass burning, and the subsequent re-deposition of these gases and their products NH_4+ and NO_3– to soils and waters; and (ii) after leaching and runoff of N, mainly as NO_3– from managed soils.

Therefore, total N_2O emitted from soils can be represented as follows:

$$N_2O\text{–}N\,(\text{Total}) = N_2O\text{–}N\,(\text{Direct}) + N_2O\text{–}N\,(\text{Indirect})$$

Using this methodology the estimates of N_2O emissions have been prepared and given the report on GHG emissions (2007). To get the estimates, India-specific emission factors have been used in place of IPCC default values (Pathak et. al 2002).

BURNING OF CROP RESIDUE

Crop residue is burnt in the fields in many Indian states such as Uttar Pradesh, Punjab, West Bengal, Haryana, Bihar, Madhya Pradesh, Himachal Pradesh, Maharashtra, Gujarat, Chhattisgarh, Jharkhand, Tamil Nadu, Uttarakhand, and Karnataka producing CO, CH_4, N_2O, NO_x, non-methane hydrocarbons (NMHCs), SO_2 and many other gases. In this report only the CH_4 and N_2O emissions estimates have been reported.

Non-CO_2 emissions from crop residue burning were calculated using the equation given as follows:

$$EBCR = \Sigma \text{ crops } (A \times B \times C \times D \times E \times F),$$

where,

$EBCR$ = emissions from residue burning
A = crop production
B = residue to crop ratio
C = dry matter fraction
D = fraction burnt
E = fraction actually oxidized
F = emission factor.

The estimation of emission of targeted species was arrived at by first estimating the amount of biomass actually burnt in the field using the IPCC-revised inventory preparation guidelines (IPCC 1996). Currently, wastes from nine crops—rice, wheat, cotton, maize, millet, sugarcane, jute, rapeseed–mustard, and groundnut—are subjected to burning.

The dry matter fraction of crop residue is taken as 0.8 (Bhattacharya and Mitra 1998), 0.25 as fraction burned (IPCC 1997) in the fields, and 0.9 as the fraction actually oxidized (IPCC 1997). Crop-specific values of carbon fraction were as per IPCC default values.

The default N/C ratios were taken from IPCC (2006). Further, the emission ratio was calculated using emission factors given by Andreae and Merlet (2001) which are the default factors mentioned in IPCC (2006) national inventory preparation guidelines.

LAND USE, LAND-USE CHANGE, AND FORESTRY

The LULUCF are a key component of the GHG emission profile.

It involves estimation of carbon stock changes, CO_2 emissions and removals, and non-CO_2 GHG emissions. The IPCC has developed three GHG inventory guidelines for the land-use sector, namely Revised 1996 Guidelines for Land-use Change and Forestry (LUCF) (IPCC 1997); IPCC Good Practice Guidelines for LULUCF (IPCC 2003); and the latest IPCC 2006 guidelines which includes Agriculture Forest and Other Land Categories (AFOLU).

India used the Revised 1996 Guidelines for LULUCF sector for preparation of GHG inventory information for its Initial National Communication. The inventory showed that the LUCF sector was a marginal source of GHG emissions (14.2 million tons of CO_2 equivalent) for the inventory year 1994. The revised 1996 IPCC Guidelines has many limitations and the inventory estimation is incomplete since all land categories are not included and the uncertainty of GHG inventory is estimated to be high. Thus IPCC developed Good Practice Guidance (GPG) for the land use sectors covering all the land use categories for the inventory. The developed countries (Annex I Countries in the United Nations Framework Convention on Climate Change (UNFCCC)) are required to use the GPG approach for LULUCF sector. Further, the developing countries (non-Annex I countries) such as India are encouraged to use the GPG approach.

WASTE

The main GHG emitted from waste management is CH_4. It is produced and released into the atmosphere as a by-product of the anaerobic decomposition of solid waste, whereby methanogenic bacteria break down organic matter in the waste. Similarly, wastewater becomes a source of CH_4 when treated or disposed anaerobically. It can also be a source of N_2O emissions as well due to protein content in domestically generated waste water.

The GHGs and their source categories considered in this document include: (i) municipal solid waste disposal resulting in CH_4 emission; (ii) domestic waste water disposal emitting CH_4 and N_2O; (iii) industrial waste water disposal leading to CH_4 emissions.

MUNICIPAL SOLID WASTE DISPOSAL RESULTING IN CH_4 EMISSION

In India, waste is only systematically collected and disposed at waste disposal sites in cities, resulting in CH_4 emission from anaerobic conditions. In rural areas, waste is scattered and as a result aerobic conditions prevail with no resulting CH_4 emission. Municipal solid waste (MSW) in Indian cities is disposed in landfills by means of open dumping; however a small fraction is used for composting in some of the cities. In mega cities such as Delhi, Mumbai, Kolkata, and Chennai, the MSW-generation rate is overriding the population growth rate. An example of CH_4 emissions from solid waste management in the mega city Chennai is given in the *GHG Emission Report, 2007*. The rate of disposal of MSW varies from city to city; therefore, the estimation of CH_4 generated from MSW at a national level becomes highly uncertain unless year-wise data on MSW generation is incorporated in the estimates. In the present estimate IPCC 2000 guidelines have been used and an average CH_4 emission factor derived from a study by the National Environmental Engineering Institute (NEERI) in 69 cities (NEERI 2005) has been applied.

DOMESTIC WASTE WATER DISPOSAL EMITTING CH_4 AND N_2O

According to the report CH_4 emission estimates have been made using the Tier-II approach of IPCC by incorporating country-specific emission factors and country-specific data. Emission estimates have been arrived at by using reliable and accepted secondary data generated by various government and private agencies working in the respective areas in the country.

INDUSTRIAL WASTE WATER DISPOSAL LEADING TO CH_4 EMISSIONS

CH_4 emission from waste water has been estimated based on the waste water produced in industries. Steel, fertilizer, beer, meat production, sugar, coffee, soft drinks, pulp and paper, petroleum refineries, rubber, and tannery industries together emit 95 per cent of the methane generated from waste water in India. These industries have been included for estimating CH_4 from industrial waste water.

The estimates of gases not covered by the report and given in the *Compendium of Environment Statistics* as follows:

(1) State-wise level of SO_2, NO_2, and RSPM in residential and industrial areas under the National Air Quality Monitoring Programme (NAMP) conducted by the CPCB.
(2) Production and consumption of ozone-depleting substances in India compiled by the Ozone Cell, MoEFCC.

Central Pollution Control Board

The CPCB has been continuously playing a key role in abatement and control of pollution in the country by generating, compiling, and collating data, providing scientific information, rendering technical inputs for formation of national policies and programmes, training and development of manpower, and through activities for promoting awareness at different levels of the government and public at large.

The main functions of CPCB are as follows:

(1) Advise the central government on any matter concerning prevention and control of water and air pollution and improvement of the quality of air.
(2) Coordinate the activities of the state boards and provide technical assistance and guidance to them, carry out and sponsor investigations and research relating to problems of water and air pollution, and for their prevention, control, or abatement.
(3) Collect, compile, and publish technical and statistical data relating to water and air pollution and the measures devised for their effective prevention, control, or abatement.
(4) Prepare manuals, codes, and guidelines relating to treatment and disposal of sewage and trade effluents as well as for stack gas cleaning devices, stacks, and ducts.
(5) Disseminate information in respect of matters relating to water and air pollution and their prevention and control.
(6) Preparation of comprehensive industry documents including environmental standards for a number of industries.

(7) Inventorization of grossly polluting industries and measures taken to control pollution.

The data on pollution are not published in any regular publication. They are generally in the form of reports or research papers. The CPCB has so far published a number of reports. Given as follows are some of the main series in which the CPCB's reports are divided:

(1) Comprehensive Industry Document Series (COINDS) containing information on pollution potential, techno-economic feasibility for pollution-control hardware, and minimal national standards for implementation in a particular industry category.
(2) Control of Urban Pollution Series (CUPS) containing reports of pollution status in and around specific geographical areas.
(3) Assessment and Development Study of River Basin Series (ADSORBS) containing reports on pollution aspects in the river basin.
(4) Ecological Impact Assessment Series (EIAS) containing reports on environmental impact assessment.
(5) Resource Recycling Series (RERES) containing reports on recycling of waste water.
(6) National Ambient Air Quality Monitoring Series (NAAQMS).
(7) Hazardous Waste Management Series (HWMS).
(8) Environment Mopping and Pollution Series (EMPS).

Details of Publications

Annual Report of the MoEFCC

The MoEFCC is the nodal agency in the administrative structure of the central government for the planning, promotion, coordination, and overseeing the implementation of India's environmental and forestry policies and programmes.

The primary concerns of the ministry are implementation of policies and programmes relating to conservation of the country's natural resources including its lakes and rivers, its biodiversity, forests and wildlife, ensuring the welfare of animals, and the prevention and abatement of pollution.[2] While implementing these

[2] The details have been discussed in State of Environment Report, compiled by MoEFCC.

policies and programmes, the ministry is guided by the principle of sustainable development and enhancement of human well-being. Some details regarding statistics are available in the Annual Report of the Ministry.

The report overviews major activities of the MoEFCC during the year. The topics covered under the annual report are: natural resources—survey and exploration conservation, environmental impact assessment, abatement of pollution, conservation of water bodies, regeneration and eco-development, research, education and awareness, centers of excellence, fellowships and awards, environmental information, legislation and institutional support, international cooperation and sustainable development, administration and civil construction, plan coordination, and budget.

Compendium of Environment Statistics

The *Compendium of Environment Statistics* is being issued by Central Statistical Office (CSO) since 1997. It broadly covers the five core parameters, namely biodiversity, atmosphere, land/soil, water and human settlements suggested by the Framework for Development

Table 14.1 NCV and CO_2 Emission Factors of Different Types of Fuel Used for Estimation

	NCV(Tj/kt)	CO_2 EF(t/Tj)
Coking coal	24.18	93.61
Non-coking Coal	19.63	95.81
Lignite	9.69	106.15
Diesel	43	74.1
Petrol	44.3	69.3
Kerosene	43.8	71.9
Fuel oil	40.4	77.4
Light distillates	43	74.1
Compressed Natural Gas (CNG)	48	56.1
Liquid Petroleum Gas (LPG)	47.3	63.1
Lubricants	40.2	73.3
Aviation Turbine Fuel (ATF)	44.1	71.5

Source: MoEFCC (2007).

of Environment Statistics (FDES) published by United Nations Statistics Division (UNSD) in 1984. The FDES sets out the scope of environment statistics by relating the components of the environment to information categories that are based on the recognition that environmental problems are the result of human activities and natural events reflecting a sequence of action, impact, and reaction.

The compendium consists of seven chapters. The first two chapters give a general introduction to environment, its degradation through different sources and their impact on human health, and the development of environment statistics in India. The remaining five chapters are on biodiversity (flora, forests, and fauna), atmosphere (air and transport, energy, industry, GHGs, noise), land/soil, water (ground water and fresh marine), and human settlements. In this chapter we have given a very brief view of biodiversity and abatement and control of pollutions.

Table 14.2 GHG Emissions in '000 tons (or Giga gram) from the Energy Sector in 2007

	CO_2	CH_4	N_2O	CO_2 equivalent
Grand total	1,497,029	20,564.2	239.31	1,727,706
Energy	9,92,836.3	4,266.05	56.88	1,100,057
Electricity generation	7,15,829.8	8.14	10.66	7,19,305.3
Other energy industries	33,787.5	1.72	0.07	33,845.32
Transport	1,38,858	23.47	8.67	1,42,038.6
Road transport	1,21,211	23	6	1,23,554
Railways	6,109	0.34	2.35	6,844.64
Aviation	10,122	0.1	0.28	10,210.9
Navigation	1,416	0.13	0.04	1,431.13
Residential	69,427	2,721.94	36.29	1,37,838.5
Commercial/Institutional	1,657	0.18	0.04	1,673.18
Agriculture/Fisheries	33,277	1.2	1.15	33,658.7
Fugitive emissions	–	–	1,509.4	31,697.3
Bunkers:	3,454	0.03	0.1	3,484.45
Aviation Bunkers	3,326	0.02	0.09	3,355.31
Marine bunkers	128	0.01	0.003	129.14

Source: MoEFCC (2007).

Bibliography

Andreae, Meinrat O. and P. Merlet. 2001. 'Emission of Trace gases and Aerosols from Biomass Burning', Global Biogeochemical Cycles, 15(4): 955–66.

Bhattacharya, S. and A.P. Mitra. 1998. *Greenhouse Gas Emission India*, base year 1990, Centre for Global Change. New Delhi: National Physical Laboratory.

Central Statistics Office (CSO). 1999. *Guide to Official Statistics*. New Delhi: Ministry of Statistics and Programme Implementation.

———. 2013. *Compendium of Environment Statistics India*. New Delhi: Ministry of Statistics and Programme Implementation.

Houghton, J.T., L.G. Meira Filho, B. Lim, K. Trenton, I. Mamaty, and Y. Bonduki (eds). 1997. *Revised 1996 IPCC Guidelines for National Greenhouse Gas Inventories*. Geneva: IPCC.

Ministry of Agriculture and Farmer's Welfare (MOAFW). 2005. *17th Indian Livestock Census*, All-India Summary Report, Department of Animal Husbandry, Dairying, and Fisheries. New Delhi: MOAFW.

Ministry of Environment, Forests and Climate Change (MoEFCC). 2007. *India: Greenhouse Gas Emissions*, Indian Network for Climate Change Assessment. New Delhi: MoEFCC.

———. 2015. *Annual Report, 2014–15*. New Delhi: MoEFCC.

———. *India: Greenhouse Gas Emissions, Indian Network for Climate Change Assessment*. New Delhi: MoEFCC.

NATCOM. 2004. *India's Initial National Communication to the UNFCC*. New Delhi: MoEFCC.

Pathak, H., A. Bhatia, Shiv Prasad Jain, M.C. Kumar, S. Singh, and U. Kumar. 2002. 'Emission of Nitrous Oxide from Soil in Rice–wheat Systems of Indo-Gangetic Plains of India', *Journal of Environmental Monitoring Assessment,* 77(2): 163–78.

Penman, J., D. Kruger, I. Galbally, T. Hiraishi, B. Nyenzi, S. Emmanul, L. Buendia et. al (eds). 2000. *Good Practice Guidance and Uncertainty Management in National Greenhouse Gas Inventories*. Tokyo: Institute for Global Environmental Strategies for IPCC.

Penman, Jim, Michael Gytarsky, Taka Hiraishi, Thelma Krug, Dina Kruger, Riitta Pipatti, Leandro Buendia et. al (eds). 2003. *Good Practice Guidance for Land Use, Land-Use Change and Forestry*. Tokyo: Institute for Global Environmental Strategies (IGES) for the IPCC.

United Nations Statistics Division. 1984. *A Framework for the Development of Environment Statistics*.

15

Housing Statistics

Population Census

The decennial censuses provide information on the number of census houses and households. Latest information is available for the 2011 Census. The definition of house varied from census to census. In the census of 1881 a house was defined as the dwelling place of one or more than one families with their servants, having a separate principal entrance from the public way. The same definition with slight modifications continued till 1951. The 1961 Census adopted, for the first time, an enlarged house listing system which continued with some modifications in 1971 and later censuses. The 1981 Census onwards, information on housing conditions and amenities such as source of drinking water, location of the source, electricity, and toilet (in case of urban areas only) was also collected. For the 1991 Census, the availability of toilet facilities was asked from rural areas also. For the 1961 Census onwards, the house was defined as a structure or part of a structure inhabited or vacant, or a dwelling, a shop-cum-dwelling or a place of business, workshop, and school with a separate main entrance. The information regarding a house is collected through a house list form. Prior to the 1961 Census each state was at liberty to design its own house list form. Differences in definitions and consequently methods led to non-comparability.

It was decided to have a standard schedule for the whole country, for the 1961 Census. The detailed data regarding housing have been collected for the 2011 Census also. The concepts and definitions applied and the information collected for this census are almost the same as those for the 2001 Census.

In the census of 2001, a new column was added in the house list schedule on the condition of the census house, that is, whether the census house is good, liveable, or dilapidated. Besides this, information on number of married couples living in the household and married couples having an independent room for sleeping were also collected. In the 2000 house list, the drinking water sources outside the premises of 1991 Census has been further sub-divided into 'near the premises' and 'away' based on distance. As regards to source of lighting, six sources of lighting were considered in the 2000 house list as against determining only availability or non-availability of electricity to the household in 1990. A new column on wastewater outlet of the census house was included in the 2000 house list. The facility of a bathroom within the census house has also been collected in 2000. Another question on facility of kitchen within the house was also added in the house list of the 2001 Census. Besides, six new columns were added regarding the availability of assets such as radio/transistor, television, telephone, bicycle, scooter/motorcycle/moped and car/jeep/van to the household. The questionnaire also probed the use of banking services by the head of the household or a member.

For the 2001 Census the following tables on houses, household amenities and assets have been prepared:

(1) Census houses and the use to which they are put.
(2) Condition of census houses used as residence and residence-cum-other use.
(3) Distribution of households by condition of census houses occupied by them. Distribution of households living in census houses by predominant material of roof, wall, and floor.
(4) Distribution of census houses used as residence and residence-cum-other use by their type of structure.
(5) Distribution of households by type of census houses occupied.
(6) Distribution of households by size and number of dwelling rooms.

(7) Distribution of households by ownership status of census houses occupied by them and number of dwelling rooms.
(8) Distribution of households by number of married couples in a household and number of dwelling rooms, total number of married couples, and number of married couples having an independent sleeping room.

Household Amenities

(1) Distribution of households by source of drinking water and its location.
(2) Distribution of households by source of lighting.
(3) Distribution of households by availability of bathroom and type of latrine within the house and type of drainage connectivity for waste water outlet.
(4) Distribution of households by availability of separate kitchen and type of fuel used for cooking.
(5) Distribution of households by source and location of drinking water and availability of electricity and latrine.

Assets

This refers to the number of households availing banking services and number of households having each of the specified asset. The tables are prepared by the Office of the Registrar General and Census Commissioner of India.

Household tables are based on 100 per cent count for small states and 20 per cent for major states. The details of data are available for all-India, state, and district level separately for rural and urban areas and each city within district.

Housing statistics are very deficient in the country. The statistics collected during different population censuses are not comparable. Some estimates of the total value of construction during different years have been prepared by following the commodity flow approach (see chapter on National Income). Some data on housing are being collected by the National Sample Survey Office (NSSO) and the National Building Organization (NBO), the details of which are given in the following sections of the chapter.

National Sample Survey Reports

Comprehensive surveys on housing conditions were carried out by NSSO in the 28th Round (October 1973–June 1974), 44th Round (July 1988–June 1989), 49th Round (January–June, 1993), and 58th Round (July–December 2002). An all-India survey of households was conducted in the 65th Round of NSS during July 2008 to June 2009 covering the subjects of (i) housing condition; (ii) domestic tourism; and (iii) condition of urban slums. Reports on conditions of urban slums and domestic tourism have already been released in May 2010 and October 2010 respectively.

Report No. 535 on housing conditions presents the results of the survey on housing conditions based on the data collected in the NSS 65th Round covering the aspects of basic type of structure, availability of separate room for married couples, and per capita floor acre and rent of hired accommodation housing amenities available to the households such as drinking water, bathroom, and electricity facilities and tenure type characteristics of the household type and conditions of the dwelling units micro-environmental elements surrounding the dwelling units like drainage and garbage disposal arrangement, and certain aspects of constructions including cost of construction undertaken by the households some aspects of housing conditions among social groups.

National Buildings Organization

The NBO was established in 1954 as an attached office under the Ministry of Housing and Urban Poverty Alleviation (earlier the Ministry of Works and Housing) for technology transfer, experimentation, development, and dissemination of housing statistics. In the context of formulation of Housing Policy and Programmes, study of socio-economic aspects of housing issues, and the increased need for housing statistics, NBO was restructured in 1992. The NBO was further restructured in March 2006 with the revised mandate keeping in view the current requirements under the National Housing Policy, and various socioeconomic and statistical functions connected with housing and building activities.

The major publications of NBO are given as follows.

Handbook of Housing Statistics—A Compendium

The publication is based mainly on the data generated as part of the census operations.

The publication contains data relating to housing stock, housing conditions, housing amenities, housing situation in metropolitan cities, housing situation in slums, tenure status, and plan investment. Under the housing stock, information on population, households, housing stock, occupied residential houses, distribution of census houses, and value of residential buildings are given. Housing conditions cover information on average number of persons per room, distribution of households by size of dwelling units, distribution of households by predominant material of wall and roof in rural and urban areas separately, housing shortage, and houseless households. Housing conditions and facilities provides information concerning drinking-water facilities, source of drinking water, availability of toilet facilities in rural and urban areas, type of toilet facilities, availability of electricity separately in rural and urban areas, and primary source of energy.

The basic purpose of bringing out the handbook is to provide information relating to housing statistics emanating from various primary sources in one compendium, thus making it easier for researchers and policy formulators.

Building Material Prices and Wages of Labour—A Compendium

The data for the publication are collected quarterly at the instance of NBO by the state governments under the three-tier scheme.

The publication contains data on selected building materials and wages of labour in respect of 248 centres spread throughout the country. The data is presented separately for four quarters for a particular year. In order to provide a comparative picture of the variations in the prices and wage rates annual average prices and wage rates for the six preceding years are also given.

The publication is useful for the public sector agencies engaged in providing housing and or related services, individual builders; persons engaged in related research, and persons in the real estate business by helping them make an assessment of the likely cost of the project.

State of Slums in India—A Statistical Compendium

This is a publication of NBO containing valuable information on slum-related statistics. It provides important data regarding state of slums and related civic facilities, namely population, health, education, and housing amenities. It provides useful information on urbanization, slums, and urban poverty-related statistics drawn from the Census of India, NSSO, Central Statistics Office (CSO), reports of commissions and other sources in a single document. The *Compendium* also tracks the evolution of the policies of the government towards slum dwellers/urban poor over the course of planned economic development in India.

Bibliography

Ministry of Housing and Urban Poverty Alleviation. 2013. *State of Slums in India—A Statistical Compendium*. New Delhi: National Buildings Organisation, Government of India.

National Buildings Organization. 2012 *Building Material Prices and Wages of Labour—A Compendium*. New Delhi: Ministry of Works and Housing.

———. 2011. *Housing in India: A Statistical Compendium*. New Delhi: National Buildings Organization.

National Sample Survey Organisation. 2010. *Housing Conditions and Amenities in India 2008–09, Report No. 535*. New Delhi: Ministry of Statistics and Programme Implementation.

———. *National Sample Survey Reports on Housing Conditions*. New Delhi: Ministry of Statistics and Programme Implementation.

Registrar General of India. 2011 *Census of India—Tables on Houses and Households*. New Delhi: Office of the Registrar General of India.

16

Education Statistics

Ministry of Education

Collection and publication of educational statistics at the all-India level is the responsibility of the Ministry of Education, now named as, Ministry of Human Resource Development (MHRD). Currently the ministry has two departments, namely: (i) Department of School Education and Literacy; and (ii) Department of Higher Education.

The earliest published statistics relate to the year 1882 when the *Report of the Indian Education Commission* was released. Since then quinquennial reviews of the *Progress of Education in India* were published for the years 1886, 1891–2 and at five-year intervals up to 1936–7. A *Decennial Review of Education* was issued for the period 1937–7, giving annual statistics for these years. Annual statistics were also published for each year from 1913–14 to 1946–7 except for those where quinquennial reports were issued. These were however, not as elaborate as the quinquennial ones. Pre-Independence statistics suffered from serious gaps in coverage as most of the princely states were not included.

In 1949–50, the basic mode of collection of data was changed. Annual and quinquennial reports were discontinued. A consolidated comprehensive form called Form A was introduced to collect detailed statistics regarding school education. For collection of statistics regarding university education two forms called Form B and Form B1 were introduced. Form B1 related to the affiliated and constituent colleges of all universities, institutions deemed to be universities, and also institutions of national importance. Form B presented consolidated statistics for individual universities including their affiliated and constituent colleges.

In 1964–5, Form A was revised and replaced by three forms called Form A, A-1 and A-2. The new Form A broadly compared with the old Form A. Form A-1 was introduced to collect data in respect of children of scheduled castes and scheduled tribes. Form A-2 was introduced to collect supplementary data required for planning. Form B was revised more than once and the latest revision was done in the year 1964–5.

To collect data, the aforementioned forms were sent to the different educational institutions. In the case of school education, the filled-in forms were received at the district offices of the Education Departments, through their *tehsil/taluka* offices in the case of primary and middle schools and directly from the institutions in case of high/higher secondary schools, teachers' training schools, vocational and technical schools, and special education schools. The district office sent the consolidated data to the state headquarters. The state headquarters, in addition, collected the returns from colleges and other departments of state governments. Statistics, after security, were sent to the Ministry of Education for publication. Different states, in addition, publish these statistics in their Statistical Abstracts. The consolidation of statistics was generally done at the district level in the case of primary and middle schools. The data for secondary schools and higher education were consolidated at the state level only. The forms for collection of data were changed from time to time, especially with the introduction of software.

Prior to 1947, the Directorate of Commercial Intelligence and Statistics collected the educational statistics and after that it was taken over by the Government of India (GoI), MHRD, or the erstwhile Ministry of Education. Besides, the National Council of Educational Research and Training (NCERT), National Institute of Educational Planning and Administration (NIEPA; now the National University of Educational Planning and Administration [NUEPA]), Registrar General of India (RGI), National Sample Survey

Office (NSSO), Central Statistical Office (CSO), and the erstwhile Planning Commission have been involved in collection and publication of the educational statistics at different points of time in the country. Each agency covers some common ground, and remaining pertinent to its specific objectives at different points of time to reveal the status of educational development as a matter of arithmetic. The major publications of statistics on education along with the contents are given as follows.

Education in India

Education in India was an annual publication of the Department of Education, MHRD. The publication had three volumes, namely, Volume I(S) and I(C), Volume II(S) and II(C), and Volume III. Like, *Selected Educational Statistics, Education in India* also disseminated state-specific information for all states and UTs. However, the information disseminated through the *Selected Educational Statistics* is provisional in nature, while that of the *Education in India* was final. The main volume presenting information on school education is available (latest) for the year 1992–3, published in 1998. The details of the information available is presented under three broad headings, namely, numeric, financial, and examination results. This publication has since been discontinued.

Selected Educational Statistics

This is an annual publication of the Department of Education, MHRD. The publication furnishes quick (provisional) estimates pertaining to numeric data, such as, number of educational institutions by management, enrolment by classes, and by stages up to university level and teachers. Statistics on enrolment and teachers are provided at district level. The detailed examination results for the board examinations are also presented. Subject-wise number of pass-outs at graduate and postgraduate levels is given. Expenditure by level of education is also available. It also presents selected data on literacy and population. Information on demographic variables in this publication is reproduced from the census publications while remaining information on educational variables is a part of its regular collection. The population projections of school-going children in the age groups of 6–11 and 11–14 years for all communities based on the projections worked out by the Expert Committee of the Planning Commission have also been provided in the publication. Over a period of time, a number of changes have taken place in terms of its coverage and presentation. Information on education of scheduled castes (SCs) and scheduled tribes (STs) in this publication is of recent origin. For the last few years, time-series information on some of the educational variables has also been produced at the all-India level. At five-year intervals, data starting from 1950–1 and annual information during the last few years on educational institutions, enrolment, percentage of girls' enrolment to total enrolment by stages, enrolment ratio, drop-out rates at primary and middle levels of education, and distribution of teachers by type of schools have also been published. The publication also contains district-wise literacy percentage in respect of total population and population belonging to SC and ST and number of schools, enrolment and teachers. An attempt has also been made to present comprehensive educational statistics of India in relation to a few selected countries. This publication also gives state-wise information on population (rural and urban), SC/ST population and its percentage to total population, and state-wise literacy rates in rural/urban areas, state-wise decadal changes in literacy rate and the male–female gap. It covers 35 states/UTs.

This publication of MHRD is available on the official website for the year 2005–6 only.[1] From 2006–7, this publication is divided into the following two publications.

Statistics of School Education

This publication is available on the official website of MHRD from the year 2006–7. It is an annual publication of MHRD. It covers number of school education institutions and number of institutions by management. It also includes data on enrolment in school education and open school education, gender enrolment ratio (GER), gender parity index (GPI), number of girls per hundred boys, dropout rates, and projected population 2010, published under three heads: all categories, scheduled caste and scheduled tribe. It gives data on

[1] Available at http://mhrd.gov.in (accessed on 19 May 2017).

teachers: number of teachers in various types of schools, percentage of trained teachers, number of female teachers per hundred male teachers, and pupil–teacher ratio.

The latest publication given on the website is for the year 2011–12. The contents followed during different years are almost the same. The contents for the last year are given in the appendix. The work related to data collection on *School Education Statistics* has been discontinued by the statistics division with effect from 2012–13. It is now being collected by the NUEPA under the Unified District Information System for Education (U-DISE).

Statistics of Higher and Technical Education

This an annual publication brought out by the Department of Higher Education, MHRD. It contains statistical data on important educational indicators, different parameters of higher and technical education and budgetary expenditure on this sector. The data on higher and technical education covers information on all the levels from under graduate to doctorate level of education, distance learning education, polytechnics, and international students.

As far as possible, different indicators in respect of SC and ST have also been given. Time series data on important parameters such as number of institutions and enrolment at the national level are provided in the statements, and graphic presentation of data has been given in the publication. An attempt has also been made to give a comparative picture of India with respect of various other countries.

This publication is available on the official website starting from the year 2006–7.[2] The sources of data are the state governments/UTs, University Grants Commission (UGC), All India Council of Technical Education (AICTE), Distance Education Council, Director General of Employment and Training (DGET), UNESCO Institute of Statistics. Since 2010–11, it is published under the name of *All India Survey on Higher Education* (AISHE), the details of which are given as follows.

[2] Available at http://mhrd.gov.in/ (accessed on 19 May 2017).

All India Survey on Higher Education

The AISHE was initiated in 2011 during which data for the year 2010–11 was collected. Data was collected on main parameters such as teachers; student enrolment: level-wise, programme-wise, and discipline-/subject-wise; examination results; education finance; and infrastructure. Indicators of educational development such as institution density, gross enrolment ratio, pupil–teacher ratio, and GPI, among others, were also calculated. These are useful in making informal policy decisions and research for development of education. The AISHE 2011–12 was started in March 2013. The AISHE 2012–13 launched on September 2013, AISHE 2013–14 in June 2014, and AISHE 2014–15 on October 2014. The AISHE 2014–15 was launched on 22 October 2014. The provisional report for this survey is already available. This survey covers all recognized institutions of higher education located within the geographical boundary of India. The institutions have been classified by three board categories, namely university and university level, college/institutions (which are affiliated to universities), and standalone institutions (not affiliated with universities).

An online module has been developed for addition and deletion and shifting of colleges from one university to another. All institutions need to register on the portal and upload their data.

Online data collection is done through questionnaires (called data capture formats) formulated as I, II, and III for universities/university-level institutions, colleges/institutions and standalone institutions respectively. These are available on the AISHE portal.[3]

Selected Information on School Education in India

This brochure is issued annually by the Department of Education since 1968–9. This publication provides state-wise information on various aspects of school education for an academic year. School education in India is characterized by a wide variation in terms of the duration of various stages of school education, age restriction for admission to Class I, medium of instruction, introduction of

[3] Available at http://aishe.gov.in/ (accessed on 19 May 2017).

compulsory education at the elementary stage, teaching of Hindi and English, number of working days in a year, academic session and vacation periods, details of public examinations by level of school education, provision of free education by type of management of schools and tuition fee charged per child per annum in government schools, adoption of no-detention policy at the elementary stage of education, and syllabus and textbooks followed, among others, in the different states and UTs. The latest publication available on the website relates to the year 2011–12. A new chapter on schemes being implemented by states/UTs for the benefits of students has been included for the year 2011–12.

National Level Educational Statistics at a Glance

The Statistics Division of the MHRD occasionally brings out a handbook *Educational Statistics at a Glance*. This handbook gives state-wise information regarding the area of a state, estimated population by sex, population by school-going children by age groups and by sex, enrolment of children of school-going age groups by sex, number of institutions by type, teachers by sex and by type of school (primary, middle, and higher secondary), intake capacity of teachers' training institutions at different levels, enrolment of SCs and STs, education budget, and distribution of budget by types of education. A new chapter on schemes being implemented by states/UTs for the benefits of students has been included for the year 2011–12.

The 2011 handbook was the fourth edition of the series. Since 2011, the MHRD has been publishing it annually. It is an attempt to present key national-level educational statistics in a compact and easy-to-carry form. It was, thus, an abstract of data contained in various publications of this department. Most of data in the handbook is already contained in various publications of the ministry. It mainly presents data on important educational indicators, different parameters of school and higher education, budgetary expenditure on education, population, and literacy. Also it includes time series data on number of institutions and enrolment as well as important indicators like GER, GPI, and pupil–teacher ratio. The latest available publication on the website is for the year 2014.

Examination Results: Results of High School and Higher Secondary Examinations

This is an annual publication of MHRD, available on their official website from the year 2005–6. The reports for years 2011, 2012, and 2013 are yet not given on the website, although the proforma are given. It is an extensive database containing important statistics of examination results of the high school, higher secondary examinations/intermediate/pre-university examinations conducted by various boards in the country. Higher secondary examinations include regular boards and open boards, and board-wise analysis. The performance of SC and ST students is also given. Various charts are given for number of students appeared and passed (category-wise, sex-wise, also given separately) as well as pass percentages among boys and girls (board-wise also). It also gives tables on annual and supplementary examination results: regular and private students (all categories, SC students, ST students), percentage-wise also given for the same. For the first time in 2010, the stream-wise (arts, science, commerce) results were also included.

The data is collected by proforma available on the ministry's website.[4] The offices of state and central boards of secondary, higher secondary and intermediate/pre-university education, National Institute of Open Schooling, state open schools supply the required data for bringing out this publication.

Analysis of Budgeted Expenditure on Education

In this annual publication of the MHRD, state-wise information is available regarding expenditure on both budgeted and actual basis. The publication gives a detailed analysis of budget provisions made by various states and central ministries for the development of education. Along with the budgeted estimates, actual and revised expenditure of previous year is also disseminated. Basically, the publication is based on the demands for grants of the central ministries and the budget documents of the states and UTs presented in the

[4] Available at http://mhrd.gov.in/ (accessed on 19 May 2017).

state legislatures. Besides giving details in respect of plan and non-plan expenditure for various sectors of education, it also disseminates expenditure incurred on research and training of both formal and non-formal education by various departments in the states and central ministries. The publication is divided into two parts. In the first part, analysis of the year under review is presented while state-wise tables are included in the second part.

The issue gives information in respect of actual expenditure for the previous year, revised estimates of the expenditure for the present year, and the budget estimates for the coming year. An analysis of the budget documents (demands for grants) for the coming year is also presented in the document.

Total expenditure on education as incurred by the centre, states, and UTs have been taken into account. Effort is also made to take precaution against double counting of expenditure because the whole of actual expenditure—both central grants and state's share under Centrally Sponsored Schemes (CSS) of the education department —is made by states/UTs and shown as such in their budget documents. The expenditure incurred on CSS of the department has been included in the central budget and has been excluded from the state budget. Special features of graphic representation of data and their analysis have been added. Bar charts and pie charts have been used as tools to portray the salient and unique features of the analysis.

District Information System for Education: NUEPA

The NUEPA publishes educational data collected under the District Primary Education Programme (DPEP). The DPEP was initiated in late 1994. The NUEPA has designed the District Information System for Education (DISE) to collect annually the educational data in districts covered under DPEP in the country. The design of data collection is institution based, and it covers elementary education (Mehta 2004). The DISE is one of the major initiatives to improve the educational management information system in India which is, at present, under implementation in all the districts of the country. More than 1.20 million schools imparting elementary education have been covered under

DISE which also maintains comprehensive profile of more than 5.2 million teachers.

District Report Card—Elementary Education in India

Since 1999, efforts are being made to share the district-level data with educational planners, administrators, and data users in the form of district report cards. In addition to print material, a variety of dissemination strategies, including card detail record (CDR) and web publishing, were adopted to improve availability of district-level data to data users. From the year 2001–2, the scope of DISE was extended to cover new data elements as well as to expand the scope to the whole of the elementary education sector. In 2005–6 all the districts of the country were covered under DISE for the first time.

The present volume presents the *District Report Cards (Volume I & II) 2014–15* and contains a comprehensive district-specific database on elementary education in India. The *District Report Cards* incorporate information on the following important areas of elementary education:

(1) Basic data on population, literacy, sex ratio, number of blocks, villages, clusters, and schools from which data is reported is presented for all districts except those created after the 2011 Census. In bifurcated districts, it is not possible to project child population in the absence of which a few key indicators are not presented for such districts.
(2) Key data on elementary education in terms of number of schools, enrolment, and teachers classified by school category and school management (government, private, and unrecognized). Details of schools and enrolment in rural areas are also available category-wise and management-wise.
(3) Grade-wise and level-wise enrolment along with percentage of over-age and under-age children at primary and upper primary levels of education in each district.
(4) Classrooms categorized into good condition, requiring minor and major repairs by school category.
(5) Distribution of regular and contractual-teachers by educational and professional qualifications and by school category and by age.

(6) Sex-wise enrolment of children with disabilities in primary and upper primary classes along with children with special needs (CWSN) enrolment by nature of disability.
(7) Gender and caste distribution of regular and contractual teachers and proportion of teachers undergoing in-service teacher training by school category.
(8) Enrolment by medium of instruction and by school category.
(9) Number of students benefited by various incentive schemes at primary and upper primary levels. Grade-specific promotion, repetition, and drop-out rates at primary and upper primary levels of education.
(10) Performance indicators in terms of school category, enrolment distribution: total, SCs, STs, other backward classes (OBC) and Muslims, percentage of girls' enrolment, GPI, number of classrooms, single-teacher schools, and schools with attached pre-primary classes.
(11) Quality indicators according to category of schools, teacher-pupil ratio, average number of teachers, availability of female teachers, school buildings, students–classroom ratio, common toilets, and girls' toilets.
(12) Number of schools received and utilized school development and teaching learning material grants by school category.

In 2011–12, DISE extended the coverage to include the unrecognized schools. As a part of the 2011–12 annual collection, data was recorded on 30 September 2011 for which a DISE Fortnight was observed during the period 1 October 2011 to 15 October 2011 across the country. In each state, data was collected by the Sarva Shiksha Abhiyan (SSA) State Implementation Society through about 70,000 cluster resource centres and 7,000 block resource centre coordinators. More than 1.3 million recognized schools imparting elementary education across the country were covered during the school census: 2011–12. In addition, unrecognized schools were also covered under the DISE during 2011–12 data collection.

Secondary Education Management Information System

When the Rashtriya Madhyamik Shiksha Abhiyan (RMSA) was launched, NUEPA was asked to extend the coverage of DISE from elementary to the secondary and higher secondary level of education in view of which NUEPA designed and developed online software especially for the secondary level of education and collected data for the first time in 2007–8.

Data for classes VIII to XII was collected under the Secondary Education Management Information System (SEMIS) and report cards were kept on the Internet. State-level data was collected on total schools, total enrolment, and total teachers under the four heads: government, private schools, schools in rural areas, and urban areas. The number of districts, blocks, villages, and schools were also mentioned for each state. Data was collected on various performance indicators such as percentage of single-classroom schools, single-teacher schools, schools with teacher's toilets and girl's toilets, drinking water facility, electricity, ramp, library facility, and labs. Data on total enrolment by age, sex, and grade and by category (SC/ST/OBC) for both secondary and higher secondary classes, and teachers by educational qualification was also collected.

Recently, the DISE software was re-designed to take care of secondary and higher secondary level of education which was launched in a workshop held at NUEPA (4 and 5 February 2012) following which all the states and UTs utilized the Unified-DISE (U-DISE) software and submitted data along with certificate issued by the state project director RMSA. Thus, 2012–13 onwards, the two (DISE and SEMIS) were merged and the data is collected under the U-DISE.[5] School education in India (NUEPA 2013–14) is the latest available report so far. For this year, 1.52 million schools spread over 662 districts across 35 states and UTs were covered. This publication covers only elementary education. For secondary education, the statistics are separately available (see under DISE publications for details).

Registrar General of India (RGI): Census of India

The RGI collects data from individual members of all households on census basis with a periodicity of 10 years on social, economic, educational, and demographic aspects. The data relating to

[5] The SEMIS website is http://semisonline.net/ (accessed on 19 May 2017).

education collected during Census 2011 pertain to the literacy, completed level of educational status of individuals whether studying or left studies, mother tongue, and child population (RGI 2011).

NSSO: National Sample Surveys

The NSSO gathers data from individual members of the household on sample basis on various facets of the economy in order to assess socio-economic planning and policy-making. The subject of education was covered in the 35th, 42nd, 50th, 52nd, 55th, 61st, and 64th Rounds of sample surveys. The aspects covered by the NSSO are literacy, present levels of education, educational status of individual (never attended, currently attending a school/college, or dropout), reasons for dropout, private expenditure on education, and number of beneficiaries under different incentive schemes provided to the children.

In addition, information on educational particulars of the individuals of a household has been regularly collected in all the surveys on employment and unemployment. In the 61st Round survey, data has been collected on educational particulars like educational level attained—both general and technical, current attendance in educational institution, type of institution, and vocational training received/being received, among others, from the household members. The highest level of education successfully completed by a person whether general education/technical education/vocational training was considered to be the general level of education of the person. Information on current attendance in educational institutions was collected from persons of age below 30 years. For those who were currently attending educational institutions, information on type of institution was collected. Information on reason for not attending educational institution was collected from those who never attended any educational institution as well as from those who ever attended but were currently not attending. From each person of age 15 to 29 years, information on formal and non-formal vocational training received and formal vocational training being received was collected. For formal vocational training received/being received, information on field of training, duration of training, source from where degree/diploma/certificate was received/to be received was also collected.

The 64th Round of NSS was a multi-subject household survey round covering 'Employment–unemployment and Migration', 'Household Consumer Expenditure', and 'Participation and Expenditure in Education'.

From each sample village or urban block, eight households were selected for the survey on 'Participation and Expenditure in Education'. For each sample household some general particulars, such as age, sex, educational level attained, current attendance, and enrolment status, were collected from all the household members. For persons of age 5–29 years, who formed the main target group of the survey, further information on current attendance and enrolment status in educational institutions was obtained. More detailed data on education was collected from the persons in the target age group who were reported to be currently attending at the primary level or above. This included information on type of education, details of course, level of current attendance, class/grade/year of study, type of management of educational institution, whether the institution is recognized, details of benefits received, if any, such as fee waiver, scholarship, free study materials, and free mid-day meals, and detailed break-up of private educational expenditure for each person. Those currently not attending any educational institution were asked whether they had ever been enrolled, and if so whether they had completed their education or discontinued midcourse, and what was the main reason for dropping out or for non-enrolment. *Report No. 532* gives the estimates of various variables relating to education.

This survey was done again during the 71st Round (January–June 2014). *Report No. 575* gives the detailed data under the following heads: household profile; literacy rates; completed educational level of population for different age groups; distance to nearest primary, upper primary, and secondary school; attendance status of persons in age group 5–29 years; attendance ratios; current attendance of students by type of education; attendance by type of courses; type of institution; students receiving free education; students receiving various incentives; private coaching; private expenditure on education; never-enrolment and discontinuance of education; access to computer and internet.

All India Educational Surveys: NCERT

Introduction

The NCERT conducts All-India Educational Surveys (AIES) after a gap of about seven or eight years. After the Independence, systematic and planned efforts were needed to fulfil the national commitment enshrined under Article 45 of the Constitution to provide free and compulsory education for children up to the age of 14 years. Certain basic inputs, such as identification of school-less habitations, their population, and distance at which schooling facility is available were required to provide schooling facilities in them. In order to fulfil the referred commitment, the first AIES was undertaken in 1957 by the then Union Ministry of Education.

The need for the survey arose because it was felt that no policies or principles were being followed for opening of new schools. At some places there were more schools than required and there were some places without any school. This survey was conducted to find out the educational facilities available and to plan the location of new schools on a rational basis. The first survey covered mainly the rural areas.

Thereafter, seven more AIESs have been conducted in the years 1965, 1973, 1978, 1986, 1993, 2002, and 2009 by the NCERT.

Eighth All India Educational Survey

The date of reference for the eighth survey was 30 September 2009. The AISE data is useful for monitoring of implementation and assessing the impact of SSA, to provide universal access, enrolment, retention, and improvement of quality in elementary education, and planning for universalization of secondary education. These surveys provided basic inputs for planning new schools, upgrading existing schools, and also for enhancing the essential facilities in them. The contribution of the AIESs to macro- as well as micro-level planning of school education has been recognized significantly. It may be pertinent to mention that, over a period of time, these surveys have acquired important status and are considered a major source of educational statistics by different organizations at the national and international levels.

Objectives of the Survey

In school education, lots of changes have taken place since 2002 in terms of schooling facilities and growth in enrolment due to various initiatives such as SSA. The objective of the survey is to develop the database to calculate and analyse a set of educational indicators for: (i) describing the current status of school education system at different levels with respect to access, enrolment, retention, participation in school process, and achievement; (ii) assessing the progress of educational development and indirectly the success of policies, programmes, and project interventions by tracking the direction and magnitude of change in the values of the indicators over time, and identifying problems or deficiencies in the system for necessary intervention; and (iii) assessing equity in educational opportunities and achievements across relevant levels and sub-populations of the education system for possible interventions needed to remove disparity by administrators, policymakers, and researchers.

The data are collected on the aspects broadly listed here:

(1) Availability of schooling facility for primary, upper-primary, secondary, and higher secondary stages within the habitations (including SC/ST) in different population slabs. In case the facility is not within the habitation, the distance at which available.
(2) Availability of basic facilities in the recognized schools such as buildings, classrooms, drinking water, electricity, urinals, lavatories, incentive schemes and beneficiaries, and medical check-up and vaccination/inoculation of students.
(3) Class-wise enrolment (total, SC, ST, OBC, Educationally Backward Minority Community [EBMC], Muslim) and children with disabilities by sex in primary, upper primary, secondary, and higher secondary stages of recognized schools.
(4) The number of children with disabilities along with degree of disability in primary, upper primary, secondary, and higher secondary schools.
(5) The subject-wise enrolment at higher secondary stage, availability of laboratories and library, physical education teachers, librarian, guidance counsellor, non-teaching staff in the recognized secondary and higher secondary schools.
(6) The position of teachers (by sex and SC/ST/OBC) with academic and professional qualifications at different school stages in recognized schools.

(7) Distribution of recognized schools in regard to languages taught and languages used as medium of instruction.
(8) Enrolment and teachers in primary/upper primary classes of unrecognized schools.
(9) The position of enrolment and instructors in schools/centres under the Education Guarantee Scheme and Alternative and Innovative Education (EGS&AIE).
(10) Number of children and teachers by sex in pre-primary schools.
(11) The position of enrolment and teachers in oriental schools, namely Maktabs, Madrasas, and Sanskrit Pathshalas.
(12) Class-wise enrolment by single age, new entrants, promotees, and repeaters in the context of universal elementary education (UEE).[6]

Operational Aspects of the Survey

At the national level, three organizations, namely the MHRD, NCERT and the National Informatics Centre (NIC) are involved. The MHRD is to provide funds for the survey and administrative support for its efficient execution. The NCERT is to share the responsibility of providing all academic inputs, management, and coordination of survey activities right from the planning of the survey to dissemination of outcomes/reports.[7]

University Grants Commission

The UGC, which came into existence on 28 December 1953, became a statutory organization by an act of Parliament in 1956. It is a national body for the coordination, determination, and maintenance of standards of university education. It serves as a coordinating body between the union and state governments and the institutions of higher learning. It also acts as an advisory body to these governments and institutions on issues relating to higher education.

[6] For more information about the AISE surveys, visit http://aises.nic.in/aboutsurvey (accessed on 19 May 2017).

[7] National- and state-level reports are available on the AISE website http://aises.nic.in (accessed on 19 May 2017).

Publications

Higher Education in India at a Glance

Higher Education in India at a Glance has been bought out by UGC. This gives data in the form of tables, charts, and diagrams at the state level regarding vital statistics pertaining to higher education in India, such as the number of higher education institutions, type of degree-awarding institutions, number of students, number of teachers in higher education, level-wise and area-wise student enrolment, and sector-wise public expenditure. This handy brochure also lists UGC interventions towards quality enhancement in higher education.[8]

Inclusive and Qualitative Expansion of Higher Education 12th Five Year Plan (2012–17)

This document contains the core of ideas towards reform initiatives in higher education. Since the reforms have to take roots at the university level, the university leadership has contributed to this document significantly in shaping the policy planning processes at the macro level and in recommending strategies for achieving the targets set. The document draws upon all the existing reports, papers, and databases on higher education and provides a synoptic view of the state of higher education. It has attempted to synthesize the data from the latest round of National Sample Survey (NSS) with the existing enrolment figures and marks a step forward in understanding of the progress and difficulties faced by higher education. It acknowledges the challenge of rising numbers, social inequalities, and the real issue of quality of teaching and learning in Indian higher education. It has reflected on the ambitious challenge of describing, analysing, and suggesting remedies for the higher education sector, and seeks to keep up the momentum of higher education through up-scaling the reforms that began in the 11th Five Year Plan.

The list of tables given in this report are on number, nature, and category of institutions, state-wise number of universities listed by

[8] It is available on the official website of UGC, for two years: February 2012 and June 2013, at http://www.ugc.ac.in/page/Other-Publications.aspx (accessed on 19 May 2017).

the UGC, colleges recognized by the UGC for financial assistance, region-wise distribution of colleges, all-India growth of student enrolment: 1984–5 to 2009–10, state-wise student enrolment in universities and colleges: 2009–10, state-wise student enrolment in university teaching department and affiliated colleges enrolment in 2009–10, student enrolment: level-wise and faculty-wise: 2009–10, state-wise number of university colleges and affiliated colleges: 2009–10, GER (18–22 years) in rural and urban areas, GER by sex and sector, 2007–8, and ratio for universities and colleges.

UGC Annual Reports

The publication of the annual report of the UGC has been a regular feature since its inception in 1953.

The annual report for 2011–12 provides not only the major initiatives taken by UGC as the apex body for coordinating and maintaining standards of higher education in the country but also provides statistics on growth of the higher education system under the following heads—institutions (number of institutions and universities, state-wise under central, state government, state private, deemed, others, and not fit for central assistance), student enrolment (like state-wise and faculty-wise by sex), faculty strength (number of teachers by categories like assistant professors/associate professors/professors/others), research degrees, growth in enrolment of women in higher education (per thousand and per hundred men over time), distribution of women enrolment by state and faculty (such as arts, science, commerce/management, law, education, and medicine) and women colleges (over the years).

It also highlights the initiatives undertaken by the UGC in promoting the general development of universities and colleges, culminating in the enhancing of access, equity, relevance and excellence.[9]

The UGC also provides the statistical data in a number of publications. Some of these are the following.

[9] The annual reports are available on the net at http://www.ugc.ac.in/page/Annual-Report.aspx (accessed on 19 May 2017), for the years 2005–6, 2007–8, 2008–9, 2009–10, and 2011–12.

University Development in India: Basic Facts and Figures

This publication is brought out annually by the Information and Statistics Division of the UGC. This publication gives a summary of important information about different universities in India. The information relates to—name of university, names of teaching departments, colleges attached with the year of establishment and location and jurisdiction; enrolment for different courses and for different years of the course for individual faculties of arts, science, commerce, engineering, agriculture, and medicine; distribution of staff by subjects and designation; number of approved hostels, their intake capacity and the number of students staying in these hostels; details of postgraduate education, and statistics for institutes deemed to be universities. The latest available report (for 1995–6 to 2000–1) was published in December 2002.

Examination Results (Annual and Supplementary)

This is an annual publication of the UGC. It gives information on examination results (out-turn of graduates and postgraduates—faculty- and sex-wise), faculty-wise/course-wise examination results (total out-turn of graduates and postgraduates), course-wise/division-wise examination results: all India by sex; university/course/division-wise examination results by sex. It also has three annexures: list of universities for which data has been included in the report; list of defaulting universities from which data has not been received; and name of the course of Indian universities for which information has been presented in this report.

Statistics of International Students in Indian Universities/Institutes of Higher Education

This publication contains useful information on foreign students studying in Indian higher education institutions. The information has broadly been provided under the faculty groups—arts, sciences, commerce and management, education, engineering and technology, medical sciences, agricultural sciences, veterinary sciences, law, and others.

This publication provides faculty-cum-gender-wise enrolment, level-cum-gender-wise, state-cum-gender and level-wise enrolments, state-cum-institution-cum-gender and level-wise enrolments, faculty-cum-level-wise (graduate, postgraduate, MPhil, PhD, diploma, certificate) enrolments and institution-cum-country-cum-gender-wise enrolment for the years 2011 to 2012.

Appendix 16A

Tables of Statistics of School Education, 2009–10

(1) Number of institutions—school education
(2) Number of institutions by management
(3) Enrolment in school education
  (a) all categories of students
  (b) SC students
  (c) ST students
  (d) rural area
(4) Percentage of SC/ST/rural area enrolment to total enrolment in schools
(5) Enrolment of CWSN
(6) Enrolment as per International Standard Classification for Education (ISCED)
(7) Number of teachers, enrolment and pupil teacher ratio by type of institutions
(8) Teacher training schools
(9) Technical/industrial/arts and craft institutes
(10) EGS/AIE centre's (ISCED1)
(11) Enrolment in open schools
  (a) All categories of students
  (b) SC students
  (c) ST students
(12) Gross enrolment ratio (GER)
  (a) all categories of students
  (b) SC students
  (c) ST students
  (d) rural area
(13) Number of girls per hundred boys
  (a) all categories of students

(b) SC students
(c) ST students

(14) Gender parity index
(a) all categories of students
(b) SC students
(c) ST students

(15) Dropout rates in classes I–V, I–VIII, and I–X
(a) all categories of students
(b) SC students
(c) ST students

(16) Examination results of boards high school examination—2010
(a) all students
(b) SC students
(c) ST students
(d) open schooling

(17) Examination results of boards class XII examination—2010
(a) all students
(b) SC students
(c) ST students
(d) open schooling
(e) population, literacy, and budget

(18) State-wise and gender-wise population in rural/urban areas

(19) State-wise scheduled caste population and its percentage to total population 2011

(20) State-wise scheduled tribes population and its percentage to total population 2011

(21) Projected population
(a) total projected population 2008
(b) projected SC population 2008
(c) projected ST population 2008
(d) rural population

(22) State-wise decadal changes in literacy rate and male female literacy gap (1991–2011)

(23) State-wise and gender-wise literacy rates in rural/urban areas Census 2011

(24) Literacy rates of scheduled castes, Census 2011

(25) Literacy rates of scheduled tribes, Census 2011

(26) Budgeted expenditure (revenue account) on education (2007–8)

(27) International comparison of key educational parameters 2008
   (a) Pre-primary education (ISCED0) and primary education (ISCED1)
   (b) Secondary and senior secondary education (ISCED 2 & 3)

Bibliography

District Information System for Education. 2009. *District Report Card—Elementary Education in India, 2008–09*. New Delhi: Ministry of Human Resource Development.

———. *School Census: 2011–12*.

Mehta, Arun C. 2004. *Elementary Education in India: Where do we stand? Analytical Report*. New Delhi: National University of Educational Planning and Administration.

Ministry of Human Resource Development (MHRD). Various issues. *Analysis of Budgeted Expenditure on Education*, 2011–12 to 2013–14, –2015. New Delhi: MHRD.

———. Various issues. *Education in India*. New Delhi: MHRD.

———. 2015. *Educational Statistics at a Glance*, 2015. New Delhi: MHRD.

———. Various issues. *Educational Statistics, District-wise*. New Delhi: MHRD.

———. 2006. *Selected Educational Statistics*, 2005–06. New Delhi: MHRD.

———. 2012. *Statistics of School Education*, 2011–12. New Delhi: MHRD.

National Council of Educational Research and Training (NCERT). 2006. *Seventh All India School Education Survey (8th AISES)*. New Delhi: NCERT.

National Sample Survey Office (NSSO). 2006. *Status of Education and Vocational Training in India 2004–05 (July 2004–June 2005), Report No. 517*. New Delhi: Ministry of Statistics and Programme Implementation.

———. 2009. *National Sample Survey (64th Round) on 'Participation and Expenditure in Education', Report No. 532*. New Delhi: Ministry of Statistics and Programme Implementation.

National University of Educational Planning and Administration (NUEPA). July 2014. *School Education in India, 2013–14*. New Delhi: NUEPA.

———. September 2005. *District Information System for Education, District Primary Education Programme (DPEP) Report, 2004*. New Delhi: NUEPA

Office of the Registrar General and Census Commissioner of India. 2011. *Census 2011*. New Delhi: Ministry of Home Affairs.

University Grants Commission (UGC). *Higher Education in India at a Glance*, 2013. New Delhi: UGC.

———. *Inclusive and Qualitative Expansion of Higher Education 12th Five-Year Plan (2012–17)*. New Delhi: UGC.

———. *UGC Annual Reports*. New Delhi: UGC.

17

Health Statistics

The collection of health statistics is mainly the responsibility of the state health directorates. The Union Ministry of Health and Family Welfare, Government of India (GoI) is responsible for implementation of various health and family welfare programmes through the state governments. The ministry implements various national programmes for control of acquired immune deficiency syndrome (AIDS), malaria, leprosy, tuberculosis, and blindness. The ministry consists of four departments—Department of Health and Family Welfare, Department of Ayurveda, Yoga and Naturopathy, Unani, Siddha and Homeopathy (AYUSH), Department of Health Research, and Department of AIDS Control.

Department of Health and Family Welfare

The Directorate General of Health Services (DGHS) is an attached office of the Department of Health and Family Welfare which has subordinate offices spread all over the country. The DGHS renders technical advice on all medical and public health matters and is involved in implementation of various health schemes. At the national level, the Central Bureau of Health Intelligence (CBHI) in the DGHS established in 1961 is there to coordinate and advise on the development of health statistics in the country. Data on health services cover medical care facilities provided to the population in the form of immunization, school health, and maternity services. Information on medical care facilities cover hospitals, dispensaries, community health centres (CHCs), primary health centres (PHCs), sub-centres, and maternity and child welfare centres. Data on manpower are derived from licence registers for various categories of doctors, dentists, pharmacists, nurses, and health visitors, and are consolidated by their respective councils. Data are available in the following publications.

Health Information of India

The CBHI brought out the first publication *Health Statistics of India: 1951–1953*. This was followed by subsequent issues covering health statistics up to the year 1975. The said publication was modified and brought out as *Pocket Book of Health Statistics of India* till the year 1980. The annual publication *Health Statistics of India* was revived from the year 1981 and continued up to the year 1985. However, 1986 onwards, this annual publication was renamed *Health Information of India* and was published up to the year 2005.

The publication gives data on the various aspects of health including the performance of national health programmes. The main data sets presented in the publication are as follows:

(1) Public health statistics: Notified cases and deaths due to cholera cases and deaths due to principal communicable and non-communicable diseases; performance of National Health Programmes for eradication of malaria, leprosy, control for filarial, *kala-azar*, Japanese encephalitis, tuberculosis, blindness, prevalence rate of goitre; admissions, discharges and deaths in specialized cancer hospitals, and specialized mental hospitals; sexually transmitted diseases (STDs) cases seen and treated, and AIDS cases detected.

(2) Medical and paramedical education: Number of medical and dental colleges; number of students admitted and qualified; out-turn of nurses, midwives, health visitors; number of training institutions for pharmacists; and number and admission capacity of colleges on Indian system of medicine.

(3) Medical and health facilities: Number of hospitals and dispensaries with bed strength rural/urban area-wise and by

category of ownership; hospital population ratio; beds; population ratio; establishment of Community Health Services such as CHCs, PHCs and sub-centres; and number of beds in specialized cancer and mental hospitals.

(4) Medical and paramedical manpower: Number of registered doctors, dentists, pharmacists, nurses, auxiliary nurses, and midwives; health visitors; and number of registered homeopaths and practitioners of Indian system of medicine.
(5) Administration of Prevention of Food Adulteration Act: Information on number of samples examined and found adulterated, including percentages.
(6) Expanded programme of immunization: Data on vaccination performance of tetanus toxoid (TT; for pregnant women); diphtheria, pertussis, and tetanus (DPT); diphtheria and tetanus (DT); polio; typhoid; measles; bacillus Calmette–Guérin (BCG); and TT (school children); and installed capacity and productions of vaccines at various units.
(7) Social security: Number of Central Government Health Scheme (CGHS) dispensaries and beneficiaries at different centres; health services under Employees State Insurance Scheme; and schemes for the workers of coal mines.
(8) Poverty: It gives state-specific poverty line in 1999–2000 (rupees per capita per month) and number of percentage of population below poverty line by states/UTs for the years 1999–2000 (30-day recall period).
(9) Disability: Information about disabled population in India in 1980 and estimated number (in thousands) of disabled population by type of disability and sex—1991 (all India) and 2002 (all India).
(10) Pattern of government investment and expenditure on health, family welfare, and AYUSH.
(11) Population and vital statistics including statistics of causes of death.
(12) International comparative statistics.
(13) Primary healthcare services (government).
(14) Secondary and tertiary medical care services.

Health Insurance Statistics

From the year 2005, the *Health Information of India* was improvized and enlarged while covering various gaps and CBHI came out with the first issue of *National Health Profile of India (NHP) 2005*. From the year 2006, *NHP* replaced *Health Information of India*.

This publication (NHP) highlights most of the relevant information for six major topics under health statistics, namely demography, socio-economic, health status, health finances, health infrastructure, and human resources for the specified calendar year, and many other relevant information required for an efficient public health system in our country. The sources as well as limitations of the data are also appropriately indicated.

Some information about these statistics is given as follows.

Demographic Statistics

Demographic characteristics of a country provide an overview of its population size, composition, territorial distribution, changes therein, and the components of changes, such as nativity, mortality, and social mobility. This section on demographic statistics has been subdivided into two parts—population statistics and vital statistics. Population statistics include statistics that measure the population size, sex ratio, density, and dependency ratio while vital statistics include statistics such as birth rate, death rate, and natural growth rate, life expectancy at birth, mortality, and fertility rates. These statistics for the country as well as states help in identifying areas that need policy and programmed interventions, setting near- and far-term goals, and deciding priorities, besides understanding them in an integrated structure. Data in this section has been taken mainly from the Census of India.

Socio-Economic Statistics

Socio-economic statistics provide a background to understand the health scenario in a country. This section on socio-economic statistics provides data on education, gender, poverty, housing and amenities like availability of bathroom and toilet facility, and facilities of drinking water, employment, and other economic statistics. These statistics for the country as well as states will help in identifying the linkages between socio-economic statistics and achievement of health goals.

Health Finance Statistics

Health finance statistics provide an understanding of patterns of investments, expenditure, sources of funding and proportion of allocation vis-à-vis other total allocation. It also provides an important tool to understand health outcomes in relation to the expenditure. Health finance statistics include allocations under five-year plans, details of expenditures on health, and trends in public and private spending.

Health Status Statistics

This chapter provides a broad overview on the incidence and prevalence of common communicable and non-communicable disease, morbidities and associated mortality, health risks, and performance of related national health programmes in the country during the calendar year. It also provides an overview of reproductive and child health in the country.

Health Infrastructure

Health infrastructure is an important statistic to understand the healthcare delivery provisions and mechanisms in a country. It also signifies the investments and priority accorded to creating the infrastructure in public and private sectors.

This section on health infrastructure statistics is subdivided into two categories, namely educational infrastructure and service infrastructure. Educational infrastructure provides details of medical colleges, students admitted to MBBS courses, postgraduate degrees/diplomas in medical and dental colleges, admissions to Bachelors in Dental Surgery and Masters in Dental Surgery courses, AYUSH institutes, nursing courses and paramedical courses.

Service infrastructure in health include details of allopathic hospitals, hospital beds, Indian system of medicine and Homeopathy hospitals, sub-centres, PHCs, CHCs, blood banks, mental hospitals, and cancer hospitals.

Human Resources in Health Sector

Human resource statistics provide an overview of availability of trained and specialized medical, nursing and paramedical personnel in the country. It also gives an idea regarding regional distribution and disparities.

Human resource statistics cover the details of allopathic doctors, dental surgeons, AYUSH doctors, nursing personnel, and various paramedical health manpower in the country.

Rural Health Statistics in India

The Rural Health Division of DGHS brings out this publication. It provides detailed statistics on rural health infrastructure in order to cater to the needs of health planners and policymakers as well as other government and non-government organizations and research institutions working in this field. This publication has two parts.

Rural Health Care System in India

This part presents, at state level, the number of sub-centres, PHCs, and CHCs, availability of manpower, buildings by tier system, and number of doctors. The sub-centre is the first contact point between the primary healthcare system and the community. The sub-centres are provided with basic drugs for minor ailments. It is the first contact point between the village community and the medical officer. The PHCs were envisaged to provide an integrated curative and preventive health care to the rural population with emphasis on preventive and promotive aspects of healthcare. The PHCs are established and maintained by the state governments under the Minimum Needs Programme (MNP)/Basic Minimum Services (BMS) programme. As per minimum requirements, a PHC is to be manned by a medical officer supported by 14 paramedical and other staff.

The CHCs are being established and maintained by the state government under the MNP/BMS programmes. As per minimum norms, a CHC is required to be manned by four medical specialists—a surgeon, a physician, a gynaecologist, and a paediatrician—supported by 21 paramedical and other staff.

Detailed Statistics

This consists of (i) demographic statistics; (ii) rural health infrastructure; (iii) health manpower in rural areas by the type of centres; (iv) status of facilities available by the type of centres; (v) training of medical and paramedical personnel; (vi) rural healthcare—some parameters of achievement; (vii) rural health infrastructure in tribal areas; and (viii) district-wise rural healthcare infrastructure, in terms of availability of different types of health centres.[1]

Family Welfare Statistics in India[2]

The *Family Welfare Statistics in India*, erstwhile *Family Welfare Programme in India Year Book*, under DGHS provides detailed family welfare performance statistics on the various facets of the family welfare programmes in India based on the reports received from states/UTs up to March of the year. The latest issue in hand is the for the year 2011. This publication provides a wide range of demographic, social, economic, and related statistics extracted from the Population Census 2011, the results of the latest Sample Registration System (SRS) released by the Registrar General of India, and large-scale surveys, namely the National Family and Health Survey (NFHS)–3 during 2005–6 and relevant data from District Level Household Survey (DLHS)–3 conducted during 2007–8, the results of which were released recently. This publication contains the following five sections.

Population and Vital Statistics

It contains tables on population growth, crude birth and death rates, and sex ratio: India 1901–2011, density and growth rate of population: Census 2011, rural and urban composition of population, basic population data, fertility and mortality statistics for all of India, and

[1] For more information, see http://mohfw.nic.in/WriteReadData/l892s/492794502RHS%202012.pdf (accessed on 22 May 2017).

[2] The Report for the year 2013 is already out. There are minor changes in the number of sections and contents. The name of the publication is changed to *Health and Family Welfare Statistics in India*.

projected population characteristics: India, 2001–26. Some statistics in this and other sections are available at the state level.

Family Programme Statistics

It gives tables on year-wise achievement of targets of medical termination of pregnancy (MTP) activities: all India, tetanus immunization for expectant mothers (ii + booster), DPT immunization for children (iii dose), DT immunization for children, prophylaxis against nutritional anaemia among women, family-planning acceptors by methods: all India, information relating to maternal health, 2007–8.

Health Management Information Systems (HMIS)—New Key Indicators

It gives data on number of pregnant women who received three ante-natal care (ANC) checkups, number of newborn visited within 24 hours of home delivery, number of still births, and number of newborns weighed at birth.

National Family Health Survey

This section gives details of key indicators of National Family Health Survey (NHFS)-III, II, and I. The Ministry of Health and Family Welfare, in collaboration with the Registrar General of India (RGI), had launched an Annual Health Survey (AHS) in the erstwhile Empowered Action Group States (Bihar, Jharkhand, Madhya Pradesh, Chhattisgarh, Uttarakhand, Uttar Pradesh, Odisha, and Rajasthan) and Assam. The aim of the survey was to provide feedback on the impact of the schemes under the National Rural Health Mission (NRHM) in reduction of total fertility rate (TFR), infant mortality rate (IMR) at the district level, and maternal mortality rate (MMR) at the regional level by estimating these rates on an annual basis for around 284 districts in these states. The results of the first round of the AHS for some of the indicators, namely crude birth rate (CBR), crude death rate (CDR), IMR, neo-natal mortality rate, under-five mortality rate, MMR, and sex ratio, have since become available and are given in this publication.

Facility Survey

This section provides data on key indicators covered in *Facility Survey: 2007–08* conducted as part of DLHS-3.

Outlay and Expenditure on Family Welfare Programmes (2010–11)

This section covers outlay and expenditure on family welfare programmes for the year 2010–11. It provides tables on year-wise budget estimates, revised estimates, and actual expenditure relating to the Department of Family Welfare, plan outlay on health and family welfare in different plan periods for centre, states, and UTs.

Integrated Disease Surveillance Programme (IDSP) and National Vector Borne Disease Control Programme (NVBDCP)

The ISDP was launched with the assistance of the World Bank in November 2004 to detect and quickly respond to disease outbreaks. Under IDSP, weekly disease surveillance data on epidemic-prone diseases are collected from reporting units such as sub-centres, PHCs, CHCs, and hospitals, including government and private sector hospitals and medical colleges. The data are being collected on 'S' (syndromic), 'P' (probable), and 'L' (laboratory) formats using standard case definitions. Presently, more than 90 per cent districts report such weekly data through e-mail/portal.[3] The weekly data are analysed by state/district surveillance units for disease trends. Whenever there is a rising trend of illnesses, it is investigated by the rapid response teams to diagnose and control the outbreak.

In addition to the IDSP, there is the National Vector Borne Disease Control Programme (NVBDCP). The directorate of NVBDCP is the central nodal agency for the prevention and control of vector borne diseases, that is, malaria, dengue, lymphatic filariasis, kala-azar, Japanese encephalitis, and chikungunya in India. It is one of the technical departments of the DGHS, GoI.

[3] Available at www.idsp.nic.in (accessed on 22 May 2017).

The data on malaria surveillance is generated at village/sub-centre level, which are compiled at the PHC/block level and sent to the districts. Districts, in turn, submit the PHC-wise data to the state from where it is compiled district-wise and transmitted to directorate of NVBDCP. As per the system, the data of the previous month is submitted to the state between the 5th and 10th of the succeeding month. The state-wise data is compiled at the central directorate, and on every 25th, the monthly epidemiological situation (MES) is generated for the previous month—for example, the MES generated on 25 April will have data till March of that year.

The method of collection and reporting for other diseases under NVBDCP is similar. The data for these diseases are also available in the annual reports of NVBDCP.

Similar details are available about blindness, cancer, and deafness.

Control Programmes

Data on the number of cases and deaths of different communicable and non-communicable diseases is available in the *National Health Profile*. This publication also gives details regarding the prevention and control of a number of diseases.

Department of AYUSH

The Department of Indian System of Medicine and Homoeopathy (ISM&H) was created in March 1995 and renamed the Department of AYUSH in November 2003 with a view to providing focused attention to development of education and research in AYUSH systems. The department continued to lay emphasis on upgrade of AYUSH educational standards, quality control, and standardization of drugs, improving the availability of medicinal plant material, research and development, and awareness generation about the efficiency of the systems, domestically and internationally. Dated 8 December 2014, the Department of AYUSH has been made the Ministry of AYUSH with focused attention on development of education and research in AYUSH systems.

Publications of AYUSH

AYUSH in India

This publication provides health-structure statistics including educational infrastructure as well as service infrastructure, details about hospitals, dispensaries, and doctors at the state level. This publication also gives data on licensed pharmacies; number of colleges; AYUSH-related foreign trade regarding value of exports and imports of Ayurvedic, Unani, Siddha, and Homoeopathic herbs and medicines; commodity-wise value of export and import of Ayurvedic, Unani, Siddha, and Homoeopathic herbs and medicines; and data on population and vital statistics.

Department of Health Research

The Department of Health Research was formally launched on 5 October 2007. So far there is no statistical publication of this department.

The following work has been allocated to the Department of Health Research.

(1) Promotion and co-ordination of basic, applied, and clinical research including clinical trials and operational research in areas related to medical, health, biomedical, and medical profession, and education through development of infrastructure, manpower, and skills in cutting edge areas and management of related information thereto.
(2) Promotion and providing guidance on research governance issues, including ethical issues in medical and health research. Inter-sectoral coordination and promotion of public–private partnership in medical, biomedical, and health research related areas.
(3) Advanced training in research areas concerning medicine and health, including grant of fellowships for such training in India and abroad.
(4) International cooperation in medical and health research, including work related to international conferences in related areas in India and abroad.
(5) Technical support for dealing with epidemics and natural calamities.

(6) Investigation of outbreaks due to new and exotic agents and development of tools for prevention.
(7) Matters relating to scientific societies and associations, charitable and religious endowments in medicine and health research areas.
(8) Coordination between organizations and institutes under the central and state governments in areas related to the subjects entrusted to the department and for the promotion of special studies in medicine and health.
(9) Administering and monitoring of Indian Council of Medical Research (ICMR).

Department of AIDS Control

The National AIDS Control Organization (NACO) collects data on cases and deaths due to AIDS/STD and publishes these in its publication, given as follows.

Core Indicators for Monitoring and Evaluation

This handbook reviews the core indicators developed for monitoring the achievements and assessing the progress of the National AIDS Control Programme—Phase III (NACP III) of India. The indicators are designed to be used at different levels of programme management and provide standardized measures of performance spanning the multiple objectives of NACP III. The collection, analysis, and use of the core statistics data is collectively referred to as strategic information management.

The purpose of the indicator handbook is to provide guidance to persons involved in the collection, reporting, and analyses of the core statistics data to ensure consistent, high quality information are available to programme managers.

From 7 August 2014, the Department of AIDS Control has been merged with Department of Health and Family Welfare.

Annual Health Survey

The Annual Health Survey was designed to yield core vital and health indicators on fertility and mortality, prevalence of disabilities, injuries, acute and chronic illness and access to health care for these morbidities, and access to maternal, child health, and family planning services, at the district level. This survey was sponsored by the Ministry of Health and Family Welfare, but was being conducted by the office of the Registrar General, Ministry of Home Affairs. The first survey was conducted with reference to 2010–11 in eight Empowered Action Group (EAG) states (Bihar, Jharkhand, Uttar Pradesh, Uttrakhand, Madhya Pradesh, Chhattisgarh, Odisha, and Rajasthan) and Assam (all 284 districts of eight EAG states and Assam). The last survey was conducted with reference to the year 2013. A representative sample of 18 million population and 3.6 million households was covered in 20,694 statistically selected PSUs in these states. Statistical Bulletins of all the states containing district level vital indicators have already been issued by 2014. Since then it has been discontinued. In fact this survey was commissioned only for this period.

Mother and Child Tracking

The details regarding children born—such as date of birth, place of delivery, blood group, caste, name of sub-centre, name and phone number of auxiliary nurse midwife (ANM) and name and phone number of associated accredited social health activist (ASHA)—and also the immunization details at birth and at different intervals of time are available on the website of the ministry since 2010. Also available are the details of pregnant women since the detection of pregnancy regarding pre-natal and anti-natal facilities available to them. Examples include details of health provider; ANC details; pregnancy outcomes; PNC details; and child details (sex, weight at birth, initiated breast feeding within one hour).

Also, details of services provided through the large network of health facilities across rural and urban areas are available on the portal up to sub-centre level (1.91 lakh health facilities reporting data during 2013–14 on various indicators). Demographic and vital indicators, maternal mortality ratio estimates, and population projection reports are put on the portal launched by the ministry in 2008.

In addition, the following three surveys have been conducted by the Ministry of Health and Family Welfare, GoI, with the

International Institute for Population Sciences, Mumbai, serving as the nodal agency. The details about the survey reports are listed as follows.

Survey Reports

National Family Health Surveys

The three NFHS conducted in 1992–3, 1998–9 and 2005–6 have collected important information on the health status of the population, family planning, fertility, and mortality as well as growth and development of children, the level of anaemia of women and children, and related parameters at the state level. The 2005–6 NFHS was the third in a series of national surveys. The fourth survey was conducted in 2015–16.

The NFHS-3 updates and evidence of trends in key population, health, and nutrition indicators, including human immunodeficiency virus (HIV) prevalence. Moreover, the survey covers a range of health-related issues, including fertility, infant and child mortality, maternal and child health, pre-natal mortality, adolescent reproductive health, high-risk sexual behaviour, safe injections, tuberculosis and malaria, non-communicable diseases, domestic violence, HIV knowledge, and attitudes towards people living with HIV. The information will enable the GoI to provide national and international agencies to monitor and evaluate policies and programmes related to population, health, nutrition, and HIV/AIDS.

In NFHS-3, 18 research organizations conducted interviews with more than 2,30,000 women aged 15–49 and men aged 15–54 throughout India. The NFHS-3 also tested more than 1,00,000 women and men for HIV and more than 2,00,000 adults and young children for anaemia. Fieldwork for NFHS-3 was conducted from December 2005 to August 2006.

Scope of NFHS-3

The NFHS-3, like NFHS-1 and NFHS-2, is a household survey which provides estimates of statistics of population, health, and nutrition by background characteristics at the national and state levels. In NFHS-3, information was collected about households, and individual interviews were conducted with women aged 15–49 and men aged 15–54. The NFHS-3 also included height and weight measurements and blood tests for HIV and anaemia.

Survey Objectives

Each successive round of the NFHS has had two specific goals: (i) to provide essential data on health and family welfare needed by the Ministry of Health and Family Welfare and other agencies for policy and programme purposes; and (ii) to provide information on important emerging health and family welfare issues.

NFHS-3 Survey

In NFHS-3, interviews were conducted with eligible respondents using a household questionnaire, a woman's questionnaire (for women aged 15–49), and a man's questionnaire (for men age 15–54).

Household Interview and Individual Respondent's Interview

This looked into measurement of height, weight, and haemoglobin content in the blood of interviewed women and men, as well as children born in January 2000 (January 2001 for the second round of interviewing) or later who were at least six months old, using the HemoCue instrument. Also as part of the household interview, cooking salt was tested for iodine content.

Collection of blood samples on filter paper cards from men aged 15–54 and women aged 15–49 for HIV testing was also done.

Data Collection

The NFHS-3 fieldwork was carried out in two phases. The first-phase activities started in August 2005 and data collection was done from December 2005 to May 2006. The second phase started in January 2006 and data collection was carried out from April to August 2006. In the first phase, 12 states were covered and in the second phase the remaining 17 states were covered.

Sampling

SAMPLE SIZE

In NFHS-3, the initial target sample size was 4,000 completed interviews for ever-married women in states with more than 30 million according to 2001 population, 3,000 completed interviews with ever-married women in states with a 2001 population between 5 and 30 million, and 1,500 completed interviews with ever-married women in states with a population of less than 5 million.

The sample size of HIV tests is estimated on the basis of the assumed HIV prevalence rate. With an assumed level of HIV prevalence of 1.25 per cent and 15 per cent relative standard error, the estimated sample size is 6,400 tests each for men and women in high HIV prevalence states.

SAMPLE DESIGN

The urban and rural samples within each state were drawn separately and, to the extent possible, the sample within each state was allocated proportionally to the size of the state's urban and rural populations. A uniform sample design was adopted in all the states. In each state, the rural sample was selected in two stages: the selection of primary sampling units (PSUs), followed by the random selection of households within each PSU in the second stage. In urban areas, a three-stage procedure was followed. In the first stage, wards were selected with PPS sampling. In the next stage, one census enumeration block (CEB) was randomly selected from each sample ward. In the final stage, households were randomly selected within each sample CEB.

Publications

Following are the NFHS-3 publications.

NUTRITION IN INDIA

This report presents key findings on the nutrition of children, women, and men in India. It supplements information published in the NFHS-3 national and state reports and provides important new information and in-depth analyses. The new features include a cross-country comparison of the nutritional status of children, a comparison of nutritional status calculated with the new World Health Organization (WHO) Child Growth Standards and the previous NCHS/WHO International Reference Population, a multivariate analysis of the nutritional status of 'elite' children, an analysis of nutrition as a contributing factor to under-five mortality, examination of the environmental links to malnutrition, the provision of a complete picture of infant and young child feeding practices by age, and an examination of geographic patterns of vegetarianism.

HEALTH AND LIVING CONDITIONS IN EIGHT INDIAN CITIES

This report provides information on a variety of topics including:

(1) The extent of poverty in the eight selected cities by slum/non-slum residence according to the census and NFHS-3 supervisor designation of these areas and by wealth status;
(2) Demographic and socioeconomic characteristics of slum/non-slum residents and the urban poor;
(3) Household living conditions; and
(4) Health and healthcare;

A PROFILE OF YOUTH IN INDIA

This report has five chapters. Chapter 1 provides a profile of youth and examines who are the youth of India. Chapter 2 discusses what youth know about selected health-related issues. Chapter 3 discusses youth attitudes toward selected population, health, and gender concerns. Chapter 4 discusses behaviour of youth in health-related spheres. Chapter 5 provides a health and nutritional profile of youth.

GENDER EQUALITY AND WOMEN'S EMPOWERMENT IN INDIA

The report provides information on (i) progress in India toward the twin goals of gender equality and women's empowerment; (ii) determinants of selected indicators of gender equality and women's empowerment; and (iii) associations of women's empowerment with selected health and nutritional outcomes.

The NFHS-4 has already been conducted. The 2015–16 National Family Health Survey (NFHS-4) is the fourth in a series of national surveys; earlier National Family Health Surveys were carried out in 1992–93 (NFHS-1), 1998–9 (NFHS-2) and 2005–6 (NFHS-3).

NFHS-4 is the first of the NFHS series that collected data in each of India's 29 states and all 7 UTs. Also, NFHS-4, for the first time, will provide estimates of most indicators at the district level for all 640 districts of the country included in the 2011 Census. In NFHS-4, women aged 15–49 years and men aged 15–54 years were interviewed. On completion of the survey throughout the country, it was predicted to cover approximately 5,70,000 households for information.

Four survey schedules—household, woman's, man's, and biomarker—were canvassed. In the household schedule, information was collected on all usual members of the household and visitors who stayed in the household the previous night as well as socio-economic characteristics of the household, water and sanitation, health insurance, and number of deaths in the household in the three years preceding the survey. Information on the woman's characteristics, marriage, fertility, children's immunizations and childcare, nutrition, contraception, reproductive health, sexual behaviour, HIV/AIDS, and domestic violence was canvassed in the woman's schedule. The man's schedule covered the man's characteristics, marriage, number of children, contraception, fertility preferences, nutrition, sexual behaviour, attitudes towards gender roles, and HIV/AIDS, among others. The biomarker schedule covered measurements of height, weight, and haemoglobin levels for children as well as measurements of height, weight, haemoglobin levels, blood pressure, and random blood glucose level for women aged 15–49 years and men aged 15–54 years. In addition, women and men were requested to provide a few drops of blood from a finger prick for laboratory testing for HIV.[4]

District Level Household Survey

In order to monitor the ongoing health and family welfare programmes, the need for a database at the district level was felt by the Government of India. For this, the DLHS-3 was undertaken. The DLHS-3 is the third in the series preceded by DLHS-1

[4] State reports and fact sheets, and district fact sheets are available online at http://rchiips.org/nfhs/factsheet_nfhs-4.shtml (accessed on 22 May 2017).

in 1998–9 and DLHS-2 in 2002–4. The DLHS-3 is one of the largest ever demographic and health surveys carried out in India, with a sample size of about seven lakh households covering all districts of the country. The DLHS-3, like the other two earlier rounds, is designed to provide estimates on maternal and child health, family planning, and other reproductive health statistics. In addition, DLHS-3 provides information related to the programmes under the NRHM.[5]

Sample Design of the Survey

A multi-stage stratified systematic sampling design was adopted for DLHS-3. In each district, 50 PSUs which were census villages for rural areas and wards for urban areas were selected in the first stage by systematic Probability Proportional to Size (PPS) sampling. In rural areas in the second stage of sampling households were drawn from the selected villages (PSUs) after house listing. Whereas in urban areas the second stage of sampling is the selection of CEBs followed by selection of households in the third stage of sampling. The numbers of households selected from the sampled PSUs of districts represented by 1,000, 1,200, and 1,500 households were 22, 27, and 33, respectively. This report is based on data collected from 7,20,320 households from 28 states and 6 UTs of India during 2007–8. From these households, 6,43,944 ever-married women aged 15–49 years and 1,66,620 unmarried women aged 15–24 years were interviewed. Separate questionnaires were circulated for households, for ever-married women in the age group of 15–49 years, unmarried women in the age-group of 15–24 years, and for villages.

The *National Report* provides detailed information on various components such as maternal and child care, family planning, knowledge and awareness of HIV/AIDS, reproductive morbidity, and health facility available. In addition, the report also provides information on other related sectors such as sanitation, drinking water, and fuel used for cooking. The report also provides status of public health facilities available in rural areas.

[5] The details about this mission are given after the details of the DLHS Survey.

The results are published in the DLHS-3 publication. The report gives the details under the following nine chapters: introduction, background characteristics of households, characteristics of women and fertility, maternal health care, child care and immunization, family planning, reproductive health problems and awareness of RTIs/STIs and HIV/AIDS, characteristics of unmarried women, and health facility: availability and quality.

In addition to the *National Report*, state-level reports as well as district factsheets are available.

The DLHS-4 has already been conducted during 2012–13. The questionnaires relate to households, ever-married women, village, and facilities.

In the household questionnaire, information on all members of the household and socio-economic characteristics of the household, assets possessed, and number of marriages and deaths in the household since January 2008 were collected. The ever-married women's questionnaire contained information on women's characteristics, maternal care, immunization and childcare, contraception and fertility references, reproductive health including knowledge about HIV/AIDS. The village questionnaire contained information on availability of health, education, and other facilities in the village, and whether the facilities were accessible throughout the year. The health facility questionnaire contained information on human resources, infrastructure, and services. For the first time, a population-linked facility survey was conducted in DLHS-4. All CHCs, district hospitals and sub-divisional hospitals were covered. Further, all sub-health centres and PHCs which serve the population of the selected PSUs were also covered.

It covers 640 districts for 36 states and UTs. The objective of the survey is to provide district-wise maternal and child health related indicators and prevalence of morbidity for a wide range of diseases covering aspects like household basic amenities, prevalence of morbidity, coverage of ante-natal services and immunization services, proportions of institutional/safe deliveries, Janani Suraksha Yojana (JSY) beneficiaries, economic burden of delivery, contraceptive prevalence rate, ASHA's involvement, unmet need for family planning, awareness about reproductive tract infections (RTI)/sexually transmitted infections (STI) and HIV/AIDS, infrastructure, manpower, equipment, drugs, services of public health facilities, and linkage between health facility and maternal and child health (MCH) indicators.

State reports, state and district fact sheets and facility survey reports are available on the survey's website.[6]

Rural Health Mission

Recognizing the importance of health in the process of economic and social development and improving the quality of life of our citizens, the GoI launched the NRHM to carry out necessary architectural correction in the basic health care delivery system. The NRHM was launched by the then prime minister Manmohan Singh on 12 April 2005, to provide accessible, affordable, and quality health care to the rural population, especially the vulnerable groups. Under the NRHM, the EAG states as well as northeastern states, Jammu and Kashmir (J&K), and Himachal Pradesh have been given the special focus. The thrust of the mission is on establishing a fully functional, community-owned, decentralized health delivery system with inter-sectoral convergence at all levels, to ensure simultaneous action on a wide range of determinants of good health such as safe drinking water, sanitation, education, nutrition, and social and gender equality. Institutional integration within the fragmented health sector was expected to provide a focus on outcomes, measured against Indian Public Health Standards for all health facilities. The plan of action includes increasing public expenditure on health, reducing regional imbalance in health infrastructure, pooling resources, integrating organizational structures, optimizing health manpower, decentralizing and district-management of health programmes, encouraging community participation and ownership of assets, encouraging induction of management and financial personnel into district health system, and operationalizing community health centres into functional hospitals meeting Indian Public Health Standards in each block of the country. The goal of the mission is to improve the availability of and access to quality healthcare by people, especially for those residing in rural areas, the poor, women, and children.

[6] Available at http://rchiips.org/ (accessed on 25 May 2017).

The National Urban Health Mission (NUHM) as a sub-mission of National Health Mission (NHM) has been approved by the cabinet on 1 May 2013. The NUHM envisages to meet health care needs of the urban population with the focus on urban poor, by making available to them essential primary healthcare services and reducing their out-of-pocket expenses for treatment. This will be achieved by strengthening the existing healthcare service delivery system, targeting the people living in slums and converging with various schemes relating to wider determinants of health like drinking water, sanitation, and school education, implemented by Ministry of Urban Development, Ministry of Housing and Urban Poverty Alleviation, Ministry of Human Resource Development (MHRD), and Ministry of Women and Child Development. The NUHM would cover all state capitals, district headquarters, and cities/towns with a population of more than 50,000. It would primarily focus on slum dwellers and other marginalized groups like rickshaw pullers, street vendors, railway and bus station coolies, homeless people, street children, and construction site workers.[7]

Coverage Evaluation Survey 2009

The CES 2009 was the latest nationwide survey conducted between November 2009 and January 2010. This survey was commissioned by UNICEF and aimed to collect and streamline data on various health issues, such as child delivery, MMR, IMR, and routine vaccination in India.

Statistical details are available regarding child immunization along with the distance travelled and time taken to reach the vaccination site, reasons for no or partial immunization, child health, and the treatment by type of government and private health facility/provider, maternal health, newborn care, breastfeeding practices during first six months, and delivery care.

[7] For more information on NRHM, visit the site http://nrhm.gov.in/nhm/nrhm.html (accessed on 22 May 2017). For more information on NUHM, visit the site http://nrhm.gov.in/nhm/nuhm.html (accessed on 22 May 2017).

The specific objectives of the survey were to:

(1) assess routine immunization;
(2) assess the level of coverage of ANC, delivery care, and post-natal care (PNC);
(3) assess accessibility, availability, and utilization of immunization and maternal care services, including JSY;
(4) identify key problems in delivery of immunization, ANC, delivery care, and PNC services;
(5) assess the care-seeking behaviour for key child morbidities, including acute respiratory infection (ARI) and diarrhoea;
(6) assess the initiation of breastfeeding, exclusive breastfeeding, and complementary feeding;
(7) assess availability and use of iodized salt and Vitamin A coverage;
(8) assess the utilization of bed-nets by pregnant women and children.

Sampling Design

The data for the CES 2009 was collected from mothers or care takers of children aged 12–23 months for childcare services and from women who delivered during 12 months preceding the survey. The samples for each state were estimated to give results at 5 per cent margin of error and 95 per cent confidence intervals. It was decided to have deep stratification that would make the samples more efficient and causing sampling biases get reduced considerably. Further, more samples were covered from bigger states. In each state, rural–urban samples were allocated in 60 to 40 ratios.

Sampling in Rural Areas

For selecting the sample in rural areas in a state, a two-stage sampling procedure was followed, that is, selection of villages at the first stage followed by the selection of households. Further, in the first stage, districts were grouped into regions considering geographical contiguity as per procedure followed in NFHS-3. The state rural sample was allocated to regions in proportion to their respective rural population sizes. All the villages in each geographical region were further stratified into three strata, namely villages with <50 households, villages with 51–200 households, and villages with more than 200 households. The number of PSUs in each region was allocated to each stratum in proportion to the total rural population in the region. In each region, the required number of villages was selected using the PPS systematic random sampling procedure using 'percentage SC/ST population' or 'percentage female literacy', both as per 2001 Census, as implicit variables.

Sampling in Urban Areas

In each state all the towns were stratified into five strata, namely metros, towns with more than 10 lakh population, towns with 5 lakh to 10 lakh population, towns with 1 lakh to 5 lakh population, and towns with less than 1 lakh population. Total state urban sample was allocated to different strata in proportion to the urban population and in each stratum, wards were selected using the PPS systematic random sampling procedure. From each ward, one CEB was selected randomly.

Selection of Households

In each selected village/CEB, complete listing of the households was done to identify households with children 12–23 months, and households with mothers who delivered during last 12 months. In each village/CEB, 10 households with children aged 12–23 months and 10 mothers who delivered in the last 12 months were selected using the systematic random sampling procedure and from the selected households all eligible mothers/caregivers were interviewed.

Separate questionnaires were prepared to gather the information required for the study—questionnaire for routine immunization coverage of children aged 12–23 months; questionnaire for maternal care services of mothers who delivered during 12 months preceding the survey; and village-information questionnaire.[8] A short explanation of the village questionnaire is as follows.

Village information was collected for each selected village. The village questionnaire collected information on road connectivity, health

[8] The details of these questionnaires are given in the report available at http://www.unicef.org/india/1_-_CES_2009_All_India_Report.pdf (accessed on 22 May 2017).

and education facilities, and amenities such as electricity, drinking water, telephone, and post office.

The all-India report, CES 2009, gives tables, figures, and maps on topics such as methodology, profile of sample households, routine immunization, maternal care services, breastfeeding practices and child nutrition, child morbidity, and care-seeking practices. In addition, state fact sheets are available on the UNICEF website.

National Sample Survey on Health

The National Sample Survey Office (NSSO) has been conducting demographic surveys at continuous intervals of time, which provide information on some aspects of mortality and morbidity and household expenditure on health services and facilities (see Table 17.1).

The National Sample Survey (NSS) made its first attempt to collect information on morbidity in the seventh round (October 1953–March 1954). This survey and the morbidity surveys conducted in the three subsequent rounds (the 11th to the 13th, 1956–8) were all exploratory in nature. The aim of these surveys was to evolve an appropriate data-collection method for studying morbidity profile in India. These surveys were followed up by a pilot survey in the 17th Round (September 1961–July 1962) to examine alternative approaches of morbidity reporting. With the aid of the findings of these exploratory surveys, a full-scale survey on morbidity was conducted in the 28th Round (October 1973–June 1974). Since then, the NSSO had not undertaken any separate morbidity survey and data on morbidity became a part of the decennial surveys on social consumption.

The NSSO carried out the first All India Survey on Social Consumption in its 35th Round (July 1980–June 1981). The items covered were the public distribution system, health services including mass immunization and family welfare programmes, and educational services. The results of the survey could not be brought out owing to some unavoidable reasons. The second Survey on Social Consumption was carried out in the 42nd Round (July 1986–June 1987) with some modifications in the coverage of subjects. Topics like problems of aged persons were included in this round. The third Survey on Social Consumption was carried out in the 52nd Round (July 1995–June 1996). Two topics, namely utilization of the public

Table 17.1 Round-wise Surveys on Health, Conducted by NSSO

Round Number	Report Number	Period of Survey	Subjects of Enquiry
71	574	January 2014–June 2014	Health, morbidity, and hospitalization
60	507	January 2004–June 2004	Morbidity and health care
52	441 and 445	July 1995–June 1996	Morbidity and health care
39		January 1984–June 1984	Births and deaths
35		July 1980–June 1981	Maternal and childcare, family planning, medical and health
34		July 1979–June 1980	Medical and health
28		October 1973–June 1974	Births and deaths, morbidity, fertility, maternal and child care, family planning, and normal health facilities in rural areas.

Source: Various NSS reports.[9]

distribution system and utilization of family planning services, were dropped, as these were covered in the NSS 50th Round and in a nationwide survey by the Ministry of Health and Family Welfare, respectively.

After a gap of about nine years, the Governing Council decided to take up a survey on 'morbidity and health care' at the request of Ministry of Health and Family Welfare, during the period January to June 2004.

[9] Available at http://mospiold.nic.in/Mospi_New/site/inner.aspx?status=3&menu_id=31 (accessed on 25 May 2017).

The results of this survey are given in *Report No. 507*. The survey covered the curative aspects of the general health care system in India and also the utilization of health care services provided by the public and private sector, together with the expenditure incurred by the households for availing these services.

This report presents the survey results relating to all these aspects, namely the utilization of the curative healthcare services, morbidity profile of the population, hospitalized and non-hospitalized treatment of ailments together with the estimates of expenditure incurred for treatment of ailments. In addition, results on problems of the aged persons are also provided separately in the report.

Geographical Coverage

The entire area of the country was covered with the exception of some interior areas of Nagaland and Andaman and Nicobar Islands, and Leh (Ladakh) and Kargil districts of J&K.

Sample Design

The sample design adopted for the survey was essentially a two-stage stratified design, with census villages and urban blocks as the first-stage units (FSUs) for the rural and urban areas respectively, and households as the second-stage units (SSUs). The survey period, January–June 2004, was split up into two sub-rounds of three months each. The rural and urban samples of FSUs were drawn independently in the form of two sub-samples and equal numbers of FSUs of each sub-sample were allocated for the two sub-rounds.

Total Sample Size (FSUs)

In all, 7,612 FSUs were allocated at the all-India level on the basis of investigator strength in different states/UTs for the central sample and 8,188 for the state sample.

This survey was done again during the 71st Round.

One of the topics covered was the determination of the prevalence rate of different diseases among different age–sex groups and the extent of use of different health services provided by the government in different regions of the country. Emphasis was given on hospitalization.

Also data were collected regarding out-of-pocket expenses for various diseases. The details were collected regarding pre-natal and post-natal care for women. Information on certain aspects of the condition of people aged 60 and above was also collected.

Bibliography

Central Bureau of Health Intelligence. Various rounds. *National Health Profile*. New Delhi: Ministry of Health and Family Welfare, Directorate General of Health Services.

Department of AYUSH. 2015 *AYUSH in India*. New Delhi: Ministry of Health and Family Welfare.

Directorate General of Health Services. Undated. *Health Information of India*. New Delhi: Ministry of Health and Family Welfare.

Ministry of Health and Family Welfare. 2015. *Bulletin on Rural Health Statistics in India*, 2014–15. New Delhi: Ministry of Health and Family Welfare.

———. Various years. *DLHS Household Surveys*. Available at http://www.rchiips.org/.

———. 2011. *Family Welfare Statistics in India*. New Delhi: Ministry of Health and Family Welfare.

———. Website. Department of Health and Family Welfare. Available at http://mohfw.nic.in/index.php.

———. *National Family Health Surveys (NFHS)*. New Delhi: Ministry of Health and Family Welfare.

———. *National Rural Health Mission*. Available at http://nrhm.gov.in/.

National Sample Survey Office (NSSO). Various Rounds. *Round wise Surveys on Health*. Ministry of Statistics and Programme Implementation. Available at http://mospi.nic.in/Mospi_New/site/home.aspx.

UNICEF. *Coverage Health Survey – 2009, All India Report*.

18

Research Organizations Conducting All-India Surveys

National Sample Survey Office (NSSO)

The National Sample Survey (NSS) was set up in 1950 in the Ministry of Finance, at the initiation of P.C. Mahalanobis, to fill the gaps in the statistics needed for planning and for the estimation of national income. It was brought under the control of the Department of Statistics, Cabinet Secretariat in 1957. The organization of the work of the NSS was reviewed by the government from time to time. In July 1960, a three-men committee consisting of B. Sivaraman, the cabinet secretary, V.M. Dandekar of Gokhale Institute of Politics and Economics, and Raghuraj Bahadur of Indian Statistical Institute (ISI), was set up to advice the government on the lines of reorganization. The committee recommended, in the main, the entrustment of all aspects of national sample survey work to a single government organization located in the cabinet secretariat and governed by a governing council. It further recommended that the council should be given sufficient independence and autonomy of decision to ensure that the collection, processing, and publication of the NSS data are free from undue influence. The government accepted the recommendations of the committee and under the Resolution of 5 March 1970, announced the decision to set up a National Sample Survey

Organization in Department of Statistics, and a governing council to govern its activities. The council was actually formed on 25 March 1970.

The governing council consisted of experts from within and outside the government and was headed by an eminent economist/statistician and the member-secretary of the council was director general and chief executive officer of NSSO. The governing council was empowered to take all technical decisions in respect of the survey work, from planning of surveys to release of survey results. After the formation of National Statistical Commission (NSC) in 2005, the governing council of NSSO was dissolved on 30 August 2006 and in its place the Steering Committee on National Sample Surveys was formed on 15 December 2006. The Steering Committee consisted of eight non-official and eight official members. The non-official members are persons of eminence in either of the fields of economics, statistics, and social sciences. The official members are all senior officers of the Ministry of Statistics and Programme Implementation (MOSPI), Planning Commission, and State Directorates of Economics and Statistics. The director general and chief executive officer (DG&CEO) of NSSO is the Convener of the Steering Committee. The name was changed to NSSO in 2010.

Since its inception, the NSSO has been conducting sample surveys on a nationwide basis for collecting statistical data, on a continuing basis, mainly of these four types: household surveys on socio-economic subjects; surveys on land holding, livestock, and agriculture; establishment surveys and enterprise surveys; and village surveys.

Under the first category come the surveys on population, birth, death, migration, fertility, family planning, morbidity, disability, employment and unemployment, agriculture and rural labour, household consumer expenditure, debt and investment, savings, construction, capital formation, housing conditions, and utilization of public services in health, education, and other sectors. Under the second are covered the surveys on land holding, land utilization, livestock number, product, and livestock enterprises. Surveys on medium and small industrial establishments and own-account enterprises (OAEs) not covered by the *Annual Survey of Industries* (*ASI*), surveys on other non-agricultural enterprises in the unorganized sector, and collection of rural retail prices from markets and shops in rural areas belong to the third category. Finally, the collection from sample villages of various types of information on the availability of infrastructure facilities in Indian villages constitutes the fourth.

These data have been used by various governmental agencies and research institutions for the formulation of development plans and for analysing various problems. Today it is the central agency for collection and independent checking of different types of socio-economic data on the basis of sample surveys on a country-wide basis.

Schedule of Surveys

Ten-Year Cycle

(1) Consumer expenditure and employment and unemployment—twice
(2) Social consumption (health and education)—twice
(3) Unorganized manufacturing—twice
(4) Unorganized services—twice
(5) Land and livestock holdings and debt and investment—once
(6) Open round—once (special surveys are also undertaken)
(7) Annual Consumer Expenditure and Employment and Unemployment Surveys (thin sample)

Recently the cycle has been revised.

(1) Consumer expenditure and employment and unemployment—twice
(2) Unincorporated non-agricultural enterprises (excluding construction)—twice
(3) Land and livestock holdings and debt and investment—once
(4) Social consumption (health and education)—once
(5) Housing conditions including slums—once (six-month survey)

There are six open rounds, four years for accommodating the requirements of other ministries/departments.

Organization

Before reorganization in March 1970, the surveys were being conducted by the ISI and the directorate of NSS. The ISI was responsible for the technical work relating to the surveys comprising the planning of the survey, preparing the details of the sample designs for the surveys, preparation of schedules, instructions and tabulation plans, training of the field staff, processing of the survey data, and preparation of the reports. There was an NSS Wing in the ISI to perform these duties. The fieldwork was done by the directorate of NSS in all the states except West Bengal and Bombay city, where it was done by the field branches of the ISI. The directorate of NSS had three main wings: (i) socio-economic wing; (ii) industrial statistics wing; and (iii) agricultural statistics wing.

The main functions of the socio-economic wing related to the collection of comprehensive data on a continuing basis regarding socio-economic and demographic conditions on a country wide basis. The industrial statistics wing dealt with the collection of statistics in the organized industrial sector. The agricultural statistics wing was responsible for the training and technical guidance to the states for conducting surveys relating to agriculture. After the reorganization the directorate of NSS has been renamed as the field operations division (FOD) of the NSSO.

Field Operations Division

The FOD has its headquarters at New Delhi and at Faridabad (agricultural wing). It has six zonal offices located at Bengaluru, Kolkata, Guwahati, Jaipur, Lucknow, and Nagpur, 49 regional offices, and 116 subregional offices located in different parts of the country. Following are the surveys of the FOD.

Urban Frame Surveys

Urban frame survey (UFS) is conducted on a continuing basis to provide an updated frame of first-stage units (FSUs) in urban areas and also in newly formed towns.

Price Collection Surveys

RURAL PRICE COLLECTION SURVEYS

The FOD of NSSO collects data from 603 villages on prices of specified commodities generally consumed by agricultural/rural labourers for compilation of consumer price index (CPI; base year 1986–7) for agricultural/rural labourers on behalf of the labour bureau. The number of items/commodities covered is about 260.

PRICE COLLECTION (URBAN)

The FOD also undertakes regular price collection work for about 1,114 quotations from 310 towns for the market survey for the CPI urban.

ANNUAL SURVEY OF INDUSTRIES

The *ASI* is an important survey of the Central Statistical Office (CSO), Ministry of Statistics and Programme Implementation (MOSPI) and the NSSO (FOD) conducts its fieldwork. This survey collects data from every individual manufacturing and repairing unit.

AGRICULTURAL SURVEYS

The FOD of NSSO has the overall responsibility of providing technical guidance to the states in developing suitable survey techniques for obtaining timely and reliable estimates of crop yield, bringing out uniformity in definitions and concepts and providing assistance in training the state field personnel. It also undertakes supervision over the primary fieldwork of the state governments in respect of area enumeration, area aggregation, and crop-cutting experiments (CCEs).

The supervision on fieldwork for qualitative improvement in agricultural statistics is carried out through well-organized sample surveys under the Improvement of Crop Statistics (ICS) scheme. The scheme aims at locating, through joint efforts of central and state agencies, the deficiencies in the state system of crop statistics and suggesting remedial measures for effecting lasting improvements. The ICS scheme is in operation in 19 land record states/UTs and 3 non-land record states.

The responsibilities of supervisory staff of the NSSO (FOD) and state governments inter alia involve sample checks in non-overlapping samples on (i) area enumeration and aggregation in about 10,000 sample villages in each season; and (ii) about 30,000 CCEs in a year carried out by state primary workers.

The findings of the sample supervision are brought out in the form of state-wise reports for two major seasons and an all-India status report titled *Review of Crop Statistics System in India through Scheme for Improvement of Crop Statistics*.

FOLLOW-UP SURVEYS OF ECONOMIC CENSUS

The surveys are conducted regarding unorganized manufactures and unorganized services.

Besides the regular socio-economic surveys of NSSO, taken up through a 10-year survey cycle, NSSO from time to time, also undertakes pilot enquiries and ad hoc or special surveys. Such surveys are conducted either for methodological studies or on the basis of specific requests received for such surveys, from other agencies. Some of the latest pilot surveys or other special surveys undertaken by NSSO are as follows given in Table 18.1.

In addition, NSSO has the following three divisions: (i) Survey Design and Research Division (SDRD); (ii) Data Processing Division (DPD); and (iii) Coordination and Publication Division (CPD).

Table 18.1 Pilot/Ad Hoc Surveys

Name of the Survey	Survey Period
Drug Abuse Survey	February 2010–May 2010
NREGA Survey	July 2009–June 2010
Gramin DAK Sevaks Survey	March–April 2008
Baseline Survey on Well-Being of Children and Women in Collaboration with UNICEF	March–May 2005
Pilot Survey on Non-profit Institutions Serving Households	July 2004–June 2005
Pilot Survey on Food Security for World Food Programme	September 2003–February 2004
Situation Assessment Survey of farmers	January–December 2003
Domestic Tourism Survey	2002–3
Diagnostic Survey on Cattle for the Use of National Commission on Cattle	April–May 2002
Pilot Survey on Suitability of Different Reference Periods for Measuring Household Consumption	January–June 2000

Source: MOSPI. Available at http://mospiold.nic.in/Mospi_New/site/inner.aspx?status=3&menu_id=59 (accessed on 22 May 2017).

Survey Design and Research Division

The SDRD is located at Kolkata. It is responsible for planning of surveys; formulation of sampling design; formulation of concepts and definitions; drawing up of survey schedules; writing of instructions to field staff; preparation of validation and tabulation programmes; finalization of survey results and release of reports; and providing technical guidance in sampling techniques to various official agencies.

Data Processing Division

The data processing division (DPD) of the NSSO, with headquarters in Kolkata and six data processing centres located at Ahmedabad, Bengaluru, Kolkata, Delhi, Giridih, and Nagpur, provide complete IT solutions from sample selection, software development, to processing and tabulation of data canvassed through various socio-economic surveys of NSSO.

The functions of the DPD are:

(1) maintenance of sampling frame and updation of UFS database;
(2) selection of samples and preparation of sample lists;
(3) manual checking of identification particulars and pre-data entry scrutiny;
(4) in-house development of validation and tabulation software;
(5) data entry and verification of filled in schedules;
(6) validation of data through various stages covering both content check and coverage check;
(7) preparation of directory and multiplier files for estimation of parameters;
(8) tabulation of validated data as per approved tabulation plan;
(9) processing and tabulation of monthly rural retail price schedules and release of quarterly bulletin;
(10) assistance to state statistical bureaus in processing of state sample data; and
(11) providing training in applications of computers and on data processing.

Coordination and Publication Division

The CPD is located at New Delhi and is responsible for:

(1) coordinating the activities of all the divisions of NSSO;
(2) dissemination of survey results and analysis through the biannual technical journal *Sarvekshana* and *National Seminars* to discuss the survey results;
(3) providing technical and secretarial assistance to the Steering Committee of National Sample Surveys;
(4) supplying survey data of various rounds to individuals, researchers, research institutions, and other private and government bodies;
(5) liaisoning with other departments/ministries on various matters concerning NSSO; and
(6) providing the technical and secretarial assistance to the DG and CEO of NSSO.

Main Features of the NSSO

The NSSO is a continuing, integrated, multi-subject survey being conducted in the form of successive rounds in which data on different topics of current interest are collected, using the method of personal interviews and direct observation. The scope, period, and programme of each round are fixed by taking into account the nature of data required and the resources available. Up to the 24th Round, the subject coverage, sample design, and tabulation programme for the surveys were finalized by the CSO in consultation with the NSSO Programme Committee and the Planning Commission. Since the 25th Round these were finalized by the governing council of the NSSO until it was replaced by the steering committee.

Geographical Coverage

The geographical coverage of the surveys extends to the entire rural and urban areas of the country with the exception of small pockets which are excluded, mainly on operational considerations. During the first two rounds, however, the surveys were conducted only in rural areas of the country and during the first seven rounds the state of Jammu and Kashmir (J&K) was excluded from these surveys.

Multi-subject and Integrated Surveys

Multi-Subject Surveys

When in a single survey operation several subjects, not necessarily very closely related, are simultaneously investigated for the sake of economy and convenience, the investigation may be called a multi-subject survey. The data on different subjects need not necessarily be obtained from the same set of sampling units, or even from the same type of units (for example, households and fields).

Integrated Surveys

In an integrated survey, data on several subjects are collected from the same set of sampling units for studying the relationship among items belonging to different subject fields.

The NSSO has been conducting multi-subject integrated sample surveys all over the country in the form of successive rounds relating to various aspects of social, economic, demographic, industrial, and agricultural statistics, in order to strike a balance between the urgent need for the data on a wide variety of topics and the constraint of following a multi-subject integrated survey system. In this system several subjects of enquiry, not necessarily closely related, are simultaneously taken up in a single survey operation to optimize the use of resources, to effect economy and operational convenience, and also to achieve better analysis of the survey results.

The integration of different subjects of enquiry is generally effected by the NSSO, at the village level in the rural sector and block level in the urban sector. Samples drawn from villages and blocks are generally different for different subjects. However, from the 19th Round (July 1964–June 1965) to the 25th Round (July 1970–June 1971), an integrated household schedule was canvassed. The information was collected from the sample households regarding demographic particulars, employment features, consumer expenditure, enterprise details, and inventory of household assets. From the 26th Round, the integrated household schedule has been discontinued.

Multi-subject integrated surveys are generally more economical and convenient than a series of uni-subject surveys. The main advantage of the multi-subject integrated surveys in the saving of the overhead costs which form an appreciable portion to the total cost. The saving can be utilized in increasing the sample size and hence the precision. The integration of different subjects, however, imposes certain restrictions on the sampling design. A compromise sampling design can of course be chosen, which can work satisfactory.

Method of Data Collection

The data are collected by specially trained, permanent, and full-time investigators in both rural and urban sectors by personally contacting the sample unit. The data are obtained by personal interviews in the case of household enquiries and by direct physical observation in the case of crop surveys. The schedule approach is applied for collection of data in preference to the questionnaire approach.

A questionnaire consists of a set of questions which the investigator is expected to ask the informant in the order in which they are given. A schedule is a list of items on which the information is to be collected; the method of questioning is left to the discretion of the investigators. The questionnaire is convenient only for asking direct and simple questions to cover all these cases. Given the items on which the information is to be collected and the necessary instructions, the investigator is in a better position to collect the data by framing and asking questions according to the exigencies of the situation.

Interpenetrating Sub-samples

The technique of interpenetrating sub-samples is being utilized by the NSSO. Two or more independent sub-samples, usually of the same size and using the same sampling techniques, are surveyed by different sets of investigators. The results of these sub-samples enable us to have more than one estimate of the same quantity and the comparison of these different estimates throws light on the accuracy of the surveys. These can also be used as a check on the performance of the different investigators.

Moving Reference Period

Since the 14th Round, each Round is of the duration of one year (except the 26th, 28th, and 60th Rounds). The total survey period is divided into four sub-rounds of three-months' duration. In each of these four sub-rounds equal numbers of sample villages/blocks (FSUs) are allotted for survey with a view to ensuring uniform spread of sample FSUs over the entire survey period. An attempt is made to survey each of the FSUs during the sub-round to which it is allotted. Due to the arduous field conditions, the restriction is not strictly enforced in Andaman and Nicobar Islands, Lakshadweep, and rural areas of Arunachal Pradesh and Nagaland.

Participation of the States

The NSSO was started as a central government agency for the collection of statistics. In view of the limitations of the NSSO, a programme of collaboration was evolved with the states. According to this programme different states are participating in the NSSO work canvassing identical schedules using same concepts and definitions in an additional sample (called state sample), of equal size so as to get fairly reliable estimates at the state level (district level also in some cases) through pooling of the state sample with the sample drawn by the NSSO (called the central sample). This programme was first started in 1954 (8th Round) in Bombay (now Mumbai) and Uttar Pradesh. Gradually it has been extended to all the states except West Bengal. In the beginning some of the states had a state sample as half of the central sample. At present the states are participating in the work of the NSSO on a full matching basis. The programme has helped in the coordination between State Statistical Bureaus and the NSSO. Also, better estimates are obtained and the checks are provided on the survey results.

Subject Coverage

The subjects covered, more or less regularly in the past few rounds, are household consumer expenditure, rural retail prices of selected commodities, employment and unemployment particulars, labour force surveys, demographic characteristics, and crop surveys. Data on subjects like small-scale enterprises (manufacture, transport, and trade), professions and services, village statistics, landholdings, and savings and indebtedness are collected periodically. Subjects such as disposal of cereals by producer households, capital formation, building construction, farming practices, economic condition of agricultural or rural labourers, animal husbandry, livestock products, family planning, and migration have also been taken up in some rounds. Besides, a few ad hoc surveys, such as income and expenditure surveys of middle class and working class and post-census surveys of population and livestock are also undertaken from time to time.

A subject-wise coverage of a few of the latest round surveys are given as follows:

The 60th Round (January–June 2004) of NSS covered the annual survey of consumer expenditure, the employment–unemployment situation, and morbidity and health care. This round onwards, a separate schedule was canvassed for employment and unemployment and consumption expenditure.

The 61st Round (July 2004–June 2005) of NSS was earmarked for surveys on 'household consumer expenditure' and 'employment and unemployment'. The survey on 'household consumer expenditure' and 'employment and unemployment' is the seventh in the series of quinquennial surveys on the subjects, the last one being conducted in the 55th Round (1999–2000) of NSS.

The 62nd Round (July 2005–June 2006) of the NSS was earmarked for surveys on (i) unorganized manufacturing enterprises under the two-digit codes 15 to 37 (Section 'D') of NIC 2004 and enterprises under cotton ginning, cleaning, and baling (NIC 2004, code 01405); (ii) survey of consumer expenditure; and (iii) survey on employment unemployment.

The 63rd Round (July 2006–June 2007) of NSS was earmarked for a survey on service sector enterprises (excluding trade and financial series). All service sector enterprises, which are not covered under the *ASI*, were under coverage of the survey. Government and public sector undertakings were not under survey coverage. Usual annual surveys on consumer expenditure and employment unemployment were also carried out during this round.

The 64th Round (July 2007–June 2008) of NSS was earmarked for surveys on 'employment–unemployment and migration', 'participation and expenditure in education', and 'household consumer expenditure'. The NSS 55th Round (July 1999–June 2000) and 49th Round (January–June 1993) were the two latest rounds where migration was taken up as one of the subjects. Detailed information on education was collected for the last time in NSS 52nd Round (July 1995–June 1996), prior to which such information were collected during the 47th Round of NSS (July–December 1991).

The 65th Round (July 2008–June 2009) of NSS was earmarked for surveys on 'domestic tourism', 'housing condition', and 'urban slums'. The NSS 54th Round (January–June 1999) and 43rd Round (July 1987–June 1988) were the two latest rounds where certain data on tourism/travel habits were collected. Detailed information on housing conditions was last collected in NSS 58th Round (July–December 2002), prior to which such information were collected during the 49th Round of NSS (January–June 1993). Survey on urban slums was last conducted during NSS 58th Round.

The 66th Round (July 2009–June 2010) of NSS was earmarked for surveys on 'household consumer expenditure' and 'employment and unemployment'. The survey on 'household consumer expenditure' and 'employment and unemployment' is the eighth quinquennial survey in the series, the last one being conducted in the 61st Round (2004–5) of NSS. The surveys have been repeated in the 68th Round (July 2011–June 2012).

In the 67th Round (July 2010–June 2011) the surveys of unincorporated non-agricultural enterprises conducted by NSSO are the primary source of data on various indicators of economic and operational characteristics of such enterprises in manufacturing, trade, and other service sector (excluding construction) at the national and state level. These are used for planning, policy formulation, decision support, and as an input for further statistical exercises by various government organizations, academicians, researchers, and scholars. During the 67th Round (July 2010–June 2011), NSSO carried out an all-India enterprise survey on economic and operational characteristics of unincorporated non-agricultural enterprises in manufacturing, trade and other service sector (excluding construction). Based on the data collected during the survey, estimates of some key economic and operational characteristics of enterprises at all-India and state levels have been presented in the report.

In the 68th Round (July 2011–June 2012), the surveys of household consumption expenditure and also employment and unemployment situation in India were conducted.

The 69th Round (July 2012–December 2012) had surveys on drinking water supply, sanitation, hygiene, and housing conditions in India and a survey on urban slums in India.

Information on housing conditions with wider coverage on the aspects of drinking water, sanitation, and hygiene was collected during NSS 69th Round (July 2012–December 2012). The information collected can be categorized into three broad groups. First, information was collected from all the selected households on the particulars of various facilities available to the sample households for decent living such as availability of drinking water, latrine, bathroom, and electricity. Second, information was collected on some of the characteristics of the houses, particulars of the dwelling unit, and the micro-environment surrounding the dwelling unit, from the households that were living in houses. Finally, information was collected on some general particulars of the households living in houses. Apart from this, some information was also collected on construction/first-hand purchase of houses or flats by the households during the last 365 days.

The *Key Indicators of Urban Slums in India* document presents estimates of some key characteristics of slums such as number of slums, approximate number of households living in the slums, proportion of slums without electricity, proportion of slums without drainage facilities, proportion of slums without a garbage disposal system, proportion of slums with the majority of the households having a *pucca* structure, proportion of slums with a tap as the major source of drinking water, and proportion of slums having a pucca road within the slum.

The 70th Round (January 2013–December 2013) had surveys covering land and livestock holdings, debt and investment, and situation assessment of farmer survey.

The 71st Round (January 2014–June 2014) had a survey on social consumption—health and education of the households.

The 72nd Round (1 July 2014–30 June 2015) had consumption expenditure survey, survey on domestic tourism expenditure, and on household expenditure on services and durable goods.

Sampling Design (Recent Rounds)[1]

The basic design followed is stratified two-stage (for smaller villages/urban blocks) or three-stage (for larger villages/blocks involving hamlet group/sub-block formation). The primary stage unit (PSU) is a village (in rural areas) or urban frame survey block (in urban areas), but the ultimate stage unit (USU) is invariably household/enterprise for household/enterprise surveys. However most of the NSS surveys being multi-subject integrated ones, detailed design varies from survey to survey.

Stratification

Each district was a basic stratum in both rural and urban areas. However, in case of urban, each city with population of 1 million or more as per Census 2001 forms a separate stratum and all other cities/towns of a district are grouped to form another stratum.

With regard to the total sample size (FSUs), a sample of 16,000 FSUs for central sample and 18,248 FSUs for state sample have been allocated at the all-India level.

Reports

The reports are prepared on the basis of final tables prepared for the topic of the survey. These reports generally give highlights about the topic of the survey, the concepts and definitions applied for the survey, sampling design adopted, and procedure of estimation, summary of findings, and detailed statistical tables. Chapter 1 is the introductory one giving details about the objective, coverage, sample design, reports to be issued regarding the subject and the contents of the report. Chapter 2 gives the concepts and definitions, while Chapter 3 onwards give the summary results. In the appendices, detailed tables

[1] The designs from the 1st to 55th Rounds are available in the paper 'Evaluation of Sample Design in the NSS from 1st to 55th Round' by S. Ray (DG&CEO, NSSO), January 2004. Available at http://mospi.nic.in/Mospi_New/upload/nsso/design_golden.pdf (accessed on 22 May 2017).

along with sample design and estimation procedure, and schedules canvassed are given. The reports are available in hard copies; in addition, these are also available at the site of MOSPI.

Before publishing, the reports are sent to different departments and ministries for their comments. National Seminars are organized to discuss and finalize the survey results. Validated unit-level data are available on magnetic media for sale.

National Council of Applied Economic Research (NCAER)

The NCAER is an independent, non-profit research institution that is committed to assist government, civil society, and the private sector to make informed policy choices. Set up in 1956 at New Delhi, as a quasi-governmental institution, it has been a significant player in the arena of capturing the socio-economic development of the country providing inputs to policy and research through sponsored projects and independent research.

It has been conducting surveys on income, investment, and savings since the early 1960s. The first surveys on savings were conducted for rural and urban areas with reference to the years 1960 and 1962. After this, the NCAER did the following surveys to obtain the estimates of income and its disposition including saving investment and wealth.

(1) All-India Rural Household Survey for the year 1961–2 (NCAER 1965).
(2) All-India Household Survey of Income, Saving and Consumer Expenditure for 1967–8 (NCAER 1972).
(3) All-India Survey on Household Income and its Disposition (NCAER 1980).
(4) The Survey on Micro Impact of Macro and Adjustment Policies (MIMAP) covering the period July 1994 to June 1995 (NCAER 1998).

Apart from these major nation-wide studies there have been other field surveys conducted by the NCAER, essentially designed to provide information on motivational and behavioural aspects of household consumption and saving. It began undertaking Market

Information Survey of Households (MISH) in 1985–6 'to estimate the size of the market for the variety of consumer goods, both durables and expendables, and also to provide a profile of consumers of such goods in terms of income, occupation, location and the like' (Lal, Mohan, and Natarajan 2001). The MISH was an annual survey conducted for all years (except for 1988–9, 1990–1, and 1991–2), the latest one being for the year 2001. In 1994, NCAER also conducted an all-India rural household survey on Human Development Profile of India (HDPI).

The last two rounds of the NCAER surveys were conducted in 2004–5 and 2010–11 respectively. A summary about these surveys is given in the following paragraphs.

National Survey on Household Income and Expenditure (NSHIE, 2004–05) was primarily aimed to generate more robust and reliable estimate of household income besides other sets of information such as demographic profile of households (religion, caste, education, and occupation), estimates of market size, and penetration of manufactured consumer goods (consumables and durables) and ownership patterns. The target population of the survey was the total population in the country, with states and urban/rural categories as sub-populations or target groups, for whom representative estimates were also sought.

Methodology

Coverage

A primary survey of households was undertaken in 24 major states/UTs of India covering both rural and urban areas of Andhra Pradesh, Assam, Bihar, Chandigarh, Chhattisgarh, Delhi, Goa, Gujarat, Haryana, Himachal Pradesh, Jharkhand, Karnataka, Kerala, Madhya Pradesh, Maharashtra, Meghalaya, Odisha, Puducherry, Punjab, Rajasthan, Tamil Nadu, Uttarakhand, Uttar Pradesh, and West Bengal. Territories excluding J&K, Sikkim, Arunachal Pradesh, Nagaland, Manipur, Mizoram, Tripura, Andaman and Nicobar Islands, Daman and Diu, Dadra and Nagar Haveli, and Lakshadweep. The remaining states were left out due to operational difficulty and account for only 3 to 4 per cent of country's total population.

Sample Design

This was a household survey and a three-stage stratified sample design was adopted in which a ready-made frame was used at least for the first two stages, and a sampling frame, that is, list of households, was developed in the last stage. Sample districts, villages, and households formed the first, second, and third stage sample units respectively for selection of the rural sample, while cities/towns, urban wards, and households were the three stages of selection for the urban sample.

Sample Size

The sample size and its distribution were determined on the basis of the accuracy required and the resources available. In rural areas, a sample of 31,446 households out of a preliminary listed sample of 2,10,439 households was covered which were spread over 1,976 villages in 250 districts and 64 NSS regions covering all major states. Similarly, in urban areas, a sample of 31,570 households, out of a preliminary listed sample of 2,40,353 households, was spread over 2,255 urban wards in 342 towns and 64 NSS regions covering 24 states.

Data Analysis

Estimates for various parameters were produced directly from the cleaned data files by weighting each sample observation with the inverse of the probability of selection of the sample household taking into account the sample design.

Cross-validation of estimates of some key parameters such as household size; sex ratio; distribution of households according to SC, ST, and others; religion; and type of dwelling; among others was done using the results from external sources such as Census 2001 and NSS 2003. Sampling errors for key estimates from the survey were also produced.

In the next round, NSHIE-2011, the agenda has been suitably carried forward with a more comprehensive view of Indian households and their life. It includes a preliminary listing survey, main survey (comprehensive Living in India data), to be followed by panel surveys covering themes in depth.

Research Objective

Income, Spending, and Savings

The research involves the study of income, spending, and savings of households, and demographics. This has been studied along with measures of related variables of debt and assets, housing, remote payments, liabilities and commitments, financial optimism, inflation, and income expectations. The survey has over the years fulfilled the need for robust estimates of income that are otherwise unavailable, and has been used for policy and corporate decision-making.

The Research Design—Living in India, 2011

The overall approach to the National Household Survey, 2011 was to meet the research objectives stated here, using the best mix of baseline-panel-longitudinal and cross-sectional surveys, in a phased manner. The research is designed as a multi-stage survey, with the listing survey canvassing over five lakh households, the main round covering around one lakh households, and subsequent panel rounds, all on the same households covered during the listing round.

The detailed objectives were derived from the agenda and primary and secondary objectives, and an intensive effort at identifying the constructs were carried out to meet these objectives. Then specific objectives at each level were stated. The chief wage earner (CWE) of the household, identified as one with the highest income, is the main respondent, for all sections except one. The data for the household level was captured for the reference period April 2010–March 2011.

Data Collection Instrument

Listing Survey Schedule

The survey schedule used for interviews in the listing phase contained ten sections, with a total of 61 items.

(1) Identification particulars of each sample village or urban block (PSU) was collected. Detailed information on state, NSS region, district, sub-district, police station, and post office was gathered.
(2) Household identification gave information on state, village name, and listing serial number.

(3) The CWE, his/her age, gender, education status, primary source of occupation was gathered in this section.
(4) Spouse of CWE and his/her age, education, and working status was recorded.
(5) Socio-economic profile of household included religion, social group, and household size, useful for later studies of development on social background, and their inclusion mainstream.
(6) Ownership of dwelling and access of infrastructure and services was also looked at. In addition to collecting information on dwelling patterns, household ownership of selected assets was obtained.
(7) Information about television ownership and usage pattern included television, cable connection, and viewing patterns.
(8) Financial inclusion entailed information about household deposit accounts, remittances sent or received, and gold purchased or sold.
(9) Health and insurance covered health insurance and health-related expenditure as well as household perceptions of health.
(10) Perceptions about well-being related to respondents' perception about economic/financial issues.

Main Survey Schedule

The schedule used in the main survey contained 23 sections. The first section contained sample identification data. The 22 sections, with 196 subsections/questions, and over 900 possible items, collected detailed information about households, given as follows. Specific items would be relevant for a given household, for example, income: out of eight subsections covering income from all types of sources as per strata, only one or two would be relevant for each household generally, and of 130 items only a few would require a response from the household.

Sample Design

The household is the target unit of the study, with states and urban/rural categories as sub-populations or target groups, for whom representative estimates were sought. The geographical coverage of the survey includes the entire country comprising major states and UTs. The sampling design is kept broadly similar to the last round, which was drawn after reviewing best international practices and proved robust and effective.

A three-stage stratified sample design has been adopted for the present survey in which a ready-made frame was used for the first two stages and a sampling frame was developed in the last stage. Districts, villages, and households form the first, second, and third stages of sampling, respectively for selection of the rural sample while cities/towns, urban blocks, and households were the three stages of selection for the urban sample. Sampling for rural as well as urban areas was done independently within each state/UTs. Following the basics of sample survey principle that geographical spread is more important than the sample size, both rural and urban samples were selected from a wide cross-section of the country. The rural sample has been selected from a representative number of districts from across the country, while the urban sample covers a range from big metropolitan cities to small towns with population below 5,000. The sample sizes at first, second, and third stages in rural and urban areas are determined on the basis of available resources and the derived level of precision for key estimates from the survey, taking into account the experience in conducting the earlier round of NSHIE 2004 survey.

Coverage

The survey was carried out in 32 states and UTs of the country. Within each state an NSS region—which is a group of districts within a state similar to each other in respect of agro-climatic features—formed the strata for both the urban and rural sample. All the 32 states are divided into 75 NSS regions which form the strata or domain of study below the level of state/UT. Each NSS region is assigned a 3-digit code where the first two digits indicate state/UT and the third indicates region number within a state/UT. The rural and urban areas are taken as defined in the census.

Sampling Frame

The list of 2001 Census districts and villages constitute the sampling frame for rural and the list of 2001 Census cities/towns for urban. In the absence of the definitive list of households (sampling frame), a specially designed listing proforma was used to list households in the selected villages and urban blocks to collect information on various auxiliary variables. In the case of large villages/urban blocks, a fraction of households was listed based on sampling fraction.

Sample Size

A total sample of 99,384 households was covered in this study. Out of this, 45,144 households spread over 2,508 villages in 292 districts and 75 NSS regions covering the 32 states/UTs was covered in rural areas. In urban areas, 54,240 households spread over 2,712 urban wards in 363 towns and 75 NSS regions were covered.

Rural Sample

In rural areas, a sample of 292 districts was allocated to the 75 NSS regions within the 32 covered states/UTs in proportion to the total number of districts in an NSS region. From each of the NSS regions, the allocated number of districts was selected, as the FSUs, with probability proportional to size and replacement, where rural population of each district as per Census 2001 was used as size measure. Villages formed the second stage of selection procedure. A total sample of 2,508 villages (SSUs) was allocated to the selected 292 districts, approximately in proportion to rural population of each selected district. The allocated number of sample villages was chosen with equal probability sampling approach. A total of 5,00,400 households were listed comprising 2,50,800 households from entire rural India.

Urban Sample

In the urban, within the 32 covered states/UTs, the 75 NSS regions were again treated as the main strata and a sample of 363 towns (first stage units) were selected covering all sample states. All the cities/towns of varying sizes (less than 5,000 to over 10 million populations) in sample districts were grouped into nine categories based on the population. Those cities/towns having population over 2,00,000 that formed first five groups (over 190 cities) were selected with a probability one. The remaining four town groups were considered as separate strata on the basis of their population size and from each stratum a sample of towns was selected independently. These town groups may be called sub-strata which are formed within the main strata of NSS regions in each state. Out of 363 sample towns in the listing survey, 189 cities and towns were selected by equal probability sampling approach from remaining four towns groups. A total sample size of 2,712 urban wards was allocated among the sample towns more or less in proportion to the number of wards in the respective towns, maintaining an equal number of wards allocated to each selected town in a town group.

Another survey was carried out by the NCAER called the *India Human Development Survey* (IHDS). The IHDS is a nationally representative, multi-topic survey of 41,554 households in 1,503 villages and 971 urban neighbourhoods across India. The first round of interviews were completed in 2004–5; data are publicly available through Interuniversity Consortium for Political and Social Research (ICPSR). A second round of IHDS is re-interviewing these households in 2011–12 to examine changes in an era of rapid economic growth. The second round also adds interviews with young people aged 15–18 to examine the process of transition to adulthood. The results of the 2004–5 survey are presented in Desai et. al (2010), which summarizes the main IHDS results.

This volume contains 14 chapters, namely: (i) introduction; (ii) income, poverty, and inequality; (iii) agriculture; (iv) employment; (v) household assets and amenities; (vi) education; (vii) health and medical care; (viii) child wellbeing; (ix) wellbeing of the older population; (x) gender and family dynamics; (xi) social integration; (xii) villages in a global world; (xiii) social safety nets in india; and (xiv) conclusion.

The survey, which involved 41,554 household interviews in 1,503 villages and 971 urban blocks in 33 states and UTs of India, was designed to be nationally representative. This survey builds on a prior survey conducted by NCAER in 1993–4. This survey is unique in that it was designed to measure different dimensions of human development, with a particular emphasis on understanding social inequalities. Unlike single-topic surveys of health, labour market behaviour, or consumption patterns, it emphasized a variety of topics of interest to a study of human development under a single rubric, providing us with a rich array of data for study.

In addition to the introduction and conclusion, the volume of this survey is divided into four sections. The first section focuses on livelihoods, with chapters exploring the level and composition of household income and poverty, agriculture and access to means of production, employment patterns and wages, and standard of living. The second section focuses on education and health, with a focus on assessing current status as well as the availability and cost of educational and health services. The third section focuses on the wellbeing of vulnerable populations: children, the elderly, and women. The fourth section is unique in its focus on the linkages between individuals and households and the broader social structures. Chapters in this section include analysis of social integration of the households into broader community networks; the level of village development in an increasingly global world; and the policy responses in the form of social safety net provisions.

Centre for Monitoring Indian Economy

The Centre for Monitoring Indian Economy (CMIE) started a survey on household income and expenditure called Consumer Pyramids. Following are the details available regarding the survey.

Consumer Pyramids

The CMIE started a survey of household income, expenditure, saving, investment, borrowings, and ownership of assets. The estimates are available for 24 states and UTs for about 300 cities, 100 homogeneous regions, and also 100 rural regions. The surveys are based on a large panel of households and are conducted quarterly. At present, the number of households on the panel is 1,58,000. The estimates of income are available. This survey makes estimates of age, gender, savings by source, and pattern of expenditure, which is tabulated by about a 100 expenditure heads. It also provides an understanding of education, occupation, health, and financial inclusion of individuals. This is the only source of estimating household incomes in India at the quarterly level. Demographic characteristics are available for over 7 lakh individuals. In this survey, the data about employment/unemployment status are collected from all members of 15 years and above of the sample households in the panel of consumer pyramids surveyed.

In addition, it provides estimates of ownership of assets such as a house, kitchen appliances, household appliances, entertainment equipment, transport equipment, and other assets.

These estimates are based on the largest household survey conducted in India. The panel is interviewed every quarter. This is the fastest frequency household survey of this size conducted in India.

It is also the only source of obtaining a comprehensive understanding of the financial health of households.

The results of these surveys are not published but are available on payment basis.

People Research on India's Consumer Economy (PRICE)

PRICE functions as a think tank, engaged in building and disseminating seminal knowledge and insight about India's consumer economy as well as India's citizen's environment. Its ICE 360° surveys are meant to guide public policy and business strategy with people-based, continuous, timely, and data-driven facts and insights about today's India.

So far, PRICE has conducted two household surveys. The first survey relates to the year 2014, and primarily focused on providing household-level details about economic and social wellbeing of Indian households. Some of the key themes of the Indian consumer economy that the survey captured included household-level income, expenditure, saving patterns, social inclusion and financial optimism, and lifestyle indicators.

The second household survey was conducted with reference to the year 2016. The scope and coverage of this survey was enlarged and following themes were also captured:

Household Characteristics: Such as type of dwelling unit and availability and access to basic amenities, ownership of durables, intention to purchase in near future, livelihood-linked seasonal migration trends, and remittance behaviour.

Social and Political Inclusion: Such as social discrimination, feeling of security within neighbourhood, areas of concern, food security, participation in social activities and political participation, membership in trade bodies, and presence in and usage of trade and social networks.

Access to Welfare: Such as awareness of and participation in flagship government programmes, method used to access information on current trade/occupation and schemes and benefits, degree of dependency on a public distribution system (PDS), life cover, and employment guarantee.

Income and Consumption: Such as volume of earned and unearned income of households from all sources, itemized consumption expenditure covering food and non-food items, utilities, debt servicing, and non-routine expenses.

Debt Situation of Households: Such as penetration of formal debt, purpose of debt (including consumption, production, for business expansion/seed capital), preferred source of credit, future intention and purpose for taking loan from formal and informal sources, and current debt-servicing costs.

Financial Optimism: Such as perception about stability in major source of household income, level of satisfaction regarding financial situation of household, perceived economic class, and expected change in household's economic situation in the next 3 years.

Saving and Investment Behaviour: Such as cross-market savings portfolios, market penetration (household) of broad investment modes, share of wallet—percentage share of total savings/investments by instruments, short- and long-term savings motivations, savings/investment plans for 2016–17, retirement outlook, and remittances, awareness, understanding, and trust in financial instruments linked to capital markets.

Labour Market Participation: Such as occupations of all members, sector of employment, job security and nature of contracting, social security and labour rights, and disguised employment.

Financial Inclusion Measure: Such as access to formal finance, sourcing of debt by purpose, debt servicing costs, bank account ownership, life insurance coverage, eligibility for accessing formal loan (proof of address, identity proof, and availability of collateral for mortgage, such as real estate, gold, and investments), and awareness of prospect of leveraging owned assets for credit from financial institutions.

Digital Connectivity: Such as penetration of smartphones, degree of comfort with using value added services, and access to and usage of internet to perform basic functions.

Access to Public Infrastructure: Such as availability and ease of access to public infrastructure, including health, education, judiciary, markets, and essential commodities.

Citizen's Report Card: Such as public opinion on direction of change of state of the nation, performance of the economy, governance, corruption, law and order, and other contemporary issues of national interest, and priority expectation from current government going forward.

Demographic Profile of All Earners: Such as age, gender, education level, occupation of the CWE, primary and secondary sources of income, unemployment by duration and profile of unemployed.

Sampling Design

The listing exercise helps to arrive at a sampling frame to conduct the Main Household Survey (ICE 360° Survey, 2016). Listing was undertaken all across the country and the sampling followed a three-stage stratified design. The listing questionnaires were canvassed in 3,00,000 households spread across 25 major Indian states.

Selection of Households in Rural Areas

For the purpose of listing, the villages were divided into various strata based on number of households. In villages with up to 1,000 households, selection of 100 households was done using systematic random sampling (SRS) considering the whole village as a single segment. The listing exercises were started from the northwest direction of the village and, using right hand rule, SRS methodology was followed until 100 households were listed. The actual selection of the household to be listed was dependent on the random starting point, the sampling interval (mentioned in the sampling sheet provided by PRICE, which details the sampling interval for each PSU), and the direction of movement which will start from a random starting point in the north-west part of the village and proceed clock-wise using the right hand rule. In each selected village, the first steps were to update the population of the village in discussion with the pradhan/sarpanch/village leader. The total population divided by 100 (the sample per village) would give the correct sampling interval. This may differ from the one in the sampling master list, as the data therein is based on Census 2011. In case the selected household, after the sampling interval, was not available on the day(s) of listing survey, then the household which was listed immediately after was considered, and the sampling interval for the selection of the next household only was adjusted by a minus one (–1). For example if the sampling interval is 8, and the 56th household to be listed as per the process is not available, then the 57th household would be considered, and the interviewer would then move to the 64th household after an interval of 7 households (just for this case) and resume the interval of 8 thereafter.

For larger villages (more than 1,000 households) a segmentation of the village was done with each segment comprising 100 households. Four segments were randomly selected and SRS was undertaken to select every fourth household starting from a random starting point, and using the north-west and onwards clockwise form of movement, in the principle of the right hand rule.

Selection of Households in Urban Areas

In the urban areas, one neighbourhood/locality was selected from the selected wards. Keeping in mind the possibilities of non-availability of household members, a total of 125 households were surveyed in each such locality to get an effective coverage of 100 listed households. Households were consecutively listed from the random starting point using the right hand rule. In the urban areas, there were instances that the housing structure is a multistoreyed building, and often a high-rise complex. The principle adopted would be that in case a multistoreyed housing structure is selected in the process of listing, and there are multiple households residing in the structure, the listing would include consecutively one after the other households, starting from the ground floor and the lowest house number and proceed on each higher storey till the listing in the structure is completed or till the required sample is exhausted. The salient features of the survey design and methodology are given in Table 18.2.

Outputs

The outputs are available in the form of various alternatives:

(1) Newspaper articles—Data views of relevance to Indian policy-making has been regularly published in leading English dailies

Table 18.2 Survey Features and Allocation

Feature	ICE 360° Survey, 2014	ICE 360° Survey, 2016
Survey type	Cross-section	Best mix of Baseline-Panel-Longitudinal and Cross-sectional
Sample design	Three-stage stratified random sampling Rural: District, Villages, and Households Urban: Towns, UFS blocks, and Households	Same as ICE 360° Survey, 2014
Coverage	21 states	25 states
Unit of selection and data collection	Households	Households
Sampling frame	1,01,534 households	3,00,000 households
Sample size	20,195 households	61,000 (12,000 panel)
Method of data collection	Face-to-face interview	Face-to-face interview and focus groups
Respondents	CWE	CWE, Housewife, Youth
Collection of primary data	September–November, 2014	Listing of households (November 2015-January 2016); Main survey (March–August 2016)

Source: PRICE (www.ice360.in, last accessed on 13 July 2017).

and are available for free download from the website of PRICE (www.ice360.in).

(2) Policy briefs—This is a collection of different policy and business briefs created from in depth analysis from the 2014 survey data and are available for free download from the website of PRICE.

(3) Infographics—A series of infographic sheets have been created using data views from the 2014 survey and are available for free download from the website of PRICE.

Bibliography

Centre for Monitoring Indian Economy. *Survey on Households' Income and Expenditure.*

Desai, Sonalde B., Amaresh Dubey, Brijlal Joshi, Mitali Sen, Abusaleh Shariff and Reeve D. Vanneman. 2010. *Human Development in India: Challenges for a Society in Transition.* New Delhi: Oxford University Press.

Lal, Deepak, Rakesh Mohan, and I. Natarajan. 2001. 'Economic Reforms and Poverty Alleviation: A Tale of Two Surveys', *Economic and Political Weekly*, 36(12): 1017–28.

Murthy, M.N. (ed.). 1970. *Proceedings of the Seminar on Data Collection Techniques in the National Sample Survey.* New Delhi: Department of Statistics, Cabinet Secretariat, Government of India.

National Council of Applied Economics Research (NCAER). 2006. *India Rural Infrastructure Report.* New Delhi: NCAER.

———. 2010. *Indian Youth: Demographics and Readership.* New Delhi: NCAER.

———. *National Survey on Household Income and Expenditure (2004–05).* New Delhi: NCAER.

National Sample Survey Organization (NSSO). 2001. *Concepts and Definitions Used in NSS*, Golden Jubilee Publication. Government of India.

———. *Note on Sample Design and Estimation Procedure NSS 66th round (July 2009–June 2010).* Government of India.

Seddey, Subhash Chand. 2011. *An Overview of National Sample Survey Organization.* National Sample Survey Organization. http://users.pop.umn.edu/~rmccaa/ipums-global/india_nsso_durban_workshop.pdf

Shukla, Rajesh. 2010. *How India Earns, Spends and Saves: Unmasking the Real India.* New Delhi: National Council of Applied Economics Research.

Shukla, Rajesh, S.K. Dwivedi and Asha Sharma with assistance from Sunil Jain. 2004. *The Great Indian Middle Class.* New Delhi: National Council of Applied Economics Research.

Index

About the Author

M.R. Saluja is a distinguished fellow at the India Development Foundation, Gurugram. He has done pioneering work in developing India's statistical system, and a social accounting matrix and input-output tables for the Indian economy. He has been an advisor to both central and state governments in India.

Saluja retired as Professor and Head of Planning Unit, Indian Statistical Institute, Delhi, India, in the year 1994. Subsequent to that he worked as consultant at the erstwhile Planning Commission of India and then as senior consultant at National Council of Applied Economic Research, New Delhi, before moving to India Development Foundation in the year 2003 as the founding member. He has also led the technical team that helped the working group revise the Planning Commission's methodology for estimating state-level poverty incidence.

He has published widely in reputed journals and his co-authored books *Household Savings and Investment Behaviour in India* (2003) and *Social Accounting Matrix for India: Concepts, Construction and Applications* (2006) are widely used reference books.